Model Tax Convention on Income and on Capital

CONDENSED VERSION

22 JULY 2010

OECD

ORGANISATION FOR ECONOMIC CO-OPERATION AND DEVELOPMENT

The OECD is a unique forum where governments work together to address the economic, social and environmental challenges of globalisation. The OECD is also at the forefront of efforts to understand and to help governments respond to new developments and concerns, such as corporate governance, the information economy and the challenges of an ageing population. The Organisation provides a setting where governments can compare policy experiences, seek answers to common problems, identify good practice and work to co-ordinate domestic and international policies.

The OECD member countries are: Australia, Austria, Belgium, Canada, Chile, the Czech Republic, Denmark, Finland, France, Germany, Greece, Hungary, Iceland, Ireland, Italy, Japan, Korea, Luxembourg, Mexico, the Netherlands, New Zealand, Norway, Poland, Portugal, the Slovak Republic, Slovenia, Spain, Sweden, Switzerland, Turkey, the United Kingdom and the United States. The European Commission takes part in the work of the OECD.

OECD Publishing disseminates widely the results of the Organisation's statistics gathering and research on economic, social and environmental issues, as well as the conventions, guidelines and standards agreed by its members.

ISBN 978-92-64-08948-8 (print)
ISBN 978-92-64-08960-0 (PDF)

Also available in French: *Modèle de Convention fiscale concernant le revenu et la fortune : Version abrégée*

Corrigenda to OECD publications may be found on line at: *www.oecd.org/publishing/corrigenda*.

FOREWORD

This is the eighth edition of the condensed version of the publication entitled *Model Tax Convention on Income and on Capital*, first published in loose-leaf format in 1992 and periodically updated since then.

This condensed version includes the text of the Model Tax Convention as it read on 22 July 2010 after the adoption of the eighth update by the Council of the OECD. Historical notes included in Volume I of the full-length version as well as the detailed list of tax conventions between OECD member countries and the background reports that are included in Volume II of the full-length version have not been reproduced in this version.

TABLE OF CONTENTS

INTRODUCTION

1.   International juridical double taxation can be generally defined as the imposition of comparable taxes in two (or more) States on the same taxpayer in respect of the same subject matter and for identical periods. Its harmful effects on the exchange of goods and services and movements of capital, technology and persons are so well known that it is scarcely necessary to stress the importance of removing the obstacles that double taxation presents to the development of economic relations between countries.

2.   It has long been recognised among the member countries of the Organisation for Economic Co-operation and Development that it is desirable to clarify, standardise, and confirm the fiscal situation of taxpayers who are engaged in commercial, industrial, financial, or any other activities in other countries through the application by all countries of common solutions to identical cases of double taxation.

3.   This is the main purpose of the OECD *Model Tax Convention on Income and on Capital*, which provides a means of settling on a uniform basis the most common problems that arise in the field of international juridical double taxation. As recommended by the Council of the OECD,[1] member countries, when concluding or revising bilateral conventions, should conform to this Model Convention as interpreted by the Commentaries thereon and having regard to the reservations contained therein and their tax authorities should follow these Commentaries, as modified from time to time and subject to their observations thereon, when applying and interpreting the provisions of their bilateral tax conventions that are based on the Model Convention.

A.   Historical background

4.   Progress had already been made towards the elimination of double taxation through bilateral conventions or unilateral measures when the Council of the Organisation for European Economic Co-operation (OEEC) adopted its first Recommendation concerning double taxation on 25 February 1955. At that time, 70 bilateral general conventions had been signed between countries that are now members of the OECD. This was to a large extent due to the work commenced in 1921 by the League of Nations. This work led to the drawing up in 1928 of the first model bilateral convention and, finally, to the Model Conventions of Mexico (1943) and London (1946), the principles of which were followed with certain variants in many of the bilateral conventions concluded or revised during the following decade. Neither of these Model Conventions, however, was fully and unanimously accepted. Moreover, in respect of several essential questions, they presented considerable dissimilarities and certain gaps.

5.   The increasing economic interdependence and co-operation of the member countries of the OEEC in the post-war period showed increasingly clearly the importance of measures for preventing international double taxation. The need was

---

1   See Annex.

recognised for extending the network of bilateral tax conventions to all member countries of the OEEC, and subsequently of the OECD, several of which had so far concluded only very few conventions and some none at all. At the same time, harmonization of these conventions in accordance with uniform principles, definitions, rules, and methods, and agreement on a common interpretation, became increasingly desirable.

6.   It was against this new background that the Fiscal Committee set to work in 1956 to establish a draft convention that would effectively resolve the double taxation problems existing between OECD member countries and that would be acceptable to all member countries. From 1958 to 1961, the Fiscal Committee prepared four interim Reports, before submitting in 1963 its final Report entitled *Draft Double Taxation Convention on Income and Capital*.[1] The Council of the OECD adopted, on 30 July 1963, a Recommendation concerning the avoidance of double taxation and called upon the Governments of member countries, when concluding or revising bilateral conventions between them, to conform to that Draft Convention.

7.   The Fiscal Committee of the OECD had envisaged, when presenting its Report in 1963, that the Draft Convention might be revised at a later stage following further study. Such a revision was also needed to take account of the experience gained by member countries in the negotiation and practical application of bilateral conventions, of changes in the tax systems of member countries, of the increase in international fiscal relations, and of the development of new sectors of business activity and the emergence of new complex business organisations at the international level. For all these reasons, the Fiscal Committee and, after 1971, its successor the Committee on Fiscal Affairs, undertook the revision of the 1963 Draft Convention and of the commentaries thereon. This resulted in the publication in 1977 of a new Model Convention and Commentaries.[2]

8.   The factors that had led to the revision of the 1963 Draft Convention continued to exert their influence and, in many ways, the pressure to update and adapt the Model Convention to changing economic conditions progressively increased. New technologies were developed and, at the same time, there were fundamental changes taking place in the ways in which cross-borders transactions were undertaken. Methods of tax avoidance and evasion became more sophisticated. The globalisation and liberalisation of OECD economies also accelerated rapidly in the 1980s. Consequently, in the course of its regular work programme, the Committee on Fiscal Affairs and, in particular, its Working Party No. 1, continued after 1977 to examine various issues directly or indirectly related to the 1977 Model Convention. This work resulted in a number of reports, some of which recommended amendments to the Model Convention and its Commentaries.[3]

---

1 *Draft Double Taxation Convention on Income and Capital*, OECD, Paris, 1963.
2 *Model Double Taxation Convention on Income and on Capital*, OECD, Paris, 1977.
3 A number of these reports were published and appear in Volume II of the full-length version of the OECD Model Tax Convention.

9.   In 1991, recognizing that the revision of the Model Convention and the Commentaries had become an ongoing process, the Committee on Fiscal Affairs adopted the concept of an ambulatory Model Convention providing periodic and more timely updates and amendments without waiting for a complete revision. It was therefore decided to publish a revised updated version of the Model Convention which would take into account the work done since 1977 by integrating many of the recommendations made in the above-mentioned reports.

10.   Because the influence of the Model Convention had extended far beyond the OECD member countries, the Committee also decided that the revision process should be opened up to benefit from the input of non-member countries, other international organisations and other interested parties. It was felt that such outside contributions would assist the Committee on Fiscal Affairs in its continuing task of updating the Model Convention to conform with the evolution of international tax rules and principles.

11.   This led to the publication in 1992 of the Model Convention in a loose-leaf format. Unlike the 1963 Draft Convention and the 1977 Model Convention, the revised Model was not the culmination of a comprehensive revision, but rather the first step of an ongoing revision process intended to produce periodic updates and thereby ensure that the Model Convention continues to reflect accurately the views of member countries at any point in time.

11.1   Through one of these updates, produced in 1997, the positions of a number of non-member countries on the Model Convention were added in a second volume in recognition of the growing influence of the Model Convention outside the OECD countries (see below). At the same time, reprints of a number of previous reports of the Committee which had resulted in changes to the Model Convention were also added.

B.   Influence of the OECD Model Convention

12.   Since 1963, the OECD Model Convention has had wide repercussions on the negotiation, application, and interpretation of tax conventions.

13.   First, OECD member countries have largely conformed to the Model Convention when concluding or revising bilateral conventions. The progress made towards eliminating double taxation between member countries can be measured by the increasing number of conventions concluded or revised since 1957 in accordance with the Recommendations of the Council of the OECD. But the importance of the Model Convention should be measured not only by the number of conventions concluded between member countries[1] but also by the fact that, in accordance with the Recommendations of the Council of the OECD, these conventions follow the pattern and, in most cases, the main provisions of the Model Convention. The existence of the Model Convention has facilitated bilateral negotiations between OECD member

---

1   See Appendix I in Volume II of the full-length version of the OECD Model Tax Convention for the list of these conventions.

countries and made possible a desirable harmonization between their bilateral conventions for the benefit of both taxpayers and national administrations.

14.   Second, the impact of the Model Convention has extended far beyond the OECD area. It has been used as a basic document of reference in negotiations between member and non-member countries and even between non-member countries, as well as in the work of other worldwide or regional international organisations in the field of double taxation and related problems. Most notably, it has been used as the basis for the original drafting and the subsequent revision of the United Nations Model Double Taxation Convention between Developed and Developing Countries,[1] which reproduces a significant part of the provisions and Commentaries of the OECD Model Convention. It is in recognition of this growing influence of the Model Convention in non-member countries that it was agreed, in 1997, to add to the Model Convention the positions of a number of these countries on its provisions and Commentaries.

15.   Third, the worldwide recognition of the provisions of the Model Convention and their incorporation into a majority of bilateral conventions have helped make the Commentaries on the provisions of the Model Convention a widely-accepted guide to the interpretation and application of the provisions of existing bilateral conventions. This has facilitated the interpretation and the enforcement of these bilateral conventions along common lines. As the network of tax conventions continues to expand, the importance of such a generally accepted guide becomes all the greater.

C.   Presentation of the Model Convention

Title of the Model Convention

16.   In both the 1963 Draft Convention and the 1977 Model Convention, the title of the Model Convention included a reference to the elimination of double taxation. In recognition of the fact that the Model Convention does not deal exclusively with the elimination of double taxation but also addresses other issues, such as the prevention of tax evasion and non-discrimination, it was subsequently decided to use a shorter title which did not include this reference. This change has been made both on the cover page of this publication and in the Model Convention itself. However, it is understood that the practice of many member countries is still to include in the title a reference to either the elimination of double taxation or to both the elimination of double taxation and the prevention of fiscal evasion.

Broad lines of the Model Convention

17.   The Model Convention first describes its scope (Chapter I) and defines some terms (Chapter II). The main part is made up of Chapters III to V, which settle to what extent each of the two Contracting States may tax income and capital and how

---

1   United Nations Model Double Taxation Convention between Developed and Developing Countries, United Nations Publications, New York, first edition 1980, second edition 2001.

international juridical double taxation is to be eliminated. Then follow the Special Provisions (Chapter VI) and the Final Provisions (entry into force and termination, Chapter VII).

Scope and definitions

18.   The Convention applies to all persons who are residents of one or both of the Contracting States (Article 1). It deals with taxes on income and on capital, which are described in a general way in Article 2. In Chapter II, some terms used in more than one Article of the Convention are defined. Other terms such as "dividends", "interest", "royalties" and "immovable property" are defined in the Articles that deal with these matters.

Taxation of income and capital

19.   For the purpose of eliminating double taxation, the Convention establishes two categories of rules. First, Articles 6 to 21 determine, with regard to different classes of income, the respective rights to tax of the State of source or situs and of the State of residence, and Article 22 does the same with regard to capital. In the case of a number of items of income and capital, an exclusive right to tax is conferred on one of the Contracting States. The other Contracting State is thereby prevented from taxing those items and double taxation is avoided. As a rule, this exclusive right to tax is conferred on the State of residence. In the case of other items of income and capital, the right to tax is not an exclusive one. As regards two classes of income (dividends and interest), although both States are given the right to tax, the amount of tax that may be imposed in the State of source is limited. Second, insofar as these provisions confer on the State of source or situs a full or limited right to tax, the State of residence must allow relief so as to avoid double taxation; this is the purpose of Articles 23 A and 23 B. The Convention leaves it to the Contracting States to choose between two methods of relief, i.e. the exemption method and the credit method.

20.   Income and capital may be classified into three classes, depending on the treatment applicable to each class in the State of source or situs:

- income and capital that may be taxed without any limitation in the State of source or situs,
  income that may be subjected to limited taxation in the State of source, and
- income and capital that may not be taxed in the State of source or situs.

21.   The following are the classes of income and capital that may be taxed without any limitation in the State of source or situs:

- income from immovable property situated in that State (including income from agriculture or forestry), gains from the alienation of such property, and capital representing it (Article 6 and paragraph 1 of Articles 13 and 22);
- profits of a permanent establishment situated in that State, gains from the alienation of such a permanent establishment, and capital representing movable property forming part of the business property of such a permanent

establishment (Article 7 and paragraph 2 of Articles 13 and 22); an exception is made, however, if the permanent establishment is maintained for the purposes of international shipping, inland waterways transport, and international air transport (see paragraph 23 below);

— income from the activities of artistes and sportsmen exercised in that State, irrespective of whether such income accrues to the artiste or sportsman himself or to another person (Article 17);

— directors' fees paid by a company that is a resident of that State (Article 16);

— remuneration in respect of an employment in the private sector, exercised in that State, unless the employee is present therein for a period not exceeding 183 days in any twelve month period commencing or ending in the fiscal year concerned and certain conditions are met; and remuneration in respect of an employment exercised aboard a ship or aircraft operated internationally or aboard a boat, if the place of effective management of the enterprise is situated in that State (Article 15);

— subject to certain conditions, remuneration and pensions paid in respect of government service (Article 19).

22.   The following are the classes of income that may be subjected to limited taxation in the State of source:

— dividends: provided the holding in respect of which the dividends are paid is not effectively connected with a permanent establishment in the State of source, that State must limit its tax to 5 per cent of the gross amount of the dividends, where the beneficial owner is a company that holds directly at least 25 per cent of the capital of the company paying the dividends, and to 15 per cent of their gross amount in other cases (Article 10);

— interest: subject to the same proviso as in the case of dividends, the State of source must limit its tax to 10 per cent of the gross amount of the interest, except for any interest in excess of a normal amount (Article 11).

23.   Other items of income or capital may not be taxed in the State of source or situs; as a rule they are taxable only in the State of residence of the taxpayer. This applies, for example, to royalties (Article 12), gains from the alienation of shares or securities (paragraph 5 of Article 13), private sector pensions (Article 18), payments received by a student for the purposes of his education or training (Article 20), and capital represented by shares or securities (paragraph 4 of Article 22). Profits from the operation of ships or aircraft in international traffic or of boats engaged in inland waterways transport, gains from the alienation of such ships, boats, or aircraft, and capital represented by them, are taxable only in the State in which the place of effective management of the enterprise is situated (Article 8 and paragraph 3 of Articles 13 and 22). Business profits that are not attributable to a permanent establishment in the State of source are taxable only in the State of residence (paragraph 1 of Article 7).

24.   Where a resident of a Contracting State receives income from sources in the other Contracting State, or owns capital situated therein, that in accordance with the

Convention is taxable only in the State of residence, no problem of double taxation arises, since the State of source or situs must refrain from taxing that income or capital.

25. Where, on the contrary, income or capital may, in accordance with the Convention, be taxed with or without limitation in the State of source or situs, the State of residence has the obligation to eliminate double taxation. This can be accomplished by one of the following two methods:

— exemption method: income or capital that is taxable in the State of source or situs is exempted in the State of residence, but it may be taken into account in determining the rate of tax applicable to the taxpayer's remaining income or capital;

— credit method: income or capital that is taxable in the State of source or situs is subject to tax in the State of residence, but the tax levied in the State of source or situs is credited against the tax levied by the State of residence on such income or capital.

Special provisions

26. There are a number of special provisions in the Convention. These provisions concern:

— the elimination of tax discrimination in various circumstances (Article 24);

— the establishment of a mutual agreement procedure for eliminating double taxation and resolving conflicts of interpretation of the Convention (Article 25);

— the exchange of information between the tax authorities of the Contracting States (Article 26);

— the assistance by Contracting States in the collection of each other's taxes (Article 27);

— the tax treatment of members of diplomatic missions and consular posts in accordance with international law (Article 28);

— the territorial extension of the Convention (Article 29).

General remarks on the Model Convention

27. The Model Convention seeks, wherever possible, to specify for each situation a single rule. On certain points, however, it was thought necessary to leave in the Convention a certain degree of flexibility, compatible with the efficient implementation of the Model Convention. Member countries therefore enjoy a certain latitude, for example, with regard to fixing the rate of tax at source on dividends and interest and the choice of method for eliminating double taxation. Moreover, for some cases, alternative or additional provisions are mentioned in the Commentaries.

Commentaries on the Articles

28.   For each Article in the Convention, there is a detailed Commentary that is intended to illustrate or interpret its provisions.

29.   As the Commentaries have been drafted and agreed upon by the experts appointed to the Committee on Fiscal Affairs by the Governments of member countries, they are of special importance in the development of international fiscal law. Although the Commentaries are not designed to be annexed in any manner to the conventions signed by member countries, which unlike the Model are legally binding international instruments, they can nevertheless be of great assistance in the application and interpretation of the conventions and, in particular, in the settlement of any disputes.

29.1 The tax administrations of member countries routinely consult the Commentaries in their interpretation of bilateral tax treaties. The Commentaries are useful both in deciding day-to-day questions of detail and in resolving larger issues involving the policies and purposes behind various provisions. Tax officials give great weight to the guidance contained in the Commentaries.

29.2 Similarly, taxpayers make extensive use of the Commentaries in conducting their businesses and planning their business transactions and investments. The Commentaries are of particular importance in countries that do not have a procedure for obtaining an advance ruling on tax matters from the tax administration as the Commentaries may be the only available source of interpretation in that case.

29.3 Bilateral tax treaties are receiving more and more judicial attention as well. The courts are increasingly using the Commentaries in reaching their decisions. Information collected by the Committee on Fiscal Affairs shows that the Commentaries have been cited in the published decisions of the courts of the great majority of member countries. In many decisions, the Commentaries have been extensively quoted and analysed, and have frequently played a key role in the judge's deliberations. The Committee expects this trend to continue as the worldwide network of tax treaties continues to grow and as the Commentaries gain even more widespread acceptance as an important interpretative reference.

30.   Observations on the Commentaries have sometimes been inserted at the request of member countries that are unable to concur in the interpretation given in the Commentary on the Article concerned. These observations thus do not express any disagreement with the text of the Convention, but usefully indicate the way in which those countries will apply the provisions of the Article in question. Since the observations are related to the interpretations of the Articles given in the Commentaries, no observation is needed to indicate a country's wish to modify the wording of an alternative or additional provision that the Commentaries allow countries to include in their bilateral conventions.

Reservations of certain member countries on some provisions of the Convention

31.   Although all member countries are in agreement with the aims and the main provisions of the Model Convention, nearly all have entered reservations on some provisions, which are recorded in the Commentaries on the Articles concerned. There has been no need for countries to make reservations indicating their intent to use the alternative or additional provisions that the Commentaries allow countries to include in their bilateral conventions or to modify the wording of a provision of the Model to confirm or incorporate an interpretation of that provision put forward in the Commentary. It is understood that insofar as a member country has entered reservations, the other member countries, in negotiating bilateral conventions with the former, will retain their freedom of action in accordance with the principle of reciprocity.

32.   The Committee on Fiscal Affairs considers that these reservations should be viewed against the background of the very wide areas of agreement that has been achieved in drafting this Convention.

Relation with previous versions

33.   When drafting the 1977 Model Convention, the Committee on Fiscal Affairs examined the problems of conflicts of interpretation that might arise as a result of changes in the Articles and Commentaries of the 1963 Draft Convention. At that time, the Committee considered that existing conventions should, as far as possible, be interpreted in the spirit of the revised Commentaries, even though the provisions of these conventions did not yet include the more precise wording of the 1977 Model Convention. It was also indicated that member countries wishing to clarify their positions in this respect could do so by means of an exchange of letters between competent authorities in accordance with the mutual agreement procedure and that, even in the absence of such an exchange of letters, these authorities could use mutual agreement procedures to confirm this interpretation in particular cases.

34.   The Committee believes that the changes to the Articles of the Model Convention and the Commentaries that have been made since 1977 should be similarly interpreted.

35.   Needless to say, amendments to the Articles of the Model Convention and changes to the Commentaries that are a direct result of these amendments are not relevant to the interpretation or application of previously concluded conventions where the provisions of those conventions are different in substance from the amended Articles. However, other changes or additions to the Commentaries are normally applicable to the interpretation and application of conventions concluded before their adoption, because they reflect the consensus of the OECD member countries as to the proper interpretation of existing provisions and their application to specific situations.

36.   Whilst the Committee considers that changes to the Commentaries should be relevant in interpreting and applying conventions concluded before the adoption of these changes, it disagrees with any form of *a contrario* interpretation that would necessarily infer from a change to an Article of the Model Convention or to the Commentaries that the previous wording resulted in consequences different from those of the modified wording. Many amendments are intended to simply clarify, not change, the meaning of the Articles or the Commentaries, and such *a contrario* interpretations would clearly be wrong in those cases.

36.1   Tax authorities in member countries follow the general principles enunciated in the preceding four paragraphs. Accordingly, the Committee on Fiscal Affairs considers that taxpayers may also find it useful to consult later versions of the Commentaries in interpreting earlier treaties.

Multilateral convention

37.   When preparing the 1963 Draft Convention and the 1977 Model Convention, the Committee on Fiscal Affairs considered whether the conclusion of a multilateral tax convention would be feasible and came to the conclusion that this would meet with great difficulties. It recognised, however, that it might be possible for certain groups of member countries to study the possibility of concluding such a convention among themselves on the basis of the Model Convention, subject to certain adaptations they might consider necessary to suit their particular purposes.

38.   The Nordic Convention on Income and Capital entered into by Denmark, Finland, Iceland, Norway and Sweden, which was concluded in 1983 and replaced in 1987, 1989 and 1996,[1] provides a practical example of such a multilateral convention between a group of member countries and follows closely the provisions of the Model Convention.

39.   Also relevant is the Convention on Mutual Administrative Assistance in Tax Matters, which was drawn up within the Council of Europe on the basis of a first draft prepared by the Committee on Fiscal Affairs. This Convention entered into force on 1 April 1995.

40.   Despite these two conventions, there are no reasons to believe that the conclusion of a multilateral tax convention involving all member countries could now be considered practicable. The Committee therefore considers that bilateral conventions are still a more appropriate way to ensure the elimination of double taxation at the international level.

Tax avoidance and evasion; improper use of conventions

41.   The Committee on Fiscal Affairs continues to examine both the improper use of tax conventions and international tax evasion. The problem is referred to in the Commentaries on several Articles. In particular, Article 26, as clarified in the Commentary, enables States to exchange information to combat these abuses.

---

1   The Faroe Islands is also a signatory of the 1989 and 1996 Conventions.

MODEL CONVENTION
WITH RESPECT TO TAXES
ON INCOME AND ON CAPITAL

SUMMARY OF THE CONVENTION

Title and Preamble

Chapter I
SCOPE OF THE CONVENTION

Chapter II
DEFINITIONS

Chapter III
TAXATION OF INCOME

Chapter IV
TAXATION OF CAPITAL

Chapter V

METHODS FOR ELIMINATION OF DOUBLE TAXATION

Chapter VI

SPECIAL PROVISIONS

Chapter VII

FINAL PROVISIONS

MODEL TAX CONVENTION (CONDENSED VERSION) – ISBN 978-92-64-08948-8 – © OECD 2010

TITLE OF THE CONVENTION

**Convention between (State A) and (State B)
with respect to taxes on income and on capital[1]**

PREAMBLE TO THE CONVENTION[2]

---

1 States wishing to do so may follow the widespread practice of including in the title a reference to either the avoidance of double taxation or to both the avoidance of double taxation and the prevention of fiscal evasion.
2 The Preamble of the Convention shall be drafted in accordance with the constitutional procedure of both Contracting States.

Chapter I
SCOPE OF THE CONVENTION

ARTICLE 1
PERSONS COVERED

This Convention shall apply to persons who are residents of one or both of the Contracting States.

ARTICLE 2
TAXES COVERED

1.   This Convention shall apply to taxes on income and on capital imposed on behalf of a Contracting State or of its political subdivisions or local authorities, irrespective of the manner in which they are levied.

2.   There shall be regarded as taxes on income and on capital all taxes imposed on total income, on total capital, or on elements of income or of capital, including taxes on gains from the alienation of movable or immovable property, taxes on the total amounts of wages or salaries paid by enterprises, as well as taxes on capital appreciation.

3.   The existing taxes to which the Convention shall apply are in particular:

   a) (in State A): ....
   b) (in State B): ....

4.   The Convention shall apply also to any identical or substantially similar taxes that are imposed after the date of signature of the Convention in addition to, or in place of, the existing taxes. The competent authorities of the Contracting States shall notify each other of any significant changes that have been made in their taxation laws.

Chapter II
DEFINITIONS

ARTICLE 3
GENERAL DEFINITIONS

1.   For the purposes of this Convention, unless the context otherwise requires:

a) the term "person" includes an individual, a company and any other body of persons;

b) the term "company" means any body corporate or any entity that is treated as a body corporate for tax purposes;

c) the term "enterprise" applies to the carrying on of any business;

d) the terms "enterprise of a Contracting State" and "enterprise of the other Contracting State" mean respectively an enterprise carried on by a resident of a Contracting State and an enterprise carried on by a resident of the other Contracting State;

e) the term "international traffic" means any transport by a ship or aircraft operated by an enterprise that has its place of effective management in a Contracting State, except when the ship or aircraft is operated solely between places in the other Contracting State;

f) the term "competent authority" means:

   (i)   (in State A): ....

   (ii)   (in State B): ....

g) the term "national", in relation to a Contracting State, means:

   (i)   any individual possessing the nationality or citizenship of that Contracting State; and

   (ii)   any legal person, partnership or association deriving its status as such from the laws in force in that Contracting State;

h) the term "business" includes the performance of professional services and of other activities of an independent character.

2.   As regards the application of the Convention at any time by a Contracting State, any term not defined therein shall, unless the context otherwise requires, have the meaning that it has at that time under the law of that State for the purposes of the taxes to which the Convention applies, any meaning under the applicable tax laws of that State prevailing over a meaning given to the term under other laws of that State.

ARTICLE 4

RESIDENT

1.   For the purposes of this Convention, the term "resident of a Contracting State" means any person who, under the laws of that State, is liable to tax therein by reason of his domicile, residence, place of management or any other criterion of a similar nature, and also includes that State and any political subdivision or local authority thereof. This term, however, does not include any person who is liable to tax in that State in respect only of income from sources in that State or capital situated therein.

2.   Where by reason of the provisions of paragraph 1 an individual is a resident of both Contracting States, then his status shall be determined as follows:

   a) he shall be deemed to be a resident only of the State in which he has a permanent home available to him; if he has a permanent home available to him in both States, he shall be deemed to be a resident only of the State with which his personal and economic relations are closer (centre of vital interests);

   b) if the State in which he has his centre of vital interests cannot be determined, or if he has not a permanent home available to him in either State, he shall be deemed to be a resident only of the State in which he has an habitual abode;

   c) if he has an habitual abode in both States or in neither of them, he shall be deemed to be a resident only of the State of which he is a national;

   d) if he is a national of both States or of neither of them, the competent authorities of the Contracting States shall settle the question by mutual agreement.

3.   Where by reason of the provisions of paragraph 1 a person other than an individual is a resident of both Contracting States, then it shall be deemed to be a resident only of the State in which its place of effective management is situated.

ARTICLE 5

PERMANENT ESTABLISHMENT

1.   For the purposes of this Convention, the term "permanent establishment" means a fixed place of business through which the business of an enterprise is wholly or partly carried on.

2.   The term "permanent establishment" includes especially:

   a) a place of management;

   b) a branch;

   c) an office;

   d) a factory;

   e) a workshop, and

   f) a mine, an oil or gas well, a quarry or any other place of extraction of natural resources.

3.   A building site or construction or installation project constitutes a permanent establishment only if it lasts more than twelve months.

4.   Notwithstanding the preceding provisions of this Article, the term "permanent establishment" shall be deemed not to include:

a) the use of facilities solely for the purpose of storage, display or delivery of goods or merchandise belonging to the enterprise;

b) the maintenance of a stock of goods or merchandise belonging to the enterprise solely for the purpose of storage, display or delivery;

c) the maintenance of a stock of goods or merchandise belonging to the enterprise solely for the purpose of processing by another enterprise;

d) the maintenance of a fixed place of business solely for the purpose of purchasing goods or merchandise or of collecting information, for the enterprise;

e) the maintenance of a fixed place of business solely for the purpose of carrying on, for the enterprise, any other activity of a preparatory or auxiliary character;

f) the maintenance of a fixed place of business solely for any combination of activities mentioned in subparagraphs a) to e), provided that the overall activity of the fixed place of business resulting from this combination is of a preparatory or auxiliary character.

5.   Notwithstanding the provisions of paragraphs 1 and 2, where a person — other than an agent of an independent status to whom paragraph 6 applies — is acting on behalf of an enterprise and has, and habitually exercises, in a Contracting State an authority to conclude contracts in the name of the enterprise, that enterprise shall be deemed to have a permanent establishment in that State in respect of any activities which that person undertakes for the enterprise, unless the activities of such person are limited to those mentioned in paragraph 4 which, if exercised through a fixed place of business, would not make this fixed place of business a permanent establishment under the provisions of that paragraph.

6.   An enterprise shall not be deemed to have a permanent establishment in a Contracting State merely because it carries on business in that State through a broker, general commission agent or any other agent of an independent status, provided that such persons are acting in the ordinary course of their business.

7.   The fact that a company which is a resident of a Contracting State controls or is controlled by a company which is a resident of the other Contracting State, or which carries on business in that other State (whether through a permanent establishment or otherwise), shall not of itself constitute either company a permanent establishment of the other.

Chapter III

TAXATION OF INCOME

ARTICLE 6

INCOME FROM IMMOVABLE PROPERTY

1.   Income derived by a resident of a Contracting State from immovable property (including income from agriculture or forestry) situated in the other Contracting State may be taxed in that other State.

2.   The term "immovable property" shall have the meaning which it has under the law of the Contracting State in which the property in question is situated. The term shall in any case include property accessory to immovable property, livestock and equipment used in agriculture and forestry, rights to which the provisions of general law respecting landed property apply, usufruct of immovable property and rights to variable or fixed payments as consideration for the working of, or the right to work, mineral deposits, sources and other natural resources; ships, boats and aircraft shall not be regarded as immovable property.

3.   The provisions of paragraph 1 shall apply to income derived from the direct use, letting, or use in any other form of immovable property.

4.   The provisions of paragraphs 1 and 3 shall also apply to the income from immovable property of an enterprise.

ARTICLE 7

BUSINESS PROFITS

1.   Profits of an enterprise of a Contracting State shall be taxable only in that State unless the enterprise carries on business in the other Contracting State through a permanent establishment situated therein. If the enterprise carries on business as aforesaid, the profits that are attributable to the permanent establishment in accordance with the provisions of paragraph 2 may be taxed in that other State.

2.   For the purposes of this Article and Article [23 A] [23B], the profits that are attributable in each Contracting State to the permanent establishment referred to in paragraph 1 are the profits it might be expected to make, in particular in its dealings with other parts of the enterprise, if it were a separate and independent enterprise engaged in the same or similar activities under the same or similar conditions, taking into account the functions performed, assets used and risks assumed by the enterprise through the permanent establishment and through the other parts of the enterprise.

3.   Where, in accordance with paragraph 2, a Contracting State adjusts the profits that are attributable to a permanent establishment of an enterprise of one of the

Contracting States and taxes accordingly profits of the enterprise that have been charged to tax in the other State, the other State shall, to the extent necessary to eliminate double taxation on these profits, make an appropriate adjustment to the amount of the tax charged on those profits. In determining such adjustment, the competent authorities of the Contracting States shall if necessary consult each other.

4.   Where profits include items of income which are dealt with separately in other Articles of this Convention, then the provisions of those Articles shall not be affected by the provisions of this Article.

ARTICLE 8

SHIPPING, INLAND WATERWAYS TRANSPORT AND AIR TRANSPORT

1.   Profits from the operation of ships or aircraft in international traffic shall be taxable only in the Contracting State in which the place of effective management of the enterprise is situated.

2.   Profits from the operation of boats engaged in inland waterways transport shall be taxable only in the Contracting State in which the place of effective management of the enterprise is situated.

3.   If the place of effective management of a shipping enterprise or of an inland waterways transport enterprise is aboard a ship or boat, then it shall be deemed to be situated in the Contracting State in which the home harbour of the ship or boat is situated, or, if there is no such home harbour, in the Contracting State of which the operator of the ship or boat is a resident.

4.   The provisions of paragraph 1 shall also apply to profits from the participation in a pool, a joint business or an international operating agency.

ARTICLE 9

ASSOCIATED ENTERPRISES

1.   Where

   a) an enterprise of a Contracting State participates directly or indirectly in the management, control or capital of an enterprise of the other Contracting State, or

   b) the same persons participate directly or indirectly in the management, control or capital of an enterprise of a Contracting State and an enterprise of the other Contracting State,

and in either case conditions are made or imposed between the two enterprises in their commercial or financial relations which differ from those which would be made between independent enterprises, then any profits which would, but for those conditions, have accrued to one of the enterprises, but, by reason of those conditions, have not so accrued, may be included in the profits of that enterprise and taxed accordingly.

2.   Where a Contracting State includes in the profits of an enterprise of that State — and taxes accordingly — profits on which an enterprise of the other Contracting State has been charged to tax in that other State and the profits so included are profits which would have accrued to the enterprise of the first-mentioned State if the conditions made between the two enterprises had been those which would have been made between independent enterprises, then that other State shall make an appropriate adjustment to the amount of the tax charged therein on those profits. In determining such adjustment, due regard shall be had to the other provisions of this Convention and the competent authorities of the Contracting States shall if necessary consult each other.

ARTICLE 10

DIVIDENDS

1.   Dividends paid by a company which is a resident of a Contracting State to a resident of the other Contracting State may be taxed in that other State.

2.   However, such dividends may also be taxed in the Contracting State of which the company paying the dividends is a resident and according to the laws of that State, but if the beneficial owner of the dividends is a resident of the other Contracting State, the tax so charged shall not exceed:

   a) 5 per cent of the gross amount of the dividends if the beneficial owner is a company (other than a partnership) which holds directly at least 25 per cent of the capital of the company paying the dividends;

   b) 15 per cent of the gross amount of the dividends in all other cases.

The competent authorities of the Contracting States shall by mutual agreement settle the mode of application of these limitations.This paragraph shall not affect the taxation of the company in respect of the profits out of which the dividends are paid.

3.   The term "dividends" as used in this Article means income from shares, "jouissance" shares or "jouissance" rights, mining shares, founders' shares or other rights, not being debt-claims, participating in profits, as well as income from other corporate rights which is subjected to the same taxation treatment as income from shares by the laws of the State of which the company making the distribution is a resident.

4.   The provisions of paragraphs 1 and 2 shall not apply if the beneficial owner of the dividends, being a resident of a Contracting State, carries on business in the other Contracting State of which the company paying the dividends is a resident through a permanent establishment situated therein and the holding in respect of which the dividends are paid is effectively connected with such permanent establishment. In such case the provisions of Article 7 shall apply.

5.   Where a company which is a resident of a Contracting State derives profits or income from the other Contracting State, that other State may not impose any tax on the dividends paid by the company, except insofar as such dividends are paid to a resident of that other State or insofar as the holding in respect of which the dividends are paid is effectively connected with a permanent establishment situated in that other State, nor subject the company's undistributed profits to a tax on the company's undistributed profits, even if the dividends paid or the undistributed profits consist wholly or partly of profits or income arising in such other State.

ARTICLE 11

INTEREST

1.   Interest arising in a Contracting State and paid to a resident of the other Contracting State may be taxed in that other State.

2.   However, such interest may also be taxed in the Contracting State in which it arises and according to the laws of that State, but if the beneficial owner of the interest is a resident of the other Contracting State, the tax so charged shall not exceed 10 per cent of the gross amount of the interest. The competent authorities of the Contracting States shall by mutual agreement settle the mode of application of this limitation.

3.   The term "interest" as used in this Article means income from debt-claims of every kind, whether or not secured by mortgage and whether or not carrying a right to participate in the debtor's profits, and in particular, income from government securities and income from bonds or debentures, including premiums and prizes attaching to such securities, bonds or debentures. Penalty charges for late payment shall not be regarded as interest for the purpose of this Article.

4.   The provisions of paragraphs 1 and 2 shall not apply if the beneficial owner of the interest, being a resident of a Contracting State, carries on business in the other Contracting State in which the interest arises through a permanent establishment situated therein and the debt-claim in respect of which the interest is paid is effectively connected with such permanent establishment. In such case the provisions of Article 7 shall apply.

5.   Interest shall be deemed to arise in a Contracting State when the payer is a resident of that State. Where, however, the person paying the interest, whether he is a resident of a Contracting State or not, has in a Contracting State a permanent establishment in connection with which the indebtedness on which the interest is paid was incurred, and such interest is borne by such permanent establishment, then such interest shall be deemed to arise in the State in which the permanent establishment is situated.

6.   Where, by reason of a special relationship between the payer and the beneficial owner or between both of them and some other person, the amount of the interest, having regard to the debt-claim for which it is paid, exceeds the amount which would

have been agreed upon by the payer and the beneficial owner in the absence of such relationship, the provisions of this Article shall apply only to the last-mentioned amount. In such case, the excess part of the payments shall remain taxable according to the laws of each Contracting State, due regard being had to the other provisions of this Convention.

ARTICLE 12

ROYALTIES

1.   Royalties arising in a Contracting State and beneficially owned by a resident of the other Contracting State shall be taxable only in that other State.

2.   The term "royalties" as used in this Article means payments of any kind received as a consideration for the use of, or the right to use, any copyright of literary, artistic or scientific work including cinematograph films, any patent, trade mark, design or model, plan, secret formula or process, or for information concerning industrial, commercial or scientific experience.

3.   The provisions of paragraph 1 shall not apply if the beneficial owner of the royalties, being a resident of a Contracting State, carries on business in the other Contracting State in which the royalties arise through a permanent establishment situated therein and the right or property in respect of which the royalties are paid is effectively connected with such permanent establishment. In such case the provisions of Article 7 shall apply.

4.   Where, by reason of a special relationship between the payer and the beneficial owner or between both of them and some other person, the amount of the royalties, having regard to the use, right or information for which they are paid, exceeds the amount which would have been agreed upon by the payer and the beneficial owner in the absence of such relationship, the provisions of this Article shall apply only to the last-mentioned amount. In such case, the excess part of the payments shall remain taxable according to the laws of each Contracting State, due regard being had to the other provisions of this Convention.

ARTICLE 13

CAPITAL GAINS

1.   Gains derived by a resident of a Contracting State from the alienation of immovable property referred to in Article 6 and situated in the other Contracting State may be taxed in that other State.

2.   Gains from the alienation of movable property forming part of the business property of a permanent establishment which an enterprise of a Contracting State has in the other Contracting State, including such gains from the alienation of such a

permanent establishment (alone or with the whole enterprise), may be taxed in that other State.

3.   Gains from the alienation of ships or aircraft operated in international traffic, boats engaged in inland waterways transport or movable property pertaining to the operation of such ships, aircraft or boats, shall be taxable only in the Contracting State in which the place of effective management of the enterprise is situated.

4.   Gains derived by a resident of a Contracting State from the alienation of shares deriving more than 50 per cent of their value directly or indirectly from immovable property situated in the other Contracting State may be taxed in that other State.

5.   Gains from the alienation of any property, other than that referred to in paragraphs 1, 2, 3 and 4, shall be taxable only in the Contracting State of which the alienator is a resident.

[ARTICLE 14 - INDEPENDENT PERSONAL SERVICES]

[Deleted]

ARTICLE 15

INCOME FROM EMPLOYMENT

1.   Subject to the provisions of Articles 16, 18 and 19, salaries, wages and other similar remuneration derived by a resident of a Contracting State in respect of an employment shall be taxable only in that State unless the employment is exercised in the other Contracting State. If the employment is so exercised, such remuneration as is derived therefrom may be taxed in that other State.

2.   Notwithstanding the provisions of paragraph 1, remuneration derived by a resident of a Contracting State in respect of an employment exercised in the other Contracting State shall be taxable only in the first-mentioned State if:

   a) the recipient is present in the other State for a period or periods not exceeding in the aggregate 183 days in any twelve month period commencing or ending in the fiscal year concerned, and

   b) the remuneration is paid by, or on behalf of, an employer who is not a resident of the other State, and

   c) the remuneration is not borne by a permanent establishment which the employer has in the other State.

3.   Notwithstanding the preceding provisions of this Article, remuneration derived in respect of an employment exercised aboard a ship or aircraft operated in international traffic, or aboard a boat engaged in inland waterways transport, may be taxed in the Contracting State in which the place of effective management of the enterprise is situated.

ARTICLE 16

DIRECTORS' FEES

Directors' fees and other similar payments derived by a resident of a Contracting State in his capacity as a member of the board of directors of a company which is a resident of the other Contracting State may be taxed in that other State.

ARTICLE 17

ARTISTES AND SPORTSMEN

1.   Notwithstanding the provisions of Articles 7 and 15, income derived by a resident of a Contracting State as an entertainer, such as a theatre, motion picture, radio or television artiste, or a musician, or as a sportsman, from his personal activities as such exercised in the other Contracting State, may be taxed in that other State.

2.   Where income in respect of personal activities exercised by an entertainer or a sportsman in his capacity as such accrues not to the entertainer or sportsman himself but to another person, that income may, notwithstanding the provisions of Articles 7 and 15, be taxed in the Contracting State in which the activities of the entertainer or sportsman are exercised.

ARTICLE 18

PENSIONS

Subject to the provisions of paragraph 2 of Article 19, pensions and other similar remuneration paid to a resident of a Contracting State in consideration of past employment shall be taxable only in that State.

ARTICLE 19

GOVERNMENT SERVICE

1. a) Salaries, wages and other similar remuneration paid by a Contracting State or a political subdivision or a local authority thereof to an individual in respect of services rendered to that State or subdivision or authority shall be taxable only in that State.

   b) However, such salaries, wages and other similar remuneration shall be taxable only in the other Contracting State if the services are rendered in that State and the individual is a resident of that State who:

   (i)   is a national of that State; or

   (ii)   did not become a resident of that State solely for the purpose of rendering the services.

MODEL TAX CONVENTION (CONDENSED VERSION) – ISBN 978-92-64-08948-8 – © OECD 2010

2. *a)* Notwithstanding the provisions of paragraph 1, pensions and other similar remuneration paid by, or out of funds created by, a Contracting State or a political subdivision or a local authority thereof to an individual in respect of services rendered to that State or subdivision or authority shall be taxable only in that State.

   b) However, such pensions and other similar remuneration shall be taxable only in the other Contracting State if the individual is a resident of, and a national of, that State.

3. The provisions of Articles 15, 16, 17, and 18 shall apply to salaries, wages, pensions, and other similar remuneration in respect of services rendered in connection with a business carried on by a Contracting State or a political subdivision or a local authority thereof.

ARTICLE 20

STUDENTS

Payments which a student or business apprentice who is or was immediately before visiting a Contracting State a resident of the other Contracting State and who is present in the first-mentioned State solely for the purpose of his education or training receives for the purpose of his maintenance, education or training shall not be taxed in that State, provided that such payments arise from sources outside that State.

ARTICLE 21

OTHER INCOME

1. Items of income of a resident of a Contracting State, wherever arising, not dealt with in the foregoing Articles of this Convention shall be taxable only in that State.

2. The provisions of paragraph 1 shall not apply to income, other than income from immovable property as defined in paragraph 2 of Article 6, if the recipient of such income, being a resident of a Contracting State, carries on business in the other Contracting State through a permanent establishment situated therein and the right or property in respect of which the income is paid is effectively connected with such permanent establishment. In such case the provisions of Article 7 shall apply.

Chapter IV

TAXATION OF CAPITAL

ARTICLE 22

CAPITAL

1.   Capital represented by immovable property referred to in Article 6, owned by a resident of a Contracting State and situated in the other Contracting State, may be taxed in that other State.

2.   Capital represented by movable property forming part of the business property of a permanent establishment which an enterprise of a Contracting State has in the other Contracting State may be taxed in that other State.

3.   Capital represented by ships and aircraft operated in international traffic and by boats engaged in inland waterways transport, and by movable property pertaining to the operation of such ships, aircraft and boats, shall be taxable only in the Contracting State in which the place of effective management of the enterprise is situated.

4.   All other elements of capital of a resident of a Contracting State shall be taxable only in that State.

Chapter V

METHODS FOR ELIMINATION OF DOUBLE TAXATION

ARTICLE 23 A

EXEMPTION METHOD

1.   Where a resident of a Contracting State derives income or owns capital which, in accordance with the provisions of this Convention, may be taxed in the other Contracting State, the first-mentioned State shall, subject to the provisions of paragraphs 2 and 3, exempt such income or capital from tax.

2.   Where a resident of a Contracting State derives items of income which, in accordance with the provisions of Articles 10 and 11, may be taxed in the other Contracting State, the first-mentioned State shall allow as a deduction from the tax on the income of that resident an amount equal to the tax paid in that other State. Such deduction shall not, however, exceed that part of the tax, as computed before the deduction is given, which is attributable to such items of income derived from that other State.

3.   Where in accordance with any provision of the Convention income derived or capital owned by a resident of a Contracting State is exempt from tax in that State, such State may nevertheless, in calculating the amount of tax on the remaining income or capital of such resident, take into account the exempted income or capital.

4.   The provisions of paragraph 1 shall not apply to income derived or capital owned by a resident of a Contracting State where the other Contracting State applies the provisions of this Convention to exempt such income or capital from tax or applies the provisions of paragraph 2 of Article 10 or 11 to such income.

ARTICLE 23 B

CREDIT METHOD

1.   Where a resident of a Contracting State derives income or owns capital which, in accordance with the provisions of this Convention, may be taxed in the other Contracting State, the first-mentioned State shall allow:

  a) as a deduction from the tax on the income of that resident, an amount equal to the income tax paid in that other State;

  b) as a deduction from the tax on the capital of that resident, an amount equal to the capital tax paid in that other State.

Such deduction in either case shall not, however, exceed that part of the income tax or capital tax, as computed before the deduction is given, which is attributable, as the case may be, to the income or the capital which may be taxed in that other State.

2.   Where in accordance with any provision of the Convention income derived or capital owned by a resident of a Contracting State is exempt from tax in that State, such State may nevertheless, in calculating the amount of tax on the remaining income or capital of such resident, take into account the exempted income or capital.

Chapter VI

SPECIAL PROVISIONS

ARTICLE 24

NON-DISCRIMINATION

1.   Nationals of a Contracting State shall not be subjected in the other Contracting State to any taxation or any requirement connected therewith, which is other or more burdensome than the taxation and connected requirements to which nationals of that other State in the same circumstances, in particular with respect to residence, are or

may be subjected. This provision shall, notwithstanding the provisions of Article 1, also apply to persons who are not residents of one or both of the Contracting States.

2.   Stateless persons who are residents of a Contracting State shall not be subjected in either Contracting State to any taxation or any requirement connected therewith, which is other or more burdensome than the taxation and connected requirements to which nationals of the State concerned in the same circumstances, in particular with respect to residence, are or may be subjected.

3.   The taxation on a permanent establishment which an enterprise of a Contracting State has in the other Contracting State shall not be less favourably levied in that other State than the taxation levied on enterprises of that other State carrying on the same activities. This provision shall not be construed as obliging a Contracting State to grant to residents of the other Contracting State any personal allowances, reliefs and reductions for taxation purposes on account of civil status or family responsibilities which it grants to its own residents.

4.   Except where the provisions of paragraph 1 of Article 9, paragraph 6 of Article 11, or paragraph 4 of Article 12, apply, interest, royalties and other disbursements paid by an enterprise of a Contracting State to a resident of the other Contracting State shall, for the purpose of determining the taxable profits of such enterprise, be deductible under the same conditions as if they had been paid to a resident of the first-mentioned State. Similarly, any debts of an enterprise of a Contracting State to a resident of the other Contracting State shall, for the purpose of determining the taxable capital of such enterprise, be deductible under the same conditions as if they had been contracted to a resident of the first-mentioned State.

5.   Enterprises of a Contracting State, the capital of which is wholly or partly owned or controlled, directly or indirectly, by one or more residents of the other Contracting State, shall not be subjected in the first-mentioned State to any taxation or any requirement connected therewith which is other or more burdensome than the taxation and connected requirements to which other similar enterprises of the first-mentioned State are or may be subjected.

6.   The provisions of this Article shall, notwithstanding the provisions of Article 2, apply to taxes of every kind and description.

ARTICLE 25

MUTUAL AGREEMENT PROCEDURE

1.   Where a person considers that the actions of one or both of the Contracting States result or will result for him in taxation not in accordance with the provisions of this Convention, he may, irrespective of the remedies provided by the domestic law of those States, present his case to the competent authority of the Contracting State of which he is a resident or, if his case comes under paragraph 1 of Article 24, to that of

the Contracting State of which he is a national. The case must be presented within three years from the first notification of the action resulting in taxation not in accordance with the provisions of the Convention.

2.   The competent authority shall endeavour, if the objection appears to it to be justified and if it is not itself able to arrive at a satisfactory solution, to resolve the case by mutual agreement with the competent authority of the other Contracting State, with a view to the avoidance of taxation which is not in accordance with the Convention. Any agreement reached shall be implemented notwithstanding any time limits in the domestic law of the Contracting States.

3.   The competent authorities of the Contracting States shall endeavour to resolve by mutual agreement any difficulties or doubts arising as to the interpretation or application of the Convention. They may also consult together for the elimination of double taxation in cases not provided for in the Convention.

4.   The competent authorities of the Contracting States may communicate with each other directly, including through a joint commission consisting of themselves or their representatives, for the purpose of reaching an agreement in the sense of the preceding paragraphs.

5.   Where,

a) under paragraph 1, a person has presented a case to the competent authority of a Contracting State on the basis that the actions of one or both of the Contracting States have resulted for that person in taxation not in accordance with the provisions of this Convention, and

b) the competent authorities are unable to reach an agreement to resolve that case pursuant to paragraph 2 within two years from the presentation of the case to the competent authority of the other Contracting State,

any unresolved issues arising from the case shall be submitted to arbitration if the person so requests. These unresolved issues shall not, however, be submitted to arbitration if a decision on these issues has already been rendered by a court or administrative tribunal of either State. Unless a person directly affected by the case does not accept the mutual agreement that implements the arbitration decision, that decision shall be binding on both Contracting States and shall be implemented notwithstanding any time limits in the domestic laws of these States. The competent authorities of the Contracting States shall by mutual agreement settle the mode of application of this paragraph.[1]

---

[1] In some States, national law, policy or administrative considerations may not allow or justify the type of dispute resolution envisaged under this paragraph. In addition, some States may only wish to include this paragraph in treaties with certain States. For these reasons, the paragraph should only be included in the Convention where each State concludes that it would be appropriate to do so based on the factors described in paragraph 65 of the Commentary on the paragraph. As mentioned in paragraph 74 of that Commentary, however, other States may be able to agree to remove from the paragraph the condition that issues may not be submitted to arbitration if a decision on these issues has already been rendered by one of their courts or administrative tribunals.

ARTICLE 26

EXCHANGE OF INFORMATION

1.   The competent authorities of the Contracting States shall exchange such information as is foreseeably relevant for carrying out the provisions of this Convention or to the administration or enforcement of the domestic laws concerning taxes of every kind and description imposed on behalf of the Contracting States, or of their political subdivisions or local authorities, insofar as the taxation thereunder is not contrary to the Convention. The exchange of information is not restricted by Articles 1 and 2.

2.   Any information received under paragraph 1 by a Contracting State shall be treated as secret in the same manner as information obtained under the domestic laws of that State and shall be disclosed only to persons or authorities (including courts and administrative bodies) concerned with the assessment or collection of, the enforcement or prosecution in respect of, the determination of appeals in relation to the taxes referred to in paragraph 1, or the oversight of the above. Such persons or authorities shall use the information only for such purposes. They may disclose the information in public court proceedings or in judicial decisions.

3.   In no case shall the provisions of paragraphs 1 and 2 be construed so as to impose on a Contracting State the obligation:

   a) to carry out administrative measures at variance with the laws and administrative practice of that or of the other Contracting State;

   b) to supply information which is not obtainable under the laws or in the normal course of the administration of that or of the other Contracting State;

   c) to supply information which would disclose any trade, business, industrial, commercial or professional secret or trade process, or information the disclosure of which would be contrary to public policy (ordre public).

4.   If information is requested by a Contracting State in accordance with this Article, the other Contracting State shall use its information gathering measures to obtain the requested information, even though that other State may not need such information for its own tax purposes. The obligation contained in the preceding sentence is subject to the limitations of paragraph 3 but in no case shall such limitations be construed to permit a Contracting State to decline to supply information solely because it has no domestic interest in such information.

5.   In no case shall the provisions of paragraph 3 be construed to permit a Contracting State to decline to supply information solely because the information is held by a bank, other financial institution, nominee or person acting in an agency or a fiduciary capacity or because it relates to ownership interests in a person.

MODEL TAX CONVENTION (CONDENSED VERSION) – ISBN 978-92-64-08948-8 – © OECD 2010

ARTICLE 27

ASSISTANCE IN THE COLLECTION OF TAXES[1]

1.   The Contracting States shall lend assistance to each other in the collection of revenue claims. This assistance is not restricted by Articles 1 and 2. The competent authorities of the Contracting States may by mutual agreement settle the mode of application of this Article.

2.   The term "revenue claim" as used in this Article means an amount owed in respect of taxes of every kind and description imposed on behalf of the Contracting States, or of their political subdivisions or local authorities, insofar as the taxation thereunder is not contrary to this Convention or any other instrument to which the Contracting States are parties, as well as interest, administrative penalties and costs of collection or conservancy related to such amount.

3.   When a revenue claim of a Contracting State is enforceable under the laws of that State and is owed by a person who, at that time, cannot, under the laws of that State, prevent its collection, that revenue claim shall, at the request of the competent authority of that State, be accepted for purposes of collection by the competent authority of the other Contracting State. That revenue claim shall be collected by that other State in accordance with the provisions of its laws applicable to the enforcement and collection of its own taxes as if the revenue claim were a revenue claim of that other State.

4.   When a revenue claim of a Contracting State is a claim in respect of which that State may, under its law, take measures of conservancy with a view to ensure its collection, that revenue claim shall, at the request of the competent authority of that State, be accepted for purposes of taking measures of conservancy by the competent authority of the other Contracting State. That other State shall take measures of conservancy in respect of that revenue claim in accordance with the provisions of its laws as if the revenue claim were a revenue claim of that other State even if, at the time when such measures are applied, the revenue claim is not enforceable in the first-mentioned State or is owed by a person who has a right to prevent its collection.

5.   Notwithstanding the provisions of paragraphs 3 and 4, a revenue claim accepted by a Contracting State for purposes of paragraph 3 or 4 shall not, in that State, be subject to the time limits or accorded any priority applicable to a revenue claim under the laws of that State by reason of its nature as such. In addition, a revenue claim accepted by a Contracting State for the purposes of paragraph 3 or 4 shall not, in that

---

1   In some countries, national law, policy or administrative considerations may not allow or justify the type of assistance envisaged under this Article or may require that this type of assistance be restricted, e.g. to countries that have similar tax systems or tax administrations or as to the taxes covered. For that reason, the Article should only be included in the Convention where each State concludes that, based on the factors described in paragraph 1 of the Commentary on the Article, they can agree to provide assistance in the collection of taxes levied by the other State.

State, have any priority applicable to that revenue claim under the laws of the other Contracting State.

6.   Proceedings with respect to the existence, validity or the amount of a revenue claim of a Contracting State shall not be brought before the courts or administrative bodies of the other Contracting State.

7.   Where, at any time after a request has been made by a Contracting State under paragraph 3 or 4 and before the other Contracting State has collected and remitted the relevant revenue claim to the first-mentioned State, the relevant revenue claim ceases to be

a) in the case of a request under paragraph 3, a revenue claim of the first-mentioned State that is enforceable under the laws of that State and is owed by a person who, at that time, cannot, under the laws of that State, prevent its collection, or

b) in the case of a request under paragraph 4, a revenue claim of the first-mentioned State in respect of which that State may, under its laws, take measures of conservancy with a view to ensure its collection

the competent authority of the first-mentioned State shall promptly notify the competent authority of the other State of that fact and, at the option of the other State, the first-mentioned State shall either suspend or withdraw its request.

8.   In no case shall the provisions of this Article be construed so as to impose on a Contracting State the obligation:

a) to carry out administrative measures at variance with the laws and administrative practice of that or of the other Contracting State;

b) to carry out measures which would be contrary to public policy (ordre public);

c) to provide assistance if the other Contracting State has not pursued all reasonable measures of collection or conservancy, as the case may be, available under its laws or administrative practice;

d) to provide assistance in those cases where the administrative burden for that State is clearly disproportionate to the benefit to be derived by the other Contracting State.

ARTICLE 28

MEMBERS OF DIPLOMATIC MISSIONS AND CONSULAR POSTS

Nothing in this Convention shall affect the fiscal privileges of members of diplomatic missions or consular posts under the general rules of international law or under the provisions of special agreements.

ARTICLE 29
TERRITORIAL EXTENSION[1]

1.   This Convention may be extended, either in its entirety or with any necessary modifications [to any part of the territory of (State A) or of (State B) which is specifically excluded from the application of the Convention or], to any State or territory for whose international relations (State A) or (State B) is responsible, which imposes taxes substantially similar in character to those to which the Convention applies. Any such extension shall take effect from such date and subject to such modifications and conditions, including conditions as to termination, as may be specified and agreed between the Contracting States in notes to be exchanged through diplomatic channels or in any other manner in accordance with their constitutional procedures.

2.   Unless otherwise agreed by both Contracting States, the termination of the Convention by one of them under Article 30 shall also terminate, in the manner provided for in that Article, the application of the Convention [to any part of the territory of (State A) or of (State B) or] to any State or territory to which it has been extended under this Article.

Chapter VII
FINAL PROVISIONS

ARTICLE 30
ENTRY INTO FORCE

1.   This Convention shall be ratified and the instruments of ratification shall be exchanged at .... as soon as possible.

2.   The Convention shall enter into force upon the exchange of instruments of ratification and its provisions shall have effect:

a) (in State A): ....
b) (in State B): ....

---

1   The words between brackets are of relevance when, by special provision, a part of the territory of a Contracting State is excluded from the application of the Convention.

ARTICLE 31

TERMINATION

This Convention shall remain in force until terminated by a Contracting State. Either Contracting State may terminate the Convention, through diplomatic channels, by giving notice of termination at least six months before the end of any calendar year after the year ...... In such event, the Convention shall cease to have effect:

a) (in State A): ....

b) (in State B): ....

TERMINAL CLAUSE[1]

---

1 The terminal clause concerning the signing shall be drafted in accordance with the constitutional procedure of both Contracting States.

COMMENTARIES ON THE ARTICLES
OF THE MODEL TAX CONVENTION

COMMENTARY ON ARTICLE 1
CONCERNING THE PERSONS COVERED BY THE CONVENTION

1.   Whereas the earliest conventions in general were applicable to "citizens" of the Contracting States, more recent conventions usually apply to "residents" of one or both of the Contracting States irrespective of nationality. Some conventions are of even wider scope because they apply more generally to "taxpayers" of the Contracting States; they are, therefore, also applicable to persons, who, although not residing in either State, are nevertheless liable to tax on part of their income or capital in each of them. It has been deemed preferable for practical reasons to provide that the Convention is to apply to persons who are residents of one or both of the Contracting States. The term "resident" is defined in Article 4.

Application of the Convention to partnerships

2.   Domestic laws differ in the treatment of partnerships. These differences create various difficulties when applying tax Conventions in relation to partnerships. These difficulties are analysed in the report by the Committee on Fiscal Affairs entitled "The Application of the OECD Model Tax Convention to Partnerships",[1] the conclusions of which have been incorporated below and in the Commentary on various other provisions of the Model Tax Convention.

3.   As discussed in that report, a main source of difficulties is the fact that some countries treat partnerships as taxable units (sometimes even as companies) whereas other countries adopt what may be referred to as the fiscally transparent approach, under which the partnership is ignored for tax purposes and the individual partners are taxed on their respective share of the partnership's income.

4.   A first difficulty is the extent to which a partnership is entitled as such to the benefits of the provisions of the Convention. Under Article 1, only persons who are residents of the Contracting States are entitled to the benefits of the tax Convention entered into by these States. While paragraph 2 of the Commentary on Article 3 explains why a partnership constitutes a person, a partnership does not necessarily qualify as a resident of a Contracting State under Article 4.

5.   Where a partnership is treated as a company or taxed in the same way, it is a resident of the Contracting State that taxes the partnership on the grounds mentioned in paragraph 1 of Article 4 and, therefore, it is entitled to the benefits of the Convention. Where, however, a partnership is treated as fiscally transparent in a State, the partnership is not "liable to tax" in that State within the meaning of paragraph 1 of Article 4, and so cannot be a resident thereof for purposes of the Convention. In such a case, the application of the Convention to the partnership as such would be refused, unless a special rule covering partnerships were provided for in the Convention. Where the application of the Convention is so refused, the partners should be entitled, with

---

1 Reproduced in Volume II of the full-length version of the OECD Model Tax Convention at page R(15)-1.

respect to their share of the income of the partnership, to the benefits provided by the Conventions entered into by the States of which they are residents to the extent that the partnership's income is allocated to them for the purposes of taxation in their State of residence (see paragraph 8.8 of the Commentary on Article 4).

6.   The relationship between the partnership's entitlement to the benefits of a tax Convention and that of the partners raises other questions.

6.1   One issue is the effect that the application of the provisions of the Convention to a partnership can have on the taxation of the partners. Where a partnership is treated as a resident of a Contracting State, the provisions of the Convention that restrict the other Contracting State's right to tax the partnership on its income do not apply to restrict that other State's right to tax the partners who are its own residents on their share of the income of the partnership. Some states may wish to include in their conventions a provision that expressly confirms a Contracting State's right to tax resident partners on their share of the income of a partnership that is treated as a resident of the other State.

6.2   Another issue is that of the effect of the provisions of the Convention on a Contracting State's right to tax income arising on its territory where the entitlement to the benefits of one, or more than one, Conventions is different for the partners and the partnership. Where, for instance, the State of source treats a domestic partnership as fiscally transparent and therefore taxes the partners on their share of the income of the partnership, a partner that is resident of a State that taxes partnerships as companies would not be able to claim the benefits of the Convention between the two States with respect to the share of the partnership's income that the State of source taxes in his hands since that income, though allocated to the person claiming the benefits of the Convention under the laws of the State of source, is not similarly allocated for purposes of determining the liability to tax on that item of income in the State of residence of that person.

6.3   The results described in the preceding paragraph should obtain even if, as a matter of the domestic law of the State of source, the partnership would not be regarded as transparent for tax purposes but as a separate taxable entity to which the income would be attributed, provided that the partnership is not actually considered as a resident of the State of source. This conclusion is founded upon the principle that the State of source should take into account, as part of the factual context in which the Convention is to be applied, the way in which an item of income, arising in its jurisdiction, is treated in the jurisdiction of the person claiming the benefits of the Convention as a resident. For States which could not agree with this interpretation of the Article, it would be possible to provide for this result in a special provision which would avoid the resulting potential double taxation where the income of the partnership is differently allocated by the two States.

6.4   Where, as described in paragraph 6.2, income has "flowed through" a transparent partnership to the partners who are liable to tax on that income in the State of their residence then the income is appropriately viewed as "paid" to the partners since it is to them and not to the partnership that the income is allocated for purposes of determining their tax liability in their State of residence. Hence the partners, in these circumstances, satisfy the condition, imposed in several Articles, that the income concerned is "paid to a resident of the other Contracting State". Similarly the requirement, imposed by some other Articles, that income or gains are "derived by a resident of the other Contracting State" is met in the circumstances described above. This interpretation avoids denying the benefits of tax Conventions to a partnership's income on the basis that neither the partnership, because it is not a resident, nor the partners, because the income is not directly paid to them or derived by them, can claim the benefits of the Convention with respect to that income. Following from the principle discussed in paragraph 6.3, the conditions that the income be paid to, or derived by, a resident should be considered to be satisfied even where, as a matter of the domestic law of the State of source, the partnership would not be regarded as transparent for tax purposes, provided that the partnership is not actually considered as a resident of the State of source.

6.5   Partnership cases involving three States pose difficult problems with respect to the determination of entitlement to benefits under Conventions. However, many problems may be solved through the application of the principles described in paragraphs 6.2 to 6.4. Where a partner is a resident of one State, the partnership is established in another State and the partner shares in partnership income arising in a third State then the partner may claim the benefits of the Convention between his State of residence and the State of source of the income to the extent that the partnership's income is allocated to him for the purposes of taxation in his State of residence. If, in addition, the partnership is taxed as a resident of the State in which it is established then the partnership may itself claim the benefits of the Convention between the State in which it is established and the State of source. In such a case of "double benefits", the State of source may not impose taxation which is inconsistent with the terms of either applicable Convention; therefore, where different rates are provided for in the two Conventions, the lower will be applied. However, Contracting States may wish to consider special provisions to deal with the administration of benefits under Conventions in situations such as these, so that the partnership may claim benefits but partners could not present concurrent claims. Such provisions could ensure appropriate and simplified administration of the giving of benefits. No benefits will be available under the Convention between the State in which the partnership is established and the State of source if the partnership is regarded as transparent for tax purposes by the State in which it is established. Similarly no benefits will be available under the Convention between the State of residence of the partner and the State of source if the income of the partnership is not allocated to the partner under the taxation law of the State of residence. If the partnership is regarded as transparent for tax purposes by the State in which it is established and the income of the partnership is not allocated to the partner under the taxation law of the State of residence of the partner, the State of source may tax partnership income allocable to the partner without restriction.

6.6   Differences in how countries apply the fiscally transparent approach may create other difficulties for the application of tax Conventions. Where a State considers that a partnership does not qualify as a resident of a Contracting State because it is not liable to tax and the partners are liable to tax in their State of residence on their share of the partnership's income, it is expected that that State will apply the provisions of the Convention as if the partners had earned the income directly so that the classification of the income for purposes of the allocative rules of Articles 6 to 21 will not be modified by the fact that the income flows through the partnership. Difficulties may arise, however, in the application of provisions which refer to the activities of the taxpayer, the nature of the taxpayer, the relationship between the taxpayer and another party to a transaction. Some of these difficulties are discussed in paragraphs 19.1 of the Commentary on Article 5 and paragraphs 6.1 and 6.2 of the Commentary on Article 15.

6.7   Finally, a number of other difficulties arise where different rules of the Convention are applied by the Contracting States to income derived by a partnership or its partners, depending on the domestic laws of these States or their interpretation of the provisions of the Convention or of the relevant facts. These difficulties relate to the broader issue of conflicts of qualification, which is dealt with in paragraphs 32.1 ff. and 56.1 ff. of the Commentary on Article 23.

Cross-Border Issues Relating to Collective Investment Vehicles

6.8   Most countries have dealt with the domestic tax issues arising from groups of small investors who pool their funds in collective investment vehicles (CIVs). In general, the goal of such systems is to provide for neutrality between direct investments and investments through a CIV. Whilst those systems generally succeed when the investors, the CIV and the investment are all located in the same country, complications frequently arise when one or more of those parties or the investments are located in different countries. These complications are discussed in the report by the Committee on Fiscal Affairs entitled "The Granting of Treaty Benefits with Respect to the Income of Collective Investment Vehicles",[1] the main conclusions of which have been incorporated below. For purposes of the Report and for this discussion, the term "CIV" is limited to funds that are widely-held, hold a diversified portfolio of securities and are subject to investor-protection regulation in the country in which they are established.

Application of the Convention to CIVs

6.9   The primary question that arises in the cross-border context is whether a CIV should qualify for the benefits of the Convention in its own right. In order to do so under treaties that, like the Convention, do not include a specific provision dealing with CIVs, a CIV would have to qualify as a "person" that is a "resident" of a Contracting

---

1   Reproduced in Volume II of the full-length version of the OECD Model Tax Convention at page R(24)-1.

State and, as regards the application of Articles 10 and 11, that is the "beneficial owner" of the income that it receives.

6.10   The determination of whether a CIV should be treated as a "person" begins with the legal form of the CIV, which differs substantially from country to country and between the various types of vehicles. In many countries, most CIVs take the form of a company. In others, the CIV typically would be a trust. In still others, many CIVs are simple contractual arrangements or a form of joint ownership. In most cases, the CIV would be treated as a taxpayer or a "person" for purposes of the tax law of the State in which it is established; for example, in some countries where the CIV is commonly established in the form of a trust, either the trust itself, or the trustees acting collectively in their capacity as such, is treated as a taxpayer or a person for domestic tax law purposes. In view of the wide meaning to be given to the term "person", the fact that the tax law of the country where such a CIV is established would treat it as a taxpayer would be indicative that the CIV is a "person" for treaty purposes. Contracting States wishing to expressly clarify that, in these circumstances, such CIVs are persons for the purposes of their conventions may agree bilaterally to modify the definition of "person" to include them.

6.11   Whether a CIV is a "resident" of a Contracting State depends not on its legal form (as long as it qualifies as a person) but on its tax treatment in the State in which it is established. Although a consistent goal of domestic CIV regimes is to ensure that there is only one level of tax, at either the CIV or the investor level, there are a number of different ways in which States achieve that goal. In some States, the holders of interests in the CIV are liable to tax on the income received by the CIV, rather than the CIV itself being liable to tax on such income. Such a fiscally transparent CIV would not be treated as a resident of the Contracting State in which it is established because it is not liable to tax therein.

6.12   By contrast, in other States, a CIV is in principle liable to tax but its income may be fully exempt, for instance, if the CIV fulfils certain criteria with regard to its purpose, activities or operation, which may include requirements as to minimum distributions, its sources of income and sometimes its sectors of operation. More frequently, CIVs are subject to tax but the base for taxation is reduced, in a variety of different ways, by reference to distributions paid to investors. Deductions for distributions will usually mean that no tax is in fact paid. Other States tax CIVs but at a special low tax rate. Finally, some States tax CIVs fully but with integration at the investor level to avoid double taxation of the income of the CIV. For those countries that adopt the view, reflected in paragraph 8.6 of the Commentary on Article 4, that a person may be liable to tax even if the State in which it is established does not impose tax, the CIV would be treated as a resident of the State in which it is established in all of these cases because the CIV is subject to comprehensive taxation in that State. Even in the case where the income of the CIV is taxed at a zero rate, or is exempt from tax, the requirements to be treated as a resident may be met if the requirements to qualify for such lower rate or exemption are sufficiently stringent.

6.13   Those countries that adopt the alternative view, reflected in paragraph 8.7 of the Commentary on Article 4, that an entity that is exempt from tax therefore is not liable to tax may not view some or all of the CIVs described in the preceding paragraph as residents of the States in which they are established. States taking the latter view, and those States negotiating with such States, are encouraged to address the issue in their bilateral negotiations.

6.14   Some countries have questioned whether a CIV, even if it is a "person" and a "resident", can qualify as the beneficial owner of the income it receives. Because a "CIV" as defined in paragraph 6.8 above must be widely-held, hold a diversified portfolio of securities and be subject to investor-protection regulation in the country in which it is established, such a CIV, or its managers, often perform significant functions with respect to the investment and management of the assets of the CIV. Moreover, the position of an investor in a CIV differs substantially, as a legal and economic matter, from the position of an investor who owns the underlying assets, so that it would not be appropriate to treat the investor in such a CIV as the beneficial owner of the income received by the CIV. Accordingly, a vehicle that meets the definition of a widely-held CIV will also be treated as the beneficial owner of the dividends and interest that it receives, so long as the managers of the CIV have discretionary powers to manage the assets generating such income (unless an individual who is a resident of that State who would have received the income in the same circumstances would not have been considered to be the beneficial owner thereof).

6.15   Because these principles are necessarily general, their application to a particular type of CIV might not be clear to the CIV, investors and intermediaries. Any uncertainty regarding treaty eligibility is especially problematic for a CIV, which must take into account amounts expected to be received, including any withholding tax benefits provided by treaty, when it calculates its net asset value ("NAV"). The NAV, which typically is calculated daily, is the basis for the prices used for subscriptions and redemptions. If the withholding tax benefits ultimately obtained by the CIV do not correspond to its original assumptions about the amount and timing of such withholding tax benefits, there will be a discrepancy between the real asset value and the NAV used by investors who have purchased, sold or redeemed their interests in the CIV in the interim.

6.16   In order to provide more certainty under existing treaties, tax authorities may want to reach a mutual agreement clarifying the treatment of some types of CIVs in their respective States. With respect to some types of CIVs, such a mutual agreement might simply confirm that the CIV satisfies the technical requirements discussed above and therefore is entitled to benefits in its own right. In other cases, the mutual agreement could provide a CIV an administratively feasible way to make claims with respect to treaty-eligible investors (see paragraphs 36 to 40 of the report "The Granting of Treaty Benefits with Respect to the Income of Collective Investment Vehicles" for a discussion of this issue). Of course, a mutual agreement could not cut back on benefits that otherwise would be available to the CIV under the terms of a treaty.

Policy issues raised by the current treatment of collective investment vehicles

6.17 The same considerations would suggest that treaty negotiators address expressly the treatment of CIVs. Thus, even if it appears that CIVs in each of the Contracting States would be entitled to benefits, it may be appropriate to confirm that position publicly (for example, through an exchange of notes) in order to provide certainty. It may also be appropriate to expressly provide for the treaty entitlement of CIVs by including, for example, a provision along the following lines:

Notwithstanding the other provisions of this Convention, a collective investment vehicle which is established in a Contracting State and which receives income arising in the other Contracting State shall be treated, for purposes of applying the Convention to such income, as an individual who is a resident of the Contracting State in which it is established and as the beneficial owner of the income it receives (provided that, if an individual who is a resident of the first-mentioned State had received the income in the same circumstances, such individual would have been considered to be the beneficial owner thereof). For purposes of this paragraph, the term "collective investment vehicle" means, in the case of [State A], a [ ] and, in the case of [State B], a [ ], as well as any other investment fund, arrangement or entity established in either Contracting State which the competent authorities of the Contracting States agree to regard as a collective investment vehicle for purposes of this paragraph.

6.18 However, in negotiating new treaties or amendments to existing treaties, the Contracting States would not be restricted to clarifying the results of the application of other treaty provisions to CIVs, but could vary those results to the extent necessary to achieve policy objectives. For example, in the context of a particular bilateral treaty, the technical analysis may result in CIVs located in one of the Contracting States qualifying for benefits, whilst CIVs in the other Contracting State may not. This may make the treaty appear unbalanced, although whether it is so in fact will depend on the specific circumstances. If it is, then the Contracting States should attempt to reach an equitable solution. If the practical result in each of the Contracting States is that most CIVs do not in fact pay tax, then the Contracting States should attempt to overcome differences in legal form that might otherwise cause those in one State to qualify for benefits and those in the other to be denied benefits. On the other hand, the differences in legal form and tax treatment in the two Contracting States may mean that it is appropriate to treat CIVs in the two States differently. In comparing the taxation of CIVs in the two States, taxation in the source State and at the investor level should be considered, not just the taxation of the CIV itself. The goal is to achieve neutrality between a direct investment and an investment through a CIV in the international context, just as the goal of most domestic provisions addressing the treatment of CIVs is to achieve such neutrality in the wholly domestic context.

6.19 A Contracting State may also want to consider whether existing treaty provisions are sufficient to prevent CIVs from being used in a potentially abusive manner. It is possible that a CIV could satisfy all of the requirements to claim treaty benefits in its own right, even though its income is not subject to much, if any, tax in practice. In that case, the CIV could present the opportunity for residents of third countries to receive treaty benefits that would not have been available had they invested directly. Accordingly, it may be appropriate to restrict benefits that might otherwise be available to such a CIV, either through generally applicable anti-abuse or anti-treaty shopping rules (as discussed under "Improper use of the Convention" below) or through a specific provision dealing with CIVs.

6.20   In deciding whether such a provision is necessary, Contracting States will want to consider the economic characteristics, including the potential for treaty shopping, presented by the various types of CIVs that are prevalent in each of the Contracting States. For example, a CIV that is not subject to any taxation in the State in which it is established may present more of a danger of treaty shopping than one in which the CIV itself is subject to an entity-level tax or where distributions to non-resident investors are subject to withholding tax.

Possible provisions modifying the treatment of CIVs

6.21   Where the Contracting States have agreed that a specific provision dealing with CIVs is necessary to address the concerns described in paragraphs 6.18 through 6.20, they could include in the bilateral treaty the following provision:

a) Notwithstanding the other provisions of this Convention, a collective investment vehicle which is established in a Contracting State and which receives income arising in the other Contracting State shall be treated for purposes of applying the Convention to such income as an individual who is a resident of the Contracting State in which it is established and as the beneficial owner of the income it receives (provided that, if an individual who is a resident of the first-mentioned State had received the income in the same circumstances, such individual would have been considered to be the beneficial owner thereof), but only to the extent that the beneficial interests in the collective investment vehicle are owned by equivalent beneficiaries.

b) For purposes of this paragraph:

(i) the term "collective investment vehicle" means, in the case of [State A], a [ ] and, in the case of [State B], a [ ], as well as any other investment fund, arrangement or entity established in either Contracting State which the competent authorities of the Contracting States agree to regard as a collective investment vehicle for purposes of this paragraph; and

(ii) the term "equivalent beneficiary" means a resident of the Contracting State in which the CIV is established, and a resident of any other State with which the Contracting State in which the income arises has an income tax convention that provides for effective and comprehensive information exchange who would, if he received the particular item of income for which benefits are being claimed under this Convention, be entitled under that convention, or under the domestic law of the Contracting State in which the income arises, to a rate of tax with respect to that item of income that is at least as low as the rate claimed under this Convention by the CIV with respect to that item of income.

6.22 It is intended that the Contracting States would provide in subdivision *b)(i)* specific cross-references to relevant tax or securities law provisions relating to CIVs. In deciding which treatment should apply with respect to particular CIVs, Contracting States should take into account the policy considerations discussed above. Negotiators may agree that economic differences in the treatment of CIVs in the two Contracting States, or even within the same Contracting State, justify differential treatment in the tax treaty. In that case, some combination of the provisions in this section might be included in the treaty.

6.23 The effect of allowing benefits to the CIV to the extent that it is owned by "equivalent beneficiaries" as defined in subdivision *b)(ii)* is to ensure that investors who would have been entitled to benefits with respect to income derived from the source State had they received the income directly are not put in a worse position by investing through a CIV located in a third country. The approach thus serves the goals of neutrality as between direct investments and investments through a CIV. It also decreases the risk of double taxation as between the source State and the State of residence of the investor, to the extent that there is a tax treaty between them. It is beneficial for investors, particularly those from small countries, who will consequently enjoy a greater choice of investment vehicles. It also increases economies of scale, which are a primary economic benefit of investing through CIVs. Finally, adopting this approach substantially simplifies compliance procedures. In many cases, nearly all of a CIV's investors will be "equivalent beneficiaries", given the extent of bilateral treaty coverage and the fact that rates in those treaties are nearly always 10-15 per cent on portfolio dividends.

6.24 At the same time, the provision prevents a CIV from being used by investors to achieve a better tax treaty position than they would have achieved by investing directly. This is achieved through the rate comparison in the definition of "equivalent beneficiary". Accordingly, the appropriate comparison is between the rate claimed by the CIV and the rate that the investor could have claimed had it received the income directly. For example, assume that a CIV established in State B receives dividends from a company resident in State A. Sixty-five per cent of the investors in the CIV are individual residents of State B; ten per cent are pension funds established in State C and 25 per cent are individual residents of State C. Under the A-B tax treaty, portfolio dividends are subject to a maximum tax rate at source of ten per cent. Under the A-C tax treaty, pension funds are exempt from taxation in the source State and other portfolio dividends are subject to tax at a maximum tax rate of 15 per cent. Both the A-B and A-C treaties include effective and comprehensive information exchange provisions. On these facts, 75 per cent of the investors in the CIV — the individual residents of State B and the pension funds established in State C — are equivalent beneficiaries.

6.25 A source State may also be concerned about the potential deferral of taxation that could arise with respect to a CIV that is subject to no or low taxation and that may accumulate its income rather than distributing it on a current basis. Such States may be tempted to limit benefits to the CIV to the proportion of the CIV's investors who are currently taxable on their share of the income of the CIV. However, such an approach has proven difficult to apply to widely-held CIVs in practice. Those States that are concerned about the possibility of such deferral may wish to negotiate provisions that extend benefits only to those CIVs that are required to distribute earnings currently. Other States may be less concerned about the potential for deferral, however. They may take the view that, even if the investor is not taxed currently on the income received by the CIV, it will be taxed eventually, either on the distribution, or on any capital gains if it sells its interest in the CIV before the CIV distributes the income. Those States may wish to negotiate provisions that grant benefits to CIVs even if they are not obliged to distribute their income on a current basis. Moreover, in many States, the tax rate with respect to investment income is not significantly higher than the treaty withholding rate on dividends, so there would be little, if any, residence State tax deferral to be achieved by earning such income through an investment fund rather than directly. In addition, many States have taken steps to ensure the current taxation of investment income earned by their residents through investment funds, regardless of whether the funds accumulate that income, further reducing the potential for such deferral. When considering the treatment of CIVs that are not required to distribute income currently, States may want to consider whether these or other factors address the concerns described above so that the type of limits described herein might not in fact be necessary.

6.26 Some States believe that taking all treaty-eligible investors, including those in third States, into account would change the bilateral nature of tax treaties. These States may prefer to allow treaty benefits to a CIV only to the extent that the investors in the CIV are residents of the Contracting State in which the CIV is established. In that case, the provision would be drafted as follows:

a) Notwithstanding the other provisions of this Convention, a collective investment vehicle which is established in a Contracting State and which receives income arising in the other Contracting State shall be treated for purposes of applying the Convention to such income as an individual who is a resident of the Contracting State in which it is established and as the beneficial owner of the income it receives (provided that, if an individual who is a resident of the first-mentioned State had received the income in the same circumstances, such individual would have been considered to be the beneficial owner thereof), but only to the extent that the beneficial interests in the collective investment vehicle are owned by residents of the Contracting State in which the collective investment vehicle is established.

b) For purposes of this paragraph, the term "collective investment vehicle" means, in the case of [State A], a [ ] and, in the case of [State B], a [ ], as well as any other investment fund, arrangement or entity established in either Contracting State which the competent authorities of the Contracting States agree to regard as a collective investment vehicle for purposes of this paragraph.

6.27   Although the purely proportionate approach set out in paragraphs 6.21 and 6.26 protects against treaty shopping, it may also impose substantial administrative burdens as a CIV attempts to determine the treaty entitlement of every single investor. A Contracting State may decide that the fact that a substantial proportion of the CIV's investors are treaty-eligible is adequate protection against treaty shopping, and thus that it is appropriate to provide an ownership threshold above which benefits would be provided with respect to all income received by the CIV. Including such a threshold would also mitigate some of the procedural burdens that otherwise might arise. If desired, therefore, the following sentence could be added at the end of subparagraph a):

> However, if at least [ ] per cent of the beneficial interests in the collective investment vehicle are owned by [equivalent beneficiaries][residents of the Contracting State in which the collective investment vehicle is established], the collective investment vehicle shall be treated as an individual who is a resident of the Contracting State in which it is established and as the beneficial owner of all of the income it receives (provided that, if an individual who is a resident of the first-mentioned State had received the income in the same circumstances, such individual would have been considered to be the beneficial owner thereof).

6.28   In some cases, the Contracting States might wish to take a different approach from that put forward in paragraphs 6.17, 6.21 and 6.26 with respect to certain types of CIVs and to treat the CIV as making claims on behalf of the investors rather than in its own name. This might be true, for example, if a large percentage of the owners of interests in the CIV as a whole, or of a class of interests in the CIV, are pension funds that are exempt from tax in the source country under terms of the relevant treaty similar to those described in paragraph 69 of the Commentary on Article 18. To ensure that the investors would not lose the benefit of the preferential rates to which they would have been entitled had they invested directly, the Contracting States might agree to a provision along the following lines with respect to such CIVs (although likely adopting one of the approaches of paragraph 6.17, 6.21 or 6.26 with respect to other types of CIVs):

a)   A collective investment vehicle described in subparagraph c) which is established in a Contracting State and which receives income arising in the other Contracting State shall not be treated as a resident of the Contracting State in which it is established, but may claim, on behalf of the owners of the beneficial interests in the collective investment vehicle, the tax reductions, exemptions or other benefits that would have been available under this Convention to such owners had they received such income directly.

b)   A collective investment vehicle may not make a claim under subparagraph a) for benefits on behalf of any owner of the beneficial interests in such collective investment vehicle if the owner has itself made an individual claim for benefits with respect to income received by the collective investment vehicle.

c) This paragraph shall apply with respect to, in the case of [State A], a [ ] and, in the case of [State B], a [ ], as well as any other investment fund, arrangement or entity established in either Contracting State to which the competent authorities of the Contracting States agree to apply this paragraph.

This provision would, however, limit the CIV to making claims on behalf of residents of the same Contracting State in which the CIV is established. If, for the reasons described in paragraph 6.23, the Contracting States deemed it desirable to allow the CIV to make claims on behalf of treaty-eligible residents of third States, that could be accomplished by replacing the words "this Convention" with "any Convention to which the other Contracting State is a party" in subparagraph a). If, as anticipated, the Contracting States would agree that the treatment provided in this paragraph would apply only to specific types of CIVs, it would be necessary to ensure that the types of CIVs listed in subparagraph c) did not include any of the types of CIVs listed in a more general provision such as that in paragraph 6.17, 6.21 or 6.26 so that the treatment of a specific type of CIV would be fixed, rather than elective. Countries wishing to allow individual CIVs to elect their treatment, either with respect to the CIV as a whole or with respect to one or more classes of interests in the CIV, are free to modify the paragraph to do so.

6.29 Under either the approach in paragraphs 6.21 and 6.26 or in paragraph 6.28, it will be necessary for the CIV to make a determination regarding the proportion of holders of interests who would have been entitled to benefits had they invested directly. Because ownership of interests in CIVs changes regularly, and such interests frequently are held through intermediaries, the CIV and its managers often do not themselves know the names and treaty status of the beneficial owners of interests. It would be impractical for the CIV to collect such information from the relevant intermediaries on a daily basis. Accordingly, Contracting States should be willing to accept practical and reliable approaches that do not require such daily tracing.

6.30 For example, in many countries the CIV industry is largely domestic, with an overwhelming percentage of investors resident in the country in which the CIV is established. In some cases, tax rules discourage foreign investment by imposing a withholding tax on distributions, or securities laws may severely restrict offerings to non-residents. Governments should consider whether these or other circumstances provide adequate protection against investment by non-treaty-eligible residents of third countries. It may be appropriate, for example, to assume that a CIV is owned by residents of the State in which it is established if the CIV has limited distribution of its shares or units to the State in which the CIV is established or to other States that provide for similar benefits in their treaties with the source State.

6.31 In other cases, interests in the CIV are offered to investors in many countries. Although the identity of individual investors will change daily, the proportion of investors in the CIV that are treaty-entitled is likely to change relatively slowly. Accordingly, it would be a reasonable approach to require the CIV to collect from other intermediaries, on specified dates, information enabling the CIV to determine the proportion of investors that are treaty-entitled. This information could be required at the end of a calendar or fiscal year or, if market conditions suggest that turnover in ownership is high, it could be required more frequently, although no more often than the end of each calendar quarter. The CIV could then make a claim on the basis of an average of those amounts over an agreed-upon time period. In adopting such procedures, care would have to be taken in choosing the measurement dates to ensure that the CIV would have enough time to update the information that it provides to other payers so that the correct amount is withheld at the beginning of each relevant period.

6.32   An alternative approach would provide that a CIV that is publicly traded in the Contracting State in which it is established will be entitled to treaty benefits without regard to the residence of its investors. This provision has been justified on the basis that a publicly-traded CIV cannot be used effectively for treaty shopping because the shareholders or unitholders of such a CIV cannot individually exercise control over it. Such a provision could read:

a)   Notwithstanding the other provisions of this Convention, a collective investment vehicle which is established in a Contracting State and which receives income arising in the other Contracting State shall be treated for purposes of applying the Convention to such income as an individual who is a resident of the Contracting State in which it is established and as the beneficial owner of the income it receives (provided that, if an individual who is a resident of the first-mentioned State had received the income in the same circumstances, such individual would have been considered to be the beneficial owner thereof), if the principal class of shares or units in the collective investment vehicle is listed and regularly traded on a regulated stock exchange in that State.

b)   For purposes of this paragraph, the term "collective investment vehicle" means, in the case of [State A], a [ ] and, in the case of [State B], a [ ], as well as any other investment fund, arrangement or entity established in either Contracting State which the competent authorities of the Contracting States agree to regard as a collective investment vehicle for purposes of this paragraph.

6.33   Each of the provisions in paragraphs 6.17, 6.21, 6.26 and 6.32 treats the CIV as the resident and the beneficial owner of the income it receives for the purposes of the application of the Convention to such income, which has the simplicity of providing for one reduced rate of withholding with respect to each type of income. These provisions should not be construed, however, as restricting in any way the right of the State of source from taxing its own residents who are investors in the CIV. Clearly, these provisions are intended to deal with the source taxation of the CIV's income and not the residence taxation of its investors (this conclusion is analogous to the one put forward in paragraph 6.1 above as regards partnerships). States that wish to confirm this point in the text of the provisions are free to amend the provisions accordingly, which could be done by adding the following sentence: "This provision shall not be construed as restricting in any way a Contracting State's right to tax the residents of that State".

6.34 Also, each of these provisions is intended only to provide that the specific characteristics of the CIV will not cause it to be treated as other than the beneficial owner of the income it receives. Therefore, a CIV will be treated as the beneficial owner of all of the income it receives. The provision is not intended, however, to put a CIV in a different or better position than other investors with respect to aspects of the beneficial ownership requirement that are unrelated to the CIV's status as such. Accordingly, where an individual receiving an item of income in certain circumstances would not be considered as the beneficial owner of that income, a CIV receiving that income in the same circumstances could not be deemed to be the beneficial owner of the income. This result is confirmed by the parenthetical limiting the application of the provision to situations in which an individual in the same circumstances would have been treated as the beneficial owner of the income.

Application of the Convention to States, their subdivisions and their wholly-owned entities

6.35 Paragraph 1 of Article 4 provides that the Contracting States themselves, their political subdivisions and their local authorities are included in the definition of a "resident of a Contracting State" and are therefore entitled to the benefits of the Convention (paragraph 8.4 of the Commentary on Article 4 explains that the inclusion of these words in 1995 confirmed the prior general understanding of most member States).

6.36 Issues may arise, however, in the case of entities set up and wholly-owned by a State or one of its political subdivisions or local authorities. Some of these entities may derive substantial income from other countries and it may therefore be important to determine whether tax treaties apply to them (this would be the case, for instance, of sovereign wealth funds: see paragraph 8.5 of the Commentary on Article 4). In many cases, these entities are totally exempt from tax and the question may arise as to whether they are entitled to the benefits of the tax treaties concluded by the State in which they are set up. In order to clarify the issue, some States modify the definition of "resident of a Contracting State" in paragraph 1 of Article 4 and include in that definition a "statutory body", an "agency or instrumentality" or a "legal person of public law" [*personne morale de droit public*] of a State, a political subdivision or local authority, which would therefore cover wholly-owned entities that are not considered to be a part of the State or its political subdivisions or local authorities.

6.37 In addition, many States include specific provisions in their bilateral conventions that grant an exemption to other States, and to some State-owned entities such as central banks, with respect to certain items of income such as interest (see paragraph 13.2 of the Commentary on Article 10 and paragraph 7.4 of the Commentary on Article 11). Treaty provisions that grant a tax exemption with respect to the income of pension funds (see paragraph 69 of the Commentary on Article 18) may similarly apply to pension funds that are wholly-owned by a State, depending on the wording of these provisions and the nature of the fund.

6.38 The application of the Convention to each Contracting State, its political subdivisions, and local authorities (and their statutory bodies, agencies or instrumentalities in the case of bilateral treaties that apply to such entities) should not be interpreted, however, as affecting in any way the possible application by each State of the customary international law principle of sovereign immunity. According to this principle, a sovereign State (including its agents, its property and activities) is, as a general rule, immune from the jurisdiction of the courts of another sovereign State. There is no international consensus, however, on the precise limits of the sovereign immunity principle. Most States, for example, would not recognise that the principle applies to business activities and many States do not recognise any application of this principle in tax matters. There are therefore considerable differences between States as regards the extent, if any, to which that principle applies to taxation. Even among States that would recognise its possible application in tax matters, some apply it only to the extent that it has been incorporated into domestic law and others apply it as customary international law but subject to important limitations. The Convention does not prejudge the issues of whether and to what extent the principle of sovereign immunity applies with respect to the persons covered under Article 1 and the taxes covered under Article 2 and each Contracting State is therefore free to apply its own interpretation of that principle as long as the resulting taxation, if any, is in conformity with the provisions of its bilateral tax conventions.

6.39 States often take account of various factors when considering whether and to what extent tax exemptions should be granted, through specific treaty or domestic law provisions or through the application of the sovereign immunity doctrine, with respect to the income derived by other States, their political subdivisions, local authorities, or their statutory bodies, agencies or instrumentalities. These factors would include, for example, whether that type of income would be exempt on a reciprocal basis, whether the income is derived from activities of a governmental nature as opposed to activities of a commercial nature, whether the assets and income of the recipient entity are used for public purposes, whether there is any possibility that these could inure to the benefit of a non-governmental person and whether the income is derived from a portfolio or direct investment.

Improper use of the Convention

7. The principal purpose of double taxation conventions is to promote, by eliminating international double taxation, exchanges of goods and services, and the movement of capital and persons. It is also a purpose of tax conventions to prevent tax avoidance and evasion.

7.1 Taxpayers may be tempted to abuse the tax laws of a State by exploiting the differences between various countries' laws. Such attempts may be countered by provisions or jurisprudential rules that are part of the domestic law of the State concerned. Such a State is then unlikely to agree to provisions of bilateral double taxation conventions that would have the effect of allowing abusive transactions that would otherwise be prevented by the provisions and rules of this kind contained in its domestic law. Also, it will not wish to apply its bilateral conventions in a way that would have that effect.

8.   It is also important to note that the extension of double taxation conventions increases the risk of abuse by facilitating the use of artificial legal constructions aimed at securing the benefits of both the tax advantages available under certain domestic laws and the reliefs from tax provided for in double taxation conventions.

9.   This would be the case, for example, if a person (whether or not a resident of a Contracting State), acts through a legal entity created in a State essentially to obtain treaty benefits that would not be available directly. Another case would be an individual who has in a Contracting State both his permanent home and all his economic interests, including a substantial shareholding in a company of that State, and who, essentially in order to sell the shares and escape taxation in that State on the capital gains from the alienation (by virtue of paragraph 5 of Article 13), transfers his permanent home to the other Contracting State, where such gains are subject to little or no tax.

9.1   This raises two fundamental questions that are discussed in the following paragraphs:

— whether the benefits of tax conventions must be granted when transactions that constitute an abuse of the provisions of these conventions are entered into (see paragraphs 9.2 and following below); and

— whether specific provisions and jurisprudential rules of the domestic law of a Contracting State that are intended to prevent tax abuse conflict with tax conventions (see paragraphs 22 and following below).

9.2   For many States, the answer to the first question is based on their answer to the second question. These States take account of the fact that taxes are ultimately imposed through the provisions of domestic law, as restricted (and in some rare cases, broadened) by the provisions of tax conventions. Thus, any abuse of the provisions of a tax convention could also be characterised as an abuse of the provisions of domestic law under which tax will be levied. For these States, the issue then becomes whether the provisions of tax conventions may prevent the application of the anti-abuse provisions of domestic law, which is the second question above. As indicated in paragraph 22.1 below, the answer to that second question is that to the extent these anti-avoidance rules are part of the basic domestic rules set by domestic tax laws for determining which facts give rise to a tax liability, they are not addressed in tax treaties and are therefore not affected by them. Thus, as a general rule, there will be no conflict between such rules and the provisions of tax conventions.

9.3   Other States prefer to view some abuses as being abuses of the convention itself, as opposed to abuses of domestic law. These States, however, then consider that a proper construction of tax conventions allows them to disregard abusive transactions, such as those entered into with the view to obtaining unintended benefits under the provisions of these conventions. This interpretation results from the object and purpose of tax conventions as well as the obligation to interpret them in good faith (see Article 31 of the *Vienna Convention on the Law of Treaties*).

9.4   Under both approaches, therefore, it is agreed that States do not have to grant the benefits of a double taxation convention where arrangements that constitute an abuse of the provisions of the convention have been entered into.

9.5   It is important to note, however, that it should not be lightly assumed that a taxpayer is entering into the type of abusive transactions referred to above. A guiding principle is that the benefits of a double taxation convention should not be available where a main purpose for entering into certain transactions or arrangements was to secure a more favourable tax position and obtaining that more favourable treatment in these circumstances would be contrary to the object and purpose of the relevant provisions.

9.6   The potential application of general anti-abuse provisions does not mean that there is no need for the inclusion, in tax conventions, of specific provisions aimed at preventing particular forms of tax avoidance. Where specific avoidance techniques have been identified or where the use of such techniques is especially problematic, it will often be useful to add to the Convention provisions that focus directly on the relevant avoidance strategy. Also, this will be necessary where a State which adopts the view described in paragraph 9.2 above believes that its domestic law lacks the anti-avoidance rules or principles necessary to properly address such strategy.

10.   For instance, some forms of tax avoidance have already been expressly dealt with in the Convention, *e.g.* by the introduction of the concept of "beneficial owner" (in Articles 10, 11, and 12) and of special provisions such as paragraph 2 of Article 17 dealing with so-called artiste-companies. Such problems are also mentioned in the Commentaries on Article 10 (paragraphs 17 and 22), Article 11 (paragraph 12) and Article 12 (paragraph 7).

10.1   Also, in some cases, claims to treaty benefits by subsidiary companies, in particular companies established in tax havens or benefiting from harmful preferential regimes, may be refused where careful consideration of the facts and circumstances of a case shows that the place of effective management of a subsidiary does not lie in its alleged state of residence but, rather, lies in the state of residence of the parent company so as to make it a resident of that latter state for domestic law and treaty purposes (this will be relevant where the domestic law of a state uses the place of management of a legal person, or a similar criterion, to determine its residence).

10.2   Careful consideration of the facts and circumstances of a case may also show that a subsidiary was managed in the state of residence of its parent in such a way that the subsidiary had a permanent establishment (*e.g.* by having a place of management) in that state to which all or a substantial part of its profits were properly attributable.

11.   A further example is provided by two particularly prevalent forms of improper use of the Convention which are discussed in two reports from the Committee on Fiscal Affairs entitled "Double Taxation Conventions and the Use of Base Companies"

and "Double Taxation Conventions and the Use of Conduit Companies".[1] As indicated in these reports, the concern expressed in paragraph 9 above has proved to be valid as there has been a growing tendency toward the use of conduit companies to obtain treaty benefits not intended by the Contracting States in their bilateral negotiations. This has led an increasing number of member countries to implement treaty provisions (both general and specific) to counter abuse and to preserve anti-avoidance legislation in their domestic laws.

12.   The treaty provisions that have been designed to cover these and other forms of abuse take different forms. The following are examples derived from provisions that have been incorporated in bilateral conventions concluded by member countries. These provide models that treaty negotiators might consider when searching for a solution to specific cases. In referring to them there should be taken into account:

— the fact that these provisions are not mutually exclusive and that various provisions may be needed in order to address different concerns;

— the degree to which tax advantages may actually be obtained by a particular avoidance strategy;

— the legal context in both Contracting States and, in particular, the extent to which domestic law already provides an appropriate response to this avoidance strategy, and

— the extent to which bona fide economic activities might be unintentionally disqualified by such provisions.

Conduit company cases

13.   Many countries have attempted to deal with the issue of conduit companies and various approaches have been designed for that purpose. One solution would be to disallow treaty benefits to a company not owned, directly or indirectly, by residents of the State of which the company is a resident. For example, such a "look-through" provision might have the following wording:

A company that is a resident of a Contracting State shall not be entitled to relief from taxation under this Convention with respect to any item of income, gains or profits if it is owned or controlled directly or through one or more companies, wherever resident, by persons who are not residents of a Contracting State.

Contracting States wishing to adopt such a provision may also want, in their bilateral negotiations, to determine the criteria according to which a company would be considered as owned or controlled by non-residents.

14.   The "look-through approach" underlying the above provision seems an adequate basis for treaties with countries that have no or very low taxation and where little substantive business activities would normally be carried on. Even in these cases it

---

1 These two reports are reproduced in Volume II of the full-length version of the OECD Model Tax Convention at pages R(5)-1 and R(6)-1.

might be necessary to alter the provision or to substitute for it another one to safeguard *bona fide* business activities.

15.   General subject-to-tax provisions provide that treaty benefits in the State of source are granted only if the income in question is subject to tax in the State of residence. This corresponds basically to the aim of tax treaties, namely to avoid double taxation. For a number of reasons, however, the Model Convention does not recommend such a general provision. Whilst this seems adequate with respect to a normal international relationship, a subject-to-tax approach might well be adopted in a typical conduit situation. A safeguarding provision of this kind could have the following wording:

> Where income arising in a Contracting State is received by a company resident of the other Contracting State and one or more persons not resident in that other Contracting State
>
>> *a)* have directly or indirectly or through one or more companies, wherever resident, a substantial interest in such company, in the form of a participation or otherwise, or
>>
>> *b)* exercise directly or indirectly, alone or together, the management or control of such company,
>
> any provision of this Convention conferring an exemption from, or a reduction of, tax shall apply only to income that is subject to tax in the last-mentioned State under the ordinary rules of its tax law.

The concept of "substantial interest" may be further specified when drafting a bilateral convention. Contracting States may express it, for instance, as a percentage of the capital or of the voting rights of the company.

16.   The subject-to-tax approach seems to have certain merits. It may be used in the case of States with a well-developed economic structure and a complex tax law. It will, however, be necessary to supplement this provision by inserting *bona fide* provisions in the treaty to provide for the necessary flexibility (see paragraph 19 below); moreover, such an approach does not offer adequate protection against advanced tax avoidance schemes such as "stepping-stone strategies".

17.   The approaches referred to above are in many ways unsatisfactory. They refer to the changing and complex tax laws of the Contracting States and not to the arrangements giving rise to the improper use of conventions. It has been suggested that the conduit problem be dealt with in a more straightforward way by inserting a provision that would single out cases of improper use with reference to the conduit arrangements themselves (the channel approach). Such a provision might have the following wording:

> Where income arising in a Contracting State is received by a company that is a resident of the other Contracting State and one or more persons who are not residents of that other Contracting State

> a) have directly or indirectly or through one or more companies, wherever resident, a substantial interest in such company, in the form of a participation or otherwise, or
>
> b) exercise directly or indirectly, alone or together, the management or control of such company

any provision of this Convention conferring an exemption from, or a reduction of, tax shall not apply if more than 50 per cent of such income is used to satisfy claims by such persons (including interest, royalties, development, advertising, initial and travel expenses, and depreciation of any kind of business assets including those on immaterial goods and processes).

18.   A provision of this kind appears to be the only effective way of combatting "stepping-stone" devices. It is found in bilateral treaties entered into by Switzerland and the United States and its principle also seems to underly the Swiss provisions against the improper use of tax treaties by certain types of Swiss companies. States that consider including a clause of this kind in their convention should bear in mind that it may cover normal business transactions and would therefore have to be supplemented by a *bona fide* clause.

19.   The solutions described above are of a general nature and they need to be accompanied by specific provisions to ensure that treaty benefits will be granted in *bona fide* cases. Such provisions could have the following wording:

a) *General bona fide provision*

"The foregoing provisions shall not apply where the company establishes that the principal purpose of the company, the conduct of its business and the acquisition or maintenance by it of the shareholding or other property from which the income in question is derived, are motivated by sound business reasons and do not have as primary purpose the obtaining of any benefits under this Convention."

b) *Activity provision*

"The foregoing provisions shall not apply where the company is engaged in substantive business operations in the Contracting State of which it is a resident and the relief from taxation claimed from the other Contracting State is with respect to income that is connected with such operations."

c) *Amount of tax provision*

"The foregoing provisions shall not apply where the reduction of tax claimed is not greater than the tax actually imposed by the Contracting State of which the company is a resident."

d) *Stock exchange provision*

"The foregoing provisions shall not apply to a company that is a resident of a Contracting State if the principal class of its shares is registered on an approved stock exchange in a Contracting State or if such company is wholly owned — directly or through one or more companies each of which is a resident of the first-mentioned State — by a company which is a resident of the first-mentioned State and the principal class of whose shares is so registered."

e) *Alternative relief provision*

In cases where an anti-abuse clause refers to non-residents of a Contracting State, it could be provided that the term "shall not be deemed to include residents of third States that have income tax conventions in force with the Contracting State from which relief from taxation is claimed and such conventions provide relief from taxation not less than the relief from taxation claimed under this Convention."

These provisions illustrate possible approaches. The specific wording of the provisions to be included in a particular treaty depends on the general approach taken in that treaty and should be determined on a bilateral basis. Also, where the competent authorities of the Contracting States have the power to apply discretionary provisions, it may be considered appropriate to include an additional rule that would give the competent authority of the source country the discretion to allow the benefits of the Convention to a resident of the other State even if the resident fails to pass any of the tests described above.

20.   Whilst the preceding paragraphs identify different approaches to deal with conduit situations, each of them deals with a particular aspect of the problem commonly referred to as "treaty shopping". States wishing to address the issue in a comprehensive way may want to consider the following example of detailed limitation-of-benefits provisions aimed at preventing persons who are not resident of either Contracting States from accessing the benefits of a Convention through the use of an entity that would otherwise qualify as a resident of one of these States, keeping in mind that adaptations may be necessary and that many States prefer other approaches to deal with treaty shopping:

1.   Except as otherwise provided in this Article, a resident of a Contracting State who derives income from the other Contracting State shall be entitled to all the benefits of this Convention otherwise accorded to residents of a Contracting State only if such resident is a "qualified person" as defined in paragraph 2 and meets the other conditions of this Convention for the obtaining of such benefits.

2.   A resident of a Contracting State is a qualified person for a fiscal year only if such resident is either:

a) an individual;

b) a qualified governmental entity;

c) a company, if

(i)   the principal class of its shares is listed on a recognised stock exchange specified in subparagraph a) or b) of paragraph 6 and is regularly traded on one or more recognised stock exchanges, or

(ii)   at least 50 per cent of the aggregate vote and value of the shares in the company is owned directly or indirectly by five or fewer companies entitled to benefits under subdivision (i) of this subparagraph, provided

that, in the case of indirect ownership, each intermediate owner is a
resident of either Contracting State;

d) a charity or other tax-exempt entity, provided that, in the case of a pension
trust or any other organization that is established exclusively to provide
pension or other similar benefits, more than 50 per cent of the person's
beneficiaries, members or participants are individuals resident in either
Contracting State; or

e) a person other than an individual, if:

(i) on at least half the days of the fiscal year persons that are qualified
persons by reason of subparagraph a), b) or d) or subdivision c) (i) of this
paragraph own, directly or indirectly, at least 50 per cent of the aggregate
vote and value of the shares or other beneficial interests in the person,
and

(ii) less than 50 per cent of the person's gross income for the taxable year is
paid or accrued, directly or indirectly, to persons who are not residents
of either Contracting State in the form of payments that are deductible
for purposes of the taxes covered by this Convention in the person's
State of residence (but not including arm's length payments in the
ordinary course of business for services or tangible property and
payments in respect of financial obligations to a bank, provided that
where such a bank is not a resident of a Contracting State such payment
is attributable to a permanent establishment of that bank located in one
of the Contracting States).

3. a) A resident of a Contracting State will be entitled to benefits of the Convention
with respect to an item of income, derived from the other State, regardless of
whether the resident is a qualified person, if the resident is actively carrying
on business in the first-mentioned State (other than the business of making or
managing investments for the resident's own account, unless these activities
are banking, insurance or securities activities carried on by a bank, insurance
company or registered securities dealer), the income derived from the other
Contracting State is derived in connection with, or is incidental to, that
business and that resident satisfies the other conditions of this Convention
for the obtaining of such benefits.

b) If the resident or any of its associated enterprises carries on a business
activity in the other Contracting State which gives rise to an item of income,
subparagraph a) shall apply to such item only if the business activity in the
first-mentioned State is substantial in relation to business carried on in the
other State. Whether a business activity is substantial for purposes of this
paragraph will be determined based on all the facts and circumstances.

c) In determining whether a person is actively carrying on business in a
Contracting State under subparagraph a), activities conducted by a
partnership in which that person is a partner and activities conducted by
persons connected to such person shall be deemed to be conducted by such

person. A person shall be connected to another if one possesses at least 50 per cent of the beneficial interest in the other (or, in the case of a company, at least 50 per cent of the aggregate vote and value of the company's shares) or another person possesses, directly or indirectly, at least 50 per cent of the beneficial interest (or, in the case of a company, at least 50 per cent of the aggregate vote and value of the company's shares) in each person. In any case, a person shall be considered to be connected to another if, based on all the facts and circumstances, one has control of the other or both are under the control of the same person or persons.

4.   Notwithstanding the preceding provisions of this Article, if a company that is a resident of a Contracting State, or a company that controls such a company, has outstanding a class of shares

a) which is subject to terms or other arrangements which entitle its holders to a portion of the income of the company derived from the other Contracting State that is larger than the portion such holders would receive absent such terms or arrangements ("the disproportionate part of the income"); and

b) 50 per cent or more of the voting power and value of which is owned by persons who are not qualified persons

the benefits of this Convention shall not apply to the disproportionate part of the income.

5.   A resident of a Contracting State that is neither a qualified person pursuant to the provisions of paragraph 2 or entitled to benefits under paragraph 3 or 4 shall, nevertheless, be granted benefits of the Convention if the competent authority of that other Contracting State determines that the establishment, acquisition or maintenance of such person and the conduct of its operations did not have as one of its principal purposes the obtaining of benefits under the Convention.

6.   For the purposes of this Article the term "recognised stock exchange" means:

a) in State A ....;

b) in State B ....; and

c) any other stock exchange which the competent authorities agree to recognise for the purposes of this Article.

Provisions which are aimed at entities benefiting from preferential tax regimes

21.   Specific types of companies enjoying tax privileges in their State of residence facilitate conduit arrangements and raise the issue of harmful tax practices. Where tax-exempt (or nearly tax-exempt) companies may be distinguished by special legal characteristics, the improper use of tax treaties may be avoided by denying the tax treaty benefits to these companies (the exclusion approach). As such privileges are granted mostly to specific types of companies as defined in the commercial law or in the tax law of a country, the most radical solution would be to exclude such companies from the scope of the treaty. Another solution would be to insert a safeguarding clause

which would apply to the income received or paid by such companies and which could be drafted along the following lines:

> No provision of the Convention conferring an exemption from, or reduction of, tax shall apply to income received or paid by a company as defined under section ... of the ... Act, or under any similar provision enacted by ... after the signature of the Convention.

The scope of this provision could be limited by referring only to specific types of income, such as dividends, interest, capital gains, or directors' fees. Under such provisions companies of the type concerned would remain entitled to the protection offered under Article 24 (non-discrimination) and to the benefits of Article 25 (mutual agreement procedure) and they would be subject to the provisions of Article 26 (exchange of information).

21.1   Exclusion provisions are clear and their application is simple, even though they may require administrative assistance in some instances. They are an important instrument by which a State that has created special privileges in its tax law may prevent those privileges from being used in connection with the improper use of tax treaties concluded by that State.

21.2   Where it is not possible or appropriate to identify the companies enjoying tax privileges by reference to their special legal characteristics, a more general formulation will be necessary. The following provision aims at denying the benefits of the Convention to entities which would otherwise qualify as residents of a Contracting State but which enjoy, in that State, a preferential tax regime restricted to foreign-held entities (i.e. not available to entities that belong to residents of that State):

> Any company, trust or partnership that is a resident of a Contracting State and is beneficially owned or controlled directly or indirectly by one or more persons who are not residents of that State shall not be entitled to the benefits of this Convention if the amount of the tax imposed on the income or capital of the company, trust or partnership by that State (after taking into account any reduction or offset of the amount of tax in any manner, including a refund, reimbursement, contribution, credit or allowance to the company, trust or partnership, or to any other person) is substantially lower than the amount that would be imposed by that State if all of the shares of the capital stock of the company or all of the interests in the trust or partnership, as the case may be, were beneficially owned by one or more residents of that State.

Provisions which are aimed at particular types of income

21.3   The following provision aims at denying the benefits of the Convention with respect to income that is subject to low or no tax under a preferential tax regime:

> 1.   The benefits of this Convention shall not apply to income which may, in accordance with the other provisions of the Convention, be taxed in a Contracting State and which is derived from activities the performance of which do not require substantial presence in that State, including:

a) such activities involving banking, shipping, financing, insurance or electronic commerce activities; or

b) activities involving headquarter or coordination centre or similar arrangements providing company or group administration, financing or other support; or

c) activities which give rise to passive income, such as dividends, interest and royalties

where, under the laws or administrative practices of that State, such income is preferentially taxed and, in relation thereto, information is accorded confidential treatment that prevents the effective exchange of information.

2.   For the purposes of paragraph 1, income is preferentially taxed in a Contracting State if, other than by reason of the preceding Articles of this Agreement, an item of income:

a) is exempt from tax; or

b) is taxable in the hands of a taxpayer but that is subject to a rate of tax that is lower than the rate applicable to an equivalent item that is taxable in the hands of similar taxpayers who are residents of that State; or

c) benefits from a credit, rebate or other concession or benefit that is provided directly or indirectly in relation to that item of income, other than a credit for foreign tax paid.

Anti-abuse rules dealing with source taxation of specific types of income

21.4   The following provision has the effect of denying the benefits of specific Articles of the convention that restrict source taxation where transactions have been entered into for the main purpose of obtaining these benefits. The Articles concerned are 10, 11, 12 and 21; the provision should be slightly modified as indicated below to deal with the specific type of income covered by each of these Articles:

The provisions of this Article shall not apply if it was the main purpose or one of the main purposes of any person concerned with the creation or assignment of the [Article 10: "shares or other rights"; Article 11: "debt-claim"; Articles 12 and 21: "rights"] in respect of which the [Article 10: "dividend"; Article 11: "interest"; Articles 12 "royalties" and Article 21: "income"] is paid to take advantage of this Article by means of that creation or assignment.

Provisions which are aimed at preferential regimes introduced after the signature of the convention

21.5   States may wish to prevent abuses of their conventions involving provisions introduced by a Contracting State after the signature of the Convention. The following provision aims to protect a Contracting State from having to give treaty benefits with respect to income benefiting from a special regime for certain offshore income introduced after the signature of the treaty:

The benefits of Articles 6 to 22 of this Convention shall not accrue to persons entitled to any special tax benefit under:

a) a law of either one of the States which has been identified in an exchange of notes between the States; or

b) any substantially similar law subsequently enacted.

22.   Other forms of abuse of tax treaties (e.g. the use of a base company) and possible ways to deal with them, including "substance-over-form", "economic substance" and general anti-abuse rules have also been analysed, particularly as concerns the question of whether these rules conflict with tax treaties, which is the second question mentioned in paragraph 9.1 above.

22.1 Such rules are part of the basic domestic rules set by domestic tax laws for determining which facts give rise to a tax liability; these rules are not addressed in tax treaties and are therefore not affected by them. Thus, as a general rule and having regard to paragraph 9.5, there will be no conflict. For example, to the extent that the application of the rules referred to in paragraph 22 results in a recharacterisation of income or in a redetermination of the taxpayer who is considered to derive such income, the provisions of the Convention will be applied taking into account these changes.

22.2 Whilst these rules do not conflict with tax conventions, there is agreement that member countries should carefully observe the specific obligations enshrined in tax treaties to relieve double taxation as long as there is no clear evidence that the treaties are being abused.

23.   The use of base companies may also be addressed through controlled foreign companies provisions. A significant number of member and non-member countries have now adopted such legislation. Whilst the design of this type of legislation varies considerably among countries, a common feature of these rules, which are now internationally recognised as a legitimate instrument to protect the domestic tax base, is that they result in a Contracting State taxing its residents on income attributable to their participation in certain foreign entities. It has sometimes been argued, based on a certain interpretation of provisions of the Convention such as paragraph 1 of Article 7 and paragraph 5 of Article 10, that this common feature of controlled foreign companies legislation conflicted with these provisions. For the reasons explained in paragraphs 14 of the Commentary on Article 7 and 37 of the Commentary on Article 10, that interpretation does not accord with the text of the provisions. It also does not hold when these provisions are read in their context. Thus, whilst some countries have felt it useful to expressly clarify, in their conventions, that controlled foreign companies legislation did not conflict with the Convention, such clarification is not necessary. It is recognised that controlled foreign companies legislation structured in this way is not contrary to the provisions of the Convention.

24.   [Deleted]

25.   [Renumbered]

26.   States that adopt controlled foreign companies provisions or the anti-abuse rules referred to above in their domestic tax laws seek to maintain the equity and neutrality of these laws in an international environment characterised by very different tax burdens, but such measures should be used only for this purpose. As a general rule, these measures should not be applied where the relevant income has been subjected to taxation that is comparable to that in the country of residence of the taxpayer.

Remittance based taxation

26.1   Under the domestic law of some States, persons who qualify as residents but who do not have what is considered to be a permanent link with the State (sometimes referred to as domicile) are only taxed on income derived from sources outside the State to the extent that this income is effectively repatriated, or remitted, thereto. Such persons are not, therefore, subject to potential double taxation to the extent that foreign income is not remitted to their State of residence and it may be considered inappropriate to give them the benefit of the provisions of the Convention on such income. Contracting States which agree to restrict the application of the provisions of the Convention to income that is effectively taxed in the hands of these persons may do so by adding the following provision to the Convention:

> Where under any provision of this Convention income arising in a Contracting State is relieved in whole or in part from tax in that State and under the law in force in the other Contracting State a person, in respect of the said income, is subject to tax by reference to the amount thereof which is remitted to or received in that other State and not by reference to the full amount thereof, then any relief provided by the provisions of this Convention shall apply only to so much of the income as is taxed in the other Contracting State.

In some States, the application of that provision could create administrative difficulties if a substantial amount of time elapsed between the time the income arose in a Contracting State and the time it were taxed by the other Contracting State in the hands of a resident of that other State. States concerned by these difficulties could subject the rule in the last part of the above provision, i.e. that the income in question will be entitled to benefits in the first-mentioned State only when taxed in the other State, to the condition that the income must be so taxed in that other State within a specified period of time from the time the income arises in the first-mentioned State.

Limitations of source taxation: procedural aspects

26.2   A number of Articles of the Convention limit the right of a State to tax income derived from its territory. As noted in paragraph 19 of the Commentary on Article 10 as concerns the taxation of dividends, the Convention does not settle procedural questions and each State is free to use the procedure provided in its domestic law in order to apply the limits provided by the Convention. A State can therefore automatically limit the tax that it levies in accordance with the relevant provisions of the Convention, subject to possible prior verification of treaty entitlement, or it can impose the tax provided for under its domestic law and subsequently refund the part of that tax that exceeds the amount that it can levy under the provisions of the Convention. As a general rule, in order to ensure expeditious implementation of taxpayers' benefits under a treaty, the first approach is the highly preferable method. If a refund system is needed, it should be based on observable difficulties in identifying entitlement to treaty benefits. Also, where the second approach is adopted, it is extremely important that the refund be made expeditiously, especially if no interest is paid on the amount of the refund, as any undue delay in making that refund is a direct cost to the taxpayer.

Observations on the Commentary

27.   *Chile* considers that some of the solutions put forward in the report "The Application of the OECD Model Tax Convention to Partnerships" and incorporated in the Commentary can only be applied if expressly incorporated in a tax convention.

27.1 The *Netherlands* will adhere to the conclusions on the application of the Convention to partnerships incorporated in the Commentary on Article 1 and in the Commentaries on the other relevant provisions of the Convention only, and to the extent to which, it is explicitly so confirmed in a specific tax treaty, as a result of mutual agreement between competent authorities as meant in Article 25 of the Convention or as unilateral policy.

27.2 *France* has expressed a number of reservations on the report on "The Application of the OECD Model Tax Convention to Partnerships". In particular, France does not agree with the interpretation put forward in paragraphs 5 and 6 above according to which if a partnership is denied the benefits of a tax convention, its members are always entitled to the benefits of the tax conventions entered into by their State of residence. France believes that this result is only possible, when France is the State of source, if its internal law authorises that interpretation or if provisions to that effect are included in the convention entered into with the State of residence of the partners.

27.3 *Portugal*, where all partnerships are taxed as such, has expressed a number of reservations on the report on "The Application of the OECD Model Tax Convention to Partnerships" and considers that the solutions put forward in that report should be incorporated in special provisions only applicable when included in tax conventions. This is the case, for example, of the treatment of the situation of partners of partnerships — a concept which is considerably fluid given the differences between States — that are fiscally transparent, including the situation where a third State is inserted between the State of source and the State of residence of the partners. The administrative difficulties resulting from some of the solutions put forward should also be noted, as indicated in the report itself in certain cases.

27.4 *Belgium* cannot share the views expressed in paragraph 23 of the Commentary. Belgium considers that the application of controlled foreign companies legislation is contrary to the provisions of paragraph 7 of Article 5, paragraph 1 of Article 7 and paragraph 5 of Article 10 of the Convention. This is especially the case where a Contracting State taxes one of its residents on income derived by a foreign entity by using a fiction attributing to that resident, in proportion to his participation in the capital of the foreign entity, the income derived by that entity. By doing so, that State increases the tax base of its resident by including in it income which has not been derived by that resident but by a foreign entity which is not taxable in that State in accordance with the Convention. That Contracting State thus disregards the legal personality of the foreign entity and therefore acts contrary to the Convention (see also paragraph 79 of the Commentary on Article 7 and paragraph 68.1 of the Commentary on Article 10).

27.5 Concerning potential conflicts between anti-abuse provisions (including controlled foreign company — CFC — provisions) in domestic law and the provisions of tax treaties, *Ireland* considers that it is not possible to have a simple general conclusion that no conflict will exist or that any conflict must be resolved in favour of the domestic law. This will depend on the nature of the domestic law provision and also on the legal and constitutional relationship in individual member countries between domestic law and international agreements and law. Also, Ireland does not agree with the deletion of the language in paragraph 26 (as it read until 2002), which stated: "It would be contrary to the general principles underlying the Model Convention and to the spirit of tax treaties in general if counteracting measures were to be extended to activities such as production, normal rendering of services or trading of companies engaged in real industrial or commercial activity, when they are clearly related to the economic environment of the country where they are resident in a situation where these activities are carried out in such a way that no tax avoidance could be suspected".

27.6 *Luxembourg* does not share the interpretation in paragraphs 9.2, 22.1 and 23 which provide that there is generally no conflict between anti-abuse provisions of the domestic law of a Contracting State and the provisions of its tax conventions. Absent an express provision in the Convention, Luxembourg therefore believes that a State can only apply its domestic anti-abuse provisions in specific cases after recourse to the mutual agreement procedure.

27.7 The *Netherlands* does not adhere to the statements in the Commentaries that as a general rule domestic anti-avoidance rules and controlled foreign companies provisions do not conflict with the provisions of tax conventions. The compatibility of such rules and provisions with tax treaties is, among other things, dependent on the nature and wording of the specific provision, the wording and purpose of the relevant treaty provision and the relationship between domestic and international law in a country. Since tax conventions are not meant to facilitate the improper use thereof, the application of national rules and provisions may be justified in specific cases of abuse or clearly unintended use. In such situations the application of domestic measures has to respect the principle of proportionality and should not go beyond what is necessary to prevent the abuse or the clearly unintended use.

27.8 [Deleted]

27.9 *Switzerland* does not share the view expressed in paragraph 7 according to which the purpose of double taxation conventions is to prevent tax avoidance and evasion. Also, this view seems to contradict the footnote to the Title of the Model Tax Convention. With respect to paragraph 22.1, Switzerland believes that domestic tax rules on abuse of tax conventions must conform to the general provisions of tax conventions, especially where the convention itself includes provisions intended to prevent its abuse. With respect to paragraph 23, Switzerland considers that controlled foreign corporation legislation may, depending on the relevant concept, be contrary to the spirit of Article 7.

27.10 *Mexico* does not agree with the interpretation put forward in paragraphs 5 and 6 above according to which if a partnership is denied the benefits of a tax convention, its members are entitled to the benefits of the tax conventions entered into by their State of residence. Mexico believes that this result is only possible, to a certain extent, if provisions to that effect are included in the convention entered into with the State where the partnership is situated.

Reservation on the Article

28.   The *United States* reserves the right, with certain exceptions, to tax its citizens and residents, including certain former citizens and long-term residents, without regard to the Convention.

MODEL TAX CONVENTION (CONDENSED VERSION) – ISBN 978-92-64-08948-8 – © OECD 2010

COMMENTARY ON ARTICLE 2
CONCERNING TAXES COVERED BY THE CONVENTION

1.   This Article is intended to make the terminology and nomenclature relating to the taxes covered by the Convention more acceptable and precise, to ensure identification of the Contracting States' taxes covered by the Convention, to widen as much as possible the field of application of the Convention by including, as far as possible, and in harmony with the domestic laws of the Contracting States, the taxes imposed by their political subdivisions or local authorities, to avoid the necessity of concluding a new convention whenever the Contracting States' domestic laws are modified, and to ensure for each Contracting State notification of significant changes in the taxation laws of the other State.

Paragraph 1

2.   This paragraph defines the scope of application of the Convention: taxes on income and on capital; the term "direct taxes" which is far too imprecise has therefore been avoided. It is immaterial on behalf of which authorities such taxes are imposed; it may be the State itself or its political subdivisions or local authorities (constituent States, regions, provinces, *départements*, cantons, districts, *arrondissements*, *Kreise*, municipalities or groups of municipalities, etc.). The method of levying the taxes is equally immaterial: by direct assessment or by deduction at the source, in the form of surtaxes or surcharges, or as additional taxes (*centimes additionnels*), etc.

Paragraph 2

3.   This paragraph gives a definition of taxes on income and on capital. Such taxes comprise taxes on total income and on elements of income, on total capital and on elements of capital. They also include taxes on profits and gains derived from the alienation of movable or immovable property, as well as taxes on capital appreciation. Finally, the definition extends to taxes on the total amounts of wages or salaries paid by undertakings ("payroll taxes"; in Germany, "*Lohnsummensteuer*"; in France, "*taxe sur les salaires*"). Social security charges, or any other charges paid where there is a direct connection between the levy and the individual benefits to be received, shall not be regarded as "taxes on the total amount of wages".

4.   Clearly a State possessing taxing powers — and it alone — may levy the taxes imposed by its legislation together with any duties or charges accessory to them: increases, costs, interest, etc. It has not been considered necessary to specify this in the Article, as it is obvious that in the levying of the tax the accessory duties or charges depend on the same rule as the principal duty. Practice among member countries varies with respect to the treatment of interest and penalties. Some countries never treat such items as taxes covered by the Article. Others take the opposite approach, especially in cases where the additional charge is computed with reference to the amount of the underlying tax. Countries are free to clarify this point in their bilateral negotiations.

5.   The Article does not mention "ordinary taxes" or "extraordinary taxes". Normally, it might be considered justifiable to include extraordinary taxes in a model convention, but experience has shown that such taxes are generally imposed in very special circumstances. In addition, it would be difficult to define them. They may be extraordinary for various reasons; their imposition, the manner in which they are levied, their rates, their objects, etc. This being so, it seems preferable not to include extraordinary taxes in the Article. But, as it is not intended to exclude extraordinary taxes from all conventions, ordinary taxes have not been mentioned either. The Contracting States are thus free to restrict the convention's field of application to ordinary taxes, to extend it to extraordinary taxes, or even to establish special provisions.

Paragraph 3

6.   This paragraph lists the taxes in force at the time of signature of the Convention. The list is not exhaustive. It serves to illustrate the preceding paragraphs of the Article. In principle, however, it will be a complete list of taxes imposed in each State at the time of signature and covered by the Convention.

6.1   Some member countries do not include paragraphs 1 and 2 in their bilateral conventions. These countries prefer simply to list exhaustively the taxes in each country to which the Convention will apply, and clarify that the Convention will also apply to subsequent taxes that are similar to those listed. Countries that wish to follow this approach might use the following wording:

1.   The taxes to which the Convention shall apply are:

a) (in State A): ....

b) (in State B): ....

2.   The Convention shall apply also to any identical or substantially similar taxes that are imposed after the date of signature of the Convention in addition to, or in place of, the taxes listed in paragraph 1. The competent authorities of the Contracting States shall notify each other of any significant changes that have been made in their taxation laws.

As mentioned in paragraph 3 above, social security charges and similar charges should be excluded from the list of taxes covered.

Paragraph 4

7.   This paragraph provides, since the list of taxes in paragraph 3 is purely declaratory, that the Convention is also to apply to all identical or substantially similar taxes that are imposed in a Contracting State after the date of signature of the Convention in addition to, or in place of, the existing taxes in that State.

8.   Each State undertakes to notify the other of any significant changes made to its taxation laws by communicating to it, for example, details of new or substituted taxes. Member countries are encouraged to communicate other significant developments as well, such as new regulations or judicial decisions; many countries already follow this

practice. Contracting States are also free to extend the notification requirement to cover any significant changes in other laws that have an impact on their obligations under the convention; Contracting states wishing to do so may replace the last sentence of the paragraph by the following:

The competent authorities of the Contracting States shall notify each other of any significant changes that have been made in their taxation laws or other laws affecting their obligations under the Convention.

9.   [Deleted]

Reservations on the Article

10.   *Canada*, *Chile* and the *United States* reserve their positions on that part of paragraph 1 which states that the Convention should apply to taxes of political subdivisions or local authorities.

11.   *Australia*, *Japan* and *Korea* reserve their position on that part of paragraph 1 which states that the Convention shall apply to taxes on capital.

12.   *Greece* holds the view that "taxes on the total amounts of wages or salaries paid by enterprises" should not be regarded as taxes on income and therefore will not be covered by the Convention.

COMMENTARY ON ARTICLE 3
CONCERNING GENERAL DEFINITIONS

1.   This Article groups together a number of general provisions required for the interpretation of the terms used in the Convention. The meaning of some important terms, however, is explained elsewhere in the Convention. Thus, the terms "resident" and "permanent establishment" are defined in Articles 4 and 5 respectively, while the interpretation of certain terms appearing in the Articles on special categories of income ("income from immovable property", "dividends", etc.) is clarified by provisions embodied in those Articles. In addition to the definitions contained in the Article, Contracting States are free to agree bilaterally on definitions of the terms "a Contracting State" and "the other Contracting State". Furthermore, Contracting States are free to agree bilaterally to include in the possible definitions of "Contracting States" a reference to continental shelves.

Paragraph 1

The term "person"

2.   The definition of the term "person" given in subparagraph a) is not exhaustive and should be read as indicating that the term "person" is used in a very wide sense (see especially Articles 1 and 4). The definition explicitly mentions individuals, companies and other bodies of persons. From the meaning assigned to the term "company" by the definition contained in subparagraph b) it follows that, in addition, the term "person" includes any entity that, although not incorporated, is treated as a body corporate for tax purposes. Thus, e.g. a foundation (fondation, Stiftung) may fall within the meaning of the term "person". Partnerships will also be considered to be "persons" either because they fall within the definition of "company" or, where this is not the case, because they constitute other bodies of persons.

The term "company"

3.   The term "company" means in the first place any body corporate. In addition, the term covers any other taxable unit that is treated as a body corporate according to the tax laws of the Contracting State in which it is organised. The definition is drafted with special regard to the Article on dividends. The term "company" has a bearing only on that Article, paragraph 7 of Article 5, and Article 16.

The term "enterprise"

4.   The question whether an activity is performed within an enterprise or is deemed to constitute in itself an enterprise has always been interpreted according to the provisions of the domestic laws of the Contracting States. No exhaustive definition of the term "enterprise" has therefore been attempted in this Article. However, it is provided that the term "enterprise" applies to the carrying on of any business. Since the term "business" is expressly defined to include the performance of professional

MODEL TAX CONVENTION (CONDENSED VERSION) – ISBN 978-92-64-08948-8 – © OECD 2010

services and of other activities of an independent character, this clarifies that the performance of professional services or other activities of an independent character must be considered to constitute an enterprise, regardless of the meaning of that term under domestic law. States which consider that such clarification is unnecessary are free to omit the definition of the term "enterprise" from their bilateral conventions.

The term "international traffic"

5.   The definition of the term "international traffic" is based on the principle set forth in paragraph 1 of Article 8 that the right to tax profits from the operation of ships or aircraft in international traffic resides only in the Contracting State in which the place of effective management is situated in view of the special nature of the international traffic business. However, as stated in the Commentary on paragraph 1 of Article 8, the Contracting States are free on a bilateral basis to insert in subparagraph e) a reference to residence, in order to be consistent with the general pattern of the other Articles. In such a case, the words "an enterprise that has its place of effective management in a Contracting State" should be replaced, by "an enterprise of a Contracting State" or "a resident of a Contracting State".

6.   The definition of the term "international traffic" is broader than is normally understood. The broader definition is intended to preserve for the State of the place of effective management the right to tax purely domestic traffic as well as international traffic between third States, and to allow the other Contracting State to tax traffic solely within its borders. This intention may be clarified by the following illustration. Suppose an enterprise of a Contracting State or an enterprise that has its place of effective management in a Contracting State, through an agent in the other Contracting State, sells tickets for a passage that is confined wholly within the first-mentioned State or alternatively, within a third State. The Article does not permit the other State to tax the profits of either voyage. The other State is allowed to tax such an enterprise of the first-mentioned State only where the operations are confined solely to places in that other State.

6.1   A ship or aircraft is operated solely between places in the other Contracting State in relation to a particular voyage if the place of departure and the place of arrival of the ship or aircraft are both in that other Contracting State. However, the definition applies where the journey of a ship or aircraft between places in the other Contracting State forms part of a longer voyage of that ship or aircraft involving a place of departure or a place of arrival which is outside that other Contracting State. For example, where, as part of the same voyage, an aircraft first flies between a place in one Contracting State to a place in the other Contracting State and then continues to another destination also located in that other Contracting State, the first and second legs of that trip will both be part of a voyage regarded as falling within the definition of "international traffic".

6.2   Some States take the view that the definition of "international traffic" should rather refer to a transport as being the journey of a passenger or cargo so that any voyage of a passenger or cargo solely between two places in the same Contracting State should not be considered as covered by the definition even if that voyage is made on a ship or plane that is used for a voyage in international traffic. Contracting States having that view may agree bilaterally to delete the reference to "the ship or aircraft" in the exception included in the definition, so as to use the following definition:

e) the term "international traffic" means any transport by a ship or aircraft operated by an enterprise that has its place of effective management in a Contracting State, except when such transport is solely between places in the other Contracting State;

6.3   The definition of "international traffic" does not apply to a transport by an enterprise which has its place of effective management in one Contracting State when the ship or aircraft is operated between two places in the other State, even if part of the transport takes place outside that State. Thus, for example, a cruise beginning and ending in that other State without a stop in a foreign port does not constitute a transport of passengers in international traffic. Contracting States wishing to expressly clarify that point in their conventions may agree bilaterally to amend the definition accordingly.

The term "competent authority"

7.   The definition of the term "competent authority" recognises that in some OECD member countries the execution of double taxation conventions does not exclusively fall within the competence of the highest tax authorities; some matters are reserved or may be delegated to other authorities. The present definition enables each Contracting State to designate one or more authorities as being competent.

The term "national"

8.   The definition of the term "national" merely stipulates that, in relation to a Contracting State, the term applies to any individual possessing the nationality or citizenship of that Contracting State. Whilst the concept of nationality covers citizenship, the latter term was also included in 2002 because it is more frequently used in some States. It was not judged necessary to include in the text of the Convention any more precise definition of the terms nationality and citizenship, nor did it seem indispensable to make any special comment on the meaning and application of these words. Obviously, in determining what is meant by "national" in the case of an individual, reference must be made to the sense in which the term is usually employed and each State's particular rules on the acquisition or loss of nationality or citizenship.

9.   Subparagraph *g)* is more specific as to legal persons, partnerships and associations. By declaring that any legal person, partnership or association deriving its status as such from the laws in force in a Contracting State is considered to be a national, the provision disposes of a difficulty that often arises. In defining the nationality of companies, certain States have regard less to the law that governs the company than to the origin of the capital with which the company was formed or the nationality of the individuals or legal persons controlling it.

10. Moreover, in view of the legal relationship created between a company and the State under whose law it is organised, which from certain points of view is closely akin to the relationship of nationality in the case of individuals, it seems justifiable not to deal with legal persons, partnerships and associations in a special provision, but to assimilate them with individuals under the term "national".

10.1 The separate mention of partnerships in subparagraph 1 g) is not inconsistent with the status of a partnership as a person under subparagraph 1 a). Under the domestic laws of some countries, it is possible for an entity to be a "person" but not a "legal person" for tax purposes. The explicit statement is necessary to avoid confusion.

The term "business"

10.2 The Convention does not contain an exhaustive definition of the term "business", which, under paragraph 2, should generally have the meaning which it has under the domestic law of the State that applies the Convention. Subparagraph h), however, provides expressly that the term includes the performance of professional services and of other activities of an independent character. This provision was added in 2000 at the same time as Article 14, which dealt with Independent Personal Services, was deleted from the Convention. This addition, which ensures that the term "business" includes the performance of the activities which were previously covered by Article 14, was intended to prevent that the term "business" be interpreted in a restricted way so as to exclude the performance of professional services, or other activities of an independent character, in States where the domestic law does not consider that the performance of such services or activities can constitute a business. Contracting States for which this is not the case are free to agree bilaterally to omit the definition.

Paragraph 2

11. This paragraph provides a general rule of interpretation for terms used in the Convention but not defined therein. However, the question arises which legislation must be referred to in order to determine the meaning of terms not defined in the Convention, the choice being between the legislation in force when the Convention was signed or that in force when the Convention is being applied, i.e. when the tax is imposed. The Committee on Fiscal Affairs concluded that the latter interpretation should prevail, and in 1995 amended the Model to make this point explicitly.

12. However, paragraph 2 specifies that this applies only if the context does not require an alternative interpretation. The context is determined in particular by the intention of the Contracting States when signing the Convention as well as the meaning given to the term in question in the legislation of the other Contracting State (an implicit reference to the principle of reciprocity on which the Convention is based). The wording of the Article therefore allows the competent authorities some leeway.

13. Consequently, the wording of paragraph 2 provides a satisfactory balance between, on the one hand, the need to ensure the permanency of commitments entered into by States when signing a convention (since a State should not be allowed

to make a convention partially inoperative by amending afterwards in its domestic law the scope of terms not defined in the Convention) and, on the other hand, the need to be able to apply the Convention in a convenient and practical way over time (the need to refer to outdated concepts should be avoided).

13.1   Paragraph 2 was amended in 1995 to conform its text more closely to the general and consistent understanding of member states. For purposes of paragraph 2, the meaning of any term not defined in the Convention may be ascertained by reference to the meaning it has for the purpose of any relevant provision of the domestic law of a Contracting State, whether or not a tax law. However, where a term is defined differently for the purposes of different laws of a Contracting State, the meaning given to that term for purposes of the laws imposing the taxes to which the Convention applies shall prevail over all others, including those given for the purposes of other tax laws. States that are able to enter into mutual agreements (under the provisions of Article 25 and, in particular, paragraph 3 thereof) that establish the meanings of terms not defined in the Convention should take those agreements into account in interpreting those terms.

Reservations on the Article

14.   *Italy* and *Portugal* reserve the right not to include the definitions in subparagraphs 1 *c)* and *h)* ("enterprise" and "business") because they reserve the right to include an article concerning the taxation of independent personal services.

15.   *Chile*, *Mexico* and the *United States* reserve the right to omit the phrase "operated by an enterprise that has its place of effective management in a Contracting State" from the definition of "international traffic" in subparagraph *e)* of paragraph 1.

COMMENTARY ON ARTICLE 4
CONCERNING THE DEFINITION OF RESIDENT

I. Preliminary remarks

1.   The concept of "resident of a Contracting State" has various functions and is of importance in three cases:

   a) in determining a convention's personal scope of application;

   b) in solving cases where double taxation arises in consequence of double residence;

   c) in solving cases where double taxation arises as a consequence of taxation in the State of residence and in the State of source or situs.

2.   The Article is intended to define the meaning of the term "resident of a Contracting State" and to solve cases of double residence. To clarify the scope of the Article some general comments are made below referring to the two typical cases of conflict, i.e. between two residences and between residence and source or situs. In both cases the conflict arises because, under their domestic laws, one or both Contracting States claim that the person concerned is resident in their territory.

3.   Generally the domestic laws of the various States impose a comprehensive liability to tax — "full tax liability" — based on the taxpayers' personal attachment to the State concerned (the "State of residence"). This liability to tax is not imposed only on persons who are "domiciled" in a State in the sense in which "domicile" is usually taken in the legislations (private law). The cases of full liability to tax are extended to comprise also, for instance, persons who stay continually, or maybe only for a certain period, in the territory of the State. Some legislations impose full liability to tax on individuals who perform services on board ships which have their home harbour in the State.

4.   Conventions for the avoidance of double taxation do not normally concern themselves with the domestic laws of the Contracting States laying down the conditions under which a person is to be treated fiscally as "resident" and, consequently, is fully liable to tax in that State. They do not lay down standards which the provisions of the domestic laws on "residence" have to fulfil in order that claims for full tax liability can be accepted between the Contracting States. In this respect the States take their stand entirely on the domestic laws.

5.   This manifests itself quite clearly in the cases where there is no conflict at all between two residences, but where the conflict exists only between residence and source or situs. But the same view applies in conflicts between two residences. The special point in these cases is only that no solution of the conflict can be arrived at by reference to the concept of residence adopted in the domestic laws of the States concerned. In these cases special provisions must be established in the Convention to determine which of the two concepts of residence is to be given preference.

6.   An example will elucidate the case. An individual has his permanent home in State A, where his wife and children live. He has had a stay of more than six months in State B and according to the legislation of the latter State he is, in consequence of the length of the stay, taxed as being a resident of that State. Thus, both States claim that he is fully liable to tax. This conflict has to be solved by the Convention.

7.   In this particular case the Article (under paragraph 2) gives preference to the claim of State A. This does not, however, imply that the Article lays down special rules on "residence" and that the domestic laws of State B are ignored because they are incompatible with such rules. The fact is quite simply that in the case of such a conflict a choice must necessarily be made between the two claims, and it is on this point that the Article proposes special rules.

II.   Commentary on the provisions of the Article

Paragraph 1

8.   Paragraph 1 provides a definition of the expression "resident of a Contracting State" for the purposes of the Convention. The definition refers to the concept of residence adopted in the domestic laws (see Preliminary remarks). As criteria for the taxation as a resident the definition mentions: domicile, residence, place of management or any other criterion of a similar nature. As far as individuals are concerned, the definition aims at covering the various forms of personal attachment to a State which, in the domestic taxation laws, form the basis of a comprehensive taxation (full liability to tax). It also covers cases where a person is deemed, according to the taxation laws of a State, to be a resident of that State and on account thereof is fully liable to tax therein (e.g. diplomats or other persons in government service).

8.1   In accordance with the provisions of the second sentence of paragraph 1, however, a person is not to be considered a "resident of a Contracting State" in the sense of the Convention if, although not domiciled in that State, he is considered to be a resident according to the domestic laws but is subject only to a taxation limited to the income from sources in that State or to capital situated in that State. That situation exists in some States in relation to individuals, e.g. in the case of foreign diplomatic and consular staff serving in their territory.

8.2   According to its wording and spirit the second sentence also excludes from the definition of a resident of a Contracting State foreign held companies exempted from tax on their foreign income by privileges tailored to attract conduit companies. It also excludes companies and other persons who are not subject to comprehensive liability to tax in a Contracting State because these persons, whilst being residents of that State under that State's tax law, are considered to be residents of another State pursuant to a treaty between these two States. The exclusion of certain companies or other persons from the definition would not of course prevent Contracting States from exchanging information about their activities (see paragraph 2 of the Commentary on

Article 26). Indeed States may feel it appropriate to develop spontaneous exchanges of information about persons who seek to obtain unintended treaty benefits.

8.3   The application of the second sentence, however, has inherent difficulties and limitations. It has to be interpreted in the light of its object and purpose, which is to exclude persons who are not subjected to comprehensive taxation (full liability to tax) in a State, because it might otherwise exclude from the scope of the Convention all residents of countries adopting a territorial principle in their taxation, a result which is clearly not intended.

8.4   It has been the general understanding of most member countries that the government of each State, as well as any political subdivision or local authority thereof, is a resident of that State for purposes of the Convention. Before 1995, the Model did not explicitly state this; in 1995, Article 4 was amended to conform the text of the Model to this understanding.

8.5   This raises the issue of the application of paragraph 1 to sovereign wealth funds, which are special purpose investment funds or arrangements created by a State or a political subdivision for macroeconomic purposes. These funds hold, manage or administer assets to achieve financial objectives, and employ a set of investment strategies which include investing in foreign financial assets. They are commonly established out of balance of payments surpluses, official foreign currency operations, the proceeds of privatisations, fiscal surpluses or receipts resulting from commodity exports.[1] Whether a sovereign wealth fund qualifies as a "resident of a Contracting State" depends on the facts and circumstances of each case. For example, when a sovereign wealth fund is an integral part of the State, it will likely fall within the scope of the expression "[the] State and any political subdivision or local authority thereof" in Article 4. In other cases, paragraphs 8.6 and 8.7 below will be relevant. States may want to address the issue in the course of bilateral negotiations, particularly in relation to whether a sovereign wealth fund qualifies as a "person" and is "liable to tax" for purposes of the relevant tax treaty (see also paragraphs 6.35 to 6.39 of the Commentary on Article 1).

8.6   Paragraph 1 refers to persons who are "liable to tax" in a Contracting State under its laws by reason of various criteria. In many States, a person is considered liable to comprehensive taxation even if the Contracting State does not in fact impose tax. For example, pension funds, charities and other organisations may be exempted from tax, but they are exempt only if they meet all of the requirements for exemption specified in the tax laws. They are, thus, subject to the tax laws of a Contracting State. Furthermore, if they do not meet the standards specified, they are also required to pay tax. Most States would view such entities as residents for purposes of the Convention (see, for example, paragraph 1 of Article 10 and paragraph 5 of Article 11).

---

1   This definition is drawn from: International Working Group of Sovereign Wealth Funds, *Sovereign Wealth Funds — Generally Accepted Principles and Practices — "Santiago Principles"*, October 2008, Annex 1.

8.7   In some States, however, these entities are not considered liable to tax if they are exempt from tax under domestic tax laws. These States may not regard such entities as residents for purposes of a convention unless these entities are expressly covered by the convention. Contracting States taking this view are free to address the issue in their bilateral negotiations.

8.8   Where a State disregards a partnership for tax purposes and treats it as fiscally transparent, taxing the partners on their share of the partnership income, the partnership itself is not liable to tax and may not, therefore, be considered to be a resident of that State. In such a case, since the income of the partnership "flows through" to the partners under the domestic law of that State, the partners are the persons who are liable to tax on that income and are thus the appropriate persons to claim the benefits of the conventions concluded by the States of which they are residents. This latter result will be achieved even if, under the domestic law of the State of source, the income is attributed to a partnership which is treated as a separate taxable entity. For States which could not agree with this interpretation of the Article, it would be possible to provide for this result in a special provision which would avoid the resulting potential double taxation where the income of the partnership is differently allocated by the two States.

Paragraph 2

9.   This paragraph relates to the case where, under the provisions of paragraph 1, an individual is a resident of both Contracting States.

10.   To solve this conflict special rules must be established which give the attachment to one State a preference over the attachment to the other State. As far as possible, the preference criterion must be of such a nature that there can be no question but that the person concerned will satisfy it in one State only, and at the same time it must reflect such an attachment that it is felt to be natural that the right to tax devolves upon that particular State. The facts to which the special rules will apply are those existing during the period when the residence of the taxpayer affects tax liability, which may be less than an entire taxable period. For example, in one calendar year an individual is a resident of State A under that State's tax laws from 1 January to 31 March, then moves to State B. Because the individual resides in State B for more than 183 days, the individual is treated by the tax laws of State B as a State B resident for the entire year. Applying the special rules to the period 1 January to 31 March, the individual was a resident of State A. Therefore, both State A and State B should treat the individual as a State A resident for that period, and as a State B resident from 1 April to 31 December.

11.   The Article gives preference to the Contracting State in which the individual has a permanent home available to him. This criterion will frequently be sufficient to solve the conflict, e.g. where the individual has a permanent home in one Contracting State and has only made a stay of some length in the other Contracting State.

12.   Subparagraph a) means, therefore, that in the application of the Convention (that is, where there is a conflict between the laws of the two States) it is considered that the residence is that place where the individual owns or possesses a home; this home

must be permanent, that is to say, the individual must have arranged and retained it for his permanent use as opposed to staying at a particular place under such conditions that it is evident that the stay is intended to be of short duration.

13.   As regards the concept of home, it should be observed that any form of home may be taken into account (house or apartment belonging to or rented by the individual, rented furnished room). But the permanence of the home is essential; this means that the individual has arranged to have the dwelling available to him at all times continuously, and not occasionally for the purpose of a stay which, owing to the reasons for it, is necessarily of short duration (travel for pleasure, business travel, educational travel, attending a course at a school, etc.).

14.   If the individual has a permanent home in both Contracting States, paragraph 2 gives preference to the State with which the personal and economic relations of the individual are closer, this being understood as the centre of vital interests. In the cases where the residence cannot be determined by reference to this rule, paragraph 2 provides as subsidiary criteria, first, habitual abode, and then nationality. If the individual is a national of both States or of neither of them, the question shall be solved by mutual agreement between the States concerned according to the procedure laid down in Article 25.

15.   If the individual has a permanent home in both Contracting States, it is necessary to look at the facts in order to ascertain with which of the two States his personal and economic relations are closer. Thus, regard will be had to his family and social relations, his occupations, his political, cultural or other activities, his place of business, the place from which he administers his property, etc. The circumstances must be examined as a whole, but it is nevertheless obvious that considerations based on the personal acts of the individual must receive special attention. If a person who has a home in one State sets up a second in the other State while retaining the first, the fact that he retains the first in the environment where he has always lived, where he has worked, and where he has his family and possessions, can, together with other elements, go to demonstrate that he has retained his centre of vital interests in the first State.

16.   Subparagraph b) establishes a secondary criterion for two quite distinct and different situations:

   a) the case where the individual has a permanent home available to him in both Contracting States and it is not possible to determine in which one he has his centre of vital interests;

   b) the case where the individual has a permanent home available to him in neither Contracting State.

Preference is given to the Contracting State where the individual has an habitual abode.

17.   In the first situation, the case where the individual has a permanent home available to him in both States, the fact of having an habitual abode in one State rather than in the other appears therefore as the circumstance which, in case of doubt as to

where the individual has his centre of vital interests, tips the balance towards the State where he stays more frequently. For this purpose regard must be had to stays made by the individual not only at the permanent home in the State in question but also at any other place in the same State.

18.   The second situation is the case of an individual who has a permanent home available to him in neither Contracting State, as for example, a person going from one hotel to another. In this case also all stays made in a State must be considered without it being necessary to ascertain the reasons for them.

19.   In stipulating that in the two situations which it contemplates preference is given to the Contracting State where the individual has an habitual abode, subparagraph b) does not specify over what length of time the comparison must be made. The comparison must cover a sufficient length of time for it to be possible to determine whether the residence in each of the two States is habitual and to determine also the intervals at which the stays take place.

20.   Where, in the two situations referred to in subparagraph b) the individual has an habitual abode in both Contracting States or in neither, preference is given to the State of which he is a national. If, in these cases still, the individual is a national of both Contracting States or of neither of them, subparagraph d) assigns to the competent authorities the duty of resolving the difficulty by mutual agreement according to the procedure established in Article 25.

Paragraph 3

21.   This paragraph concerns companies and other bodies of persons, irrespective of whether they are or are not legal persons. It may be rare in practice for a company, etc. to be subject to tax as a resident in more than one State, but it is, of course, possible if, for instance, one State attaches importance to the registration and the other State to the place of effective management. So, in the case of companies, etc., also, special rules as to the preference must be established.

22.   It would not be an adequate solution to attach importance to a purely formal criterion like registration. Therefore paragraph 3 attaches importance to the place where the company, etc. is actually managed.

23.   The formulation of the preference criterion in the case of persons other than individuals was considered in particular in connection with the taxation of income from shipping, inland waterways transport and air transport. A number of conventions for the avoidance of double taxation on such income accord the taxing power to the State in which the "place of management" of the enterprise is situated; other conventions attach importance to its "place of effective management", others again to the "fiscal domicile of the operator".

24.   As a result of these considerations, the "place of effective management" has been adopted as the preference criterion for persons other than individuals. The place of effective management is the place where key management and commercial decisions that are necessary for the conduct of the entity's business as a whole are in substance

made. All relevant facts and circumstances must be examined to determine the place of effective management. An entity may have more than one place of management, but it can have only one place of effective management at any one time.

24.1 Some countries, however, consider that cases of dual residence of persons who are not individuals are relatively rare and should be dealt with on a case-by-case basis. Some countries also consider that such a case-by-case approach is the best way to deal with the difficulties in determining the place of effective management of a legal person that may arise from the use of new communication technologies. These countries are free to leave the question of the residence of these persons to be settled by the competent authorities, which can be done by replacing the paragraph by the following provision:

3.   Where by reason of the provisions of paragraph 1 a person other than an individual is a resident of both Contracting States, the competent authorities of the Contracting States shall endeavour to determine by mutual agreement the Contracting State of which such person shall be deemed to be a resident for the purposes of the Convention, having regard to its place of effective management, the place where it is incorporated or otherwise constituted and any other relevant factors. In the absence of such agreement, such person shall not be entitled to any relief or exemption from tax provided by this Convention except to the extent and in such manner as may be agreed upon by the competent authorities of the Contracting State.

Competent authorities having to apply such a provision to determine the residence of a legal person for purposes of the Convention would be expected to take account of various factors, such as where the meetings of its board of directors or equivalent body are usually held, where the chief executive officer and other senior executives usually carry on their activities, where the senior day-to-day management of the person is carried on, where the person's headquarters are located, which country's laws govern the legal status of the person, where its accounting records are kept, whether determining that the legal person is a resident of one of the Contracting States but not of the other for the purpose of the Convention would carry the risk of an improper use of the provisions of the Convention etc. Countries that consider that the competent authorities should not be given the discretion to solve such cases of dual residence without an indication of the factors to be used for that purpose may want to supplement the provision to refer to these or other factors that they consider relevant. Also, since the application of the provision would normally be requested by the person concerned through the mechanism provided for under paragraph 1 of Article 25, the request should be made within three years from the first notification to that person that its taxation is not in accordance with the Convention since it is considered to be a resident of both Contracting States. Since the facts on which a decision will be based may change over time, the competent authorities that reach a decision under that provision should clarify which period of time is covered by that decision.

Observations on the Commentary

25.   As regards paragraphs 24 and 24.1, *Italy* holds the view that the place where the main and substantial activity of the entity is carried on is also to be taken into account when determining the place of effective management of a person other than an individual.

26.   *Spain*, due to the fact that according to its internal law the fiscal year coincides with the calendar year and there is no possibility of concluding the fiscal period by reason of the taxpayer's change of residence, will not be able to proceed in accordance with paragraph 10 of the Commentary on Article 4. In this case, a mutual agreement procedure will be needed to ascertain the date from which the taxpayer will be deemed to be a resident of one of the Contracting States.

26.1 *Mexico* does not agree with the general principle expressed in paragraph 8.8 of the Commentary according to which if tax owed by a partnership is determined on the basis of the personal characteristics of the partners, these partners are entitled to the benefits of tax conventions entered into by the States of which they are residents as regards income that "flows through" that partnership.

26.2 [Deleted]

26.3 *France* considers that the definition of the place of effective management in paragraph 24, according to which "the place of effective management is the place where key management and commercial decisions that are necessary for the conduct of the entity's business as a whole are in substance made", will generally correspond to the place where the person or group of persons who exercises the most senior functions (for example a board of directors or management board) makes its decisions. It is the place where the organs of direction, management and control of the entity are, in fact, mainly located.

26.4 As regards paragraph 24, *Hungary* is of the opinion that in determining the place of effective management, one should not only consider the place where key management and commercial decisions that are necessary for the conduct of the entity's business as a whole are in substance made, but should also take into account the place where the chief executive officer and other senior executives usually carry on their activities as well as the place where the senior day-to-day management of the enterprise is usually carried on.

Reservations on the Article

27.   *Canada* reserves the right to use as the test for paragraph 3 the place of incorporation or organisation with respect to a company and, failing that, to deny dual resident companies the benefits under the Convention.

28.   *Japan* and *Korea* reserve their position on the provisions in this and other Articles in the Model Tax Convention which refer directly or indirectly to the place of effective management. Instead of the term "place of effective management", these countries wish to use in their conventions the term "head or main office".

MODEL TAX CONVENTION (CONDENSED VERSION) – ISBN 978-92-64-08948-8 – © OECD 2010

29.   France does not agree with the general principle according to which if tax owed by a partnership is determined on the basis of the personal characteristics of the partners, these partners are entitled to the benefits of tax conventions entered into by the States of which they are residents as regards income that "flows through" that partnership. For this reason, France reserves the right to amend the Article in its tax conventions in order to specify that French partnerships must be considered as residents of France in view of their legal and tax characteristics and to indicate in which situations and under which conditions flow-through partnerships located in the other Contracting State or in a third State will be entitled to benefit from the recognition by France of their flow-through nature.

30.   *Turkey* reserves the right to use the "registered office" criterion (legal head office) as well as the "place of effective management" criterion for determining the residence of a person, other than an individual, which is a resident of both Contracting States because of the provisions of paragraph 1 of the Article.

31.   The *United States* reserves the right to use a place of incorporation test for determining the residence of a corporation, and, failing that, to deny dual resident companies certain benefits under the Convention.

32.   *Germany* reserves the right to include a provision under which a partnership that is not a resident of a Contracting State according to the provisions of paragraph 1 is deemed to be a resident of the Contracting State where the place of its effective management is situated, but only to the extent that the income derived from the other Contracting State or the capital situated in that other State is liable to tax in the first-mentioned State.

COMMENTARY ON ARTICLE 5
CONCERNING THE DEFINITION OF PERMANENT ESTABLISHMENT

1.   The main use of the concept of a permanent establishment is to determine the right of a Contracting State to tax the profits of an enterprise of the other Contracting State. Under Article 7 a Contracting State cannot tax the profits of an enterprise of the other Contracting State unless it carries on its business through a permanent establishment situated therein.

1.1   Before 2000, income from professional services and other activities of an independent character was dealt under a separate Article, *i.e.* Article 14. The provisions of that Article were similar to those applicable to business profits but it used the concept of fixed base rather than that of permanent establishment since it had originally been thought that the latter concept should be reserved to commercial and industrial activities. The elimination of Article 14 in 2000 reflected the fact that there were no intended differences between the concepts of permanent establishment, as used in Article 7, and fixed base, as used in Article 14, or between how profits were computed and tax was calculated according to which of Article 7 or 14 applied. The elimination of Article 14 therefore meant that the definition of permanent establishment became applicable to what previously constituted a fixed base.

Paragraph 1

2.   Paragraph 1 gives a general definition of the term "permanent establishment" which brings out its essential characteristics of a permanent establishment in the sense of the Convention, *i.e.* a distinct "situs", a "fixed place of business". The paragraph defines the term "permanent establishment" as a fixed place of business, through which the business of an enterprise is wholly or partly carried on. This definition, therefore, contains the following conditions:

— the existence of a "place of business", *i.e.* a facility such as premises or, in certain instances, machinery or equipment;

— this place of business must be "fixed", *i.e.* it must be established at a distinct place with a certain degree of permanence;

— the carrying on of the business of the enterprise through this fixed place of business. This means usually that persons who, in one way or another, are dependent on the enterprise (personnel) conduct the business of the enterprise in the State in which the fixed place is situated.

3.   It could perhaps be argued that in the general definition some mention should also be made of the other characteristic of a permanent establishment to which some importance has sometimes been attached in the past, namely that the establishment must have a productive character, *i.e.* contribute to the profits of the enterprise. In the present definition this course has not been taken. Within the framework of a well-run business organisation it is surely axiomatic to assume that each part contributes to the productivity of the whole. It does not, of course, follow in every case that because in the

MODEL TAX CONVENTION (CONDENSED VERSION) – ISBN 978-92-64-08948-8 – © OECD 2010

wider context of the whole organisation a particular establishment has a "productive character" it is consequently a permanent establishment to which profits can properly be attributed for the purpose of tax in a particular territory (see Commentary on paragraph 4).

4.   The term "place of business" covers any premises, facilities or installations used for carrying on the business of the enterprise whether or not they are used exclusively for that purpose. A place of business may also exist where no premises are available or required for carrying on the business of the enterprise and it simply has a certain amount of space at its disposal. It is immaterial whether the premises, facilities or installations are owned or rented by or are otherwise at the disposal of the enterprise. A place of business may thus be constituted by a pitch in a market place, or by a certain permanently used area in a customs depot (e.g. for the storage of dutiable goods). Again the place of business may be situated in the business facilities of another enterprise. This may be the case for instance where the foreign enterprise has at its constant disposal certain premises or a part thereof owned by the other enterprise.

4.1   As noted above, the mere fact that an enterprise has a certain amount of space at its disposal which is used for business activities is sufficient to constitute a place of business. No formal legal right to use that place is therefore required. Thus, for instance, a permanent establishment could exist where an enterprise illegally occupied a certain location where it carried on its business.

4.2   Whilst no formal legal right to use a particular place is required for that place to constitute a permanent establishment, the mere presence of an enterprise at a particular location does not necessarily mean that that location is at the disposal of that enterprise. These principles are illustrated by the following examples where representatives of one enterprise are present on the premises of another enterprise. A first example is that of a salesman who regularly visits a major customer to take orders and meets the purchasing director in his office to do so. In that case, the customer's premises are not at the disposal of the enterprise for which the salesman is working and therefore do not constitute a fixed place of business through which the business of that enterprise is carried on (depending on the circumstances, however, paragraph 5 could apply to deem a permanent establishment to exist).

4.3   A second example is that of an employee of a company who, for a long period of time, is allowed to use an office in the headquarters of another company (e.g. a newly acquired subsidiary) in order to ensure that the latter company complies with its obligations under contracts concluded with the former company. In that case, the employee is carrying on activities related to the business of the former company and the office that is at his disposal at the headquarters of the other company will constitute a permanent establishment of his employer, provided that the office is at his disposal for a sufficiently long period of time so as to constitute a "fixed place of business" (see paragraphs 6 to 6.3) and that the activities that are performed there go beyond the activities referred to in paragraph 4 of the Article.

4.4   A third example is that of a road transportation enterprise which would use a delivery dock at a customer's warehouse every day for a number of years for the purpose of delivering goods purchased by that customer. In that case, the presence of the road transportation enterprise at the delivery dock would be so limited that that enterprise could not consider that place as being at its disposal so as to constitute a permanent establishment of that enterprise.

4.5   A fourth example is that of a painter who, for two years, spends three days a week in the large office building of its main client. In that case, the presence of the painter in that office building where he is performing the most important functions of his business (i.e. painting) constitute a permanent establishment of that painter.

4.6   The words "through which" must be given a wide meaning so as to apply to any situation where business activities are carried on at a particular location that is at the disposal of the enterprise for that purpose. Thus, for instance, an enterprise engaged in paving a road will be considered to be carrying on its business "through" the location where this activity takes place.

5.   According to the definition, the place of business has to be a "fixed" one. Thus in the normal way there has to be a link between the place of business and a specific geographical point. It is immaterial how long an enterprise of a Contracting State operates in the other Contracting State if it does not do so at a distinct place, but this does not mean that the equipment constituting the place of business has to be actually fixed to the soil on which it stands. It is enough that the equipment remains on a particular site (but see paragraph 20 below).

5.1   Where the nature of the business activities carried on by an enterprise is such that these activities are often moved between neighbouring locations, there may be difficulties in determining whether there is a single "place of business" (if two places of business are occupied and the other requirements of Article 5 are met, the enterprise will, of course, have two permanent establishments). As recognised in paragraphs 18 and 20 below a single place of business will generally be considered to exist where, in light of the nature of the business, a particular location within which the activities are moved may be identified as constituting a coherent whole commercially and geographically with respect to that business.

5.2   This principle may be illustrated by examples. A mine clearly constitutes a single place of business even though business activities may move from one location to another in what may be a very large mine as it constitutes a single geographical and commercial unit as concerns the mining business. Similarly, an "office hotel" in which a consulting firm regularly rents different offices may be considered to be a single place of business of that firm since, in that case, the building constitutes a whole geographically and the hotel is a single place of business for the consulting firm. For the same reason, a pedestrian street, outdoor market or fair in different parts of which a trader regularly sets up his stand represents a single place of business for that trader.

5.3   By contrast, where there is no commercial coherence, the fact that activities may be carried on within a limited geographic area should not result in that area being considered as a single place of business. For example, where a painter works successively under a series of unrelated contracts for a number of unrelated clients in a large office building so that it cannot be said that there is one single project for repainting the building, the building should not be regarded as a single place of business for the purpose of that work. However, in the different example of a painter who, under a single contract, undertakes work throughout a building for a single client, this constitutes a single project for that painter and the building as a whole can then be regarded as a single place of business for the purpose of that work as it would then constitute a coherent whole commercially and geographically.

5.4   Conversely, an area where activities are carried on as part of a single project which constitutes a coherent commercial whole may lack the necessary geographic coherence to be considered as a single place of business. For example, where a consultant works at different branches in separate locations pursuant to a single project for training the employees of a bank, each branch should be considered separately. However if the consultant moves from one office to another within the same branch location, he should be considered to remain in the same place of business. The single branch location possesses geographical coherence which is absent where the consultant moves between branches in different locations.

5.5   Clearly, a permanent establishment may only be considered to be situated in a Contracting State if the relevant place of business is situated in the territory of that State. The question of whether a satellite in geostationary orbit could constitute a permanent establishment for the satellite operator relates in part to how far the territory of a State extends into space. No member country would agree that the location of these satellites can be part of the territory of a Contracting State under the applicable rules of international law and could therefore be considered to be a permanent establishment situated therein. Also, the particular area over which a satellite's signals may be received (the satellite's "footprint") cannot be considered to be at the disposal of the operator of the satellite so as to make that area a place of business of the satellite's operator.

6.   Since the place of business must be fixed, it also follows that a permanent establishment can be deemed to exist only if the place of business has a certain degree of permanency, i.e. if it is not of a purely temporary nature. A place of business may, however, constitute a permanent establishment even though it exists, in practice, only for a very short period of time because the nature of the business is such that it will only be carried on for that short period of time. It is sometimes difficult to determine whether this is the case. Whilst the practices followed by member countries have not been consistent in so far as time requirements are concerned, experience has shown that permanent establishments normally have not been considered to exist in situations where a business had been carried on in a country through a place of business that was maintained for less than six months (conversely, practice shows that there were many cases where a permanent establishment has been considered to exist where the place of business was maintained for a period longer than six months). One exception has been where the activities were of a recurrent nature; in such cases, each

period of time during which the place is used needs to be considered in combination with the number of times during which that place is used (which may extend over a number of years). Another exception has been made where activities constituted a business that was carried on exclusively in that country; in this situation, the business may have short duration because of its nature but since it is wholly carried on in that country, its connection with that country is stronger. For ease of administration, countries may want to consider these practices when they address disagreements as to whether a particular place of business that exists only for a short period of time constitutes a permanent establishment.

6.1   As mentioned in paragraphs 11 and 19, temporary interruptions of activities do not cause a permanent establishment to cease to exist. Similarly, as discussed in paragraph 6, where a particular place of business is used for only very short periods of time but such usage takes place regularly over long periods of time, the place of business should not be considered to be of a purely temporary nature.

6.2   Also, there may be cases where a particular place of business would be used for very short periods of time by a number of similar businesses carried on by the same or related persons in an attempt to avoid that the place be considered to have been used for more than purely temporary purposes by each particular business. The remarks of paragraph 18 on arrangements intended to abuse the twelve month period provided for in paragraph 3 would equally apply to such cases.

6.3   Where a place of business which was, at the outset, designed to be used for such a short period of time that it would not have constituted a permanent establishment but is in fact maintained for such a period that it can no longer be considered as a temporary one, it becomes a fixed place of business and thus — retrospectively — a permanent establishment. A place of business can also constitute a permanent establishment from its inception even though it existed, in practice, for a very short period of time, if as a consequence of special circumstances (*e.g.* death of the taxpayer, investment failure), it was prematurely liquidated.

7.   For a place of business to constitute a permanent establishment the enterprise using it must carry on its business wholly or partly through it. As stated in paragraph 3 above, the activity need not be of a productive character. Furthermore, the activity need not be permanent in the sense that there is no interruption of operation, but operations must be carried out on a regular basis.

8.   Where tangible property such as facilities, industrial, commercial or scientific (ICS) equipment, buildings, or intangible property such as patents, procedures and similar property, are let or leased to third parties through a fixed place of business maintained by an enterprise of a Contracting State in the other State, this activity will, in general, render the place of business a permanent establishment. The same applies if capital is made available through a fixed place of business. If an enterprise of a State lets or leases facilities, ICS equipment, buildings or intangible property to an enterprise of the other State without maintaining for such letting or leasing activity a fixed place of business in the other State, the leased facility, ICS

equipment, building or intangible property, as such, will not constitute a permanent establishment of the lessor provided the contract is limited to the mere leasing of the ICS equipment, etc. This remains the case even when, for example, the lessor supplies personnel after installation to operate the equipment provided that their responsibility is limited solely to the operation or maintenance of the ICS equipment under the direction, responsibility and control of the lessee. If the personnel have wider responsibilities, for example, participation in the decisions regarding the work for which the equipment is used, or if they operate, service, inspect and maintain the equipment under the responsibility and control of the lessor, the activity of the lessor may go beyond the mere leasing of ICS equipment and may constitute an entrepreneurial activity. In such a case a permanent establishment could be deemed to exist if the criterion of permanency is met. When such activity is connected with, or is similar in character to, those mentioned in paragraph 3, the time limit of twelve months applies. Other cases have to be determined according to the circumstances.

9.   The leasing of containers is one particular case of the leasing of industrial or commercial equipment which does, however, have specific features. The question of determining the circumstances in which an enterprise involved in the leasing of containers should be considered as having a permanent establishment in another State is more fully discussed in a report entitled "The Taxation of Income Derived from the Leasing of Containers."[1]

9.1   Another example where an enterprise cannot be considered to carry on its business wholly or partly through a place of business is that of a telecommunications operator of a Contracting State who enters into a "roaming" agreement with a foreign operator in order to allow its users to connect to the foreign operator's telecommunications network. Under such an agreement, a user who is outside the geographical coverage of that user's home network can automatically make and receive voice calls, send and receive data or access other services through the use of the foreign network. The foreign network operator then bills the operator of that user's home network for that use. Under a typical roaming agreement, the home network operator merely transfers calls to the foreign operator's network and does not operate or have physical access to that network. For these reasons, any place where the foreign network is located cannot be considered to be at the disposal of the home network operator and cannot, therefore, constitute a permanent establishment of that operator.

10.   The business of an enterprise is carried on mainly by the entrepreneur or persons who are in a paid-employment relationship with the enterprise (personnel). This personnel includes employees and other persons receiving instructions from the enterprise (e.g. dependent agents). The powers of such personnel in its relationship with third parties are irrelevant. It makes no difference whether or not the dependent agent is authorised to conclude contracts if he works at the fixed place of business (see paragraph 35 below). But a permanent establishment may nevertheless exist if the

---

1   Reproduced in Volume II of the full-length version of the OECD Model Tax Convention at page R(3)-1.

business of the enterprise is carried on mainly through automatic equipment, the activities of the personnel being restricted to setting up, operating, controlling and maintaining such equipment. Whether or not gaming and vending machines and the like set up by an enterprise of a State in the other State constitute a permanent establishment thus depends on whether or not the enterprise carries on a business activity besides the initial setting up of the machines. A permanent establishment does not exist if the enterprise merely sets up the machines and then leases the machines to other enterprises. A permanent establishment may exist, however, if the enterprise which sets up the machines also operates and maintains them for its own account. This also applies if the machines are operated and maintained by an agent dependent on the enterprise.

11.   A permanent establishment begins to exist as soon as the enterprise commences to carry on its business through a fixed place of business. This is the case once the enterprise prepares, at the place of business, the activity for which the place of business is to serve permanently. The period of time during which the fixed place of business itself is being set up by the enterprise should not be counted, provided that this activity differs substantially from the activity for which the place of business is to serve permanently. The permanent establishment ceases to exist with the disposal of the fixed place of business or with the cessation of any activity through it, that is when all acts and measures connected with the former activities of the permanent establishment are terminated (winding up current business transactions, maintenance and repair of facilities). A temporary interruption of operations, however, cannot be regarded as a closure. If the fixed place of business is leased to another enterprise, it will normally only serve the activities of that enterprise instead of the lessor's; in general, the lessor's permanent establishment ceases to exist, except where he continues carrying on a business activity of his own through the fixed place of business.

Paragraph 2

12.   This paragraph contains a list, by no means exhaustive, of examples, each of which can be regarded, *prima facie*, as constituting a permanent establishment. As these examples are to be seen against the background of the general definition given in paragraph 1, it is assumed that the Contracting States interpret the terms listed, "a place of management", "a branch", "an office", etc. in such a way that such places of business constitute permanent establishments only if they meet the requirements of paragraph 1.

13.   The term "place of management" has been mentioned separately because it is not necessarily an "office". However, where the laws of the two Contracting States do not contain the concept of "a place of management" as distinct from an "office", there will be no need to refer to the former term in their bilateral convention.

14.   Subparagraph *f)* provides that mines, oil or gas wells, quarries or any other place of extraction of natural resources are permanent establishments. The term "any other

place of extraction of natural resources" should be interpreted broadly. It includes, for example, all places of extraction of hydrocarbons whether on or off-shore.

15.   Subparagraph *f)* refers to the extraction of natural resources, but does not mention the exploration of such resources, whether on or off shore. Therefore, whenever income from such activities is considered to be business profits, the question whether these activities are carried on through a permanent establishment is governed by paragraph 1. Since, however, it has not been possible to arrive at a common view on the basic questions of the attribution of taxation rights and of the qualification of the income from exploration activities, the Contracting States may agree upon the insertion of specific provisions. They may agree, for instance, that an enterprise of a Contracting State, as regards its activities of exploration of natural resources in a place or area in the other Contracting State:

a) shall be deemed not to have a permanent establishment in that other State; or

b) shall be deemed to carry on such activities through a permanent establishment in that other State; or

c) shall be deemed to carry on such activities through a permanent establishment in that other State if such activities last longer than a specified period of time.

The Contracting States may moreover agree to submit the income from such activities to any other rule.

Paragraph 3

16.   The paragraph provides expressly that a building site or construction or installation project constitutes a permanent establishment only if it lasts more than twelve months. Any of those items which does not meet this condition does not of itself constitute a permanent establishment, even if there is within it an installation, for instance an office or a workshop within the meaning of paragraph 2, associated with the construction activity. Where, however, such an office or workshop is used for a number of construction projects and the activities performed therein go beyond those mentioned in paragraph 4, it will be considered a permanent establishment if the conditions of the Article are otherwise met even if none of the projects involve a building site or construction or installation project that lasts more than twelve months. In that case, the situation of the workshop or office will therefore be different from that of these sites or projects, none of which will constitute a permanent establishment, and it will be important to ensure that only the profits properly attributable to the functions performed through that office or workshop, taking into account the assets used and the risks assumed through that office or workshop, are attributed to the permanent establishment. This could include profits attributable to functions performed in relation to the various construction sites but only to the extent that these functions are properly attributable to the office.

17.   The term "building site or construction or installation project" includes not only the construction of buildings but also the construction of roads, bridges or canals, the renovation (involving more than mere maintenance or redecoration) of buildings, roads, bridges or canals, the laying of pipe-lines and excavating and dredging.

Additionally, the term "installation project" is not restricted to an installation related to a construction project; it also includes the installation of new equipment, such as a complex machine, in an existing building or outdoors. On-site planning and supervision of the erection of a building are covered by paragraph 3. States wishing to modify the text of the paragraph to provide expressly for that result are free to do so in their bilateral conventions.

18.   The twelve month test applies to each individual site or project. In determining how long the site or project has existed, no account should be taken of the time previously spent by the contractor concerned on other sites or projects which are totally unconnected with it. A building site should be regarded as a single unit, even if it is based on several contracts, provided that it forms a coherent whole commercially and geographically. Subject to this proviso, a building site forms a single unit even if the orders have been placed by several persons (e.g. for a row of houses). The twelve month threshold has given rise to abuses; it has sometimes been found that enterprises (mainly contractors or subcontractors working on the continental shelf or engaged in activities connected with the exploration and exploitation of the continental shelf) divided their contracts up into several parts, each covering a period less than twelve months and attributed to a different company which was, however, owned by the same group. Apart from the fact that such abuses may, depending on the circumstances, fall under the application of legislative or judicial anti-avoidance rules, countries concerned with this issue can adopt solutions in the framework of bilateral negotiations.

19.   A site exists from the date on which the contractor begins his work, including any preparatory work, in the country where the construction is to be established, e.g. if he installs a planning office for the construction. In general, it continues to exist until the work is completed or permanently abandoned. A site should not be regarded as ceasing to exist when work is temporarily discontinued. Seasonal or other temporary interruptions should be included in determining the life of a site. Seasonal interruptions include interruptions due to bad weather. Temporary interruption could be caused, for example, by shortage of material or labour difficulties. Thus, for example, if a contractor started work on a road on 1 May, stopped on 1 November because of bad weather conditions or a lack of materials but resumed work on 1 February the following year, completing the road on 1 June, his construction project should be regarded as a permanent establishment because thirteen months elapsed between the date he first commenced work (1 May) and the date he finally finished (1 June of the following year). If an enterprise (general contractor) which has undertaken the performance of a comprehensive project subcontracts parts of such a project to other enterprises (subcontractors), the period spent by a subcontractor working on the building site must be considered as being time spent by the general contractor on the building project. The subcontractor himself has a permanent establishment at the site if his activities there last more than twelve months.

19.1 In the case of fiscally transparent partnerships, the twelve month test is applied at the level of the partnership as concerns its own activities. If the period of time spent on the site by the partners and the employees of the partnership exceeds twelve months, the enterprise carried on by the partnership will therefore be considered to have a permanent establishment. Each partner will thus be considered to have a permanent establishment for purposes of the taxation of his share of the business profits derived by the partnership regardless of the time spent by himself on the site.

20.   The very nature of a construction or installation project may be such that the contractor's activity has to be relocated continuously or at least from time to time, as the project progresses. This would be the case for instance where roads or canals were being constructed, waterways dredged, or pipe-lines laid. Similarly, where parts of a substantial structure such as an offshore platform are assembled at various locations within a country and moved to another location within the country for final assembly, this is part of a single project. In such cases, the fact that the work force is not present for twelve months in one particular location is immaterial. The activities performed at each particular spot are part of a single project, and that project must be regarded as a permanent establishment if, as a whole, it lasts more than twelve months.

Paragraph 4

21.   This paragraph lists a number of business activities which are treated as exceptions to the general definition laid down in paragraph 1 and which are not permanent establishments, even if the activity is carried on through a fixed place of business. The common feature of these activities is that they are, in general, preparatory or auxiliary activities. This is laid down explicitly in the case of the exception mentioned in subparagraph e), which actually amounts to a general restriction of the scope of the definition contained in paragraph 1. Moreover subparagraph f) provides that combinations of activities mentioned in subparagraphs a) to e) in the same fixed place of business shall be deemed not to be a permanent establishment, provided that the overall activity of the fixed place of business resulting from this combination is of a preparatory or auxiliary character. Thus the provisions of paragraph 4 are designed to prevent an enterprise of one State from being taxed in the other State, if it carries on in that other State, activities of a purely preparatory or auxiliary character.

22.   Subparagraph a) relates only to the case in which an enterprise acquires the use of facilities for storing, displaying or delivering its own goods or merchandise. Subparagraph b) relates to the stock of merchandise itself and provides that the stock, as such, shall not be treated as a permanent establishment if it is maintained for the purpose of storage, display or delivery. Subparagraph c) covers the case in which a stock of goods or merchandise belonging to one enterprise is processed by a second enterprise, on behalf of, or for the account of, the first-mentioned enterprise. The reference to the collection of information in subparagraph d) is intended to include the case of the newspaper bureau which has no purpose other than to act as one of many "tentacles" of the parent body; to exempt such a bureau is to do no more than to extend the concept of "mere purchase".

23.   Subparagraph e) provides that a fixed place of business through which the enterprise exercises solely an activity which has for the enterprise a preparatory or auxiliary character, is deemed not to be a permanent establishment. The wording of this subparagraph makes it unnecessary to produce an exhaustive list of exceptions. Furthermore, this subparagraph provides a generalised exception to the general definition in paragraph 1 and, when read with that paragraph, provides a more selective test, by which to determine what constitutes a permanent establishment. To a considerable degree it limits that definition and excludes from its rather wide scope a number of forms of business organisations which, although they are carried on through a fixed place of business, should not be treated as permanent establishments. It is recognised that such a place of business may well contribute to the productivity of the enterprise, but the services it performs are so remote from the actual realisation of profits that it is difficult to allocate any profit to the fixed place of business in question. Examples are fixed places of business solely for the purpose of advertising or for the supply of information or for scientific research or for the servicing of a patent or a know-how contract, if such activities have a preparatory or auxiliary character.

24.   It is often difficult to distinguish between activities which have a preparatory or auxiliary character and those which have not. The decisive criterion is whether or not the activity of the fixed place of business in itself forms an essential and significant part of the activity of the enterprise as a whole. Each individual case will have to be examined on its own merits. In any case, a fixed place of business whose general purpose is one which is identical to the general purpose of the whole enterprise, does not exercise a preparatory or auxiliary activity. Where, for example, the servicing of patents and know-how is the purpose of an enterprise, a fixed place of business of such enterprise exercising such an activity cannot get the benefits of subparagraph e). A fixed place of business which has the function of managing an enterprise or even only a part of an enterprise or of a group of the concern cannot be regarded as doing a preparatory or auxiliary activity, for such a managerial activity exceeds this level. If enterprises with international ramifications establish a so-called "management office" in States in which they maintain subsidiaries, permanent establishments, agents or licensees, such office having supervisory and coordinating functions for all departments of the enterprise located within the region concerned, a permanent establishment will normally be deemed to exist, because the management office may be regarded as an office within the meaning of paragraph 2. Where a big international concern has delegated all management functions to its regional management offices so that the functions of the head office of the concern are restricted to general supervision (so-called polycentric enterprises), the regional management offices even have to be regarded as a "place of management" within the meaning of subparagraph a) of paragraph 2. The function of managing an enterprise, even if it only covers a certain area of the operations of the concern, constitutes an essential part of the business operations of the enterprise and therefore can in no way be regarded as an activity which has a preparatory or auxiliary character within the meaning of subparagraph e) of paragraph 4.

MODEL TAX CONVENTION (CONDENSED VERSION) – ISBN 978-92-64-08948-8 – © OECD 2010

25.   A permanent establishment could also be constituted if an enterprise maintains a fixed place of business for the delivery of spare parts to customers for machinery supplied to those customers where, in addition, it maintains or repairs such machinery, as this goes beyond the pure delivery mentioned in subparagraph *a)* of paragraph 4. Since these after-sale organisations perform an essential and significant part of the services of an enterprise vis-à-vis its customers, their activities are not merely auxiliary ones. Subparagraph *e)* applies only if the activity of the fixed place of business is limited to a preparatory or auxiliary one. This would not be the case where, for example, the fixed place of business does not only give information but also furnishes plans etc. specially developed for the purposes of the individual customer. Nor would it be the case if a research establishment were to concern itself with manufacture.

26.   Moreover, subparagraph *e)* makes it clear that the activities of the fixed place of business must be carried on for the enterprise. A fixed place of business which renders services not only to its enterprise but also directly to other enterprises, for example to other companies of a group to which the company owning the fixed place belongs, would not fall within the scope of subparagraph *e)*.

26.1   Another example is that of facilities such as cables or pipelines that cross the territory of a country. Apart from the fact that income derived by the owner or operator of such facilities from their use by other enterprises is covered by Article 6 where they constitute immovable property under paragraph 2 of Article 6, the question may arise as to whether paragraph 4 applies to them. Where these facilities are used to transport property belonging to other enterprises, subparagraph *a)*, which is restricted to delivery of goods or merchandise belonging to the enterprise that uses the facility, will not be applicable as concerns the owner or operator of these facilities. Subparagraph *e)* also will not be applicable as concerns that enterprise since the cable or pipeline is not used solely for the enterprise and its use is not of preparatory or auxiliary character given the nature of the business of that enterprise. The situation is different, however, where an enterprise owns and operates a cable or pipeline that crosses the territory of a country solely for purposes of transporting its own property and such transport is merely incidental to the business of that enterprise, as in the case of an enterprise that is in the business of refining oil and that owns and operates a pipeline that crosses the territory of a country solely to transport its own oil to its refinery located in another country. In such case, subparagraph *a)* would be applicable. An additional question is whether the cable or pipeline could also constitute a permanent establishment for the customer of the operator of the cable or pipeline, *i.e.* the enterprise whose data, power or property is transmitted or transported from one place to another. In such a case, the enterprise is merely obtaining transmission or transportation services provided by the operator of the cable or pipeline and does not have the cable or pipeline at its disposal. As a consequence, the cable or pipeline cannot be considered to be a permanent establishment of that enterprise.

27.   As already mentioned in paragraph 21 above, paragraph 4 is designed to provide for exceptions to the general definition of paragraph 1 in respect of fixed places of

business which are engaged in activities having a preparatory or auxiliary character. Therefore, according to subparagraph *f)* of paragraph 4, the fact that one fixed place of business combines any of the activities mentioned in the subparagraphs *a)* to *e)* of paragraph 4 does not mean of itself that a permanent establishment exists. As long as the combined activity of such a fixed place of business is merely preparatory or auxiliary a permanent establishment should be deemed not to exist. Such combinations should not be viewed on rigid lines, but should be considered in the light of the particular circumstances. The criterion "preparatory or auxiliary character" is to be interpreted in the same way as is set out for the same criterion of subparagraph *e)* (see paragraphs 24 and 25 above). States which want to allow any combination of the items mentioned in subparagraphs *a)* to *e)*, disregarding whether or not the criterion of the preparatory or auxiliary character of such a combination is met, are free to do so by deleting the words "provided" to "character" in subparagraph *f)*.

27.1   Subparagraph *f)* is of no importance in a case where an enterprise maintains several fixed places of business within the meaning of subparagraphs *a)* to *e)* provided that they are separated from each other locally and organisationally, as in such a case each place of business has to be viewed separately and in isolation for deciding whether a permanent establishment exists. Places of business are not "separated organisationally" where they each perform in a Contracting State complementary functions such as receiving and storing goods in one place, distributing those goods through another etc. An enterprise cannot fragment a cohesive operating business into several small operations in order to argue that each is merely engaged in a preparatory or auxiliary activity.

28.   The fixed places of business mentioned in paragraph 4 cannot be deemed to constitute permanent establishments so long as their activities are restricted to the functions which are the prerequisite for assuming that the fixed place of business is not a permanent establishment. This will be the case even if the contracts necessary for establishing and carrying on the business are concluded by those in charge of the places of business themselves. The employees of places of business within the meaning of paragraph 4 who are authorised to conclude such contracts should not be regarded as agents within the meaning of paragraph 5. A case in point would be a research institution the manager of which is authorised to conclude the contracts necessary for maintaining the institution and who exercises this authority within the framework of the functions of the institution. A permanent establishment, however, exists if the fixed place of business exercising any of the functions listed in paragraph 4 were to exercise them not only on behalf of the enterprise to which it belongs but also on behalf of other enterprises. If, for instance, an advertising agency maintained by an enterprise were also to engage in advertising for other enterprises, it would be regarded as a permanent establishment of the enterprise by which it is maintained.

29.   If a fixed place of business under paragraph 4 is deemed not to be a permanent establishment, this exception applies likewise to the disposal of movable property forming part of the business property of the place of business at the termination of the enterprise's activity in such installation (see paragraph 11 above and paragraph 2 of

Article 13). Since, for example, the display of merchandise is excepted under subparagraphs *a)* and *b)*, the sale of the merchandise at the termination of a trade fair or convention is covered by this exception. The exception does not, of course, apply to sales of merchandise not actually displayed at the trade fair or convention.

30.   A fixed place of business used both for activities which rank as exceptions (paragraph 4) and for other activities would be regarded as a single permanent establishment and taxable as regards both types of activities. This would be the case, for instance, where a store maintained for the delivery of goods also engaged in sales.

Paragraph 5

31.   It is a generally accepted principle that an enterprise should be treated as having a permanent establishment in a State if there is under certain conditions a person acting for it, even though the enterprise may not have a fixed place of business in that State within the meaning of paragraphs 1 and 2. This provision intends to give that State the right to tax in such cases. Thus paragraph 5 stipulates the conditions under which an enterprise is deemed to have a permanent establishment in respect of any activity of a person acting for it. The paragraph was redrafted in the 1977 Model Convention to clarify the intention of the corresponding provision of the 1963 Draft Convention without altering its substance apart from an extension of the excepted activities of the person.

32.   Persons whose activities may create a permanent establishment for the enterprise are so-called dependent agents *i.e.* persons, whether or not employees of the enterprise, who are not independent agents falling under paragraph 6. Such persons may be either individuals or companies and need not be residents of, nor have a place of business in, the State in which they act for the enterprise. It would not have been in the interest of international economic relations to provide that the maintenance of any dependent person would lead to a permanent establishment for the enterprise. Such treatment is to be limited to persons who in view of the scope of their authority or the nature of their activity involve the enterprise to a particular extent in business activities in the State concerned. Therefore, paragraph 5 proceeds on the basis that only persons having the authority to conclude contracts can lead to a permanent establishment for the enterprise maintaining them. In such a case the person has sufficient authority to bind the enterprise's participation in the business activity in the State concerned. The use of the term "permanent establishment" in this context presupposes, of course, that that person makes use of this authority repeatedly and not merely in isolated cases.

32.1   Also, the phrase "authority to conclude contracts in the name of the enterprise" does not confine the application of the paragraph to an agent who enters into contracts literally in the name of the enterprise; the paragraph applies equally to an agent who concludes contracts which are binding on the enterprise even if those contracts are not actually in the name of the enterprise. Lack of active involvement by an enterprise in transactions may be indicative of a grant of authority to an agent. For example, an agent may be considered to possess actual authority to conclude contracts where he solicits and receives (but does not formally finalise) orders which are sent directly to a warehouse from which goods are delivered and where the foreign enterprise routinely approves the transactions.

33.   The authority to conclude contracts must cover contracts relating to operations which constitute the business proper of the enterprise. It would be irrelevant, for instance, if the person had authority to engage employees for the enterprise to assist that person's activity for the enterprise or if the person were authorised to conclude, in the name of the enterprise, similar contracts relating to internal operations only. Moreover the authority has to be habitually exercised in the other State; whether or not this is the case should be determined on the basis of the commercial realities of the situation. A person who is authorised to negotiate all elements and details of a contract in a way binding on the enterprise can be said to exercise this authority "in that State", even if the contract is signed by another person in the State in which the enterprise is situated or if the first person has not formally been given a power of representation. The mere fact, however, that a person has attended or even participated in negotiations in a State between an enterprise and a client will not be sufficient, by itself, to conclude that the person has exercised in that State an authority to conclude contracts in the name of the enterprise. The fact that a person has attended or even participated in such negotiations could, however, be a relevant factor in determining the exact functions performed by that person on behalf of the enterprise. Since, by virtue of paragraph 4, the maintenance of a fixed place of business solely for purposes listed in that paragraph is deemed not to constitute a permanent establishment, a person whose activities are restricted to such purposes does not create a permanent establishment either.

33.1 The requirement that an agent must "habitually" exercise an authority to conclude contracts reflects the underlying principle in Article 5 that the presence which an enterprise maintains in a Contracting State should be more than merely transitory if the enterprise is to be regarded as maintaining a permanent establishment, and thus a taxable presence, in that State. The extent and frequency of activity necessary to conclude that the agent is "habitually exercising" contracting authority will depend on the nature of the contracts and the business of the principal. It is not possible to lay down a precise frequency test. Nonetheless, the same sorts of factors considered in paragraph 6 would be relevant in making that determination.

34.   Where the requirements set out in paragraph 5 are met, a permanent establishment of the enterprise exists to the extent that the person acts for the latter, i.e. not only to the extent that such a person exercises the authority to conclude contracts in the name of the enterprise.

35.   Under paragraph 5, only those persons who meet the specific conditions may create a permanent establishment; all other persons are excluded. It should be borne in mind, however, that paragraph 5 simply provides an alternative test of whether an enterprise has a permanent establishment in a State. If it can be shown that the enterprise has a permanent establishment within the meaning of paragraphs 1 and 2

(subject to the provisions of paragraph 4), it is not necessary to show that the person in charge is one who would fall under paragraph 5.

Paragraph 6

36.   Where an enterprise of a Contracting State carries on business dealings through a broker, general commission agent or any other agent of an independent status, it cannot be taxed in the other Contracting State in respect of those dealings if the agent is acting in the ordinary course of his business (see paragraph 32 above). Although it stands to reason that such an agent, representing a separate enterprise, cannot constitute a permanent establishment of the foreign enterprise, paragraph 6 has been inserted in the Article for the sake of clarity and emphasis.

37.   A person will come within the scope of paragraph 6, i.e. he will not constitute a permanent establishment of the enterprise on whose behalf he acts only if:

a) he is independent of the enterprise both legally and economically, and

b) he acts in the ordinary course of his business when acting on behalf of the enterprise.

38.   Whether a person is independent of the enterprise represented depends on the extent of the obligations which this person has vis-à-vis the enterprise. Where the person's commercial activities for the enterprise are subject to detailed instructions or to comprehensive control by it, such person cannot be regarded as independent of the enterprise. Another important criterion will be whether the entrepreneurial risk has to be borne by the person or by the enterprise the person represents.

38.1   In relation to the test of legal dependence, it should be noted that the control which a parent company exercises over its subsidiary in its capacity as shareholder is not relevant in a consideration of the dependence or otherwise of the subsidiary in its capacity as an agent for the parent. This is consistent with the rule in paragraph 7 of Article 5. But, as paragraph 41 of the Commentary indicates, the subsidiary may be considered a dependent agent of its parent by application of the same tests which are applied to unrelated companies.

38.2   The following considerations should be borne in mind when determining whether an agent may be considered to be independent.

38.3   An independent agent will typically be responsible to his principal for the results of his work but not subject to significant control with respect to the manner in which that work is carried out. He will not be subject to detailed instructions from the principal as to the conduct of the work. The fact that the principal is relying on the special skill and knowledge of the agent is an indication of independence.

38.4   Limitations on the scale of business which may be conducted by the agent clearly affect the scope of the agent's authority. However such limitations are not relevant to dependency which is determined by consideration of the extent to which the agent exercises freedom in the conduct of business on behalf of the principal within the scope of the authority conferred by the agreement.

38.5   It may be a feature of the operation of an agreement that an agent will provide substantial information to a principal in connection with the business conducted under the agreement. This is not in itself a sufficient criterion for determination that the agent is dependent unless the information is provided in the course of seeking approval from the principal for the manner in which the business is to be conducted. The provision of information which is simply intended to ensure the smooth running of the agreement and continued good relations with the principal is not a sign of dependence.

38.6   Another factor to be considered in determining independent status is the number of principals represented by the agent. Independent status is less likely if the activities of the agent are performed wholly or almost wholly on behalf of only one enterprise over the lifetime of the business or a long period of time. However, this fact is not by itself determinative. All the facts and circumstances must be taken into account to determine whether the agent's activities constitute an autonomous business conducted by him in which he bears risk and receives reward through the use of his entrepreneurial skills and knowledge. Where an agent acts for a number of principals in the ordinary course of his business and none of these is predominant in terms of the business carried on by the agent legal dependence may exist if the principals act in concert to control the acts of the agent in the course of his business on their behalf.

38.7   Persons cannot be said to act in the ordinary course of their own business if, in place of the enterprise, such persons perform activities which, economically, belong to the sphere of the enterprise rather than to that of their own business operations. Where, for example, a commission agent not only sells the goods or merchandise of the enterprise in his own name but also habitually acts, in relation to that enterprise, as a permanent agent having an authority to conclude contracts, he would be deemed in respect of this particular activity to be a permanent establishment, since he is thus acting outside the ordinary course of his own trade or business (namely that of a commission agent), unless his activities are limited to those mentioned at the end of paragraph 5.

38.8   In deciding whether or not particular activities fall within or outside the ordinary course of business of an agent, one would examine the business activities customarily carried out within the agent's trade as a broker, commission agent or other independent agent rather than the other business activities carried out by that agent. Whilst the comparison normally should be made with the activities customary to the agent's trade, other complementary tests may in certain circumstances be used concurrently or alternatively, for example where the agent's activities do not relate to a common trade.

39.   According to the definition of the term "permanent establishment" an insurance company of one State may be taxed in the other State on its insurance business, if it has a fixed place of business within the meaning of paragraph 1 or if it carries on business through a person within the meaning of paragraph 5. Since agencies of foreign insurance companies sometimes do not meet either of the above requirements,

it is conceivable that these companies do large-scale business in a State without being taxed in that State on their profits arising from such business. In order to obviate this possibility, various conventions concluded by OECD member countries include a provision which stipulates that insurance companies of a State are deemed to have a permanent establishment in the other State if they collect premiums in that other State through an agent established there — other than an agent who already constitutes a permanent establishment by virtue of paragraph 5 — or insure risks situated in that territory through such an agent. The decision as to whether or not a provision along these lines should be included in a convention will depend on the factual and legal situation prevailing in the Contracting States concerned. Frequently, therefore, such a provision will not be contemplated. In view of this fact, it did not seem advisable to insert a provision along these lines in the Model Convention.

Paragraph 7

40.   It is generally accepted that the existence of a subsidiary company does not, of itself, constitute that subsidiary company a permanent establishment of its parent company. This follows from the principle that, for the purpose of taxation, such a subsidiary company constitutes an independent legal entity. Even the fact that the trade or business carried on by the subsidiary company is managed by the parent company does not constitute the subsidiary company a permanent establishment of the parent company.

41.   A parent company may, however, be found, under the rules of paragraphs 1 or 5 of the Article, to have a permanent establishment in a State where a subsidiary has a place of business. Thus, any space or premises belonging to the subsidiary that is at the disposal of the parent company (see paragraphs 4, 5 and 6 above) and that constitutes a fixed place of business through which the parent carries on its own business will constitute a permanent establishment of the parent under paragraph 1, subject to paragraphs 3 and 4 of the Article (see for instance, the example in paragraph 4.3 above). Also, under paragraph 5, a parent will be deemed to have a permanent establishment in a State in respect of any activities that its subsidiary undertakes for it if the subsidiary has, and habitually exercises, in that State an authority to conclude contracts in the name of the parent (see paragraphs 32, 33 and 34 above), unless these activities are limited to those referred to in paragraph 4 of the Article or unless the subsidiary acts in the ordinary course of its business as an independent agent to which paragraph 6 of the Article applies.

41.1 The same principles apply to any company forming part of a multinational group so that such a company may be found to have a permanent establishment in a State where it has at its disposal (see paragraphs 4, 5 and 6 above) and uses premises belonging to another company of the group, or if the former company is deemed to have a permanent establishment under paragraph 5 of the Article (see paragraphs 32, 33 and 34 above). The determination of the existence of a permanent establishment under the rules of paragraphs 1 or 5 of the Article must, however, be done separately for each company of the group. Thus, the existence in one State of a permanent establishment of one company of the group will not have any relevance as to whether another company of the group has itself a permanent establishment in that State.

42.   Whilst premises belonging to a company that is a member of a multinational group can be put at the disposal of another company of the group and may, subject to the other conditions of Article 5, constitute a permanent establishment of that other company if the business of that other company is carried on through that place, it is important to distinguish that case from the frequent situation where a company that is a member of a multinational group provides services (*e.g.* management services) to another company of the group as part of its own business carried on in premises that are not those of that other company and using its own personnel. In that case, the place where those services are provided is not at the disposal of the latter company and it is not the business of that company that is carried on through that place. That place cannot, therefore, be considered to be a permanent establishment of the company to which the services are provided. Indeed, the fact that a company's own activities at a given location may provide an economic benefit to the business of another company does not mean that the latter company carries on its business through that location: clearly, a company that merely purchases parts produced or services supplied by another company in a different country would not have a permanent establishment because of that, even though it may benefit from the manufacturing of these parts or the supplying of these services.

Electronic commerce

42.1   There has been some discussion as to whether the mere use in electronic commerce operations of computer equipment in a country could constitute a permanent establishment. That question raises a number of issues in relation to the provisions of the Article.

42.2   Whilst a location where automated equipment is operated by an enterprise may constitute a permanent establishment in the country where it is situated (see below), a distinction needs to be made between computer equipment, which may be set up at a location so as to constitute a permanent establishment under certain circumstances, and the data and software which is used by, or stored on, that equipment. For instance, an Internet web site, which is a combination of software and electronic data, does not in itself constitute tangible property. It therefore does not have a location that can constitute a "place of business" as there is no "facility such as premises or, in certain instances, machinery or equipment" (see paragraph 2 above) as far as the software and data constituting that web site is concerned. On the other hand, the server on which the web site is stored and through which it is accessible is a piece of equipment having a physical location and such location may thus constitute a "fixed place of business" of the enterprise that operates that server.

42.3   The distinction between a web site and the server on which the web site is stored and used is important since the enterprise that operates the server may be different from the enterprise that carries on business through the web site. For example, it is common for the web site through which an enterprise carries on its business to be hosted on the server of an Internet Service Provider (ISP). Although the fees paid to the ISP under such arrangements may be based on the amount of disk space used to store the software and data required by the web site, these contracts typically do not result in the server and its location being at the disposal of the enterprise (see paragraph 4 above), even if the enterprise has been able to determine that its web site should be hosted on a particular server at a particular location. In such a case, the enterprise does not even have a physical presence at that location since the web site is not tangible. In these cases, the enterprise cannot be considered to have acquired a place of business by virtue of that hosting arrangement. However, if the enterprise carrying on business through a web site has the server at its own disposal, for example it owns (or leases) and operates the server on which the web site is stored and used, the place where that server is located could constitute a permanent establishment of the enterprise if the other requirements of the Article are met.

42.4   Computer equipment at a given location may only constitute a permanent establishment if it meets the requirement of being fixed. In the case of a server, what is relevant is not the possibility of the server being moved, but whether it is in fact moved. In order to constitute a fixed place of business, a server will need to be located at a certain place for a sufficient period of time so as to become fixed within the meaning of paragraph 1.

42.5   Another issue is whether the business of an enterprise may be said to be wholly or partly carried on at a location where the enterprise has equipment such as a server at its disposal. The question of whether the business of an enterprise is wholly or partly carried on through such equipment needs to be examined on a case-by-case basis, having regard to whether it can be said that, because of such equipment, the enterprise has facilities at its disposal where business functions of the enterprise are performed.

42.6   Where an enterprise operates computer equipment at a particular location, a permanent establishment may exist even though no personnel of that enterprise is required at that location for the operation of the equipment. The presence of personnel is not necessary to consider that an enterprise wholly or partly carries on its business at a location when no personnel are in fact required to carry on business activities at that location. This conclusion applies to electronic commerce to the same extent that it applies with respect to other activities in which equipment operates automatically, *e.g.* automatic pumping equipment used in the exploitation of natural resources.

42.7   Another issue relates to the fact that no permanent establishment may be considered to exist where the electronic commerce operations carried on through computer equipment at a given location in a country are restricted to the preparatory or auxiliary activities covered by paragraph 4. The question of whether particular activities performed at such a location fall within paragraph 4 needs to be examined on a case-by-case basis having regard to the various functions performed by the enterprise through that equipment. Examples of activities which would generally be regarded as preparatory or auxiliary include:

— providing a communications link — much like a telephone line — between suppliers and customers;

— advertising of goods or services;

— relaying information through a mirror server for security and efficiency purposes;

— gathering market data for the enterprise;

— supplying information.

42.8   Where, however, such functions form in themselves an essential and significant part of the business activity of the enterprise as a whole, or where other core functions of the enterprise are carried on through the computer equipment, these would go beyond the activities covered by paragraph 4 and if the equipment constituted a fixed place of business of the enterprise (as discussed in paragraphs 42.2 to 42.6 above), there would be a permanent establishment.

42.9   What constitutes core functions for a particular enterprise clearly depends on the nature of the business carried on by that enterprise. For instance, some ISPs are in the business of operating their own servers for the purpose of hosting web sites or other applications for other enterprises. For these ISPs, the operation of their servers in order to provide services to customers is an essential part of their commercial activity and cannot be considered preparatory or auxiliary. A different example is that of an enterprise (sometimes referred to as an "e-tailer") that carries on the business of selling products through the Internet. In that case, the enterprise is not in the business of operating servers and the mere fact that it may do so at a given location is not enough to conclude that activities performed at that location are more than preparatory and auxiliary. What needs to be done in such a case is to examine the nature of the activities performed at that location in light of the business carried on by the enterprise. If these activities are merely preparatory or auxiliary to the business of selling products on the Internet (for example, the location is used to operate a server that hosts a web site which, as is often the case, is used exclusively for advertising, displaying a catalogue of products or providing information to potential customers), paragraph 4 will apply and the location will not constitute a permanent establishment. If, however, the typical functions related to a sale are performed at that location (for example, the conclusion of the contract with the customer, the processing of the payment and the delivery of the products are performed automatically through the equipment located there), these activities cannot be considered to be merely preparatory or auxiliary.

42.10   A last issue is whether paragraph 5 may apply to deem an ISP to constitute a permanent establishment. As already noted, it is common for ISPs to provide the service of hosting the web sites of other enterprises on their own servers. The issue may then arise as to whether paragraph 5 may apply to deem such ISPs to constitute permanent establishments of the enterprises that carry on electronic commerce through web sites operated through the servers owned and operated by these ISPs. Whilst this could be the case in very unusual circumstances, paragraph 5 will generally not be applicable because the ISPs will not constitute an agent of the enterprises to which the web sites belong, because they will not have authority to conclude contracts in the name of these enterprises and will not regularly conclude such contracts or because they will constitute independent agents acting in the ordinary course of their business, as evidenced by the fact that they host the web sites of many different enterprises. It is also clear that since the web site through which an enterprise carries on its business is not itself a "person" as defined in Article 3, paragraph 5 cannot apply to deem a permanent establishment to exist by virtue of the web site being an agent of the enterprise for purposes of that paragraph.

The taxation of services

42.11 The combined effect of this Article and Article 7 is that the profits from services performed in the territory of a Contracting State by an enterprise of the other Contracting State are not taxable in the first-mentioned State if they are not attributable to a permanent establishment situated therein (as long as they are not covered by other Articles of the Convention that would allow such taxation). This result, under which these profits are only taxable in the other State, is supported by various policy and administrative considerations. It is consistent with the principle of Article 7 that until an enterprise of one State sets up a permanent establishment in another State, it should not be regarded as participating in the economic life of that State to such an extent that it comes within the taxing jurisdiction of that other State. Also, the provision of services should, as a general rule subject to a few exceptions for some types of service (e.g. those covered by Article 8 and 17), be treated the same way as other business activities and, therefore, the same permanent establishment threshold of taxation should apply to all business activities, including the provision of independent services.

42.12 One of the administrative considerations referred to above is that the extension of the cases where source taxation of profits from services performed in the territory of a Contracting State by an enterprise of the other Contracting State would be allowed would increase the compliance and administrative burden of enterprises and tax administrations. This would be especially problematic with respect to services provided to non-business consumers, which would not need to be disclosed to the source country's tax administration for purposes of claiming a business expense deduction. Since the rules that have typically been designed for that purpose are based on the amount of time spent in a State, both tax administrations and enterprises would need to take account of the time spent in a country by personnel of service enterprises and these enterprises would face the risk of having a permanent establishment in unexpected circumstances in cases where they would be unable to determine in advance how long personnel would be present in a particular country (e.g. in situations where that presence would be extended because of unforeseen difficulties or at the request of a client). These cases create particular compliance difficulties as they require an enterprise to retroactively comply with a number of administrative requirements associated with a permanent establishment. These concerns relate to the need to maintain books and records, the taxation of the employees (*e.g.* the need to make source deductions in another country) as well as other non-income tax requirements.

42.13 Also, the source taxation of profits from services performed in the territory of a Contracting State by an enterprise of the other Contracting State that does not have a fixed place of business in the first-mentioned State would create difficulties concerning the determination of the profits to be taxed and the collection of the relevant tax. In most cases, the enterprise would not have the accounting records and assets typically associated with a permanent establishment and there would be no dependent agent which could comply with information and collection requirements. Moreover, whilst it is a common feature of States' domestic law to tax profits from services performed in their territory, it does not necessarily represent optimal tax treaty policy.

42.14 Some States, however, are reluctant to adopt the principle of exclusive residence taxation of services that are not attributable to a permanent establishment situated in their territory but that are performed in that territory. These States propose changes to the Article in order to preserve source taxation rights, in certain circumstances, with respect to the profits from such services. States that believe that additional source taxation rights should be allocated under a treaty with respect to services performed in their territory rely on various arguments to support their position.

42.15 These States may consider that profits from services performed in a given state should be taxable in that state on the basis of the generally-accepted policy principles for determining when business profits should be considered to have their source within a jurisdiction. They consider that, from the exclusive angle of the pure policy question of where business profits originate, the State where services are performed should have a right to tax even when these services are not attributable to a permanent establishment as defined in Article 5. They would note that the domestic law of many countries provides for the taxation of services performed in these countries even in the absence of a permanent establishment (even though services performed over very short periods of time may not always be taxed in practice).

42.16 These States are concerned that some service businesses do not require a fixed place of business in their territory in order to carry on a substantial level of business activities therein and consider that these additional rights are therefore appropriate.

42.17 Also, these States consider that even if the taxation of profits of enterprises carried on by non-residents that are not attributable to a permanent establishment raises certain compliance and administrative difficulties, these difficulties do not justify exempting from tax the profits from all services performed on their territory by such enterprises. Those who support that view may refer to mechanisms that are already in place in some States to ensure taxation of services performed in these States but not attributable to permanent establishments (such mechanisms are based on requirements for resident payers to report, and possibly withhold tax on, payments to non-residents for services performed in these States).

42.18 It should be noted, however, that all member States agree that a State should not have source taxation rights on income derived from the provision of services performed by a non-resident outside that State. Under tax conventions, the profits from the sale of goods that are merely imported by a resident of a country and that are neither produced nor distributed through a permanent establishment in that country are not taxable therein and the same principle should apply in the case of services. The mere fact that the payer of the consideration for services is a resident of a State, or that such consideration is borne by a permanent establishment situated in that State or that the result of the services is used within the State does not constitute a sufficient nexus to warrant allocation of income taxing rights to that State.

42.19 Another fundamental issue on which there is general agreement relates to the determination of the amount on which tax should be levied. In the case of non-employment services (and subject to possible exceptions such as Article 17) only the profits derived from the services should be taxed. Thus, provisions that are sometimes included in bilateral conventions and that allow a State to tax the gross amount of the fees paid for certain services if the payer of the fees is a resident of that State do not seem to provide an appropriate way of taxing services. First, because these provisions are not restricted to services performed in the State of source, they have the effect of allowing a State to tax business activities that do not take place in that State. Second, these rules allow taxation of the gross payments for services as opposed to the profits therefrom.

42.20 Also, member States agree that it is appropriate, for compliance and other reasons, not to allow a State to tax the profits from services performed in their territory in certain circumstances (e.g. when such services are provided during a very short period of time).

42.21 The Committee therefore considered that it was important to circumscribe the circumstances in which States that did not agree with the conclusion in paragraph 42.11 above could, if they wished to, provide that profits from services performed in the territory of a Contracting State by an enterprise of the other Contracting State would be taxable by that State even if there was no permanent establishment, as defined in Article 5, to which the profits were attributable.

42.22 Clearly, such taxation should not extend to services performed outside the territory of a State and should apply only to the profits from these services rather than to the payments for them. Also, there should be a minimum level of presence in a State before such taxation is allowed.

42.23 The following is an example of a provision that would conform to these requirements; States are free to agree bilaterally to include such a provision in their tax treaties:

Notwithstanding the provisions of paragraphs 1, 2 and 3, where an enterprise of a Contracting State performs services in the other Contracting State

a) through an individual who is present in that other State for a period or periods exceeding in the aggregate 183 days in any twelve month period, and more

> than 50 per cent of the gross revenues attributable to active business activities of the enterprise during this period or periods are derived from the services performed in that other State through that individual, or
>
> b) for a period or periods exceeding in the aggregate 183 days in any twelve month period, and these services are performed for the same project or for connected projects through one or more individuals who are present and performing such services in that other State
>
> the activities carried on in that other State in performing these services shall be deemed to be carried on through a permanent establishment of the enterprise situated in that other State, unless these services are limited to those mentioned in paragraph 4 which, if performed through a fixed place of business, would not make this fixed place of business a permanent establishment under the provisions of that paragraph. For the purposes of this paragraph, services performed by an individual on behalf of one enterprise shall not be considered to be performed by another enterprise through that individual unless that other enterprise supervises, directs or controls the manner in which these services are performed by the individual.

42.24 That alternative provision constitutes an extension of the permanent establishment definition that allows taxation of income from services provided by enterprises carried on by non-residents but does so in conformity with the principles described in paragraph 42.22. The following paragraphs discuss various aspects of the alternative provision; clearly these paragraphs are not relevant in the case of treaties that do not include such a provision and do not, therefore, allow a permanent establishment to be found merely because the conditions described in this provision have been met.

42.25 The provision has the effect of deeming a permanent establishment to exist where one would not otherwise exist under the definition provided in paragraph 1 and the examples of paragraph 2. It therefore applies notwithstanding these paragraphs. As is the case of paragraph 5 of the Article, the provision provides a supplementary basis under which an enterprise may be found to have a permanent establishment in a State; it could apply, for example, where a consultant provides services over a long period in a country but at different locations that do not meet the conditions of paragraph 1 to constitute one or more permanent establishments. If it can be shown that the enterprise has a permanent establishment within the meaning of paragraphs 1 and 2 (subject to the provisions of paragraph 4), it is not necessary to apply the provision in order to find a permanent establishment. Since the provision simply creates a permanent establishment when none would otherwise exist, it does not provide an alternative definition of the concept of permanent establishment and obviously cannot limit the scope of the definition in paragraph 1 and of the examples in paragraph 2.

42.26 The provision also applies notwithstanding paragraph 3. Thus, an enterprise may be deemed to have a permanent establishment because it performs services in a country for the periods of time provided for in the suggested paragraph even if the various locations where these services are performed do not constitute permanent establishments pursuant to paragraph 3. The following example illustrates that result. A self-employed individual resident of one Contracting State provides services and is present in the other Contracting State for more than 183 days during a twelve month period but his services are performed for equal periods of time at a location that is not a construction site (and are not in relation to a construction or installation project) as well as on two unrelated building sites which each lasts less than the period of time provided for in paragraph 3. Whilst paragraph 3 would deem the two sites not to constitute permanent establishments, the proposed paragraph, which applies notwithstanding paragraph 3, would deem the enterprise carried on by that person to have a permanent establishment (since the individual is self-employed, it must be assumed that the 50 per cent of gross revenues test will be met with respect to his enterprise).

42.27 Another example is that of a large construction enterprise that carries on a single construction project in a country. If the project is carried on at a single site, the provision should not have a significant impact as long as the period required for the site to constitute a permanent establishment is not substantially different from the period required for the provision to apply. States that wish to use the alternative provision may therefore wish to consider referring to the same periods of time in that provision and in paragraph 3 of Article 5; if a shorter period is used in the alternative provision, this will reduce, in practice, the scope of application of paragraph 3.

42.28 The situation, however, may be different if the project, or connected projects, are carried out in different parts of a country. If the individual sites where a single project is carried on do not last sufficiently long for each of them to constitute a permanent establishment (see, however, paragraph 20 above), a permanent establishment will still be deemed to exist if the conditions of the alternative provision are met. That result is consistent with the purpose of the provision, which is to subject to source taxation foreign enterprises that are present in a country for a sufficiently long period of time notwithstanding the fact that their presence at any particular location in that country is not sufficiently long to make that location a fixed place of business of the enterprise. Some States, however, may consider that paragraph 3 should prevail over the alternative provision and may wish to amend the provision accordingly.

42.29 The suggested paragraph only applies to services. Other types of activities that do not constitute services are therefore excluded from its scope. Thus, for instance, the paragraph would not apply to a foreign enterprise that carries on fishing activities in the territorial waters of a State and derives revenues from selling its catches (in some treaties, however, activities such as fishing and oil extraction may be covered by specific provisions).

42.30 The provision applies to services performed by an enterprise. Thus, services must be provided by the enterprise to third parties. Clearly, the provision could not have the effect of deeming an enterprise to have a permanent establishment merely because services are provided to that enterprise. For example, services might be provided by an individual to his employer without that employer performing any services (e.g. an employee who provides manufacturing services to an enterprise that sells manufactured products). Another example would be where the employees of one enterprise provide services in one country to an associated enterprise under detailed instructions and close supervision of the latter enterprise; in that case, assuming the services in question are not for the benefit of any third party, the latter enterprise does not itself perform any services to which the provision could apply.

42.31 Also, the provision only applies to services that are performed in a State by a foreign enterprise. Whether or not the relevant services are furnished to a resident of the State does not matter; what matters is that the services are performed in the State through an individual present in that State.

42.32 The alternative provision does not specify that the services must be provided "through employees or other personnel engaged by the enterprise", a phrase that is sometimes found in bilateral treaties. It simply provides that the services must be performed by an enterprise. As explained in paragraph 10, the business of an enterprise (which, in the context of the paragraph, would include the services performed in a Contracting State) "is carried on mainly by the entrepreneur or persons who are in paid-employment relationship with the enterprise (personnel). This personnel includes employees and other persons receiving instructions from the enterprise (e.g. dependent agents)." For the purposes of the alternative provision, the individuals through which an enterprise provides services will therefore be the individuals referred to in paragraph 10, subject to the exception included in the last sentence of that provision (see paragraph 42.43 below).

42.33 The alternative provision will apply in two different sets of circumstances. Subparagraph a) looks at the duration of the presence of the individual through whom an enterprise derives most of its revenues in a way that is similar to that of subparagraph 2 a) of Article 15; subparagraph b) looks at the duration of the activities of the individuals through whom the services are performed.

42.34 Subparagraph a) deals primarily with the situation of an enterprise carried on by a single individual. It also covers, however, the case of an enterprise which, during the relevant period or periods, derives most of its revenues from services provided by one individual. Such extension is necessary to avoid a different treatment between, for example, a case where services are provided by an individual and a case where similar services are provided by a company all the shares of which are owned by the only employee of that company.

42.35 The subparagraph may apply in different situations where an enterprise performs services through an individual, such as when the services are performed by a sole proprietorship, by the partner of a partnership, by the employee of a company etc. The main conditions are that

— the individual through whom the services are performed be present in a State for a period or periods exceeding in the aggregate 183 days in any twelve month period, and

— more than 50 per cent of the gross revenues attributable to active business activities of the enterprise during the period or periods of presence be derived from the services performed in that State through that individual.

42.36 The first condition refers to the days of presence of an individual. Since the formulation is identical to that of subparagraph 2 a) of Article 15, the principles applicable to the computation of the days of presence for purposes of that last subparagraph are also applicable to the computation of the days of presence for the purpose of the suggested paragraph.

42.37 For the purposes of the second condition, according to which more than 50 per cent of the gross revenues attributable to active business activities of the enterprise during the relevant period or periods must be derived from the services performed in that State through that individual, the gross revenues attributable to active business activities of the enterprise would represent what the enterprise has charged or should charge for its active business activities, regardless of when the actual billing will occur or of domestic law rules concerning when such revenues should be taken into account for tax purposes. Such active business activities are not restricted to activities related to the provision of services. Gross revenues attributable to "active business activities" would clearly exclude income from passive investment activities, including, for example, receiving interest and dividends from investing surplus funds. States may, however, prefer to use a different test, such as "50 per cent of the business profits of the enterprise during this period or periods is derived from the services" or "the services represent the most important part of the business activities of the enterprise", in order to identify an enterprise that derives most of its revenues from services performed by an individual on their territory.

42.38 The following examples illustrate the application of subparagraph a) (assuming that the alternative provision has been included in a treaty between States R and S):

— Example 1: W, a resident of State R, is a consultant who carries on her business activities in her own name (i.e. that enterprise is a sole proprietorship). Between 2 February 00 and 1 February 01, she is present in State S for a period or periods of 190 days and during that period all the revenues from her business activities are derived from services that she performs in State S. Since subparagraph a) applies in that situation, these services shall be deemed to be performed through a permanent establishment in State S.

— Example 2: X, a resident of State R, is one of the two shareholders and employees of XCO, a company resident of State R that provides engineering services. Between 20 December 00 and 19 December 01, X is present in State S for a period or periods of 190 days and during that period, 70 per cent of all the gross revenues of XCO attributable to active business activities are derived from the services that X performs in State S. Since subparagraph a) applies in that situation, these services shall be deemed to be performed through a permanent establishment of XCO in State S.

— Example 3: X and Y, who are residents of State R, are the two partners of X&Y, a partnership established in State R which provides legal services. For tax purposes, State R treats partnerships as transparent entities. Between 15 July 00 and 14 July 01, Y is present in State S for a period or periods of 240 days and during that period, 55 per cent of all the fees of X&Y attributable to X&Y's active business activities are derived from the services that Y performs in State S. Subparagraph a) applies in that situation and, for the purposes of the taxation of X and Y, the services performed by Y are deemed to be performed through a permanent establishment in State S.

— Example 4: Z, a resident of State R, is one of 10 employees of ACO, a company resident of State R that provides accounting services. Between 10 April 00 and 9 April 01, Z is present in State S for a period or periods of 190 days and during that period, 12 per cent of all the gross revenues of ACO attributable to its active business activities are derived from the services that Z performs in State S. Subparagraph a) does not apply in that situation and, unless subparagraph b) applies to ACO, the alternative provision will not deem ACO to have a permanent establishment in State S.

42.39 Subparagraph b) addresses the situation of an enterprise that performs services in a Contracting State in relation to a particular project (or for connected projects) and which performs these through one or more individuals over a substantial period. The period or periods referred to in the subparagraph apply in relation to the enterprise and not to the individuals. It is therefore not necessary that it be the same individual or individuals who perform the services and are present throughout these periods. As long as, on a given day, the enterprise is performing its services through at least one individual who is doing so and is present in the State, that day would be included in the period or periods referred to in the subparagraph. Clearly, however, that day will count as a single day regardless of how many individuals are performing such services for the enterprise during that day.

42.40 The reference to an "enterprise ... performing these services for the same project" should be interpreted from the perspective of the enterprise that provides the services. Thus, an enterprise may have two different projects to provide services to a single customer (e.g. to provide tax advice and to provide training in an area unrelated to tax) and whilst these may be related to a single project of the customer, one should not consider that the services are performed for the same project.

42.41 The reference to "connected projects" is intended to cover cases where the services are provided in the context of separate projects carried on by an enterprise but these projects have a commercial coherence (see paragraphs 5.3 and 5.4 above). The determination of whether projects are connected will depend on the facts and circumstances of each case but factors that would generally be relevant for that purpose include:

— whether the projects are covered by a single master contract;
— where the projects are covered by different contracts, whether these different contracts were concluded with the same person or with related persons and whether the conclusion of the additional contracts would reasonably have been expected when concluding the first contract;
— whether the nature of the work involved under the different projects is the same;

— whether the same individuals are performing the services under the different projects.

42.42 Subparagraph b) requires that during the relevant periods, the enterprise is performing services through individuals who are performing such services in that other State. For that purpose, a period during which individuals are performing services means a period during which the services are actually provided, which would normally correspond to the working days of these individuals. An enterprise that agrees to keep personnel available in case a client needs the services of such personnel and charges the client standby charges for making such personnel available is performing services through the relevant individuals even though they are idle during the working days when they remain available.

42.43 As indicated in paragraph 42.32, for the purposes of the alternative provision, the individuals through whom an enterprise provides services will be the individuals referred to in paragraph 10 above. If, however, an individual is providing the services on behalf of one enterprise, the exception included in the last sentence of the provision clarifies that the services performed by that individual will only be taken into account for another enterprise if the work of that individual is exercised under the supervision, direction or control of the last-mentioned enterprise. Thus, for example, where a company that has agreed by contract to provide services to third parties provides these services through the employees of a separate enterprise (e.g. an enterprise providing outsourced services), the services performed through these employees will not be taken into account for purposes of the application of subparagraph b) to the company that entered into the contract to provide services to third parties. This rule applies regardless of whether the separate enterprise is associated to, or independent from, the company that entered into the contract.

42.44 The following examples illustrate the application of subparagraph b) (assuming that the alternative provision has been included in a treaty between States R and S):

— Example 1: X, a company resident of State R, has agreed with company Y to carry on geological surveys in various locations in State S where company Y owns exploration rights. Between 15 May 00 and 14 May 01, these surveys are carried on over 185 working days by employees of X as well as by self-employed individuals to whom X has sub-contracted part of the work but who work under the direction, supervision or control of X. Since subparagraph b) applies in that situation, these services shall be deemed to be performed through a permanent establishment of X in State S.

— Example 2: Y, a resident of State T, is one of the two shareholders and employees of WYCO, a company resident of State R that provides training services. Between 10 June 00 and 9 June 01, Y performs services in State S under a contract that WYCO has concluded with a company which is a resident of State S to train the employees of that company. These services are performed in State S over 185 working days. During the period of Y's presence in State S, the revenues from these services account for 40 per cent of the gross revenues of WYCO from its active business activities. Whilst subparagraph a) does not apply in that situation, subparagraph *b)* applies and these services shall be deemed to be performed through a permanent establishment of WYCO in State S.

— Example 3: ZCO, a resident of State R, has outsourced to company OCO, which is a resident of State S, the technical support that it provides by telephone to its clients. OCO operates a call centre for a number of companies similar to ZCO. During the period of 1 January 00 to 31 December 00, the employees of OCO provide technical support to various clients of ZCO. Since the employees of OCO are not under the supervision, direction or control of ZCO, it cannot be considered, for the purposes of subparagraph *b)*, that ZCO is performing services in State S through these employees. Additionally, whilst the services provided by OCO's employees to the various clients of ZCO are similar, these are provided under different contracts concluded by ZCO with unrelated clients: these services cannot, therefore, be considered to be rendered for the same or connected projects.

42.45   The 183-day thresholds provided for in the alternative provision may give rise to the same type of abuse as is described in paragraph 18 above. As indicated in that paragraph, legislative or judicial anti-avoidance rules may apply to prevent such abuses. Some States, however, may prefer to deal with them by including a specific provision in the Article. Such a provision could be drafted along the following lines:

For the purposes of paragraph [x], where an enterprise of a Contracting State that is performing services in the other Contracting State is, during a period of time, associated with another enterprise that performs substantially similar services in that other State for the same project or for connected projects through one or more individuals who, during that period, are present and performing such services in that State, the first-mentioned enterprise shall be deemed, during that period of time, to be performing services in the other State for that same project or for connected projects through these individuals. For the purpose of the preceding sentence, an enterprise shall be associated with another enterprise if one is controlled directly or indirectly by the other, or both are controlled directly or indirectly by the same persons, regardless of whether or not these persons are residents of one of the Contracting States.

42.46   According to the provision, the activities carried on in the other State by the individuals referred to in subparagraph *a)* or *b)* through which the services are performed by the enterprise during the period or periods referred to in these subparagraphs are deemed to be carried on through a permanent establishment that the enterprise has in that other State. The enterprise is therefore deemed to have a permanent establishment in that other State for the purposes of all the provisions of the Convention (including, for example, paragraph 5 of Article 11 and paragraph 2 of Article 15) and the profits derived from the activities carried on in the other State in providing these services are attributable to that permanent establishment and are therefore taxable in that State pursuant to Article 7.

42.47   By deeming the activities carried on in performing the relevant services to be carried on through a permanent establishment that the enterprise has in a Contracting

State, the provision allows the application of Article 7 and therefore, the taxation, by that State, of the profits attributable to these activities. As a general rule, it is important to ensure that only the profits derived from the activities carried on in performing the services are taxed; whilst there may be certain exceptions, it would be detrimental to the cross-border trade in services if payments received for these services were taxed regardless of the direct or indirect expenses incurred for the purpose of performing these services.

42.48   This alternative provision will not apply if the services performed are limited to those mentioned in paragraph 4 of the Article 5 which, if performed through a fixed place of business, would not make this fixed place of business a permanent establishment under the provisions of that paragraph. Since the provision refers to the performance of services by the enterprise and this would not cover services provided to the enterprise itself, most of the provisions of paragraph 4 would not appear to be relevant. It may be, however, that the services that are performed are exclusively of a preparatory or auxiliary character (e.g. the supply of information to prospective customers when this is merely preparatory to the conduct of the ordinary business activities of the enterprise; see paragraph 23 above) and in that case, it is logical not to consider that the performance of these services will constitute a permanent establishment.

Observations on the Commentary

43.   Concerning paragraph 26.1, *Germany* reserves its position on whether and under which circumstances the acquisition of a right of disposal over the transport capacity of pipelines or the capacity of technical installations, lines and cables for the transmission of electrical power or communications (including the distribution of radio and television programs) owned by an unrelated third party could result in disposal over the pipeline, cable or line as a fixed place of business.

44.   The *Czech Republic* and the *Slovak Republic* would add to paragraph 25 their view that when an enterprise has established an office (such as a commercial representation office) in a country, and the employees working at that office are substantially involved in the negotiation of contracts for the import of products or services into that country, the office will in most cases not fall within paragraph 4 of Article 5. Substantial involvement in the negotiations exists when the essential parts of the contract — the type, quality, and amount of goods, for example, and the time and terms of delivery — are determined by the office. These activities form a separate and indispensable part of the business activities of the foreign enterprise, and are not simply activities of an auxiliary or preparatory character.

45.   Regarding paragraph 38, *Mexico* believes that the arm's length principle should also be considered in determining whether or not an agent is of an independent status for purposes of paragraph 6 of the Article and wishes, when necessary, to add wording to its conventions to clarify that this is how the paragraph should be interpreted.

45.1   [Deleted]

45.2   *Italy* and *Portugal* deem as essential to take into consideration that — irrespective of the meaning given to the third sentence of paragraph 1.1 — as far as the method for computing taxes is concerned, national systems are not affected by the new wording of the model, *i.e.* by the elimination of Article 14.

45.3   The *Czech Republic* has expressed a number of explanations and reservations on the report on "Issues Arising Under Article 5 of the OECD Model Tax Convention". In particular, the Czech Republic does not agree with the interpretation mentioned in paragraphs 5.3 (first part of the paragraph) and 5.4 (first part of the paragraph). According to its policy, these examples could also be regarded as constituting a permanent establishment if the services are furnished on its territory over a substantial period of time.

45.4   As regards paragraph 17, the *Czech Republic* adopts a narrower interpretation of the term "installation project" and therefore, it restricts it to an installation and assembly related to a construction project. Furthermore, the Czech Republic adheres to an interpretation that supervisory activities will be automatically covered by paragraph 3 of Article 5 only if they are carried on by the building contractor. Otherwise, they will be covered by it, but only if they are expressly mentioned in this special provision. In the case of an installation project not in relation with a construction project and in the case that supervisory activity is carried on by an enterprise other than the building contractor and it is not expressly mentioned in paragraph 3 of Article 5, then these activities are automatically subject to the rules concerning the taxation of income derived from the provision of other services.

45.5   In relation to paragraphs 42.1 to 42.10, the *United Kingdom* takes the view that a server used by an e-tailer, either alone or together with web sites, could not as such constitute a permanent establishment.

45.6   *Chile* and *Greece* do not adhere to all the interpretations in paragraphs 42.1 to 42.10.

45.7   *Germany* does not agree with the interpretation of the "painter example" in paragraph 4.5 which it regards as inconsistent with the principle stated in the first sentence of paragraph 4.2, thus not giving rise to a permanent establishment under Article 5 paragraph 1 of the Model Convention. As regards the example described in paragraph 5.4, Germany would require that the consultant has disposal over the offices used apart from his mere presence during the training activities.

45.8   *Germany* reserves its position concerning the scope and limits of application of guidance in sentences 2 and 5 to 7 in paragraph 6, taking the view that in order to permit the assumption of a fixed place of business, the necessary degree of permanency requires a certain minimum period of presence during the year concerned, irrespective of the recurrent or other nature of an activity. Germany does in particular not agree with the criterion of economic nexus — as described in sentence 6 of paragraph 6 — to justify an exception from the requirements of qualifying presence and duration.

45.9 *Germany*, as regards paragraph 33.1 (with reference to paragraphs 32 and 6), attaches increased importance to the requirement of minimum duration of representation of the enterprise under Article 5 paragraph 5 of the Model Convention in the absence of a residence and/or fixed place of business of the agent in the source country. Germany therefore in these cases takes a particularly narrow view on the applicability of the factors mentioned in paragraph 6.

45.10 *Italy* wishes to clarify that, with respect to paragraphs 33, 41, 41.1 and 42, its jurisprudence is not to be ignored in the interpretation of cases falling in the above paragraphs.

45.11 *Portugal* wishes to reserve its right not to follow the position expressed in paragraphs 42.1 to 42.10.

Reservations on the Article

Paragraph 1

46. *Australia* reserves the right to treat an enterprise as having a permanent establishment in a State if it carries on activities relating to natural resources or operates substantial equipment in that State with a certain degree of continuity, or a person — acting in that State on behalf of the enterprise — manufactures or processes in that State goods or merchandise belonging to the enterprise.

47. Considering the special problems in applying the provisions of the Model Convention to offshore hydrocarbon exploration and exploitation and related activities, *Canada*, *Denmark*, *Ireland*, *Norway* and the *United Kingdom* reserve the right to insert in a special article provisions related to such activities.

48. *Chile* reserves the right to deem an enterprise to have a permanent establishment in certain circumstances where services are provided.

49. The *Czech Republic* and the *Slovak Republic*, whilst agreeing with the "fixed place of business" requirement of paragraph 1, reserve the right to propose in bilateral negotiations specific provisions clarifying the application of this principle to arrangements for the performance of services over a substantial period of time.

50. *Greece* reserves the right to treat an enterprise as having a permanent establishment in Greece if the enterprise carries on planning, supervisory or consultancy activities in connection with a building site or construction or installation project lasting more than six months, if scientific equipment or machinery is used in Greece for more than three months by the enterprise in the exploration or extraction of natural resources or if the enterprise carries out more than one separate project, each one lasting less than six months, in the same period of time (i.e. within a calendar year).

51. *Greece* reserves the right to insert special provisions relating to offshore activities.

52. *Mexico* reserves the right to tax individuals performing professional services or other activities of an independent character if they are present in Mexico for a period

or periods exceeding in the aggregate 183 days in any twelve month period.

53.   *New Zealand* reserves the right to insert provisions that deem a permanent establishment to exist if, for more than six months, an enterprise conducts activities relating to the exploration or exploitation of natural resources or uses or leases substantial equipment.

54.   *Turkey* reserves the right to treat a person as having a permanent establishment in Turkey if the person performs professional services and other activities of independent character, including planning, supervisory or consultancy activities, with a certain degree of continuity either directly or through the employees of a separate enterprise.

Paragraph 2

55.   *Canada* and *Chile* reserve the right in subparagraph 2 *f)* to replace the words "of extraction" with the words "relating to the exploration for or the exploitation".

56.   *Greece* reserves the right to include paragraph 2 of Article 5 as it was drafted in the 1963 Draft Convention.

Paragraph 3

57.   *Australia, Chile, Greece, Korea, New Zealand, Portugal* and *Turkey* reserve their positions on paragraph 3, and consider that any building site or construction or installation project which lasts more than six months should be regarded as a permanent establishment.

58.   *Australia* reserves the right to treat an enterprise as having a permanent establishment in a State if it carries on in that State supervisory or consultancy activities for more than 183 days in any twelve month period in connection with a building site or construction or installation project in that State.

59.   *Korea* reserves its position so as to be able to tax an enterprise which carries on supervisory activities for more than six months in connection with a building site or construction or installation project lasting more than six months.

60.   *Slovenia* reserves the right to include connected supervisory or consultancy activities in paragraph 3 of the Article.

61.   *Mexico* and the *Slovak Republic* reserve the right to tax an enterprise that carries on supervisory activities for more than six months in connection with a building site or a construction, assembly, or installation project.

62.   *Mexico* and the *Slovak Republic* reserve their position on paragraph 3 and consider that any building site or construction, assembly, or installation project that lasts more than six months should be regarded as a permanent establishment.

63.   *Poland* and *Slovenia* reserve the right to replace "construction or installation project" with "construction, assembly, or installation project".

64.   *Portugal* reserves the right to treat an enterprise as having a permanent establishment in Portugal if the enterprise carries on an activity consisting of planning, supervising, consulting, any auxiliary work or any other activity in connection with a building site or construction or installation project lasting more than six months, if such activities or work also last more than six months.

65.   The *United States* reserves the right to add "a drilling rig or ship used for the exploration of natural resources" to the activities covered by the twelve month threshold test in paragraph 3.

Paragraph 4

66.   *Chile* reserves the right to amend paragraph 4 by eliminating subparagraph *f)* and replacing subparagraph *e)* with the corresponding text of the 1963 Draft Model Tax Convention.

67.   *Mexico* reserves the right to exclude subparagraph *f)* of paragraph 4 of the Article to consider that a permanent establishment could exist where a fixed place of business is maintained for any combination of activities mentioned in subparagraphs *a)* to *e)* of paragraph 4.

Paragraph 6

68.   *Slovenia* reserves the right to amend paragraph 6 to make clear that an agent whose activities are conducted wholly or almost wholly on behalf of a single enterprise will not be considered an agent of an independent status.

COMMENTARY ON ARTICLE 6
CONCERNING THE TAXATION OF INCOME FROM IMMOVABLE PROPERTY

1.   Paragraph 1 gives the right to tax income from immovable property to the State of source, that is, the State in which the property producing such income is situated. This is due to the fact that there is always a very close economic connection between the source of this income and the State of source. Although income from agriculture or forestry is included in Article 6, Contracting States are free to agree in their bilateral conventions to treat such income under Article 7. Article 6 deals only with income which a resident of a Contracting State derives from immovable property situated in the other Contracting State. It does not, therefore, apply to income from immovable property situated in the Contracting State of which the recipient is a resident within the meaning of Article 4 or situated in a third State; the provisions of paragraph 1 of Article 21 shall apply to such income.

2.   Defining the concept of immovable property by reference to the law of the State in which the property is situated, as is provided in paragraph 2, will help to avoid difficulties of interpretation over the question whether an asset or a right is to be regarded as immovable property or not. The paragraph, however, specifically mentions the assets and rights which must always be regarded as immovable property. In fact such assets and rights are already treated as immovable property according to the laws or the taxation rules of most OECD member countries. Conversely, the paragraph stipulates that ships, boats and aircraft shall never be considered as immovable property. No special provision has been included as regards income from indebtedness secured by immovable property, as this question is settled by Article 11.

3.   Paragraph 3 indicates that the general rule applies irrespective of the form of exploitation of the immovable property. Paragraph 4 makes it clear that the provisions of paragraphs 1 and 3 apply also to income from immovable property of industrial, commercial and other enterprises. Income in the form of distributions from Real Estate Investment Trusts (REITs), however, raises particular issues which are discussed in paragraphs 67.1 to 67.7 of the Commentary on Article 10.

4.   It should be noted in this connection that the right to tax of the State of source has priority over the right to tax of the other State and applies also where, in the case of an enterprise, income is only indirectly derived from immovable property. This does not prevent income from immovable property, when derived through a permanent establishment, from being treated as income of an enterprise, but secures that income from immovable property will be taxed in the State in which the property is situated also in the case where such property is not part of a permanent establishment situated in that State. It should further be noted that the provisions of the Article do not prejudge the application of domestic law as regards the manner in which income from immovable property is to be taxed.

MODEL TAX CONVENTION (CONDENSED VERSION) – ISBN 978-92-64-08948-8 – © OECD 2010

Reservations on the Article

5.   *Finland* reserves the right to tax income of shareholders in Finnish companies from the direct use, letting, or use in any other form of the right to enjoyment of immovable property situated in Finland and held by the company, where such right is based on the ownership of shares or other corporate rights in the company.

6.   *France* wishes to retain the possibility of applying the provisions in its domestic laws relative to the taxation of income from shares or rights, which are treated therein as income from immovable property.

7.   *Spain* reserves its right to tax income from any form of use of a right to enjoyment of immovable property situated in Spain when such right derives from the holding of shares or other corporate rights in the company owning the property.

8.   *Canada* reserves the right to include in paragraph 3 a reference to income from the alienation of immovable property.

9.   *New Zealand* reserves the right to include fishing and rights relating to all natural resources under this Article.

10.   The *United States* reserves the right to add a paragraph to Article 6 allowing a resident of a Contracting State to elect to be taxed by the other Contracting State on a net basis on income from real property.

11.   *Australia* reserves the right to include rights relating to all natural resources under this Article.

12.   *Mexico* reserves the right to treat as immovable property any right that allows the use or enjoyment of immovable property situated in a Contracting State where that use or enjoyment relates to time sharing since under its domestic law such right is not considered to constitute immovable property.

COMMENTARY ON ARTICLE 7
CONCERNING THE TAXATION OF BUSINESS PROFITS

I. Preliminary remarks

1. This Article allocates taxing rights with respect to the business profits of an enterprise of a Contracting State to the extent that these profits are not subject to different rules under other Articles of the Convention. It incorporates the basic principle that unless an enterprise of a Contracting State has a permanent establishment situated in the other State, the business profits of that enterprise may not be taxed by that other State unless these profits fall into special categories of income for which other Articles of the Convention give taxing rights to that other State.

2. Article 5, which includes the definition of the concept of permanent establishment, is therefore relevant to the determination of whether the business profits of an enterprise of a Contracting State may be taxed in the other State. That Article, however, does not itself allocate taxing rights: when an enterprise of a Contracting State carries on business in the other Contracting State through a permanent establishment situated therein, it is necessary to determine what, if any, are the profits that the other State may tax. Article 7 provides the answer to that question by determining that the other State may tax the profits that are attributable to the permanent establishment.

3. The principles underlying Article 7, and in particular paragraph 2 of the Article, have a long history. When the OECD first examined what criteria should be used in attributing profits to a permanent establishment, this question had previously been addressed in a large number of tax conventions and in various models developed by the League of Nations. The separate entity and arm's length principles, on which paragraph 2 is based, had already been incorporated in these conventions and models and the OECD considered that it was sufficient to restate these principles with some slight amendments and modifications for the main purpose of clarification.

4. Practical experience has shown, however, that there was considerable variation in the interpretation of these general principles and of other provisions of earlier versions of Article 7. This lack of a common interpretation created problems of double taxation and non-taxation. Over the years, the Committee on Fiscal Affairs spent considerable time and effort trying to ensure a more consistent interpretation and application of the rules of the Article. Minor changes to the wording of the Article and a number of changes to the Commentary were made when the 1977 Model Tax Convention was adopted. A report that addressed that question in the specific case of banks was published in 1984.[1] In 1987, noting that the determination of profits attributable to a permanent establishment could give rise to some uncertainty, the Committee undertook a review of the question which led to the adoption, in 1993, of

---

1 "The Taxation of Multinational Banking Enterprises", in *Transfer Pricing and Multinational Enterprises: Three Taxation Issues*, OECD, Paris, 1984.

the report entitled "Attribution of Income to Permanent Establishments"[1] and to subsequent changes to the Commentary.

5.   Despite that work, the practices of OECD and non-OECD countries regarding the attribution of profits to permanent establishments and these countries' interpretation of Article 7 continued to vary considerably. The Committee acknowledged the need to provide more certainty to taxpayers: in its report *Transfer Pricing Guidelines for Multinational Enterprises and Tax Administrations*[2] (the "OECD Transfer Pricing Guidelines"), it indicated that further work would address the application of the arm's length principle to permanent establishments. That work resulted, in 2008, in a report entitled *Attribution of Profits to Permanent Establishments*[3] (the "2008 Report").

6.   The approach developed in the 2008 Report was not constrained by either the original intent or by the historical practice and interpretation of Article 7. Instead, the focus was on formulating the most preferable approach to attributing profits to a permanent establishment under Article 7 given modern-day multinational operations and trade. When it approved the 2008 Report, the Committee considered that the guidance included therein represented a better approach to attributing profits to permanent establishments than had previously been available. It also recognised, however, that there were differences between some of the conclusions of the 2008 Report and the interpretation of Article 7 previously given in this Commentary.

7.   In order to provide maximum certainty on how profits should be attributed to permanent establishments, the Committee therefore decided that the 2008 Report's full conclusions should be reflected in a new version of Article 7, together with accompanying Commentary, to be used in the negotiation of future treaties and the amendment of existing treaties. In addition, in order to provide improved certainty for the interpretation of treaties that had already been concluded on the basis of the previous wording of Article 7, the Committee decided that a revised Commentary for that previous version of the Article should also be prepared, to take into account those aspects of the report that did not conflict with the Commentary as it read before the adoption of the 2008 Report.

8.   The new version of the Article, which now appears in the Model Tax Convention, was adopted in 2010. At the same time, the Committee adopted a revised version of the 2008 Report in order to ensure that the conclusions of that report could be read harmoniously with the new wording and modified numbering of this new version of the Article. Whilst the conclusions and interpretations included in the revised report that was thus adopted in 2010[4] (hereinafter referred to as "the Report") are identical to

---

1   *Attribution of Income to Permanent Establishments*, Issues in International Taxation No. 5, OECD, Paris, 1994; reproduced in Volume II of the full-length version of the OECD Model Tax Convention at page R(13)-1.
2   The original version of that report was approved by the Council of the OECD on 27 June 1995 and was updated a number of times since then. Published by the OECD as *OECD Transfer Pricing Guidelines for Multinational Enterprises and Tax Administrations*.
3   Available at http://www.oecd.org/dataoecd/20/36/41031455.pdf.
4   *Attribution of Profits to Permanent Establishments*, OECD, Paris, 2010.

those of the 2008 Report, that revised version takes account of the drafting of the Article as it now reads (the Annex to this Commentary includes, for historical reference, the text of the previous wording of Article 7 and that revised Commentary, as they read before the adoption of the current version of the Article).

9.   The current version of the Article therefore reflects the approach developed in the Report and must be interpreted in light of the guidance contained in it. The Report deals with the attribution of profits both to permanent establishments in general (Part I of the Report) and, in particular, to permanent establishments of businesses operating in the financial sector, where trading through a permanent establishment is widespread (Part II of the Report, which deals with permanent establishments of banks, Part III, which deals with permanent establishments of enterprises carrying on global trading and Part IV, which deals with permanent establishments of enterprises carrying on insurance activities).

II.   Commentary on the provisions of the Article

Paragraph 1

10.   Paragraph 1 incorporates the rules for the allocation of taxing rights on the business profits of enterprises of each Contracting State. First, it states that unless an enterprise of a Contracting State has a permanent establishment situated in the other State, the business profits of that enterprise may not be taxed by that other State. Second, it provides that if such an enterprise carries on business in the other State through a permanent establishment situated therein, the profits that are attributable to the permanent establishment, as determined in accordance with paragraph 2, may be taxed by that other State. As explained below, however, paragraph 4 restricts the application of these rules by providing that Article 7 does not affect the application of other Articles of the Convention that provide special rules for certain categories of profits (e.g. those derived from the operation of ships and aircraft in international traffic) or for certain categories of income that may also constitute business profits (e.g. income derived by an enterprise in respect of personal activities of an entertainer or sportsman).

11.   The first principle underlying paragraph 1, i.e. that the profits of an enterprise of one Contracting State shall not be taxed in the other State unless the enterprise carries on business in that other State through a permanent establishment situated therein, has a long history and reflects the international consensus that, as a general rule, until an enterprise of one State has a permanent establishment in another State, it should not properly be regarded as participating in the economic life of that other State to such an extent that the other State should have taxing rights on its profits.

12.   The second principle, which is reflected in the second sentence of the paragraph, is that the right to tax of the State where the permanent establishment is situated does not extend to profits that the enterprise may derive from that State but that are not attributable to the permanent establishment. This is a question on which there have historically been differences of view, a few countries having some time ago pursued a

principle of general "force of attraction" according to which income such as other business profits, dividends, interest and royalties arising from sources in their territory was fully taxable by them if the beneficiary had a permanent establishment therein even though such income was clearly not attributable to that permanent establishment. Whilst some bilateral tax conventions include a limited anti-avoidance rule based on a restricted force of attraction approach that only applies to business profits derived from activities similar to those carried on by a permanent establishment, the general force of attraction approach described above has now been rejected in international tax treaty practice. The principle that is now generally accepted in double taxation conventions is based on the view that in taxing the profits that a foreign enterprise derives from a particular country, the tax authorities of that country should look at the separate sources of profit that the enterprise derives from their country and should apply to each the permanent establishment test, subject to the possible application of other Articles of the Convention. This solution allows simpler and more efficient tax administration and compliance, and is more closely adapted to the way in which business is commonly carried on. The organisation of modern business is highly complex. There are a considerable number of companies each of which is engaged in a wide diversity of activities and is carrying on business extensively in many countries. A company may set up a permanent establishment in another country through which it carries on manufacturing activities whilst a different part of the same company sells different goods in that other country through independent agents. That company may have perfectly valid commercial reasons for doing so: these may be based, for example, on the historical pattern of its business or on commercial convenience. If the country in which the permanent establishment is situated wished to go so far as to try to determine, and tax, the profit element of each of the transactions carried on through independent agents, with a view to aggregating that profit with the profits of the permanent establishment, that approach would interfere seriously with ordinary commercial activities and would be contrary to the aims of the Convention.

13.   As indicated in the second sentence of paragraph 1, the profits that are attributable to the permanent establishment are determined in accordance with the provisions of paragraph 2, which provides the meaning of the phrase "profits that are attributable to the permanent establishment" found in paragraph 1. Since paragraph 1 grants taxing rights to the State in which the permanent establishment is situated only with respect to the profits that are attributable to that permanent establishment, the paragraph therefore prevents that State, subject to the application of other Articles of the Convention, from taxing the enterprise of the other Contracting State on profits that are not attributable to the permanent establishment.

14.   The purpose of paragraph 1 is to limit the right of one Contracting State to tax the business profits of enterprises of the other Contracting State. The paragraph does not limit the right of a Contracting State to tax its own residents under controlled foreign companies provisions found in its domestic law even though such tax imposed on these residents may be computed by reference to the part of the profits of an enterprise

that is resident of the other Contracting State that is attributable to these residents' participation in that enterprise. Tax so levied by a State on its own residents does not reduce the profits of the enterprise of the other State and may not, therefore, be said to have been levied on such profits (see also paragraph 23 of the Commentary on Article 1 and paragraphs 37 to 39 of the Commentary on Article 10).

Paragraph 2

15.   Paragraph 2 provides the basic rule for the determination of the profits that are attributable to a permanent establishment. According to the paragraph, these profits are the profits that the permanent establishment might be expected to make if it were a separate and independent enterprise engaged in the same or similar activities under the same or similar conditions, taking into account the functions performed, assets used and risks assumed through the permanent establishment and through other parts of the enterprise. In addition, the paragraph clarifies that this rule applies with respect to the dealings between the permanent establishment and the other parts of the enterprise.

16.   The basic approach incorporated in the paragraph for the purposes of determining what are the profits that are attributable to the permanent establishment is therefore to require the determination of the profits under the fiction that the permanent establishment is a separate enterprise and that such an enterprise is independent from the rest of the enterprise of which it is a part as well as from any other person. The second part of that fiction corresponds to the arm's length principle which is also applicable, under the provisions of Article 9, for the purpose of adjusting the profits of associated enterprises (see paragraph 1 of the Commentary on Article 9).

17.   Paragraph 2 does not seek to allocate the overall profits of the whole enterprise to the permanent establishment and its other parts but, instead, requires that the profits attributable to a permanent establishment be determined as if it were a separate enterprise. Profits may therefore be attributed to a permanent establishment even though the enterprise as a whole has never made profits. Conversely, paragraph 2 may result in no profits being attributed to a permanent establishment even though the enterprise as a whole has made profits.

18.   Clearly, however, where an enterprise of a Contracting State has a permanent establishment in the other Contracting State, the first State has an interest in the directive of paragraph 2 being correctly applied by the State where the permanent establishment is located. Since that directive applies to both Contracting States, the State of the enterprise must, in accordance with either Article 23 A or 23 B, eliminate double taxation on the profits properly attributable to the permanent establishment (see paragraph 27 below). In other words, if the State where the permanent establishment is located attempts to tax profits that are not attributable to the permanent establishment under Article 7, this may result in double taxation of profits that should properly be taxed only in the State of the enterprise.

19.   As indicated in paragraphs 8 and 9 above, Article 7, as currently worded, reflects the approach developed in the Report adopted by the Committee on Fiscal Affairs

in 2010. The Report dealt primarily with the application of the separate and independent enterprise fiction that underlies paragraph 2 and the main purpose of the changes made to that paragraph following the adoption of the Report was to ensure that the determination of the profits attributable to a permanent establishment followed the approach put forward in that Report. The Report therefore provides a detailed guide as to how the profits attributable to a permanent establishment should be determined under the provisions of paragraph 2.

20.   As explained in the Report, the attribution of profits to a permanent establishment under paragraph 2 will follow from the calculation of the profits (or losses) from all its activities, including transactions with independent enterprises, transactions with associated enterprises (with direct application of the OECD Transfer Pricing Guidelines) and dealings with other parts of the enterprise. This analysis involves two steps which are described below. The order of the listing of items within each of these two steps is not meant to be prescriptive, as the various items may be interrelated (*e.g.* risk is initially attributed to a permanent establishment as it performs the significant people functions relevant to the assumption of that risk but the recognition and characterisation of a subsequent dealing between the permanent establishment and another part of the enterprise that manages the risk may lead to a transfer of the risk and supporting capital to the other part of the enterprise).

21.   Under the first step, a functional and factual analysis is undertaken which will lead to:

— the attribution to the permanent establishment, as appropriate, of the rights and obligations arising out of transactions between the enterprise of which the permanent establishment is a part and separate enterprises;

— the identification of significant people functions relevant to the attribution of economic ownership of assets, and the attribution of economic ownership of assets to the permanent establishment;

— the identification of significant people functions relevant to the assumption of risks, and the attribution of risks to the permanent establishment;

— the identification of other functions of the permanent establishment;

— the recognition and determination of the nature of those dealings between the permanent establishment and other parts of the same enterprise that can appropriately be recognised, having passed the threshold test referred to in paragraph 26; and

— the attribution of capital based on the assets and risks attributed to the permanent establishment.

22.   Under the second step, any transactions with associated enterprises attributed to the permanent establishment are priced in accordance with the guidance of the OECD Transfer Pricing Guidelines and these Guidelines are applied by analogy to dealings between the permanent establishment and the other parts of the enterprise of which it is a part. The process involves the pricing on an arm's length basis of these recognised dealings through:

— the determination of comparability between the dealings and uncontrolled transactions, established by applying the Guidelines' comparability factors directly (characteristics of property or services, economic circumstances and business strategies) or by analogy (functional analysis, contractual terms) in light of the particular factual circumstances of the permanent establishment; and

— the application by analogy of one of the Guidelines' methods to arrive at an arm's length compensation for the dealings between the permanent establishment and the other parts of the enterprise, taking into account the functions performed by and the assets and risks attributed to the permanent establishment and the other parts of the enterprise.

23.   Each of these operations is discussed in greater detail in the Report, in particular as regards the attribution of profits to permanent establishments of businesses operating in the financial sector, where trading through a permanent establishment is widespread (see Part II of the Report, which deals with permanent establishments of banks; Part III, which deals with permanent establishments of enterprises carrying on global trading, and Part IV, which deals with permanent establishments of enterprises carrying on insurance activities).

24.   Paragraph 2 refers specifically to the dealings between the permanent establishment and other parts of the enterprise of which the permanent establishment is a part in order to emphasise that the separate and independent enterprise fiction of the paragraph requires that these dealings be treated the same way as similar transactions taking place between independent enterprises. That specific reference to dealings between the permanent establishment and other parts of the enterprise does not, however, restrict the scope of the paragraph. Where a transaction that takes place between the enterprise and an associated enterprise affects directly the determination of the profits attributable to the permanent establishment (e.g. the acquisition by the permanent establishment from an associated enterprise of goods that will be sold through the permanent establishment), paragraph 2 also requires that, for the purpose of computing the profits attributable to the permanent establishment, the conditions of the transaction be adjusted, if necessary, to reflect the conditions of a similar transaction between independent enterprises. Assume, for instance, that the permanent establishment situated in State S of an enterprise of State R acquires property from an associated enterprise of State T. If the price provided for in the contract between the two associated enterprises exceeds what would have been agreed to between independent enterprises, paragraph 2 of Article 7 of the treaty between State R and State S will authorise State S to adjust the profits attributable to the permanent establishment to reflect what a separate and independent enterprise would have paid for that property. In such a case, State R will also be able to adjust the profits of the enterprise of State R under paragraph 1 of Article 9 of the treaty between State R and State T, which will trigger the application of the corresponding adjustment mechanism of paragraph 2 of Article 9 of that treaty.

25.   Dealings between the permanent establishment and other parts of the enterprise of which it is a part have no legal consequences for the enterprise as a whole. This

implies a need for greater scrutiny of these dealings than of transactions between two associated enterprises. This also implies a greater scrutiny of documentation (in the inevitable absence, for example, of legally binding contracts) that might otherwise exist.

26.   It is generally not intended that more burdensome documentation requirements be imposed in connection with such dealings than apply to transactions between associated enterprises. Moreover, as in the case of transfer pricing documentation referred to in the OECD Transfer Pricing Guidelines, the requirements should not be applied in such a way as to impose on taxpayers costs and burdens disproportionate to the circumstances. Nevertheless, considering the uniqueness of the nature of a dealing, countries would wish to require taxpayers to demonstrate clearly that it would be appropriate to recognise the dealing. Thus, for example, an accounting record and contemporaneous documentation showing a dealing that transfers economically significant risks, responsibilities and benefits would be a useful starting point for the purposes of attributing profits. Taxpayers are encouraged to prepare such documentation, as it may reduce substantially the potential for controversies regarding application of the approach. Tax administrations would give effect to such documentation, notwithstanding its lack of legal effect, to the extent that:

— the documentation is consistent with the economic substance of the activities taking place within the enterprise as revealed by the functional and factual analysis;

— the arrangements documented in relation to the dealing, viewed in their entirety, do not differ from those which would have been adopted by comparable independent enterprises behaving in a commercially rational manner, or if they do, the structure as presented in the taxpayer's documentation does not practically impede the tax administration from determining an appropriate transfer price; and

— the dealing presented in the taxpayer's documentation does not violate the principles of the approach put forward in the Report by, for example, purporting to transfer risks in a way that segregates them from functions.

27.   The opening words of paragraph 2 and the phrase "in each Contracting State" indicate that paragraph 2 applies not only for the purposes of determining the profits that the Contracting State in which the permanent establishment is situated may tax in accordance with the last sentence of paragraph 1 but also for the application of Articles 23 A and 23 B by the other Contracting State. Where an enterprise of one State carries on business through a permanent establishment situated in the other State, the first-mentioned State must either exempt the profits that are attributable to the permanent establishment (Article 23 A) or give a credit for the tax levied by the other State on these profits (Article 23 B). Under both these Articles, that State must therefore determine the profits attributable to the permanent establishment in order to provide relief from double taxation and is required to follow the provisions of paragraph 2 for that purpose.

28.   The separate and independent enterprise fiction that is mandated by paragraph 2 is restricted to the determination of the profits that are attributable to a permanent establishment. It does not extend to create notional income for the enterprise which a Contracting State could tax as such under its domestic law by arguing that such income is covered by another Article of the Convention which, in accordance with paragraph 4 of Article 7, allows taxation of that income notwithstanding paragraph 1 of Article 7. Assume, for example, that the circumstances of a particular case justify considering that the economic ownership of a building used by the permanent establishment should be attributed to the head office (see paragraph 75 of Part I of the Report). In such a case, paragraph 2 could require the deduction of a notional rent in determining the profits of the permanent establishment. That fiction, however, could not be interpreted as creating income from immovable property for the purposes of Article 6. Indeed, the fiction mandated by paragraph 2 does not change the nature of the income derived by the enterprise; it merely applies to determine the profits attributable to the permanent establishment for the purposes of Articles 7, 23 A and 23 B. Similarly, the fact that, under paragraph 2, a notional interest charge could be deducted in determining the profits attributable to a permanent establishment does not mean that any interest has been paid to the enterprise of which the permanent establishment is a part for the purposes of paragraphs 1 and 2 of Article 11. The separate and independent enterprise fiction does not extend to Article 11 and, for the purposes of that Article, one part of an enterprise cannot be considered to have made an interest payment to another part of the same enterprise. Clearly, however, if interest paid by an enterprise to a different person is paid on indebtedness incurred in connection with a permanent establishment of the enterprise and is borne by that permanent establishment, this real interest payment may, under paragraph 2 of Article 11, be taxed by the State in which the permanent establishment is located. Also, where a transfer of assets between a permanent establishment and the rest of the enterprise is treated as a dealing for the purposes of paragraph 2 of Article 7, Article 13 does not prevent States from taxing profits or gains from such a dealing as long as such taxation is in accordance with Article 7 (see paragraphs 4, 8 and 10 of the Commentary on Article 13).

29.   Some States consider that, as a matter of policy, the separate and independent enterprise fiction that is mandated by paragraph 2 should not be restricted to the application of Articles 7, 23 A and 23 B but should also extend to the interpretation and application of other Articles of the Convention, so as to ensure that permanent establishments are, as far as possible, treated in the same way as subsidiaries. These States may therefore consider that notional charges for dealings which, pursuant to paragraph 2, are deducted in computing the profits of a permanent establishment should be treated, for the purposes of other Articles of the Convention, in the same way as payments that would be made by a subsidiary to its parent company. These States may therefore wish to include in their tax treaties provisions according to which charges for internal dealings should be recognised for the purposes of Articles 6 and 11 (it should be noted, however, that tax will be levied in accordance with such provisions only to the extent provided for under domestic law). Alternatively, these States may

wish to provide that no internal dealings will be recognised in circumstances where an equivalent transaction between two separate enterprises would give rise to income covered by Article 6 or 11 (in that case, however, it will be important to ensure that an appropriate share of the expenses related to what would otherwise have been recognised as a dealing be attributed to the relevant part of the enterprise). States considering these alternatives should, however, take account of the fact that, due to special considerations applicable to internal interest charges between different parts of a financial enterprise (*e.g.* a bank), dealings resulting in such charges have long been recognised, even before the adoption of the present version of the Article.

30. Paragraph 2 determines the profits that are attributable to a permanent establishment for the purposes of the rule in paragraph 1 that allocates taxing rights on these profits. Once the profits that are attributable to a permanent establishment have been determined in accordance with paragraph 2 of Article 7, it is for the domestic law of each Contracting State to determine whether and how such profits should be taxed as long as there is conformity with the requirements of paragraph 2 and the other provisions of the Convention. Paragraph 2 does not deal with the issue of whether expenses are deductible when computing the taxable income of the enterprise in either Contracting State. The conditions for the deductibility of expenses are a matter to be determined by domestic law, subject to the provisions of the Convention and, in particular, paragraph 3 of Article 24 (see paragraphs 33 and 34 below).

31. Thus, for example, whilst domestic law rules that would ignore the recognition of dealings that should be recognised for the purposes of determining the profits attributable to a permanent establishment under paragraph 2 or that would deny the deduction of expenses not incurred exclusively for the benefit of the permanent establishment would clearly be in violation of paragraph 2, rules that prevent the deduction of certain categories of expenses (*e.g.* entertainment expenses) or that provide when a particular expense should be deducted are not affected by paragraph 2. In making that distinction, however, some difficult questions may arise as in the case of domestic law restrictions based on when an expense or element of income is actually paid. Since, for instance, an internal dealing will not involve an actual transfer or payment between two different persons, the application of such domestic law restrictions should generally take into account the nature of the dealing and, therefore, treat the relevant transfer or payment as if it had been made between two different persons.

32. Variations between the domestic laws of the two States concerning matters such as depreciation rates, the timing of the recognition of income and restrictions on the deductibility of certain expenses will normally result in a different amount of taxable income in each State even though, for the purposes of the Convention, the amount of profits attributable to the permanent establishment will have been computed on the basis of paragraph 2 in both States (see also paragraphs 39-43 of the Commentary on Articles 23 A and 23 B). Thus, even though paragraph 2 applies equally to the Contracting State in which the permanent establishment is situated (for the purposes

of paragraph 1) and to the other Contracting State (for the purposes of Articles 23 A or 23 B), it is likely that the amount of taxable income on which an enterprise of a Contracting State will be taxed in the State where the enterprise has a permanent establishment will, for a given taxable period, be different from the amount of taxable income with respect to which the first State will have to provide relief pursuant to Articles 23 A or 23 B. Also, to the extent that the difference results from domestic law variations concerning the types of expenses that are deductible, as opposed to timing differences in the recognition of these expenses, the difference will be permanent.

33.   In taxing the profits attributable to a permanent establishment situated on its territory, a Contracting State will, however, have to take account of the provisions of paragraph 3 of Article 24. That paragraph requires, among other things, that expenses be deductible under the same conditions whether they are incurred for the purposes of a permanent establishment situated in a Contracting State or for the purposes of an enterprise of that State. As stated in paragraph 40 of the Commentary on Article 24:

> Permanent establishments must be accorded the same right as resident enterprises to deduct the trading expenses that are, in general, authorised by the taxation law to be deducted from taxable profits. Such deductions should be allowed without any restrictions other than those also imposed on resident enterprises.

34.   The requirement imposed by paragraph 3 of Article 24 is the same regardless of how expenses incurred by an enterprise for the benefit of a permanent establishment are taken into account for the purposes of paragraph 2 of Article 7. In some cases, it will not be appropriate to consider that a dealing has taken place between different parts of the enterprise. In such cases, expenses incurred by an enterprise for the purposes of the activities performed by the permanent establishment will be directly deducted in determining the profits of the permanent establishment (*e.g.* the salary of a local construction worker hired and paid locally to work exclusively on a construction site that constitutes a permanent establishment of a foreign enterprise). In other cases, expenses incurred by the enterprise will be attributed to functions performed by other parts of the enterprise wholly or partly for the benefit of the permanent establishment and an appropriate charge will be deducted in determining the profits attributable to the permanent establishment (*e.g.* overhead expenses related to administrative functions performed by the head office for the benefit of the permanent establishment). In both cases, paragraph 3 of Article 24 will require that, as regards the permanent establishment, the expenses be deductible under the same conditions as those applicable to an enterprise of that State. Thus, any expense incurred by the enterprise directly or indirectly for the benefit of the permanent establishment must not, for tax purposes, be treated less favourably than a similar expense incurred by an enterprise of that State. That rule will apply regardless of whether or not, for the purposes of paragraph 2 of this Article 7, the expense is directly attributed to the permanent establishment (first example) or is attributed to another part of the enterprise but reflected in a notional charge to the permanent establishment (second example).

35.   Paragraph 3 of Article 5 sets forth a special rule for a fixed place of business that is a building site or a construction or installation project. Such a fixed place of business is a permanent establishment only if it lasts more than twelve months. Experience has shown that these types of permanent establishments can give rise to special problems in attributing income to them under Article 7.

36.   These problems arise chiefly where goods are provided, or services performed, by the other parts of the enterprise or a related party in connection with the building site or construction or installation project. Whilst these problems can arise with any permanent establishment, they are particularly acute for building sites and construction or installation projects. In these circumstances, it is necessary to pay close attention to the general principle that income is attributable to a permanent establishment only when it results from activities carried on by the enterprise through that permanent establishment.

37.   For example, where such goods are supplied by the other parts of the enterprise, the profits arising from that supply do not result from the activities carried on through the permanent establishment and are not attributable to it. Similarly, profits resulting from the provision of services (such as planning, designing, drawing blueprints, or rendering technical advice) by the parts of the enterprise operating outside the State where the permanent establishment is located do not result from the activities carried on through the permanent establishment and are not attributable to it.

38.   Article 7, as it read before 2010, included the following paragraph 3:

In determining the profits of a permanent establishment, there shall be allowed as deductions expenses which are incurred for the purposes of the permanent establishment, including executive and general administrative expenses so incurred, whether in the State in which the permanent establishment is situated or elsewhere.

Whilst that paragraph was originally intended to clarify that paragraph 2 required expenses incurred directly or indirectly for the benefit of a permanent establishment to be taken into account in determining the profits of the permanent establishment even if these expenses had been incurred outside the State in which the permanent establishment was located, it had sometimes been read as limiting the deduction of expenses that indirectly benefited the permanent establishment to the actual amount of the expenses.

39.   This was especially the case of general and administrative expenses, which were expressly mentioned in that paragraph. Under the previous version of paragraph 2, as interpreted in the Commentary, this was generally not a problem since a share of the general and administrative expenses of the enterprise could usually only be allocated to a permanent establishment on a cost-basis.

40.   As now worded, however, paragraph 2 requires the recognition and arm's length pricing of the dealings through which one part of the enterprise performs functions for the benefit of the permanent establishment (e.g. through the provision of assistance in day-to-day management). The deduction of an arm's length charge for these dealings,

as opposed to a deduction limited to the amount of the expenses, is required by paragraph 2. The previous paragraph 3 has therefore been deleted to prevent it from being misconstrued as limiting the deduction to the amount of the expenses themselves. That deletion does not affect the requirement, under paragraph 2, that in determining the profits attributable to a permanent establishment, all relevant expenses of the enterprise, wherever incurred, be taken into account. Depending on the circumstances, this will be done through the deduction of all or part of the expenses or through the deduction of an arm's length charge in the case of a dealing between the permanent establishment and another part of the enterprise.

41. Article 7, as it read before 2010, also included a provision that allowed the attribution of profits to a permanent establishment to be done on the basis of an apportionment of the total profits of the enterprise to its various parts. That method, however, was only to be applied to the extent that its application had been customary in a Contracting State and that the result was in accordance with the principles of Article 7. For the Committee, methods other than an apportionment of total profits of an enterprise can be applied even in the most difficult cases. The Committee therefore decided to delete that provision because its application had become very exceptional and because of concerns that it was extremely difficult to ensure that the result of its application would be in accordance with the arm's length principle.

42. At the same time, the Committee also decided to eliminate another provision that was found in the previous version of the Article and according to which the profits to be attributed to the permanent establishment were to be "determined by the same method year by year unless there is good and sufficient reason to the contrary." That provision, which was intended to ensure continuous and consistent treatment, was appropriate as long as it was accepted that the profits attributable to a permanent establishment could be determined through direct or indirect methods or even on the basis of an apportionment of the total profits of the enterprise to its various parts. The new approach developed by the Committee, however, does not allow for the application of such fundamentally different methods and therefore avoids the need for such a provision.

43. A final provision that was deleted from the Article at the same time provided that "[n]o profits shall be attributed to a permanent establishment by reason of the mere purchase by that permanent establishment of goods or merchandise for the enterprise." Subparagraph 4 d) of Article 5 recognises that where an enterprise of a Contracting State maintains in the other State a fixed place of business exclusively for the purpose of purchasing goods for itself, its activity at that location should not be considered to have reached a level that justifies taxation in that other State. Where, however, subparagraph 4 d) is not applicable because other activities are carried on by the enterprise through that place of business, which therefore constitutes a permanent establishment, it is appropriate to attribute profits to all the functions performed at that location. Indeed, if the purchasing activities were performed by an independent enterprise, the purchaser would be remunerated on an arm's length basis for its services. Also, since a tax exemption restricted to purchasing activities undertaken for

the enterprise would require that expenses incurred for the purposes of performing these activities be excluded in determining the profits of the permanent establishment, such an exemption would raise administrative problems. The Committee therefore considered that a provision according to which no profits should be attributed to a permanent establishment by reason of the mere purchase of goods or merchandise for the enterprise was not consistent with the arm's length principle and should not be included in the Article.

Paragraph 3

44.   The combination of Articles 7 (which restricts the taxing rights of the State in which the permanent establishment is situated) and 23 A and 23 B (which oblige the other State to provide relief from double taxation) ensures that there is no unrelieved double taxation of the profits that are properly attributable to the permanent establishment. This result may require that the two States resolve differences based on different interpretations of paragraph 2 and it is important that mechanisms be available to resolve all such differences to the extent necessary to eliminate double taxation.

45.   As already indicated, the need for the two Contracting States to reach a common understanding as regards the application of paragraph 2 in order to eliminate risks of double taxation has led the Committee to develop detailed guidance on the interpretation of that paragraph. This guidance is reflected in the Report, which draws on the principles of the OECD Transfer Pricing Guidelines.

46.   Risks of double taxation will usually be avoided because the taxpayer will determine the profits attributable to the permanent establishment in the same manner in each Contracting State and in accordance with paragraph 2 as interpreted by the Report, which will ensure the same result for the purposes of Articles 7 and 23 A or 23 B (see, however, paragraph 66). Insofar as each State agrees that the taxpayer has done so, it should refrain from adjusting the profits in order to reach a different result under paragraph 2. This is illustrated in the following example.

47.   Example. A manufacturing plant located in State R of an enterprise of State R has transferred goods for sale to a permanent establishment of the enterprise situated in State S. For the purpose of determining the profits attributable to the permanent establishment under paragraph 2, the Report provides that a dealing must be recognised and a notional arm's length price must be determined for that dealing. The enterprise's documentation, which is consistent with the functional and factual analysis and which has been used by the taxpayer as the basis for the computation of its taxable income in each State, shows that a dealing in the nature of a sale of the goods by the plant in State R to the permanent establishment in State S has occurred and that a notional arm's length price of 100 has been used to determine the profits attributable to the permanent establishment. Both States agree that the recognition of the dealing and the price used by the taxpayer are in conformity with the principles of the Report and of the OECD Transfer Pricing Guidelines. In this case, both States should refrain from adjusting the profits on the basis that a different arm's length price should

have been used; as long as there is agreement that the taxpayer has conformed with paragraph 2, the tax administrations of both States cannot substitute their judgment for that of the taxpayer as to what are the arm's length conditions. In this example, the fact that the same arm's length price has been used in both States and that both States will recognise that price for the purposes of the application of the Convention will ensure that any double taxation related to that dealing will be eliminated under Article 23 A or 23 B.

48.   In the previous example, both States agreed that the recognition of the dealing and the price used by the taxpayer were in conformity with the principles of the Report and of the OECD Transfer Pricing Guidelines. The Contracting States, however, may not always reach such an agreement. In some cases, the Report and the OECD Transfer Pricing Guidelines may allow different interpretations of paragraph 2 and, to the extent that double taxation would otherwise result from these different interpretations, it is essential to ensure that such double taxation is relieved. Paragraph 3 provides the mechanism that guarantees that outcome.

49.   For example, as explained in paragraphs 105-171 of Part I of the Report, paragraph 2 permits different approaches for determining, on the basis of the attribution of "free" capital to a permanent establishment, the interest expense attributable to that permanent establishment. The Committee recognised that this could create problems, in particular for financial institutions. It concluded that in this and other cases where the two Contracting States have interpreted paragraph 2 differently and it is not possible to conclude that either interpretation is not in accordance with paragraph 2, it is important to ensure that any double taxation that would otherwise result from that difference will be eliminated.

50.   Paragraph 3 will ensure that this result is achieved. It is important to note, however, that the cases where it will be necessary to have recourse to that paragraph are fairly limited.

51.   First, as explained in paragraph 46 above, where the taxpayer has determined the profits attributable to the permanent establishment in the same manner in each Contracting State and both States agree that the taxpayer has done so in accordance with paragraph 2 as interpreted by the Report, no adjustments should be made to the profits in order to reach a different result under paragraph 2.

52.   Second, paragraph 3 is not intended to limit in any way the remedies already available to ensure that each Contracting State conforms with its obligations under Articles 7 and 23 A or 23 B. For example, if the determination, by a Contracting State, of the profits attributable to a permanent establishment situated in that State is not in conformity with paragraph 2, the taxpayer will be able to use the available domestic legal remedies and the mutual agreement procedure provided for by Article 25 to address the fact that the taxpayer has not been taxed by that State in accordance with the Convention. Similarly, these remedies will also be available if the other State does not, for the purposes of Article 23 A or 23 B, determine the profits attributable to the

permanent establishment in conformity with paragraph 2 and therefore does not comply with the provisions of this Article.

53.   Where, however, the taxpayer has not determined the profits attributable to the permanent establishment in conformity with paragraph 2, each State is entitled to make an adjustment in order to ensure conformity with that paragraph. Where one State makes an adjustment in conformity with paragraph 2, that paragraph certainly permits the other State to make a reciprocal adjustment so as to avoid any double taxation through the combined application of paragraph 2 and of Article 23 A or 23 B (see paragraph 65 below). It may be, however, that the domestic law of that other State (e.g. the State where the permanent establishment is located) may not allow it to make such a change or that State may have no incentive to do it on its own if the effect is to reduce the amount of profits that was previously taxable in that State. It may also be that, as indicated above, the two Contracting States will adopt different interpretations of paragraph 2 and it is not possible to conclude that either interpretation is not in accordance with paragraph 2.

54.   Such concerns are addressed by paragraph 3. The following example illustrates the application of that paragraph.

55.   Example. A manufacturing plant located in State R of an enterprise of State R has transferred goods for sale to a permanent establishment of the enterprise situated in State S. For the purpose of determining the profits attributable to the permanent establishment under paragraph 2, a dealing must be recognised and a notional arm's length price must be determined for that dealing. The enterprise's documentation, which is consistent with the functional and factual analysis and which has been used by the taxpayer as the basis for the computation of its taxable income in each State, shows that a dealing in the nature of a sale of the goods by the plant in State R to the permanent establishment in State S has occurred and that a notional price of 90 has been used to determine the profits attributable to the permanent establishment. State S accepts the amount used by the taxpayer but State R considers that the amount is below what is required by its domestic law and the arm's length principle of paragraph 2. It considers that the appropriate arm's length price that should have been used is 110 and adjusts the amount of tax payable in State R accordingly after reducing the amount of the exemption (Article 23 A) or the credit (Article 23 B) claimed by the taxpayer with respect to the profits attributable to the permanent establishment. In that situation, since the price of the same dealing will have been determined as 90 in State S and 110 in State R, profits of 20 may be subject to double taxation. Paragraph 3 will address that situation by requiring State S, to the extent that there is indeed double taxation and that the adjustment made by State R is in conformity with paragraph 2, to provide a corresponding adjustment to the tax payable in State S on the profits that are taxed in both States.

56.   If State S, however, does not agree that the adjustment by State R was warranted by paragraph 2, it will not consider that it has to make the adjustment. In such a case, the issue of whether State S should make the adjustment under paragraph 3 (if the adjustment by State R is justified under paragraph 2) or whether State R should refrain

from making the initial adjustment (if it is not justified under paragraph 2) will be solved under a mutual agreement procedure pursuant to paragraph 1 of Article 25 using, if necessary, the arbitration provision of paragraph 5 of Article 25 (since it involves the question of whether the actions of one or both of the Contracting States have resulted or will result for the taxpayer in taxation not in accordance with the Convention). Through that procedure, the two States will be able to agree on the same arm's length price, which may be one of the prices put forward by the taxpayer and the two States or a different one.

57.   As shown by the example in paragraph 55, paragraph 3 addresses the concern that the Convention might not provide adequate protection against double taxation in some situations where the two Contracting States adopt different interpretations of paragraph 2 of Article 7 and each State could be considered to be taxing "in accordance with" the Convention. Paragraph 3 ensures that relief of double taxation will be provided in such a case, which is consistent with the overall objectives of the Convention.

58.   Paragraph 3 shares the main features of paragraph 2 of Article 9. First, it applies to each State with respect to an adjustment made by the other State. It therefore applies reciprocally whether the initial adjustment has been made by the State where the permanent establishment is situated or by the other State. Also, it does not apply unless there is an adjustment by one of the States.

59.   As is the case for paragraph 2 of Article 9, a corresponding adjustment is not automatically to be made under paragraph 3 simply because the profits attributed to the permanent establishment have been adjusted by one of the Contracting States. The corresponding adjustment is required only if the other State considers that the adjusted profits conform with paragraph 2. In other words, paragraph 3 may not be invoked and should not be applied where the profits attributable to the permanent establishment are adjusted to a level that is different from what they would have been if they had been correctly computed in accordance with the principles of paragraph 2. Regardless of which State makes the initial adjustment, the other State is obliged to make an appropriate corresponding adjustment only if it considers that the adjusted profits correctly reflect what the profits would have been if the permanent establishment's dealings had been transactions at arm's length. The other State is therefore committed to make such a corresponding adjustment only if it considers that the initial adjustment is justified both in principle and as regards the amount.

60.   Paragraph 3 does not specify the method by which a corresponding adjustment is to be made. Where the initial adjustment is made by the State in which the permanent establishment is situated, the adjustment provided for by paragraph 3 could be granted in the other State through the adjustment of the amount of income that must be exempted under Article 23 A or of the credit that must be granted under Article 23 B. Where the initial adjustment is made by that other State, the adjustment provided for by paragraph 3 could be made by the State in which the permanent establishment is situated by re-opening the assessment of the enterprise of the other State in order to reduce the taxable income by an appropriate amount.

61.   The issue of so-called "secondary adjustments", which is discussed in paragraph 8 of the Commentary on Article 9, does not arise in the case of an adjustment under paragraph 3. As indicated in paragraph 28 above, the determination of the profits attributable to a permanent establishment is only relevant for the purposes of Articles 7 and 23 A and 23 B and does not affect the application of other Articles of the Convention.

62.   Like paragraph 2 of Article 9, paragraph 3 leaves open the question whether there should be a period of time after the expiration of which a State would not be obliged to make an appropriate adjustment to the profits attributable to a permanent establishment following an upward revision of these profits in the other State. Some States consider that the commitment should be open-ended — in other words, that however many years the State making the initial adjustment has gone back, the enterprise should in equity be assured of an appropriate adjustment in the other State. Other States consider that an open-ended commitment of this sort is unreasonable as a matter of practical administration. This problem has not been dealt with in the text of either paragraph 2 of Article 9 or paragraph 3 but Contracting States are left free in bilateral conventions to include, if they wish, provisions dealing with the length of time during which a State should be obliged to make an appropriate adjustment (see on this point paragraphs 39, 40 and 41 of the Commentary on Article 25).

63.   There may be cases where the initial adjustment made by one State will not immediately require a corresponding adjustment to the amount of tax charged on profits in the other State (e.g. where the initial adjustment by one State of the profits attributable to the permanent establishment will affect the determination of the amount of a loss attributable to the rest of the enterprise in the other State). The competent authorities may, in accordance with the second sentence of paragraph 3, determine the future impact that the initial adjustment will have on the tax that will be payable in the other State before that tax is actually levied; in fact, in order to avoid the problem described in the preceding paragraph, competent authorities may wish to use the mutual agreement procedure at the earliest opportunity in order to determine to what extent a corresponding adjustment may be required in the other State at a later stage.

64.   If there is a dispute between the parties concerned over the amount and character of the appropriate adjustment, the mutual agreement procedure provided for under Article 25 should be implemented, as is the case for an adjustment under paragraph 2 of Article 9. Indeed, as shown in the example in paragraph 55 above, if one of the two Contracting States adjusts the profits attributable to a permanent establishment without the other State granting a corresponding adjustment to the extent needed to avoid double taxation, the taxpayer will be able to use the mutual agreement procedure of paragraph 1 of Article 25, and if necessary the arbitration provision of paragraph 5 of Article 25, to require the competent authorities to agree that either the initial adjustment by one State or the failure by the other State to make a corresponding adjustment is not in accordance with the provisions of the Convention (the arbitration provision of paragraph 5 of Article 25 will play a critical role in cases

where the competent authorities would otherwise be unable to agree as it will ensure that the issues that prevent an agreement are resolved through arbitration).

65.   Paragraph 3 only applies to the extent necessary to eliminate the double taxation of profits that result from the adjustment. Assume, for instance, that the State where the permanent establishment is situated adjusts the profits that the taxpayer attributed to the permanent establishment to reflect the fact that the price of a dealing between the permanent establishment and the rest of the enterprise did not conform with the arm's length principle. Assume that the other State also agrees that the price used by the taxpayer was not at arm's length. In that case, the combined application of paragraph 2 and of Article 23 A or 23 B will require that other State to attribute to the permanent establishment, for the purposes of providing relief of double taxation, adjusted profits that would reflect an arm's length price. In such a case, paragraph 3 will only be relevant to the extent that States adopt different interpretations of what the correct arm's length price should be.

66.   Paragraph 3 only applies with respect to differences in the determination of the profits attributed to a permanent establishment that result in the same part of the profits being attributed to different parts of the enterprise in conformity with the Article. As already explained (see paragraphs 30 and 31 above), Article 7 does not deal with the computation of taxable income but, instead, with the attribution of profits for the purpose of the allocation of taxing rights between the two Contracting States. The Article therefore only serves to allocate revenues and expenses for the purposes of allocating taxing rights and does not prejudge the issue of which revenues are taxable and which expenses are deductible, which is a matter of domestic law as long as there is conformity with paragraph 2. Where the profits attributed to the permanent establishment are the same in each State, the amount that will be included in the taxable income on which tax will be levied in each State for a given taxable period may be different given differences in domestic law rules, *e.g.* for the recognition of income and the deduction of expenses. Since these different domestic law rules only apply to the profits attributed to each State, they do not, by themselves, result in double taxation for the purposes of paragraph 3.

67.   Also, paragraph 3 does not apply to affect the computation of the exemption or credit under Article 23 A or 23 B except for the purposes of providing what would otherwise be unavailable double taxation relief for the tax paid to the Contracting State in which the permanent establishment is situated on the profits that have been attributed to the permanent establishment in that State. This paragraph will therefore not apply where these profits have been fully exempted by the other State or where the tax paid in the first-mentioned State has been fully credited against the other State's tax under the domestic law of that other State and in accordance with Article 23 A or 23 B.

68.   Some States may prefer that the cases covered by paragraph 3 be resolved through the mutual agreement procedure (a failure to do so triggering the application of the arbitration provision of paragraph 5 of Article 25) if a State does not unilaterally agree to make a corresponding adjustment, without any deference being given to the

adjusting State's preferred position as to the arm's length price or method. These States would therefore prefer a provision that would always give the possibility for a State to negotiate with the adjusting State over the arm's length price or method to be applied. States that share that view may prefer to use the following alternative version of paragraph 3:

> Where, in accordance with paragraph 2, a Contracting State adjusts the profits that are attributable to a permanent establishment of an enterprise of one of the Contracting States and taxes accordingly profits of the enterprise that have been charged to tax in the other State, the other Contracting State shall, to the extent necessary to eliminate double taxation, make an appropriate adjustment if it agrees with the adjustment made by the first-mentioned State; if the other Contracting State does not so agree, the Contracting States shall eliminate any double taxation resulting therefrom by mutual agreement.

69. This alternative version is intended to ensure that the State being asked to give a corresponding adjustment would always be able to require that to be done through the mutual agreement procedure. This version differs significantly from paragraph 3 in that it does not create a legal obligation on that State to agree to give a corresponding adjustment, even where it considers the adjustment made by the other State to have been made in accordance with paragraph 2. The provision would always give the possibility for a State to negotiate with the other State over what is the most appropriate arm's length price or method. Where the State in question does not unilaterally agree to make the corresponding adjustment, this version of paragraph 3 would ensure that the taxpayer has the right to access the mutual agreement procedure to have the case resolved. Moreover, where the mutual agreement procedure is triggered in such a case, the provision imposes a reciprocal legal obligation on the Contracting States to eliminate the double taxation by mutual agreement even though it does not provide a substantive standard to govern which State has the obligation to compromise its position to achieve that mutual agreement. If the two Contracting States do not reach an agreement to eliminate the double taxation, they will both be in violation of their treaty obligation. The obligation to eliminate such cases of double taxation by mutual agreement is therefore stronger than the standard of paragraph 2 of Article 25, which merely requires the competent authorities to "endeavour" to resolve a case by mutual agreement.

70. If Contracting States agree bilaterally to replace paragraph 3 by the alternative above, the comments made in paragraphs 66 and 67 as regards paragraph 3 will also apply with respect to that provision.

Paragraph 4

71. Although it has not been found necessary in the Convention to define the term "profits", it should nevertheless be understood that the term when used in this Article and elsewhere in the Convention has a broad meaning including all income derived in carrying on an enterprise. Such a broad meaning corresponds to the use of the term made in the tax laws of most OECD member countries.

72.   Absent paragraph 4, this interpretation of the term "profits" could have given rise to some uncertainty as to the application of the Convention. If the profits of an enterprise include categories of income which are dealt with separately in other Articles of the Convention, *e.g.* dividends, the question would have arisen as to which Article should apply to these categories of income, *e.g.* in the case of dividends, this Article or Article 10.

73.   To the extent that an application of this Article and the special Article concerned would result in the same tax treatment, there is little practical significance to this question. Further, it should be noted that some of the special Articles contain specific provisions giving priority to a specific Article (see paragraph 4 of Article 6, paragraph 4 of Articles 10 and 11, paragraph 3 of Article 12, and paragraph 2 of Article 21).

74.   The question, however, could arise with respect to other types of income and it has therefore been decided to include a rule of interpretation that ensures that Articles applicable to specific categories of income will have priority over Article 7. It follows from this rule that Article 7 will be applicable to business profits which do not belong to categories of income covered by these other Articles, and, in addition, to income which under paragraph 4 of Articles 10 and 11, paragraph 3 of Article 12 and paragraph 2 of Article 21, fall within Article 7. This rule does not, however, govern the manner in which the income will be classified for the purposes of domestic law; thus, if a Contracting State may tax an item of income pursuant to other Articles of this Convention, that State may, for its own domestic tax purposes, characterise such income as it wishes (*i.e.* as business profits or as a specific category of income) provided that the tax treatment of that item of income is in accordance with the provisions of the Convention. It should also be noted that where an enterprise of a Contracting State derives income from immovable property through a permanent establishment situated in the other State, that other State may not tax that income if it is derived from immovable property situated in the first-mentioned State or in a third State (see paragraph 4 of the Commentary on Article 21 and paragraphs 9 and 10 of the Commentary on Articles 23 A and 23 B).

75.   It is open to Contracting States to agree bilaterally upon special explanations or definitions concerning the term "profits" with a view to clarifying the distinction between this term and *e.g.* the concept of dividends. It may in particular be found appropriate to do so where in a convention under negotiation a deviation has been made from the definitions in the Articles on dividends, interest and royalties.

76.   Finally, it should be noted that two categories of profits that were previously covered by other Articles of the Convention are now covered by Article 7. First, whilst the definition of "royalties" in paragraph 2 of Article 12 of the 1963 Draft Convention and 1977 Model Convention included payments "for the use of, or the right to use, industrial, commercial, or scientific equipment", the reference to these payments was subsequently deleted from that definition in order to ensure that income from the leasing of industrial, commercial or scientific equipment, including the income from the leasing of containers, falls under the provisions of Article 7 or Article 8 (see paragraph 9 of the Commentary on that Article), as the case may be, rather than under

those of Article 12, a result that the Committee on Fiscal Affairs considers appropriate given the nature of such income.

77.   Second, before 2000, income from professional services and other activities of an independent character was dealt with under a separate Article, i.e. Article 14. The provisions of that Article were similar to those applicable to business profits but Article 14 used the concept of fixed base rather than that of permanent establishment since it had originally been thought that the latter concept should be reserved to commercial and industrial activities. However, it was not always clear which activities fell within Article 14 as opposed to Article 7. The elimination of Article 14 in 2000 reflected the fact that there were no intended differences between the concepts of permanent establishment, as used in Article 7, and fixed base, as used in Article 14, or between how profits were computed and tax was calculated according to which of Article 7 or 14 applied. The effect of the deletion of Article 14 is that income derived from professional services or other activities of an independent character is now dealt with under Article 7 as business profits. This was confirmed by the addition, in Article 3, of a definition of the term "business" which expressly provides that this term includes professional services or other activities of an independent character.

Observations on the Commentary

78.   *Italy* and *Portugal* deem as essential to take into consideration that — irrespective of the meaning given to the fourth sentence of paragraph 77 — as far as the method for computing taxes is concerned, national systems are not affected by the new wording of the model, i.e. by the elimination of Article 14.

79.   *Belgium* cannot share the views expressed in paragraph 14 of the Commentary. Belgium considers that the application of controlled foreign companies legislation is contrary to the provisions of paragraph 1 of Article 7. This is especially the case where a Contracting State taxes one of its residents on income derived by a foreign entity by using a fiction attributing to that resident, in proportion to his participation in the capital of the foreign entity, the income derived by that entity. By doing so, that State increases the tax base of its resident by including in it income which has not been derived by that resident but by a foreign entity which is not taxable in that State in accordance with paragraph 1 of Article 7. That Contracting State thus disregards the legal personality of the foreign entity and acts contrary to paragraph 1 of Article 7.

80.   *Luxembourg* does not share the interpretation in paragraph 14 which provides that paragraph 1 of Article 7 does not restrict a Contracting State's right to tax its own residents under controlled foreign companies provisions found in its domestic law as this interpretation challenges the fundamental principle contained in paragraph 1 of Article 7.

81.   With reference to paragraph 14, *Ireland* notes its general observation in paragraph 27.5 of the Commentary on Article 1.

82.   *Sweden* wishes to clarify that it does not consider that the different approaches for attributing "free" capital that are included in the Report *Attribution of Profits to*

Permanent Establishments will necessarily lead to a result in accordance with the arm's length principle. Consequently, Sweden would, when looking at the facts and circumstances of each case, in many cases not consider that the amount of interest deduction resulting from the application of these approaches conforms to the arm's length principle. When the different views on attributing "free" capital will lead to double taxation, the mutual agreement procedure provided for in Article 25 will have to be used.

83. With reference to paragraphs 27 and 65, the *United States* wishes to clarify how it will relieve double taxation arising due to the application of paragraph 2 of Article 7. Where a taxpayer can demonstrate to the competent authority of the United States that such double taxation has been left unrelieved after the application of mechanisms under the United States' domestic law such as the utilisation of foreign tax credit limitation created by other transactions, the United States will relieve such additional double taxation.

84. *Turkey* does not share the views expressed in paragraph 28 of the Commentary on Article 7.

Reservations on the Article

85. *Australia* reserves the right to include a provision that will permit its domestic law to apply in relation to the taxation of profits from any form of insurance.

86. *Australia* reserves the right to include a provision clarifying its right to tax a share of business profits to which a resident of the other Contracting State is beneficially entitled where those profits are derived by a trustee of a trust estate (other than certain unit trusts that are treated as companies for Australian tax purposes) from the carrying on of a business in Australia through a permanent establishment.

87. *Korea* and *Portugal* reserve the right to tax persons performing professional services or other activities of an independent character if they are present on their territory for a period or periods exceeding in the aggregate 183 days in any twelve month period, even if they do not have a permanent establishment (or a fixed base) available to them for the purpose of performing such services or activities.

88. *Italy* and *Portugal* reserve the right to tax persons performing independent personal services under a separate article which corresponds to Article 14 as it stood before its elimination in 2000.

89. The *United States* reserves the right to amend Article 7 to provide that, in applying paragraphs 1 and 2 of the Article, any income or gain attributable to a permanent establishment during its existence may be taxable by the Contracting State in which the permanent establishment exists even if the payments are deferred until after the permanent establishment has ceased to exist. The United States also wishes to note that it reserves the right to apply such a rule, as well, under Articles 11, 12, 13 and 21.

90. *Turkey* reserves the right to subject income from the leasing of containers to a withholding tax at source in all cases. In case of the application of Articles 5 and 7 to

such income, Turkey would like to apply the permanent establishment rule to the simple depot, depot-agency and operational branch cases.

91.   *Norway* and the *United States* reserve the right to treat income from the use, maintenance or rental of containers used in international traffic under Article 8 in the same manner as income from shipping and air transport.

92.   *Australia* and *Portugal* reserve the right to propose in bilateral negotiations a provision to the effect that, if the information available to the competent authority of a Contracting State is inadequate to determine the profits to be attributed to the permanent establishment of an enterprise, the competent authority may apply to that enterprise for that purpose the provisions of the taxation law of that State, subject to the qualification that such law will be applied, so far as the information available to the competent authority permits, in accordance with the principles of this Article.

93.   *Mexico* reserves the right to tax in the State where the permanent establishment is situated business profits derived from the sale of goods or merchandise carried out directly by its home office situated in the other Contracting State, provided that those goods and merchandise are of the same or similar kind as the ones sold through that permanent establishment. The Government of Mexico will apply this rule only as a safeguard against abuse and not as a general "force of attraction" principle; thus, the rule will not apply when the enterprise proves that the sales have been carried out for reasons other than obtaining a benefit under the Convention.

94.   The *Czech Republic* reserves the right to add to paragraph 3 a provision limiting the potential corresponding adjustments to *bona fide* cases.

95.   *New Zealand* reserves the right to use the previous version of Article 7 taking into account its observation and reservations on that version (*i.e.* the version included in the Model Tax Convention immediately before the 2010 update of the Model Tax Convention) because it does not agree with the approach reflected in Part I of the 2010 Report *Attribution of Profits to Permanent Establishments*. It does not, therefore, endorse the changes to the Commentary on the Article made through that update.

96.   *Chile*, *Greece*, *Mexico* and *Turkey* reserve the right to use the previous version of Article 7, i.e. the version that was included in the Model Tax Convention immediately before the 2010 update of the Model Tax Convention. They do not, therefore, endorse the changes to the Commentary on the Article made through that update.

97.   *Portugal* reserves its right to continue to adopt in its conventions the text of the Article as it read before 2010 until its domestic law is adapted in order to apply the new approach.

98.   *Slovenia* reserves the right to specify that a potential adjustment will be made under paragraph 3 only if it is considered justified.

ANNEX

PREVIOUS VERSION OF ARTICLE 7 AND ITS COMMENTARY

The following is the text of Article 7 and its Commentary as they read before 22 July 2010. That previous version of the Article and Commentary is provided below for historical reference as it will continue to be relevant for the application and interpretation of bilateral tax conventions concluded before that date.

Article 7
BUSINESS PROFITS

1.   The profits of an enterprise of a Contracting State shall be taxable only in that State unless the enterprise carries on business in the other Contracting State through a permanent establishment situated therein. If the enterprise carries on business as aforesaid, the profits of the enterprise may be taxed in the other State but only so much of them as is attributable to that permanent establishment.

2.   Subject to the provisions of paragraph 3, where an enterprise of a Contracting State carries on business in the other Contracting State through a permanent establishment situated therein, there shall in each Contracting State be attributed to that permanent establishment the profits which it might be expected to make if it were a distinct and separate enterprise engaged in the same or similar activities under the same or similar conditions and dealing wholly independently with the enterprise of which it is a permanent establishment.

3.   In determining the profits of a permanent establishment, there shall be allowed as deductions expenses which are incurred for the purposes of the permanent establishment, including executive and general administrative expenses so incurred, whether in the State in which the permanent establishment is situated or elsewhere.

4.   Insofar as it has been customary in a Contracting State to determine the profits to be attributed to a permanent establishment on the basis of an apportionment of the total profits of the enterprise to its various parts, nothing in paragraph 2 shall preclude that Contracting State from determining the profits to be taxed by such an apportionment as may be customary; the method of apportionment adopted shall, however, be such that the result shall be in accordance with the principles contained in this Article.

5.   No profits shall be attributed to a permanent establishment by reason of the mere purchase by that permanent establishment of goods or merchandise for the enterprise.

6.   For the purposes of the preceding paragraphs, the profits to be attributed to the permanent establishment shall be determined by the same method year by year unless there is good and sufficient reason to the contrary.

7.   Where profits include items of income which are dealt with separately in other Articles of this Convention, then the provisions of those Articles shall not be affected by the provisions of this Article.

COMMENTARY ON ARTICLE 7
CONCERNING THE TAXATION OF BUSINESS PROFITS

I. Preliminary remarks

1.   This Article is in many respects a continuation of, and a corollary to, Article 5 on the definition of the concept of permanent establishment. The permanent establishment criterion is commonly used in international double taxation conventions to determine whether a particular kind of income shall or shall not be taxed in the country from which it originates but the criterion does not of itself provide a complete solution to the problem of the double taxation of business profits; in order to prevent such double taxation it is necessary to supplement the definition of permanent establishment by adding to it an agreed set of rules by reference to which the profits attributable to the permanent establishment are to be calculated. To put the matter in a slightly different way, when an enterprise of a Contracting State carries on business in the other Contracting State the authorities of that second State have to ask themselves two questions before they levy tax on the profits of the enterprise: the first question is whether the enterprise has a permanent establishment in their country; if the answer is in the affirmative the second question is what, if any, are the profits on which that permanent establishment should pay tax. It is with the rules to be used in determining the answer to this second question that Article 7 is concerned. Rules for ascertaining the profits of an enterprise of a Contracting State which is trading with an enterprise of the other Contracting State when both enterprises are associated are dealt with in Article 9.

2.   Articles 7 and 9 are not particularly detailed and were not strikingly novel when they were adopted by the OECD. The question of what criteria should be used in attributing profits to a permanent establishment, and of how to allocate profits from transactions between associated enterprises, has had to be dealt with in a large number of double taxation conventions and in various models developed by the League of Nations before the OECD first dealt with it and the solutions adopted have generally conformed to a standard pattern.

3.   It is generally recognised that the essential principles on which this standard pattern is based are well founded, and, when the OECD first examined that question, it was thought sufficient to restate them with some slight amendments and modifications primarily aimed at producing greater clarity. The two Articles incorporate a number of directives. They do not, nor in the nature of things could they be expected to, lay down a series of precise rules for dealing with every kind of problem that may arise when an enterprise of one State makes profits in another. Modern commerce organises itself in an infinite variety of ways, and it would be quite impossible within the fairly narrow limits of an Article in a double taxation convention to specify an exhaustive set of rules for dealing with every kind of problem that may arise.

4.   It must be acknowledged, however, that there has been considerable variation in the interpretation of the general directives of Article 7 and of the provisions of earlier conventions and models on which the wording of the Article is based. This lack of a common interpretation of Article 7 can lead to problems of double taxation and non-taxation. For that reason, it is important for tax authorities to agree on mutually consistent methods of dealing with these problems, using, where appropriate, the mutual agreement procedure provided for in Article 25.

5.   Over the years, the Committee on Fiscal Affairs has therefore spent considerable time and effort trying to ensure a more consistent interpretation and application of the rules of the Article. Minor changes to the wording of the Article and a number of changes to the Commentary were made when the 1977 Model Tax Convention was adopted. A report that addressed that question in the specific case of banks was published in 1984.[1] In 1987, noting that the determination of profits attributable to a permanent establishment could give rise to some uncertainty, the Committee undertook a review of the question which led to the adoption, in 1993, of the report entitled "Attribution of Income to Permanent Establishments"[2] and to subsequent changes to the Commentary.

6.   Despite that work, the practices of OECD and non-OECD countries regarding the attribution of profits to permanent establishments and these countries' interpretation of Article 7 continued to vary considerably. The Committee acknowledged the need to provide more certainty to taxpayers: in its report *Transfer Pricing Guidelines for Multinational Enterprises and Tax Administrations*, adopted in 1995, it indicated that further work would address the application of the arm's length principle to permanent establishments. That work resulted, in 2008, in a report entitled *Attribution of Profits to Permanent Establishments*. The approach developed in that report was not constrained by either the original intent or by the historical practice and interpretation of Article 7. Instead, the focus has been on formulating the most preferable approach to attributing profits to a permanent establishment under Article 7 given modern-day multinational operations and trade.

7.   The approach put forward in that Report deals with the attribution of profits both to permanent establishments in general (Part I of the Report) and, in particular, to permanent establishments of businesses operating in the financial sector, where trading through a permanent establishment is widespread (Part II of the Report, which deals with permanent establishments of banks, Part III, which deals with permanent establishments of enterprises carrying on global trading and Part IV, which deals with permanent establishments of enterprises carrying on insurance activities). The Committee considers that the guidance included in the Report represents a better approach to attributing profits to permanent establishments than has previously been available. It does recognise, however, that there are differences between some of the conclusions of the Report and the interpretation of the Article previously given in this Commentary. For that reason, this Commentary has been amended to incorporate a number of conclusions of the Report that did not conflict with the previous version of this Commentary, which prescribed specific approaches in some areas and left considerable leeway in others. The Report therefore represents internationally agreed principles and, to the extent that it does not conflict with this Commentary, provides guidelines for the application of the arm's length principle incorporated in the Article.

8.   Before 2000, income from professional services and other activities of an independent character was dealt with under a separate Article, i.e. Article 14. The provisions of that Article were similar to those applicable to business profits but it used the concept of fixed base rather than that of permanent establishment since it had originally been thought that the latter concept should be reserved to commercial and

---

1   "The Taxation of Multinational Banking Enterprises", in *Transfer Pricing and Multinational Enterprises Three Taxation Issues*, OECD, Paris, 1984.
2   Reproduced in Volume II of the loose-leaf version of the OECD Model Tax Convention at page R(13)-1.

industrial activities. However, it was not always clear which activities fell within Article 14 as opposed to Article 7. The elimination of Article 14 in 2000 reflected the fact that there were no intended differences between the concepts of permanent establishment, as used in Article 7, and fixed base, as used in Article 14, or between how profits were computed and tax was calculated according to which of Article 7 or 14 applied. The effect of the deletion of Article 14 is that income derived from professional services or other activities of an independent character is now dealt with under Article 7 as business profits. This was confirmed by the addition of a definition of the term "business" which expressly provides that this term includes professional services or other activities of an independent character.

II.   Commentary on the provisions of the Article

Paragraph 1

9.   This paragraph is concerned with two questions. First, it restates the generally accepted principle of double taxation conventions that an enterprise of one State shall not be taxed in the other State unless it carries on business in that other State through a permanent establishment situated therein. It is hardly necessary to argue here the merits of this principle. It is perhaps sufficient to say that it has come to be accepted in international fiscal matters that until an enterprise of one State sets up a permanent establishment in another State it should not properly be regarded as participating in the economic life of that other State to such an extent that it comes within the jurisdiction of that other State's taxing rights.

10.   The second principle, which is reflected in the second sentence of the paragraph, is that the right to tax of the State where the permanent establishment is situated does not extend to profits that the enterprise may derive from that State but that are not attributable to the permanent establishment. This is a question on which there have historically been differences of view, a few countries having some time ago pursued a principle of general "force of attraction" according to which income such as other business profits, dividends, interest and royalties arising from sources in their territory was fully taxable by them if the beneficiary had a permanent establishment therein even though such income was clearly not attributable to that permanent establishment. Whilst some bilateral tax conventions include a limited anti-avoidance rule based on a restricted force of attraction approach that only applies to business profits derived from activities similar to those carried on by a permanent establishment, the general force of attraction approach described above has now been rejected in international tax treaty practice. The principle that is now generally accepted in double taxation conventions is based on the view that in taxing the profits that a foreign enterprise derives from a particular country, the tax authorities of that country should look at the separate sources of profit that the enterprise derives from their country and should apply to each the permanent establishment test, subject to the possible application of other Articles of the Convention. This solution allows simpler and more efficient tax administration and compliance, and is more closely adapted to the way in which business is commonly carried on. The organisation of modern business is highly complex. There are a considerable number of companies each of which is engaged in a wide diversity of activities and is carrying on business extensively in many countries. A company may set up a permanent establishment in another country through which it carries on manufacturing activities whilst a different part of the same company sells different goods or manufactures in that other country through independent agents. That company may have perfectly valid commercial

reasons for doing so: these may be based, for example, on the historical pattern of its business or on commercial convenience. If the country in which the permanent establishment is situated wished to go so far as to try to determine, and tax, the profit element of each of the transactions carried on through independent agents, with a view to aggregating that profit with the profits of the permanent establishment, that approach would interfere seriously with ordinary commercial activities and would be contrary to the aims of the Convention.

11.   When referring to the part of the profits of an enterprise that is attributable to a permanent establishment, the second sentence of paragraph 1 refers directly to paragraph 2, which provides the directive for determining what profits should be attributed to a permanent establishment. As paragraph 2 is part of the context in which the sentence must be read, that sentence should not be interpreted in a way that could contradict paragraph 2, *e.g.* by interpreting it as restricting the amount of profits that can be attributed to a permanent establishment to the amount of profits of the enterprise as a whole. Thus, whilst paragraph 1 provides that a Contracting State may only tax the profits of an enterprise of the other Contracting State to the extent that they are attributable to a permanent establishment situated in the first State, it is paragraph 2 that determines the meaning of the phrase "profits attributable to a permanent establishment". In other words, the directive of paragraph 2 may result in profits being attributed to a permanent establishment even though the enterprise as a whole has never made profits; conversely, that directive may result in no profits being attributed to a permanent establishment even though the enterprise as a whole has made profits.

12.   Clearly, however, the Contracting State of the enterprise has an interest in the directive of paragraph 2 being correctly applied by the State where the permanent establishment is located. Since that directive applies to both Contracting States, the State of the enterprise must, in accordance with Article 23, eliminate double taxation on the profits properly attributable to the permanent establishment. In other words, if the State where the permanent establishment is located attempts to tax profits that are not attributable to the permanent establishment under Article 7, this may result in double taxation of profits that should properly be taxed only in the State of the enterprise.

13.   The purpose of paragraph 1 is to provide limits to the right of one Contracting State to tax the business profits of enterprises of the other Contracting State. The paragraph does not limit the right of a Contracting State to tax its own residents under controlled foreign companies provisions found in its domestic law even though such tax imposed on these residents may be computed by reference to the part of the profits of an enterprise that is resident of the other Contracting State that is attributable to these residents' participation in that enterprise. Tax so levied by a State on its own residents does not reduce the profits of the enterprise of the other State and may not, therefore, be said to have been levied on such profits (see also paragraph 23 of the Commentary on Article 1 and paragraphs 37 to 39 of the Commentary on Article 10).

Paragraph 2

14.   This paragraph contains the central directive on which the attribution of profits to a permanent establishment is intended to be based. The paragraph incorporates the view that the profits to be attributed to a permanent establishment are those which that permanent establishment would have made if, instead of dealing with the rest of the enterprise, it had been dealing with an entirely separate enterprise under

conditions and at prices prevailing in the ordinary market. This corresponds to the "arm's length principle" discussed in the Commentary on Article 9. Normally, the profits so determined would be the same profits that one would expect to be determined by the ordinary processes of good business accountancy.

15.   The paragraph requires that this principle be applied in each Contracting State. Clearly, this does not mean that the amount on which the enterprise will be taxed in the source State will, for a given period of time, be exactly the same as the amount of income with respect to which the other State will have to provide relief pursuant to Articles 23 A or 23 B. Variations between the domestic laws of the two States concerning matters such as depreciation rates, the timing of the recognition of income and restrictions on the deductibility of certain expenses that are in accordance with paragraph 3 of this Article will normally result in a different amount of taxable income in each State.

16.   In the great majority of cases, trading accounts of the permanent establishment — which are commonly available if only because a well-run business organisation is normally concerned to know what is the profitability of its various branches — will be used to ascertain the profit properly attributable to that establishment. Exceptionally there may be no separate accounts (cf. paragraphs 51 to 55 below). But where there are such accounts they will naturally form the starting point for any processes of adjustment in case adjustment is required to produce the amount of profits that are properly attributable to the permanent establishment under the directive contained in paragraph 2. It should perhaps be emphasised that this directive is no justification to construct hypothetical profit figures in vacuo; it is always necessary to start with the real facts of the situation as they appear from the business records of the permanent establishment and to adjust as may be shown to be necessary the profit figures which those facts produce. As noted in paragraph 19 below and as explained in paragraph 39 of Part I of the Report *Attribution of Profits to Permanent Establishments*, however, records and documentation must satisfy certain requirements in order to be considered to reflect the real facts of the situation.

17.   In order to determine whether such an adjustment is required by paragraph 2, it will be necessary to determine the profits that would have been realised if the permanent establishment had been a separate and distinct enterprise engaged in the same or similar activities under the same or similar conditions and dealing wholly independently with the rest of the enterprise. Sections D-2 and D-3 of Part I of the Report *Attribution of Profits to Permanent Establishments* describe the two-step approach through which this should be done. This approach will allow the calculation of the profits attributable to all the activities carried on through the permanent establishment, including transactions with other independent enterprises, transactions with associated enterprises and dealings (*e.g.* the internal transfer of capital or property or the internal provision of services — see for instance paragraphs 31 and 32) with other parts of the enterprise (under the second step referred to above), in accordance with the directive of paragraph 2.

18.   The first step of that approach requires the identification of the activities carried on through the permanent establishment. This should be done through a functional and factual analysis (the guidance found in the *Transfer Pricing Guidelines for Multinational Enterprises and Tax Administrations*[1] will be relevant for that purpose). Under that first step, the economically significant activities and responsibilities undertaken through the permanent establishment will be identified. This analysis

should, to the extent relevant, consider the activities and responsibilities undertaken through the permanent establishment in the context of the activities and responsibilities undertaken by the enterprise as a whole, particularly those parts of the enterprise that engage in dealings with the permanent establishment. Under the second step of that approach, the remuneration of any such dealings will be determined by applying by analogy the principles developed for the application of the arm's length principle between associated enterprises (these principles are articulated in the *Transfer Pricing Guidelines for Multinational Enterprises and Tax Administrations*) by reference to the functions performed, assets used and risk assumed by the enterprise through the permanent establishment and through the rest of the enterprise.

19.   A question that may arise is to what extent accounting records should be relied upon when they are based on agreements between the head office and its permanent establishments (or between the permanent establishments themselves). Clearly, such internal agreements cannot qualify as legally binding contracts. However, to the extent that the trading accounts of the head office and the permanent establishments are both prepared symmetrically on the basis of such agreements and that those agreements reflect the functions performed by the different parts of the enterprise, these trading accounts could be accepted by tax authorities. Accounts should not be regarded as prepared symmetrically, however, unless the values of transactions or the methods of attributing profits or expenses in the books of the permanent establishment corresponded exactly to the values or methods of attribution in the books of the head office in terms of the national currency or functional currency in which the enterprise recorded its transactions. Also, as explained in paragraph 16, records and documentation must satisfy certain requirements in order to be considered to reflect the real facts of the situation. For example, where trading accounts are based on internal agreements that reflect purely artificial arrangements instead of the real economic functions of the different parts of the enterprise, these agreements should simply be ignored and the accounts corrected accordingly. One such case would be where a permanent establishment involved in sales were, under such an internal agreement, given the role of principal (accepting all the risks and entitled to all the profits from the sales) when in fact the permanent establishment concerned was nothing more than an intermediary or agent (incurring limited risks and entitled to receive only a limited share of the resulting income) or, conversely, were given the role of intermediary or agent when in reality it was a principal.

20.   It may therefore be concluded that accounting records and contemporaneous documentation that meet the above-mentioned requirements constitute a useful starting point for the purposes of attributing profits to a permanent establishment. Taxpayers are encouraged to prepare such documentation, as it may reduce substantially the potential for controversies. Section D-2 (*vi*)*b*) of Part I of the Report *Attribution of Profits to Permanent Establishments* discusses the conditions under which tax administrations would give effect to such documentation.

21.   There may be a realisation of a taxable profit when an asset, whether or not trading stock, forming part of the business property of a permanent establishment situated within a State's territory is transferred to a permanent establishment or the head office of the same enterprise situated in another State. Article 7 allows the former

---

1   The original version of that report was approved by the Council of the OECD on 27 June 1995. Published in a full format as *Transfer Pricing Guidelines for Multinational Enterprises and Tax Administrations*, OECD, Paris, 1995.

State to tax profits deemed to arise in connection with such a transfer. Such profits may be determined as indicated below. In cases where such transfer takes place, whether or not it is a permanent one, the question arises as to when taxable profits are realised. In practice, where such property has a substantial market value and is likely to appear on the balance sheet of the importing permanent establishment or other part of the enterprise after the taxation year during that in which the transfer occurred, the realisation of the taxable profits will not, so far as the enterprise as a whole is concerned, necessarily take place in the taxation year of the transfer under consideration. However, the mere fact that the property leaves the purview of a tax jurisdiction may trigger the taxation of the accrued gains attributable to that property as the concept of realisation depends on each country's domestic law.

22.   Where the countries in which the permanent establishments operate levy tax on the profits accruing from an internal transfer as soon as it is made, even when these profits are not actually realised until a subsequent commercial year, there will be inevitably a time lag between the moment when tax is paid abroad and the moment it can be taken into account in the country where the enterprise's head office is located. A serious problem is inherent in the time lag, especially when a permanent establishment transfers fixed assets or — in the event that it is wound up — its entire operating equipment stock, to some other part of the enterprise of which it forms part. In such cases, it is up to the head office country to seek, on a case by case basis, a bilateral solution with the outward country where there is serious risk of overtaxation.

23.   Paragraph 3 of Article 5 sets forth a special rule for a fixed place of business that is a building site or a construction or installation project. Such a fixed place of business is a permanent establishment only if it lasts more than twelve months. Experience has shown that these types of permanent establishments can give rise to special problems in attributing income to them under Article 7.

24.   These problems arise chiefly where goods are provided, or services performed, by the other parts of the enterprise or a related party in connection with the building site or construction or installation project. Whilst these problems can arise with any permanent establishment, they are particularly acute for building sites and construction or installation projects. In these circumstances, it is necessary to pay close attention to the general principle that income is attributable to a permanent establishment only when it results from activities carried on by the enterprise through that permanent establishment.

25.   For example, where such goods are supplied by the other parts of the enterprise, the profits arising from that supply do not result from the activities carried on through the permanent establishment and are not attributable to it. Similarly, profits resulting from the provision of services (such as planning, designing, drawing blueprints, or rendering technical advice) by the parts of the enterprise operating outside the State where the permanent establishment is located do not result from the activities carried on through the permanent establishment and are not attributable to it.

26.   Where, under paragraph 5 of Article 5, a permanent establishment of an enterprise of a Contracting State is deemed to exist in the other Contracting State by reason of the activities of a so-called dependent agent (see paragraph 32 of the Commentary on Article 5), the same principles used to attribute profits to other types of permanent establishment will apply to attribute profits to that deemed permanent establishment. As a first step, the activities that the dependent agent undertakes for the enterprise will be identified through a functional and factual analysis that will

determine the functions undertaken by the dependent agent both on its own account and on behalf of the enterprise. The dependent agent and the enterprise on behalf of which it is acting constitute two separate potential taxpayers. On the one hand, the dependent agent will derive its own income or profits from the activities that it performs on its own account for the enterprise; if the agent is itself a resident of either Contracting State, the provisions of the Convention (including Article 9 if that agent is an enterprise associated to the enterprise on behalf of which it is acting) will be relevant to the taxation of such income or profits. On the other hand, the deemed permanent establishment of the enterprise will be attributed the assets and risks of the enterprise relating to the functions performed by the dependent agent on behalf of that enterprise (i.e. the activities that the dependent agent undertakes for that enterprise), together with sufficient capital to support those assets and risks. Profits will then be attributed to the deemed permanent establishment on the basis of those assets, risks and capital; these profits will be separate from, and will not include, the income or profits that are properly attributable to the dependent agent itself (see section D-5 of Part I of the Report *Attribution of Profits to Permanent Establishments*).

Paragraph 3

27.   This paragraph clarifies, in relation to the expenses of a permanent establishment, the general directive laid down in paragraph 2. The paragraph specifically recognises that in calculating the profits of a permanent establishment allowance is to be made for expenses, wherever incurred, that were incurred for the purposes of the permanent establishment. Clearly in some cases it will be necessary to estimate or to calculate by conventional means the amount of expenses to be taken into account. In the case, for example, of general administrative expenses incurred at the head office of the enterprise, it may be appropriate to take into account a proportionate part based on the ratio that the permanent establishment's turnover (or perhaps gross profits) bears to that of the enterprise as a whole. Subject to this, it is considered that the amount of expenses to be taken into account as incurred for the purposes of the permanent establishment should be the actual amount so incurred. The deduction allowable to the permanent establishment for any of the expenses of the enterprise attributed to it does not depend upon the actual reimbursement of such expenses by the permanent establishment.

28.   It has sometimes been suggested that the need to reconcile paragraphs 2 and 3 created practical difficulties as paragraph 2 required that prices between the permanent establishment and the head office be normally charged on an arm's length basis, giving to the transferring entity the type of profit which it might have been expected to make were it dealing with an independent enterprise, whilst the wording of paragraph 3 suggested that the deduction for expenses incurred for the purposes of permanent establishments should be the actual cost of those expenses, normally without adding any profit element.

29.   In fact, whilst the application of paragraph 3 may raise some practical difficulties, especially in relation to the separate enterprise and arm's length principles underlying paragraph 2, there is no difference of principle between the two paragraphs. Paragraph 3 indicates that in determining the profits of a permanent establishment, certain expenses must be allowed as deductions whilst paragraph 2 provides that the profits determined in accordance with the rule contained in paragraph 3 relating to the deduction of expenses must be those that a separate and distinct enterprise engaged in the same or similar activities under the same or similar conditions would have made.

Thus, whilst paragraph 3 provides a rule applicable for the determination of the profits of the permanent establishment, paragraph 2 requires that the profits so determined correspond to the profits that a separate and independent enterprise would have made.

30.   Also, paragraph 3 only determines which expenses should be attributed to the permanent establishment for purposes of determining the profits attributable to that permanent establishment. It does not deal with the issue of whether those expenses, once attributed, are deductible when computing the taxable income of the permanent establishment since the conditions for the deductibility of expenses are a matter to be determined by domestic law, subject to the rules of Article 24 on Non-discrimination (in particular, paragraphs 3 and 4 of that Article).

31.   In applying these principles to the practical determination of the profits of a permanent establishment, the question may arise as to whether a particular cost incurred by an enterprise can truly be considered as an expense incurred for the purposes of the permanent establishment, keeping in mind the separate and independent enterprise principles of paragraph 2. Whilst in general independent enterprises in their dealings with each other will seek to realise a profit and, when transferring property or providing services to each other, will charge such prices as the open market would bear, nevertheless, there are also circumstances where it cannot be considered that a particular property or service would have been obtainable from an independent enterprise or when independent enterprises may agree to share between them the costs of some activity which is pursued in common for their mutual benefit. In these particular circumstances, it may be appropriate to treat any relevant costs incurred by the enterprise as an expense incurred for the permanent establishment. The difficulty arises in making a distinction between these circumstances and the cases where a cost incurred by an enterprise should not be considered as an expense of the permanent establishment and the relevant property or service should be considered, on the basis of the separate and independent enterprises principle, to have been transferred between the head office and the permanent establishment at a price including an element of profit. The question must be whether the internal transfer of property and services, be it temporary or final, is of the same kind as those which the enterprise, in the normal course of its business, would have charged to a third party at an arm's length price, i.e. by normally including in the sale price an appropriate profit.

32.   On the one hand, the answer to that question will be in the affirmative if the expense is initially incurred in performing a function the direct purpose of which is to make sales of a specific good or service and to realise a profit through a permanent establishment. On the other hand, the answer will be in the negative if, on the basis of the facts and circumstances of the specific case, it appears that the expense is initially incurred in performing a function the essential purpose of which is to rationalise the overall costs of the enterprise or to increase in a general way its sales.[1]

33.   Where goods are supplied for resale whether in a finished state or as raw materials or semi-finished goods, it will normally be appropriate for the provisions of paragraph 2 to apply and for the supplying part of the enterprise to be allocated a profit, measured by reference to arm's length principles. But there may be exceptions even here. One example might be where goods are not supplied for resale but for

---

1   Internal transfers of financial assets, which are primarily relevant for banks and other financial institutions, raise specific issues which have been dealt with in Parts II and III of the Report *Attribution of Profits to Permanent Establishments*.

temporary use in the trade so that it may be appropriate for the parts of the enterprise which share the use of the material to bear only their share of the cost of such material e.g. in the case of machinery, the depreciation costs that relate to its use by each of these parts. It should of course be remembered that the mere purchase of goods does not constitute a permanent establishment (subparagraph 4 d) of Article 5) so that no question of attribution of profit arises in such circumstances.

34.   In the case of intangible rights, the rules concerning the relations between enterprises of the same group (e.g. payment of royalties or cost sharing arrangements) cannot be applied in respect of the relations between parts of the same enterprise. Indeed, it may be extremely difficult to allocate "ownership" of the intangible right solely to one part of the enterprise and to argue that this part of the enterprise should receive royalties from the other parts as if it were an independent enterprise. Since there is only one legal entity it is not possible to allocate legal ownership to any particular part of the enterprise and in practical terms it will often be difficult to allocate the costs of creation exclusively to one part of the enterprise. It may therefore be preferable for the costs of creation of intangible rights to be regarded as attributable to all parts of the enterprise which will make use of them and as incurred on behalf of the various parts of the enterprise to which they are relevant accordingly. In such circumstances it would be appropriate to allocate between the various parts of the enterprise the actual costs of the creation or acquisition of such intangible rights, as well as the costs subsequently incurred with respect to these intangible rights, without any mark-up for profit or royalty. In so doing, tax authorities must be aware of the fact that the possible adverse consequences deriving from any research and development activity (e.g. the responsibility related to the products and damages to the environment) shall also be allocated to the various parts of the enterprise, therefore giving rise, where appropriate, to a compensatory charge.

35.   The area of services is the one in which difficulties may arise in determining whether in a particular case a service should be charged between the various parts of a single enterprise at its actual cost or at that cost plus a mark-up to represent a profit to the part of the enterprise providing the service. The trade of the enterprise, or part of it, may consist of the provision of such services and there may be a standard charge for their provision. In such a case it will usually be appropriate to charge a service at the same rate as is charged to the outside customer.

36.   Where the main activity of a permanent establishment is to provide specific services to the enterprise to which it belongs and where these services provide a real advantage to the enterprise and their costs represent a significant part of the expenses of the enterprise, the host country may require that a profit margin be included in the amount of the costs. As far as possible, the host country should then try to avoid schematic solutions and rely on the value of these services in the given circumstances of each case.

37.   However, more commonly the provision of services is merely part of the general management activity of the company taken as a whole as where, for example, the enterprise conducts a common system of training and employees of each part of the enterprise benefit from it. In such a case it would usually be appropriate to treat the cost of providing the service as being part of the general administrative expenses of the enterprise as a whole which should be allocated on an actual cost basis to the various parts of the enterprise to the extent that the costs are incurred for the purposes of that

part of the enterprise, without any mark-up to represent profit to another part of the enterprise.

38.   The treatment of services performed in the course of the general management of an enterprise raises the question whether any part of the total profits of an enterprise should be deemed to arise from the exercise of good management. Consider the case of a company that has its head office in one country but carries on all its business through a permanent establishment situated in another country. In the extreme case it might well be that only the directors' meetings were held at the head office and that all other activities of the company apart from purely formal legal activities, were carried on in the permanent establishment. In such a case there is something to be said for the view that at least part of the profits of the whole enterprise arose from the skillful management and business acumen of the directors and that part of the profits of the enterprise ought, therefore, to be attributed to the country in which the head office was situated. If the company had been managed by a managing agency, then that agency would doubtless have charged a fee for its services and the fee might well have been a simple percentage participation in the profits of the enterprise. But whatever the theoretical merits of such a course, practical considerations weigh heavily against it. In the kind of case quoted the expenses of management would, of course, be set against the profits of the permanent establishment in accordance with the provisions of paragraph 3, but when the matter is looked at as a whole, it is thought that it would not be right to go further by deducting and taking into account some notional figure for "profits of management". In cases identical to the extreme case mentioned above, no account should therefore be taken in determining taxable profits of the permanent establishment of any notional figure such as profits of management.

39.   It may be, of course, that countries where it has been customary to allocate some proportion of the total profits of an enterprise to the head office of the enterprise to represent the profits of good management will wish to continue to make such an allocation. Nothing in the Article is designed to prevent this. Nevertheless it follows from what is said in paragraph 38 above that a country in which a permanent establishment is situated is in no way required to deduct when calculating the profits attributable to that permanent establishment an amount intended to represent a proportionate part of the profits of management attributable to the head office.

40.   It might well be that if the country in which the head office of an enterprise is situated allocates to the head office some percentage of the profits of the enterprise only in respect of good management, while the country in which the permanent establishment is situated does not, the resulting total of the amounts charged to tax in the two countries would be greater than it should be. In any such case the country in which the head office of the enterprise is situated should take the initiative in arranging for such adjustments to be made in computing the taxation liability in that country as may be necessary to ensure that any double taxation is eliminated.

41.   The treatment of interest charges raises particular issues. First, there might be amounts which, under the name of interest, are charged by a head office to its permanent establishment with respect to internal "loans" by the former to the latter. Except for financial enterprises such as banks, it is generally agreed that such internal "interest" need not be recognised. This is because:

— From the legal standpoint, the transfer of capital against payment of interest and an undertaking to repay in full at the due date is really a formal act incompatible with the true legal nature of a permanent establishment.

— From the economic standpoint, internal debts and receivables may prove to be non existent, since if an enterprise is solely or predominantly equity funded it ought not to be allowed to deduct interest charges that it has manifestly not had to pay. Whilst, admittedly, symmetrical charges and returns will not distort the enterprise's overall profits, partial results may well be arbitrarily changed.

42.   For these reasons, the ban on deductions for internal debts and receivables should continue to apply generally, subject to the special situation of banks, as mentioned below.

43.   A different issue, however, is that of the deduction of interest on debts actually incurred by the enterprise. Such debts may relate in whole or in part to the activities of the permanent establishment; indeed, loans contracted by an enterprise will serve either the head office, the permanent establishment or both. The question that arises in relation to these debts is how to determine the part of the interest that should be deducted in computing the profits attributable to the permanent establishment.

44.   The approach suggested in this Commentary before 1994, namely the direct and indirect apportionment of actual debt charges, did not prove to be a practical solution, notably since it was unlikely to be applied in a uniform manner. Also, it is well known that the indirect apportionment of total interest payment charges, or of the part of interest that remains after certain direct allocations, comes up against practical difficulties. It is also well known that direct apportionment of total interest expense may not accurately reflect the cost of financing the permanent establishment because the taxpayer may be able to control where loans are booked and adjustments may need to be made to reflect economic reality, in particular the fact that an independent enterprise would normally be expected to have a certain level of "free" capital.

45.   Consequently, the majority of member countries consider that it would be preferable to look for a practicable solution that would take into account a capital structure appropriate to both the organization and the functions performed. This appropriate capital structure will take account of the fact that in order to carry out its activities, the permanent establishment requires a certain amount of funding made up of "free" capital and interest bearing debt. The objective is therefore to attribute an arm's length amount of interest to the permanent establishment after attributing an appropriate amount of "free" capital in order to support the functions, assets and risks of the permanent establishment. Under the arm's length principle a permanent establishment should have sufficient capital to support the functions it undertakes, the assets it economically owns and the risks it assumes. In the financial sector regulations stipulate minimum levels of regulatory capital to provide a cushion in the event that some of the risks inherent in the business crystallise into financial loss. Capital provides a similar cushion against crystallisation of risk in non-financial sectors.

46.   As explained in section D-2 (v)b) of Part I of the Report *Attribution of Profits to Permanent Establishments*, there are different acceptable approaches for attributing "free" capital that are capable of giving an arm's length result. Each approach has its own strengths and weaknesses, which become more or less material depending on the facts and circumstances of particular cases. Different methods adopt different starting points for determining the amount of "free" capital attributable to a permanent establishment, which either put more emphasis on the actual structure of the enterprise of which the permanent establishment is a part or alternatively, on the capital structures of comparable independent enterprises. The key to attributing "free" capital is to recognise:

- the existence of strengths and weaknesses in any approach and when these are likely to be present;
- that there is no single arm's length amount of "free" capital, but a range of potential capital attributions within which it is possible to find an amount of "free" capital that can meet the basic principle set out above.

47.   It is recognised, however, that the existence of different acceptable approaches for attributing "free" capital to a permanent establishment which are capable of giving an arm's length result can give rise to problems of double taxation. The main concern, which is especially acute for financial institutions, is that if the domestic law rules of the State where the permanent establishment is located and of the State of the enterprise require different acceptable approaches for attributing an arm's length amount of free capital to the permanent establishment, the amount of profits calculated by the State of the permanent establishment may be higher than the amount of profits calculated by the State of the enterprise for purposes of relief of double taxation.

48.   Given the importance of that issue, the Committee has looked for a practical solution. OECD member countries have therefore agreed to accept, for the purposes of determining the amount of interest deduction that will be used in computing double taxation relief, the attribution of capital derived from the application of the approach used by the State in which the permanent establishment is located if the following two conditions are met: first, if the difference in capital attribution between that State and the State of the enterprise results from conflicting domestic law choices of capital attribution methods, and second, if there is agreement that the State in which the permanent establishment is located has used an authorised approach to the attribution of capital and there is also agreement that that approach produces a result consistent with the arm's length principle in the particular case. OECD member countries consider that they are able to achieve that result either under their domestic law, through the interpretation of Articles 7 and 23 or under the mutual agreement procedure of Article 25 and, in particular, the possibility offered by that Article to resolve any issues concerning the application or interpretation of their tax treaties.

49.   As already mentioned, special considerations apply to internal interest charges on advances between different parts of a financial enterprise (e.g. a bank), in view of the fact that making and receiving advances is closely related to the ordinary business of such enterprises. This problem, as well as other problems relating to the application of Article 7 to the permanent establishments of banks and enterprises carrying on global trading, is discussed in Parts II and III of the Report Attribution of Profits to Permanent Establishments.

50.   The determination of the investment assets attributable to a permanent establishment through which insurance activities are carried on also raises particular issues, which are discussed in Part IV of the Report.

51.   It is usually found that there are, or there can be constructed, adequate accounts for each part or section of an enterprise so that profits and expenses, adjusted as may be necessary, can be allocated to a particular part of the enterprise with a considerable degree of precision. This method of allocation is, it is thought, to be preferred in general wherever it is reasonably practicable to adopt it. There are, however, circumstances in which this may not be the case and paragraphs 2 and 3 are in no way intended to imply that other methods cannot properly be adopted where appropriate in order to arrive at the profits of a permanent establishment on a "separate enterprise" footing. It may well

be, for example, that profits of insurance enterprises can most conveniently be ascertained by special methods of computation, *e.g.* by applying appropriate co-efficients to gross premiums received from policy holders in the country concerned. Again, in the case of a relatively small enterprise operating on both sides of the border between two countries, there may be no proper accounts for the permanent establishment nor means of constructing them. There may, too, be other cases where the affairs of the permanent establishment are so closely bound up with those of the head office that it would be impossible to disentangle them on any strict basis of branch accounts. Where it has been customary in such cases to estimate the arm's length profit of a permanent establishment by reference to suitable criteria, it may well be reasonable that that method should continue to be followed, notwithstanding that the estimate thus made may not achieve as high a degree of accurate measurement of the profit as adequate accounts. Even where such a course has not been customary, it may, exceptionally, be necessary for practical reasons to estimate the arm's length profits based on other methods.

Paragraph 4

52.   It has in some cases been the practice to determine the profits to be attributed to a permanent establishment not on the basis of separate accounts or by making an estimate of arm's length profit, but simply by apportioning the total profits of the enterprise by reference to various formulae. Such a method differs from those envisaged in paragraph 2, since it contemplates not an attribution of profits on a separate enterprise footing, but an apportionment of total profits; and indeed it might produce a result in figures which would differ from that which would be arrived at by a computation based on separate accounts. Paragraph 4 makes it clear that such a method may continue to be employed by a Contracting State if it has been customary in that State to adopt it, even though the figure arrived at may at times differ to some extent from that which would be obtained from separate accounts, provided that the result can fairly be said to be in accordance with the principles contained in the Article. It is emphasised, however, that in general the profits to be attributed to a permanent establishment should be determined by reference to the establishment's accounts if these reflect the real facts. It is considered that a method of allocation which is based on apportioning total profits is generally not as appropriate as a method which has regard only to the activities of the permanent establishment and should be used only where, exceptionally, it has as a matter of history been customary in the past and is accepted in the country concerned both by the taxation authorities and taxpayers generally there as being satisfactory. It is understood that paragraph 4 may be deleted where neither State uses such a method. Where, however, Contracting States wish to be able to use a method which has not been customary in the past the paragraph should be amended during the bilateral negotiations to make this clear.

53.   It would not, it is thought, be appropriate within the framework of this Commentary to attempt to discuss at length the many various methods involving apportionment of total profits that have been adopted in particular fields for allocating profits. These methods have been well documented in treatises on international taxation. It may, however, not be out of place to summarise briefly some of the main types and to lay down some very general directives for their use.

54.   The essential character of a method involving apportionment of total profits is that a proportionate part of the profits of the whole enterprise is allocated to a part thereof, all parts of the enterprise being assumed to have contributed on the basis of

the criterion or criteria adopted to the profitability of the whole. The difference between one such method and another arises for the most part from the varying criteria used to determine what is the correct proportion of the total profits. It is fair to say that the criteria commonly used can be grouped into three main categories, namely those which are based on the receipts of the enterprise, its expenses or its capital structure. The first category covers allocation methods based on turnover or on commission, the second on wages and the third on the proportion of the total working capital of the enterprise allocated to each branch or part. It is not, of course, possible to say *in vacuo* that any of these methods is intrinsically more accurate than the others; the appropriateness of any particular method will depend on the circumstances to which it is applied. In some enterprises, such as those providing services or producing proprietary articles with a high profit margin, net profits will depend very much on turnover. For insurance enterprises it may be appropriate to make an apportionment of total profits by reference to premiums received from policy holders in each of the countries concerned. In the case of an enterprise manufacturing goods with a high cost raw material or labour content, profits may be found to be related more closely to expenses. In the case of banking and financial concerns the proportion of total working capital may be the most relevant criterion. It is considered that the general aim of any method involving apportionment of total profits ought to be to produce figures of taxable profit that approximate as closely as possible to the figures that would have been produced on a separate accounts basis, and that it would not be desirable to attempt in this connection to lay down any specific directive other than that it should be the responsibility of the taxation authority, in consultation with the authorities of other countries concerned, to use the method which in the light of all the known facts seems most likely to produce that result.

55.   The use of any method which allocates to a part of an enterprise a proportion of the total profits of the whole does, of course, raise the question of the method to be used in computing the total profits of the enterprise. This may well be a matter which will be treated differently under the laws of different countries. This is not a problem which it would seem practicable to attempt to resolve by laying down any rigid rule. It is scarcely to be expected that it would be accepted that the profits to be apportioned should be the profits as they are computed under the laws of one particular country; each country concerned would have to be given the right to compute the profits according to the provisions of its own laws.

Paragraph 5

56.   In paragraph 4 of Article 5 there are listed a number of examples of activities which, even though carried on at a fixed place of business, are deemed not to be included in the term "permanent establishment". In considering rules for the allocation of profits to a permanent establishment the most important of these examples is the activity mentioned in paragraph 5 of this Article, i.e. the purchasing office.

57.   Paragraph 5 is not, of course, concerned with the organisation established solely for purchasing; such an organisation is not a permanent establishment and the profits allocation provisions of this Article would not therefore come into play. The paragraph is concerned with a permanent establishment which, although carrying on other business, also carries on purchasing for its head office. In such a case the paragraph provides that the profits of the permanent establishment shall not be increased by adding to them a notional figure for profits from purchasing. It follows, of course, that

any expenses that arise from the purchasing activities will also be excluded in calculating the taxable profits of the permanent establishment.

Paragraph 6

58.   This paragraph is intended to lay down clearly that a method of allocation once used should not be changed merely because in a particular year some other method produces more favourable results. One of the purposes of a double taxation convention is to give an enterprise of a Contracting State some degree of certainty about the tax treatment that will be accorded to its permanent establishment in the other Contracting State as well as to the part of it in its home State which is dealing with the permanent establishment; for this reason, paragraph 6 gives an assurance of continuous and consistent tax treatment.

Paragraph 7

59.   Although it has not been found necessary in the Convention to define the term "profits", it should nevertheless be understood that the term when used in this Article and elsewhere in the Convention has a broad meaning including all income derived in carrying on an enterprise. Such a broad meaning corresponds to the use of the term made in the tax laws of most OECD member countries.

60.   This interpretation of the term "profits", however, may give rise to some uncertainty as to the application of the Convention. If the profits of an enterprise include categories of income which are treated separately in other Articles of the Convention, e.g. dividends, it may be asked whether the taxation of those profits is governed by the special Article on dividends etc., or by the provisions of this Article.

61.   To the extent that an application of this Article and the special Article concerned would result in the same tax treatment, there is little practical significance to this question. Further, it should be noted that some of the special Articles contain specific provisions giving priority to a specific Article (cf. paragraph 4 of Article 6, paragraph 4 of Articles 10 and 11, paragraph 3 of Article 12, and paragraph 2 of Article 21).

62.   It has seemed desirable, however, to lay down a rule of interpretation in order to clarify the field of application of this Article in relation to the other Articles dealing with a specific category of income. In conformity with the practice generally adhered to in existing bilateral conventions, paragraph 7 gives first preference to the special Articles on dividends, interest etc. It follows from the rule that this Article will be applicable to business profits which do not belong to categories of income covered by the special Articles, and, in addition, to dividends, interest etc. which under paragraph 4 of Articles 10 and 11, paragraph 3 of Article 12 and paragraph 2 of Article 21, fall within this Article (cf. paragraphs 12 to 18 of the Commentary on Article 12 which discuss the principles governing whether, in the particular case of computer software, payments should be classified as business profits within Article 7 or as a capital gain within Article 13 on the one hand or as royalties within Article 12 on the other). It is understood that the items of income covered by the special Articles may, subject to the provisions of the Convention, be taxed either separately, or as business profits, in conformity with the tax laws of the Contracting States.

63.   It is open to Contracting States to agree bilaterally upon special explanations or definitions concerning the term "profits" with a view to clarifying the distinction between this term and e.g. the concept of dividends. It may in particular be found appropriate to do so where in a convention under negotiation a deviation has been made from the definitions in the special Articles on dividends, interest and royalties. It

may also be deemed desirable if the Contracting States wish to place on notice, that, in agreement with the domestic tax laws of one or both of the States, the term "profits" includes special classes of receipts such as income from the alienation or the letting of a business or of movable property used in a business. In this connection it may have to be considered whether it would be useful to include also additional rules for the allocation of such special profits.

64.   It should also be noted that, whilst the definition of "royalties" in paragraph 2 of Article 12 of the 1963 Draft Convention and 1977 Model Convention included payments "for the use of, or the right to use, industrial, commercial, or scientific equipment", the reference to these payments was subsequently deleted from that definition in order to ensure that income from the leasing of industrial, commercial or scientific equipment, including the income from the leasing of containers, falls under the provisions of Article 7 rather than those of Article 12, a result that the Committee on Fiscal Affairs considers to be appropriate given the nature of such income.

Observations on the Commentary

65.   *Italy* and *Portugal* deem as essential to take into consideration that — irrespective of the meaning given to the fourth sentence of paragraph 8 — as far as the method for computing taxes is concerned, national systems are not affected by the new wording of the model, *i.e.* by the elimination of Article 14.

66.   *Belgium* cannot share the views expressed in paragraph 13 of the Commentary. Belgium considers that the application of controlled foreign companies legislation is contrary to the provisions of paragraph 1 of Article 7. This is especially the case where a Contracting State taxes one of its residents on income derived by a foreign entity by using a fiction attributing to that resident, in proportion to his participation in the capital of the foreign entity, the income derived by that entity. By doing so, that State increases the tax base of its resident by including in it income which has not been derived by that resident but by a foreign entity which is not taxable in that State in accordance with paragraph 1 of Article 7. That Contracting State thus disregards the legal personality of the foreign entity and acts contrary to paragraph 1 of Article 7.

67.   *Luxembourg* does not share the interpretation in paragraph 13 which provides that paragraph 1 of Article 7 does not restrict a Contracting State's right to tax its own residents under controlled foreign companies provisions found in its domestic law as this interpretation challenges the fundamental principle contained in paragraph 1 of Article 7.

68.   With reference to paragraph 13, *Ireland* notes its general observation in paragraph 27.5 of the Commentary on Article 1.

69.   With regard to paragraph 45, *Greece* notes that the Greek internal law does not foresee any rules or methods for attributing "free" capital to permanent establishments. Concerning loans contracted by an enterprise that relate in whole or in part to the activities of the permanent establishment, Greece allows as deduction the part of the interest which corresponds to the amount of a loan contracted by the head office and actually remitted to the permanent establishment.

70.   *Portugal* wishes to reserve its right not to follow the position expressed in paragraph 45 of the Commentary on Article 7 except whenever there are specific domestic provisions foreseeing certain levels of "free" capital for permanent establishments.

71.   With regard to paragraph 46, *Sweden* wishes to clarify that it does not consider that the different approaches for attributing "free" capital that the paragraph refers to as being "acceptable" will necessarily lead to a result in accordance with the arm's length principle. Consequently, when looking at the facts and circumstances of each case in order to determine whether the amount of interest deduction resulting from the application of these approaches conforms to the arm's length principle, Sweden in many cases would not consider that the other States' approach conforms to the arm's length principle. Sweden is of the opinion that double taxation will therefore often occur, requiring the use of the mutual agreement procedure.

72.   *Portugal* wishes to reserve its right not to follow the "symmetry" approach described in paragraph 48 of the Commentary on Article 7, insofar as the Portuguese internal law does not foresee any rules or methods for attributing "free" capital to permanent establishments. In eliminating double taxation according to Article 23, Portugal, as the home country, determines the amount of profits attributable to a permanent establishment according to the domestic law.

73.   *Germany, Japan* and the *United States*, whilst agreeing to the practical solution described in paragraph 48, wish to clarify how this agreement will be implemented. Neither Germany, nor Japan, nor the United States can automatically accept for all purposes all calculations by the State in which the permanent establishment is located. In cases involving Germany or Japan, the second condition described in paragraph 48 has to be satisfied through a mutual agreement procedure under Article 25. In the case of Japan and the United States, a taxpayer who seeks to obtain additional foreign tax credit limitation must do so through a mutual agreement procedure in which the taxpayer would have to prove to the Japanese or the United States competent authority, as the case may be, that double taxation of the permanent establishment profits which resulted from the conflicting domestic law choices of capital attribution methods has been left unrelieved after applying mechanisms under their respective domestic tax law such as utilisation of foreign tax credit limitation created by other transactions.

74.   With reference to paragraphs 6 and 7, *New Zealand* notes that it does not agree with the approach put forward on the attribution of profits to permanent establishments in general, as reflected in Part I of the Report *Attribution of Profits to Permanent Establishments*.

Reservations on the Commentary

75.   *Australia, Chile*[1] and *New Zealand* reserve the right to include a provision that will permit their domestic law to apply in relation to the taxation of profits from any form of insurance.

76.   *Australia* and *New Zealand* reserve the right to include a provision clarifying their right to tax a share of business profits to which a resident of the other Contracting State is beneficially entitled where those profits are derived by a trustee of a trust estate (other than certain unit trusts that are treated as companies for Australian and New Zealand tax purposes) from the carrying on of a business in Australia or New Zealand, as the case may be, through a permanent establishment.

77.   *Korea* and *Portugal* reserve the right to tax persons performing professional services or other activities of an independent character if they are present on their

---

1   Chile was added to this reservation when it joined the OECD in 2010.

territory for a period or periods exceeding in the aggregate 183 days in any twelve month period, even if they do not have a permanent establishment (or a fixed base) available to them for the purpose of performing such services or activities.

78.   Chile,[1] Italy and Portugal reserve the right to tax persons performing independent personal services under a separate article which corresponds to Article 14 as it stood before its elimination in 2000.

79.   The United States reserves the right to amend Article 7 to provide that, in applying paragraphs 1 and 2 of the Article, any income or gain attributable to a permanent establishment during its existence may be taxable by the Contracting State in which the permanent establishment exists even if the payments are deferred until after the permanent establishment has ceased to exist. The United States also wishes to note that it reserves the right to apply such a rule, as well, under Articles 11, 12, 13 and 21.

80.   Turkey reserves the right to subject income from the leasing of containers to a withholding tax at source in all cases. In case of the application of Articles 5 and 7 to such income, Turkey would like to apply the permanent establishment rule to the simple depot, depot-agency and operational branches cases.

81.   Norway and the United States reserve the right to treat income from the use, maintenance or rental of containers used in international traffic under Article 8 in the same manner as income from shipping and air transport.

82.   Australia and Portugal reserve the right to propose in bilateral negotiations a provision to the effect that, if the information available to the competent authority of a Contracting State is inadequate to determine the profits to be attributed to the permanent establishment of an enterprise, the competent authority may apply to that enterprise for that purpose the provisions of the taxation law of that State, subject to the qualification that such law will be applied, so far as the information available to the competent authority permits, in accordance with the principles of this Article.

83.   Mexico reserves the right to tax in the State where the permanent establishment is situated business profits derived from the sale of goods or merchandise carried out directly by its home office situated in the other Contracting State, provided that those goods and merchandise are of the same or similar kind as the ones sold through that permanent establishment. The Government of Mexico will apply this rule only as a safeguard against abuse and not as a general "force of attraction" principle; thus, the rule will not apply when the enterprise proves that the sales have been carried out for reasons other than obtaining a benefit under the Convention.

---

1   Chile was added to this reservation when it joined the OECD in 2010.

COMMENTARY ON ARTICLE 8
CONCERNING THE TAXATION OF PROFITS FROM SHIPPING, INLAND WATERWAYS TRANSPORT AND AIR TRANSPORT

Paragraph 1

1.   The object of paragraph 1 concerning profits from the operation of ships or aircraft in international traffic is to secure that such profits will be taxed in one State alone. The provision is based on the principle that the taxing right shall be left to the Contracting State in which the place of effective management of the enterprise is situated. The term "international traffic" is defined in subparagraph *e)* of paragraph 1 of Article 3.

2.   In certain circumstances the Contracting State in which the place of effective management is situated may not be the State of which an enterprise operating ships or aircraft is a resident, and some States therefore prefer to confer the exclusive taxing right on the State of residence. Such States are free to substitute a rule on the following lines:

> Profits of an enterprise of a Contracting State from the operation of ships or aircraft in international traffic shall be taxable only in that State.

3.   Some other States, on the other hand, prefer to use a combination of the residence criterion and the place of effective management criterion by giving the primary right to tax to the State in which the place of effective management is situated while the State of residence eliminates double taxation in accordance with Article 23, so long as the former State is able to tax the total profits of the enterprise, and by giving the primary right to tax to the State of residence when the State of effective management is not able to tax total profits. States wishing to follow that principle are free to substitute a rule on the following lines:

> Profits of an enterprise of a Contracting State from the operation of ships or aircraft, other than those from transport by ships or aircraft operated solely between places in the other Contracting State, shall be taxable only in the first-mentioned State. However, where the place of effective management of the enterprise is situated in the other State and that other State imposes tax on the whole of the profits of the enterprise from the operation of ships or aircraft, the profits from the operation of ships or aircraft, other than those from transport by ships or aircraft operated solely between places in the first-mentioned State, may be taxed in that other State.

4.   The profits covered consist in the first place of the profits directly obtained by the enterprise from the transportation of passengers or cargo by ships or aircraft (whether owned, leased or otherwise at the disposal of the enterprise) that it operates in international traffic. However, as international transport has evolved, shipping and air transport enterprises invariably carry on a large variety of activities to permit, facilitate or support their international traffic operations. The paragraph also covers profits from activities directly connected with such operations as well as profits from activities

MODEL TAX CONVENTION (CONDENSED VERSION) – ISBN 978-92-64-08948-8 – © OECD 2010

which are not directly connected with the operation of the enterprise's ships or aircraft in international traffic as long as they are ancillary to such operation.

4.1   Any activity carried on primarily in connection with the transportation, by the enterprise, of passengers or cargo by ships or aircraft that it operates in international traffic should be considered to be directly connected with such transportation.

4.2   Activities that the enterprise does not need to carry on for the purposes of its own operation of ships or aircraft in international traffic but which make a minor contribution relative to such operation and are so closely related to such operation that they should not be regarded as a separate business or source of income of the enterprise should be considered to be ancillary to the operation of ships and aircraft in international traffic.

4.3   In light of these principles, the following paragraphs discuss the extent to which paragraph 1 applies with respect to some particular types of activities that may be carried on by an enterprise engaged in the operation of ships or aircraft in international traffic.

5.   Profits obtained by leasing a ship or aircraft on charter fully equipped, crewed and supplied must be treated like the profits from the carriage of passengers or cargo. Otherwise, a great deal of business of shipping or air transport would not come within the scope of the provision. However, Article 7, and not Article 8, applies to profits from leasing a ship or aircraft on a bare boat charter basis except when it is an ancillary activity of an enterprise engaged in the international operation of ships or aircraft.

6.   Profits derived by an enterprise from the transportation of passengers or cargo otherwise than by ships or aircraft that it operates in international traffic are covered by the paragraph to the extent that such transportation is directly connected with the operation, by that enterprise, of ships or aircraft in international traffic or is an ancillary activity. One example would be that of an enterprise engaged in international transport that would have some of its passengers or cargo transported internationally by ships or aircraft operated by other enterprises, *e.g.* under code-sharing or slot-chartering arrangements or to take advantage of an earlier sailing. Another example would be that of an airline company that operates a bus service connecting a town with its airport primarily to provide access to and from that airport to the passengers of its international flights.

7.   A further example would be that of an enterprise that transports passengers or cargo by ships or aircraft operated in international traffic which undertakes to have those passengers or that cargo picked up in the country where the transport originates or transported or delivered in the country of destination by any mode of inland transportation operated by other enterprises. In such a case, any profits derived by the first enterprise from arranging such transportation by other enterprises are covered by the paragraph even though the profits derived by the other enterprises that provide such inland transportation would not be.

8.   An enterprise will frequently sell tickets on behalf of other transport enterprises at a location that it maintains primarily for purposes of selling tickets for

transportation on ships or aircraft that it operates in international traffic. Such sales of tickets on behalf of other enterprises will either be directly connected with voyages aboard ships or aircraft that the enterprise operates (*e.g.* sale of a ticket issued by another enterprise for the domestic leg of an international voyage offered by the enterprise) or will be ancillary to its own sales. Profits derived by the first enterprise from selling such tickets are therefore covered by the paragraph.

8.1   Advertising that the enterprise may do for other enterprises in magazines offered aboard ships or aircraft that it operates or at its business locations (*e.g.* ticket offices) is ancillary to its operation of these ships or aircraft and profits generated by such advertising fall within the paragraph.

9.   Containers are used extensively in international transport. Such containers frequently are also used in inland transport. Profits derived by an enterprise engaged in international transport from the lease of containers are usually either directly connected or ancillary to its operation of ships or aircraft in international traffic and in such cases fall within the scope of the paragraph. The same conclusion would apply with respect to profits derived by such an enterprise from the short-term storage of such containers (*e.g.* where the enterprise charges a customer for keeping a loaded container in a warehouse pending delivery) or from detention charges for the late return of containers.

10.   An enterprise that has assets or personnel in a foreign country for purposes of operating its ships or aircraft in international traffic may derive income from providing goods or services in that country to other transport enterprises. This would include (for example) the provision of goods and services by engineers, ground and equipment-maintenance staff, cargo handlers, catering staff and customer services personnel. Where the enterprise provides such goods to, or performs services for, other enterprises and such activities are directly connected or ancillary to the enterprise's operation of ships or aircraft in international traffic, the profits from the provision of such goods or services to other enterprises will fall under the paragraph.

10.1   For example, enterprises engaged in international transport may enter into pooling arrangements for the purposes of reducing the costs of maintaining facilities needed for the operation of their ships or aircraft in other countries. For instance, where an airline enterprise agrees, under an International Airlines Technical Pool agreement, to provide spare parts or maintenance services to other airlines landing at a particular location (which allows it to benefit from these services at other locations), activities carried on pursuant to that agreement will be ancillary to the operation of aircraft in international traffic.

11.   [Deleted]

12.   The paragraph does not apply to a shipbuilding yard operated in one country by a shipping enterprise having its place of effective management in another country.

13.   [Renumbered]

14.   Investment income of shipping or air transport enterprises (*e.g.* income from stocks, bonds, shares or loans) is to be subjected to the treatment ordinarily applied to this class of income, except where the investment that generates the income is made as an integral part of the carrying on of the business of operating the ships or aircraft in international traffic in the Contracting State so that the investment may be considered to be directly connected with such operation. Thus, the paragraph would apply to interest income generated, for example, by the cash required in a Contracting State for the carrying on of that business or by bonds posted as security where this is required by law in order to carry on the business: in such cases, the investment is needed to allow the operation of the ships or aircraft at that location. The paragraph would not apply, however, to interest income derived in the course of the handling of cash-flow or other treasury activities for permanent establishments of the enterprise to which the income is not attributable or for associated enterprises, regardless of whether these are located within or outside that Contracting State, or for the head office (centralisation of treasury and investment activities), nor would it apply to interest income generated by the short-term investment of the profits generated by the local operation of the business where the funds invested are not required for that operation.

Paragraph 2

15.   The rules with respect to the taxing right of the State of residence as set forth in paragraphs 2 and 3 above apply also to this paragraph of the Article.

16.   The object of this paragraph is to apply the same treatment to transport on rivers, canals and lakes as to shipping and air transport in international traffic. The provision applies not only to inland waterways transport between two or more countries, but also to inland waterways transport carried on by an enterprise of one country between two points in another country.

16.1   Paragraphs 4 to 14 above provide guidance with respect to the profits that may be considered to be derived from the operation of ships or aircraft in international traffic. The principles and examples included in these paragraphs are applicable, with the necessary adaptations, for purposes of determining which profits may be considered to be derived from the operation of boats engaged in inland waterways transport.

17.   The provision does not prevent specific tax problems which may arise in connection with inland waterways transport, in particular between adjacent countries, from being settled specially by bilateral agreement.

17.1   It may also be agreed bilaterally that profits from the operation of vessels engaged in fishing, dredging or hauling activities on the high seas be treated as income falling under this Article.

Enterprises not exclusively engaged in shipping, inland waterways transport or air transport

18.   It follows from the wording of paragraphs 1 and 2 that enterprises not exclusively engaged in shipping, inland waterways transport or air transport nevertheless come within the provisions of these paragraphs as regards profits arising to them from the operation of ships, boats or aircraft belonging to them.

19.   If such an enterprise has in a foreign country permanent establishments exclusively concerned with the operation of its ships or aircraft, there is no reason to treat such establishments differently from the permanent establishments of enterprises engaged exclusively in shipping, inland waterways transport or air transport.

20.   Nor does any difficulty arise in applying the provisions of paragraphs 1 and 2 if the enterprise has in another State a permanent establishment which is not exclusively engaged in shipping, inland waterways transport or air transport. If its goods are carried in its own ships to a permanent establishment belonging to it in a foreign country, it is right to say that none of the profit obtained by the enterprise through acting as its own carrier can properly be taxed in the State where the permanent establishment is situated. The same must be true even if the permanent establishment maintains installations for operating the ships or aircraft (e.g. consignment wharves) or incurs other costs in connection with the carriage of the enterprise's goods (e.g. staff costs). In this case, even though certain functions related to the operation of ships and aircraft in international traffic may be performed by the permanent establishment, the profits attributable to these functions are taxable exclusively in the State where the place of effective management of the enterprise is situated. Any expenses, or part thereof, incurred in performing such functions must be deducted in computing that part of the profit that is not taxable in the State where the permanent establishment is located and will not, therefore, reduce the part of the profits attributable to the permanent establishment which may be taxed in that State pursuant to Article 7.

21.   Where ships or aircraft are operated in international traffic, the application of the Article to the profits arising from such operation will not be affected by the fact that the ships or aircraft are operated by a permanent establishment which is not the place of effective management of the whole enterprise; thus, even if such profits could be attributed to the permanent establishment under Article 7, they will only be taxable in the State in which the place of effective management of the enterprise is situated (a result that is confirmed by paragraph 4 of Article 7).

Paragraph 3

22.   This paragraph deals with the particular case where the place of effective management of the enterprise is aboard a ship or a boat. In this case tax will only be charged by the State where the home harbour of the ship or boat is situated. It is

provided that if the home harbour cannot be determined, tax will be charged only in the Contracting State of which the operator of the ship or boat is a resident.

Paragraph 4

23.   Various forms of international co-operation exist in shipping or air transport. In this field international co-operation is secured through pooling agreements or other conventions of a similar kind which lay down certain rules for apportioning the receipts (or profits) from the joint business.

24.   In order to clarify the taxation position of the participant in a pool, joint business or in an international operating agency and to cope with any difficulties which may arise the Contracting States may bilaterally add the following, if they find it necessary:

... but only to so much of the profits so derived as is attributable to the participant in proportion to its share in the joint operation.

25.   [Renumbered]

Observations on the Commentary

26.   [Renumbered]

27.   [Deleted]

28.   *Greece* and *Portugal* reserve their position as to the application of this Article to income from ancillary activities (see paragraphs 4 to 10.1).

29.   *Germany, Greece* and *Turkey* reserve their position as to the application of the Article to income from inland transportation of passengers or cargo and from container services (see paragraphs 4, 6, 7 and 9 above).

30.   *Greece* will apply Article 12 to payments from leasing a ship or aircraft on a bareboat charter basis.

Reservations on the Article

31.   *Canada, Hungary, Mexico* and *New Zealand* reserve the right to tax as profits from internal traffic, profits from the carriage of passengers or cargo taken on board at one place in a respective country for discharge at another place in the same country. New Zealand also reserves the right to tax as profits from internal traffic profits from other coastal and continental shelf activities.

32.   *Belgium, Canada, Greece, Mexico, Turkey,* the *United Kingdom* and the *United States* reserve the right not to extend the scope of the Article to cover inland transportation in bilateral conventions (paragraph 2 of the Article).

33.   *Denmark, Norway* and *Sweden* reserve the right to insert special provisions regarding profits derived by the air transport consortium Scandinavian Airlines System (SAS).

34.   [Deleted]

35.   In view of its particular situation in relation to shipping, *Greece* will retain its freedom of action with regard to the provisions in the Convention relating to profits from the operation of ships in international traffic.

36.   *Mexico* reserves the right to tax at source profits derived from the provision of accommodation.

37.   [Deleted]

38.   *Australia* reserves the right to tax profits from the carriage of passengers or cargo taken on board at one place in Australia for discharge in Australia.

39.   The *United States* reserves the right to include within the scope of paragraph 1, income from the rental of ships and aircraft on a full basis, and on a bareboat basis if either the ships or aircraft are operated in international traffic by the lessee, or if the rental income is incidental to profits from the operation of ships or aircraft in international traffic. The United States also reserves the right to include within the scope of the paragraph, income from the use, maintenance or rental of containers used in international traffic.

40.   The *Slovak Republic* reserves the right to tax under Article 12 profits from the leasing of ships, aircraft and containers.

41.   *Ireland* reserves the right to include within the scope of the Article income from the rental of ships or aircraft on a bareboat basis if either the ships or aircraft are operated in international traffic by the lessee or if the rental income is incidental to profits from the operation of ships or aircraft in international traffic.

42.   *Turkey* reserves the right in exceptional cases to apply the permanent establishment rule in taxation of profit from international transport. Turkey also reserves the right to broaden the scope of the Article to cover transport by road vehicle and to make a corresponding change to the definition of "international traffic" in Article 3.

43.   *Chile* and *Slovenia* reserve the right not to extend the scope of the Article to cover inland waterways transportation in bilateral conventions and to make corresponding modifications to paragraph 3 of Articles 13, 15 and 22.

MODEL TAX CONVENTION (CONDENSED VERSION) – ISBN 978-92-64-08948-8 – © OECD 2010

COMMENTARY ON ARTICLE 9
CONCERNING THE TAXATION OF ASSOCIATED ENTERPRISES

1.   This Article deals with adjustments to profits that may be made for tax purposes where transactions have been entered into between associated enterprises (parent and subsidiary companies and companies under common control) on other than arm's length terms. The Committee has spent considerable time and effort (and continues to do so) examining the conditions for the application of this Article, its consequences and the various methodologies which may be applied to adjust profits where transactions have been entered into on other than arm's length terms. Its conclusions are set out in the report entitled *Transfer Pricing Guidelines for Multinational Enterprises and Tax Administrations*,[1] which is periodically updated to reflect the progress of the work of the Committee in this area. That report represents internationally agreed principles and provides guidelines for the application of the arm's length principle of which the Article is the authoritative statement.

Paragraph 1

2.   This paragraph provides that the taxation authorities of a Contracting State may, for the purpose of calculating tax liabilities of associated enterprises, re-write the accounts of the enterprises if, as a result of the special relations between the enterprises, the accounts do not show the true taxable profits arising in that State. It is evidently appropriate that adjustment should be sanctioned in such circumstances. The provisions of this paragraph apply only if special conditions have been made or imposed between the two enterprises. No re-writing of the accounts of associated enterprises is authorised if the transactions between such enterprises have taken place on normal open market commercial terms (on an arm's length basis).

3.   As discussed in the Committee on Fiscal Affairs' Report on "Thin Capitalisation",[2] there is an interplay between tax treaties and domestic rules on thin capitalisation relevant to the scope of the Article. The Committee considers that:

   a) the Article does not prevent the application of national rules on thin capitalisation insofar as their effect is to assimilate the profits of the borrower to an amount corresponding to the profits which would have accrued in an arm's length situation;

   b) the Article is relevant not only in determining whether the rate of interest provided for in a loan contract is an arm's length rate, but also whether a *prima facie* loan can be regarded as a loan or should be regarded as some other kind of payment, in particular a contribution to equity capital;

---

1   The original version of that report was approved by the Council of the OECD on 27 June 1995. Published in a loose-leaf format as *Transfer Pricing Guidelines for Multinational Enterprises and Tax Administrations*, OECD, Paris, 1995.
2   Adopted by the Council of the OECD on 26 November 1986 and reproduced in Volume II of the full-length version of the OECD Model Tax Convention at page R(4)-1.

c) the application of rules designed to deal with thin capitalisation should normally not have the effect of increasing the taxable profits of the relevant domestic enterprise to more than the arm's length profit, and that this principle should be followed in applying existing tax treaties.

4.   The question arises as to whether special procedural rules which some countries have adopted for dealing with transactions between related parties are consistent with the Convention. For instance, it may be asked whether the reversal of the burden of proof or presumptions of any kind which are sometimes found in domestic laws are consistent with the arm's length principle. A number of countries interpret the Article in such a way that it by no means bars the adjustment of profits under national law under conditions that differ from those of the Article and that it has the function of raising the arm's length principle at treaty level. Also, almost all member countries consider that additional information requirements which would be more stringent than the normal requirements, or even a reversal of the burden of proof, would not constitute discrimination within the meaning of Article 24. However, in some cases the application of the national law of some countries may result in adjustments to profits at variance with the principles of the Article. Contracting States are enabled by the Article to deal with such situations by means of corresponding adjustments (see below) and under mutual agreement procedures.

Paragraph 2

5.   The re-writing of transactions between associated enterprises in the situation envisaged in paragraph 1 may give rise to economic double taxation (taxation of the same income in the hands of different persons), insofar as an enterprise of State A whose profits are revised upwards will be liable to tax on an amount of profit which has already been taxed in the hands of its associated enterprise in State B. Paragraph 2 provides that in these circumstances, State B shall make an appropriate adjustment so as to relieve the double taxation.

6.   It should be noted, however, that an adjustment is not automatically to be made in State B simply because the profits in State A have been increased; the adjustment is due only if State B considers that the figure of adjusted profits correctly reflects what the profits would have been if the transactions had been at arm's length. In other words, the paragraph may not be invoked and should not be applied where the profits of one associated enterprise are increased to a level which exceeds what they would have been if they had been correctly computed on an arm's length basis. State B is therefore committed to make an adjustment of the profits of the affiliated company only if it considers that the adjustment made in State A is justified both in principle and as regards the amount.

7.   The paragraph does not specify the method by which an adjustment is to be made. OECD member countries use different methods to provide relief in these circumstances and it is therefore left open for Contracting States to agree bilaterally on any specific rules which they wish to add to the Article. Some States, for example, would prefer the system under which, where the profits of enterprise X in State A are

increased to what they would have been on an arm's length basis, the adjustment would be made by re-opening the assessment on the associated enterprise Y in State B containing the doubly taxed profits in order to reduce the taxable profit by an appropriate amount. Some other States, on the other hand, would prefer to provide that, for the purposes of Article 23, the doubly taxed profits should be treated in the hands of enterprise Y of State B as if they may be taxed in State A; accordingly, the enterprise of State B is entitled to relief in State B, under Article 23, in respect of tax paid by its associate enterprise in State A.

8.   It is not the purpose of the paragraph to deal with what might be called "secondary adjustments". Suppose that an upward revision of taxable profits of enterprise X in State A has been made in accordance with the principle laid down in paragraph 1 and suppose also that an adjustment is made to the profits of enterprise Y in State B in accordance with the principle laid down in paragraph 2. The position has still not been restored exactly to what it would have been had the transactions taken place at arm's length prices because, as a matter of fact, the money representing the profits which are the subject of the adjustment is found in the hands of enterprise Y instead of in those of enterprise X. It can be argued that if arm's length pricing had operated and enterprise X had subsequently wished to transfer these profits to enterprise Y, it would have done so in the form of, for example, a dividend or a royalty (if enterprise Y were the parent of enterprise X) or in the form of, for example, a loan (if enterprise X were the parent of enterprise Y) and that in those circumstances there could have been other tax consequences (e.g. the operation of a withholding tax) depending upon the type of income concerned and the provisions of the Article dealing with such income.

9.   These secondary adjustments, which would be required to establish the situation exactly as it would have been if transactions had been at arm's length, depend on the facts of the individual case. It should be noted that nothing in paragraph 2 prevents such secondary adjustments from being made where they are permitted under the domestic laws of Contracting States.

10.   The paragraph also leaves open the question whether there should be a period of time after the expiration of which State B would not be obliged to make an appropriate adjustment to the profits of enterprise Y following an upward revision of the profits of enterprise X in State A. Some States consider that State B's commitment should be open-ended — in other words, that however many years State A goes back to revise assessments, enterprise Y should in equity be assured of an appropriate adjustment in State B. Other States consider that an open-ended commitment of this sort is unreasonable as a matter of practical administration. In the circumstances, therefore, this problem has not been dealt with in the text of the Article; but Contracting States are left free in bilateral conventions to include, if they wish, provisions dealing with the length of time during which State B is to be under obligation to make an appropriate adjustment (see on this point paragraphs 39, 40 and 41 of the Commentary on Article 25).

11.   If there is a dispute between the parties concerned over the amount and character of the appropriate adjustment, the mutual agreement procedure provided for under Article 25 should be implemented; the Commentary on that Article contains a number of considerations applicable to adjustments of the profits of associated enterprises carried out on the basis of the present Article (following, in particular, adjustment of transfer prices) and to the corresponding adjustments which must then be made in pursuance of paragraph 2 thereof (see in particular paragraphs 10, 11, 12, 33, 34, 40 and 41 of the Commentary on Article 25).

Observation on the Commentary

12.   [Renumbered]

13.   [Deleted]

14.   [Deleted]

15.   The *United States* observes that there may be reasonable ways to address cases of thin capitalisation other than changing the character of the financial instrument from debt to equity and the character of the payment from interest to a dividend. For instance, in appropriate cases, the character of the instrument (as debt) and the character of the payment (as interest) may be unchanged, but the taxing State may defer the deduction for interest paid that otherwise would be allowed in computing the borrower's net income.

Reservations on the Article

16.   The *Czech Republic* and *Hungary* reserve the right not to insert paragraph 2 in their conventions but are prepared in the course of negotiations to accept this paragraph and at the same time to add a third paragraph limiting the potential corresponding adjustment to *bona fide* cases.

17.   *Germany* reserves the right not to insert paragraph 2 in its conventions but is prepared in the course of negotiations to accept this paragraph based on Germany's long-standing and unaltered understanding that the other Contracting State is only obliged to make an adjustment to the amount of tax to the extent that it agrees, unilaterally or in a mutual agreement procedure, with the adjustment of profits by the first-mentioned State.

17.1   *Italy* reserves the right to insert in its treaties a provision according to which it will make adjustments under paragraph 2 of Article 9 only in accordance with the procedure provided for by the mutual agreement article of the relevant treaty.

18.   *Australia* reserves the right to propose a provision to the effect that, if the information available to the competent authority of a Contracting State is inadequate to determine the profits to be attributed to an enterprise, the competent authority may apply to that enterprise for that purpose the provisions of the taxation law of that State, subject to the qualification that such law will be applied, as far as the

information available to the competent authority permits, in accordance with the principles of this Article.

19.   *Slovenia* reserves the right to specify in paragraph 2 that a correlative adjustment will be made only if it considers that the primary adjustment is justified.

COMMENTARY ON ARTICLE 10
CONCERNING THE TAXATION OF DIVIDENDS

I.   Preliminary remarks

1.   By "dividends" is generally meant the distribution of profits to the shareholders by companies limited by shares,[1] limited partnerships with share capital,[2] limited liability companies[3] or other joint stock companies.[4] Under the laws of the OECD member countries, such joint stock companies are legal entities with a separate juridical personality distinct from all their shareholders. On this point, they differ from partnerships insofar as the latter do not have juridical personality in most countries.

2.   The profits of a business carried on by a partnership are the partners' profits derived from their own exertions; for them they are business profits. So the partner is ordinarily taxed personally on his share of the partnership capital and partnership profits.

3.   The position is different for the shareholder; he is not a trader and the company's profits are not his; so they cannot be attributed to him. He is personally taxable only on those profits which are distributed by the company (apart from the provisions in certain countries' laws relating to the taxation of undistributed profits in special cases). From the shareholders' standpoint, dividends are income from the capital which they have made available to the company as its shareholders.

II.   Commentary on the provisions of the Article

Paragraph 1

4.   Paragraph 1 does not prescribe the principle of taxation of dividends either exclusively in the State of the beneficiary's residence or exclusively in the State of which the company paying the dividends is a resident.

5.   Taxation of dividends exclusively in the State of source is not acceptable as a general rule. Furthermore, there are some States which do not have taxation of dividends at the source, while as a general rule, all the States tax residents in respect of dividends they receive from non-resident companies.

6.   On the other hand, taxation of dividends exclusively in the State of the beneficiary's residence is not feasible as a general rule. It would be more in keeping with the nature of dividends, which are investment income, but it would be unrealistic to suppose that there is any prospect of it being agreed that all taxation of dividends at the source should be relinquished.

---

1   *Sociétés anonymes.*
2   *Sociétés en commandite par actions.*
3   *Sociétés à responsabilité limitée.*
4   *Sociétés de capitaux.*

7.   For this reason, paragraph 1 states simply that dividends may be taxed in the State of the beneficiary's residence. The term "paid" has a very wide meaning, since the concept of payment means the fulfilment of the obligation to put funds at the disposal of the shareholder in the manner required by contract or by custom.

8.   The Article deals only with dividends paid by a company which is a resident of a Contracting State to a resident of the other Contracting State. It does not, therefore, apply to dividends paid by a company which is a resident of a third State or to dividends paid by a company which is a resident of a Contracting State which are attributable to a permanent establishment which an enterprise of that State has in the other Contracting State (for these cases, see paragraphs 4 to 6 of the Commentary on Article 21).

Paragraph 2

9.   Paragraph 2 reserves a right to tax to the State of source of the dividends, *i.e.* to the State of which the company paying the dividends is a resident; this right to tax, however, is limited considerably. The rate of tax is limited to 15 per cent, which appears to be a reasonable maximum figure. A higher rate could hardly be justified since the State of source can already tax the company's profits.

10.   On the other hand, a lower rate (5 per cent) is expressly provided in respect of dividends paid by a subsidiary company to its parent company. If a company of one of the States owns directly a holding of at least 25 per cent in a company of the other State, it is reasonable that payments of profits by the subsidiary to the foreign parent company should be taxed less heavily to avoid recurrent taxation and to facilitate international investment. The realisation of this intention depends on the fiscal treatment of the dividends in the State of which the parent company is a resident (see paragraphs 49 to 54 of the Commentary on Articles 23 A and 23 B).

11.   If a partnership is treated as a body corporate under the domestic laws applying to it, the two Contracting States may agree to modify subparagraph *a)* of paragraph 2 in a way to give the benefits of the reduced rate provided for parent companies also to such partnership.

12.   The requirement of beneficial ownership was introduced in paragraph 2 of Article 10 to clarify the meaning of the words "paid ... to a resident" as they are used in paragraph 1 of the Article. It makes plain that the State of source is not obliged to give up taxing rights over dividend income merely because that income was immediately received by a resident of a State with which the State of source had concluded a convention. The term "beneficial owner" is not used in a narrow technical sense, rather, it should be understood in its context and in light of the object and purposes of the Convention, including avoiding double taxation and the prevention of fiscal evasion and avoidance.

12.1   Where an item of income is received by a resident of a Contracting State acting in the capacity of agent or nominee it would be inconsistent with the object and purpose of the Convention for the State of source to grant relief or exemption merely on account of the status of the immediate recipient of the income as a resident of the other Contracting State. The immediate recipient of the income in this situation qualifies as a resident but no potential double taxation arises as a consequence of that status since the recipient is not treated as the owner of the income for tax purposes in the State of residence. It would be equally inconsistent with the object and purpose of the Convention for the State of source to grant relief or exemption where a resident of a Contracting State, otherwise than through an agency or nominee relationship, simply acts as a conduit for another person who in fact receives the benefit of the income concerned. For these reasons, the report from the Committee on Fiscal Affairs entitled "Double Taxation Conventions and the Use of Conduit Companies"[1] concludes that a conduit company cannot normally be regarded as the beneficial owner if, though the formal owner, it has, as a practical matter, very narrow powers which render it, in relation to the income concerned, a mere fiduciary or administrator acting on account of the interested parties.

12.2 Subject to other conditions imposed by the Article, the limitation of tax in the State of source remains available when an intermediary, such as an agent or nominee located in a Contracting State or in a third State, is interposed between the beneficiary and the payer but the beneficial owner is a resident of the other Contracting State (the text of the Model was amended in 1995 to clarify this point, which has been the consistent position of all member countries). States which wish to make this more explicit are free to do so during bilateral negotiations.

13. The tax rates fixed by the Article for the tax in the State of source are maximum rates. The States may agree, in bilateral negotiations, on lower rates or even on taxation exclusively in the State of the beneficiary's residence. The reduction of rates provided for in paragraph 2 refers solely to the taxation of dividends and not to the taxation of the profits of the company paying the dividends.

13.1 Under the domestic laws of many States, pension funds and similar entities are generally exempt from tax on their investment income. In order to achieve neutrality of treatment as regards domestic and foreign investments by these entities, some States provide bilaterally that income, including dividends, derived by such an entity resident of the other State shall be exempt from source taxation. States wishing to do so may agree bilaterally on a provision drafted along the lines of the provision found in paragraph 69 of the Commentary on Article 18.

13.2 Similarly, some States refrain from levying tax on dividends paid to other States and some of their wholly-owned entities, at least to the extent that such dividends are derived from activities of a governmental nature. Some States are able to grant such an exemption under their interpretation of the sovereign immunity principle (see paragraphs 6.38 and 6.39 of the Commentary on Article 1); others may do it pursuant to provisions of their domestic law. States wishing to do so may confirm or clarify, in their bilateral conventions, the scope of these exemptions or grant such an exemption in

---

1 Reproduced in Volume II of the full-length version of the OECD Model Tax Convention at page R(6)-1.

cases where it would not otherwise be available. This may be done by adding to the Article an additional paragraph drafted along the following lines:

Notwithstanding the provisions of paragraph 2, dividends referred to in paragraph 1 shall be taxable only in the Contracting State of which the recipient is a resident if the beneficial owner of the dividends is that State or a political subdivision or local authority thereof.

14.   The two Contracting States may also, during bilateral negotiations, agree to a holding percentage lower than that fixed in the Article. A lower percentage is, for instance, justified in cases where the State of residence of the parent company, in accordance with its domestic law, grants exemption to such a company for dividends derived from a holding of less than 25 per cent in a non-resident subsidiary.

15.   In subparagraph a) of paragraph 2, the term "capital" is used in relation to the taxation treatment of dividends, i.e. distributions of profits to shareholders. The use of this term in this context implies that, for the purposes of subparagraph a), it should be used in the sense in which it is used for the purposes of distribution to the shareholder (in the particular case, the parent company).

a) As a general rule, therefore, the term "capital" in subparagraph a) should be understood as it is understood in company law. Other elements, in particular the reserves, are not to be taken into account.

b) Capital, as understood in company law, should be indicated in terms of par value of all shares which in the majority of cases will be shown as capital in the company's balance sheet.

c) No account need be taken of differences due to the different classes of shares issued (ordinary shares, preference shares, plural voting shares, non-voting shares, bearer shares, registered shares, etc.), as such differences relate more to the nature of the shareholder's right than to the extent of his ownership of the capital.

d) When a loan or other contribution to the company does not, strictly speaking, come as capital under company law but when on the basis of internal law or practice ("thin capitalisation", or assimilation of a loan to share capital), the income derived in respect thereof is treated as dividend under Article 10, the value of such loan or contribution is also to be taken as "capital" within the meaning of subparagraph a).

e) In the case of bodies which do not have a capital within the meaning of company law, capital for the purpose of subparagraph a) is to be taken as meaning the total of all contributions to the body which are taken into account for the purpose of distributing profits.

In bilateral negotiations, Contracting States may depart from the criterion of "capital" used in subparagraph a) of paragraph 2 and use instead the criterion of "voting power".

16.   Subparagraph a) of paragraph 2 does not require that the company receiving the dividends must have owned at least 25 per cent of the capital for a relatively long time before the date of the distribution. This means that all that counts regarding the

holding is the situation prevailing at the time material for the coming into existence of the liability to the tax to which paragraph 2 applies, i.e. in most cases the situation existing at the time when the dividends become legally available to the shareholders. The primary reason for this resides in the desire to have a provision which is applicable as broadly as possible. To require the parent company to have possessed the minimum holding for a certain time before the distribution of the profits could involve extensive inquiries. Internal laws of certain OECD member countries provide for a minimum period during which the recipient company must have held the shares to qualify for exemption or relief in respect of dividends received. In view of this, Contracting States may include a similar condition in their conventions.

17.   The reduction envisaged in subparagraph a) of paragraph 2 should not be granted in cases of abuse of this provision, for example, where a company with a holding of less than 25 per cent has, shortly before the dividends become payable, increased its holding primarily for the purpose of securing the benefits of the above-mentioned provision, or otherwise, where the qualifying holding was arranged primarily in order to obtain the reduction. To counteract such manoeuvres Contracting States may find it appropriate to add to subparagraph a) a provision along the following lines:

>   provided that this holding was not acquired primarily for the purpose of taking advantage of this provision.

18.   Paragraph 2 lays down nothing about the mode of taxation in the State of source. It therefore leaves that State free to apply its own laws and, in particular, to levy the tax either by deduction at source or by individual assessment.

19.   The paragraph does not settle procedural questions. Each State should be able to use the procedure provided in its own laws. It can either forthwith limit its tax to the rates given in the Article or tax in full and make a refund (see, however, paragraph 26.2 of the Commentary on Article 1). Specific questions arise with triangular cases (see paragraph 71 of the Commentary on Article 24).

20.   It does not specify whether or not the relief in the State of source should be conditional upon the dividends being subject to tax in the State of residence. This question can be settled by bilateral negotiations.

21.   The Article contains no provisions as to how the State of the beneficiary's residence should make allowance for the taxation in the State of source of the dividends. This question is dealt with in Articles 23 A and 23 B.

22.   Attention is drawn generally to the following case: the beneficial owner of the dividends arising in a Contracting State is a company resident of the other Contracting State; all or part of its capital is held by shareholders resident outside that other State; its practice is not to distribute its profits in the form of dividends; and it enjoys preferential taxation treatment (private investment company, base company). The question may arise whether in the case of such a company it is justifiable to allow in the State of source of the dividends the limitation of tax which is provided in paragraph 2. It may be appropriate, when bilateral negotiations are being conducted, to

agree upon special exceptions to the taxing rule laid down in this Article, in order to define the treatment applicable to such companies.

Paragraph 3

23.　In view of the great differences between the laws of OECD member countries, it is impossible to define "dividends" fully and exhaustively. Consequently, the definition merely mentions examples which are to be found in the majority of the member countries' laws and which, in any case, are not treated differently in them. The enumeration is followed up by a general formula. In the course of the revision of the 1963 Draft Convention, a thorough study has been undertaken to find a solution that does not refer to domestic laws. This study has led to the conclusion that, in view of the still remaining dissimilarities between member countries in the field of company law and taxation law, it did not appear to be possible to work out a definition of the concept of dividends that would be independent of domestic laws. It is open to the Contracting States, through bilateral negotiations, to make allowance for peculiarities of their laws and to agree to bring under the definition of "dividends" other payments by companies falling under the Article.

24.　The notion of dividends basically concerns distributions by companies within the meaning of subparagraph b) of paragraph 1 of Article 3. Therefore the definition relates, in the first instance, to distributions of profits the title to which is constituted by shares, that is holdings in a company limited by shares (joint stock company). The definition assimilates to shares all securities issued by companies which carry a right to participate in the companies' profits without being debt-claims; such are, for example, "jouissance" shares or "jouissance" rights, founders' shares or other rights participating in profits. In bilateral conventions, of course, this enumeration may be adapted to the legal situation in the Contracting States concerned. This may be necessary in particular, as regards income from "jouissance" shares and founders' shares. On the other hand, debt-claims participating in profits do not come into this category (see paragraph 19 of the Commentary on Article 11); likewise interest on convertible debentures is not a dividend.

25.　Article 10 deals not only with dividends as such but also with interest on loans insofar as the lender effectively shares the risks run by the company, i.e. when repayment depends largely on the success or otherwise of the enterprise's business. Articles 10 and 11 do not therefore prevent the treatment of this type of interest as dividends under the national rules on thin capitalisation applied in the borrower's country. The question whether the contributor of the loan shares the risks run by the enterprise must be determined in each individual case in the light of all the circumstances, as for example the following:

— the loan very heavily outweighs any other contribution to the enterprise's capital (or was taken out to replace a substantial proportion of capital which has been lost) and is substantially unmatched by redeemable assets;

— the creditor will share in any profits of the company;

— repayment of the loan is subordinated to claims of other creditors or to the payment of dividends;

— the level or payment of interest would depend on the profits of the company;

— the loan contract contains no fixed provisions for repayment by a definite date.

26.   The laws of many of the States put participations in a *société à responsabilité limitée* (limited liability company) on the same footing as shares. Likewise, distributions of profits by co-operative societies are generally regarded as dividends.

27.   Distributions of profits by partnerships are not dividends within the meaning of the definition, unless the partnerships are subject, in the State where their place of effective management is situated, to a fiscal treatment substantially similar to that applied to companies limited by shares (for instance, in Belgium, Portugal and Spain, also in France as regards distributions to *commanditaires* in the *sociétés en commandite simple*). On the other hand, clarification in bilateral conventions may be necessary in cases where the taxation law of a Contracting State gives the owner of holdings in a company a right to opt, under certain conditions, for being taxed as a partner of a partnership, or, vice versa, gives the partner of a partnership the right to opt for taxation as the owner of holdings in a company.

28.   Payments regarded as dividends may include not only distributions of profits decided by annual general meetings of shareholders, but also other benefits in money or money's worth, such as bonus shares, bonuses, profits on a liquidation and disguised distributions of profits. The reliefs provided in the Article apply so long as the State of which the paying company is a resident taxes such benefits as dividends. It is immaterial whether any such benefits are paid out of current profits made by the company or are derived, for example, from reserves, *i.e.* profits of previous financial years. Normally, distributions by a company which have the effect of reducing the membership rights, for instance, payments constituting a reimbursement of capital in any form whatever, are not regarded as dividends.

29.   The benefits to which a holding in a company confer entitlement are, as a general rule, available solely to the shareholders themselves. Should, however, certain of such benefits be made available to persons who are not shareholders within the meaning of company law, they may constitute dividends if:

— the legal relations between such persons and the company are assimilated to a holding in a company ("concealed holdings"); and

— the persons receiving such benefits are closely connected with a shareholder; this is the case, for example, where the recipient is a relative of the shareholder or is a company belonging to the same group as the company owning the shares.

30.   When the shareholder and the person receiving such benefits are residents of two different States with which the State of source has concluded conventions, differences of views may arise as to which of these conventions is applicable. A similar problem may arise when the State of source has concluded a convention with one of the States but not with the other. This, however, is a conflict which may affect other

types of income, and the solution to it can be found only through an arrangement under the mutual agreement procedure.

Paragraph 4

31. Certain States consider that dividends, interest and royalties arising from sources in their territory and payable to individuals or legal persons who are residents of other States fall outside the scope of the arrangement made to prevent them from being taxed both in the State of source and in the State of the beneficiary's residence when the beneficiary has a permanent establishment in the former State. Paragraph 4 is not based on such a conception which is sometimes referred to as "the force of attraction of the permanent establishment". It does not stipulate that dividends flowing to a resident of a Contracting State from a source situated in the other State must, by a kind of legal presumption, or fiction even, be related to a permanent establishment which that resident may have in the latter State, so that the said State would not be obliged to limit its taxation in such a case. The paragraph merely provides that in the State of source the dividends are taxable as part of the profits of the permanent establishment there owned by the beneficiary which is a resident of the other State, if they are paid in respect of holdings forming part of the assets of the permanent establishment or otherwise effectively connected with that establishment. In that case, paragraph 4 relieves the State of source of the dividends from any limitations under the Article. The foregoing explanations accord with those in the Commentary on Article 7.

32. It has been suggested that the paragraph could give rise to abuses through the transfer of shares to permanent establishments set up solely for that purpose in countries that offer preferential treatment to dividend income. Apart from the fact that such abusive transactions might trigger the application of domestic anti-abuse rules, it must be recognised that a particular location can only constitute a permanent establishment if a business is carried on therein and, as explained below, that the requirement that a shareholding be "effectively connected" to such a location requires more than merely recording the shareholding in the books of the permanent establishment for accounting purposes.

32.1 A holding in respect of which dividends are paid will be effectively connected with a permanent establishment, and will therefore form part of its business assets, if the "economic" ownership of the holding is allocated to that permanent establishment under the principles developed in the Committee's report entitled *Attribution of Profits to Permanent Establishments*[1] (see in particular paragraphs 72-97 of Part I of the report) for the purposes of the application of paragraph 2 of Article 7. In the context of that paragraph, the "economic" ownership of a holding means the equivalent of ownership for income tax purposes by a separate enterprise, with the attendant benefits and burdens (*e.g.* the right to the dividends attributable to the ownership of the holding and

---

1 *Attribution of Profits to Permanent Establishments*, OECD, Paris, 2010.

the potential exposure to gains or losses from the appreciation or depreciation of the holding).

32.2 In the case of the permanent establishment of an enterprise carrying on insurance activities, the determination of whether a holding is effectively connected with the permanent establishment shall be made by giving due regard to the guidance set forth in Part IV of the Committee's report with respect to whether the income on or gain from that holding is taken into account in determining the permanent establishment's yield on the amount of investment assets attributed to it (see in particular paragraphs 165-170 of Part IV). That guidance being general in nature, tax authorities should consider applying a flexible and pragmatic approach which would take into account an enterprise's reasonable and consistent application of that guidance for purposes of identifying the specific assets that are effectively connected with the permanent establishment.

Paragraph 5

33. The Article deals only with dividends paid by a company which is a resident of a Contracting State to a resident of the other State. Certain States, however, tax not only dividends paid by companies resident therein but even distributions by non-resident companies of profits arising within their territory. Each State, of course, is entitled to tax profits arising in its territory which are made by non-resident companies, to the extent provided in the Convention (in particular in Article 7). The shareholders of such companies should not be taxed as well at any rate, unless they are residents of the State and so naturally subject to its fiscal sovereignty.

34. Paragraph 5 rules out the extra-territorial taxation of dividends, i.e. the practice by which States tax dividends distributed by a non-resident company solely because the corporate profits from which the distributions are made originated in their territory (for example, realised through a permanent establishment situated therein). There is, of course, no question of extra-territorial taxation when the country of source of the corporate profits taxes the dividends because they are paid to a shareholder who is a resident of that State or to a permanent establishment situated in that State.

35. Moreover, it can be argued that such a provision does not aim at, or cannot result in, preventing a State from subjecting the dividends to a withholding tax when distributed by foreign companies if they are cashed in its territory. Indeed, in such a case, the criterion for tax liability is the fact of the payment of the dividends, and not the origin of the corporate profits allotted for distribution. But if the person cashing the dividends in a Contracting State is a resident of the other Contracting State (of which the distributing company is a resident), he may under Article 21 obtain exemption from, or refund of, the withholding tax of the first-mentioned State. Similarly, if the beneficiary of the dividends is a resident of a third State which had concluded a double taxation convention with the State where the dividends are cashed, he may, under Article 21 of that convention, obtain exemption from, or refund of, the withholding tax of the last-mentioned State.

36.   Paragraph 5 further provides that non-resident companies are not to be subjected to special taxes on undistributed profits.

37.   It might be argued that where the taxpayer's country of residence, pursuant to its controlled foreign companies legislation or other rules with similar effect seeks to tax profits which have not been distributed, it is acting contrary to the provisions of paragraph 5. However, it should be noted that the paragraph is confined to taxation at source and, thus, has no bearing on the taxation at residence under such legislation or rules. In addition, the paragraph concerns only the taxation of the company and not that of the shareholder.

38.   The application of such legislation or rules may, however, complicate the application of Article 23. If the income were attributed to the taxpayer then each item of the income would have to be treated under the relevant provisions of the Convention (business profits, interest, royalties). If the amount is treated as a deemed dividend then it is clearly derived from the base company thus constituting income from that company's country. Even then, it is by no means clear whether the taxable amount is to be regarded as a dividend within the meaning of Article 10 or as "other income" within the meaning of Article 21. Under some of these legislation or rules the taxable amount is treated as a dividend with the result that an exemption provided for by a tax convention, e.g. an affiliation exemption, is also extended to it. It is doubtful whether the Convention requires this to be done. If the country of residence considers that this is not the case it may face the allegation that it is obstructing the normal operation of the affiliation exemption by taxing the dividend (in the form of "deemed dividend") in advance.

39.   Where dividends are actually distributed by the base company, the provisions of a bilateral convention regarding dividends have to be applied in the normal way because there is dividend income within the meaning of the convention. Thus, the country of the base company may subject the dividend to a withholding tax. The country of residence of the shareholder will apply the normal methods for the elimination of double taxation (i.e. tax credit or tax exemption is granted). This implies that the withholding tax on the dividend should be credited in the shareholder's country of residence, even if the distributed profit (the dividend) has been taxed years before under controlled foreign companies legislation or other rules with similar effect. However, the obligation to give credit in that case remains doubtful. Generally the dividend as such is exempted from tax (as it was already taxed under the relevant legislation or rules) and one might argue that there is no basis for a tax credit. On the other hand, the purpose of the treaty would be frustrated if the crediting of taxes could be avoided by simply anticipating the dividend taxation under counteracting legislation. The general principle set out above would suggest that the credit should be granted, though the details may depend on the technicalities of the relevant legislation or rules) and the system for crediting foreign taxes against domestic tax, as well as on the particularities of the case (e.g. time lapsed since the taxation of the "deemed dividend"). However, taxpayers who have recourse to artificial arrangements are taking risks against which they cannot fully be safeguarded by tax authorities.

III. Effects of special features of the domestic tax laws of certain countries

40.   Certain countries' laws seek to avoid or mitigate economic double taxation i.e. the simultaneous taxation of the company's profits at the level of the company and of the dividends at the level of the shareholder. There are various ways of achieving this:

— company tax in respect of distributed profits may be charged at a lower rate than that on retained profits;

— relief may be granted in computing the shareholder's personal tax;

— dividends may bear only one tax, the distributed profits not being taxed at the level of the company.

The Committee on Fiscal Affairs has examined the question whether the special features of the tax laws of the member countries would justify solutions other than those contained in the Model Convention.

A.   Dividends distributed to individuals

41.   In contrast to the notion of juridical double taxation, which has, generally, a quite precise meaning, the concept of economic double taxation is less certain. Some States do not accept the validity of this concept and others, more numerously, do not consider it necessary to relieve economic double taxation at the national level (dividends distributed by resident companies to resident shareholders). Consequently, as the concept of economic double taxation was not sufficiently well defined to serve as a basis for the analysis, it seemed appropriate to study the problem from a more general economic standpoint, i.e. from the point of view of the effects which the various systems for alleviating such double taxation can have on the international flow of capital. For this purpose, it was necessary to see, among other things, what distortions and discriminations the various national systems could create; but it was necessary to have regard also to the implications for States' budgets and for effective fiscal verification, without losing sight of the principle of reciprocity that underlies every convention. In considering all these aspects, it became apparent that the burden represented by company tax could not be wholly left out of account.

1.   States with the classical system

42.   The Committee has recognised that economic double taxation need not be relieved at the international level when such double taxation remains unrelieved at the national level. It therefore considers that in relations between two States with the classical system, i.e. States which do not relieve economic double taxation, the respective levels of company tax in the Contracting States should have no influence on the rate of withholding tax on the dividend in the State of source (rate limited to 15 per cent by subparagraph b) of paragraph 2 of Article 10). Consequently, the solution recommended in the Model Convention remains fully applicable in the present case.

2. States applying a split rate company tax

43. These States levy company tax at different rates according to what the company does with its profits: the high rate is charged on any profits retained and the lower rate on those distributed.

44. None of these States, in negotiating double taxation conventions, has obtained, on the grounds of its split rate of company tax, the right to levy with- holding tax of more than 15 per cent (see subparagraph b) of paragraph 2 of Article 10) on dividends paid by its companies to a shareholder who is an individual resident in the other State.

45. The Committee considered whether such a State (State B) should not be recognised as being entitled to levy withholding tax exceeding 15 per cent on dividends distributed by its companies to residents of a State with a classical system (State A), with the proviso that the excess over 15 per cent, which would be designed to offset, in relation to the shareholder concerned, the effects of the lower rate of company tax on distributed profits of companies of State B, would not be creditable against the tax payable by the shareholder in State A of which he is a resident.

46. Most member countries considered that in State B regard should be had to the average level of company tax, and that such average level should be considered as the counterpart to the charge levied in the form of a single-rate tax on companies resident of State A. The levy by State B of an additional withholding tax not credited in State A would, moreover, create twofold discrimination: on the one hand, dividends, distributed by a company resident of State B would be more heavily taxed when distributed to residents of State A than when distributed to residents of State B, and, on the other hand, the resident of State A would pay higher personal tax on his dividends from State B than on his dividends from State A. The idea of a "balancing tax" was not, therefore, adopted by the Committee.

3. States which provide relief at the shareholder's level

47. In these States, the company is taxed on its total profits, whether distributed or not, and the dividends are taxed in the hands of the resident shareholder (an individual); the latter, however, is entitled to relief, usually as a tax credit against his personal tax, on the grounds that — in the normal course at least — the dividend has borne company tax as part of the company's profits.

48. Internal law of these States does not provide for the extension of the tax relief to the international field. Relief is allowed only to residents and only in respect of dividends of domestic sources. However, as indicated below, some States have, in some conventions, extended the right to the tax credit provided for in their legislation to residents of the other Contracting State.

49. In many States that provide relief at the shareholder's level, the resident shareholder receives a credit in recognition of the fact that the profits out of which the dividends are paid have already been taxed in the hands of the company. The resident shareholder is taxed on his dividend grossed up by the tax credit; this credit is set off against the tax payable and can possibly give rise to a refund. In some double taxation

conventions, some countries that apply this system have agreed to extend the credit to shareholders who are residents of the other Contracting State. Whilst most States that have agreed to such extensions have done so on a reciprocal basis, a few countries have concluded conventions where they unilaterally extend the benefits of the credit to residents of the other Contracting State.

50.   Some States that also provide relief at the shareholder's level claim that under their systems the company tax remains in its entirety a true company tax, in that it is charged by reference solely to the company's own situation, without any regard to the person and the residence of the shareholder, and in that, having been so charged, it remains appropriated to the Treasury. The tax credit given to the shareholder is designed to relieve his personal tax liability and in no way constitutes an adjustment of the company's tax. No refund, therefore, is given if the tax credit exceeds that personal tax.

51.   The Committee could not reach a general agreement on whether the systems of the States referred to in paragraph 50 above display a fundamental difference that could justify different solutions at the international level.

52.   Some member countries were of the opinion that such a fundamental difference does not exist. This opinion leaves room for the conclusion that the States referred to in paragraph 50 above should agree to extend the tax credit to non-resident shareholders, at least on a reciprocal basis, in the same way as some of the countries referred to in paragraph 49 above do. Such a solution tends to ensure neutrality as regards dividends distributed by companies of these countries, the same treatment being given to resident and non-resident shareholders. On the other hand, it would in relation to shareholders who are residents of a Contracting State (a State with a classical system in particular) encourage investment in a State that provides relief at the shareholder's level since residents of the first State would receive a tax credit (in fact a refund of company tax) for dividends from the other State while they do not receive one for dividends from their own country. However, these effects are similar to those which present themselves between a State applying a split rate company tax and a State with a classical system or between two States with a classical system one of which has a lower company tax rate than the other (paragraphs 42 and 43 to 46 above).

53.   On the other hand, many member countries stressed the fact that a determination of the true nature of the tax relief given under the systems of the States referred to in paragraph 50 above reveals a mere alleviation of the shareholder's personal income tax in recognition of the fact that his dividend will normally have borne company tax. The tax credit is given once and for all (*forfaitaire*) and is therefore not in exact relation to the actual company tax appropriate to the profits out of which the dividend is paid. There is no refund if the tax credit exceeds the personal income tax.

54.   As the relief in essence is not a refund of company tax but an alleviation of the personal income tax, the extension of the relief to non-resident shareholders who are not subject to personal income tax in the countries concerned does not come into

consideration. On the other hand, however, on this line of reasoning, the question whether States which provide relief at the shareholder's level should give relief against personal income tax levied from resident shareholders on foreign dividends deserves attention. In this respect it should be observed that the answer is in the affirmative if the question is looked at from the standpoint of neutrality as regards the source of the dividends; otherwise, residents of these States will be encouraged to acquire shares in their own country rather than abroad. But such an extension of the tax credit would be contrary to the principle of reciprocity: not only would the State concerned thereby be making a unilateral budgetary sacrifice (allowing the tax credit over and above the withholding tax levied in the other State), but it would do so without receiving any economic compensation, since it would not be encouraging residents of the other State to acquire shares in its own territory.

55.   To overcome these objections, it might be a conceivable proposition, amongst other possibilities, that the State of source — which will have collected company tax on dividends distributed by resident companies — should bear the cost of the tax credit that a State which provides relief at the shareholder's level would allow, by transferring funds to that State. As, however, such transfers are hardly favoured by the States this might be more simply achieved by means of a "compositional" arrangement under which the State of source would relinquish all withholding tax on dividends paid to residents of the other State, and the latter would then allow against its own tax, not the 15 per cent withholding tax (abolished in the State of source) but a tax credit similar to that which it gives on dividends of domestic source.

56.   When everything is fully considered, it seems that the problem can be solved only in bilateral negotiations, where one is better placed to evaluate the sacrifices and advantages which the Convention must bring for each Contracting State.

57.   [Deleted]

58.   [Deleted]

B.   *Dividends distributed to companies*

59.   Comments above relating to dividends paid to individuals are generally applicable to dividends paid to companies which hold less than 25 per cent of the capital of the company paying the dividends. The treatment of dividends paid to collective investment vehicles raises particular issues which are addressed in paragraphs 6.8 to 6.34 of the Commentary on Article 1.

60.   In respect of dividends paid to companies which hold at least 25 per cent of the capital of the company paying the dividends, the Committee has examined the incidence which the particular company taxation systems quoted in paragraphs 42 and following have on the tax treatment of dividends paid by the subsidiary.

61.   Various opinions were expressed in the course of the discussion. Opinions diverge even when the discussion is limited to the taxation of subsidiaries and parent companies. They diverge still more if the discussion takes into account

more general economic considerations and extends to the taxation of shareholders of the parent company.

62.   In their bilateral conventions States have adopted different solutions, which were motivated by the economic objectives and the peculiarities of the legal situation of those States, by budgetary considerations, and by a whole series of other factors. Accordingly, no generally accepted principles have emerged. The Committee did nevertheless consider the situation for the more common systems of company taxation.

1.   Classical system in the State of the subsidiary
(paragraph 42 above)

63.   The provisions of the Convention have been drafted to apply when the State of which the distributing company is a resident has a so-called "classical" system of company taxation, namely one under which distributed profits are not entitled to any benefit at the level either of the company or of the shareholder (except for the purpose of avoiding recurrent taxation of inter-company dividends).

2.   Split-rate company tax system in the State of the subsidiary
(paragraph 43 to 46 above)

64.   States of this kind collect company tax on distributed profits at a lower rate than on retained profits which results in a lower company tax burden on profits distributed by a subsidiary to its parent company. In view of this situation, most of these States have obtained, in their conventions, rates of tax at source of 10 or 15 per cent, and in some cases even above 15 per cent. It has not been possible in the Committee to get views to converge on this question, the solution of which is left to bilateral negotiations.

3.   Imputation system in the State of the subsidiary
(paragraph 47 and following)

65.   In such States, a company is liable to tax on the whole of its profits, whether distributed or not; the shareholders resident of the State of which the distributing company is itself a resident are subject to tax on dividends distributed to them, but receive a tax credit in consideration of the fact that the profits distributed have been taxed at company level.

66.   The question has been considered whether States of this kind should extend the benefit of the tax credit to the shareholders of parent companies resident of another State, or even to grant the tax credit directly to such parent companies. It has not been possible in the Committee to get views to converge on this question, the solution of which is left to bilateral negotiations.

67.   If, in such a system, profits, whether distributed or not, are taxed at the same rate, the system is not different from a "classical" one at the level of the distributing

company. Consequently, the State of which the subsidiary is a resident can only levy a tax at source at the rate provided in subparagraph *a)* of paragraph 2.

IV. Distributions by Real Estate Investment Trusts

67.1 In many States, a large part of portfolio investment in immovable property is done through Real Estate Investment Trusts (REITs). A REIT may be loosely described as a widely held company, trust or contractual or fiduciary arrangement that derives its income primarily from long-term investment in immovable property, distributes most of that income annually and does not pay income tax on the income related to immovable property that is so distributed. The fact that the REIT vehicle does not pay tax on that income is the result of tax rules that provide for a single-level of taxation in the hands of the investors in the REIT.

67.2 The importance and the globalisation of investments in and through REITs have led the Committee on Fiscal Affairs to examine the tax treaty issues that arise from such investments. The results of that work appear in a report entitled "Tax Treaty Issues Related to REITS."[1]

67.3 One issue discussed in the report is the tax treaty treatment of cross-border distributions by a REIT. In the case of a small investor in a REIT, the investor has no control over the immovable property acquired by the REIT and no connection to that property. Notwithstanding the fact that the REIT itself will not pay tax on its distributed income, it may therefore be appropriate to consider that such an investor has not invested in immovable property but, rather, has simply invested in a company and should be treated as receiving a portfolio dividend. Such a treatment would also reflect the blended attributes of a REIT investment, which combines the attributes of both shares and bonds. In contrast, a larger investor in a REIT would have a more particular interest in the immovable property acquired by the REIT; for that investor, the investment in the REIT may be seen as a substitute for an investment in the underlying property of the REIT. In this situation, it would not seem appropriate to restrict the source taxation of the distribution from the REIT since the REIT itself will not pay tax on its income.

67.4 States that wish to achieve that result may agree bilaterally to replace paragraph 2 of the Article by the following:

2.   However, such dividends may also be taxed in the Contracting State of which the company paying the dividends is a resident and according to the laws of that State, but if the beneficial owner of the dividends is a resident of the other Contracting State (other than a beneficial owner of dividends paid by a company which is a REIT in which such person holds, directly or indirectly, capital that represents at least 10 per cent of the value of all the capital in that company), the tax so charged shall not exceed:

---

1   Reproduced in Volume II of the full-length version of the OECD Model Tax Convention at R(23)-1.

a) 5 per cent of the gross amount of the dividends if the beneficial owner is a company (other than a partnership) which holds directly at least 25 per cent of the capital of the company paying the dividends (other than a paying company that is a REIT);

b) 15 per cent of the gross amount of the dividends in all other cases.

According to this provision, a large investor in a REIT is an investor holding, directly or indirectly, capital that represents at least 10 per cent of the value of all the REIT's capital. States may, however, agree bilaterally to use a different threshold. Also, the provision applies to all distributions by a REIT; in the case of distributions of capital gains, however, the domestic law of some countries provides for a different threshold to differentiate between a large investor and a small investor entitled to taxation at the rate applicable to portfolio dividends and these countries may wish to amend the provision to preserve that distinction in their treaties. Finally, because it would be inappropriate to restrict the source taxation of a REIT distribution to a large investor, the drafting of subparagraph a) excludes dividends paid by a REIT from its application; thus, the subparagraph can never apply to such dividends, even if a company that did not hold capital representing 10 per cent or more of the value of the capital of a REIT held at least 25 per cent of its capital as computed in accordance with paragraph 15 above. The State of source will therefore be able to tax such distributions to large investors regardless of the restrictions in subparagraphs a) and b).

67.5   Where, however, the REITs established in one of the Contracting States do not qualify as companies that are residents of that Contracting State, the provision will need to be amended to ensure that it applies to distributions by such REITs.

67.6   For example, if the REIT is a company that does not qualify as a resident of the State, paragraphs 1 and 2 of the Article will need to be amended as follows to achieve that result:

1.   Dividends paid by a company which is a resident, or a REIT organised under the laws, of a Contracting State to a resident of the other Contracting State may be taxed in that other State.

2.   However, such dividends may also be taxed in, and according to the laws of, the Contracting State of which the company paying the dividends is a resident or, in the case of a REIT, under the laws of which it has been organised, but if the beneficial owner of the dividends is a resident of the other Contracting State (other than a beneficial owner of dividends paid by a company which is a REIT in which such person holds, directly or indirectly, capital that represents at least 10 per cent of the value of all the capital in that company), the tax so charged shall not exceed:

a) 5 per cent of the gross amount of the dividends if the beneficial owner is a company (other than a partnership) which holds directly at least 25 per cent of the capital of the company paying the dividends (other than a paying company that is a REIT);

b) 15 per cent of the gross amount of the dividends in all other cases.

67.7   Similarly, in order to achieve that result where the REIT is structured as a trust or as a contractual or fiduciary arrangement and does not qualify as a company, States may agree bilaterally to add to the alternative version of paragraph 2 set forth in paragraph 67.4 above an additional provision drafted along the following lines:

> For the purposes of this Convention, where a REIT organised under the laws of a Contracting State makes a distribution of income to a resident of the other Contracting State who is the beneficial owner of that distribution, the distribution of that income shall be treated as a dividend paid by a company resident of the first-mentioned State.

Under this additional provision, the relevant distribution would be treated as a dividend and not, therefore, as another type of income (e.g. income from immovable property or capital gain) for the purposes of applying Article 10 and the other Articles of the Convention. Clearly, however, that would not change the characterisation of that distribution for purposes of domestic law so that domestic law treatment would not be affected except for the purposes of applying the limitations imposed by the relevant provisions of the Convention.

Observations on the Commentary

68.   Canada and the United Kingdom do not adhere to paragraph 24 above. Under their law, certain interest payments are treated as distributions, and are therefore included in the definition of dividends.

68.1   Belgium cannot share the views expressed in paragraph 37 of the Commentary. Belgium considers that paragraph 5 of Article 10 is a particular application of a general principle underlying various provisions of the Convention (paragraph 7 of Article 5, paragraph 1 of Article 7, and paragraphs 1 and 5 of Article 10), which is the prohibition for a Contracting State, except in exceptional cases expressly provided for in the Convention, to levy a tax on the profits of a company which is a resident of the other Contracting State. Paragraph 5, which deals with taxation where the income has its source, confirms this general prohibition and provides that the prohibition applies even where the undistributed profits derived by the entity that is a resident of the other Contracting State arise from business carried out in the State of source. Paragraph 5 prohibits the taxation of the undistributed profits of the foreign entity even where the State where those profits arise taxes them in the hands of a resident shareholder. The fact that a Contracting State taxes one of its residents on profits that are beneficially owned by a resident of the other State cannot change the nature of the profits, their beneficiary and, therefore, the allocation of the taxing rights on these profits.

68.2   With reference to paragraph 37, Ireland notes its general observation in paragraph 27.5 of the Commentary on Article 1.

Reservations on the Article

Paragraph 2

69. [Deleted]

70. [Deleted]

71. [Deleted]

72. The *United States* reserves the right to provide that shareholders of certain pass-through entities, such as Regulated Investment Companies and Real Estate Investment Trusts, will not be granted the direct dividend investment rate, even if they would qualify based on their percentage ownership.

73. [Deleted]

74. In view of its particular taxation system, *Chile* retains its freedom of action with regard to the provisions in the Convention relating to the rate and form of distribution of profits by companies.

75. *Mexico*, *Portugal* and *Turkey* reserve their positions on the rates of tax in paragraph 2.

76. [Deleted]

77. *Poland* reserves its position on the minimum percentage for the holding (25 per cent) and the rates of tax (5 per cent and 15 per cent).

Paragraph 3

78. *Belgium* reserves the right to broaden the definition of dividends in paragraph 3 so as to cover expressly income — even when paid in the form of interest — which is subjected to the same taxation treatment as income from shares by its internal law.

79. *Denmark* reserves the right, in certain cases, to consider as dividends the selling price derived from the sale of shares.

80. *France* and *Mexico* reserve the right to amplify the definition of dividends in paragraph 3 so as to cover all income subjected to the taxation treatment of distributions.

81. *Canada* and *Germany* reserve the right to amplify the definition of dividends in paragraph 3 so as to cover certain interest payments which are treated as distributions under their domestic law.

81.1 *Portugal* reserves the right to amplify the definition of dividends in paragraph 3 so as to cover certain payments, made under profit participation arrangements, which are treated as distributions under its domestic law.

81.2 *Chile* and *Luxembourg* reserve the right to expand the definition of dividends in paragraph 3 in order to cover certain payments which are treated as distributions of dividends under their domestic law.

82. [Deleted]

Paragraph 5

83.   *Canada* and the *United States* reserve the right to impose their branch tax on the earnings of a company attributable to a permanent establishment situated in these countries. Canada also reserves the right to impose this tax on profits attributable to the alienation of immovable property situated in Canada by a company carrying on a trade in immovable property.

84.   [Deleted]

85.   *Turkey* reserves the right to tax, in a manner corresponding to that provided by paragraph 2 of the Article, the part of the profits of a company of the other Contracting State that carries on business through a permanent establishment situated in Turkey that remains after taxation pursuant to Article 7.

COMMENTARY ON ARTICLE 11
CONCERNING THE TAXATION OF INTEREST

I. Preliminary remarks

1. "Interest" is generally taken to mean remuneration on money lent, being remuneration coming within the category of "income from movable capital" (*revenus de capitaux mobiliers*). Unlike dividends, interest does not suffer economic double taxation, that is, it is not taxed both in the hands of the debtor and in the hands of the creditor. Unless it is provided to the contrary by the contract, payment of the tax charged on interest falls on the recipient. If it happens that the debtor undertakes to bear any tax chargeable at the source, this is as though he had agreed to pay his creditor additional interest corresponding to such tax.

2. But, like dividends, interest on bonds or debentures or loans usually attracts tax charged by deduction at the source when the interest is paid. This method is, in fact, commonly used for practical reasons, as the tax charged at the source can constitute an advance of the tax payable by the recipient in respect of his total income or profits. If in such a case the recipient is a resident of the country which practises deduction at the source, any double taxation he suffers is remedied by internal measures. But the position is different if he is a resident of another country: he is then liable to be taxed twice on the interest, first by the State of source and then by the State of which he is a resident. It is clear that his double charge of tax can reduce considerably the interest on the money lent and so hamper the movement of capital and the development of international investment.

3. A formula reserving the exclusive taxation of interest to one State, whether the State of the beneficiary's residence or the State of source, could not be sure of receiving general approval. Therefore a compromise solution was adopted. It provides that interest may be taxed in the State of residence, but leaves to the State of source the right to impose a tax if its laws so provide, it being implicit in this right that the State of source is free to give up all taxation on interest paid to non-residents. Its exercise of this right will however be limited by a ceiling which its tax cannot exceed but, it goes without saying, the Contracting States can agree to adopt an even lower rate of taxation in the State of source. The sacrifice that the latter would accept in such conditions will be matched by a relief to be given by the State of residence, in order to take into account the tax levied in the State of source (see Article 23 A or 23 B).

4. Certain countries do not allow interest paid to be deducted for the purposes of the payer's tax unless the recipient also resides in the same State or is taxable in that State. Otherwise they forbid the deduction. The question whether the deduction should also be allowed in cases where the interest is paid by a resident of a Contracting State to a resident of the other State, is dealt with in paragraph 4 of Article 24.

II. Commentary on the provisions of the Article

Paragraph 1

5.   Paragraph 1 lays down the principle that interest arising in a Contracting State and paid to a resident of the other Contracting State may be taxed in the latter. In doing so, it does not stipulate an exclusive right to tax in favour of the State of residence. The term "paid" has a very wide meaning, since the concept of payment means the fulfilment of the obligation to put funds at the disposal of the creditor in the manner required by contract or by custom.

6.   The Article deals only with interest arising in a Contracting State and paid to a resident of the other Contracting State. It does not, therefore, apply to interest arising in a third State or to interest arising in a Contracting State which is attributable to a permanent establishment which an enterprise of that State has in the other Contracting State (for these cases, see paragraphs 4 to 6 of the Commentary on Article 21).

Paragraph 2

7.   Paragraph 2 reserves a right to tax interest to the State in which the interest arises; but it limits the exercise of that right by determining a ceiling for the tax, which may not exceed 10 per cent. This rate may be considered a reasonable maximum bearing in mind that the State of source is already entitled to tax profits or income produced on its territory by investments financed out of borrowed capital. The Contracting States may agree in bilateral negotiations upon a lower tax or on exclusive taxation in the State of the beneficiary's residence with respect to all interest payments or, as explained below, as regards some specific categories of interest.

7.1   In certain cases, the approach adopted in paragraph 2, which is to allow source taxation of payments of interest, can constitute an obstacle to international trade or may be considered inappropriate for other reasons. For instance, when the beneficiary of the interest has borrowed in order to finance the operation which earns the interest, the profit realised by way of interest will be much smaller than the nominal amount of interest received; if the interest paid is equal to or exceeds the interest received, there will be either no profit at all or even a loss. The problem, in that case, cannot be solved by the State of residence, since little or no tax will be levied in that State where the beneficiary is taxed on the net profit derived from the transaction. That problem arises because the tax in the State of source is typically levied on the gross amount of the interest regardless of expenses incurred in order to earn such interest. In order to avoid that problem, creditors will, in practice, tend to shift to the debtor the burden of the tax levied by the State of source on the interest and therefore increase the rate of interest charged to the debtor, whose financial burden is then increased by an amount corresponding to the tax payable to the State of source.

7.2   The Contracting States may wish to add an additional paragraph to provide for the exclusive taxation in the State of the beneficiary's residence of certain interest. The preamble of that paragraph, which would be followed by subparagraphs describing the various interest subject to that treatment (see below), might be drafted along the following lines:

> 3.   Notwithstanding the provisions of paragraph 2, interest referred to in paragraph 1 shall be taxable only in the Contracting State of which the recipient is a resident if the beneficial owner of the interest is a resident of that State, and:
>
> > a) [description of the relevant category of interest] ...

7.3   The following are some of the categories of interest that Contracting States may wish to consider for the purposes of paragraph 7.2 above.

Interest paid to a State, its political subdivisions and to central banks

7.4   Some States refrain from levying tax on income derived by other States and some of their wholly-owned entities (e.g. a central bank established as a separate entity), at least to the extent that such income is derived from activities of a governmental nature. Some States are able to grant such an exemption under their interpretation of the sovereign immunity principle (see paragraphs 6.38 and 6.39 of the Commentary on Article 1); others may do it pursuant to provisions of their domestic law. In their bilateral conventions, many States wish to confirm or clarify the scope of these exemptions with respect to interest or to grant such an exemption in cases where it would not otherwise be available. States wishing to do so may therefore agree to include the following category of interest in a paragraph providing for exemption of certain interest from taxation in the State of source:

> a)   is that State or the central bank, a political subdivision or local authority thereof;

Interest paid by a State or its political subdivisions

7.5   Where the payer of the interest happens to be the State itself, a political subdivision or a statutory body, the end result may well be that the tax levied at source may actually be borne by that State if the lender increases the interest rate to recoup the tax levied at source. In that case, any benefits for the State taxing the interest at source will be offset by the increase of its borrowing costs. For that reason, many States provide that such interest will be exempt from any tax at source. States wishing to do so may agree to include the following category of interest in a paragraph providing for exemption of certain interest from taxation in the State of source:

> b)   if the interest is paid by the State in which the interest arises or by a political subdivision, a local authority or statutory body thereof;

In this suggested provision, the phrase "statutory body" refers to any public sector institution. Depending on their domestic law and terminology, some States may prefer to use phrases such as "agency or instrumentality" or "legal person of public law" [personne morale de droit public] to refer to such an institution.

Interest paid pursuant to export financing programmes

7.6   In order to promote international trade, many States have established export financing programmes or agencies which may either provide export loans directly or insure or guarantee export loans granted by commercial lenders. Since that type of financing is supported by public funds, a number of States provide bilaterally that interest arising from loans covered by these programmes shall be exempt from source taxation. States wishing to do so may agree to include the following category of interest in a paragraph providing for exemption of certain interest from taxation in the State of source:

c)   if the interest is paid in respect of a loan, debt-claim or credit that is owed to, or made, provided, guaranteed or insured by, that State or a political subdivision, local authority or export financing agency thereof;

Interest paid to financial institutions

7.7   The problem described in paragraph 7.1, which essentially arises because taxation by the State of source is typically levied on the gross amount of the interest and therefore ignores the real amount of income derived from the transaction for which the interest is paid, is particularly important in the case of financial institutions. For instance, a bank generally finances the loan which it grants with funds lent to it and, in particular, funds accepted on deposit. Since the State of source, in determining the amount of tax payable on the interest, will usually ignore the cost of funds for the bank, the amount of tax may prevent the transaction from occurring unless the amount of that tax is borne by the debtor. For that reason, many States provide that interest paid to a financial institution such as a bank will be exempt from any tax at source. States wishing to do so may agree to include the following interest in a paragraph providing from exemption of certain interest from taxation in the State of source:

d)   is a financial institution;

Interest on sales on credit

7.8   The disadvantages described in paragraph 7.1 also arise frequently in the case of sales on credit of equipment and other commercial credit sales. The supplier in such cases very often merely passes on to the customer, without any additional charge, the price he will himself have had to pay to a bank or an export finance agency to finance the credit. In these cases, the interest is more an element of the selling price than income from invested capital. In fact, in many cases, the interest incorporated in the amounts of instalments to be paid will be difficult to separate from the actual sale price. States may therefore wish to include interest arising from such sales on credit in a paragraph providing for exemption of certain interest from taxation in the State of source, which they can do by adding the following subparagraph:

e)   if the interest is paid with respect to indebtedness arising as a consequence of the sale on credit of any equipment, merchandise or services;

7.9   The types of sales on credit referred to in this suggested provision comprise not only sales of complete units, but also sales of separate components thereof. Sales financed through a general line of credit provided by a seller to a customer constitute sales on credit as well for the purposes of the provision. Also, it is immaterial whether the interest is stipulated separately in addition to the sale price or is included from the outset in the price payable by instalments.

Interest paid to some tax-exempt entities (e.g. pension funds)

7.10   Under the domestic laws of many States, pension funds and similar entities are generally exempt from tax on their investment income. In order to achieve neutrality of treatment as regards domestic and foreign investments by these entities, some States provide bilaterally that income, including interest, derived by such an entity resident of the other State shall also be exempt from source taxation. States wishing to do so may agree bilaterally on a provision drafted along the lines of the provision found in paragraph 69 of the Commentary on Article 18.

7.11   If the Contracting States do not wish to exempt completely any or all of the above categories of interest from taxation in the State of source, they may wish to apply to them a lower rate of tax than that provided for in paragraph 2 (that solution would not, however, seem very practical in the case of interest paid by a State or its political subdivision or statutory body). In that case, paragraph 2 might be drafted along the following lines:

2.   However, such interest may also be taxed in the Contracting State in which it arises and according to the laws of that State, but if the beneficial owner of the interest is a resident of the other Contracting State, the tax so charged shall not exceed:

a) *[lower rate of tax]* per cent of the gross amount of the interest in the case of interest paid *[description of the relevant category of interest]* ...

b) 10 per cent of the gross amount of the interest in all other cases.

The competent authorities of the Contracting States shall by mutual agreement settle the mode of application of this limitation.

If the Contracting States agree to exempt some of the above categories of interest, this alternative provision would be followed by a paragraph 3 as suggested in paragraph 7.2 above.

7.12   Contracting States may add to the categories of interest enumerated in the paragraphs above, other categories in regard to which the imposition of a tax in the State of source might appear to them to be undesirable.

8.   Attention is drawn generally to the following case: the beneficial owner of interest arising in a Contracting State is a company resident in the other Contracting State; all or part of its capital is held by shareholders resident outside that other State; its practice is not to distribute its profits in the form of dividends; and it enjoys preferential taxation treatment (private investment company, base company). The question may arise whether, in the case of such a company, it is justifiable to allow in

the State of source of the interest the limitation of tax which is provided in paragraph 2. It may be appropriate, when bilateral negotiations are being conducted, to agree upon special exceptions to the taxing rule laid down in this Article, in order to define the treatment applicable to such companies.

9.   The requirement of beneficial ownership was introduced in paragraph 2 of Article 11 to clarify the meaning of the words "paid to a resident" as they are used in paragraph 1 of the Article. It makes plain that the State of source is not obliged to give up taxing rights over interest income merely because that income was immediately received by a resident of a State with which the State of source had concluded a convention. The term "beneficial owner" is not used in a narrow technical sense, rather, it should be understood in its context and in light of the object and purposes of the Convention, including avoiding double taxation and the prevention of fiscal evasion and avoidance.

10.   Relief or exemption in respect of an item of income is granted by the State of source to a resident of the other Contracting State to avoid in whole or in part the double taxation that would otherwise arise from the concurrent taxation of that income by the State of residence. Where an item of income is received by a resident of a Contracting State acting in the capacity of agent or nominee it would be inconsistent with the object and purpose of the Convention for the State of source to grant relief or exemption merely on account of the status of the immediate recipient of the income as a resident of the other Contracting State. The immediate recipient of the income in this situation qualifies as a resident but no potential double taxation arises as a consequence of that status since the recipient is not treated as the owner of the income for tax purposes in the State of residence. It would be equally inconsistent with the object and purpose of the Convention for the State of source to grant relief or exemption where a resident of a Contracting State, otherwise than through an agency or nominee relationship, simply acts as a conduit for another person who in fact receives the benefit of the income concerned. For these reasons, the report from the Committee on Fiscal Affairs entitled "Double Taxation Conventions and the Use of Conduit Companies"[1] concludes that a conduit company cannot normally be regarded as the beneficial owner if, though the formal owner, it has, as a practical matter, very narrow powers which render it, in relation to the income concerned, a mere fiduciary or administrator acting on account of the interested parties.

11.   Subject to other conditions imposed by the Article, the limitation of tax in the State of source remains available when an intermediary, such as an agent or nominee located in a Contracting State or in a third State, is interposed between the beneficiary and the payer but the beneficial owner is a resident of the other Contracting State (the text of the Model was amended in 1995 to clarify this point, which has been the consistent position of all member countries). States which wish to make this more explicit are free to do so during bilateral negotiations.

---

1   Reproduced in Volume II of the full-length version of the OECD Model Tax Convention at page R(6)-1.

12.   The paragraph lays down nothing about the mode of taxation in the State of source. It therefore leaves that State free to apply its own laws and, in particular, to levy the tax either by deduction at source or by individual assessment. Procedural questions are not dealt with in this Article. Each State should be able to apply the procedure provided in its own law (see, however, paragraph 26.2 of the Commentary on Article 1). Specific questions arise with triangular cases (see paragraph 71 of the Commentary on Article 24).

13.   It does not specify whether or not the relief in the State of source should be conditional upon the interest being subject to tax in the State of residence. This question can be settled by bilateral negotiations.

14.   The Article contains no provisions as to how the State of the beneficiary's residence should make allowance for the taxation in the State of source of the interest. This question is dealt with in Articles 23 A and 23 B.

15.   [Deleted]

16.   [Renumbered]

17.   [Renumbered]

Paragraph 3

18.   Paragraph 3 specifies the meaning to be attached to the term "interest" for the application of the taxation treatment defined by the Article. The term designates, in general, income from debt-claims of every kind, whether or not secured by mortgage and whether or not carrying a right to participate in profits. The term "debt-claims of every kind" obviously embraces cash deposits and security in the form of money, as well as government securities, and bonds and debentures, although the three latter are specially mentioned because of their importance and of certain peculiarities that they may present. It is recognised, on the one hand, that mortgage interest comes within the category of income from movable capital (*revenus de capitaux mobiliers*), even though certain countries assimilate it to income from immovable property. On the other hand, debt-claims, and bonds and debentures in particular, which carry a right to participate in the debtor's profits are nonetheless regarded as loans if the contract by its general character clearly evidences a loan at interest.

19.   Interest on participating bonds should not normally be considered as a dividend, and neither should interest on convertible bonds until such time as the bonds are actually converted into shares. However, the interest on such bonds should be considered as a dividend if the loan effectively shares the risks run by the debtor company (see *inter alia* paragraph 25 of the Commentary on Article 10). In situations of presumed thin capitalisation, it is sometimes difficult to distinguish between dividends and interest and in order to avoid any possibility of overlap between the categories of income dealt with in Article 10 and Article 11 respectively, it should be noted that the term "interest" as used in Article 11 does not include items of income which are dealt with under Article 10.

MODEL TAX CONVENTION (CONDENSED VERSION) – ISBN 978-92-64-08948-8 – © OECD 2010

20.   As regards, more particularly, government securities, and bonds and debentures, the text specifies that premiums or prizes attaching thereto constitute interest. Generally speaking, what constitutes interest yielded by a loan security, and may properly be taxed as such in the State of source, is all that the institution issuing the loan pays over and above the amount paid by the subscriber, that is to say, the interest accruing plus any premium paid at redemption or at issue. It follows that when a bond or debenture has been issued at a premium, the excess of the amount paid by the subscriber over that repaid to him may constitute negative interest which should be deducted from the interest that is taxable. On the other hand, any profit or loss which a holder of such a security realises by the sale thereof to another person does not enter into the concept of interest. Such profit or loss may, depending on the case, constitute either a business profit or a loss, a capital gain or a loss, or income falling under Article 21.

21.   Moreover, the definition of interest in the first sentence of paragraph 3 is, in principle, exhaustive. It has seemed preferable not to include a subsidiary reference to domestic laws in the text; this is justified by the following considerations:

   a) the definition covers practically all the kinds of income which are regarded as interest in the various domestic laws;

   b) the formula employed offers greater security from the legal point of view and ensures that conventions would be unaffected by future changes in any country's domestic laws;

   c) in the Model Convention references to domestic laws should as far as possible be avoided.

It nevertheless remains understood that in a bilateral convention two Contracting States may widen the formula employed so as to include in it any income which is taxed as interest under either of their domestic laws but which is not covered by the definition and in these circumstances may find it preferable to make reference to their domestic laws.

21.1   The definition of interest in the first sentence of paragraph 3 does not normally apply to payments made under certain kinds of nontraditional financial instruments where there is no underlying debt (for example, interest rate swaps). However, the definition will apply to the extent that a loan is considered to exist under a "substance over form" rule, an "abuse of rights" principle, or any similar doctrine.

22.   The second sentence of paragraph 3 excludes from the definition of interest penalty charges for late payment but Contracting States are free to omit this sentence and treat penalty charges as interest in their bilateral conventions. Penalty charges, which may be payable under the contract, or by customs or by virtue of a judgement, consist either of payments calculated *pro rata temporis* or else of fixed sums; in certain cases they may combine both forms of payment. Even if they are determined *pro rata temporis* they constitute not so much income from capital as a special form of compensation for the loss suffered by the creditor through the debtor's delay in meeting his obligations. Moreover, considerations of legal security and practical

convenience make it advisable to place all penalty charges of this kind, in whatever form they be paid, on the same footing for the purposes of their taxation treatment. On the other hand, two Contracting States may exclude from the application of Article 11 any kinds of interest which they intend to be treated as dividends.

23. Finally, the question arises whether annuities ought to be assimilated to interest; it is considered that they ought not to be. On the one hand, annuities granted in consideration of past employment are referred to in Article 18 and are subject to the rules governing pensions. On the other hand, although it is true that instalments of purchased annuities include an interest element on the purchase capital as well as return of capital, such instalments thus constituting *"fruits civils"* which accrue from day to day, it would be difficult for many countries to make a distinction between the element representing income from capital and the element representing a return of capital in order merely to tax the income element under the same category as income from movable capital. Taxation laws often contain special provisions classifying annuities in the category of salaries, wages and pensions, and taxing them accordingly.

Paragraph 4

24. Certain States consider that dividends, interest and royalties arising from sources in their territory and payable to individuals or legal persons who are residents of other States fall outside the scope of the arrangement made to prevent them from being taxed both in the State of source and in the State of the beneficiary's residence when the beneficiary has a permanent establishment in the former State. Paragraph 4 is not based on such a conception which is sometimes referred to as "the force of attraction of the permanent establishment". It does not stipulate that interest arising to a resident of a Contracting State from a source situated in the other State must, by a kind of legal presumption, or fiction even, be related to a permanent establishment which that resident may have in the latter State, so that the said State would not be obliged to limit its taxation in such a case. The paragraph merely provides that in the State of source the interest is taxable as part of the profits of the permanent establishment there owned by the beneficiary which is a resident in the other State, if it is paid in respect of debt-claims forming part of the assets of the permanent establishment or otherwise effectively connected with that establishment. In that case, paragraph 4 relieves the State of source of the interest from any limitation under the Article. The foregoing explanations accord with those in the Commentary on Article 7.

25. It has been suggested that the paragraph could give rise to abuses through the transfer of loans to permanent establishments set up solely for that purpose in countries that offer preferential treatment to interest income. Apart from the fact that such abusive transactions might trigger the application of domestic anti-abuse rules, it must be recognised that a particular location can only constitute a permanent establishment if a business is carried on therein and, as explained below, that the requirement that a debt-claim be "effectively connected" to such a location requires

more than merely recording the debt-claim in the books of the permanent establishment for accounting purposes.

25.1 A debt-claim in respect of which interest is paid will be effectively connected with a permanent establishment, and will therefore form part of its business assets, if the "economic" ownership of the debt-claim is allocated to that permanent establishment under the principles developed in the Committee's report entitled *Attribution of Profits to Permanent Establishments*[1] (see in particular paragraphs 72-97 of Part I of the report) for the purposes of the application of paragraph 2 of Article 7. In the context of that paragraph, the "economic" ownership of a debt-claim means the equivalent of ownership for income tax purposes by a separate enterprise, with the attendant benefits and burdens (*e.g.* the right to the interest attributable to the ownership of the debt-claim and the potential exposure to gains or losses from the appreciation or depreciation of the debt-claim).

25.2 In the case of the permanent establishment of an enterprise carrying on insurance activities, the determination of whether a debt-claim is effectively connected with the permanent establishment shall be made by giving due regard to the guidance set forth in Part IV of the Committee's report with respect to whether the income on or gain from that debt-claim is taken into account in determining the permanent establishment's yield on the amount of investment assets attributed to it (see in particular paragraphs 165-170 of Part IV). That guidance being general in nature, tax authorities should consider applying a flexible and pragmatic approach which would take into account an enterprise's reasonable and consistent application of that guidance for purposes of identifying the specific assets that are effectively connected with the permanent establishment.

Paragraph 5

26.   This paragraph lays down the principle that the State of source of the interest is the State of which the payer of the interest is a resident. It provides, however, for an exception to this rule in the case of interest-bearing loans which have an obvious economic link with a permanent establishment owned in the other Contracting State by the payer of the interest. If the loan was contracted for the requirements of that establishment and the interest is borne by the latter, the paragraph determines that the source of the interest is in the Contracting State in which the permanent establishment is situated, leaving aside the place of residence of the owner of the permanent establishment, even when he resides in a third State.

27.   In the absence of an economic link between the loan on which the interest arises and the permanent establishment, the State where the latter is situated cannot on that account be regarded as the State where the interest arises; it is not entitled to tax such interest, not even within the limits of a "taxable quota" proportional to the importance of the permanent establishment. Such a practice would be incompatible with paragraph 5. Moreover, any departure from the rule fixed in the first sentence of

---

1   *Attribution of Profits to Permanent Establishments*, OECD, Paris, 2010

paragraph 5 is justified only where the economic link between the loan and the permanent establishment is sufficiently clear-cut. In this connection, a number of possible cases may be distinguished:

a) The management of the permanent establishment has contracted a loan which it uses for the specific requirements of the permanent establishment; it shows it among its liabilities and pays the interest thereon directly to the creditor.

b) The head office of the enterprise has contracted a loan the proceeds of which are used solely for the purposes of a permanent establishment situated in another country. The interest is serviced by the head office but is ultimately borne by the permanent establishment.

c) The loan is contracted by the head office of the enterprise and its proceeds are used for several permanent establishments situated in different countries.

In cases a) and b) the conditions laid down in the second sentence of paragraph 5 are fulfilled, and the State where the permanent establishment is situated is to be regarded as the State where the interest arises. Case c), however, falls outside the provisions of paragraph 5, the text of which precludes the attribution of more than one source to the same loan. Such a solution, moreover, would give rise to considerable administrative complications and make it impossible for lenders to calculate in advance the taxation that interest would attract. It is, however, open to two Contracting States to restrict the application of the final provision in paragraph 5 to case a) or to extend it to case c).

28.   Paragraph 5 provides no solution for the case, which it excludes from its provisions, where both the beneficiary and the payer are indeed residents of the Contracting States, but the loan was borrowed for the requirements of a permanent establishment owned by the payer in a third State and the interest is borne by that establishment. As paragraph 5 now stands, therefore, only its first sentence will apply in such a case. The interest will be deemed to arise in the Contracting State of which the payer is a resident and not in the third State in whose territory is situated the permanent establishment for the account of which the loan was effected and by which the interest is payable. Thus the interest will be taxed both in the Contracting State of which the payer is a resident and in the Contracting State of which the beneficiary is a resident. But, although double taxation will be avoided between these two States by the arrangements provided in the Article, it will not be avoided between them and the third State if the latter taxes the interest on the loan at the source when it is borne by the permanent establishment in its territory.

29.   It has been decided not to deal with that case in the Convention. The Contracting State of the payer's residence does not, therefore, have to relinquish its tax at the source in favour of the third State in which is situated the permanent establishment for the account of which the loan was effected and by which the interest is borne. If this were not the case and the third State did not subject the interest borne by the permanent establishment to source taxation, there could be attempts to avoid source taxation in the Contracting State through the use of a permanent establishment situated in such a third State. States for which this is not a concern and that wish to address the issue described in the paragraph above may do so by agreeing to use, in

their bilateral convention, the alternative formulation of paragraph 5 suggested in paragraph 30 below. The risk of double taxation just referred to could also be avoided through a multilateral convention. Also, if in the case described in paragraph 28, the State of the payer's residence and the third State in which is situated the permanent establishment for the account of which the loan is effected and by which the interest is borne, together claim the right to tax the interest at the source, there would be nothing to prevent those two States together with, where appropriate, the State of the beneficiary's residence, from concerting measures to avoid the double taxation that would result from such claims using, where necessary, the mutual agreement procedure (as envisaged in paragraph 3 of Article 25).

30.   As mentioned in paragraph 29, any such double taxation could be avoided either through a multilateral convention or if the State of the beneficiary's residence and the State of the payer's residence agreed to word the second sentence of paragraph 5 in the following way, which would have the effect of ensuring that paragraphs 1 and 2 of the Article did not apply to the interest, which would then typically fall under Article 7 or 21:

> Where, however, the person paying the interest, whether he is a resident of a Contracting State or not, has in a State other than that of which he is a resident a permanent establishment in connection with which the indebtedness on which the interest is paid was incurred, and such interest is borne by such permanent establishment, then such interest shall be deemed to arise in the State in which the permanent establishment is situated.

31.   If two Contracting States agree in bilateral negotiations to reserve to the State where the beneficiary of the income resides the exclusive right to tax such income, then ipso facto there is no value in inserting in the convention which fixes their relations that provision in paragraph 5 which defines the State of source of such income. But it is equally obvious that double taxation would not be fully avoided in such a case if the payer of the interest owned, in a third State which charged its tax at the source on the interest, a permanent establishment for the account of which the loan had been borrowed and which bore the interest payable on it. The case would then be just the same as is contemplated in paragraphs 28 to 30 above.

Paragraph 6

32.   The purpose of this paragraph is to restrict the operation of the provisions concerning the taxation of interest in cases where, by reason of a special relationship between the payer and the beneficial owner or between both of them and some other person, the amount of the interest paid exceeds the amount which would have been agreed upon by the payer and the beneficial owner had they stipulated at arm's length. It provides that in such a case the provisions of the Article apply only to that last-mentioned amount and that the excess part of the interest shall remain taxable according to the laws of the two Contracting States, due regard being had to the other provisions of the Convention.

33.   It is clear from the text that for this clause to apply the interest held excessive must be due to a special relationship between the payer and the beneficial owner or between both of them and some other person. There may be cited as examples cases where interest is paid to an individual or legal person who directly or indirectly controls the payer, or who is directly or indirectly controlled by him or is subordinate to a group having common interest with him. These examples, moreover, are similar or analogous to the cases contemplated by Article 9.

34.   On the other hand, the concept of special relationship also covers relationship by blood or marriage and, in general, any community of interests as distinct from the legal relationship giving rise to the payment of the interest.

35.   With regard to the taxation treatment to be applied to the excess part of the interest, the exact nature of such excess will need to be ascertained according to the circumstances of each case, in order to determine the category of income in which it should be classified for the purposes of applying the provisions of the tax laws of the States concerned and the provisions of the Convention. This paragraph permits only the adjustment of the rate at which interest is charged and not the reclassification of the loan in such a way as to give it the character of a contribution to equity capital. For such an adjustment to be possible under paragraph 6 of Article 11 it would be necessary as a minimum to remove the limiting phrase "having regard to the debt-claim for which it is paid". If greater clarity of intent is felt appropriate, a phrase such as "for whatever reason" might be added after "exceeds". Either of these alternative versions would apply where some or all of an interest payment is excessive because the amount of the loan or the terms relating to it (including the rate of interest) are not what would have been agreed upon in the absence of the special relationship. Nevertheless, this paragraph can affect not only the recipient but also the payer of excessive interest and if the law of the State of source permits, the excess amount can be disallowed as a deduction, due regard being had to other applicable provisions of the Convention. If two Contracting States should have difficulty in determining the other provisions of the Convention applicable, as cases require, to the excess part of the interest, there would be nothing to prevent them from introducing additional clarifications in the last sentence of paragraph 6, as long as they do not alter its general purport.

36.   Should the principles and rules of their respective laws oblige the two Contracting States to apply different Articles of the Convention for the purpose of taxing the excess, it will be necessary to resort to the mutual agreement procedure provided by the Convention in order to resolve the difficulty.

Observation on the Commentary

37.   *Canada* and the *United Kingdom* do not adhere to paragraph 18 above. Under their domestic legislation, certain interest payments are treated as distributions, and are therefore dealt with under Article 10.

MODEL TAX CONVENTION (CONDENSED VERSION) – ISBN 978-92-64-08948-8 – © OECD 2010

Reservations on the Article

Paragraph 2

38.   *Chile, Hungary, Mexico, Portugal,* the *Slovak Republic* and *Turkey* reserve their positions on the rate provided in paragraph 2.

39.   [Deleted]

40.   The *United States* reserves the right to tax certain forms of contingent interest at the rate applicable to portfolio dividends under subparagraph *b)* of paragraph 2 of Article 10. It also reserves the right to tax under its law a form of interest that is "an excess inclusion with respect to residual interest in a real estate mortgage investment conduit".

Paragraph 3

41.   *Mexico* reserves the right to consider as interest other types of income, such as income derived from financial leasing and factoring contracts.

42.   *Belgium, Canada* and *Ireland* reserve the right to amend the definition of interest so as to secure that interest payments treated as distributions under their domestic law fall within Article 10.

43.   *Canada, Chile* and *Norway* reserve the right to delete the reference to debt-claims carrying the right to participate in the debtor's profits.

44.   *Greece, Portugal* and *Spain* reserve the right to widen the definition of interest by including a reference to their domestic law in line with the definition contained in the 1963 Draft Convention.

45.   [Deleted]

Paragraph 6

46.   *Mexico* reserves the right to include a provision regarding the treatment of interest derived from back-to-back loans, as a safeguard against abuse.

COMMENTARY ON ARTICLE 12
CONCERNING THE TAXATION OF ROYALTIES

I.   Preliminary remarks

1.   In principle, royalties in respect of licences to use patents and similar property and similar payments are income to the recipient from a letting. The letting may be granted in connection with an enterprise (*e.g.* the use of literary copyright granted by a publisher or the use of a patent granted by the inventor) or quite independently of any activity of the grantor (*e.g.* use of a patent granted by the inventor's heirs).

2.   Certain countries do not allow royalties paid to be deducted for the purposes of the payer's tax unless the recipient also resides in the same State or is taxable in that State. Otherwise they forbid the deduction. The question whether the deduction should also be allowed in cases where the royalties are paid by a resident of a Contracting State to a resident of the other State, is dealt with in paragraph 4 of Article 24.

II.   Commentary on the provisions of the Article

Paragraph 1

3.   Paragraph 1 lays down the principle of exclusive taxation of royalties in the State of the beneficial owner's residence. The only exception to this principle is that made in the cases dealt with in paragraph 3.

4.   The requirement of beneficial ownership was introduced in paragraph 1 of Article 12 to clarify how the Article applies in relation to payments made to intermediaries. It makes plain that the State of source is not obliged to give up taxing rights over royalty income merely because that income was immediately received by a resident of a State with which the State of source had concluded a convention. The term "beneficial owner" is not used in a narrow technical sense, rather, it should be understood in its context and in light of the object and purposes of the Convention, including avoiding double taxation and the prevention of fiscal evasion and avoidance.

4.1   Relief or exemption in respect of an item of income is granted by the State of source to a resident of the other Contracting State to avoid in whole or in part the double taxation that would otherwise arise from the concurrent taxation of that income by the State of residence. Where an item of income is received by a resident of a Contracting State acting in the capacity of agent or nominee it would be inconsistent with the object and purpose of the Convention for the State of source to grant relief or exemption merely on account of the status of the immediate recipient of the income as a resident of the other Contracting State. The immediate recipient of the income in this situation qualifies as a resident but no potential double taxation arises as a consequence of that status since the recipient is not treated as the owner of the income for tax purposes in the State of residence. It would be equally inconsistent with the object and purpose of the Convention for the State of source to grant relief or exemption where a resident of a Contracting State, otherwise than through an agency or nominee relationship, simply acts as a conduit for another person who in fact receives the benefit of the income concerned. For these reasons, the report from the Committee on Fiscal Affairs entitled "Double Taxation Conventions and the Use of Conduit Companies"[1] concludes that a conduit company cannot normally be regarded as the beneficial owner if, though the formal owner, it has, as a practical matter, very narrow powers which render it, in relation to the income concerned, a mere fiduciary or administrator acting on account of the interested parties.

4.2   Subject to other conditions imposed by the Article, the limitation of tax in the State of source remains available when an intermediary, such as an agent or nominee, is interposed between the beneficiary and the payer, in those cases where the beneficial owner is a resident of the other Contracting State (the text of the Model was amended in 1995 to clarify this point, which has been the consistent position of all member countries). States which wish to make this more explicit are free to do so during bilateral negotiations.

5.   The Article deals only with royalties arising in a Contracting State and beneficially owned by a resident of the other Contracting State. It does not, therefore, apply to royalties arising in a third State as well as to royalties arising in a Contracting State which are attributable to a permanent establishment which an enterprise of that State has in the other Contracting State (for these cases see paragraphs 4 to 6 of the Commentary on Article 21). Procedural questions are not dealt with in this Article. Each State should be able to apply the procedure provided in its own law. Specific questions arise with triangular cases (see paragraph 71 of the Commentary on Article 24).

6.   The paragraph does not specify whether or not the exemption in the State of source should be conditional upon the royalties being subject to tax in the State of residence. This question can be settled by bilateral negotiations.

7.   Attention is drawn generally to the following case: the beneficial owner of royalties arising in a Contracting State is a company resident in the other Contracting State; all or part of its capital is held by shareholders resident outside that other State; its practice is not to distribute its profits in the form of dividends; and it enjoys preferential taxation treatment (private investment company, base company). The question may arise whether in the case of such a company it is justifiable to allow in the State of source of the royalties the tax exemption which is provided in paragraph 1. It may be appropriate, when bilateral negotiations are being conducted, to agree upon special exceptions to the taxing rule laid down in this Article, in order to define the treatment applicable to such companies.

---

1   Reproduced in Volume II of the full-length version of the OECD Model Tax Convention at page R(6)-1.

Paragraph 2

8.   Paragraph 2 contains a definition of the term "royalties". These relate, in general, to rights or property constituting the different forms of literary and artistic property, the elements of intellectual property specified in the text and information concerning industrial, commercial or scientific experience. The definition applies to payments for the use of, or the entitlement to use, rights of the kind mentioned, whether or not they have been, or are required to be, registered in a public register. The definition covers both payments made under a license and compensation which a person would be obliged to pay for fraudulently copying or infringing the right.

8.1   The definition does not, however, apply to payments that, whilst based on the number of times a right belonging to someone is used, are made to someone else who does not himself own the right or the right to use it (see, for instance, paragraph 18 below).

8.2   Where a payment is in consideration for the transfer of the full ownership of an element of property referred to in the definition, the payment is not in consideration "for the use of, or the right to use" that property and cannot therefore represent a royalty. As noted in paragraphs 15 and 16 below as regards software, difficulties can arise in the case of a transfer of rights that could be considered to form part of an element of property referred to in the definition where these rights are transferred in a way that is presented as an alienation. For example, this could involve the exclusive granting of all rights to an intellectual property for a limited period or all rights to the property in a limited geographical area in a transaction structured as a sale. Each case will depend on its particular facts and will need to be examined in the light of the national intellectual property law applicable to the relevant type of property and the national law rules as regards what constitutes an alienation but in general, if the payment is in consideration for the alienation of rights that constitute distinct and specific property (which is more likely in the case of geographically-limited than time limited rights), such payments are likely to be business profits within Article 7 or a capital gain within Article 13 rather than royalties within Article 12. That follows from the fact that where the ownership of rights has been alienated, the consideration cannot be for the use of the rights. The essential character of the transaction as an alienation cannot be altered by the form of the consideration, the payment of the consideration in instalments or, in the view of most countries, by the fact that the payments are related to a contingency.

8.3   The word "payment", used in the definition, has a very wide meaning since the concept of payment means the fulfilment of the obligation to put funds at the disposal of the creditor in the manner required by contract or by custom.

8.4   As a guide, certain explanations are given below in order to define the scope of Article 12 in relation to that of other Articles of the Convention, as regards, in particular, the provision of information.

8.5   Where information referred to in paragraph 2 is supplied or where the use or the right to use a type of property referred to in that paragraph is granted, the person who owns that information or property may agree not to supply or grant to anyone else that information or right. Payments made as consideration for such an agreement constitute payments made to secure the exclusivity of that information or an exclusive right to use that property, as the case may be. These payments being payments "of any kind received as a consideration for … the right to use" the property "or for information", fall under the definition of royalties.

9.   Whilst the definition of the term "royalties" in the 1963 Draft Convention and the 1977 Model Convention included payments "for the use of, or the right to use, industrial, commercial or scientific equipment", the reference to these payments was subsequently deleted from the definition. Given the nature of income from the leasing of industrial, commercial or scientific equipment, including the leasing of containers, the Committee on Fiscal Affairs decided to exclude income from such leasing from the definition of royalties and, consequently, to remove it from the application of Article 12 in order to make sure that it would fall under the rules for the taxation of business profits, as defined in Articles 5 and 7.

9.1   Satellite operators and their customers (including broadcasting and telecommunication enterprises) frequently enter into "transponder leasing" agreements under which the satellite operator allows the customer to utilise the capacity of a satellite transponder to transmit over large geographical areas. Payments made by customers under typical "transponder leasing" agreements are made for the use of the transponder transmitting capacity and will not constitute royalties under the definition of paragraph 2: these payments are not made in consideration for the use of, or right to use, property, or for information, that is referred to in the definition (they cannot be viewed, for instance, as payments for information or for the use of, or right to use, a secret process since the satellite technology is not transferred to the customer). As regards treaties that include the leasing of industrial, commercial or scientific (ICS) equipment in the definition of royalties, the characterisation of the payment will depend to a large extent on the relevant contractual arrangements. Whilst the relevant contracts often refer to the "lease" of a transponder, in most cases the customer does not acquire the physical possession of the transponder but simply its transmission capacity: the satellite is operated by the lessor and the lessee has no access to the transponder that has been assigned to it. In such cases, the payments made by the customers would therefore be in the nature of payments for services, to which Article 7 applies, rather than payments for the use, or right to use, ICS equipment. A different, but much less frequent, transaction would be where the owner of the satellite leases it to another party so that the latter may operate it and either use it for its own purposes or offer its data transmission capacity to third parties. In such a case, the payment made by the satellite operator to the satellite owner could well be considered as a payment for the leasing of industrial, commercial or scientific equipment. Similar considerations apply to payments made to lease or purchase the capacity of cables for the transmission of electrical power or communications (*e.g.* through a contract granting an indefeasible right of use of such capacity) or pipelines (*e.g.* for the transportation of gas or oil).

9.2   Also, payments made by a telecommunications network operator to another network operator under a typical "roaming" agreement (see paragraph 9.1 of the Commentary on Article 5) will not constitute royalties under the definition of paragraph 2 since these payments are not made in consideration for the use of, or right to use, property, or for information, referred to in the definition (they cannot be viewed, for instance, as payments for the use of, or right to use, a secret process since no secret technology is used or transferred to the operator). This conclusion holds true even in the case of treaties that include the leasing of industrial, commercial or scientific (ICS) equipment in the definition of royalties since the operator that pays a charge under a roaming agreement is not paying for the use, or the right to use, the visited network, to which it does not have physical access, but rather for the telecommunications services provided by the foreign network operator.

9.3   Payments for the use of, or the right to use, some or all of part of the radio frequency spectrum (e.g. pursuant to a so-called "spectrum license" that allows the holder to transmit media content over designated frequency ranges of the electromagnetic spectrum) do not constitute payments for the use of, or the right to use, property, or for information, that is referred in the definition of royalties in paragraph 2. This conclusion holds true even in the case of treaties that include the leasing of industrial, commercial or scientific (ICS) equipment in the definition of royalties since the payment is not for the use, or the right to use, any equipment.

10.   Rents in respect of cinematograph films are also treated as royalties, whether such films are exhibited in cinemas or on the television. It may, however, be agreed through bilateral negotiations that rents in respect of cinematograph films shall be treated as business profits and, in consequence, subjected to the provisions of Articles 7 and 9.

10.1   Payments that are solely made in consideration for obtaining the exclusive distribution rights of a product or service in a given territory do not constitute royalties as they are not made in consideration for the use of, or the right to use, an element of property included in the definition. These payments, which are best viewed as being made to increase sales receipts, would rather fall under Article 7. An example of such a payment would be that of a distributor of clothes resident in one Contracting State who pays a certain sum of money to a manufacturer of branded shirts, who is a resident of the other Contracting State, as consideration for the exclusive right to sell in the first State the branded shirts manufactured abroad by that manufacturer. In that example, the resident distributor does not pay for the right to use the trade name or trade mark under which the shirts are sold; he merely obtains the exclusive right to sell in his State of residence shirts that he will buy from the manufacturer.

10.2   A payment cannot be said to be "for the use of, or the right to use" a design, model or plan if the payment is for the development of a design, model or plan that does not already exist. In such a case, the payment is made in consideration for the services that will result in the development of that design, model or plan and would thus fall under Article 7. This will be the case even if the designer of the design, model or plan (e.g. an architect) retains all rights, including the copyright, in that design,

MODEL TAX CONVENTION (CONDENSED VERSION) – ISBN 978-92-64-08948-8 – © OECD 2010

model or plan. Where, however, the owner of the copyright in previously-developed plans merely grants someone the right to modify or reproduce these plans without actually performing any additional work, the payment received by that owner in consideration for granting the right to such use of the plans would constitute royalties.

11.   In classifying as royalties payments received as consideration for information concerning industrial, commercial or scientific experience, paragraph 2 is referring to the concept of "know-how". Various specialist bodies and authors have formulated definitions of know-how. The words "payments ... for information concerning industrial, commercial or scientific experience" are used in the context of the transfer of certain information that has not been patented and does not generally fall within other categories of intellectual property rights. It generally corresponds to undivulged information of an industrial, commercial or scientific nature arising from previous experience, which has practical application in the operation of an enterprise and from the disclosure of which an economic benefit can be derived. Since the definition relates to information concerning previous experience, the Article does not apply to payments for new information obtained as a result of performing services at the request of the payer.

11.1   In the know-how contract, one of the parties agrees to impart to the other, so that he can use them for his own account, his special knowledge and experience which remain unrevealed to the public. It is recognised that the grantor is not required to play any part himself in the application of the formulas granted to the licensee and that he does not guarantee the result thereof.

11.2   This type of contract thus differs from contracts for the provision of services, in which one of the parties undertakes to use the customary skills of his calling to execute work himself for the other party. Payments made under the latter contracts generally fall under Article 7.

11.3   The need to distinguish these two types of payments, i.e. payments for the supply of know-how and payments for the provision of services, sometimes gives rise to practical difficulties. The following criteria are relevant for the purpose of making that distinction:

— Contracts for the supply of know-how concern information of the kind described in paragraph 11 that already exists or concern the supply of that type of information after its development or creation and include specific provisions concerning the confidentiality of that information.

— In the case of contracts for the provision of services, the supplier undertakes to perform services which may require the use, by that supplier, of special knowledge, skill and expertise but not the transfer of such special knowledge, skill or expertise to the other party.

— In most cases involving the supply of know-how, there would generally be very little more which needs to be done by the supplier under the contract other than to supply existing information or reproduce existing material. On the other hand, a contract for the performance of services would, in the majority of cases, involve a very much greater level of expenditure by the supplier in order to perform his contractual obligations. For instance, the supplier, depending on the nature of the services to be rendered, may have to incur salaries and wages for employees engaged in researching, designing, testing, drawing and other associated activities or payments to sub-contractors for the performance of similar services.

11.4   Examples of payments which should therefore not be considered to be received as consideration for the provision of know-how but, rather, for the provision of services, include:

— payments obtained as consideration for after-sales service,

— payments for services rendered by a seller to the purchaser under a warranty,

— payments for pure technical assistance,

— payments for a list of potential customers, when such a list is developed specifically for the payer out of generally available information (a payment for the confidential list of customers to which the payee has provided a particular product or service would, however, constitute a payment for know-how as it would relate to the commercial experience of the payee in dealing with these customers),

— payments for an opinion given by an engineer, an advocate or an accountant, and

— payments for advice provided electronically, for electronic communications with technicians or for accessing, through computer networks, a trouble-shooting database such as a database that provides users of software with non-confidential information in response to frequently asked questions or common problems that arise frequently.

11.5   In the particular case of a contract involving the provision, by the supplier, of information concerning computer programming, as a general rule the payment will only be considered to be made in consideration for the provision of such information so as to constitute know-how where it is made to acquire information constituting ideas and principles underlying the program, such as logic, algorithms or programming languages or techniques, where this information is provided under the condition that the customer not disclose it without authorisation and where it is subject to any available trade secret protection.

11.6   In business practice, contracts are encountered which cover both know-how and the provision of technical assistance. One example, amongst others, of contracts of this kind is that of franchising, where the franchisor imparts his knowledge and experience to the franchisee and, in addition, provides him with varied technical assistance, which, in certain cases, is backed up with financial assistance and the supply of goods. The appropriate course to take with a mixed contract is, in principle, to break down, on the basis of the information contained in the contract or by means of a reasonable apportionment, the whole amount of the stipulated consideration according to the various parts of what is being provided under the contract, and then to apply to each part of it so determined the taxation treatment proper thereto. If, however, one part of what is being provided constitutes by far the principal purpose of the contract and the other parts stipulated therein are only of an ancillary and largely unimportant character, then the treatment applicable to the principal part should generally be applied to the whole amount of the consideration.

12.   Whether payments received as consideration for computer software may be classified as royalties poses difficult problems but is a matter of considerable importance in view of the rapid development of computer technology in recent years and the extent of transfers of such technology across national borders. In 1992, the Commentary was amended to describe the principles by which such classification should be made. Paragraphs 12 to 17 were further amended in 2000 to refine the analysis by which business profits are distinguished from royalties in computer software transactions. In most cases, the revised analysis will not result in a different outcome.

12.1 Software may be described as a program, or series of programs, containing instructions for a computer required either for the operational processes of the computer itself (operational software) or for the accomplishment of other tasks (application software). It can be transferred through a variety of media, for example in writing or electronically, on a magnetic tape or disk, or on a laser disk or CD-Rom. It may be standardised with a wide range of applications or be tailor-made for single users. It can be transferred as an integral part of computer hardware or in an independent form available for use on a variety of hardware.

12.2 The character of payments received in transactions involving the transfer of computer software depends on the nature of the rights that the transferee acquires under the particular arrangement regarding the use and exploitation of the program. The rights in computer programs are a form of intellectual property. Research into the practices of OECD member countries has established that all but one protect rights in computer programs either explicitly or implicitly under copyright law. Although the term "computer software" is commonly used to describe both the program — in which the intellectual property rights (copyright) subsist — and the medium on which it is embodied, the copyright law of most OECD member countries recognises a distinction between the copyright in the program and software which incorporates a copy of the copyrighted program. Transfers of rights in relation to software occur in many different ways ranging from the alienation of the entire rights in the copyright in a program to the sale of a product which is subject to restrictions on the use to which it is put. The consideration paid can also take numerous forms. These factors may make it difficult to determine where the boundary lies between software payments that are properly to be regarded as royalties and other types of payment. The difficulty of determination is compounded by the ease of reproduction of computer software, and by the fact that acquisition of software frequently entails the making of a copy by the acquirer in order to make possible the operation of the software.

13.   The transferee's rights will in most cases consist of partial rights or complete rights in the underlying copyright (see paragraphs 13.1 and 15 below), or they may be (or be equivalent to) partial or complete rights in a copy of the program (the "program copy"), whether or not such copy is embodied in a material medium or provided

electronically (see paragraphs 14 to 14.2 below). In unusual cases, the transaction may represent a transfer of "know-how" or secret formula (paragraph 14.3).

13.1 Payments made for the acquisition of partial rights in the copyright (without the transferor fully alienating the copyright rights) will represent a royalty where the consideration is for granting of rights to use the program in a manner that would, without such license, constitute an infringement of copyright. Examples of such arrangements include licenses to reproduce and distribute to the public software incorporating the copyrighted program, or to modify and publicly display the program. In these circumstances, the payments are for the right to use the copyright in the program (i.e. to exploit the rights that would otherwise be the sole prerogative of the copyright holder). It should be noted that where a software payment is properly to be regarded as a royalty there may be difficulties in applying the copyright provisions of the Article to software payments since paragraph 2 requires that software be classified as a literary, artistic or scientific work. None of these categories seems entirely apt. The copyright laws of many countries deal with this problem by specifically classifying software as a literary or scientific work. For other countries treatment as a scientific work might be the most realistic approach. Countries for which it is not possible to attach software to any of those categories might be justified in adopting in their bilateral treaties an amended version of paragraph 2 which either omits all references to the nature of the copyrights or refers specifically to software.

14. In other types of transactions, the rights acquired in relation to the copyright are limited to those necessary to enable the user to operate the program, for example, where the transferee is granted limited rights to reproduce the program. This would be the common situation in transactions for the acquisition of a program copy. The rights transferred in these cases are specific to the nature of computer programs. They allow the user to copy the program, for example onto the user's computer hard drive or for archival purposes. In this context, it is important to note that the protection afforded in relation to computer programs under copyright law may differ from country to country. In some countries the act of copying the program onto the hard drive or random access memory of a computer would, without a license, constitute a breach of copyright. However, the copyright laws of many countries automatically grant this right to the owner of software which incorporates a computer program. Regardless of whether this right is granted under law or under a license agreement with the copyright holder, copying the program onto the computer's hard drive or random access memory or making an archival copy is an essential step in utilising the program. Therefore, rights in relation to these acts of copying, where they do no more than enable the effective operation of the program by the user, should be disregarded in analysing the character of the transaction for tax purposes. Payments in these types of transactions would be dealt with as commercial income in accordance with Article 7.

14.1 The method of transferring the computer program to the transferee is not relevant. For example, it does not matter whether the transferee acquires a computer disk containing a copy of the program or directly receives a copy on the hard disk of her computer via a modem connection. It is also of no relevance that there may be restrictions on the use to which the transferee can put the software.

14.2 The ease of reproducing computer programs has resulted in distribution arrangements in which the transferee obtains rights to make multiple copies of the program for operation only within its own business. Such arrangements are commonly referred to as "site licences", "enterprise licenses", or "network licences". Although these arrangements permit the making of multiple copies of the program, such rights are generally limited to those necessary for the purpose of enabling the operation of the program on the licensee's computers or network, and reproduction for any other purpose is not permitted under the license. Payments under such arrangements will in most cases be dealt with as business profits in accordance with Article 7.

14.3 Another type of transaction involving the transfer of computer software is the more unusual case where a software house or computer programmer agrees to supply information about the ideas and principles underlying the program, such as logic, algorithms or programming languages or techniques. In these cases, the payments may be characterised as royalties to the extent that they represent consideration for the use of, or the right to use, secret formulas or for information concerning industrial, commercial or scientific experience which cannot be separately copyrighted. This contrasts with the ordinary case in which a program copy is acquired for operation by the end user.

14.4 Arrangements between a software copyright holder and a distribution intermediary frequently will grant to the distribution intermediary the right to distribute copies of the program without the right to reproduce that program. In these transactions, the rights acquired in relation to the copyright are limited to those necessary for the commercial intermediary to distribute copies of the software program. In such transactions, distributors are paying only for the acquisition of the software copies and not to exploit any right in the software copyrights. Thus, in a transaction where a distributor makes payments to acquire and distribute software copies (without the right to reproduce the software), the rights in relation to these acts of distribution should be disregarded in analysing the character of the transaction for tax purposes. Payments in these types of transactions would be dealt with as business profits in accordance with Article 7. This would be the case regardless of whether the copies being distributed are delivered on tangible media or are distributed electronically (without the distributor having the right to reproduce the software), or whether the software is subject to minor customisation for the purposes of its installation.

15. Where consideration is paid for the transfer of the full ownership of the rights in the copyright, the payment cannot represent a royalty and the provisions of the Article are not applicable. Difficulties can arise where there is a transfer of rights involving:

— exclusive right of use of the copyright during a specific period or in a limited geographical area;

— additional consideration related to usage;

— consideration in the form of a substantial lump sum payment.

16.   Each case will depend on its particular facts but in general if the payment is in consideration for the transfer of rights that constitute a distinct and specific property (which is more likely in the case of geographically-limited than time limited rights), such payments are likely to be business profits within Article 7 or a capital gain within Article 13 rather than royalties within Article 12. That follows from the fact that where the ownership of rights has been alienated, the consideration cannot be for the use of the rights. The essential character of the transaction as an alienation cannot be altered by the form of the consideration, the payment of the consideration in instalments or, in the view of most countries, by the fact that the payments are related to a contingency.

17.   Software payments may be made under mixed contracts. Examples of such contracts include sales of computer hardware with built-in software and concessions of the right to use software combined with the provision of services. The methods set out in paragraph 11 above for dealing with similar problems in relation to patent royalties and know-how are equally applicable to computer software. Where necessary the total amount of the consideration payable under a contract should be broken down on the basis of the information contained in the contract or by means of a reasonable apportionment with the appropriate tax treatment being applied to each apportioned part.

17.1   The principles expressed above as regards software payments are also applicable as regards transactions concerning other types of digital products such as images, sounds or text. The development of electronic commerce has multiplied the number of such transactions. In deciding whether or not payments arising in these transactions constitute royalties, the main question to be addressed is the identification of that for which the payment is essentially made.

17.2   Under the relevant legislation of some countries, transactions which permit the customer to electronically download digital products may give rise to use of copyright by the customer, e.g. because a right to make one or more copies of the digital content is granted under the contract. Where the consideration is essentially for something other than for the use of, or right to use, rights in the copyright (such as to acquire other types of contractual rights, data or services), and the use of copyright is limited to such rights as are required to enable downloading, storage and operation on the customer's computer, network or other storage, performance or display device, such use of copyright should not affect the analysis of the character of the payment for purposes of applying the definition of "royalties".

17.3   This is the case for transactions that permit the customer (which may be an enterprise) to electronically download digital products (such as software, images, sounds or text) for that customer's own use or enjoyment. In these transactions, the payment is essentially for the acquisition of data transmitted in the form of a digital signal and therefore does not constitute royalties but falls within Article 7 or Article 13, as the case may be. To the extent that the act of copying the digital signal onto the customer's hard disk or other non-temporary media involves the use of a copyright by the customer under the relevant law and contractual arrangements, such copying is merely the means by which the digital signal is captured and stored. This use of copyright is not important for classification purposes because it does not correspond to what the payment is essentially in consideration for (i.e. to acquire data transmitted in the form of a digital signal), which is the determining factor for the purposes of the definition of royalties. There also would be no basis to classify such transactions as "royalties" if, under the relevant law and contractual arrangements, the creation of a copy is regarded as a use of copyright by the provider rather than by the customer.

17.4   By contrast, transactions where the essential consideration for the payment is the granting of the right to use a copyright in a digital product that is electronically downloaded for that purpose will give rise to royalties. This would be the case, for example, of a book publisher who would pay to acquire the right to reproduce a copyrighted picture that it would electronically download for the purposes of including it on the cover of a book that it is producing. In this transaction, the essential consideration for the payment is the acquisition of rights to use the copyright in the digital product, i.e. the right to reproduce and distribute the picture, and not merely for the acquisition of the digital content.

18.   The suggestions made above regarding mixed contracts could also be applied in regard to certain performances by artists and, in particular, in regard to an orchestral concert given by a conductor or a recital given by a musician. The fee for the musical performance, together with that paid for any simultaneous radio broadcasting thereof, seems to fall under Article 17. Where, whether under the same contract or under a separate one, the musical performance is recorded and the artist has stipulated that he, on the basis of his copyright in the sound recording, be paid royalties on the sale or public playing of the records, then so much of the payment received by him as consists of such royalties falls to be treated under Article 12. Where, however, the copyright in a sound recording, because of either the relevant copyright law or the terms of contract, belongs to a person with whom the artist has contractually agreed to provide his services (i.e. a musical performance during the recording), or to a third party, the payments made under such a contract fall under Articles 7 (e.g. if the performance takes place outside the State of source of the payment) or 17 rather than under this article, even if these payments are contingent on the sale of the recordings.

19.   It is further pointed out that variable or fixed payments for the working of mineral deposits, sources or other natural resources are governed by Article 6 and do not, therefore, fall within the present Article.

Paragraph 3

20.   Certain States consider that dividends, interest and royalties arising from sources in their territory and payable to individuals or legal persons who are residents of other States fall outside the scope of the arrangement made to prevent them from being taxed both in the State of source and in the State of the beneficiary's residence when the beneficiary has a permanent establishment in the former State. Paragraph 3 is not based on such a conception which is sometimes referred to as "the force of attraction of the permanent establishment". It does not stipulate that royalties arising

to a resident of a Contracting State from a source situated in the other State must, by a kind of legal presumption, or fiction even, be related to a permanent establishment which that resident may have in the latter State, so that the said State would not be obliged to limit its taxation in such a case. The paragraph merely provides that in the State of source the royalties are taxable as part of the profits of the permanent establishment there owned by the beneficiary which is a resident of the other State, if they are paid in respect of rights or property forming part of the assets of the permanent establishment or otherwise effectively connected with that establishment. In that case, paragraph 3 relieves the State of source of the royalties from any limitations under the Article. The foregoing explanations accord with those in the Commentary on Article 7.

21.   It has been suggested that the paragraph could give rise to abuses through the transfer of rights or property to permanent establishments set up solely for that purpose in countries that offer preferential treatment to royalty income. Apart from the fact that such abusive transactions might trigger the application of domestic anti-abuse rules, it must be recognised that a particular location can only constitute a permanent establishment if a business is carried on therein and, as explained below, that the requirement that a right or property be "effectively connected" to such a location requires more than merely recording the right or property in the books of the permanent establishment for accounting purposes.

21.1   A right or property in respect of which royalties are paid will be effectively connected with a permanent establishment, and will therefore form part of its business assets, if the "economic" ownership of that right or property is allocated to that permanent establishment under the principles developed in the Committee's report entitled *Attribution of Profits to Permanent Establishments*[1] (see in particular paragraphs 72-97 of Part I of the report) for the purposes of the application of paragraph 2 of Article 7. In the context of that paragraph, the "economic" ownership of a right or property means the equivalent of ownership for income tax purposes by a separate enterprise, with the attendant benefits and burdens (*e.g.* the right to the royalties attributable to the ownership of the right or property, the right to any available depreciation and the potential exposure to gains or losses from the appreciation or depreciation of that right or property).

21.2   In the case of the permanent establishment of an enterprise carrying on insurance activities, the determination of whether a right or property is effectively connected with the permanent establishment shall be made by giving due regard to the guidance set forth in Part IV of the Committee's report with respect to whether the income on or gain from that right or property is taken into account in determining the permanent establishment's yield on the amount of investment assets attributed to it (see in particular paragraphs 165-170 of Part IV). That guidance being general in nature, tax authorities should consider applying a flexible and pragmatic approach which would take into account an enterprise's reasonable and consistent application of that

---

1   *Attribution of Profits to Permanent Establishments*, OECD, Paris, 2010.

guidance for purposes of identifying the specific assets that are effectively connected with the permanent establishment.

Paragraph 4

22.   The purpose of this paragraph is to restrict the operation of the provisions concerning the taxation of royalties in cases where, by reason of a special relationship between the payer and the beneficial owner or between both of them and some other person, the amount of the royalties paid exceeds the amount which would have been agreed upon by the payer and the beneficial owner had they stipulated at arm's length. It provides that in such a case the provisions of the Article apply only to that last-mentioned amount and that the excess part of the royalty shall remain taxable according to the laws of the two Contracting States due regard being had to the other provisions of the Convention. The paragraph permits only the adjustment of the amount of royalties and not the reclassification of the royalties in such a way as to give it a different character, e.g. a contribution to equity capital. For such an adjustment to be possible under paragraph 4 of Article 12 it would be necessary as a minimum to remove the limiting phrase "having regard to the use, right or information for which they are paid". If greater clarity of intent is felt appropriate, a phrase such as "for whatever reason" might be added after "exceeds".

23.   It is clear from the text that for this clause to apply the payment held excessive must be due to a special relationship between the payer and the beneficial owner or between both of them and some other person. There may be cited as examples cases where royalties are paid to an individual or legal person who directly or indirectly controls the payer, or who is directly or indirectly controlled by him or is subordinate to a group having common interest with him. These examples, moreover, are similar or analogous to the cases contemplated by Article 9.

24.   On the other hand, the concept of special relationship also covers relationship by blood or marriage and, in general, any community of interests as distinct from the legal relationship giving rise to the payment of the royalty.

25.   With regard to the taxation treatment to be applied to the excess part of the royalty, the exact nature of such excess will need to be ascertained according to the circumstances of each case, in order to determine the category of income in which it should be classified for the purpose of applying the provisions of the tax laws of the States concerned and the provisions of the Convention. If two Contracting States should have difficulty in determining the other provisions of the Convention applicable, as cases required, to the excess part of the royalties, there would be nothing to prevent them from introducing additional clarifications in the last sentence of paragraph 4, as long as they do not alter its general purport.

26.   Should the principles and rules of their respective laws oblige the two Contracting States to apply different Articles of the Convention for the purpose of taxing the excess, it will be necessary to resort to the mutual agreement procedure provided by the Convention in order to resolve the difficulty.

233

Observations on the Commentary

27.   *Italy* and *Spain* do not adhere to the interpretation in paragraph 8.2. They hold the view that payments in consideration for the transfer of the ownership of an element referred to in the definition of royalties fall within the scope of this Article where less than the full ownership is transferred. Italy also takes that view with respect to paragraphs 15 and 16.

27.1 As regards paragraph 10.1, *Italy* considers that where contracts grant exclusive distribution rights of a product or a service together with other rights referred to in the definition of royalties, the part of the payment made, under these contracts, in consideration for the exclusive distribution rights of a product or a service may, depending on the circumstances, be covered by the Article.

28.   *Mexico*, *Portugal* and *Spain* do not adhere to the interpretation in paragraphs 14, 14.4, 15, 16 and 17.1 to 17.4. Mexico, Portugal and Spain hold the view that payments relating to software fall within the scope of the Article where less than the full rights to software are transferred either if the payments are in consideration for the right to use a copyright on software for commercial exploitation (except payments for the right to distribute standardised software copies, not comprising the right neither to customise nor to reproduce them) or if they relate to software acquired for the business use of the purchaser, when, in this last case, the software is not absolutely standardised but somehow adapted to the purchaser.

29.   *Mexico* does not adhere to the interpretation in paragraph 8.2. Mexico holds the view that payments in consideration for the transfer of rights presented as an alienation (*e.g.* geographically limited or time limited rights) fall within the scope of this Article because less than the full rights inherent to an element of property referred to in the definition are transferred.

30.   The *Slovak Republic* does not adhere to the interpretation in paragraphs 14, 15 and 17. The Slovak Republic holds the view that payments relating to software fall within the scope of the Article where less than the full rights to software are transferred, either if the payments are in consideration for the right to use a copyright on software for commercial exploitation or if they relate to software acquired for the personal or business use of the purchaser when, in this last case, the software is not absolutely standardised but somehow adapted to the purchaser.

31.   *Greece* does not adhere to the interpretation in paragraphs 14 and 15 above. Greece takes the view that payments related to software fall within the scope of this Article, whether the payments are in consideration for the use of (or the right to use) software for commercial exploitation or for the personal or business use of the purchaser.

31.1 With respect to paragraph 14, *Korea* is of the opinion that the paragraph may neglect the fact that know-how can be transferred in the form of computer software. Therefore, Korea considers know-how imparted by non-residents through software or computer program to be treated in accordance with Article 12.

31.2   *Italy* does not agree that the interpretation in paragraph 14.4 will apply in all cases. It will examine each case taking into account all circumstances, including the rights granted in relation to the acts of distribution.

Reservations on the Article

Paragraph 1

32.   Concerning paragraph 9.1, *Germany* reserves its position on whether and under which circumstances payments made for the acquisition of the right of disposal over the transport capacity of pipelines or the capacity of technical installations, lines or cables for the transmission of electrical power or communications (including the distribution of radio and television programs) could be regarded as payments made for the leasing of industrial, commercial or scientific equipment.

32.1   *Greece* reserves the right to include the payments referred to in paragraphs 9.1, 9.2 and 9.3 in the definition of royalties.

33.   *Greece* is unable to accept a provision which would preclude it, in bilateral conventions for the avoidance of double taxation, from stipulating a clause conferring on it the right to tax royalties at a rate of up to 10 per cent.

34.   The *Czech Republic* reserves the right to tax at a rate of 10 per cent royalties that, under Czech law, have a source in the Czech Republic. The Czech Republic also reserves the right to subject payments for the use of, or the right to use, software rights to a tax regime different from that provided for copyrights.

35.   *Canada* reserves its position on paragraph 1 and wishes to retain a 10 per cent rate of tax at source in its bilateral conventions. However, Canada would be prepared to provide an exemption from tax for copyright royalties in respect of cultural, dramatic, musical or artistic work, but not including royalties in respect of motion picture films and works on films or video tape or other means of reproduction for use in connection with television. Canada would also be prepared in most circumstances to provide an exemption for royalties in respect of computer software, patents and know-how.

36.   *Australia*, *Chile*, *Korea*, *Mexico*, *New Zealand*, *Poland*, *Portugal*, the *Slovak Republic*, *Slovenia* and *Turkey* reserve the right to tax royalties at source.

37.   *Italy* reserves the right to tax royalties at source, but is prepared to grant favourable treatment to certain royalties (*e.g.* copyright royalties). Italy also reserves the right to subject the use of, or the right to use, software rights to a tax regime different from that provided for copyright.

Paragraph 2

38.   [Deleted]

39.   *Australia* reserves the right to amend the definition of royalties to include payments or credits which are treated as royalties under its domestic law.

40.   *Canada, Chile,* the *Czech Republic, Hungary, Korea* and the *Slovak Republic* reserve the right to add the words "for the use of, or the right to use, industrial, commercial or scientific equipment" to paragraph 2.

41.   *Greece, Italy* and *Mexico* reserve the right to continue to include income derived from the leasing of industrial, commercial or scientific equipment and of containers in the definition of "royalties" as provided for in paragraph 2 of Article 12 of the 1977 Model Convention.

41.1   *Poland* reserves the right to include in the definition of "royalties" income derived from the use of, or the right to use, industrial, commercial or scientific equipment and containers.

42.   *New Zealand* reserves the right to tax at source payments from the leasing of industrial, commercial or scientific equipment and of containers.

43.   [Deleted]

43.1   *Portugal* reserves the right to tax at source as royalties income from the leasing of industrial, commercial or scientific equipment and of containers, as well as income arising from technical assistance in connection with the use of, or the right to use, such equipment and containers.

44.   *Portugal* reserves the right to tax at source as royalties income arising from technical assistance in connection with the use of, or right to use, rights or information of the type referred to in paragraph 2 of the Article.

45.   *Spain* reserves its right to continue to adhere in its conventions to a definition of royalties which includes income from the leasing of industrial, commercial or scientific equipment and of containers.

46.   *Turkey* reserves the right to tax at source income from the leasing of industrial, commercial or scientific equipment.

46.1   *Mexico* and the *United States* reserve the right to treat as a royalty a gain derived from the alienation of a property described in paragraph 2 of the Article, provided that the gain is contingent on the productivity, use or disposition of the property.

46.2   *Greece* does not adhere to the interpretation in the sixth dash of paragraph 11.4 and takes the view that all concerning payments are falling within the scope of the Article.

46.3   *Greece* does not adhere to the interpretation in paragraphs 17.2 and 17.3 because the payments related to downloading of computer software ought to be considered as royalties even if those products are acquired for the personal or business use of the purchaser.

47.   [Deleted]

Other reservations

48.   *Australia, Belgium, Canada, Chile,* the *Czech Republic, France, Mexico,* the *Slovak Republic* and *Slovenia* reserve the right, in order to fill what they consider as a gap in the

Article, to propose a provision defining the source of royalties by analogy with the provisions of paragraph 5 of Article 11, which deals with the same problem in the case of interest.

49.   *Mexico* reserves the right to propose a provision considering that royalties will be deemed to arise in a Contracting State where such royalties relate to the use of, or the right to use, in that Contracting State, any property or right described in paragraph 2 of Article 12.

50.   The *Slovak Republic* reserves the right to subject payments for the use of, or the right to use, software rights to a tax regime different from that provided for copyrights.

COMMENTARY ON ARTICLE 13
CONCERNING THE TAXATION OF CAPITAL GAINS

I. Preliminary remarks

1.   A comparison of the tax laws of the OECD member countries shows that the taxation of capital gains varies considerably from country to country:

— in some countries capital gains are not deemed to be taxable income;

— in other countries capital gains accrued to an enterprise are taxed, but capital gains made by an individual outside the course of his trade or business are not taxed;

— even where capital gains made by an individual outside the course of his trade or business are taxed, such taxation often applies only in specified cases, *e.g.* profits from the sale of immovable property or speculative gains (where an asset was bought to be resold).

2.   Moreover, the taxes on capital gains vary from country to country. In some OECD member countries, capital gains are taxed as ordinary income and therefore added to the income from other sources. This applies especially to the capital gains made by the alienation of assets of an enterprise. In a number of OECD member countries, however, capital gains are subjected to special taxes, such as taxes on profits from the alienation of immovable property, or general capital gains taxes, or taxes on capital appreciation (increment taxes). Such taxes are levied on each capital gain or on the sum of the capital gains accrued during a year, mostly at special rates, which do not take into account the other income (or losses) of the taxpayer. It does not seem necessary to describe all those taxes.

3.   The Article does not deal with the above-mentioned questions. It is left to the domestic law of each Contracting State to decide whether capital gains should be taxed and, if they are taxable, how they are to be taxed. The Article can in no way be construed as giving a State the right to tax capital gains if such right is not provided for in its domestic law. The Article does not specify to what kind of tax it applies. It is understood that the Article must apply to all kinds of taxes levied by a Contracting State on capital gains. The wording of Article 2 is large enough to achieve this aim and to include also special taxes on capital gains.

II. Commentary on the provisions of the Article

General remarks

4.   It is normal to give the right to tax capital gains on a property of a given kind to the State which under the Convention is entitled to tax both the property and the income derived therefrom. The right to tax a gain from the alienation of a business asset must be given to the same State without regard to the question whether such gain is a capital gain or a business profit. Accordingly, no distinction between capital gains and commercial profits is made nor is it necessary to have special provisions as

MODEL TAX CONVENTION (CONDENSED VERSION) – ISBN 978-92-64-08948-8 – © OECD 2010

to whether the Article on capital gains or Article 7 on the taxation of business profits should apply. It is however left to the domestic law of the taxing State to decide whether a tax on capital gains or on ordinary income must be levied. The Convention does not prejudge this question.

5.   The Article does not give a detailed definition of capital gains. This is not necessary for the reasons mentioned above. The words "alienation of property" are used to cover in particular capital gains resulting from the sale or exchange of property and also from a partial alienation, the expropriation, the transfer to a company in exchange for stock, the sale of a right, the gift and even the passing of property on death.

6.   Most States taxing capital gains do so when an alienation of capital assets takes place. Some of them, however, tax only so-called realised capital gains. Under certain circumstances, though there is an alienation no realised capital gain is recognised for tax purposes (e.g. when the alienation proceeds are used for acquiring new assets). Whether or not there is a realisation has to be determined according to the applicable domestic tax law. No particular problems arise when the State which has the right to tax does not exercise it at the time the alienation takes place.

7.   As a rule, appreciation in value not associated with the alienation of a capital asset is not taxed, since, as long as the owner still holds the asset in question, the capital gain exists only on paper. There are, however, tax laws under which capital appreciation and revaluation of business assets are taxed even if there is no alienation.

8.   Special circumstances may lead to the taxation of the capital appreciation of an asset that has not been alienated. This may be the case if the value of a capital asset has increased in such a manner that the owner proceeds to the revaluation of this asset in his books. Such revaluation of assets in the books may also occur in the case of a depreciation of the national currency. A number of States levy special taxes on such book profits, amounts put into reserve, an increase in the paid-up capital and other revaluations resulting from the adjustment of the book-value to the intrinsic value of a capital asset. These taxes on capital appreciation (increment taxes) are covered by the Convention according to Article 2.

9.   Where capital appreciation and revaluation of business assets are taxed, the same principle should, as a rule, apply as in the case of the alienation of such assets. It has not been found necessary to mention such cases expressly in the Article or to lay down special rules. The provisions of the Article as well as those of Articles 6, 7 and 21, seem to be sufficient. As a rule, the right to tax is conferred by the above-mentioned provisions on the State of which the alienator is a resident, except that in the cases of immovable property or of movable property forming part of the business property of a permanent establishment, the prior right to tax belongs to the State where such property is situated. Special attention must be drawn, however, to the cases dealt with in paragraphs 13 to 17 below.

10.   In some States the transfer of an asset from a permanent establishment situated in the territory of such State to a permanent establishment or the head office of the

same enterprise situated in another State is assimilated to an alienation of property. The Article does not prevent these States from taxing profits or gains deemed to arise in connection with such a transfer, provided, however, that such taxation is in accordance with Article 7.

11.   The Article does not distinguish as to the origin of the capital gain. Therefore all capital gains, those accruing over a long term, parallel to a steady improvement in economic conditions, as well as those accruing in a very short period (speculative gains) are covered. Also capital gains which are due to depreciation of the national currency are covered. It is, of course, left to each State to decide whether or not such gains should be taxed.

12.   The Article does not specify how to compute a capital gain, this being left to the domestic law applicable. As a rule, capital gains are calculated by deducting the cost from the selling price. To arrive at cost all expenses incidental to the purchase and all expenditure for improvements are added to the purchase price. In some cases the cost after deduction of the depreciation allowances already given is taken into account. Some tax laws prescribe another base instead of cost, e.g. the value previously reported by the alienator of the asset for capital tax purposes.

13.   Special problems may arise when the basis for the taxation of capital gains is not uniform in the two Contracting States. The capital gain from the alienation of an asset computed in one State according to the rules mentioned in paragraph 12 above, may not necessarily coincide with the capital gain computed in the other State under the accounting rules used there. This may occur when one State has the right to tax capital gains because it is the State of situs while the other State has the right to tax because the enterprise is a resident of that other State.

14.   The following example may illustrate this problem: an enterprise of State A bought immovable property situated in State B. The enterprise may have entered depreciation allowances in the books kept in State A. If such immovable property is sold at a price which is above cost, a capital gain may be realised and, in addition, the depreciation allowances granted earlier may be recovered. State B, in which the immovable property is situated and where no books are kept, does not have to take into account, when taxing the income from the immovable property, the depreciation allowances booked in State A. Neither can State B substitute the value of the immovable property shown in the books kept in State A for the cost at the time of the alienation. State B cannot, therefore, tax the depreciation allowances realised in addition to the capital gain as mentioned in paragraph 12 above.

15.   On the other hand, State A of which the alienator is a resident, cannot be obliged in all cases to exempt such book profits fully from its taxes under paragraph 1 of the Article and Article 23 A (there will be hardly any problems for States applying the tax credit method). To the extent that such book profits are due to the realisation of the depreciation allowances previously claimed in State A and which had reduced the income or profits taxable in such State A, that State cannot be prevented from taxing

such book profits. The situation corresponds to that dealt with in paragraph 44 of the Commentary on Article 23 A.

16.   Further problems may arise in connection with profits due to changes of the rate of exchange between the currencies of State A and State B. After the devaluation of the currency of State A, enterprises of such State A may, or may have to, increase the book value of the assets situated outside the territory of State A. Apart from any devaluation of the currency of a State, the usual fluctuations of the rate of exchange may give rise to so-called currency gains or losses. Take for example an enterprise of State A having bought and sold immovable property situated in State B. If the cost and the selling price, both expressed in the currency of State B, are equal, there will be no capital gain in State B. When the value of the currency of State B has risen between the purchase and the sale of the asset in relation to the currency of State A, in the currency of that State a profit will accrue to such enterprise. If the value of the currency of State B has fallen in the meantime, the alienator will sustain a loss which will not be recognised in State B. Such currency gains or losses may also arise in connection with claims and debts contracted in a foreign currency. If the balance sheet of a permanent establishment situated in State B of an enterprise of State A shows claims and debts expressed in the currency of State B, the books of the permanent establishment do not show any gain or loss when repayments are made. Changes of the rate of exchange may be reflected, however, in the accounts of the head office. If the value of the currency of State B has risen (fallen) between the time the claim has originated and its repayment, the enterprise, as a whole, will realise a gain (sustain a loss). This is true also with respect to debts if between the time they have originated and their repayment, the currency of State B has fallen (risen) in value.

17.   The provisions of the Article do not settle all questions regarding the taxation of such currency gains. Such gains are in most cases not connected with an alienation of the asset; they may often not even be determined in the State on which the right to tax capital gains is conferred by the Article. Accordingly, the question, as a rule, is not whether the State in which a permanent establishment is situated has a right to tax, but whether the State of which the taxpayer is a resident must, if applying the exemption method, refrain from taxing such currency gains which, in many cases, cannot be shown but in the books kept in the head office. The answer to that latter question depends not only on the Article but also on Article 7 and on Article 23 A. If in a given case differing opinions of two States should result in an actual double taxation, the case should be settled under the mutual agreement procedure provided for by Article 25.

18.   Moreover the question arises which Article should apply when there is paid for property sold an annuity during the lifetime of the alienator and not a fixed price. Are such annuity payments, as far as they exceed costs, to be dealt with as a gain from the alienation of the property or as "income not dealt with" according to Article 21? Both opinions may be supported by arguments of equivalent weight, and it seems difficult to give one rule on the matter. In addition such problems are rare in practice, so it therefore seems unnecessary to establish a rule for insertion in the Convention. It may

be left to Contracting States who may be involved in such a question to adopt a solution in the mutual agreement procedure provided for by Article 25.

19.   The Article is not intended to apply to prizes in a lottery or to premiums and prizes attaching to bonds or debentures.

20.   The Article deals first with the gains which may be taxed in the State where the alienated property is situated. For all other capital gains, paragraph 5 gives the right to tax to the State of which the alienator is a resident.

21.   As capital gains are not taxed by all States, it may be considered reasonable to avoid only actual double taxation of capital gains. Therefore, Contracting States are free to supplement their bilateral convention in such a way that a State has to forego its right to tax conferred on it by the domestic laws only if the other State on which the right to tax is conferred by the Convention makes use thereof. In such a case, paragraph 5 of the Article should be supplemented accordingly. Besides, a modification of Article 23 A as suggested in paragraph 35 of the Commentary on Article 23 A is needed.

Paragraph 1

22.   Paragraph 1 states that gains from the alienation of immovable property may be taxed in the State in which it is situated. This rule corresponds to the provisions of Article 6 and of paragraph 1 of Article 22. It applies also to immovable property forming part of the assets of an enterprise. For the definition of immovable property paragraph 1 refers to Article 6. Paragraph 1 of Article 13 deals only with gains which a resident of a Contracting State derives from the alienation of immovable property situated in the other Contracting State. It does not, therefore, apply to gains derived from the alienation of immovable property situated in the Contracting State of which the alienator is a resident in the meaning of Article 4 or situated in a third State; the provisions of paragraph 5 shall apply to such gains (and not, as was mentioned in this Commentary before 2002, those of paragraph 1 of Article 21).

23.   The rules of paragraph 1 are supplemented by those of paragraph 4, which applies to gains from the alienation of all or part of the shares in a company holding immovable property (see paragraphs 28.3 to 28.8 below).

Paragraph 2

24.   Paragraph 2 deals with movable property forming part of the business property of a permanent establishment of an enterprise. The term "movable property" means all property other than immovable property which is dealt with in paragraph 1. It includes also incorporeal property, such as goodwill, licences, etc. Gains from the alienation of such assets may be taxed in the State in which the permanent establishment is situated, which corresponds to the rules for business profits (Article 7).

25.   The paragraph makes clear that its rules apply when movable property of a permanent establishment is alienated as well as when the permanent establishment as such (alone or with the whole enterprise) is alienated. If the whole enterprise is

alienated, then the rule applies to such gains which are deemed to result from the alienation of movable property forming part of the business property of the permanent establishment. The rules of Article 7 should then apply *mutatis mutandis* without express reference thereto. For the transfer of an asset from a permanent establishment in one State to a permanent establishment (or the head office) in another State, see paragraph 10 above.

26.   On the other hand, paragraph 2 may not always be applicable to capital gains from the alienation of a participation in an enterprise. The provision applies only to property which was owned by the alienator, either wholly or jointly with another person. Under the laws of some countries, capital assets of a partnership are considered to be owned by the partners. Under some other laws, however, partnerships and other associations are treated as body corporate for tax purposes, distinct from their partners (members), which means that participations in such entities are dealt with in the same way as shares in a company. Capital gains from the alienation of such participations, like capital gains from the alienation of shares, are therefore taxable only in the State of residence of the alienator. Contracting States may agree bilaterally on special rules governing the taxation of capital gains from the alienation of a participation in a partnership.

27.   Certain States consider that all capital gains arising from sources in their territory should be subject to their taxes according to their domestic laws, if the alienator has a permanent establishment within their territory. Paragraph 2 is not based on such a conception which is sometimes referred to as "the force of attraction of the permanent establishment". The paragraph merely provides that gains from the alienation of movable property forming part of the business property of a permanent establishment may be taxed in the State where the permanent establishment is situated. The gains from the alienation of all other movable property are taxable only in the State of residence of the alienator as provided in paragraph 5. The foregoing explanations accord with those in the Commentary on Article 7.

27.1 For the purposes of the paragraph, property will form part of the business property of a permanent establishment if the "economic" ownership of the property is allocated to that permanent establishment under the principles developed in the Committee's report entitled *Attribution of Profits to Permanent Establishments*[1] (see in particular paragraphs 72-97 of Part I of the report) for the purposes of the application of paragraph 2 of Article 7. In the context of that paragraph, the "economic" ownership of property means the equivalent of ownership for income tax purposes by a separate enterprise, with the attendant benefits and burdens (*e.g.* the right to any income attributable to the ownership of that property, the right to any available depreciation and the potential exposure to gains or losses from the appreciation or depreciation of that property). The mere fact that the property has been recorded, for accounting purposes, on a balance sheet prepared for the permanent establishment will therefore

---

1   *Attribution of Profits to Permanent Establishments*, OECD, Paris, 2010.

not be sufficient to conclude that it is effectively connected with that permanent establishment.

27.2 In the case of the permanent establishment of an enterprise carrying on insurance activities, the determination of whether property will form part of the business property of the permanent establishment shall be made by giving due regard to the guidance set forth in Part IV of the Committee's report with respect to whether the income on or gain from that property is taken into account in determining the permanent establishment's yield on the amount of investment assets attributed to it (see in particular paragraphs 165-170 of Part IV). That guidance being general in nature, tax authorities should consider applying a flexible and pragmatic approach which would take into account an enterprise's reasonable and consistent application of that guidance for purposes of identifying the specific assets that form part of the business property of the permanent establishment.

Paragraph 3

28. An exception from the rule of paragraph 2 is provided for ships and aircraft operated in international traffic and for boats engaged in inland waterways transport and movable property pertaining to the operation of such ships, aircraft and boats. Normally, gains from the alienation of such assets are taxable only in the State in which the place of effective management of the enterprise operating such ships, aircraft and boats is situated. This rule corresponds to the provisions of Article 8 and of paragraph 3 of Article 22. It is understood that paragraph 3 of Article 8 is applicable if the place of effective management of such enterprise is aboard a ship or a boat. Contracting States which would prefer to confer the exclusive taxing right on the State of residence or to use a combination of the residence criterion and the place of effective management criterion are free, in bilateral conventions, to substitute for paragraph 3 a provision corresponding to those proposed in paragraphs 2 and 3 of the Commentary on Article 8.

28.1 Paragraph 3 applies where the enterprise that alienates the property operates itself the boats, ships or aircraft referred to in the paragraph, whether for its own transportation activities or when leasing the boats, ships or aircraft on charter fully equipped, manned and supplied. It does not apply, however, where the enterprise owning the boats, ships or aircraft does not operate them (for example, where the enterprise leases the property to another person, other than in the case of an occasional bare boat lease as referred to in paragraph 5 of the Commentary on Article 8). In such a case, the gains accruing to the true owner of the property, or connected moveable property, will be covered by paragraph 2 or 5.

28.2 In their bilateral conventions, member countries are free to clarify further the application of Article 13 in this situation. They might adopt the following alternative version of paragraph 3 of the Article (see also paragraphs 4.1 and 4.2 of the Commentary on Article 22):

3. Gains from the alienation of property forming part of the business property of an enterprise and consisting of ships or aircraft operated by that enterprise in

international traffic or movable property pertaining to the operation of such ships or aircraft, shall be taxable only in the Contracting State in which the place of effective management of the enterprise is situated.

Paragraph 4

28.3 By providing that gains from the alienation of shares deriving more than 50 per cent of their value directly or indirectly from immovable property situated in a Contracting State may be taxed in that State, paragraph 4 provides that gains from the alienation of such shares and gains from the alienation of the underlying immovable property, which are covered by paragraph 1, are equally taxable in that State.

28.4 Paragraph 4 allows the taxation of the entire gain attributable to the shares to which it applies even where part of the value of the share is derived from property other than immovable property located in the source State. The determination of whether shares of a company derive more than 50 per cent of their value directly or indirectly from immovable property situated in a Contracting State will normally be done by comparing the value of such immovable property to the value of all the property owned by the company without taking into account debts or other liabilities of the company (whether or not secured by mortgages on the relevant immovable property).

28.5 In their bilateral conventions, many States either broaden or narrow the scope of the paragraph. For instance, some States consider that the provision should not only cover gains from shares but also gains from the alienation of interests in other entities, such as partnerships or trusts, that do not issue shares, as long as the value of these interests is similarly derived principally from immovable property. States wishing to extend the scope of the paragraph to cover such interests are free to amend the paragraph as follows:

> 4.   Gains derived by a resident of a Contracting State from the alienation of shares or comparable interests deriving more than 50 per cent of their value directly or indirectly from immovable property situated in the other Contracting State may be taxed in that other State.

28.6 It is also possible for States to increase or reduce the percentage of the value of the shares that must be derived directly or indirectly from immovable property for the provision to apply. This would simply be done by replacing "50 per cent" by the percentage that these States would agree to. Another change that some States may agree to make is to restrict the application of the provision to cases where the alienator holds a certain level of participation in the entity.

28.7 Also, some States consider that the paragraph should not apply to gains derived from the alienation of shares of companies that are listed on an approved stock exchange of one of the States, to gains derived from the alienation of shares in the course of a corporate reorganisation or where the immovable property from which the shares derive their value is immovable property (such as a mine or a hotel) in which a business is carried on. States wishing to provide for one or more of these exceptions are free to do so.

28.8 Another possible exception relates to shares held by pension funds and similar entities. Under the domestic laws of many States, pension funds and similar entities are generally exempt from tax on their investment income. In order to achieve neutrality of treatment as regards domestic and foreign investments by these entities, some States provide bilaterally that income derived by such an entity resident of the other State, which would include capital gains on shares referred to in paragraph 4, shall be exempt from source taxation. States wishing to do so may agree bilaterally on a provision drafted along the lines of the provision found in paragraph 69 of the Commentary on Article 18.

28.9 Finally, a further possible exception relates to shares and similar interests in a Real Estate Investment Trust (see paragraphs 67.1 to 67.7 of the Commentary on Article 10 for background information on REITs). Whilst it would not seem appropriate to make an exception to paragraph 4 in the case of the alienation of a large investor's interests in a REIT, which could be considered to be the alienation of a substitute for a direct investment in immovable property, an exception to paragraph 4 for the alienation of a small investor's interest in a REIT may be considered to be appropriate.

28.10 As discussed in paragraph 67.3 of the Commentary on Article 10, it may be appropriate to consider a small investor's interest in a REIT as a security rather than as an indirect holding in immovable property. In this regard, in practice it would be very difficult to administer the application of source taxation of gains on small interests in a widely held REIT. Moreover, since REITs, unlike other entities deriving their value primarily from immovable property, are required to distribute most of their profits, it is unlikely that there would be significant residual profits to which the capital gain tax would apply (as compared to other companies). States that share this view may agree bilaterally to add, before the phrase "may be taxed in that other State", words such as "except shares held by a person who holds, directly or indirectly, interests representing less than 10 per cent of all the interests in a company if that company is a REIT". (If paragraph 4 is amended along the lines of paragraph 28.5 above to cover interests similar to shares, these words should be amended accordingly.)

28.11 Some States, however, consider that paragraph 4 was intended to apply to any gain on the alienation of shares in a company that derives its value primarily from immovable property and that there would be no reason to distinguish between a REIT and a publicly held company with respect to the application of that paragraph, especially since a REIT is not taxed on its income. These States consider that as long as there is no exception for the alienation of shares in companies quoted on a stock exchange (see paragraph 28.7 above), there should not be a special exception for interests in a REIT.

28.12 Since the domestic laws of some States do not allow them to tax the gains covered by paragraph 4, States that adopt the exemption method should be careful to ensure that the inclusion of the paragraph does not result in a double exemption of these gains. These States may wish to exclude these gains from exemption and apply the credit method, as suggested by paragraph 35 of the Commentary on Articles 23 A and 23 B.

Paragraph 5

29.   As regards gains from the alienation of any property other than that referred to in paragraphs 1, 2, 3 and 4, paragraph 5 provides that they are taxable only in the State of which the alienator is a resident. This corresponds to the rules laid down in Article 22.

30.   The Article does not contain special rules for gains from the alienation of shares in a company (other than shares of a company dealt with in paragraph 4) or of securities, bonds, debentures and the like. Such gains are, therefore, taxable only in the State of which the alienator is a resident.

31.   If shares are sold by a shareholder to the issuing company in connection with the liquidation of such company or the reduction of its paid-up capital, the difference between the selling price and the par value of the shares may be treated in the State of which the company is a resident as a distribution of accumulated profits and not as a capital gain. The Article does not prevent the State of residence of the company from taxing such distributions at the rates provided for in Article 10: such taxation is permitted because such difference is covered by the definition of the term "dividends" contained in paragraph 3 of Article 10 and interpreted in paragraph 28 of the Commentary relating thereto. The same interpretation may apply if bonds or debentures are redeemed by the debtor at a price which is higher than the par value or the value at which the bonds or debentures have been issued; in such a case, the difference may represent interest and, therefore, be subjected to a limited tax in the State of source of the interest in accordance with Article 11 (see also paragraphs 20 and 21 of the Commentary on Article 11).

32.   There is a need to distinguish the capital gain that may be derived from the alienation of shares acquired upon the exercise of a stock-option granted to an employee or member of a board of directors from the benefit derived from the stock-option that is covered by Articles 15 or 16. The principles on which that distinction is based are discussed in paragraphs 12.2 to 12.5 of the Commentary on Article 15 and paragraph 3.1 of the Commentary on Article 16.

Reservations on the Article

33.   *Spain* reserves its right to tax gains from the alienation of shares or other rights where the ownership of such shares or rights entitles, directly or indirectly, to the enjoyment of immovable property situated in Spain.

34.   [Deleted]

35.   *Finland* reserves the right to tax gains from the alienation of shares or other corporate rights in Finnish companies, where the ownership of such shares or other

corporate rights entitles to the enjoyment of immovable property situated in Finland and held by the company.

36.   *France* can accept the provisions of paragraph 5, but wishes to retain the possibility of applying the provisions in its laws relative to the taxation of gains from the alienation of shares or rights which are part of a substantial participation in a company which is a resident of France.

37.   [Deleted]

38.   *New Zealand* reserves its position on paragraphs 3 and 5.

39.   *Chile* and *Sweden* reserve the right to tax gains from the alienation of shares or other corporate rights in their companies.

40.   *Turkey* reserves the right, in accordance with its legislation, to tax capital gains from the alienation, within its territory, of movable capital and any property other than those mentioned in paragraph 2 if the delay between their acquisition and their alienation is less than two years.

41.   Notwithstanding paragraph 5 of this Article, where the selling price of shares is considered to be dividends under Danish legislation, *Denmark* reserves the right to tax this selling price as dividends in accordance with paragraph 2 of Article 10.

42.   *Japan* reserves the right to tax gains from the alienation of a Japanese financial institution's shares if these shares were previously acquired by the alienator from the Government of Japan which had itself previously acquired the shares as part of the bail-out of the financial institution due to its insolvency.

43.   *Denmark, Ireland, Norway* and the *United Kingdom* reserve the right to insert in a special article provisions regarding capital gains relating to offshore hydrocarbon exploration and exploitation and related activities.

43.1   *Greece* reserves the right to insert in a special article provisions regarding capital gains relating to offshore exploration and exploitation and related activities.

44.   *Denmark, Norway* and *Sweden* reserve the right to insert special provisions regarding capital gains derived by the air transport consortium Scandinavian Airlines System (SAS).

45.   *Korea* reserves the right to tax gains from the alienation of shares or other rights forming part of a substantial participation in a company which is a resident.

46.   The *United States* wants to reserve its right to apply its tax on certain real estate gains under the Foreign Investment in Real Property Tax Act.

47.   In view of its particular situation in relation to shipping, *Greece* will retain its freedom of action with regard to the provisions in the Convention relating to capital gains from the alienation of ships in international traffic and movable property pertaining to the operation of such ships.

48.   *Ireland* reserves the right to tax gains from the alienation of property by an individual who was a resident of Ireland at any time during the five years preceding such alienation.

49.   *Mexico* reserves its position to retain the possibility of applying the provisions in its laws relative to the taxation of gains from the alienation of shares or similar rights in a company that is a resident of Mexico.

50.   The *United States* reserves the right to include gains from the alienation of containers within the scope of paragraph 3 of the Article.

51.   *Belgium*, *Luxembourg*, the *Netherlands* and *Switzerland* reserve the right not to include paragraph 4 in their conventions.

COMMENTARY ON ARTICLE 14
CONCERNING THE TAXATION OF INDEPENDENT PERSONAL SERVICES

[Article 14 was deleted from the Model Tax Convention on 29 April 2000 on the basis of the report entitled "Issues Related to Article 14 of the OECD Model Tax Convention" (adopted by the Committee on Fiscal Affairs on 27 January 2000 and reproduced in Volume II of the full-length version of the Model Tax Convention at page R(16)-1). That decision reflected the fact that there were no intended differences between the concepts of permanent establishment, as used in Article 7, and fixed base, as used in Article 14, or between how profits were computed and tax was calculated according to which of Article 7 or 14 applied. In addition, it was not always clear which activities fell within Article 14 as opposed to Article 7. The effect of the deletion of Article 14 is that income derived from professional services or other activities of an independent character is now dealt with under Article 7 as business profits.]

MODEL TAX CONVENTION (CONDENSED VERSION) – ISBN 978-92-64-08948-8 – © OECD 2010

COMMENTARY ON ARTICLE 15
CONCERNING THE TAXATION OF INCOME FROM EMPLOYMENT[1]

1.   Paragraph 1 establishes the general rule as to the taxation of income from employment (other than pensions), namely, that such income is taxable in the State where the employment is actually exercised. The issue of whether or not services are provided in the exercise of an employment may sometimes give rise to difficulties which are discussed in paragraphs 8.1 ff. Employment is exercised in the place where the employee is physically present when performing the activities for which the employment income is paid. One consequence of this would be that a resident of a Contracting State who derived remuneration, in respect of an employment, from sources in the other State could not be taxed in that other State in respect of that remuneration merely because the results of this work were exploited in that other State.

2.   The general rule is subject to exception only in the case of pensions (Article 18) and of remuneration and pensions in respect of government service (Article 19). Non-employment remuneration of members of boards of directors of companies is the subject of Article 16.

2.1   Member countries have generally understood the term "salaries, wages and other similar remuneration" to include benefits in kind received in respect of an employment (e.g. stock-options, the use of a residence or automobile, health or life insurance coverage and club memberships).

2.2   The condition provided by the Article for taxation by the State of source is that the salaries, wages or other similar remuneration be derived from the exercise of employment in that State. This applies regardless of when that income may be paid to, credited to or otherwise definitively acquired by the employee.

3.   Paragraph 2 contains, however, a general exception to the rule in paragraph 1. This exception covers all individuals rendering services in the course of an employment (sales representatives, construction workers, engineers, etc.), to the extent that their remuneration does not fall under the provisions of other Articles, such as those applying to government services or artistes and sportsmen.

4.   The three conditions prescribed in this paragraph must be satisfied for the remuneration to qualify for the exemption. The first condition is that the exemption is limited to the 183 day period. It is further stipulated that this time period may not be exceeded "in any twelve month period commencing or ending in the fiscal year concerned". This contrasts with the 1963 Draft Convention and the 1977 Model

---

1   Before 2000, the title of Article 15 referred to "Dependent Personal Services" by contrast to the title of Article 14 which referred to "Independent Personal Services". As a result of the elimination of the latter Article (see the history of Article 14 in the full-length version of the Model Tax Convention), the title of Article 15 was changed to refer to "Employment", a term that is more commonly used to describe the activities to which the Article applies. This change was not intended to affect the scope of the Article in any way.

Convention which provided that the 183 day period should not be exceeded "in the fiscal year concerned", a formulation that created difficulties where the fiscal years of the Contracting States did not coincide and which opened up opportunities in the sense that operations were sometimes organised in such a way that, for example, workers stayed in the State concerned for the last 5 1/2 months of one year and the first 5 1/2 months of the following year. The present wording of subparagraph 2 *a)* does away with such opportunities for tax avoidance. In applying that wording, all possible periods of twelve consecutive months must be considered, even periods which overlap others to a certain extent. For instance, if an employee is present in a State during 150 days between 1 April 01 and 31 March 02 but is present there during 210 days between 1 August 01 and 31 July 02, the employee will have been present for a period exceeding 183 days during the second 12 month period identified above even though he did not meet the minimum presence test during the first period considered and that first period partly overlaps the second.

5.   Although various formulas have been used by member countries to calculate the 183 day period, there is only one way which is consistent with the wording of this paragraph: the "days of physical presence" method. The application of this method is straightforward as the individual is either present in a country or he is not. The presence could also relatively easily be documented by the taxpayer when evidence is required by the tax authorities. Under this method the following days are included in the calculation: part of a day, day of arrival, day of departure and all other days spent inside the State of activity such as Saturdays and Sundays, national holidays, holidays before, during and after the activity, short breaks (training, strikes, lock-out, delays in supplies), days of sickness (unless they prevent the individual from leaving and he would have otherwise qualified for the exemption) and death or sickness in the family. However, days spent in the State of activity in transit in the course of a trip between two points outside the State of activity should be excluded from the computation. It follows from these principles that any entire day spent outside the State of activity, whether for holidays, business trips, or any other reason, should not be taken into account. A day during any part of which, however brief, the taxpayer is present in a State counts as a day of presence in that State for purposes of computing the 183 day period.

5.1   Days during which the taxpayer is a resident of the source State should not, however, be taken into account in the calculation. Subparagraph *a)* has to be read in the context of the first part of paragraph 2, which refers to "remuneration derived by a resident of a Contracting State in respect of an employment exercised in the other Contracting State", which does not apply to a person who resides and works in the same State. The words "the recipient is present", found in subparagraph *a)*, refer to the recipient of such remuneration and, during a period of residence in the source State, a person cannot be said to be the recipient of remuneration derived by a resident of a Contracting State in respect of an employment exercised in the other Contracting State. The following examples illustrate this conclusion:

— Example 1: From January 01 to December 01, X lives in, and is a resident of, State S. On 1 January 02, X is hired by an employer who is a resident of State R and moves to State R where he becomes a resident. X is subsequently sent to State S by his employer from 15 to 31 March 02. In that case, X is present in State S for 292 days between 1 April 01 and 31 March 02 but since he is a resident of State S between 1 April 01 and 31 December 01, this first period is not taken into account for purposes of the calculation of the periods referred to in subparagraph a).

— Example 2: From 15 to 31 October 01, Y, a resident of State R, is present in State S to prepare the expansion in that country of the business of ACO, also a resident of State R. On 1 May 02, Y moves to State S where she becomes a resident and works as the manager of a newly created subsidiary of ACO resident of State S. In that case, Y is present in State S for 184 days between 15 October 01 and 14 October 02 but since she is a resident of State S between 1 May and 14 October 02, this last period is not taken into account for purposes of the calculation of the periods referred to in subparagraph a).

6.   The second condition is that the employer paying the remuneration must not be a resident of the State in which the employment is exercised. Some member countries may, however, consider that it is inappropriate to extend the exception of paragraph 2 to cases where the employer is not a resident of the State of residence of the employee, as there might then be administrative difficulties in determining the employment income of the employee or in enforcing withholding obligations on the employer. Contracting States that share this view are free to adopt bilaterally the following alternative wording of subparagraph 2 b):

   b)   the remuneration is paid by, or on behalf of, an employer who is a resident of the first-mentioned State, and

6.1   The application of the second condition in the case of fiscally transparent partnerships presents difficulties since such partnerships cannot qualify as a resident of a Contracting State under Article 4 (see paragraph 8.2 of the Commentary on Article 4). While it is clear that such a partnership could qualify as an "employer" (especially under the domestic law definitions of the term in some countries, e.g. where an employer is defined as a person liable for a wage tax), the application of the condition at the level of the partnership regardless of the situation of the partners would therefore render the condition totally meaningless.

6.2   The object and purpose of subparagraphs b) and c) of paragraph 2 are to avoid the source taxation of short-term employments to the extent that the employment income is not allowed as a deductible expense in the State of source because the employer is not taxable in that State as he neither is a resident nor has a permanent establishment therein. These subparagraphs can also be justified by the fact that imposing source deduction requirements with respect to short-term employments in a given State may be considered to constitute an excessive administrative burden where the employer neither resides nor has a permanent establishment in that State. In order to achieve a meaningful interpretation of subparagraph b) that would accord with its context and its object, it should therefore be considered that, in the case of fiscally transparent partnerships, that subparagraph applies at the level of the partners. Thus, the concepts of "employer" and "resident", as found in subparagraph b), are applied at the level of the partners rather than at the level of a fiscally transparent partnership. This approach is consistent with that under which other provisions of tax conventions must be applied at the partners' rather than at the partnership's level. While this interpretation could create difficulties where the partners reside in different States, such difficulties could be addressed through the mutual agreement procedure by determining, for example, the State in which the partners who own the majority of the interests in the partnership reside (i.e. the State in which the greatest part of the deduction will be claimed).

7.   Under the third condition, if the employer has a permanent establishment in the State in which the employment is exercised, the exemption is given on condition that the remuneration is not borne by that permanent establishment. The phrase "borne by" must be interpreted in the light of the underlying purpose of subparagraph c) of the Article, which is to ensure that the exception provided for in paragraph 2 does not apply to remuneration that could give rise to a deduction, having regard to the principles of Article 7 and the nature of the remuneration, in computing the profits of a permanent establishment situated in the State in which the employment is exercised.

7.1   The fact that the employer has, or has not, actually claimed a deduction for the remuneration in computing the profits attributable to the permanent establishment is not necessarily conclusive since the proper test is whether any deduction otherwise available with respect to that remuneration should be taken into account in determining the profits attributable to the permanent establishment. That test would be met, for instance, even if no amount were actually deducted as a result of the permanent establishment being exempt from tax in the source country or of the employer simply deciding not to claim a deduction to which he was entitled. The test would also be met where the remuneration is not deductible merely because of its nature (e.g. where the State takes the view that the issuing of shares pursuant to an employee stock-option does not give rise to a deduction) rather than because it should not be allocated to the permanent establishment.

7.2   For the purpose of determining the profits attributable to a permanent establishment pursuant to paragraph 2 of Article 7, the remuneration paid to an employee of an enterprise of a Contracting State for employment services rendered in the other State for the benefit of a permanent establishment of the enterprise situated in that other State may, given the circumstances, either give rise to a direct deduction or give rise to the deduction of a notional charge, e.g. for services rendered to the permanent establishment by another part of the enterprise. In the latter case, since the notional charge required by the legal fiction of the separate and independent enterprise that is applicable under paragraph 2 of Article 7 is merely a mechanism provided for by that paragraph for the sole purpose of determining the profits attributable to the permanent establishment, this fiction does not affect the

 MODEL TAX CONVENTION (CONDENSED VERSION) – ISBN 978-92-64-08948-8 – © OECD 2010

determination of whether or not the remuneration is borne by the permanent establishment.

8.   There is a direct relationship between the principles underlying the exception of paragraph 2 and Article 7. Article 7 is based on the principle that an enterprise of a Contracting State should not be subjected to tax in the other State unless its business presence in that other State has reached a level sufficient to constitute a permanent establishment. The exception of paragraph 2 of Article 15 extends that principle to the taxation of the employees of such an enterprise where the activities of these employees are carried on in the other State for a relatively short period. Subparagraphs b) and c) make it clear that the exception is not intended to apply where the employment services are rendered to an enterprise the profits of which are subjected to tax in a State either because it is carried on by a resident of that State or because it has a permanent establishment therein to which the services are attributable.

8.1   It may be difficult, in certain cases, to determine whether the services rendered in a State by an individual resident of another State, and provided to an enterprise of the first State (or that has a permanent establishment in that State), constitute employment services, to which Article 15 applies, or services rendered by a separate enterprise, to which Article 7 applies or, more generally, whether the exception applies. While the Commentary previously dealt with cases where arrangements were structured for the main purpose of obtaining the benefits of the exception of paragraph 2 of Article 15, it was found that similar issues could arise in many other cases that did not involve tax-motivated transactions and the Commentary was amended to provide a more comprehensive discussion of these questions.

8.2   In some States, a formal contractual relationship would not be questioned for tax purposes unless there were some evidence of manipulation and these States, as a matter of domestic law, would consider that employment services are only rendered where there is a formal employment relationship.

8.3   If States where this is the case are concerned that such approach could result in granting the benefits of the exception provided for in paragraph 2 in unintended situations (e.g. in so-called "hiring-out of labour" cases), they are free to adopt bilaterally a provision drafted along the following lines:

Paragraph 2 of this Article shall not apply to remuneration derived by a resident of a Contracting State in respect of an employment exercised in the other Contracting State and paid by, or on behalf of, an employer who is not a resident of that other State if:

a) the recipient renders services in the course of that employment to a person other than the employer and that person, directly or indirectly, supervises, directs or controls the manner in which those services are performed; and

b) those services constitute an integral part of the business activities carried on by that person.

8.4   In many States, however, various legislative or jurisprudential rules and criteria (*e.g.* substance over form rules) have been developed for the purpose of distinguishing cases where services rendered by an individual to an enterprise should be considered to be rendered in an employment relationship (contract of service) from cases where such services should be considered to be rendered under a contract for the provision of services between two separate enterprises (contract for services). That distinction keeps its importance when applying the provisions of Article 15, in particular those of subparagraphs 2 *b*) and *c*). Subject to the limit described in paragraph 8.11 and unless the context of a particular convention requires otherwise, it is a matter of domestic law of the State of source to determine whether services rendered by an individual in that State are provided in an employment relationship and that determination will govern how that State applies the Convention.

8.5   In some cases, services rendered by an individual to an enterprise may be considered to be employment services for purposes of domestic tax law even though these services are provided under a formal contract for services between, on the one hand, the enterprise that acquires the services, and, on the other hand, either the individual himself or another enterprise by which the individual is formally employed or with which the individual has concluded another formal contract for services.

8.6   In such cases, the relevant domestic law may ignore the way in which the services are characterised in the formal contracts. It may prefer to focus primarily on the nature of the services rendered by the individual and their integration into the business carried on by the enterprise that acquires the services to conclude that there is an employment relationship between the individual and that enterprise.

8.7   Since the concept of employment to which Article 15 refers is to be determined according to the domestic law of the State that applies the Convention (subject to the limit described in paragraph 8.11 and unless the context of a particular convention requires otherwise), it follows that a State which considers such services to be employment services will apply Article 15 accordingly. It will, therefore, logically conclude that the enterprise to which the services are rendered is in an employment relationship with the individual so as to constitute his employer for purposes of subparagraph 2 *b*) and *c*). That conclusion is consistent with the object and purpose of paragraph 2 of Article 15 since, in that case, the employment services may be said to be rendered to a resident of the State where the services are performed.

8.8   As mentioned in paragraph 8.2, even where the domestic law of the State that applies the Convention does not offer the possibility of questioning a formal contractual relationship and therefore does not allow the State to consider that services rendered to a local enterprise by an individual who is formally employed by a non-resident are rendered in an employment relationship (contract of service) with that local enterprise, it is possible for that State to deny the application of the exception of paragraph 2 in abusive cases.

8.9   The various approaches that are available to States that want to deal with such abusive cases are discussed in the section "Improper use of the Convention" in the

Commentary on Article 1. As explained in paragraph 9.4 of that Commentary, it is agreed that States do not have to grant the benefits of a tax convention where arrangements that constitute an abuse of the Convention have been entered into. As noted in paragraphs 9.5 of that Commentary, however, it should not be lightly assumed that this is the case (see also paragraph 22.2 of that Commentary).

8.10   The approach described in the previous paragraphs therefore allows the State in which the activities are exercised to reject the application of paragraph 2 in abusive cases and in cases where, under that State's domestic law concept of employment, services rendered to a local enterprise by an individual who is formally employed by a non-resident are rendered in an employment relationship (contract of service) with that local enterprise. This approach ensures that relief of double taxation will be provided in the State of residence of the individual even if that State does not, under its own domestic law, consider that there is an employment relationship between the individual and the enterprise to which the services are provided. Indeed, as long as the State of residence acknowledges that the concept of employment in the domestic tax law of the State of source or the existence of arrangements that constitute an abuse of the Convention allows that State to tax the employment income of an individual in accordance with the Convention, it must grant relief for double taxation pursuant to the obligations incorporated in Articles 23 A and 23 B (see paragraphs 32.1 to 32.7 of the Commentary on these articles). The mutual agreement procedure provided by paragraph 1 of Article 25 will be available to address cases where the State of residence does not agree that the other State has correctly applied the approach described above and, therefore, does not consider that the other State has taxed the relevant income in accordance with the Convention.

8.11   The conclusion that, under domestic law, a formal contractual relationship should be disregarded must, however, be arrived at on the basis of objective criteria. For instance, a State could not argue that services are deemed, under its domestic law, to constitute employment services where, under the relevant facts and circumstances, it clearly appears that these services are rendered under a contract for the provision of services concluded between two separate enterprises. The relief provided under paragraph 2 of Article 15 would be rendered meaningless if States were allowed to deem services to constitute employment services in cases where there is clearly no employment relationship or to deny the quality of employer to an enterprise carried on by a non-resident where it is clear that that enterprise provides services, through its own personnel, to an enterprise carried on by a resident. Conversely, where services rendered by an individual may properly be regarded by a State as rendered in an employment relationship rather than as under a contract for services concluded between two enterprises, that State should logically also consider that the individual is not carrying on the business of the enterprise that constitutes that individual's formal employer; this could be relevant, for example, for purposes of determining whether that enterprise has a permanent establishment at the place where the individual performs his activities.

8.12 It will not always be clear, however, whether services rendered by an individual may properly be regarded by a State as rendered in an employment relationship rather than as under a contract for services concluded between two enterprises. Any disagreement between States as to whether this is the case should be solved having regard to the following principles and examples (using, where appropriate, the mutual agreement procedure).

8.13 The nature of the services rendered by the individual will be an important factor since it is logical to assume that an employee provides services which are an integral part of the business activities carried on by his employer. It will therefore be important to determine whether the services rendered by the individual constitute an integral part of the business of the enterprise to which these services are provided. For that purpose, a key consideration will be which enterprise bears the responsibility or risk for the results produced by the individual's work. Clearly, however, this analysis will only be relevant if the services of an individual are rendered directly to an enterprise. Where, for example, an individual provides services to a contract manufacturer or to an enterprise to which business is outsourced, the services of that individual are not rendered to enterprises that will obtain the products or services in question.

8.14 Where a comparison of the nature of the services rendered by the individual with the business activities carried on by his formal employer and by the enterprise to which the services are provided points to an employment relationship that is different from the formal contractual relationship, the following additional factors may be relevant to determine whether this is really the case:

— who has the authority to instruct the individual regarding the manner in which the work has to be performed;

— who controls and has responsibility for the place at which the work is performed;

— the remuneration of the individual is directly charged by the formal employer to the enterprise to which the services are provided (see paragraph 8.15 below);

— who puts the tools and materials necessary for the work at the individual's disposal;

— who determines the number and qualifications of the individuals performing the work;

— who has the right to select the individual who will perform the work and to terminate the contractual arrangements entered into with that individual for that purpose;

— who has the right to impose disciplinary sanctions related to the work of that individual;

— who determines the holidays and work schedule of that individual.

8.15 Where an individual who is formally an employee of one enterprise provides services to another enterprise, the financial arrangements made between the two enterprises will clearly be relevant, although not necessarily conclusive, for the purposes of determining whether the remuneration of the individual is directly charged by the formal employer to the enterprise to which the services are provided.

For instance, if the fees charged by the enterprise that formally employs the individual represent the remuneration, employment benefits and other employment costs of that individual for the services that he provided to the other enterprise, with no profit element or with a profit element that is computed as a percentage of that remuneration, benefits and other employment costs, this would be indicative that the remuneration of the individual is directly charged by the formal employer to the enterprise to which the services are provided. That should not be considered to be the case, however, if the fee charged for the services bears no relationship to the remuneration of the individual or if that remuneration is only one of many factors taken into account in the fee charged for what is really a contract for services (*e.g.* where a consulting firm charges a client on the basis of an hourly fee for the time spent by one of its employee to perform a particular contract and that fee takes account of the various costs of the enterprise), provided that this is in conformity with the arm's length principle if the two enterprises are associated. It is important to note, however, that the question of whether the remuneration of the individual is directly charged by the formal employer to the enterprise to which the services are provided is only one of the subsidiary factors that are relevant in determining whether services rendered by that individual may properly be regarded by a State as rendered in an employment relationship rather than as under a contract for services concluded between two enterprises.

8.16   Example 1: Aco, a company resident of State A, concludes a contract with Bco, a company resident of State B, for the provision of training services. Aco is specialised in training people in the use of various computer software and Bco wishes to train its personnel to use recently acquired software. X, an employee of Aco who is a resident of State A, is sent to Bco's offices in State B to provide training courses as part of the contract.

8.17   In that case, State B could not argue that X is in an employment relationship with Bco or that Aco is not the employer of X for purposes of the convention between States A and B. X is formally an employee of Aco whose own services, when viewed in light of the factors in paragraphs 8.13 and 8.14, form an integral part of the business activities of Aco. The services that he renders to Bco are rendered on behalf of Aco under the contract concluded between the two enterprises. Thus, provided that X is not present in State B for more than 183 days during any relevant twelve month period and that Aco does not have in State B a permanent establishment which bears the cost of X's remuneration, the exception of paragraph 2 of Article 15 will apply to X's remuneration.

8.18   Example 2: Cco, a company resident of State C, is the parent company of a group of companies that includes Dco, a company resident of State D. Cco has developed a new worldwide marketing strategy for the products of the group. In order to ensure that the strategy is well understood and followed by Dco, which sells the group's products, Cco sends X, one of its employees who has worked on the development of the strategy, to work in Dco's headquarters for four months in order to advise Dco with respect to its marketing and to ensure that Dco's communications department understands and complies with the worldwide marketing strategy.

8.19   In that case, Cco's business includes the management of the worldwide marketing activities of the group and X's own services are an integral part of that business activity. While it could be argued that an employee could have been easily hired by Dco to perform the function of advising the company with respect to its marketing, it is clear that such function is frequently performed by a consultant, especially where specialised knowledge is required for a relatively short period of time. Also, the function of monitoring the compliance with the group's worldwide marketing strategy belongs to the business of Cco rather than to that of Dco. The exception of paragraph 2 of Article 15 should therefore apply provided that the other conditions for that exception are satisfied.

8.20   Example 3: A multinational owns and operates hotels worldwide through a number of subsidiaries. Eco, one of these subsidiaries, is a resident of State E where it owns and operates a hotel. X is an employee of Eco who works in this hotel. Fco, another subsidiary of the group, owns and operates a hotel in State F where there is a shortage of employees with foreign language skills. For that reason, X is sent to work for five months at the reception desk of Fco's hotel. Fco pays the travel expenses of X, who remains formally employed and paid by Eco, and pays Eco a management fee based on X's remuneration, social contributions and other employment benefits for the relevant period.

8.21   In that case, working at the reception desk of the hotel in State F, when examined in light of the factors in paragraphs 8.13 and 8.14, may be viewed as forming an integral part of Fco's business of operating that hotel rather than of Eco's business. Under the approach described above, if, under the domestic law of State F, the services of X are considered to have been rendered to Fco in an employment relationship, State F could then logically consider that Fco is the employer of X and the exception of paragraph 2 of Article 15 would not apply.

8.22   Example 4: Gco is a company resident of State G. It carries on the business of filling temporary business needs for highly specialised personnel. Hco is a company resident of State H which provides engineering services on building sites. In order to complete one of its contracts in State H, Hco needs an engineer for a period of five months. It contacts Gco for that purpose. Gco recruits X, an engineer resident of State X, and hires him under a five month employment contract. Under a separate contract between Gco and Hco, Gco agrees to provide the services of X to Hco during that period. Under these contracts, Gco will pay X's remuneration, social contributions, travel expenses and other employment benefits and charges.

8.23   In that case, X provides engineering services while Gco is in the business of filling short-term business needs. By their nature the services rendered by X are not an integral part of the business activities of his formal employer. These services are, however, an integral part of the business activities of Hco, an engineering firm. In light of the factors in paragraphs 8.13 and 8.14, State H could therefore consider that, under the approach described above, the exception of paragraph 2 of Article 15 would not apply with respect to the remuneration for the services of the engineer that will be rendered in that State.

8.24 Example 5: Ico is a company resident of State I specialised in providing engineering services. Ico employs a number of engineers on a full time basis. Jco, a smaller engineering firm resident of State J, needs the temporary services of an engineer to complete a contract on a construction site in State J. Ico agrees with Jco that one of Ico's engineers, who is a resident of State I momentarily not assigned to any contract concluded by Ico, will work for four months on Jco's contract under the direct supervision and control of one of Jco's senior engineers. Jco will pay Ico an amount equal to the remuneration, social contributions, travel expenses and other employment benefits of that engineer for the relevant period, together with a 5 per cent commission. Jco also agrees to indemnify Ico for any eventual claims related to the engineer's work during that period of time.

8.25 In that case, even if Ico is in the business of providing engineering services, it is clear that the work performed by the engineer on the construction site in State J is performed on behalf of Jco rather than Ico. The direct supervision and control exercised by Jco over the work of the engineer, the fact that Jco takes over the responsibility for that work and that it bears the cost of the remuneration of the engineer for the relevant period are factors that could support the conclusion that the engineer is in an employment relationship with Jco. Under the approach described above, State J could therefore consider that the exception of paragraph 2 of Article 15 would not apply with respect to the remuneration for the services of the engineer that will be rendered in that State.

8.26 Example 6: Kco, a company resident of State K, and Lco, a company resident of State L, are part of the same multinational group of companies. A large part of the activities of that group are structured along function lines, which requires employees of different companies of the group to work together under the supervision of managers who are located in different States and employed by other companies of the group. X is a resident of State K employed by Kco; she is a senior manager in charge of supervising human resources functions within the multinational group. Since X is employed by Kco, Kco acts as a cost centre for the human resource costs of the group; periodically, these costs are charged out to each of the companies of the group on the basis of a formula that takes account of various factors such as the number of employees of each company. X is required to travel frequently to other States where other companies of the group have their offices. During the last year, X spent three months in State L in order to deal with human resources issues at Lco.

8.27 In that case, the work performed by X is part of the activities that Kco performs for its multinational group. These activities, like other activities such as corporate communication, strategy, finance and tax, treasury, information management and legal support, are often centralised within a large group of companies. The work that X performs is thus an integral part of the business of Kco. The exception of paragraph 2 of Article 15 should therefore apply to the remuneration derived by X for her work in State L provided that the other conditions for that exception are satisfied.

8.28 Where, in accordance with the above principles and examples, a State properly considers that the services rendered on its territory by an individual have been rendered in an employment relationship rather than under a contract for services concluded between two enterprises, there will be a risk that the enterprises would be required to withhold tax at source in two jurisdictions on the remuneration of that individual even though double taxation should ultimately be avoided (see paragraph 8.10 above). This compliance difficulty may be partly reduced by tax administrations making sure that their domestic rules and practices applicable to employment are clear and well understood by employers and are easily accessible. Also, the problem can be alleviated if the State of residence allows enterprises to quickly adjust the amount of tax to be withheld to take account of any relief for double taxation that will likely be available to the employee.

9.   Paragraph 3 applies to the remuneration of crews of ships or aircraft operated in international traffic, or of boats engaged in inland waterways transport, a rule which follows up to a certain extent the rule applied to the income from shipping, inland waterways transport and air transport, that is, to tax them in the Contracting State in which the place of effective management of the enterprise concerned is situated. In the Commentary on Article 8, it is indicated that Contracting States may agree to confer the right to tax such income on the State of the enterprise operating the ships, boats or aircraft. The reasons for introducing that possibility in the case of income from shipping, inland waterways and air transport operations are valid also in respect of remuneration of the crew. Accordingly Contracting States are left free to agree on a provision which gives the right to tax such remuneration to the State of the enterprise. Such a provision, as well as that of paragraph 3 of Article 15, assumes that the domestic laws of the State on which the right to tax is conferred allows it to tax the remuneration of a person in the service of the enterprise concerned, irrespective of his residence. It is understood that paragraph 3 of Article 8 is applicable if the place of effective management of a shipping enterprise or of an inland waterways transport enterprise is aboard a ship or a boat. According to the domestic laws of some member countries, tax is levied on remuneration received by non-resident members of the crew in respect of employment aboard ships only if the ship has the nationality of such a State. For that reason conventions concluded between these States provide that the right to tax such remuneration is given to the State of the nationality of the ship. On the other hand many States cannot make use of such a taxation right and the provision could in such cases lead to non-taxation. However, States having that taxation principle in their domestic laws may agree bilaterally to confer the right to tax remuneration in respect of employment aboard ships on the State of the nationality of the ship.

10.   It should be noted that no special rules regarding the taxation of income of frontier workers or of employees working on trucks and trains travelling between States are included as it would be more suitable for the problems created by local conditions to be solved directly between the States concerned.

11.   No special provision has been made regarding remuneration derived by visiting professors or students employed with a view to their acquiring practical experience. Many conventions contain rules of some kind or other concerning such cases, the main

purpose of which is to facilitate cultural relations by providing for a limited tax exemption. Sometimes, tax exemption is already provided under domestic taxation laws. The absence of specific rules should not be interpreted as constituting an obstacle to the inclusion of such rules in bilateral conventions whenever this is felt desirable.

The treatment of employee stock-options

12.   The different country rules for taxing employee stock-options create particular problems which are discussed below. While many of these problems arise with respect to other forms of employee remuneration, particularly those that are based on the value of shares of the employer or a related company, they are particularly acute in the case of stock-options. This is largely due to the fact that stock-options are often taxed at a time (*e.g.* when the option is exercised or the shares sold) that is different from the time when the employment services that are remunerated through these options are rendered.

12.1   As noted in paragraph 2.2, the Article allows the State of source to tax the part of the stock-option benefit that constitutes remuneration derived from employment exercised in that State even if the tax is levied at a later time when the employee is no longer employed in that State.

12.2   While the Article applies to the employment benefit derived from a stock-option granted to an employee regardless of when that benefit is taxed, there is a need to distinguish that employment benefit from the capital gain that may be derived from the alienation of shares acquired upon the exercise of the option. This Article, and not Article 13, will apply to any benefit derived from the option itself until it has been exercised, sold or otherwise alienated (*e.g.* upon cancellation or acquisition by the employer or issuer). Once the option is exercised or alienated, however, the employment benefit has been realised and any subsequent gain on the acquired shares (*i.e.* the value of the shares that accrues after exercise) will be derived by the employee in his capacity of investor-shareholder and will be covered by Article 13. Indeed, it is at the time of exercise that the option, which is what the employee obtained from his employment, disappears and the recipient obtains the status of shareholder (and usually invests money in order to do so). Where, however, the option that has been exercised entitles the employee to acquire shares that will not irrevocably vest until the end of a period of required employment, it will be appropriate to apply this Article to the increase in value, if any, until the end of the required period of employment that is subsequent to the exercise of the option.

12.3   The fact that the Article does not apply to a benefit derived after the exercise or alienation of the option does not imply in any way that taxation of the employment income under domestic law must occur at the time of that exercise or alienation. As already noted, the Article does not impose any restriction as to when the relevant income may be taxed by the State of source. Thus, the State of source could tax the relevant income at the time the option is granted, at the time the option is exercised (or alienated), at the time the share is sold or at any other time. The State of source, however, may only tax the benefits attributable to the option itself and not what is attributable to the subsequent holding of shares acquired upon the exercise of that option (except in the circumstances described in the last sentence of the preceding paragraph).

12.4 Since paragraph 1 must be interpreted to apply to any benefit derived from the option until it has been exercised, sold or otherwise alienated, it does not matter how such benefit, or any part thereof, is characterised for domestic tax purposes. As a result, whilst the Article will be interpreted to allow the State of source to tax the benefits accruing up to the time when the option has been exercised, sold or otherwise alienated, it will be left to that State to decide how to tax such benefits, *e.g.* as either employment income or capital gain. If the State of source decides, for example, to impose a capital gains tax on the option when the employee ceases to be a resident of that country, that tax will be allowed under the Article. The same will be true in the State of residence. For example, while that State will have sole taxation right on the increase of value of the share obtained after exercise since this will be considered to fall under Article 13 of the Convention, it may well decide to tax such increase as employment income rather than as a capital gain under its domestic law.

12.5 The benefits resulting from a stock-option granted to an employee will not, as a general rule, fall under either Article 21, which does not apply to income covered by other Articles, or Article 18, which only applies to pension and other similar remuneration, even if the option is exercised after termination of the employment or retirement.

12.6 Paragraph 1 allows the State of source to tax salaries, wages and other similar remuneration derived from employment exercised in that State. The determination of whether and to what extent an employee stock-option is derived from employment exercised in a particular State must be done in each case on the basis of all the relevant facts and circumstances, including the contractual conditions associated with that option (*e.g.* the conditions under which the option granted may be exercised or disposed of). The following general principles should be followed for that purpose.

12.7 The first principle is that, as a general rule, an employee stock-option should not be considered to relate to any services rendered after the period of employment that is required as a condition for the employee to acquire the right to exercise that option. Thus, where a stock-option is granted to an employee on the condition that he provides employment services to the same employer (or an associated enterprise) for a period of three years, the employment benefit derived from that option should generally not be attributed to services performed after that three year period.

12.8 In applying the above principle, however, it is important to distinguish between a period of employment that is required to obtain the right to exercise an employee stock-option and a period of time that is merely a delay before such option may be exercised (a blocking period). Thus, for example, an option that is granted to an employee on the condition that he remains employed by the same employer (or an associated enterprise) during a period of three years can be considered to be derived from the services performed during these three years while an option that is granted, without any condition of subsequent employment, to an employee on a given date but which, under its terms and conditions, can only be exercised after a delay of three years, should not be considered to relate to the employment performed during these years as the benefit of such an option would accrue to its recipient even if he were to leave his employment immediately after receiving it and waited the required three years before exercising it.

12.9 It is also important to distinguish between a situation where a period of employment is required as a condition for the acquisition of the right to exercise an option, i.e. the vesting of the option, and a situation where an option that has already vested may be forfeited if it is not exercised before employment is terminated (or within a short period after). In the latter situation, the benefit of the option should not be considered to relate to services rendered after vesting since the employee has already obtained the benefit and could in fact realise it at any time. A condition under which the vested option may be forfeited if employment is terminated is not a condition for the acquisition of the benefit but, rather, one under which the benefit already acquired may subsequently be lost. The following examples illustrate this distinction:

— Example 1: On 1 January of year 1, a stock-option is granted to an employee. The acquisition of the option is conditional on the employee continuing to be employed by the same employer until 1 January of year 3. The option, once this condition is met, will be exercisable from 1 January of year 3 until 1 January of year 10 (a so-called "American" option[1]). It is further provided, however, that any option not previously exercised will be lost upon cessation of employment. In that example, the right to exercise that option has been acquired on 1 January of year 3 (i.e. the date of vesting) since no further period of employment is then required for the employee to obtain the right to exercise the option.

— Example 2: On 1 January of year 1, a stock-option is granted to an employee. The option is exercisable on 1 January of year 5 (a so-called "European" option). The option has been granted subject to the condition that it can only be exercised on 1 January of year 5 if employment is not terminated before that date. In that example, the right to exercise that option is not acquired until 1 January of year 5, which is the date of exercise, since employment until that date is required to acquire the right to exercise the option (i.e. for the option to vest).

12.10 There are cases where that first principle might not apply. One such case could be where the stock-option is granted without any condition to an employee at the time he either takes up an employment, is transferred to a new country or is given significant new responsibilities and, in each case, the option clearly relates to the new

---

1 Under an "American" stock-option, the right to acquire a share may be exercised during a certain period (typically a number of years) whilst under a European stock-option, that right may only be exercised at a given moment (i.e. on a particular date).

functions to be performed by the employee during a specific future period. In that case, it may be appropriate to consider that the option relates to these new functions even if the right to exercise the option is acquired before these are performed. There are also cases where an option vested technically but where that option entitles the employee to acquire shares which will not vest until the end of a period of required employment. In such cases, it may be appropriate to consider that the benefit of the option relates to the services rendered in the whole period between the grant of the option and the vesting of the shares.

12.11 The second principle is that an employee stock-option should only be considered to relate to services rendered before the time when it is granted to the extent that such grant is intended to reward the provision of such services by the recipient for a specific period. This would be the case, for example, where the remuneration is demonstrably based on the employee's past performance during a certain period or is based on the employer's past financial results and is conditional on the employee having been employed by the employer or an associated enterprise during a certain period to which these financial results relate. Also, in some cases, there may be objective evidence demonstrating that during a period of past employment, there was a well-founded expectation among participants to an employee stock-option plan that part of their remuneration for that period would be provided through the plan by having stock-options granted at a later date. This evidence might include, for example, the consistent practice of an employer that has granted similar levels of stock-options over a number of years, as long as there was no indication that this practice might be discontinued. Depending on other factors, such evidence may be highly relevant for purposes of determining if and to what extent the stock-option relates to such a period of past employment.

12.12 Where a period of employment is required to obtain the right to exercise an employee's stock-option but such requirement is not applied in certain circumstances, e.g. where the employment is terminated by the employer or where the employee reaches retirement age, the stock-option benefit should be considered to relate only to the period of services actually performed when these circumstances have in fact occurred.

12.13 Finally, there may be situations in which some factors may suggest that an employee stock-option is rewarding past services but other factors seem to indicate that it relates to future services. In cases of doubt, it should be recognised that employee stock-options are generally provided as an incentive to future performance or as a way to retain valuable employees. Thus, employee stock-options are primarily related to future services. However, all relevant facts and circumstances will need to be taken into account before such a determination can be made and there may be cases where it can be shown that a stock-option is related to combined specific periods of previous and future services (e.g. options are granted on the basis of the employee having achieved specific performance targets for the previous year, but they become exercisable only if the employee remains employed for another three years).

12.14 Where, based on the preceding principles, a stock-option is considered to be derived from employment exercised in more than one State, it will be necessary to determine which part of the stock-option benefit is derived from employment exercised in each State for purposes of the application of the Article and of Articles 23 A and 23 B. In such a case, the employment benefit attributable to the stock-option should be considered to be derived from a particular country in proportion of the number of days during which employment has been exercised in that country to the total number of days during which the employment services from which the stock-option is derived has been exercised. For that purpose, the only days of employment that should be taken into account are those that are relevant for the stock-option plan, e.g. those during which services are rendered to the same employer or to other employers the employment by whom would be taken into account to satisfy a period of employment required to acquire the right to exercise the option.

12.15 It is possible for member countries to depart from the case-by-case application of the above principles (in paragraphs 12.7 to 12.14) by agreeing to a specific approach in a bilateral context. For example, two countries that tax predominantly at exercise of an option may agree, as a general principle, to attribute the income from an option that relates primarily to future services to the services performed by an employee in the two States between date of grant and date of exercise. Thus, in the case of options that do not become exercisable until the employee has performed services for the employer for a specific period of time, two States could agree to an approach that attributes the income from the option to each State based on the number of days worked in each State by the employee for the employer in the period between date of grant and date of exercise. Another example would be for two countries that have similar rules for the tax treatment of employee stock-options to adopt provisions that would give to one of the Contracting States exclusive taxation rights on the employment benefit even if a minor part of the employment services to which the option relates have been rendered in the other State. Of course, member countries should be careful in adopting such approaches because they may result in double taxation or double non-taxation if part of the employment is exercised in a third State that does not apply a similar approach.

Observations on the Commentary

13. *France* considers that paragraph 8.13 should not be interpreted as being sufficient in itself to question a formal contractual relationship. If, with respect to paragraph 8.13, the services rendered by an individual constitute an integral part of the business of the enterprise to which these services are provided, the situation should then be analysed in accordance with the provisions of paragraph 8.14.

13.1 With respect to paragraph 6.2, *Germany* holds the view that a partnership as such should be considered as the employer (as under the national law of most OECD member States even if these States do not tax the partnership as such). The residence of the partnership would then have to be determined hypothetically as if the partnership were liable to tax by reason of one of the criteria mentioned in paragraph 1.

Reservations on the Article

14.   *Slovenia* reserves the right to add an article which addresses the situation of teachers, professors and researchers, subject to various conditions, and to make a corresponding modification to paragraph 1 of Article 15.

15.   *Denmark, Norway* and *Sweden* reserve the right to insert special provisions regarding remuneration derived in respect of an employment exercised aboard an aircraft operated in international traffic by the air transport consortium Scandinavian Airlines System (SAS).

16.   *Germany* and *Norway* reserve the right to include an express reference in paragraph 2 to income earned by hired-out personnel of one Contracting State working in the other Contracting State, in order to clarify the understanding that the exception in paragraph 2 does not apply in situations of "international hiring-out of labour".

17.   *Ireland, Norway* and the *United Kingdom* reserve the right to insert in a special article provisions regarding income derived from employment relating to offshore hydrocarbon exploration and exploitation and related activities.

18.   [Deleted]

19.   *Switzerland* reserves its position on subparagraph *a)* of paragraph 2 and wishes to insert in its conventions the words "in the fiscal year concerned" instead of the words "in any twelve month period commencing or ending in the fiscal year concerned".

20.   In view of its particular situation in relation to shipping, *Greece* will retain its freedom of action with regard to the provisions in the Convention relating to remuneration of crews of ships in international traffic.

21.   *Greece* reserves the right to insert special provisions regarding income from employment relating to offshore activities.

COMMENTARY ON ARTICLE 16
CONCERNING THE TAXATION OF DIRECTORS' FEES

1.   This Article relates to remuneration received by a resident of a Contracting State, whether an individual or a legal person, in the capacity of a member of a board of directors of a company which is a resident of the other Contracting State. Since it might sometimes be difficult to ascertain where the services are performed, the provision treats the services as performed in the State of residence of the company.

1.1   Member countries have generally understood the term "fees and other similar payments" to include benefits in kind received by a person in that person's capacity as a member of the board of directors of a company (e.g. stock-options, the use of a residence or automobile, health or life insurance coverage and club memberships).

2.   A member of the board of directors of a company often also has other functions with the company, e.g. as ordinary employee, adviser, consultant, etc. It is clear that the Article does not apply to remuneration paid to such a person on account of such other functions.

3.   In some countries organs of companies exist which are similar in function to the board of directors. Contracting States are free to include in bilateral conventions such organs of companies under a provision corresponding to Article 16.

3.1   Many of the issues discussed under paragraphs 12 to 12.15 of the Commentary on Article 15 in relation to stock-options granted to employees will also arise in the case of stock-options granted to members of the board of directors of companies. To the extent that stock-options are granted to a resident of a Contracting State in that person's capacity as a member of the board of directors of a company which is a resident of the other State, that other State will have the right to tax the part of the stock-option benefit that constitutes director's fees or a similar payment (see paragraph 1.1 above) even if the tax is levied at a later time when the person is no longer a member of that board. While the Article applies to the benefit derived from a stock-option granted to a member of the board of directors regardless of when that benefit is taxed, there is a need to distinguish that benefit from the capital gain that may be derived from the alienation of shares acquired upon the exercise of the option. This Article, and not Article 13, will apply to any benefit derived from the option itself until it has been exercised, sold or otherwise alienated (e.g. upon cancellation or acquisition by the company or issuer). Once the option is exercised or alienated, however, the benefit taxable under this Article has been realised and any subsequent gain on the acquired shares (i.e. the value of the shares that accrues after exercise) will be derived by the member of the board of directors in his capacity of investor-shareholder and will be covered by Article 13. Indeed, it is at the time of exercise that the option, which is what the director obtained in his capacity as such, disappears and the recipient obtains the status of shareholder (and usually invests money in order to do so).

Reservations on the Article

4.   [Deleted]

5.   The *United States* will require that any tax imposed on such fees be limited to the income earned from services performed in the country of source.

6.   *Belgium* reserves the right to state that remuneration that a person dealt with in Article 16 receives in respect of daily activities as well as remuneration that a partner of a company, other than a company with share capital, receives in respect of his personal activities for the company shall be taxable in accordance with the provisions of Article 15.

7.   *Greece* reserves the right to apply Article 16 to remuneration of a partner who acts in the capacity of a manager of a Greek limited liability company or of a Greek partnership.

COMMENTARY ON ARTICLE 17
CONCERNING THE TAXATION OF ARTISTES AND SPORTSMEN

Paragraph 1

1.　Paragraph 1 provides that artistes and sportsmen who are residents of a Contracting State may be taxed in the other Contracting State in which their personal activities as such are performed, whether these are of a business or employment nature. This provision is an exception to the rules in Article 7 and to that in paragraph 2 of Article 15, respectively.

2.　This provision makes it possible to avoid the practical difficulties which often arise in taxing artistes and sportsmen performing abroad. Moreover, too strict provisions might in certain cases impede cultural exchanges. In order to overcome this disadvantage, the States concerned may, by common agreement, limit the application of paragraph 1 to business activities. To achieve this it would be sufficient to amend the text of the Article so that an exception is made only to the provisions of Article 7. In such a case, artistes and sportsmen performing in the course of an employment would automatically come within Article 15 and thus be entitled to the exemptions provided for in paragraph 2 of that Article.

3.　Paragraph 1 refers to artistes and sportsmen. It is not possible to give a precise definition of "artiste", but paragraph 1 includes examples of persons who would be regarded as such. These examples should not be considered as exhaustive. On the one hand, the term "artiste" clearly includes the stage performer, film actor, actor (including for instance a former sportsman) in a television commercial. The Article may also apply to income received from activities which involve a political, social, religious or charitable nature, if an entertainment character is present. On the other hand, it does not extend to a visiting conference speaker or to administrative or support staff (e.g. cameramen for a film, producers, film directors, choreographers, technical staff, road crew for a pop group etc.). In between there is a grey area where it is necessary to review the overall balance of the activities of the person concerned.

4.　An individual may both direct a show and act in it, or may direct and produce a television programme or film and take a role in it. In such cases it is necessary to look at what the individual actually does in the State where the performance takes place. If his activities in that State are predominantly of a performing nature, the Article will apply to all the resulting income he derives in that State. If, however, the performing element is a negligible part of what he does in that State, the whole of the income will fall outside the Article. In other cases an apportionment should be necessary.

5.　Whilst no precise definition is given of the term "sportsmen" it is not restricted to participants in traditional athletic events (e.g. runners, jumpers, swimmers). It also covers, for example, golfers, jockeys, footballers, cricketers and tennis players, as well as racing drivers.

6.   The Article also applies to income from other activities which are usually regarded as of an entertainment character, such as those deriving from billiards and snooker, chess and bridge tournaments.

7.   Income received by impresarios, etc. for arranging the appearance of an artiste or sportsman is outside the scope of the Article, but any income they receive on behalf of the artiste or sportsman is of course covered by it.

8.   Paragraph 1 applies to income derived directly and indirectly by an individual artiste or sportsman. In some cases the income will not be paid directly to the individual or his impresario or agent. For instance, a member of an orchestra may be paid a salary rather than receive payment for each separate performance: a Contracting State where a performance takes place is entitled, under paragraph 1, to tax the proportion of the musician's salary which corresponds to such a performance. Similarly, where an artiste or sportsman is employed by e.g. a one person company, the State where the performance takes place may tax an appropriate proportion of any remuneration paid to the individual. In addition, where its domestic laws "look through" such entities and treat the income as accruing directly to the individual, paragraph 1 enables that State to tax income derived from appearances in its territory and accruing in the entity for the individual's benefit, even if the income is not actually paid as remuneration to the individual.

9.   Besides fees for their actual appearances, artistes and sportsmen often receive income in the form of royalties or of sponsorship or advertising fees. In general, other Articles would apply whenever there was no direct link between the income and a public exhibition by the performer in the country concerned. Royalties for intellectual property rights will normally be covered by Article 12 rather than Article 17 (see paragraph 18 of the Commentary on Article 12), but in general advertising and sponsorship fees will fall outside the scope of Article 12. Article 17 will apply to advertising or sponsorship income, etc. which is related directly or indirectly to performances or appearances in a given State. Similar income which could not be attributed to such performances or appearances would fall under the standard rules of Article 7 or Article 15, as appropriate. Payments received in the event of the cancellation of a performance are also outside the scope of Article 17, and fall under Articles 7 or 15, as the case may be.

10.   The Article says nothing about how the income in question is to be computed. It is for a Contracting State's domestic law to determine the extent of any deductions for expenses. Domestic laws differ in this area, and some provide for taxation at source, at a low rate based on the gross amount paid to artistes and sportsmen. Such rules may also apply to income paid to groups or incorporated teams, troupes, etc. Some States, however, may consider that the taxation of the gross amount may be inappropriate in some circumstances even if the applicable rate is low. These States may want to give the option to the taxpayer to be taxed on a net basis. This could be done through the inclusion of a paragraph drafted along the following lines:

> Where a resident of a Contracting State derives income referred to in paragraph 1 or 2 and such income is taxable in the other Contracting State on a gross basis, that

person may, within [period to be determined by the Contracting States] request the other State in writing that the income be taxable on a net basis in that other State. Such request shall be allowed by that other State. In determining the taxable income of such resident in the other State, there shall be allowed as deductions those expenses deductible under the domestic laws of the other State which are incurred for the purposes of the activities exercised in the other State and which are available to a resident of the other State exercising the same or similar activities under the same or similar conditions.

Paragraph 2

11.   Paragraph 1 of the Article deals with income derived by individual artistes and sportsmen from their personal activities. Paragraph 2 deals with situations where income from their activities accrues to other persons. If the income of an entertainer or sportsman accrues to another person, and the State of source does not have the statutory right to look through the person receiving the income to tax it as income of the performer, paragraph 2 provides that the portion of the income which cannot be taxed in the hands of the performer may be taxed in the hands of the person receiving the remuneration. If the person receiving the income carries on business activities, tax may be applied by the source country even if the income is not attributable to a permanent establishment there. But it will not always be so. There are three main situations of this kind:

a) The first is the management company which receives income for the appearance of *e.g.* a group of sportsmen (which is not itself constituted as a legal entity).

b) The second is the team, troupe, orchestra, etc. which is constituted as a legal entity. Income for performances may be paid to the entity. Individual members of the team, orchestra, etc. will be liable to tax under paragraph 1, in the State in which a performance is given, on any remuneration (or income accruing for their benefit) as a counterpart to the performance; however, if the members are paid a fixed periodic remuneration and it would be difficult to allocate a portion of that income to particular performances, member countries may decide, unilaterally or bilaterally, not to tax it. The profit element accruing from a performance to the legal entity would be liable to tax under paragraph 2.

c) The third situation involves certain tax avoidance devices in cases where remuneration for the performance of an artiste or sportsman is not paid to the artiste or sportsman himself but to another person, *e.g.* a so-called artiste company, in such a way that the income is taxed in the State where the activity is performed neither as personal service income to the artiste or sportsman nor as profits of the enterprise, in the absence of a permanent establishment. Some countries "look through" such arrangements under their domestic law and deem the income to be derived by the artiste or sportsman; where this is so, paragraph 1 enables them to tax income resulting from activities in their territory. Other countries cannot do this. Where a performance takes place in such a country, paragraph 2 permits it to impose a tax on the profits diverted from the income of the artiste or sportsman to the enterprise. It may be, however, that the domestic laws of some States do not enable them to apply such a provision. Such States are free to agree to other solutions or to leave paragraph 2 out of their bilateral conventions.

11.1 The application of paragraph 2 is not restricted to situations where both the entertainer or sportsman and the other person to whom the income accrues, e.g. a star-company, are residents of the same Contracting State. The paragraph allows the State in which the activities of an entertainer or sportsman are exercised to tax the income derived from these activities and accruing to another person regardless of other provisions of the Convention that may otherwise be applicable. Thus, notwithstanding the provisions of Article 7, the paragraph allows that State to tax the income derived by a star-company resident of the other Contracting State even where the entertainer or sportsman is not a resident of that other State. Conversely, where the income of an entertainer resident in one of the Contracting States accrues to a person, e.g. a star-company, who is a resident of a third State with which the State of source does not have a tax convention, nothing will prevent the Contracting State from taxing that person in accordance with its domestic laws.

11.2 As a general rule it should be noted, however, that, regardless of Article 17, the Convention would not prevent the application of general anti-avoidance rules of the domestic law of the State of source which would allow that State to tax either the entertainer/sportsman or the star-company in abusive cases, as is recognised in paragraph 24 of the Commentary on Article 1.

Additional considerations relating to paragraphs 1 and 2

12.   Where, in the cases dealt with in paragraphs 1 and 2, the exemption method for relieving double taxation is used by the State of residence of the person receiving the income, that State would be precluded from taxing such income even if the State where the activities were performed could not make use of its right to tax. It is therefore understood that the credit method should be used in such cases. The same result could be achieved by stipulating a subsidiary right to tax for the State of residence of the person receiving the income, if the State where the activities are performed cannot make use of the right conferred on it by paragraphs 1 and 2. Contracting States are free to choose any of these methods in order to ensure that the income does not escape taxation.

13.   Article 17 will ordinarily apply when the artiste or sportsman is employed by a Government and derives income from that Government; see paragraph 6 of the Commentary on Article 19. Certain conventions contain provisions excluding artistes and sportsmen employed in organisations which are subsidised out of public funds from the application of Article 17.

14.   Some countries may consider it appropriate to exclude from the scope of the Article events supported from public funds. Such countries are free to include a provision to achieve this but the exemptions should be based on clearly definable and

objective criteria to ensure that they are given only where intended. Such a provision might read as follows:

> The provisions of paragraphs 1 and 2 shall not apply to income derived from activities performed in a Contracting State by artistes or sportsmen if the visit to that State is wholly or mainly supported by public funds of one or both of the Contracting States or political subdivisions or local authorities thereof. In such a case, the income is taxable only in the Contracting State in which the artiste or the sportsman is a resident.

Observations on the Commentary

15. Concerning paragraphs 8 and 9, *Germany*, considering paragraph 18 of the Commentary on Article 12, takes the view that payments made as remuneration for live broadcasting rights of an event are income of the performing or appearing sportspersons or artistes under paragraph 1 of Article 17. This income may be taxed in accordance with paragraph 2 of Article 17 in the case of payments made to any other third party in the context of an economic exploitation of the live broadcasting rights.

15.1 *France* considers that the statement in the first sentence of paragraph 13, which is at variance with the wording prior to the 1995 revision, is incorrect, because it does not conform with reality to characterise *a priori* as business the public activities at issue — and in particular cultural activities — that do not ordinarily have a profit motive. In addition, this statement is not consistent with the second sentence of the same paragraph or with paragraph 14, which explicitly provides the right to apply a special exemption regime to the public activities in question: if applied generally to business activities, such a regime would be unjustified, because it would then be contrary to fiscal neutrality and tax equality.

Reservations on the Article

16. *Canada, Switzerland* and the *United States* are of the opinion that paragraph 2 of the Article should apply only to cases mentioned in subparagraph 11 c) above and these countries reserve the right to propose an amendment to that effect.

17. [Deleted]

18. [Deleted]

19. [Deleted]

20. The *United States* reserves the right to limit paragraph 1 to situations where the entertainer or sportsman earns a specified amount.

COMMENTARY ON ARTICLE 18
CONCERNING THE TAXATION OF PENSIONS

1.   According to this Article, pensions paid in respect of private employment are taxable only in the State of residence of the recipient. Various policy and administrative considerations support the principle that the taxing right with respect to this type of pension, and other similar remuneration, should be left to the State of residence. For instance, the State of residence of the recipient of a pension is in a better position than any other State to take into account the recipient's overall ability to pay tax, which mostly depends on worldwide income and personal circumstances such as family responsibilities. This solution also avoids imposing on the recipient of this type of pension the administrative burden of having to comply with tax obligations in States other than that recipient's State of residence.

2.   Some States, however, are reluctant to adopt the principle of exclusive residence taxation of pensions and propose alternatives to the Article. Some of these alternatives and the issues that they raise are discussed in paragraphs 12 to 21 below, which deal with the various considerations related to the allocation of taxing rights with respect to pension benefits and the reasons supporting the Article as drafted.

Scope of the Article

3.   The types of payment that are covered by the Article include not only pensions directly paid to former employees but also to other beneficiaries (e.g. surviving spouses, companions or children of the employees) and other similar payments, such as annuities, paid in respect of past employment. The Article also applies to pensions in respect of services rendered to a State or a political subdivision or local authority thereof which are not covered by the provisions of paragraph 2 of Article 19. The Article only applies, however, to payments that are in consideration of past employment; it would therefore not apply, for example, to an annuity acquired directly by the annuitant from capital that has not been funded from an employment pension scheme. The Article applies regardless of the tax treatment of the scheme under which the relevant payments are made; thus, a payment made under a pension plan that is not eligible for tax relief could nevertheless constitute a "pension or other similar remuneration" (the tax mismatch that could arise in such a situation is discussed below).

4.   Various payments may be made to an employee following cessation of employment. Whether or not such payments fall under the Article will be determined by the nature of the payments, having regard to the facts and circumstances in which they are made, as explained in the following two paragraphs.

5.   While the word "pension", under the ordinary meaning of the word, covers only periodic payments, the words "other similar remuneration" are broad enough to cover non-periodic payments. For instance, a lump-sum payment in lieu of periodic pension payments that is made on or after cessation of employment may fall within the Article.

MODEL TAX CONVENTION (CONDENSED VERSION) – ISBN 978-92-64-08948-8 – © OECD 2010

6.   Whether a particular payment is to be considered as other remuneration similar to a pension or as final remuneration for work performed falling under Article 15 is a question of fact. For example, if it is shown that the consideration for the payment is the commutation of the pension or the compensation for a reduced pension then the payment may be characterised as "other similar remuneration" falling under the Article. This would be the case where a person was entitled to elect upon retirement between the payment of a pension or a lump-sum computed either by reference to the total amount of the contributions or to the amount of pension to which that person would otherwise be entitled under the rules in force for the pension scheme. The source of the payment is an important factor; payments made from a pension scheme would normally be covered by the Article. Other factors which could assist in determining whether a payment or series of payments fall under the Article include: whether a payment is made on or after the cessation of the employment giving rise to the payment, whether the recipient continues working, whether the recipient has reached the normal age of retirement with respect to that particular type of employment, the status of other recipients who qualify for the same type of lump-sum payment and whether the recipient is simultaneously eligible for other pension benefits. Reimbursement of pension contributions (e.g. after temporary employment) does not constitute "other similar remuneration" under Article 18. Where cases of difficulty arise in the taxation of such payments, the Contracting States should solve the matter by recourse to the provisions of Article 25.

7.   Since the Article applies only to pensions and other similar remuneration that are paid in consideration for past employment, it does not cover other pensions such as those that are paid with respect to previous independent personal services. Some States, however, extend the scope of the Article to cover all types of pensions, including Government pensions; States wishing to do so are free to agree bilaterally to include provisions to that effect.

Cross-border issues related to pensions

8.   The globalisation of the economy and the development of international communications and transportation have considerably increased the international mobility of individuals, both for work-related and personal reasons. This has significantly increased the importance of cross-border issues arising from the interaction of the different pension arrangements which exist in various States and which were primarily designed on the basis of purely domestic policy considerations. As these issues often affect large numbers of individuals, it is desirable to address them in tax conventions so as to remove obstacles to the international movement of persons, and employees in particular.

9.   Many such issues relate to mismatches resulting from differences in the general tax policy that States adopt with respect to retirement savings. In many States, tax incentives are provided for pension contributions. Such incentives frequently take the form of a tax deferral so that the part of the income of an individual that is contributed to a pension arrangement as well as the income earned in the scheme or any pension

rights that accrue to the individual are exempt from tax. Conversely, the pension benefits from these arrangements are taxable upon receipt. Other States, however, treat pension contributions like other forms of savings and neither exempt these contributions nor the return thereon; logically, therefore, they do not tax pension benefits. Between these two approaches exist a variety of systems where contributions, the return thereon, the accrual of pension rights or pension benefits are partially taxed or exempt.

10.   Other issues arise from the existence of very different arrangements to provide retirement benefits. These arrangements are often classified under the following three broad categories:

— statutory social security schemes;

— occupational pension schemes;

— individual retirement schemes.

The interaction between these three categories of arrangements presents particular difficulties. These difficulties are compounded by the fact that each State may have different tax rules for the arrangements falling in each of these categories as well as by the fact that there are considerable differences in the extent to which States rely on each of these categories to ensure retirement benefits to individuals (*e.g.* some States provide retirement benefits almost exclusively through their social security system while others rely primarily on occupational pension schemes or individual retirement schemes).

11.   The issues arising from all these differences need to be fully considered in the course of bilateral negotiations, in particular to avoid double taxation or non-taxation, and, where appropriate, addressed through specific provisions. The following sections examine some of these cross-border issues.

Allocation of taxing rights with respect to pension benefits

12.   As explained in paragraph 9 above, many States have adopted the approach under which, subject to various restrictions, tax is totally or partially deferred on contributions to, and earnings in, pension schemes or on the accrual of pension rights, but is recovered when pension benefits are paid.

13.   Some of these States consider that because a deduction for pension contributions is a deferral of tax on the part of the employment income that is saved towards retirement, they should be able to recover the tax so deferred where the individual has ceased to be a resident before the payment of all or part of the pension benefits. This view is particularly prevalent where the benefits are paid through a lump-sum amount or over a short period of time as this increases risks of double non-taxation.

14.   If the other State of which that individual then becomes a resident has adopted a similar approach and therefore taxes these pension benefits when received, the issue is primarily one of allocation of taxing rights between the two States. If, however, the

individual becomes a resident of a State which adopts a different approach so as not to tax pension benefits, the mismatch in the approaches adopted by the two States will result in a situation where no tax will ever be payable on the relevant income.

15. For these reasons, some States seek to include in their tax conventions alternative provisions designed to secure either exclusive or limited source taxation rights with respect to pensions in consideration of past employment. The following are examples of provisions that some members have adopted in consequence of these policy and administrative considerations; States are free to agree bilaterally to include such provisions:

a) *Provisions allowing exclusive source taxation of pension payments*

Under such a provision, the Article is drafted along the following lines:

Subject to the provisions of paragraph 2 of Article 19, pensions and other similar remuneration arising in a Contracting State and paid to a resident of the other Contracting State in consideration of past employment shall be taxable only in the first-mentioned State.

b) *Provisions allowing non-exclusive source taxation of pension payments*

Under such a provision, the State of source is given the right to tax pension payments and the rules of Articles 23 A or 23 B results in that right being either exclusive or merely prior to that of the State of residence. The Article is then drafted along the following lines:

Subject to the provisions of paragraph 2 of Article 19, pensions and other similar remuneration paid to a resident of a Contracting State in consideration of past employment shall be taxable only in that State. However such pensions and other similar remuneration may also be taxed in the other Contracting State if they arise in that State.

c) *Provisions allowing limited source taxation of pension*

Under such a provision, the State of source is given the right to tax pension payments but that right is subjected to a limit, usually expressed as a percentage of the payment. The Article is then drafted along the following lines:

1. Subject to the provisions of paragraph 2 of Article 19, pensions and other similar remuneration paid to a resident of a Contracting State in consideration of past employment may be taxed in that State.

2. However such pensions and other similar remuneration may also be taxed in the Contracting State in which they arise and according to the laws of that State but the tax so charged shall not exceed [percentage] of the gross amount of the payment.

Where such a provision is used, a reference to paragraph 2 of Article 18 is added to paragraph 2 of Article 23 A to ensure that the residence State, if it applies the exemption method, is allowed to tax the pension payments but needs to provide a credit for the tax levied by the source State.

d) *Provisions allowing source taxation of pension payments only where the State of residence does not tax these payments*

Such a provision is used by States that are primarily concerned with the structural mismatch described in paragraph 14 above. A paragraph 2 is then added along the following lines:

> 2. However such pensions and other similar remuneration may also be taxed in the Contracting State in which they arise if these payments are not subject to tax in the other Contracting State under the ordinary rules of its tax law.

16.   Apart from the reasons presented in paragraphs 13 and 14 above, various policy and administrative considerations should be taken into account when considering such provisions.

17.   First, the State of residence is in a better position to provide for adequate taxation of pension payments as it is easier for that State to take into account the worldwide income, and therefore the overall ability to pay tax, of the recipient so as to apply appropriate rates and personal allowances. By contrast, the source taxation of pensions may well result in excessive taxation where the source State imposes a final withholding tax on the gross amount paid. If little or no tax is levied in the residence State (*e.g.* because of available allowances), the pensioner may not be able to claim a credit in the residence State for the tax paid. However, some States have sought to relieve that problem by extending their personal allowances to non-residents who derive almost all their income from these States. Also, some States have allowed the pension payments made to non-resident recipients to be taxed at the marginal rate that would be applicable if that recipient were taxed on worldwide income (that system, however, involves administrative difficulties as it requires a determination of the worldwide income of the non-resident only for the purpose of determining the applicable rate of tax).

18.   Second, equity considerations could be relevant since the level of pensions paid in the source State will generally have been set factoring local rates of tax. In this situation, an individual who has emigrated to another State with different tax rates will either be advantaged or disadvantaged by receiving an after-tax pension that will be different from that envisaged under the pension scheme.

19.   Third, alternative provisions under which there is either exclusive or limited source taxation rights with respect to pensions require a determination of the State of source of pensions. Since a mere reference to a pension "arising in" a Contracting State could be construed as meaning either a pension paid by a fund established in that State or a pension derived from work performed in a State, States using such wording should clarify how it should be interpreted and applied.

19.1   Conceptually, the State of source might be considered to be the State in which the fund is established, the State where the relevant work has been performed or the State where deductions have been claimed. Each of these approaches would raise difficulties in the case of individuals who work in more than one State, change residence during their career or derive pensions from funds established in a State other than that in which they have worked. For example, many individuals now spend significant parts of their careers outside the State in which their pension funds are established and from which their pension benefits are ultimately paid. In such a case, treating the State in which the fund is established as the State of source would seem difficult to justify. The alternative of considering as the State of source the State where the work has been performed or deductions claimed would address that issue but would raise administrative difficulties for both taxpayers and tax authorities, particularly in the case of individuals who have worked in many States during their career, since it would create the possibility of different parts of the same pension having different States of source.

19.2 States that wish to use provisions under which there is either exclusive or limited source taxation rights with respect to pensions should take account of these issues related to the determination of the State of source of pensions. They should then address the administrative difficulties that will arise from the rule that they adopt for that purpose, for example to avoid situations where two States would claim to have source taxation rights on the same pension.

20.   Fourth, another argument against these alternative provisions is that exclusive taxation by the State of residence means that pensioners only need to comply with the tax rules of their State of residence as regards payments covered by Article 18. Where, however, limited or exclusive source taxation of pensions is allowed, the pensioner will need to comply with the tax rules of both Contracting States.

21.   Exclusive residence taxation may, however, give rise to concerns about the non-reporting of foreign pension income. Exchange of information coupled with adequate taxpayer compliance systems will, however, reduce the incidence of non-reporting of foreign pension payments.

Exempt pensions

22.   As mentioned in paragraph 9 above, some States do not tax pension payments generally or otherwise exempt particular categories or parts of pension payments. In these cases, the provisions of the Article, which provides for taxation of pensions in the State of residence, may result in the taxation by that State of pensions which were designed not to be taxed and the amount of which may well have been determined having regard to that exemption. This may result in undue financial hardship for the recipient of the pension.

23.   To avoid the problems resulting from this type of mismatch, some States include in their tax treaties provisions to preserve the exempt treatment of pensions when the recipient is a resident of the other Contracting State. These provisions may be restricted to specific categories of pensions or may address the issue in a more comprehensive way. An example of that latter approach would be a provision drafted along the following lines:

Notwithstanding any provision of this Convention, any pension or other similar remuneration paid to a resident of a Contracting State in respect of past employment exercised in the other Contracting State shall be exempt from tax in the first-mentioned State if that pension or other remuneration would be exempt from tax in the other State if the recipient were a resident of that other State.

Issues related to statutory social security schemes

24.   Depending on the circumstances, social security payments can fall under this Article as "pensions and other similar remuneration in consideration of past employment", under Article 19 as "pension[s] paid by, or out of funds created by, a Contracting State ... in respect of services rendered to that State..." or under Article 21 as "items of income ... not dealt with in the foregoing Articles". Social security pensions fall under this Article when they are paid in consideration of past employment, unless paragraph 2 of Article 19 applies (see below). A social security pension may be said to be "in consideration of past employment" if employment is a condition for that pension. For instance, this will be the case where, under the relevant social security scheme:

— the amount of the pension is determined on the basis of either or both the period of employment and the employment income so that years when the individual was not employed do not give rise to pension benefits,

— the amount of the pension is determined on the basis of contributions to the scheme that are made under the condition of employment and in relation to the period of employment, or

— the amount of the pension is determined on the basis of the period of employment and either or both the contributions to the scheme and the investment income of the scheme.

25.   Paragraph 2 of Article 19 will apply to a social security pension that would fall within Article 18 except for the fact that the past employment in consideration of which it is paid constituted services rendered to a State or a political subdivision or a local authority thereof, other than services referred to in paragraph 3 of Article 19.

26.   Social security payments that do not fall within Articles 18 or 19 fall within Article 21. This would be the case, for instance, for payments made to self-employed persons as well as a pension purely based on resources, on age or disability which would be paid regardless of past employment or factors related to past employment (such as years of employment or contributions made during employment).

27.   Some States, however, consider pensions paid out under a public pension scheme which is part of their social security system similar to Government pensions. Such States argue on that basis that the State of source, i.e. the State from which the pension is paid, should have a right to tax all such pensions. Many conventions concluded by these States contain provisions to that effect, sometimes including also other payments made under the social security legislation of the State of source. Contracting States having that view may agree bilaterally on an additional paragraph to the Article giving the State of source a right to tax payments made under its social security legislation. A paragraph of that kind could be drafted along the following lines:

Notwithstanding the provisions of paragraph 1, pensions and other payments made under the social security legislation of a Contracting State may be taxed in that State.

Where the State of which the recipient of such payments is a resident applies the exemption method the payments will be taxable only in the State of source while States using the credit method may tax the payments and give credit for the tax levied in the State of source. Some States using the credit method as the general method in their conventions may, however, consider that the State of source should have an exclusive right to tax such payments. Such States should then substitute the words "shall be taxable only" for the words "may be taxed" in the above draft provision.

28.   Although the above draft provision refers to the social security legislation of each Contracting State, there are limits to what it covers. "Social security" generally refers to a system of mandatory protection that a State puts in place in order to provide its population with a minimum level of income or retirement benefits or to mitigate the financial impact of events such as unemployment, employment-related injuries, sickness or death. A common feature of social security systems is that the level of benefits is determined by the State. Payments that may be covered by the provision include retirement pensions available to the general public under a public pension scheme, old age pension payments as well as unemployment, disability, maternity, survivorship, sickness, social assistance, and family protection payments that are made by the State or by public entities constituted to administer the funds to be distributed. As there may be substantial differences in the social security systems of the Contracting States, it is important for the States that intend to use the draft provision to verify, during the course of bilateral negotiations, that they have a common understanding of what will be covered by the provision.

Issues related to individual retirement schemes

29.   In many States, preferential tax treatment (usually in the form of the tax deferral described in paragraph 9 above) is available to certain individual private saving schemes established to provide retirement benefits. These individual retirement schemes are usually available to individuals who do not have access to occupational pension schemes; they may also, however, be available to employees who wish to supplement the retirement benefits that they will derive from their social security and occupational pension schemes. These schemes take various legal forms. For example, they may be bank savings accounts, individual investment funds or individually subscribed full life insurance policies. Their common feature is a preferential tax treatment which is subject to certain contribution limits.

30.   These schemes raise many of the cross-border issues that arise in the case of occupational schemes, such as the tax treatment, in one Contracting State, of contributions to such a scheme established in the other State (see paragraphs 31 to 65 below). There may be, however, issues that are specific to individual retirement schemes and which may need to be addressed separately during the negotiation of a bilateral convention. One such issue is the tax treatment, in each State, of income

accruing in such a scheme established in the other State. Many States have rules (such as foreign investment funds (FIF) rules, rules that attribute the income of a trust to a settlor or beneficiary in certain circumstances or rules that provide for the accrual taxation of income with respect to certain types of investment, including full life insurance policies) that may, in certain circumstances, result in the taxation of income accruing in an individual retirement scheme established abroad. States which consider that result inappropriate in light of their approach to the taxation of retirement savings may wish to prevent such taxation. A provision dealing with the issue and restricted to those schemes which are recognised as individual retirement schemes could be drafted along the following lines:

> For purposes of computing the tax payable in a Contracting State by an individual who is a resident of that State and who was previously a resident of the other Contracting State, any income accruing under an arrangement
>
> a) entered into with a person established outside the first-mentioned State in order to secure retirement benefits for that individual,
>
> b) in which the individual participates and had participated when the individual was a resident of the other State,
>
> c) that is accepted by the competent authority of the first-mentioned State as generally corresponding to an individual retirement scheme recognised as such for tax purposes by that State,
>
> shall be treated as income accruing in an individual retirement scheme established in that State. This paragraph shall not restrict in any manner the taxation of any benefit distributed under the arrangement.

The tax treatment of contributions to foreign pension schemes

A.   General comments

31.   It is characteristic of multinational enterprises that their staff are expected to be willing to work outside their home country from time to time. The terms of service under which staff are sent to work in other countries are of keen interest and importance to both the employer and the employee. One consideration is the pension arrangements that are made for the employee in question. Similarly, individuals who move to other countries to provide independent services are often confronted with cross-border tax issues related to the pension arrangements that they have established in their home country.

32.   Individuals working abroad will often wish to continue contributing to a pension scheme (including a social security scheme that provides pension benefits) in their home country during their absence abroad. This is both because switching schemes can lead to a loss of rights and benefits, and because many practical difficulties can arise from having pension arrangements in a number of countries.

33.   The tax treatment accorded to pension contributions made by or for individuals working outside their home country varies both from country to country and

depending on the circumstances of the individual case. Before taking up an overseas assignment or contract, pension contributions made by or for these individuals commonly qualify for tax relief in the home country. When the individual works abroad, the contributions in some cases continue to qualify for relief. Where the individual, for example, remains resident and fully taxable in the home country, pension contributions made to a pension scheme established in the home country will generally continue to qualify for relief there. But frequently, contributions paid in the home country by an individual working abroad do not qualify for relief under the domestic laws of either the home country or the host country. Where this is the case it can become expensive, if not prohibitive, to maintain membership of a pension scheme in the home country during a foreign assignment or contract. Paragraph 37 below suggests a provision which member countries can, if they wish, include in bilateral treaties to provide reliefs for the pension contributions made by or for individuals working outside their home country.

34.   However, some member countries may not consider that the solution to the problem lies in a treaty provision, preferring, for example, the pension scheme to be amended to secure deductibility of contributions in the host State. Other countries may be opposed to including the provision below in treaties where domestic legislation allows relief only with respect to contributions paid to residents. In such cases it may be inappropriate to include the suggested provision in a bilateral treaty.

35.   The suggested provision covers contributions made to all forms of pension schemes, including individual retirement schemes as well as social security schemes. Many member countries have entered into bilateral social security totalisation agreements which may help to partially avoid the problem with respect to contributions to social security schemes; these agreements, however, usually do not deal with the tax treatment of cross-border contributions. In the case of an occupational scheme to which both the employer and the employees contribute, the provision covers both these contributions. Also, the provision is not restricted to the issue of the deductibility of the contributions as it deals with all aspects of the tax treatment of the contributions as regards the individual who derive benefits from a pension scheme. Thus the provision deals with issues such as whether or not the employee should be taxed on the employment benefit that an employer's contribution constitutes and whether or not the investment income derived from the contributions should be taxed in the hands of the individual. It does not, however, deal with the taxation of the pension fund on its income (this issue is dealt with in paragraph 69 below). Contracting States wishing to modify the scope of the provision with respect to any of these issues may do so in their bilateral negotiations.

B.   Aim of the provision

36.   The aim of the provision is to ensure that, as far as possible, individuals are not discouraged from taking up overseas work by the tax treatment of their contributions to a home country pension scheme. The provision seeks, first, to determine the general equivalence of pension plans in the two countries and then to establish limits to the

contributions to which the tax relief applies based on the limits in the laws of both countries.

C. *Suggested provision*

37.   The following is the suggested text of the provision that could be included in bilateral conventions to deal with the problem identified above:

1.   Contributions to a pension scheme established in and recognised for tax purposes in a Contracting State that are made by or on behalf of an individual who renders services in the other Contracting State shall, for the purposes of determining the individual's tax payable and the profits of an enterprise which may be taxed in that State, be treated in that State in the same way and subject to the same conditions and limitations as contributions made to a pension scheme that is recognised for tax purposes in that State, provided that:

   a) the individual was not a resident of that State, and was participating in the pension scheme, immediately before beginning to provide services in that State, and

   b) the pension scheme is accepted by the competent authority of that State as generally corresponding to a pension scheme recognised as such for tax purposes by that State.

2.   For the purposes of paragraph 1:

   a) the term "a pension scheme" means an arrangement in which the individual participates in order to secure retirement benefits payable in respect of the services referred to in paragraph 1 and

   b) a pension scheme is recognised for tax purposes in a State if the contributions to the scheme would qualify for tax relief in that State.

38.   The above provision is restricted to pension schemes established in one of the two Contracting States. As it is not unusual for individuals to work in a number of different countries in succession, some States may wish to extend the scope of the provision to cover situations where an individual moves from one Contracting State to another while continuing to make contributions to a pension scheme established in a third State. Such an extension may, however, create administrative difficulties if the host State cannot have access to information concerning the pension scheme (*e.g.* through the exchange of information provisions of a tax convention concluded with the third State); it may also create a situation where relief would be given on a non-reciprocal basis because the third State would not grant similar relief to an individual contributing to a pension scheme established in the host State. States which, notwithstanding these difficulties, want to extend the suggested provision to funds established in third States can do so by adopting an alternative version of the suggested provision drafted along the following lines:

1.   Contributions made by or on behalf of an individual who renders services in a Contracting State to a pension scheme

   a) recognised for tax purposes in the other Contracting State,

b) in which the individual participated immediately before beginning to provide services in the first-mentioned State,

c) in which the individual participated at a time when that individual was providing services in, or was a resident of, the other State, and

d) that is accepted by the competent authority of the first-mentioned State as generally corresponding to a pension scheme recognised as such for tax purposes by that State,

shall, for the purposes of

e) determining the individual's tax payable in the first-mentioned State, and

f) determining the profits of an enterprise which may be taxed in the first-mentioned State,

be treated in that State in the same way and subject to the same conditions and limitations as contributions made to a pension scheme that is recognised for tax purposes in that first-mentioned State.

2.   For the purposes of paragraph 1:

a) the term "a pension scheme" means an arrangement in which the individual participates in order to secure retirement benefits payable in respect of the services referred to in paragraph 1; and

b) a pension scheme is recognised for tax purposes in a State if the contributions to the scheme would qualify for tax relief in that State.

D.   *Characteristics of the suggested provision*

39.   The following paragraphs discuss the main characteristics of the suggested provision found in paragraph 37 above.

40.   Paragraph 1 of the suggested provision lays down the characteristics of both the individual and the contributions in respect of which the provision applies. It also provides the principle that contributions made by or on behalf of an individual rendering services in one Contracting State (the host State) to a defined pension scheme in the other Contracting State (the home State) are to be treated for tax purposes in the host State in the same way and subject to the same conditions and limitations as contributions to domestic pension schemes of the host State.

41.   Tax relief with respect to contributions to the home country pension scheme under the conditions outlined can be given by either the home country, being the country where the pension scheme is situated or by the host country, where the economic activities giving rise to the contributions are carried out.

42.   A solution in which relief would be given by the home country might not be effective, since the individual might have no or little taxable income in that country. Practical considerations therefore suggest that it would be preferable for relief to be given by the host country and this is the solution adopted in the suggested provision.

43.   In looking at the characteristics of the individual, paragraph 1 makes it clear that, in order to get the relief from taxation in the host State, the individual must not have been resident in the host State immediately prior to working there.

44.   Paragraph 1 does not, however, limit the application of the provision to individuals who become resident in the host State. In many cases, individuals working abroad who remain resident in their home State will continue to qualify for relief there, but this will not be so in all cases. The suggested provision therefore applies to non-residents working in the host State as well as to individuals who attain residence status there. In some member countries the domestic legislation may restrict deductibility to contributions borne by residents, and these member countries may wish to restrict the suggested provision to cater for this. Also, States with a special regime for non-residents (*e.g.* taxation at a special low rate) may, in bilateral negotiations, wish to agree on a provision restricted to residents.

45.   In the case where individuals temporarily cease to be resident in the host country in order to join a pension scheme in a country with more relaxed rules, individual States may want a provision which would prevent the possibility of abuse. One form such a provision could take would be a nationality test which could exclude from the suggested provision individuals who are nationals of the host State.

46.   As already noted, it is not unusual for individuals to work in a number of different countries in succession; for that reason, the suggested provision is not limited to individuals who are residents of the home State immediately prior to providing services in the host State. The provision covers an individual coming to the host State from a third country as it is only limited to individuals who were not resident in the host country before starting to work there. However, Article 1 restricts the scope of the Convention to residents of one or both Contracting States. An individual who is neither a resident of the host State nor of the home State where the pension scheme is established is therefore outside the scope of the Convention between the two States.

47.   The suggested provision places no limits on the length of time for which an individual can work in a host State. It could be argued that, if an individual works in the host State for long enough, it in effect becomes his home country and the provision should no longer apply. Indeed, some host countries already restrict relief for contributions to foreign pension schemes to cases where the individuals are present on a temporary basis.

48.   In addition, the inclusion of a time limit may be helpful in preventing the possibility of abuse outlined in paragraph 45 above. In bilateral negotiations, individual countries may find it appropriate to include a limit on the length of time for which an individual may provide services in the host State after which reliefs granted by the suggested provision would no longer apply.

49.   In looking at the characteristics of the contributions, paragraph 1 provides a number of tests. It makes it clear that the provision applies only to contributions made by or on behalf of an individual to a pension scheme established in and recognised for

tax purposes in the home State. The phrase "recognised for tax purposes" is further defined in subparagraph 2 *b)* of the suggested provision. The phrase "made by or on behalf of" is intended to apply to contributions that are made directly by the individual as well as to those that are made for that individual's benefit by an employer or another party (*e.g.* a spouse). While paragraph 4 of Article 24 ensures that the employer's contributions to a pension fund resident of the other Contracting State are deductible under the same conditions as contributions to a resident pension fund, that provision may not be sufficient to ensure the similar treatment of employer's contributions to domestic and foreign pension funds. This will be the case, for example, where the employer's contributions to the foreign fund are treated as a taxable benefit in the hands of the employee or where the deduction of the employer's contributions is not dependent on the fund being a resident but, rather, on other conditions (*e.g.* registration with tax authorities or the presence of offices) which have the effect of generally excluding foreign pension funds. For these reasons, employer's contributions are covered by the suggested provision even though paragraph 4 of Article 24 may already ensure a similar relief in some cases.

50.   The second test applied to the characteristics of the contributions is that the contributions should be made to a home State scheme recognised by the competent authority of the host State as generally corresponding to a scheme recognised as such for tax purposes by the host State. This operates on the premise that only contributions to recognised schemes qualify for relief in member countries. This limitation does not, of course, necessarily secure equivalent tax treatment of contributions paid where an individual was working abroad and of contributions while working in the home country. If the host State's rules for recognising pension schemes were narrower than those of the home State, the individual could find that contributions to his home country pension scheme were less favourably treated when he was working in the host country than when working in the home country.

51.   However, it would not be in accordance with the stated aim of securing, as far as possible, equivalent tax treatment of contributions to foreign schemes to give relief for contributions which do not — at least broadly — correspond to domestically recognised schemes. To do so would mean that the amount of relief in the host State would become dependent on legislation in the home State. In addition, it could be hard to defend treating individuals working side by side differently depending on whether their pension scheme was at home or abroad (and if abroad, whether it was one country rather than another). By limiting the suggested provision to schemes which generally correspond to those in the host country such difficulties are avoided.

52.   The suggested provision makes it clear that it is for the competent authority of the host State to determine whether the scheme in the home State generally corresponds to recognised schemes in the host State. Individual States may wish, in bilateral negotiations, to specify expressly to which existing schemes the provision will apply or to establish what interpretation the competent authority places on the term "generally corresponding"; for example how widely it is interpreted and what tests are imposed.

53.   The contributions covered by the provision are limited to payments to schemes in which the individual was participating before beginning to provide services in the host State. This means that contributions to new pension schemes which an individual joins while in the host State are excluded from the suggested provision.

54.   It is, however, recognised that special rules may be needed to cover cases where new pension schemes are substituted for previous ones. For instance, in some member countries the common practice may be that, if a company employer is taken over by another company, the existing company pension scheme for its employees may be ended and a new scheme opened by the new employer. In bilateral negotiations, therefore, individual States may wish to supplement the provision to cover such substitution schemes; this could be done by adding the following subparagraph to paragraph 2 of the suggested provision:

   c)   a pension scheme that is substituted for, but is substantially similar to, a pension scheme accepted by the competent authority of a Contracting State under subparagraph b) of paragraph 1 shall be deemed to be the pension scheme that was so accepted.

55.   Paragraph 1 also sets out the relief to be given by the host State if the characteristics of the individual and the contributions fall within the terms of the provision. In brief, the contributions must be treated for tax purposes in a way which corresponds to the manner in which they would be treated if these contributions were to a scheme established in the host State. Thus, the contributions will qualify for the same tax relief (e.g. be deductible), for both the individual and the employer (where the individual is employed and contributions are made by the employer) as if these contributions had been made to a scheme in the host State. Also, the same treatment has to be given as regards the taxation of an employee on the employment benefit derived from an employer's contribution to either a foreign or a local scheme (see paragraph 58 below).

56.   This measure of relief does not, of course, necessarily secure equivalent tax treatment given to contributions paid when an individual is working abroad and contributions paid when he is working in the home country. Similar considerations apply here to those discussed in paragraphs 50 and 51 above. The measure does, however, ensure equivalent treatment of the contributions of co-workers. The following example is considered. The home country allows relief for pension contributions subject to a limit of 18 per cent of income. The host country allows relief subject to a limit of 20 per cent. The suggested provision in paragraph 37 would require the host country to allow relief up to its domestic limit of 20 per cent. Countries wishing to adopt the limit in the home country would need to amend the wording of the provision appropriately.

57.   The amount and method of giving the relief would depend upon the domestic tax treatment of pension contributions by the host State. This would settle such questions as whether contributions qualify for relief in full, or only in part, and whether relief should be given as a deduction in computing taxable income (and if so, which income,

e.g. in the case of an individual, only employment or business income or all income) or as a tax credit.

58.   For an individual who participates in an occupational pension scheme, being assigned to work abroad may not only mean that this employee's contributions to a pension scheme in his home country cease to qualify for tax relief. It may also mean that contributions to the pension scheme by the employer are regarded as the employee's income for tax purposes. In some member countries employees are taxed on employer's contributions to domestic schemes whilst working in the home country whereas in others these contributions remain exempt. Since it applies to both employees' and employers' contributions, the suggested provision ensures that employers' contributions in the context of the employees' tax liability are accorded the same treatment that such contributions to domestic schemes would receive.

59.   Subparagraph 2 *a)* defines a pension scheme for the purposes of paragraph 1. It makes it clear that, for these purposes, a pension scheme is an arrangement in which the individual who makes the payments participates in order to secure retirement benefits. These benefits must be payable in respect of services provided in the host State. All the above conditions must apply to the pension scheme before it can qualify for relief under the suggested provision.

60.   Subparagraph 2 *a)* refers to the participation of the individual in the pension scheme in order to secure retirement benefits. This definition is intended to ensure that the proportion of contributions made to secure benefits other than periodic pension payments on retirement, *e.g.* a lump sum on retirement, will also qualify for relief under the provision.

61.   The initial definition of a pension scheme is "an arrangement". This is a widely drawn term, the use of which is intended to encompass the various forms which pension schemes (whether social security, occupational or individual retirement schemes) may take in different member countries.

62.   Although subparagraph 2 *a)* sets out that participation in this scheme has to be by the individual who provides services referred to in paragraph 1 there is no reference to the identity of the recipient of the retirement benefits secured by participation in the scheme. This is to ensure that any proportion of contributions intended to generate a pension for other beneficiaries (*e.g.* surviving spouses, companions or children) may be eligible for relief under the suggested provision.

63.   The definition of a pension scheme makes no distinction between pensions paid from State-run occupational pension schemes and similar privately-run schemes. Both are covered by the scope of the provision. Social security schemes are therefore covered by the provision to the extent that contributions to such schemes can be considered to be with respect to the services provided in the host State by an individual, whether as an employee or in an independent capacity.

64.   Subparagraph 2 *b)* further defines the phrase "recognised for tax purposes". As the aim of the provision is, so far as possible, to ensure that contributions are neither more nor less favourably treated for tax purposes than they would be if the individual

were resident in his home State, it is right to limit the scope of the provision to contributions which would have qualified for relief if the individual had remained in the home State. The provision seeks to achieve this aim by limiting its scope to contributions made to a scheme only if contributions to this scheme would qualify for tax relief in that State.

65.   This method of attempting to achieve parity of treatment assumes that in all member countries only contributions to recognised pension schemes qualify for relief. The tax treatment of contributions to pension schemes under member countries' tax systems may differ from this assumption. It is recognised that, in bilateral negotiations, individual countries may wish to further define the qualifying pension schemes in terms that match the respective domestic laws of the treaty partners. They may also wish to define other terms used in the provision, such as "renders services" and "provides services".

Tax obstacles to the portability of pension rights

66.   Another issue, which also relates to international labour mobility, is that of the tax consequences that may arise from the transfer of pension rights from a pension scheme established in one Contracting State to another scheme located in the other Contracting State. When an individual moves from one employer to another, it is frequent for the pension rights that this individual accumulated in the pension scheme covering the first employment to be transferred to a different scheme covering the second employment. Similar arrangements may exist to allow for the portability of pension rights to or from an individual retirement scheme.

67.   Such transfers usually give rise to a payment representing the actuarial value, at the time of the transfer, of the pension rights of the individual or representing the value of the contributions and earnings that have accumulated in the scheme with respect to the individual. These payments may be made directly from the first scheme to the second one; alternatively, they may be made by requiring the individual to contribute to the new pension scheme all or part of the amount received upon withdrawing from the previous scheme. In both cases, it is frequent for tax systems to allow such transfers, when they are purely domestic, to take place on a tax-free basis.

68.   Problems may arise, however, where the transfer is made from a pension scheme located in one Contracting State to a scheme located in the other State. In such a case, the Contracting State where the individual resides may consider that the payment arising upon the transfer is a taxable benefit. A similar problem arises when the payment is made from a scheme established in a State to which the relevant tax convention gives source taxing rights on pension payments arising therefrom as that State may want to apply that taxing right to any benefit derived from the scheme. Contracting States that wish to address that issue are free to include a provision drafted along the following lines:

> Where pension rights or amounts have accumulated in a pension scheme
> established in and recognised for tax purposes in one Contracting State for the

benefit of an individual who is a resident of the other Contracting State, any transfer of these rights or amounts to a pension scheme established in and recognised for tax purposes in that other State shall, in each State, be treated for tax purposes in the same way and subject to the same conditions and limitations as if it had been made from one pension scheme established in and recognised for tax purposes in that State to another pension scheme established in and recognised for tax purposes in the same State.

The above provision could be modified to also cover transfers to or from pensions funds established and recognised in third States (this, however, could raise similar concerns as those described in the preamble of paragraph 38 above).

Exemption of the income of a pension fund

69.   Where, under their domestic law, two States follow the same approach of generally exempting from tax the investment income of pension funds established in their territory, these States, in order to achieve greater neutrality with respect to the location of capital, may want to extend that exemption to the investment income that a pension fund established in one State derives from the other State. In order to do so, States sometimes include in their conventions a provision drafted along the following lines:

Notwithstanding any provision of this Convention, income arising in a Contracting State that is derived by a resident of the other Contracting State that was constituted and is operated exclusively to administer or provide pension benefits and has been accepted by the competent authority of the first-mentioned State as generally corresponding to a pension scheme recognised as such for tax purposes by that State, shall be exempt from tax in that State.

Observation on the Commentary

70.   With regard to paragraphs 24 and 26, the *Netherlands* is of the opinion that social security payments can in some circumstances fall within Article 15 if they are paid whilst the employment still continues.

COMMENTARY ON ARTICLE 19
CONCERNING THE TAXATION OF REMUNERATION IN RESPECT OF GOVERNMENT SERVICE

1.   This Article applies to salaries, wages, and other similar remuneration, and pensions, in respect of government service. Similar provisions in old bilateral conventions were framed in order to conform with the rules of international courtesy and mutual respect between sovereign States. They were therefore rather limited in scope. However, the importance and scope of Article 19 has increased on account of the fact that, consequent on the growth of the public sector in many countries, governmental activities abroad have been considerably extended. According to the original version of paragraph 1 of Article 19 in the 1963 Draft Convention the paying State had a right to tax payments made for services rendered to that State or political subdivision or local authority thereof. The expression "may be taxed" was used and this did not connote an exclusive right of taxation.

2.   In the 1977 Model Convention, paragraph 1 was split into two paragraphs, paragraph 1 concerning salaries, wages, and other similar remuneration other than a pension and paragraph 2 concerning pensions, respectively. Unlike the original provision, subparagraph a) of paragraphs 1 and 2 are both based on the principle that the paying State shall have an exclusive right to tax the payments. Countries using the credit method as the general method for relieving double taxation in their conventions are thus, as an exception to that method, obliged to exempt from tax such payments to their residents as are dealt with under paragraphs 1 and 2. If both Contracting States apply the exemption method for relieving double taxation, they can continue to use the expression "may be taxed" instead of "shall be taxable only". In relation to such countries the effect will of course be the same irrespective of which of these expressions they use. It is understood that the expression "shall be taxable only" shall not prevent a Contracting State from taking into account the income exempted under subparagraph a) of paragraphs 1 and 2 in determining the rate of tax to be imposed on income derived by its residents from other sources. The principle of giving the exclusive taxing right to the paying State is contained in so many of the existing conventions between OECD member countries that it can be said to be already internationally accepted. It is also in conformity with the conception of international courtesy which is at the basis of the Article and with the provisions of the *Vienna Conventions on Diplomatic and Consular Relations*. It should, however, be observed that the Article is not intended to restrict the operation of any rules originating from international law in the case of diplomatic missions and consular posts (see Article 28) but deals with cases not covered by such rules.

2.1   In 1994, a further amendment was made to paragraph 1 by replacing the term "remuneration" by the words "salaries, wages, and other similar remuneration". This amendment was intended to clarify the scope of the Article, which only applies to State employees and to persons deriving pensions from past employment by a State,

MODEL TAX CONVENTION (CONDENSED VERSION) – ISBN 978-92-64-08948-8 – © OECD 2010

COMMENTARY ON ARTICLE 19

and not to persons rendering independent services to a State or deriving pensions related to such services.

2.2   Member countries have generally understood the term "salaries, wages and other similar remuneration ... paid" to include benefits in kind received in respect of services rendered to a State or political subdivision or local authority thereof (*e.g.* the use of a residence or automobile, health or life insurance coverage and club memberships).

3.   The provisions of the Article apply to payments made not only by a State but also by its political subdivisions and local authorities (constituent states, regions, provinces, *départements*, cantons, districts, *arrondissements*, *Kreise*, municipalities, or groups of municipalities, etc.).

4.   An exception from the principle of giving exclusive taxing power to the paying State is contained in subparagraph *b*) of paragraph 1. It is to be seen against the background that, according to the Vienna Conventions mentioned above, the receiving State is allowed to tax remuneration paid to certain categories of personnel of foreign diplomatic missions and consular posts, who are permanent residents or nationals of that State. Given that pensions paid to retired government officials ought to be treated for tax purposes in the same way as salaries or wages paid to such employees during their active time, an exception like the one in subparagraph *b*) of paragraph 1 is incorporated also in subparagraph *b*) of paragraph 2 regarding pensions. Since the condition laid down in subdivision *b*)(ii) of paragraph 1 cannot be valid in relation to a pensioner, the only prerequisite for the receiving State's power to tax the pension is that the pensioner must be one of its own residents and nationals.

5.   According to Article 19 of the 1963 Draft Convention, the services rendered to the State, political subdivision or local authority had to be rendered "in the discharge of functions of a governmental nature". That expression was deleted in the 1977 Model Convention. Some OECD member countries, however, thought that the exclusion would lead to a widening of the scope of the Article. Contracting States who are of that view and who feel that such a widening is not desirable may continue to use, and preferably specify, the expression "in the discharge of functions of a governmental nature" in their bilateral conventions.

5.1   Whilst the word "pension", under the ordinary meaning of the word, covers only periodic payments, the words "other similar remuneration", which were added to paragraph 2 in 2005, are broad enough to cover non-periodic payments. For example, a lump-sum payment in lieu of periodic pension payments that is made to a former State employee after cessation of employment may fall within paragraph 2 of the Article. Whether a particular lump-sum payment made in these circumstances is to be considered as other remuneration similar to a pension falling under paragraph 2 or as final remuneration for work performed falling under paragraph 1 is a question of fact which can be resolved in light of the factors presented in paragraph 5 of the Commentary on Article 18.

MODEL TAX CONVENTION (CONDENSED VERSION) – ISBN 978-92-64-08948-8 – © OECD 2010   295

5.2   It should be noted that the expression "out of funds created by" in subparagraph *a*) of paragraph 2 covers the situation where the pension is not paid directly by the State, a political subdivision or a local authority but out of separate funds created by a government body. In addition, the original capital of the fund would not need to be provided by the State, a political subdivision or a local authority. The phrase would cover payments from a privately administered fund established for the government body.

5.3   An issue arises where pensions are paid for combined private and government services. This issue may frequently arise where a person has been employed in both the private and public sector and receives one pension in respect of both periods of employment. This may occur either because the person participated in the same scheme throughout the employment or because the person's pension rights were portable. A trend towards greater mobility between private and public sectors may increase the significance of this issue.

5.4   Where a civil servant having rendered services to a State has transferred a right to a pension from a public scheme to a private scheme the pension payments would be taxed only under Article 18 because such payment would not meet the technical requirement of subparagraph 2 *a*).

5.5   Where the transfer is made in the opposite direction and the pension rights are transferred from a private scheme to a public scheme, some States tax the whole pension payments under Article 19. Other States, however, apportion the pension payments based on the relative source of the pension entitlement so that part is taxed under Article 18 and another part under Article 19. In so doing, some States consider that if one source has provided by far the principal amount of the pension, then the pension should be treated as having been paid exclusively from that source. Nevertheless, it is recognised that apportionment often raises significant administrative difficulties.

5.6   Contracting States may be concerned about the revenue loss or the possibility of double non-taxation if the treatment of pensions could be changed by transferring the fund between public and private schemes. Apportionment may counter this; however, to enable apportionment to be applied to pensions rights that are transferred from a public scheme to a private scheme, Contracting States may, in bilateral negotiations, consider extending subparagraph 2 *a*) to cover the part of any pension or other similar remuneration that it is paid in respect of services rendered to a Contracting State or a political subdivision or a local authority thereof. Such a provision could be drafted as follows:

   2. *a*)   Notwithstanding the provisions of paragraph 1, the part of any pension or other similar remuneration that is paid in respect of services rendered to a Contracting State or a political subdivision or a local authority thereof shall be taxable only in that Contracting State.

Alternatively Contracting States may address the concern by subjecting all pensions to a common treatment.

MODEL TAX CONVENTION (CONDENSED VERSION) – ISBN 978-92-64-08948-8 – © OECD 2010

6.   Paragraphs 1 and 2 do not apply if the services are performed in connection with business carried on by the State, or one of its political subdivisions or local authorities, paying the salaries, wages, pensions or other similar remuneration. In such cases the ordinary rules apply: Article 15 for wages and salaries, Article 16 for directors' fees and other similar payments, Article 17 for artistes and sportsmen, and Article 18 for pensions. Contracting States, wishing for specific reasons to dispense with paragraph 3 in their bilateral conventions, are free to do so thus bringing in under paragraphs 1 and 2 also services rendered in connection with business. In view of the specific functions carried out by certain public bodies, *e.g.* State Railways, the Post Office, State-owned theatres etc., Contracting States wanting to keep paragraph 3 may agree in bilateral negotiations to include under the provisions of paragraphs 1 and 2 salaries, wages, pensions, and other similar remuneration paid by such bodies, even if they could be said to be performing business activities.

Observation on the Commentary

7.   The *Netherlands* does not adhere to the interpretation in paragraphs 5.4 and 5.6. Apportionment of pension payments on the base of the relative source of the pension entitlements, private or government employment, is in the Netherlands view also possible if pension rights are transferred from a public pension scheme to a private scheme.

Reservations on the Article

8.   [Deleted]

9.   The *United States* reserves the right to modify the text to indicate that its application is not limited by Article 1.

10.   [Deleted]

11.   *France* reserves the right to specify in its conventions that salaries, wages, and other similar remuneration paid by a Contracting State or a political subdivision or local authority thereof to an individual in respect of services rendered to that State or subdivision or authority shall be taxable only in that State if the individual is a national of both Contracting States. Also, France reserves its position concerning subdivision b)(ii) of paragraph 1 in view of the difficulties raised by this provision.

12.   [Deleted]

13.   *France* considers that the scope of the application of Article 19 should cover:

— remuneration paid by public legal entities of the State or a political subdivision or local authority thereof, because the identity of the payer is less significant than the public nature of the income;

— public remuneration of artistes and sportsmen in conformity with the wording of the Model prior to 1995 (without applying the criterion of business activity, seldom relevant in these cases), as long as Article 17 does not contain a provision along the lines suggested in paragraph 14 of the Commentary on Article 17.

COMMENTARY ON ARTICLE 20
CONCERNING THE TAXATION OF STUDENTS

1.   The rule established in this Article concerns certain payments received by students or business apprentices for the purpose of their maintenance, education or training. All such payments received from sources outside the State in which the student or business apprentice concerned is staying shall be exempted from tax in that State.

2.   The word "immediately" was inserted in the 1977 Model Convention in order to make clear that the Article does not cover a person who has once been a resident of a Contracting State but has subsequently moved his residence to a third State before visiting the other Contracting State.

3.   The Article covers only payments received for the purpose of the recipient's maintenance, education or training. It does not, therefore, apply to a payment, or any part thereof, that is remuneration for services rendered by the recipient and which is covered by Article 15 (or by Article 7 in the case of independent services). Where the recipient's training involves work experience, however, there is a need to distinguish between a payment for services and a payment for the recipient's maintenance, education or training. The fact that the amount paid is similar to that paid to persons who provide similar services and are not students or business apprentices would generally indicate that the payment is a remuneration for services. Also, payments for maintenance, education or training should not exceed the level of expenses that are likely to be incurred to ensure the recipient's maintenance, education or training.

4.   For the purpose of the Article, payments that are made by or on behalf of a resident of a Contracting State or that are borne by a permanent establishment which a person has in that State are not considered to arise from sources outside that State.

MODEL TAX CONVENTION (CONDENSED VERSION) – ISBN 978-92-64-08948-8 – © OECD 2010

COMMENTARY ON ARTICLE 21
CONCERNING THE TAXATION OF OTHER INCOME

1.   This Article provides a general rule relating to income not dealt with in the foregoing Articles of the Convention. The income concerned is not only income of a class not expressly dealt with but also income from sources not expressly mentioned. The scope of the Article is not confined to income arising in a Contracting State; it extends also to income from third States. Where, for instance, a person who would be a resident of two Contracting States under the provisions of paragraph 1 of Article 4 is deemed to be a resident of only one of these States pursuant to the provisions of paragraph 2 or 3 of that Article, this Article will prevent the other State from taxing the person on income arising in third states even if the person is resident of this other State for domestic law purposes (see also paragraph 8.2 of the Commentary on Article 4 as regards the effect of paragraphs 2 and 3 of Article 4 for purposes of the conventions concluded between this other State and third states).

Paragraph 1

2.   Under this paragraph the exclusive right to tax is given to the State of residence. In cases of conflict between two residences, Article 4 will also allocate the taxation right in respect of third State income.

3.   The rule set out in the paragraph applies irrespective of whether the right to tax is in fact exercised by the State of residence, and thus, when the income arises in the other Contracting State, that State cannot impose tax even if the income is not taxed in the first-mentioned State. Likewise, when income arises in a third State and the recipient of this income is considered as a resident by both Contracting States under their domestic law, the application of Article 4 will result in the recipient being treated as a resident of one Contracting State only and being liable to comprehensive taxation ("full tax liability") in that State only. In this case, the other Contracting State may not impose tax on the income arising from the third State, even if the recipient is not taxed by the State of which he is considered a resident under Article 4. In order to avoid non-taxation, Contracting States may agree to limit the scope of the Article to income which is taxed in the Contracting State of which the recipient is a resident and may modify the provisions of the paragraph accordingly. In fact, this problem is merely a special aspect of the general problem dealt with in paragraphs 34 and 35 of the Commentary on Article 23 A.

Paragraph 2

4.   This paragraph provides for an exception from the provisions of paragraph 1 where the income is associated with the activity of a permanent establishment which a resident of a Contracting State has in the other Contracting State. The paragraph includes income from third States. In such a case, a right to tax is given to the Contracting State in which the permanent establishment is situated. Paragraph 2 does not apply to immovable property for which, according to paragraph 4 of Article 6, the

State of situs has a primary right to tax (see paragraphs 3 and 4 of the Commentary on Article 6). Therefore, immovable property situated in a Contracting State and forming part of the business property of a permanent establishment of an enterprise of that State situated in the other Contracting State shall be taxable only in the first-mentioned State in which the property is situated and of which the recipient of the income is a resident. This is in consistency with the rules laid down in Articles 13 and 22 in respect of immovable property since paragraph 2 of those Articles applies only to movable property of a permanent establishment.

5.   The paragraph also covers the case where the beneficiary and the payer of the income are both residents of the same Contracting State, and the income is attributed to a permanent establishment which the beneficiary of the income has in the other Contracting State. In such a case a right to tax is given to the Contracting State in which the permanent establishment is situated. Where double taxation occurs, the State of residence should give relief under the provisions of Article 23 A or 23 B. However, a problem may arise as regards the taxation of dividends and interest in the State of residence as the State of source: the combination of Articles 7 and 23 A prevents that State from levying tax on that income, whereas if it were paid to a resident of the other State, the first State, being the State of source of the dividends or interest, could tax such dividends or interest at the rates provided for in paragraph 2 of Articles 10 and 11. Contracting States which find this position unacceptable may include in their conventions a provision according to which the State of residence would be entitled, as State of source of the dividends or interest, to levy a tax on such income at the rates provided for in paragraph 2 of Articles 10 and 11. The State where the permanent establishment is situated would give a credit for such tax on the lines of the provisions of paragraph 2 of Article 23 A or of paragraph 1 of Article 23 B; of course, this credit should not be given in cases where the State in which the permanent establishment is situated does not tax the dividends or interest attributed to the permanent establishment, in accordance with its domestic laws.

5.1   For the purposes of the paragraph, a right or property in respect of which income is paid will be effectively connected with a permanent establishment if the "economic" ownership of that right or property is allocated to that permanent establishment under the principles developed in the Committee's report entitled *Attribution of Profits to Permanent Establishments*[1] (see in particular paragraphs 72-97 of Part I of the report) for the purposes of the application of paragraph 2 of Article 7. In the context of that paragraph, the "economic" ownership of a right or property means the equivalent of ownership for income tax purposes by a separate enterprise, with the attendant benefits and burdens (*e.g.* the right to the income attributable to the ownership of the right or property, the right to any available depreciation and the potential exposure to gains or losses from the appreciation or depreciation of that right or property).

5.2   In the case of the permanent establishment of an enterprise carrying on insurance activities, the determination of whether a right or property is effectively

---

1 *Attribution of Profits to Permanent Establishments*, OECD, Paris, 2010.

connected with the permanent establishment shall be made by giving due regard to the guidance set forth in Part IV of the Committee's report with respect to whether the income on or gain from that right or property is taken into account in determining the permanent establishment's yield on the amount of investment assets attributed to it (see in particular paragraphs 165-170 of Part IV). That guidance being general in nature, tax authorities should consider applying a flexible and pragmatic approach which would take into account an enterprise's reasonable and consistent application of that guidance for purposes of identifying the specific assets that are effectively connected with the permanent establishment.

6.   Some States which apply the exemption method (Article 23 A) may have reason to suspect that the treatment accorded in paragraph 2 may provide an inducement to an enterprise of a Contracting State to attach assets such as shares, bonds or patents, to a permanent establishment situated in the other Contracting State in order to obtain more favourable tax treatment there. To counteract such arrangements which they consider would represent abuse, some States might take the view that the transaction is artificial and, for this reason, would regard the assets as not effectively connected with the permanent establishment. Some other States may strengthen their position by adding in paragraph 2 a condition providing that the paragraph shall not apply to cases where the arrangements were primarily made for the purpose of taking advantage of this provision. Also, the requirement that a right or property be "effectively connected" with such a location requires more than merely recording the right or property in the books of the permanent establishment for accounting purposes.

7.   Some countries have encountered difficulties in dealing with income arising from certain nontraditional financial instruments when the parties to the instrument have a special relationship. These countries may wish to add the following paragraph to Article 21:

> 3.   Where, by reason of a special relationship between the person referred to in paragraph 1 and some other person, or between both of them and some third person, the amount of the income referred to in paragraph 1 exceeds the amount (if any) which would have been agreed upon between them in the absence of such a relationship, the provisions of this Article shall apply only to the last mentioned amount. In such a case, the excess part of the income shall remain taxable according to the laws of each Contracting State, due regard being had to the other applicable provisions of this Convention.

The inclusion of this additional paragraph should carry no implication about the treatment of innovative financial transactions between independent persons or under other provisions of the Convention.

8.   This paragraph restricts the operation of the provisions concerning the taxation of income not dealt with in other Articles in the same way that paragraph 6 of Article 11 restricts the operation of the provisions concerning the taxation of interest. In general, the principles enunciated in paragraphs 32-34 of the Commentary on Article 11 apply to this paragraph as well.

9.   Although the restriction could apply to any income otherwise subject to Article 21, it is not envisaged that in practice it is likely to be applied to payments such as alimony payments or social security payments but rather that it is likely to be most relevant where certain nontraditional financial instruments are entered into in circumstances and on terms such that they would not have been entered into in the absence of the special relationship (see paragraph 21.1 of the Commentary to Article 11).

10.   The restriction of Article 21 differs from the restriction of Article 11 in two important respects. First, the paragraph permits, where the necessary circumstances exist, all of the payments under a nontraditional financial instrument to be regarded as excessive. Second, income that is removed from the operation of the interest Article might still be subject to some other Article of the Convention, as explained in paragraphs 35-36 of the Commentary on Article 11. Income to which Article 21 would otherwise apply is by definition not subject to any other Article. Therefore, if the Article 21 restriction removes a portion of income from the operation of that Article, then Articles 6 through 20 of the Convention are not applicable to that income at all, and each Contracting State may tax it under its domestic law.

11.   Other provisions of the Convention, however, will continue to be applicable to such income, such as Article 23 (Relief from Double Taxation), Article 25 (Mutual Agreement Procedure) and Article 26 (Exchange of Information).

12.   [Deleted]

Reservations on the Article

13.   *Australia, Canada, Chile, Mexico, New Zealand, Portugal* and the *Slovak Republic* reserve their positions on this Article and would wish to maintain the right to tax income arising from sources in their own country.

14.   *Finland* and *Sweden* would wish to retain the right to tax certain annuities and similar payments to non-residents, where such payments are made on account of a pension insurance issued in their respective country.

15.   The *United Kingdom* wishes to maintain the right to tax income paid by its residents to non-residents in the form of income from a trust or from estates of deceased persons in the course of administration.

16.   In order to avoid non-taxation, *Belgium* reserves the right to allow the State in which income arises to tax that income where the State of residence, which would otherwise have the exclusive right to tax that income, does not effectively exercise that right.

17.   The *United States* reserves the right to provide for exemption in both States of child support payments.

COMMENTARY ON ARTICLE 22
CONCERNING THE TAXATION OF CAPITAL

1.   This Article deals only with taxes on capital, to the exclusion of taxes on estates and inheritances and on gifts and of transfer duties. Taxes on capital to which the Article applies are those referred to in Article 2.

2.   Taxes on capital generally constitute complementary taxation of income from capital. Consequently, taxes on a given element of capital can be levied, in principle, only by the State which is entitled to tax the income from this element of capital. However, it is not possible to refer purely and simply to the rules relating to the taxation of such class of income, for not all items of income are subject to taxation exclusively in one State.

3.   The Article, therefore, enumerates first property which may be taxed in the State in which they are situated. To this category belong immovable property referred to in Article 6 which a resident of a Contracting State owns and which is situated in the other Contracting State (paragraph 1) and movable property forming part of the business property of a permanent establishment which an enterprise of a Contracting State has in the other Contracting State (paragraph 2).

3.1   For the purposes of paragraph 2, property will form part of the business property of a permanent establishment if the "economic" ownership of the property is allocated to that permanent establishment under the principles developed in the Committee's report entitled *Attribution of Profits to Permanent Establishments*[1] (see in particular paragraphs 72-97 of Part I of the report) for the purposes of the application of paragraph 2 of Article 7. In the context of that paragraph, the "economic" ownership of property means the equivalent of ownership for income tax purposes by a separate enterprise, with the attendant benefits and burdens (*e.g.* the right to any income attributable to the ownership of that property, the right to any available depreciation and the potential exposure to gains or losses from the appreciation or depreciation of that property). The mere fact that the property has been recorded, for accounting purposes, on a balance sheet prepared for the permanent establishment will therefore not be sufficient to conclude that it is effectively connected with that permanent establishment.

3.2   In the case of the permanent establishment of an enterprise carrying on insurance activities, the determination of whether property will form part of the business property of the permanent establishment shall be made by giving due regard to the guidance set forth in Part IV of the Committee's report with respect to whether the income on or gain from that property is taken into account in determining the permanent establishment's yield on the amount of investment assets attributed to it (see in particular paragraphs 165-170 of Part IV). That guidance being general in nature, tax authorities should consider applying a flexible and pragmatic approach which would take into account an enterprise's reasonable and consistent application of that

---

1   *Attribution of Profits to Permanent Establishments*, OECD, Paris, 2010.

guidance for purposes of identifying the specific assets that form part of the business property of the permanent establishment.

4.   Normally, ships and aircraft operated in international traffic and boats engaged in inland waterways transport and movable property pertaining to the operation of such ships, boats or aircraft shall be taxable only in the State in which the place of effective management of the enterprise is situated (paragraph 3). This rule corresponds to the provisions of Article 8 and of paragraph 3 of Article 13. It is understood that paragraph 3 of Article 8 is applicable if the place of effective management of a shipping enterprise or of an inland waterways transport enterprise is aboard a ship or boat. Contracting States which would prefer to confer the exclusive taxing right on the State of residence or to use a combination of the residence criterion and the place of effective management criterion are free in bilateral conventions to substitute for paragraph 3 a provision corresponding to those proposed in paragraphs 2 and 3 of the Commentary on Article 8. Immovable property pertaining to the operation of ships, boats or aircraft may be taxed in the State in which they are situated in accordance with the rule laid down in paragraph 1.

4.1   Paragraph 3 applies where the enterprise that owns the property operates itself the boats, ships or aircraft referred to in the paragraph, whether for its own transportation activities or when leasing the boats, ships or aircraft on charter fully equipped, manned and supplied. It does not apply, however, where the enterprise owning the boats, ships or aircraft does not operate them (for example, where the enterprise leases the property to another person, other than in the case of an occasional bare boat lease as referred to in paragraph 5 of the Commentary on Article 8). In such a case, the capital will be covered by paragraph 2 or 4.

4.2   In their bilateral conventions, member countries are free to clarify further the application of Article 22 in this situation. They might adopt the following alternative version of paragraph 3 of the Article (see also paragraphs 28.1 and 28.2 of the Commentary on Article 13):

    3.   Capital represented by property forming part of the business property of an enterprise the place of effective management of which is situated in a Contracting State, and consisting of ships and aircraft operated by such enterprise in international traffic and of movable property pertaining to the operation of such ships and aircraft shall be taxable only in that State.

5.   As regards elements of capital other than those listed in paragraphs 1 to 3, the Article provides that they are taxable only in the Contracting State of which the person to whom they belong is a resident (paragraph 4).

6.   If, when the provisions of paragraph 4 are applied to elements of movable property under usufruct, double taxation subsists because of the disparity between domestic laws, the States concerned may resort to the mutual agreement procedure or settle the question by means of bilateral negotiations.

7.   The Article does not provide any rule about the deductions of debts. The laws of OECD member countries are too different to allow a common solution for such a

MODEL TAX CONVENTION (CONDENSED VERSION) – ISBN 978-92-64-08948-8 – © OECD 2010

deduction. The problem of the deduction of debts which could arise when the taxpayer and the creditor are not residents of the same State is dealt with in paragraph 4 of Article 24.

8.   [Renumbered]

Reservations on the Article

9.   *Finland* reserves the right to tax shares or other corporate rights in Finnish companies, where the ownership of such shares or other corporate rights entitles to the enjoyment of immovable property situated in Finland and held by the company.

10.   *New Zealand, Portugal* and *Turkey* reserve their positions on this Article if and when they impose taxes on capital.

11.   *France* can accept the provisions of paragraph 4 but wishes to retain the possibility of applying the provisions of its law relative to the taxation of shares or rights which are part of a substantial participation in a company which is a resident of France, or of shares or rights of companies the assets of which consist mainly of immovable property situated in France.

12.   *Denmark, Norway* and *Sweden* reserve the right to insert special provisions regarding capital represented by aircraft operated in international traffic, when owned by the air transport consortium Scandinavian Airlines System (SAS).

13.   *Spain* reserves its right to tax capital represented by shares or other rights in a company whose assets consist mainly of immovable property situated in Spain, by shares or other corporate rights which entitle its owner to a right of enjoyment of immovable property situated in Spain or by shares or other rights constituting a substantial participation in a company which is a resident of Spain.

14.   In view of its particular situation in relation to shipping, *Greece* will retain its freedom of action with regard to the provisions in the Convention relating to capital represented by ships in international traffic and by movable property pertaining to the operation of such ships.

COMMENTARY ON ARTICLES 23 A AND 23 B CONCERNING THE METHODS FOR ELIMINATION OF DOUBLE TAXATION

I. Preliminary remarks

A. *The scope of the Articles*

1.   These Articles deal with the so-called juridical double taxation where the same income or capital is taxable in the hands of the same person by more than one State.

2.   This case has to be distinguished especially from the so-called economic double taxation, i.e. where two different persons are taxable in respect of the same income or capital. If two States wish to solve problems of economic double taxation, they must do so in bilateral negotiations.

3.   International juridical double taxation may arise in three cases:

   a) where each Contracting State subjects the same person to tax on his worldwide income or capital (concurrent full liability to tax, see paragraph 4 below);

   b) where a person is a resident of a Contracting State (R)[1] and derives income from, or owns capital in, the other Contracting State (S or E) and both States impose tax on that income or capital (see paragraph 5 below);

   c) where each Contracting State subjects the same person, not being a resident of either Contracting State to tax on income derived from, or capital owned in, a Contracting State; this may result, for instance, in the case where a non-resident person has a permanent establishment in one Contracting State (E) through which he derives income from, or owns capital in, the other Contracting State (S) (concurrent limited tax liability, see paragraph 11 below).

4.   The conflict in case a) is reduced to that of case b) by virtue of Article 4. This is because that Article defines the term "resident of a Contracting State" by reference to the liability to tax of a person under domestic law by reason of his domicile, residence, place of management or any other criterion of a similar nature (paragraph 1 of Article 4) and by listing special criteria for the case of double residence to determine which of the two States is the State of residence (R) within the meaning of the Convention (paragraphs 2 and 3 of Article 4).

4.1   Article 4, however, only deals with cases of concurrent full liability to tax. The conflict in case a) may therefore not be solved if the same item of income is subject to the full liability to tax of two countries but at different times. The following example illustrates that problem. Assume that a resident of State R1 derives a taxable benefit from an employee stock-option that is granted to that person. State R1 taxes that benefit when the option is granted. The person subsequently becomes a resident of State R2,

---

1   Throughout the Commentary on Articles 23 A and 23 B, the letter "R" stands for the State of residence within the meaning of the Convention, "S" for the State of source or situs, and "E" for the State where a permanent establishment is situated.

MODEL TAX CONVENTION (CONDENSED VERSION) – ISBN 978-92-64-08948-8 – © OECD 2010

which taxes the benefit at the time of its subsequent exercise. In that case, the person is taxed by each State at a time when he is a resident of that State and Article 4 does not deal with the issue as there is no concurrent residence in the two States.

4.2   The conflict in that situation will be reduced to that of case b) and solved accordingly to the extent that the employment services to which the option relates have been rendered in one of the Contracting States so as to be taxable by that State under Article 15 because it is the State where the relevant employment is exercised. Indeed, in such a case, the State in which the services have been rendered will be the State of source for purposes of elimination of double taxation by the other State. It does not matter that the first State does not levy tax at the same time (see paragraph 32.8). It also does not matter that that State considers that it levies tax as a State of residence as opposed to a State of source (see the last sentence of paragraph 8).

4.3   Where, however, the relevant employment services have not been rendered in either State, the conflict will not be one of source-residence double taxation. The mutual agreement procedure could be used to deal with such a case. One possible basis to solve the case would be for the competent authorities of the two States to agree that each State should provide relief as regards the residence-based tax that was levied by the other State on the part of the benefit that relates to services rendered during the period while the employee was a resident of that other State. Thus, in the above example, if the relevant services were rendered in a third State before the person became a resident of State R2, it would be logical for the competent authority of State R2 to agree to provide relief (either through the credit or exemption method) for the State R1 tax that has been levied on the part of the employment benefit that relates to services rendered in the third State since, at the time when these services were rendered, the taxpayer was a resident of State R1 and not of State R2 for purposes of the convention between these two States.

5.   The conflict in case b) may be solved by allocation of the right to tax between the Contracting States. Such allocation may be made by renunciation of the right to tax either by the State of source or situs (S) or of the situation of the permanent establishment (E), or by the State of residence (R), or by a sharing of the right to tax between the two States. The provisions of the Chapters III and IV of the Convention, combined with the provisions of Article 23 A or 23 B, govern such allocation.

6.   For some items of income or capital, an exclusive right to tax is given to one of the Contracting States, and the relevant Article states that the income or capital in question "shall be taxable only" in a Contracting State.[1] The words "shall be taxable only" in a Contracting State preclude the other Contracting State from taxing, thus double taxation is avoided. The State to which the exclusive right to tax is given is normally the State of which the taxpayer is a resident within the meaning of Article 4,

---

[1] See first sentence of paragraph 1 of Article 7, paragraphs 1 and 2 of Article 8, paragraph 1 of Article 12, paragraphs 3 and 5 of Article 13, first sentence of paragraph 1 and paragraph 2 of Article 15, Article 18, paragraphs 1 and 2 of Article 19, paragraph 1 of Article 21 and paragraphs 3 and 4 of Article 22.

that is State R, but in four Articles[1] the exclusive right may be given to the other Contracting State (S) of which the taxpayer is not a resident within the meaning of Article 4.

7.   For other items of income or capital, the attribution of the right to tax is not exclusive, and the relevant Article then states that the income or capital in question "may be taxed" in the Contracting State (S or E) of which the taxpayer is not a resident within the meaning of Article 4. In such case the State of residence (R) must give relief so as to avoid the double taxation. Paragraphs 1 and 2 of Article 23 A and paragraph 1 of Article 23 B are designed to give the necessary relief.

8.   Articles 23 A and 23 B apply to the situation in which a resident of State R derives income from, or owns capital in, the other Contracting State E or S (not being the State of residence within the meaning of the Convention) and that such income or capital, in accordance with the Convention, may be taxed in such other State E or S. The Articles, therefore, apply only to the State of residence and do not prescribe how the other Contracting State E or S has to proceed.

9.   Where a resident of the Contracting State R derives income from the same State R through a permanent establishment which he has in the other Contracting State E, State E may tax such income (except income from immovable property situated in State R) if it is attributable to the said permanent establishment (paragraph 2 of Article 21). In this instance too, State R must give relief under Article 23 A or Article 23 B for income attributable to the permanent establishment situated in State E, notwithstanding the fact that the income in question originally arises in State R (see paragraph 5 of the Commentary on Article 21). However, where the Contracting States agree to give to State R which applies the exemption method a limited right to tax as the State of source of dividends or interest within the limits fixed in paragraph 2 of the Articles 10 or 11 (see paragraph 5 of the Commentary on Article 21), then the two States should also agree upon a credit to be given by State E for the tax levied by State R, along the lines of paragraph 2 of Article 23 A or of paragraph 1 of Article 23 B.

10.   Where a resident of State R derives income from a third State through a permanent establishment which he has in State E, such State E may tax such income (except income from immovable property situated in the third State) if it is attributable to such permanent establishment (paragraph 2 of Article 21). State R must give relief under Article 23 A or Article 23 B in respect of income attributable to the permanent establishment in State E. There is no provision in the Convention for relief to be given by Contracting State E for taxes levied in the third State where the income arises; however, under paragraph 3 of Article 24 any relief provided for in the domestic laws of State E (double taxation conventions excluded) for residents of State E is also to be granted to a permanent establishment in State E of an enterprise of State R (see paragraphs 67 to 72 of the Commentary on Article 24).

---

1 See paragraphs 1 and 2 of Article 8, paragraph 3 of Article 13, subparagraph a) of paragraphs 1 and 2 of Article 19 and paragraph 3 of Article 22.

11.   The conflict in case c) of paragraph 3 above is outside the scope of the Convention as, under Article 1, it applies only to persons who are residents of one or both of the States. It can, however, be settled by applying the mutual agreement procedure (see also paragraph 10 above).

B.   Description of methods for elimination of double taxation

12.   In the existing conventions, two leading principles are followed for the elimination of double taxation by the State of which the taxpayer is a resident. For purposes of simplicity, only income tax is referred to in what follows; but the principles apply equally to capital tax.

1.   The principle of exemption

13.   Under the principle of exemption, the State of residence R does not tax the income which according to the Convention may be taxed in State E or S (nor, of course, also income which shall be taxable only in State E or S; see paragraph 6 above).

14.   The principle of exemption may be applied by two main methods:

a) the income which may be taxed in State E or S is not taken into account at all by State R for the purposes of its tax; State R is not entitled to take the income so exempted into consideration when determining the tax to be imposed on the rest of the income; this method is called "full exemption";

b) the income which may be taxed in State E or S is not taxed by State R, but State R retains the right to take that income into consideration when determining the tax to be imposed on the rest of the income; this method is called "exemption with progression".

2.   The principle of credit

15.   Under the principle of credit, the State of residence R calculates its tax on the basis of the taxpayer's total income including the income from the other State E or S which, according to the Convention, may be taxed in that other State (but not including income which shall be taxable only in State S; see paragraph 6 above). It then allows a deduction from its own tax for the tax paid in the other State.

16.   The principle of credit may be applied by two main methods:

a) State R allows the deduction of the total amount of tax paid in the other State on income which may be taxed in that State, this method is called "full credit";

b) the deduction given by State R for the tax paid in the other State is restricted to that part of its own tax which is appropriate to the income which may be taxed in the other State; this method is called "ordinary credit".

17.   Fundamentally, the difference between the methods is that the exemption methods look at income, while the credit methods look at tax.

C. Operation and effects of the methods

18. An example in figures will facilitate the explanation of the effects of the various methods. Suppose the total income to be 100,000, of which 80,000 is derived from one State (State of residence R) and 20,000 from the other State (State of source S). Assume that in State R the rate of tax on an income of 100,000 is 35 per cent and on an income of 80,000 is 30 per cent. Assume further that in State S the rate of tax is either 20 per cent — case (i) — or 40 per cent — case (ii) — so that the tax payable therein on 20,000 is 4,000 in case (i) or 8,000 in case (ii), respectively.

19. If the taxpayer's total income of 100,000 arises in State R, his tax would be 35,000. If he had an income of the same amount, but derived in the manner set out above, and if no relief is provided for in the domestic laws of State R and no conventions exists between State R and State S, then the total amount of tax would be, in case (i): 35,000 plus 4,000 = 39,000, and in case (ii): 35,000 plus 8,000 = 43,000.

1. Exemption methods

20. Under the exemption methods, State R limits its taxation to that part of the total income which, in accordance with the various Articles of the Convention, it has a right to tax, i.e. 80,000.

a) Full exemption

State R imposes tax on 80,000 at the rate of tax applicable to 80,000, i.e. at 30 per cent.

	Case (i)	Case (ii)
Tax in State R, 30% of 80,000	24,000	24,000
Plus tax in State S	4,000	8,000
Total taxes	28,000	32,000
Relief has been given by State R in the amount of	11,000	11,000

b) Exemption with progression

State R imposes tax on 80,000 at the rate of tax applicable to total income wherever it arises (100,000), i.e. at 35 per cent.

	Case (i)	Case (ii)
Tax in State R, 35% of 80,000	28,000	28,000
Plus tax in State S	4,000	8,000
Total taxes	32,000	36,000
Relief has been given by State R in the amount of	7,000	7,000

21. In both cases, the level of tax in State S does not affect the amount of tax given up by State R. If the tax on the income from State S is lower in State S than the relief to

be given by State R — cases *a* (i), *a* (ii), and *b* (i) — then the taxpayer will fare better than if his total income were derived solely from State R. In the converse case — case *b* (ii) — the taxpayer will be worse off.

22.   The example shows also that the relief given where State R applies the full exemption method may be higher than the tax levied in State S, even if the rates of tax in State S are higher than those in State R. This is due to the fact that under the full exemption method, not only the tax of State R on the income from State S is surrendered (35 per cent of 20,000 = 7,000; as under the exemption with progression), but that also the tax on remaining income (80,000) is reduced by an amount corresponding to the differences in rates at the two income levels in State R (35 less 30 = 5 per cent applied to 80,000 = 4,000).

2.   Credit methods

23.   Under the credit methods, State R retains its right to tax the total income of the taxpayer, but against the tax so imposed, it allows a deduction.

a) Full credit

State R computes tax on total income of 100,000 at the rate of 35 per cent and allows the deduction of the tax due in State S on the income from S.

	Case (i)	Case (ii)
Tax in State R, 35% of 100,000	35,000	35,000
less tax in State S	- 4,000	- 8,000
Tax due	31,000	27,000
Total taxes	35,000	35,000
Relief has been given by State R in the amount of	4,000	8,000

b) Ordinary credit

State R computes tax on total income of 100,000 at the rate of 35 per cent and allows the deduction of the tax due in State S on the income from S, but in no case it allows more than the portion of tax in State R attributable to the income from S (maximum deduction). The maximum deduction would be 35 per cent of 20,000 = 7,000.

	Case (i)	Case (ii)
Tax in State R, 35% of 100,000	35,000	35,000
less tax in State S	- 4,000	
less maximum tax		- 7,000
Tax due	31,000	28,000
Total taxes	35,000	36,000
Relief has been given by State R in the amount of	4,000	7,000

24. A characteristic of the credit methods compared with the exemption methods is that State R is never obliged to allow a deduction of more than the tax due in State S.

25. Where the tax due in State S is lower than the tax of State R appropriate to the income from State S (maximum deduction), the taxpayer will always have to pay the same amount of taxes as he would have had to pay if he were taxed only in State R, i.e. as if his total income were derived solely from State R.

26. The same result is achieved, where the tax due in State S is the higher while State R applies the full credit, at least as long as the total tax due to State R is as high or higher than the amount of the tax due in State S.

27. Where the tax due in State S is higher and where the credit is limited (ordinary credit), the taxpayer will not get a deduction for the whole of the tax paid in State S. In such event the result would be less favourable to the taxpayer than if his whole income arose in State R, and in these circumstances the ordinary credit method would have the same effect as the method of exemption with progression.

Table 23-1 Total amount of tax in the different cases illustrated above

A. All income arising in State R	Total tax = 35,000	
B. Income arising in two States, viz. 80,000 in State R and 20,000 in State S	Total tax if tax in State S is	
	4,000 (case (i))	8,000 (case (ii))
No convention (19)[1]	39,000	43,000
Full exemption (20a)	28,000	32,000
Exemption with progression (20b)	32,000	36,000
Full credit (23a)	35,000	35,000
Ordinary credit (23b)	35,000	36,000

1. Numbers in brackets refer to paragraphs in this Commentary.

Table 23-2 Amount of tax given up by the state of residence

	If tax in State S is	
	4,000 (case (i))	8,000 (case (ii))
No convention	0	0
Full exemption (20a)[1]	11,000	11,000
Exemption with progression (20b)	7,000	7,000
Full credit (23a)	4,000	8,000
Ordinary credit (23b)	4,000	7,000

1. Numbers in brackets refer to paragraphs in this Commentary.

MODEL TAX CONVENTION (CONDENSED VERSION) – ISBN 978-92-64-08948-8 – © OECD 2010

D.   *The methods proposed in the Articles*

28.   In the conventions concluded between OECD member countries both leading principles have been followed. Some States have a preference for the first one, some for the other. Theoretically a single principle could be held to be more desirable, but, on account of the preferences referred to, each State has been left free to make its own choice.

29.   On the other hand, it has been found important to limit the number of methods based on each leading principle to be employed. In view of this limitation, the Articles have been drafted so that member countries are left free to choose between two methods:

— the exemption method with progression (Article 23 A), and

— the ordinary credit method (Article 23 B).

30.   If two Contracting States both adopt the same method, it will be sufficient to insert the relevant Article in the convention. On the other hand, if the two Contracting States adopt different methods, both Articles may be amalgamated in one, and the name of the State must be inserted in each appropriate part of the Article, according to the method adopted by that State.

31.   Contracting States may use a combination of the two methods. Such combination is indeed necessary for a Contracting State R which generally adopts the exemption method in the case of income which under Articles 10 and 11 may be subjected to a limited tax in the other Contracting State S. For such case, Article 23 A provides in paragraph 2 a credit for the limited tax levied in the other Contracting State S (adjustments to paragraphs 1 and 2 of Article 23 A may, however, be required in the case of distributions from Real Estate Investment Trusts (REITs) where provisions similar to those referred to in paragraphs 67.1 to 67.7 of the Commentary on Article 10 have been adopted by the Contracting States). Moreover, States which in general adopt the exemption method may wish to exclude specific items of income from exemption and to apply to such items the credit method. In such case, paragraph 2 of Article 23 A could be amended to include these items of income.

31.1 One example where paragraph 2 could be so amended is where a State that generally adopts the exemption method considers that that method should not apply to items of income that benefit from a preferential tax treatment in the other State by reason of a tax measure that has been introduced in that State after the date of signature of the Convention. In order to include these items of income, paragraph 2 could be amended as follows:

2.   Where a resident of a Contracting State derives an item of income which

a)   in accordance with the provisions of Articles 10 and 11, may be taxed in the other Contracting State, or

b)   in accordance with the provisions of this Convention, may be taxed in the other Contracting State but which benefits from a preferential tax treatment in that other State by reason of a tax measure

(i) that has been introduced in the other Contracting State after the date of signature of the Convention, and

(ii) in respect of which that State has notified the competent authorities of the other Contracting State, before the item of income is so derived and after consultation with that other State, that this paragraph shall apply,

the first-mentioned State shall allow as a deduction from the tax on the income of that resident an amount equal to the tax paid in that other State. Such deduction shall not, however, exceed that part of the tax, as computed before the deduction is given, which is attributable to such item of income derived from that other State.

32. The two Articles are drafted in a general way and do not give detailed rules on how the exemption or credit is to be computed, this being left to the domestic laws and practice applicable. Contracting States which find it necessary to settle any problem in the Convention itself are left free to do so in bilateral negotiations.

E. *Conflicts of qualification*

32.1 Both Articles 23 A and 23 B require that relief be granted, through the exemption or credit method, as the case may be, where an item of income or capital may be taxed by the State of source in accordance with the provisions of the Convention. Thus, the State of residence has the obligation to apply the exemption or credit method in relation to an item of income or capital where the Convention authorises taxation of that item by the State of source.

32.2 The interpretation of the phrase "in accordance with the provisions of this Convention, may be taxed", which is used in both Articles, is particularly important when dealing with cases where the State of residence and the State of source classify the same item of income or capital differently for purposes of the provisions of the Convention.

32.3 Different situations need to be considered in that respect. Where, due to differences in the domestic law between the State of source and the State of residence, the former applies, with respect to a particular item of income or capital, provisions of the Convention that are different from those that the State of residence would have applied to the same item of income or capital, the income is still being taxed in accordance with the provisions of the Convention, as interpreted and applied by the State of source. In such a case, therefore, the two Articles require that relief from double taxation be granted by the State of residence notwithstanding the conflict of qualification resulting from these differences in domestic law.

32.4 This point may be illustrated by the following example. A business is carried on through a permanent establishment in State E by a partnership established in that State. A partner, resident in State R, alienates his interest in that partnership. State E treats the partnership as fiscally transparent whereas State R treats it as taxable entity. State E therefore considers that the alienation of the interest in the partnership is, for the purposes of its Convention with State R, an alienation by the partner of the underlying assets of the business carried on by the partnership, which may be taxed by that State in accordance with paragraph 1 or 2 of Article 13. State R, as it treats the partnership as a taxable entity, considers that the alienation of the interest in the partnership is akin to the alienation of a share in a company, which could not be taxed by State E by reason of paragraph 5 of Article 13. In such a case, the conflict of qualification results exclusively from the different treatment of partnerships in the domestic laws of the two States and State E must be considered by State R to have taxed the gain from the alienation "in accordance with the provisions of the Convention" for purposes of the application of Article 23 A or Article 23 B. State R must therefore grant an exemption pursuant to Article 23 A or give a credit pursuant to Article 23 B irrespective of the fact that, under its own domestic law, it treats the alienation gain as income from the disposition of shares in a corporate entity and that, if State E's qualification of the income were consistent with that of State R, State R would not have to give relief under Article 23 A or Article 23 B. No double taxation will therefore arise in such a case.

32.5   Article 23 A and Article 23 B, however, do not require that the State of residence eliminate double taxation in all cases where the State of source has imposed its tax by applying to an item of income a provision of the Convention that is different from that which the State of residence considers to be applicable. For instance, in the example above, if, for purposes of applying paragraph 2 of Article 13, State E considers that the partnership carried on business through a fixed place of business but State R considers that paragraph 5 applies because the partnership did not have a fixed place of business in State E, there is actually a dispute as to whether State E has taxed the income in accordance with the provisions of the Convention. The same may be said if State E, when applying paragraph 2 of Article 13, interprets the phrase "forming part of the business property" so as to include certain assets which would not fall within the meaning of that phrase according to the interpretation given to it by State R. Such conflicts resulting from different interpretation of facts or different interpretation of the provisions of the Convention must be distinguished from the conflicts of qualification described in the above paragraph where the divergence is based not on different interpretations of the provisions of the Convention but on different provisions of domestic law. In the former case, State R can argue that State E has not imposed its tax in accordance with the provisions of the Convention if it has applied its tax based on what State R considers to be a wrong interpretation of the facts or a wrong interpretation of the Convention. States should use the provisions of Article 25 (Mutual Agreement Procedure), and in particular paragraph 3 thereof, in order to resolve this type of conflict in cases that would otherwise result in unrelieved double taxation.

32.6   The phrase "in accordance with the provisions of this Convention, may be taxed" must also be interpreted in relation to possible cases of double non-taxation that can arise under Article 23 A. Where the State of source considers that the provisions of the Convention preclude it from taxing an item of income or capital which it would otherwise have had the right to tax, the State of residence should, for purposes of applying paragraph 1 of Article 23 A, consider that the item of income may not be taxed by the State of source in accordance with the provisions of the Convention, even though the State of residence would have applied the Convention differently so as to have the right to tax that income if it had been in the position of the State of source. Thus the State of residence is not required by paragraph 1 to exempt the item of income, a result which is consistent with the basic function of Article 23 which is to eliminate double taxation.

32.7 This situation may be illustrated by reference to a variation of the example described above. A business is carried on through a fixed place of business in State E by a partnership established in that State and a partner, resident in State R, alienates his interest in that partnership. Changing the facts of the example, however, it is now assumed that State E treats the partnership as a taxable entity whereas State R treats it as fiscally transparent; it is further assumed that State R is a State that applies the exemption method. State E, as it treats the partnership as a corporate entity, considers that the alienation of the interest in the partnership is akin to the alienation of a share in a company, which it cannot tax by reason of paragraph 5 of Article 13. State R, on the other hand, considers that the alienation of the interest in the partnership should have been taxable by State E as an alienation by the partner of the underlying assets of the business carried on by the partnership to which paragraphs 1 or 2 of Article 13 would have been applicable. In determining whether it has the obligation to exempt the income under paragraph 1 of Article 23 A, State R should nonetheless consider that, given the way that the provisions of the Convention apply in conjunction with the domestic law of State E, that State may not tax the income in accordance with the provisions of the Convention. State R is thus under no obligation to exempt the income.

F. Timing mismatch

32.8 The provisions of the Convention that allow the State of source to tax particular items of income or capital do not provide any restriction as to when such tax is to be levied (see, for instance, paragraph 2.2 of the Commentary on Article 15). Since both Articles 23 A and 23 B require that relief be granted where an item of income or capital may be taxed by the State of source in accordance with the provisions of the Convention, it follows that such relief must be provided regardless of when the tax is levied by the State of source. The State of residence must therefore provide relief of double taxation through the credit or exemption method with respect to such item of income or capital even though the State of source taxes it in an earlier or later year. Some States, however, do not follow the wording of Article 23 A or 23 B in their bilateral conventions and link the relief of double taxation that they give under tax conventions to what is provided under their domestic laws. These countries, however, would be expected to seek other ways (the mutual agreement procedure, for example) to relieve the double taxation which might otherwise arise in cases where the State of source levies tax in a different taxation year.

II. Commentary on the provisions of Article 23 A (exemption method)

Paragraph 1

A. The obligation of the State of residence to give exemption

33.   In the Article it is laid down that the State of residence R shall exempt from tax income and capital which in accordance with the Convention "may be taxed" in the other State E or S.

34.   The State of residence must accordingly exempt income and capital which may be taxed by the other State in accordance with the Convention whether or not the right to tax is in effect exercised by that other State. This method is regarded as the most practical one since it relieves the State of residence from undertaking investigations of the actual taxation position in the other State.

34.1   The obligation imposed on the State of residence to exempt a particular item of income or capital depends on whether this item may be taxed by the State of source in accordance with the Convention. Paragraphs 32.1 to 32.7 above discuss how this condition should be interpreted. Where the condition is met, however, the obligation may be considered as absolute, subject to the exceptions of paragraphs 2 and 4 of Article 23 A. Paragraph 2 addresses the case, already mentioned in paragraph 31 above, of items of income which may only be subjected to a limited tax in the State of source. For such items of income, the paragraph provides for the credit method (see paragraph 47 below). Paragraph 4 addresses the case of certain conflicts of qualification which would result in double non-taxation as a consequence of the application of the Convention if the State of residence were obliged to give exemption (see paragraphs 56.1 to 56.3 below).

35.   Occasionally, negotiating States may find it reasonable in certain circumstances, in order to avoid double non-taxation, to make an exception to the absolute obligation on the State of residence to give exemption in cases where neither paragraph 3 or 4 would apply. Such may be the case where no tax on specific items of income or capital is provided under the domestic laws of the State of source, or tax is not effectively collected owing to special circumstances such as the set-off of losses, a mistake, or the statutory time limit having expired. To avoid such double non-taxation of specific items of income, Contracting States may agree to amend the relevant Article itself (see paragraph 9 of the Commentary on Article 15 and paragraph 12 of the Commentary on Article 17; for the converse case where relief in the State of source is subject to actual taxation in the State of residence, see paragraph 20 of the Commentary on Article 10, paragraph 10 of the Commentary on Article 11, paragraph 6 of the Commentary on Article 12, paragraph 21 of the Commentary on Article 13 and paragraph 3 of the Commentary on Article 21). One might also make an exception to the general rule, in order to achieve a certain reciprocity, where one of the States adopts the exemption method and the other the credit method. Finally, another exception to the general rule

may be made where a State wishes to apply to specific items of income the credit method rather than exemption (see paragraph 31 above).

36. [Deleted]

B. Alternative formulation of the Article

37. An effect of the exemption method as it is drafted in the Article is that the taxable income or capital in the State of residence is reduced by the amount exempted in that State. If in a particular State the amount of income as determined for income tax purposes is used as a measure for other purposes, *e.g.* social benefits, the application of the exemption method in the form proposed may have the effect that such benefits may be given to persons who ought not to receive them. To avoid such consequences, the Article may be altered so that the income in question is included in the taxable income in the State of residence. The State of residence must, in such cases, give up that part of the total tax appropriate to the income concerned. This procedure would give the same result as the Article in the form proposed. States can be left free to make such modifications in the drafting of the Article. If a State wants to draft the Article as indicated above, paragraph 1 may be drafted as follows:

Where a resident of a Contracting State derives income or owns capital which, in accordance with the provisions of this Convention, shall be taxable only or may be taxed in the other Contracting State, the first-mentioned State shall, subject to the provisions of paragraph 2, allow as a deduction from the income tax or capital tax that part of the income tax or capital tax, respectively, which is applicable, as the case may be, to the income derived from or the capital owned in that other State.

If the Article is so drafted, paragraph 3 would not be necessary and could be omitted.

C. Miscellaneous problems

38. Article 23 A contains the principle that the State of residence has to give exemption, but does not give detailed rules on how the exemption has to be implemented. This is consistent with the general pattern of the Convention. Articles 6 to 22 too lay down rules attributing the right to tax in respect of the various types of income or capital without dealing, as a rule, with the determination of taxable income or capital, deductions, rate of tax, etc. (see, however, Article 24). Experience has shown that many problems may arise. This is especially true with respect to Article 23 A. Some of them are dealt with in the following paragraphs. In the absence of a specific provision in the Convention, the domestic laws of each Contracting State are applicable. Some conventions contain an express reference to the domestic laws but of course this would not help where the exemption method is not used in the domestic laws. In such cases, Contracting States which face this problem should establish rules for the application of Article 23 A, if necessary, after having consulted with the competent authority of the other Contracting State (paragraph 3 of Article 25).

MODEL TAX CONVENTION (CONDENSED VERSION) – ISBN 978-92-64-08948-8 – © OECD 2010

1. Amount to be exempted

39. The amount of income to be exempted from tax by the State of residence is the amount which, but for the Convention, would be subjected to domestic income tax according to the domestic laws governing such tax. It may, therefore, differ from the amount of income subjected to tax by the State of source according to its domestic laws.

40. Normally, the basis for the calculation of income tax is the total net income, i.e. gross income less allowable deductions. Therefore, it is the gross income derived from the State of source less any allowable deductions (specified or proportional) connected with such income which is to be exempted.

41. Problems arise from the fact that most countries provide in their respective taxation laws for additional deductions from total income or specific items of income to arrive at the income subject to tax. A numerical example may illustrate the problem:

a)	Domestic income (gross less allowable expenses)	100
b)	Income from the other State (gross less allowable expenses)	100
c)	Total income	200
d)	Deductions for other expenses provided for under the laws of the State of residence which are not connected with any of the income under a or b, such as insurance premiums, contributions to welfare institutions	-20
e)	"Net" income	180
f)	Personal and family allowances	-30
g)	Income subject to tax	150

The question is, what amount should be exempted from tax, e.g.

— 100 (line b), leaving a taxable amount of 50;

— 90 (half of line e, according to the ratio between line b and line c), leaving 60 (line f being fully deducted from domestic income);

— 75 (half of line g, according to the ratio between line b and line c), leaving 75;

— or any other amount.

42. A comparison of the laws and practices of the OECD member countries shows that the amount to be exempted varies considerably from country to country. The solution adopted by a State will depend on the policy followed by that State and its tax structure. It may be the intention of a State that its residents always enjoy the full benefit of their personal and family allowances and other deductions. In other States these tax free amounts are apportioned. In many States personal or family allowances form part of the progressive scale, are granted as a deduction from tax, or are even unknown, the family status being taken into account by separate tax scales.

43. In view of the wide variety of fiscal policies and techniques in the different States regarding the determination of tax, especially deductions, allowances and similar benefits, it is preferable not to propose an express and uniform solution in the Convention, but to leave each State free to apply its own legislation and technique.

Contracting States which prefer to have special problems solved in their convention are, of course, free to do so in bilateral negotiations. Finally, attention is drawn to the fact that the problem is also of importance for States applying the credit method (see paragraph 62 below).

2. Treatment of losses

44. Several States in applying Article 23 A treat losses incurred in the other State in the same manner as they treat income arising in that State: as State of residence (State R), they do not allow deduction of a loss incurred from immovable property or a permanent establishment situated in the other State (E or S). Provided that this other State allows carry-over of such loss, the taxpayer will not be at any disadvantage as he is merely prevented from claiming a double deduction of the same loss namely in State E (or S) and in State R. Other States may, as State of residence R, allow a loss incurred in State E (or S) as a deduction from the income they assess. In such a case State R should be free to restrict the exemption under paragraph 1 of Article 23 A for profits or income which are made subsequently in the other State E (or S) by deducting from such subsequent profits or income the amount of earlier losses which the taxpayer can carry over in State E (or S). As the solution depends primarily on the domestic laws of the Contracting States and as the laws of the OECD member countries differ from each other substantially, no solution can be proposed in the Article itself, it being left to the Contracting States, if they find it necessary, to clarify the above-mentioned question and other problems connected with losses (see paragraph 62 below for the credit method) bilaterally, either in the Article itself or by way of a mutual agreement procedure (paragraph 3 of Article 25).

3. Taxation of the rest of the income

45. Apart from the application of progressive tax rates which is now dealt with in paragraph 3 of the Article (see paragraphs 55 and 56 below), some problems may arise from specific provisions of the tax laws. Thus, *e.g.* some tax laws provide that taxation starts only if a minimum amount of taxable income is reached or exceeded (tax exempt threshold). Total income before application of the Convention may clearly exceed such tax free threshold, but by virtue of the exemption resulting from the application of the Convention which leads to a deduction of the tax exempt income from total taxable income, the remaining taxable income may be reduced to an amount below this threshold. For the reasons mentioned in paragraph 43 above, no uniform solution can be proposed. It may be noted, however, that the problem will not arise, if the alternative formulation of paragraph 1 of Article 23 A (as set out in paragraph 37 above) is adopted.

46. Certain States have introduced special systems for taxing corporate income (see paragraphs 40 to 67 of the Commentary on Article 10). In States applying a split rate corporation tax (paragraph 43 of the said Commentary), the problem may arise whether the income to be exempted has to be deducted from undistributed income (to which the normal rate of tax applies) or from distributed income (to which the reduced

rate applies) or whether the income to be exempted has to be attributed partly to distributed and partly to undistributed income. Where, under the laws of a State applying the split rate corporation tax, a supplementary tax is levied in the hands of a parent company on dividends which it received from a domestic subsidiary company but which it does not redistribute (on the grounds that such supplementary tax is a compensation for the benefit of a lower tax rate granted to the subsidiary on the distributions), the problem arises, whether such supplementary tax may be charged where the subsidiary pays its dividends out of income exempt from tax by virtue of the Convention. Finally a similar problem may arise in connection with taxes (*précompte*, Advance Corporation Tax) which are levied on distributed profits of a corporation in order to cover the tax credit attributable to the shareholders (see paragraph 47 of the Commentary on Article 10). The question is whether such special taxes connected with the distribution of profits, could be levied insofar as distributions are made out of profits exempt from tax. It is left to Contracting States to settle these questions by bilateral negotiations.

Paragraph 2

47.   In Articles 10 and 11 the right to tax dividends and interest is divided between the State of residence and the State of source. In these cases, the State of residence is left free not to tax if it wants to do so (see *e.g.* paragraphs 72 to 78 below) and to apply the exemption method also to the above-mentioned items of income. However, where the State of residence prefers to make use of its right to tax such items of income, it cannot apply the exemption method to eliminate the double taxation since it would thus give up fully its right to tax the income concerned. For the State of residence, the application of the credit method would normally seem to give a satisfactory solution. Moreover, as already indicated in paragraph 31 above, States which in general apply the exemption method may wish to apply to specific items of income the credit method rather than exemption. Consequently, the paragraph is drafted in accordance with the ordinary credit method. The Commentary on Article 23 B hereafter applies *mutatis mutandis* to paragraph 2 of Article 23 A.

48.   In the cases referred to in the previous paragraph, certain maximum percentages are laid down for tax reserved to the State of source. In such cases, the rate of tax in the State of residence will very often be higher than the rate in the State of source. The limitation of the deduction which is laid down in the second sentence of paragraph 2 and which is in accordance with the ordinary credit method is therefore of consequence only in a limited number of cases. If, in such cases, the Contracting States prefer to waive the limitation and to apply the full credit method, they can do so by deleting the second sentence of paragraph 2 (see also paragraph 63 below).

Dividends from substantial holdings by a company

49.   The combined effect of paragraphs 1 and 2 of Article 10 and Article 23 (Article 23 A and 23 B as appropriate) is that the State of residence of the shareholder is allowed to tax dividends arising in the other State, but that it must credit against its

own tax on such dividends the tax which has been collected by the State where the dividends arise at a rate fixed under paragraph 2 of Article 10. This regime equally applies when the recipient of the dividends is a parent company receiving dividends from a subsidiary; in this case, the tax withheld in the State of the subsidiary — and credited in the State of the parent company — is limited to 5 per cent of the gross amount of the dividends by the application of subparagraph a) of paragraph 2 of Article 10.

50.   These provisions effectively avoid the juridical double taxation of dividends but they do not prevent recurrent corporate taxation on the profits distributed to the parent company: first at the level of the subsidiary and again at the level of the parent company. Such recurrent taxation creates a very important obstacle to the development of international investment. Many States have recognised this and have inserted in their domestic laws provisions designed to avoid this obstacle. Moreover, provisions to this end are frequently inserted in double taxation conventions.

51.   The Committee on Fiscal Affairs has considered whether it would be appropriate to modify Article 23 of the Convention in order to settle this question. Although many States favoured the insertion of such a provision in the Model Convention this met with many difficulties, resulting from the diverse opinions of States and the variety of possible solutions. Some States, fearing tax evasion, preferred to maintain their freedom of action and to settle the question only in their domestic laws.

52.   In the end, it appeared preferable to leave States free to choose their own solution to the problem. For States preferring to solve the problem in their conventions, the solutions would most frequently follow one of the principles below:

a) *Exemption with progression*

The State of which the parent company is a resident exempts the dividends it receives from its subsidiary in the other State, but it may nevertheless take these dividends into account in computing the tax due by the parent company on the remaining income (such a provision will frequently be favoured by States applying the exemption method specified in Article 23 A).

b) *Credit for underlying taxes*

As regards dividends received from the subsidiary, the State of which the parent company is a resident gives credit as provided for in paragraph 2 of Article 23 A or in paragraph 1 of Article 23 B, as appropriate, not only for the tax on dividends as such, but also for the tax paid by the subsidiary on the profits distributed (such a provision will frequently be favoured by States applying as a general rule the credit method specified in Article 23 B).

c) *Exemption with progression*

The dividends that the parent company derives from a foreign subsidiary are treated, in the State of the parent company, in the same way for tax purposes as dividends received from a subsidiary which is a resident of that State.

53.   When the State of the parent company levies taxes on capital, a similar solution should also be applied to such taxes.

54.   Moreover, States are free to fix the limits and methods of application of these provisions (definition and minimum duration of holding of the shares, proportion of the dividends deemed to be taken up by administrative or financial expenses) or to make the relief granted under the special regime subject to the condition that the subsidiary is carrying out a genuine economic activity in the State of which it is a resident, or that it derives the major part of its income from that State or that it is subject to a substantial taxation on profits therein.

Paragraph 3

55.   The 1963 Draft Convention reserved expressly the application of the progressive scale of tax rates by the State of residence (last sentence of paragraph 1 of Article 23 A) and most conventions concluded between OECD member countries which adopt the exemption method follow this principle. According to paragraph 3 of Article 23 A, the State of residence retains the right to take the amount of exempted income or capital into consideration when determining the tax to be imposed on the rest of the income or capital. The rule applies even where the exempted income (or items of capital) and the taxable income (or items of capital) accrue to those persons (*e.g.* husband and wife) whose incomes (or items of capital) are taxed jointly according to the domestic laws. This principle of progression applies to income or capital exempted by virtue of paragraph 1 of Article 23 A as well as to income or capital which under any other provision of the Convention "shall be taxable only" in the other Contracting State (see paragraph 6 above). This is the reason why, in the 1977 Model Convention, the principle of progression was transferred from paragraph 1 of Article 23 A to a new paragraph 3 of the said Article, and reference was made to exemption "in accordance with any provision of the Convention".

56.   Paragraph 3 of Article 23 A relates only to the State of residence. The form of the Article does not prejudice the application by the State of source of the provisions of its domestic laws concerning the progression.

Paragraph 4

56.1   The purpose of this paragraph is to avoid double non taxation as a result of disagreements between the State of residence and the State of source on the facts of a case or on the interpretation of the provisions of the Convention. The paragraph applies where, on the one hand, the State of source interprets the facts of a case or the provisions of the Convention in such a way that an item of income or capital falls under a provision of the Convention that eliminates its right to tax that item or limits the tax that it can impose while, on the other hand, the State of residence adopts a different interpretation of the facts or of the provisions of the Convention and thus considers that the item may be taxed in the State of source in accordance with the Convention, which, absent this paragraph, would lead to an obligation for the State of residence to give exemption under the provisions of paragraph 1.

56.2   The paragraph only applies to the extent that the State of source has applied the provisions of the Convention to exempt an item of income or capital or has applied the provisions of paragraph 2 of Article 10 or 11 to an item of income. The paragraph would therefore not apply where the State of source considers that it may tax an item of income or capital in accordance with the provisions of the Convention but where no tax is actually payable on such income or capital under the provisions of the domestic laws of the State of source. In such a case, the State of residence must exempt that item of income under the provisions of paragraph 1 because the exemption in the State of source does not result from the application of the provisions of the Convention but, rather, from the domestic law of the State of source (see paragraph 34 above). Similarly, where the source and residence States disagree not only with respect to the qualification of the income but also with respect to the amount of such income, paragraph 4 applies only to that part of the income that the State of source exempts from tax through the application of the Convention or to which that State applies paragraph 2 of Article 10 or 11.

56.3   Cases where the paragraph applies must be distinguished from cases where the qualification of an item of income under the domestic law of the State of source interacts with the provisions of the Convention to preclude that State from taxing an item of income or capital in circumstances where the qualification of that item under the domestic law of the State of residence would not have had the same result. In such a case, which is discussed in paragraphs 32.6 and 32.7 above, paragraph 1 does not impose an obligation on the State of residence to give exemption because the item of income may not be taxed in the State of source in accordance with the Convention. Since paragraph 1 does not apply, the provisions of paragraph 4 are not required in such a case to ensure the taxation right of the State of residence.

III.   Commentary on the provisions of Article 23 B (credit method)

Paragraph 1

A.   Methods

57.   Article 23 B, based on the credit principle, follows the ordinary credit method: the State of residence (R) allows, as a deduction from its own tax on the income or capital of its resident, an amount equal to the tax paid in the other State E (or S) on the income derived from, or capital owned in, that other State E (or S), but the deduction is restricted to the appropriate proportion of its own tax.

58.   The ordinary credit method is intended to apply also for a State which follows the exemption method but has to give credit, under paragraph 2 of Article 23 A, for the tax levied at limited rates in the other State on dividends and interest (see paragraph 47 above). The possibility of some modification as mentioned in paragraphs 47 and 48 above (full credit) could, of course, also be of relevance in the case

of dividends and interest paid to a resident of a State which adopted the ordinary credit method (see also paragraph 63 below).

59.   The obligation imposed by Article 23 B on a State R to give credit for the tax levied in the other State E (or S) on an item of income or capital depends on whether this item may be taxed by the State E (or S) in accordance with the Convention. Paragraphs 32.1 to 32.7 above discuss how this condition should be interpreted. Items of income or capital which according to Article 8, to paragraph 3 of Article 13, to subparagraph a) of paragraphs 1 and 2 of Article 19 and to paragraph 3 of Article 22, "shall be taxable only" in the other State, are from the outset exempt from tax in State R (see paragraph 6 above), and the Commentary on Article 23 A applies to such exempted income and capital. As regards progression, reference is made to paragraph 2 of the Article (and paragraph 79 below).

60.   Article 23 B sets out the main rules of the credit method, but does not give detailed rules on the computation and operation of the credit. This is consistent with the general pattern of the Convention. Experience has shown that many problems may arise. Some of them are dealt with in the following paragraphs. In many States, detailed rules on credit for foreign tax already exist in their domestic laws. A number of conventions, therefore, contain a reference to the domestic laws of the Contracting States and further provide that such domestic rules shall not affect the principle laid down in Article 23 B. Where the credit method is not used in the domestic laws of a Contracting State, this State should establish rules for the application of Article 23 B, if necessary after consultation with the competent authority of the other Contracting State (paragraph 3 of Article 25).

61.   The amount of foreign tax for which a credit has to be allowed is the tax effectively paid in accordance with the Convention in the other Contracting State. Problems may arise, e.g. where such tax is not calculated on the income of the year for which it is levied but on the income of a preceding year or on the average income of two of more preceding years. Other problems may arise in connection with different methods of determining the income or in connection with changes in the currency rates (devaluation or revaluation). However, such problems could hardly be solved by an express provision in the Convention.

62.   According to the provisions of the second sentence of paragraph 1 of Article 23 B, the deduction which the State of residence (R) is to allow is restricted to that part of the income tax which is appropriate to the income derived from the State S, or E (so-called "maximum deduction"). Such maximum deduction may be computed either by apportioning the total tax on total income according to the ratio between the income for which credit is to be given and the total income, or by applying the tax rate for total income to the income for which credit is to be given. In fact, in cases where the tax in State E (or S) equals or exceeds the appropriate tax of State R, the credit method will have the same effect as the exemption method with progression. Also under the credit method, similar problems as regards the amount of income, tax rate, etc. may arise as are mentioned in the Commentary on Article 23 A (see especially paragraphs 39 to 41 and 44 above). For the same reasons mentioned in paragraphs 42 and 43 above, it is

preferable also for the credit method not to propose an express and uniform solution in the Convention, but to leave each State free to apply its own legislation and technique. This is also true for some further problems which are dealt with below.

63.   The maximum deduction is normally computed as the tax on net income, i.e. on the income from State E (or S) less allowable deductions (specified or proportional) connected with such income (see paragraph 40 above). For such reason, the maximum deduction in many cases may be lower than the tax effectively paid in State E (or S). This may especially be true in the case where, for instance, a resident of State R deriving interest from State S has borrowed funds from a third person to finance the interest-producing loan. As the interest due on such borrowed money may be offset against the interest derived from State S, the amount of net income subject to tax in State R may be very small, or there may even be no net income at all. This problem could be solved by using the full credit method in State R as mentioned in paragraph 48 above. Another solution would be to exempt such income from tax in State S, as it is proposed in the Commentary in respect of interest on credit sales and on loans granted by banks (see paragraph 15 of the Commentary on Article 11).

64.   If a resident of State R derives income of different kinds from State S, and the latter State, according to its tax laws imposes tax only on one of these items, the maximum deduction which State R is to allow will normally be that part of its tax which is appropriate only to that item of income which is taxed in State S. However, other solutions are possible, especially in view of the following broader problem: the fact that credit has to be given, e.g. for several items of income on which tax at different rates is levied in State S, or for income from several States, with or without conventions, raises the question whether the maximum deduction or the credit has to be calculated separately for each item of income, or for each country, or for all foreign income qualifying for credit under domestic laws and under conventions. Under an "overall credit" system, all foreign income is aggregated, and the total of foreign taxes is credited against the domestic tax appropriate to the total foreign income.

65.   Further problems may arise in case of losses. A resident of State R, deriving income from State E (or S), may have a loss in State R, or in State E (or S) or in a third State. For purposes of the tax credit, in general, a loss in a given State will be set off against other income from the same State. Whether a loss suffered outside State R (e.g. in a permanent establishment) may be deducted from other income, whether derived from State R or not depends on the domestic laws of State R. Here similar problems may arise, as mentioned in the Commentary on Article 23 A (paragraph 44 above). When the total income is derived from abroad, and no income but a loss not exceeding the income from abroad arises in State R, then the total tax charged in State R will be appropriate to the income from State S, and the maximum deduction which State R is to allow will consequently be the tax charged in State R. Other solutions are possible.

66.   The aforementioned problems depend very much on domestic laws and practice, and the solution must, therefore, be left to each State. In this context, it may be noted that some States are very liberal in applying the credit method. Some States are also considering or have already adopted the possibility of carrying over unused tax credits.

Contracting States are, of course, free in bilateral negotiations to amend the Article to deal with any of the aforementioned problems.

67.   In so-called "thin capitalisation" situations, the Model Convention allows the State of the borrower company, under certain conditions, to treat an interest payment as a distribution of dividends in accordance with its domestic legislation; the essential condition is that the contributor of the loan should effectively share the risks run by the borrower company. This gives rise to two consequences:

— the taxing at source of such "interest" at the rate for dividends (paragraph 2 of Article 10);

— the inclusion of such "interest" in the taxable profits of the lender company.

68.   If the relevant conditions are met, the State of residence of the lender would be obliged to give relief for any juridical or economic double taxation of the interest as if the payment was in fact a dividend. It should then give credit for tax effectively withheld on this interest in the State of residence of the borrower at the rate applicable to dividends and, in addition, if the lender is the parent company of the borrower company, apply to such "interest" any additional relief under its parent/subsidiary regime. This obligation may result:

a) from the actual wording of Article 23 of the Convention, when it grants relief in respect of income defined as dividends in Article 10 or of items of income dealt with in Article 10;

b) from the context of the Convention, i.e. from a combination of Articles 9, 10, 11, and 23 and if need be, by way of the mutual agreement procedure:

— where the interest has been treated in the country of residence of the borrower company as a dividend under rules which are in accordance with paragraph 1 of Article 9 or paragraph 6 of Article 11 and where the State of residence of the lender agrees that it has been properly so treated and is prepared to apply a corresponding adjustment;

— when the State of residence of the lender applies similar thin capitalisation rules and would treat the payment as a dividend in a reciprocal situation, i.e. if the payment were made by a company established in its territory to a resident in the other Contracting State;

— in all other cases where the State of residence of the lender recognises that it was proper for the State of residence of the borrower to treat the interest as a dividend.

69.   As regards dividends from a substantial holding by a company, reference is made to paragraphs 49 to 54 above.

69.1 Problems may arise where Contracting States treat entities such as partnerships in a different way. Assume, for example, that the State of source treats a partnership as a company and the State of residence of a partner treats it as fiscally transparent. The State of source may, subject to the applicable provisions of the Convention, tax the partnership on its income when that income is realised and, subject to the limitations of paragraph 2 of Article 10, may also tax the distribution of profits by the partnership to its non-resident partners. The State of residence, however, will only tax the partner on his share of the partnership's income when that income is realised by the partnership.

69.2 The first issue that arises in this case is whether the State of residence, which taxes the partner on his share in the partnership's income, is obliged, under the Convention, to give credit for the tax that is levied in the State of source on the partnership, which that latter State treats as a separate taxable entity. The answer to that question must be affirmative. To the extent that the State of residence flows through the income of the partnership to the partner for the purpose of taxing him, it must adopt a coherent approach and flow through to the partner the tax paid by the partnership for the purposes of eliminating double taxation arising from its taxation of the partner. In other words, if the corporate status given to the partnership by the State of source is ignored by the State of residence for purposes of taxing the partner on his share of the income, it should likewise be ignored for purposes of the foreign tax credit.

69.3 A second issue that arises in this case is the extent to which the State of residence must provide credit for the tax levied by the State of source on the distribution, which is not taxed in the State of residence. The answer to that question lies in that last fact. Since the distribution is not taxed in the State of residence, there is simply no tax in the State of residence against which to credit the tax levied by the State of source upon the distribution. A clear distinction must be made between the generation of profits and the distribution of those profits and the State of residence should not be expected to credit the tax levied by the State of source upon the distribution against its own tax levied upon generation (see the first sentence of paragraph 64 above).

B. *Remarks concerning capital tax*

70. As paragraph 1 is drafted, credit is to be allowed for income tax only against income tax and for capital tax only against capital tax. Consequently, credit for or against capital tax will be given only if there is a capital tax in both Contracting States.

71. In bilateral negotiations, two Contracting States may agree that a tax called a capital tax is of a nature closely related to income tax and may, therefore, wish to allow credit for it against income tax and vice versa. There are cases where, because one State does not impose a capital tax or because both States impose capital taxes only on domestic assets, no double taxation of capital will arise. In such cases it is, of course, understood that the reference to capital taxation may be deleted. Furthermore, States may find it desirable, regardless of the nature of the taxes under the convention, to allow credit for the total amount of tax in the State of source or situs against the total amount of tax in the State of residence. Where, however, a convention includes both real capital taxes and capital taxes which are in their nature income taxes, the States may wish to allow credit against income tax only for the latter capital taxes. In such cases, States are free to alter the proposed Article so as to achieve the desired effect.

C. Tax sparing

72.   Some States grant different kinds of tax incentives to foreign investors for the purpose of attracting foreign investment. When the State of residence of a foreign investor applies the credit method, the benefit of the incentive granted by a State of source may be reduced to the extent that the State of residence, when taxing income that has benefited from the incentive, will allow a deduction only for the tax actually paid in the State of source. Similarly, if the State of residence applies the exemption method but subject the application of that method to a certain level of taxation by the State of source, the granting of a tax reduction by the State of source may have the effect of denying the investor the application of the exemption method in his State of residence.

73.   To avoid any such effect in the State of residence, some States that have adopted tax incentive programmes wish to include provisions, usually referred to as "tax sparing" provisions, in their conventions. The purpose of these provisions is to allow non-residents to obtain a foreign tax credit for the taxes that have been "spared" under the incentive programme of the source State or to ensure that these taxes will be taken into account for the purposes of applying certain conditions that may be attached to exemption systems.

74.   Tax sparing provisions constitute a departure from the provisions of Articles 23 A and 23 B. Tax sparing provisions may take different forms, as for example:

a) the State of residence will allow as a deduction the amount of tax which the State of source could have imposed in accordance with its general legislation or such amount as limited by the Convention (e.g. limitations of rates provided for dividends and interest in Articles 10 and 11) even if the State of source has waived all or part of that tax under special provisions for the promotion of its economic development;

b) as a counterpart for the tax reduction by the State of the State of residence agrees to allow a deduction against its own tax of an amount (in part fictitious) fixed at a higher rate;

c) the State of residence exempts the income which has benefited from tax incentives in the State of source.

75.   A 1998 report by the Committee of Fiscal Affairs, entitled "Tax Sparing a Reconsideration",[1] analyses the tax policy considerations that underlie tax sparing provisions as well as their drafting. The report identifies a number of concerns that put into question the overall usefulness of the granting of tax sparing relief. These concerns relate in particular to:

—   the potential for abuse offered by tax sparing;

—   the effectiveness of tax sparing as an instrument of foreign aid to promote economic development of the source country; and

---

1   Reproduced in Volume II of the full-length version of the OECD Model Tax Convention at page R(14)-1.

— general concerns with the way in which tax sparing may encourage States to use tax incentives.

76. Experience has shown that tax sparing is very vulnerable to taxpayer abuse, which can be very costly in terms of lost revenue to both the State of residence and the State of source. This kind of abuse is difficult to detect. In addition, even where it is detected, it is difficult for the State of residence to react quickly against such abuse. The process of removing or modifying existing tax sparing provisions to prevent such abuses is often slow and cumbersome.

77. Furthermore, tax sparing is not necessarily an effective tool to promote economic development. A reduction or elimination of the benefit of the tax incentive by the State of residence will, in most cases, only occur to the extent that profits are repatriated. By promoting the repatriation of profits, tax sparing may therefore provide an inherent incentive to foreign investors to engage in short-term investment projects and a disincentive to operate in the source State on a long-term basis. Also, foreign tax credit systems are usually designed in a way that allows a foreign investor, in computing its foreign tax credit, to offset to some extent the reduction of taxes resulting from a particular tax incentive with the higher taxes paid in that or other country so that, ultimately, no additional taxes are levied by the State of residence as a result of the tax incentive.

78. Finally, the accelerating integration of national economies has made many segments of the national tax bases increasingly geographically mobile. These developments have induced some States to adopt tax regimes that have as their primary purpose the erosion of the tax bases of other countries. These types of tax incentives are specifically tailored to target highly mobile financial and other services that are particularly sensitive to tax differentials. The potentially harmful effects of such regimes may be aggravated by the existence of ill-designed tax sparing provisions in treaties. This is particularly so where a State adopts a tax regime subsequent to the conclusion of treaties and tailors this regime so as to ensure that it is covered by the scope of the existing tax sparing provision.

78.1 The Committee concluded that member States should not necessarily refrain from adopting tax sparing provisions. The Committee expressed the view, however, that tax sparing should be considered only in regard to States the economic level of which is considerably below that of OECD member States. Member States should employ objective economic criteria to define States eligible for tax sparing. Where States agree to insert a tax sparing provision, they are therefore encouraged to follow the guidance set out in section VI of the tax sparing report. The use of these "best practices" will minimise the potential for abuse of such provisions by ensuring that they apply exclusively to genuine investments aimed at developing the domestic infrastructure of the source State. A narrow provision applying to real investment would also discourage harmful tax competition for geographically mobile activities.

Paragraph 2

79.   This paragraph has been added to enable the State of residence to retain the right to take the amount of income or capital exempted in that State into consideration when determining the tax to be imposed on the rest of the income or capital. The right so retained extends to income or capital which "shall be taxable only" in the other State. The principle of progression is thus safeguarded for the State of residence, not only in relation to income or capital which "may be taxed" in the other State, but also for income or capital which "shall be taxable only" in that other State. The Commentary on paragraph 3 of Article 23 A in relation to the State of source also applies to paragraph 2 of Article 23 B.

Observations on the Commentary

80.   The *Netherlands* in principle is in favour of solving situations of both double taxation and double non-taxation due to conflicts of qualification between Contracting States, since in the Netherlands view such situations are not intended by the Contracting States and moreover go against the object and purpose of a tax treaty. However, the Netherlands does not agree with the interpretation given in paragraphs 32.4 and 32.6 to the phrase "in accordance with the provisions of this Convention" in Articles 23 A and 23 B of the Convention that in cases of conflicts of qualification that are due to differences in domestic law between the State of source and the State of residence as a rule the qualification given by the State of source would prevail for purposes of the application by the State of residence of Article 23 A or 23 B. The Netherlands wishes to preserve its right to subject a solution and its modalities for a certain conflict of qualification to the circumstances of the cases at hand and to the relationship with the Contracting State concerned. The Netherlands therefore will adhere to said interpretation in paragraphs 32.4 and 32.6 only, and to the extent which, it is explicitly so confirmed in a specific tax treaty, as a result of mutual agreement between competent authorities as meant in Article 25 of the Convention or as unilateral policy.

81.   *Switzerland* reserves its right not to apply the rules laid down in paragraph 32 in cases where a conflict of qualification results from a modification to the internal law of the State of source subsequent to the conclusion of a Convention.

COMMENTARY ON ARTICLE 24
CONCERNING NON-DISCRIMINATION

General remarks

1.   This Article deals with the elimination of tax discrimination in certain precise circumstances. All tax systems incorporate legitimate distinctions based, for example, on differences in liability to tax or ability to pay. The non-discrimination provisions of the Article seek to balance the need to prevent unjustified discrimination with the need to take account of these legitimate distinctions. For that reason, the Article should not be unduly extended to cover so-called "indirect" discrimination. For example, whilst paragraph 1, which deals with discrimination on the basis of nationality, would prevent a different treatment that is really a disguised form of discrimination based on nationality such as a different treatment of individuals based on whether or not they hold, or are entitled to, a passport issued by the State, it could not be argued that non-residents of a given State include primarily persons who are not nationals of that State to conclude that a different treatment based on residence is indirectly a discrimination based on nationality for purposes of that paragraph.

2.   Likewise, the provisions of the Article cannot be interpreted as to require most-favoured-nation treatment. Where a State has concluded a bilateral or multilateral agreement which affords tax benefits to nationals or residents of the other Contracting State(s) party to that agreement, nationals or residents of a third State that is not a Contracting State of the treaty may not claim these benefits by reason of a similar non-discrimination provision in the double taxation convention between the third State and the first-mentioned State. As tax conventions are based on the principle of reciprocity, a tax treatment that is granted by one Contracting State under a bilateral or multilateral agreement to a resident or national of another Contracting State party to that agreement by reason of the specific economic relationship between those Contracting States may not be extended to a resident or national of a third State under the non-discrimination provision of the tax convention between the first State and the third State.

3.   The various provisions of Article 24 prevent differences in tax treatment that are solely based on certain specific grounds (e.g. nationality, in the case of paragraph 1). Thus, for these paragraphs to apply, other relevant aspects must be the same. The various provisions of Article 24 use different wording to achieve that result (e.g. "in the same circumstances" in paragraphs 1 and 2; "carrying on the same activities" in paragraph 3; "similar enterprises" in paragraph 5). Also, whilst the Article seeks to eliminate distinctions that are solely based on certain grounds, it is not intended to provide foreign nationals, non-residents, enterprises of other States or domestic enterprises owned or controlled by non-residents with a tax treatment that is better than that of nationals, residents or domestic enterprises owned or controlled by residents (see, for example, paragraph 34 below).

4.   Finally, as illustrated by paragraph 79 below, the provisions of the Article must be read in the context of the other Articles of the Convention so that measures that are mandated or expressly authorised by the provisions of these Articles cannot be considered to violate the provisions of the Article even if they only apply, for example, as regards payments to non-residents. Conversely, however, the fact that a particular measure does not constitute a violation of the provisions of the Article does not mean that it is authorised by the Convention since that measure could violate other Articles of the Convention.

Paragraph 1

5.   This paragraph establishes the principle that for purposes of taxation discrimination on the grounds of nationality is forbidden, and that, subject to reciprocity, the nationals of a Contracting State may not be less favourably treated in the other Contracting State than nationals of the latter State in the same circumstances.

6.   It is noteworthy that the principle of non-discrimination, under various descriptions and with a more or less wide scope, was applied in international fiscal relations well before the appearance, at the end of the 19th Century, of the classic type of double taxation conventions. Thus, in a great many agreements of different kinds (consular or establishment conventions, treaties of friendship or commerce, etc.) concluded by States, especially in the 19th Century, in order to extend and strengthen the diplomatic protection of their nationals wherever resident, there are clauses under which each of the two Contracting States undertakes to accord nationals of the other State equality of treatment with its own nationals. The fact that such clauses subsequently found their way into double taxation conventions has in no way affected their original justification and scope. The text of paragraph 1 provides that the application of this paragraph is not restricted by Article 1 to nationals solely who are residents of a Contracting State, but on the contrary, extends to all nationals of each Contracting State, whether or not they be residents of one of them. In other words, all nationals of a Contracting State are entitled to invoke the benefit of this provision as against the other Contracting State. This holds good, in particular, for nationals of the Contracting States who are not residents of either of them but of a third State.

7.   The expression "in the same circumstances" refers to taxpayers (individuals, legal persons, partnerships and associations) placed, from the point of view of the application of the ordinary taxation laws and regulations, in substantially similar circumstances both in law and in fact. The expression "in particular with respect to residence" makes clear that the residence of the taxpayer is one of the factors that are relevant in determining whether taxpayers are placed in similar circumstances. The expression "in the same circumstances" would be sufficient by itself to establish that a taxpayer who is a resident of a Contracting State and one who is not a resident of that State are not in the same circumstances. In fact, whilst the expression "in particular with respect to residence" did not appear in the 1963 Draft Convention or in the 1977 Model Convention, the member countries have consistently held, in applying and

interpreting the expression "in the same circumstances", that the residence of the taxpayer must be taken into account. However, in revising the Model Convention, the Committee on Fiscal Affairs felt that a specific reference to the residence of the taxpayers would be a useful clarification as it would avoid any possible doubt as to the interpretation to be given to the expression "in the same circumstances" in this respect.

8.   In applying paragraph 1, therefore, the underlying question is whether two persons who are residents of the same State are being treated differently solely by reason of having a different nationality. Consequently if a Contracting State, in giving relief from taxation on account of family responsibilities, distinguishes between its own nationals according to whether they reside in its territory or not, that State cannot be obliged to give nationals of the other State who do not reside in its territory the same treatment as it gives its resident nationals but it undertakes to extend to them the same treatment as is available to its nationals who reside in the other State. Similarly, paragraph 1 does not apply where a national of a Contracting State (State R) who is also a resident of State R is taxed less favourably in the other Contracting State (State S) than a national of State S residing in a third State (for instance, as a result of the application of provisions aimed at discouraging the use of tax havens) as the two persons are not in the same circumstances with respect to their residence.

9.   The expression "in the same circumstances" can in some cases refer to a person's tax situation. This would be the case, for example, where a country would subject its nationals, or some of them, to a more comprehensive tax liability than non-nationals (this, for example, is a feature of the United States tax system). As long as such treatment is not itself a violation of paragraph 1, it could not be argued that persons who are not nationals of that State are in the same circumstances as its nationals for the purposes of the application of the other provisions of the domestic tax law of that State with respect to which the comprehensive or limited liability to tax of a taxpayer would be relevant (e.g. the granting of personal allowances).

10.   Likewise, the provisions of paragraph 1 are not to be construed as obliging a State which accords special taxation privileges to its own public bodies or services as such, to extend the same privileges to the public bodies and services of the other State.

11.   Neither are they to be construed as obliging a State which accords special taxation privileges to private institutions not for profit whose activities are performed for purposes of public benefit, which are specific to that State, to extend the same privileges to similar institutions whose activities are not for its benefit.

12.   To take the first of these two cases, if a State accords immunity from taxation to its own public bodies and services, this is justified because such bodies and services are integral parts of the State and at no time can their circumstances be comparable to those of the public bodies and services of the other State. Nevertheless, this reservation is not intended to apply to State corporations carrying on gainful undertakings. To the extent that these can be regarded as being on the same footing as private business undertakings, the provisions of paragraph 1 will apply to them.

13.   As for the second case, if a State accords taxation privileges to certain private institutions not for profit, this is clearly justified by the very nature of these institutions' activities and by the benefit which that State and its nationals will derive from those activities.

14.   Furthermore, paragraph 1 has been deliberately framed in a negative form. By providing that the nationals of a Contracting State may not be subjected in the other Contracting State to any taxation or any requirement connected therewith which is other or more burdensome than the taxation and connected requirements to which nationals of the other Contracting State in the same circumstances are or may be subjected, this paragraph has the same mandatory force as if it enjoined the Contracting States to accord the same treatment to their respective nationals. But since the principal object of this clause is to forbid discrimination in one State against the nationals of the other, there is nothing to prevent the first State from granting to persons of foreign nationality, for special reasons of its own, or in order to comply with a special stipulation in a double taxation convention, such as, notably, the requirement that profits of permanent establishments are to be taxed in accordance with Article 7, certain concessions or facilities which are not available to its own nationals. As it is worded, paragraph 1 would not prohibit this.

15.   Subject to the foregoing observation, the words "… shall not be subjected … to any taxation or any requirement connected therewith which is other or more burdensome …" mean that when a tax is imposed on nationals and foreigners in the same circumstances, it must be in the same form as regards both the basis of charge and the method of assessment, its rate must be the same and, finally, the formalities connected with the taxation (returns, payment, prescribed times, etc.) must not be more onerous for foreigners than for nationals.

16.   In view of the legal relationship created between the company and the State under whose law it is constituted, which from certain points of view is closely akin to the relationship of nationality in the case of individuals, it seems justifiable not to deal with legal persons, partnerships and associations in a special provision, but to assimilate them with individuals under paragraph 1. This result is achieved through the definition of the term "national" in subparagraph g) of paragraph 1 of Article 3.

17.   By virtue of that definition, in the case of a legal person such as a company, "national of a Contracting State" means a legal person "deriving its status as such from the laws in force in that Contracting State". A company will usually derive its status as such from the laws in force in the State in which it has been incorporated or registered. Under the domestic law of many countries, however, incorporation or registration constitutes the criterion, or one of the criteria, to determine the residence of companies for the purposes of Article 4. Since paragraph 1 of Article 24 prevents different treatment based on nationality but only with respect to persons or entities "in the same circumstances, in particular with respect to residence", it is therefore important to distinguish, for purposes of that paragraph, a different treatment that is solely based on nationality from a different treatment that relates to other circumstances and, in particular, residence. As explained in paragraphs 7 and 8 above,

paragraph 1 only prohibits discrimination based on a different nationality and requires that all other relevant factors, including the residence of the entity, be the same. The different treatment of residents and non-residents is a crucial feature of domestic tax systems and of tax treaties; when Article 24 is read in the context of the other Articles of the Convention, most of which provide for a different treatment of residents and non-residents, it is clear that two companies that are not residents of the same State for purposes of the Convention (under the rules of Article 4) are usually not in the same circumstances for purposes of paragraph 1.

18.   Whilst residents and non-residents are usually not in the same circumstances for the purposes of paragraph 1, it is clear, however, that this is not the case where residence has no relevance whatsoever with respect to the different treatment under consideration.

19.   The following examples illustrate these principles.

20.   Example 1: Under the domestic income tax law of State A, companies incorporated in that State or having their place of effective management in that State are residents thereof. The State A - State B tax convention is identical to this Model Tax Convention. The domestic tax law of State A provides that dividends paid to a company incorporated in that country by another company incorporated in that country are exempt from tax. Since a company incorporated in State B that would have its place of effective management in State A would be a resident of State A for purposes of the State A - State B Convention, the fact that dividends paid to such a company by a company incorporated in State A would not be eligible for this exemption, even though the recipient company is in the same circumstances as a company incorporated in State A with respect to its residence, would constitute a breach of paragraph 1 absent other relevant different circumstances.

21.   Example 2: Under the domestic income tax law of State A, companies incorporated in that State are residents thereof and companies incorporated abroad are non-residents. The State A - State B tax convention is identical to this Model Tax Convention except that paragraph 3 of Article 4 provides that if a legal person is a resident of both States under paragraph 1 of that Article, that legal person shall be deemed to be a resident of the State in which it has been incorporated. The domestic tax law of State A provides that dividends paid to a company incorporated in that country by another company incorporated in that country are exempt from tax. Paragraph 1 does not extend that treatment to dividends paid to a company incorporated in State B. Even if a company incorporated in State A and a company incorporated in State B that receive such dividends are treated differently, these companies are not in the same circumstances with regards to their residence and residence is a relevant factor in this case (as can be concluded, for example, from paragraph 5 of Article 10, which would prevent the subsequent taxation of dividends paid by a non-resident company but not those paid by a resident company).

22.   Example 3: Under the domestic income tax law of State A, companies that are incorporated in that State are residents thereof. Under the domestic tax law of State B,

    MODEL TAX CONVENTION (CONDENSED VERSION) – ISBN 978-92-64-08948-8 – © OECD 2010

companies that have their place of effective management in that State are residents thereof. The State A - State B tax convention is identical to this Model Tax Convention. The domestic tax law of State A provides that a non-resident company that is a resident of a State with which State A does not have a tax treaty that allows for the exchange of tax information is subject to an annual tax equal to 3 per cent of the value of its immovable property instead of a tax on the net income derived from that property. A company incorporated in State B but which is a resident of a State with which State A does not have a tax treaty that allows for the exchange of tax information cannot claim that paragraph 1 prevents the application of the 3 per cent tax levied by State A because it is treated differently from a company incorporated in State A. In that case, such a company would not be in the same circumstances, with respect to its residence, as a company incorporated in State A and the residence of the company would be relevant (e.g. for purposes of accessing the information necessary to verify the net income from immovable property derived by a non-resident taxpayer).

23.   Example 4: Under the domestic income tax law of State A, companies incorporated in that State are residents of State A and companies incorporated abroad are non-residents. The State A - State B tax convention is identical to this Model Tax Convention except that paragraph 3 of Article 4 provides that if a legal person is a resident of both States under paragraph 1 of that Article, that legal person shall be deemed to be a resident of the State in which it has been incorporated. Under State A's payroll tax law, all companies that employ resident employees are subject to a payroll tax that does not make any distinction based on the residence of the employer but that provides that only companies incorporated in State A shall benefit from a lower rate of payroll tax. In that case, the fact that a company incorporated in State B will not have the same residence as a company incorporated in State A for the purposes of the A-B convention has no relevance at all with respect to the different tax treatment under the payroll tax and that different treatment would therefore be in violation of paragraph 1 absent other relevant different circumstances.

24.   Example 5: Under the domestic income tax law of State A, companies incorporated in that State or which have their place of effective management in that State are residents of the State and companies that do not meet one of these two conditions are non-residents. Under the domestic income tax law of State B, companies incorporated in that State are residents of that State. The State A - State B tax convention is identical to this Model Tax Convention except that paragraph 3 of Article 4 provides that if a legal person is a resident of both States under paragraph 1 of that Article, that legal person shall be deemed to be a resident only of the State in which it has been incorporated. The domestic tax law of State A further provides that companies that have been incorporated and that have their place of effective management in that State are entitled to consolidate their income for tax purposes if they are part of a group of companies that have common shareholders. Company X, which was incorporated in State B, belongs to the same group as two companies incorporated in State A and all these companies are effectively managed in State A.

Since it was not incorporated in State A, company X is not allowed to consolidate its income with that of the two other companies.

25. In that case, even if company X is a resident of State A under the domestic law of that State, it is not a resident of State A for purposes of the Convention by virtue of paragraph 3 of Article 4. It will therefore not be in the same circumstances as the other companies of the group as regards residence and paragraph 1 will not allow it to obtain the benefits of consolidation even if the different treatment results from the fact that company X has not been incorporated in State A. The residence of company X is clearly relevant with respect to the benefits of consolidation since certain provisions of the Convention, such as Articles 7 and 10, would prevent State A from taxing certain types of income derived by company X.

Paragraph 2

26. On 28 September 1954, a number of States concluded in New York a Convention relating to the status of stateless persons, under Article 29 of which stateless persons must be accorded national treatment. The signatories of the Convention include several OECD member countries.

27. It should, however, be recognised that the provisions of paragraph 2 will, in a bilateral convention, enable national treatment to be extended to stateless persons who, because they are in one of the situations enumerated in paragraph 2 of Article 1 of the above-mentioned Convention of 28 September 1954, are not covered by that Convention. This is mainly the case, on the one hand, of persons receiving at the time of signature of that Convention, protection or assistance from organs or agencies of the United Nations other than the United Nations High Commissioner for Refugees, and, on the other hand, of persons who are residents of a country and who there enjoy and are subject to the rights and obligations attaching to the possession of that country's nationality.

28. The purpose of paragraph 2 is to limit the scope of the clause concerning equality of treatment with nationals of a Contracting State solely to stateless persons who are residents of that or of the other Contracting State.

29. By thus excluding stateless persons who are residents of neither Contracting State, such a clause prevents their being privileged in one State as compared with nationals of the other State.

30. However, if States were to consider it desirable in their bilateral relations to extend the application of paragraph 2 to all stateless persons, whether residents of a Contracting State or not, so that in all cases they enjoy the most favourable treatment accorded to nationals of the State concerned, in order to do this they would need only to adopt the following text which contains no condition as to residence in a Contracting State:

Notwithstanding the provisions of Article 1, stateless persons shall not be subjected in a Contracting State to any taxation or any requirement connected therewith which is other or more burdensome than the taxation and connected requirements to which nationals of that State in the same circumstances, in particular with respect to residence, are or may be subjected.

31.   It is possible that in the future certain States will take exception to the provisions of paragraph 2 as being too liberal insofar as they entitle stateless persons who are residents of one State to claim equality of treatment not only in the other State but also in their State of residence and thus benefit in particular in the latter from the provisions of double taxation conventions concluded by it with third States. If such States wished to avoid this latter consequence, they would have to modify paragraph 2 as follows:

> Stateless persons who are residents of a Contracting State shall not be subjected in the other Contracting State to any taxation or any requirement connected therewith which is other or more burdensome than the taxation and connected requirements to which nationals of that other State in the same circumstances, in particular with respect to residence, are or may be subjected.

32.   Finally, it should be understood that the definition of the term "stateless person" to be used for the purposes of such a clause can only be that laid down in paragraph 1 of Article 1 of the Convention of 28 September 1954, which defines a stateless person as "a person who is not considered as a national by any State under the operation of its law".

Paragraph 3

33.   Strictly speaking, the type of discrimination which this paragraph is designed to end is discrimination based not on nationality but on the actual situs of an enterprise. It therefore affects without distinction, and irrespective of their nationality, all residents of a Contracting State who have a permanent establishment in the other Contracting State.

34.   It appears necessary first to make it clear that the wording of the first sentence of paragraph 3 must be interpreted in the sense that it does not constitute discrimination to tax non-resident persons differently, for practical reasons, from resident persons, as long as this does not result in more burdensome taxation for the former than for the latter. In the negative form in which the provision concerned has been framed, it is the result alone which counts, it being permissible to adapt the mode of taxation to the particular circumstances in which the taxation is levied. For example, paragraph 3 does not prevent the application of specific mechanisms that apply only for the purposes of determining the profits that are attributable to a permanent establishment. The paragraph must be read in the context of the Convention and, in particular, of paragraph 2 of Article 7 which provides that the profits attributable to the permanent establishment are those that a separate and independent enterprise engaged in the same or similar activities under the same or similar conditions would have been expected to make. Clearly, rules or administrative practices that seek to determine the profits that are attributable to a permanent establishment on the basis required by paragraph 2 of Article 7 cannot be considered to violate paragraph 3, which is based on the same principle since it requires that the

taxation on the permanent establishment be not less favourable than that levied on a domestic enterprise carrying on similar activities.

35.   By the terms of the first sentence of paragraph 3, the taxation of a permanent establishment shall not be less favourably levied in the State concerned than the taxation levied on enterprises of that State carrying on the same activities. The purpose of this provision is to end all discrimination in the treatment of permanent establishments as compared with resident enterprises belonging to the same sector of activities, as regards taxes based on business activities, and especially taxes on business profits.

36.   However, the second sentence of paragraph 3 specifies the conditions under which the principle of equal treatment set forth in the first sentence should be applied to individuals who are residents of a Contracting State and have a permanent establishment in the other State. It is designed mainly to ensure that such persons do not obtain greater advantages than residents, through entitlement to personal allowances and reliefs for family responsibilities, both in the State of which they are residents, by the application of its domestic laws, and in the other State by virtue of the principle of equal treatment. Consequently, it leaves it open to the State in which the permanent establishment is situated whether or not to give personal allowances and reliefs to the persons concerned in the proportion which the amount of the permanent establishment's profits bears to the world income taxable in the other State.

37.   It is also clear that, for purposes of paragraph 3, the tax treatment in one Contracting State of the permanent establishment of an enterprise of the other Contracting State should be compared to that of an enterprise of the first-mentioned State that has a legal structure that is similar to that of the enterprise to which the permanent establishment belongs. Thus, for example, paragraph 3 does not require a State to apply to the profits of the permanent establishment of an enterprise carried on by a non-resident individual the same rate of tax as is applicable to an enterprise of that State that is carried on by a resident company.

38.   Similarly, regulated and unregulated activities would generally not constitute the "same activities" for the purposes of paragraph 3. Thus, for instance, paragraph 3 would not require that the taxation on a permanent establishment whose activities include the borrowing and lending of money but which is not registered as a bank be not less favourably levied than that of domestic banks since the permanent establishment does not carry on the same activities. Another example would be that of activities carried on by a State or its public bodies, which, since they are controlled by the State, could not be considered, for the purposes of paragraph 3, to be similar to activities that an enterprise of the other State performs through a permanent establishment.

39.   As regards the first sentence, experience has shown that it was difficult to define clearly and completely the substance of the principle of equal treatment and this has led to wide differences of opinion with regard to the many implications of this principle. The main reason for difficulty seems to reside in the actual nature of the

permanent establishment, which is not a separate legal entity but only a part of an enterprise that has its head office in another State. The situation of the permanent establishment is different from that of a domestic enterprise, which constitutes a single entity all of whose activities, with their fiscal implications, can be fully brought within the purview of the State where it has its head office. The implications of the equal treatment clause will be examined below under several aspects of the levying of tax.

A.   Assessment of tax

40.   With regard to the basis of assessment of tax, the principle of equal treatment normally has the following implications:

a) Permanent establishments must be accorded the same right as resident enterprises to deduct the trading expenses that are, in general, authorised by the taxation law to be deducted from taxable profits. Such deductions should be allowed without any restrictions other than those also imposed on resident enterprises (see also paragraphs 33 and 34 of the Commentary on Article 7).

b) Permanent establishments must be accorded the same facilities with regard to depreciation and reserves. They should be entitled to avail themselves without restriction not only of the depreciation facilities which are customarily available to enterprises (straight line depreciation, declining balance depreciation), but also of the special systems that exist in a number of countries ("wholesale" writing down, accelerated depreciation, etc.). As regards reserves, it should be noted that these are sometimes authorised for purposes other than the offsetting — in accordance with commercial accounting principles — of depreciation on assets, expenses or losses which have not yet occurred but which circumstances make likely to occur in the near future. Thus, in certain countries, enterprises are entitled to set aside, out of taxable profit, provisions or "reserves" for investment. When such a right is enjoyed by all enterprises, or by all enterprises in a given sector of activity, it should normally also be enjoyed, under the same conditions, by non-resident enterprises with respect to their permanent establishments situated in the State concerned, insofar, that is, as the activities to which such provisions or reserves would pertain are taxable in that State.

c) Permanent establishments should also have the option that is available in most countries to resident enterprises of carrying forward or backward a loss brought out at the close of an accounting period within a certain period of time (e.g. 5 years). It is hardly necessary to specify that in the case of permanent establishments it is the loss on their own business activities which will qualify for such carry-forward.

d) Permanent establishments should further have the same rules applied to resident enterprises, with regard to the taxation of capital gains realised on the alienation of assets, whether during or on the cessation of business.

41.   As clearly stated in subparagraph c) above, the equal treatment principle of paragraph 3 only applies to the taxation of the permanent establishment's own

activities. That principle, therefore, is restricted to a comparison between the rules governing the taxation of the permanent establishment's own activities and those applicable to similar business activities carried on by an independent resident enterprise. It does not extend to rules that take account of the relationship between an enterprise and other enterprises (*e.g.* rules that allow consolidation, transfer of losses or tax-free transfers of property between companies under common ownership) since the latter rules do not focus on the taxation of an enterprise's own business activities similar to those of the permanent establishment but, instead, on the taxation of a resident enterprise as part of a group of associated enterprises. Such rules will often operate to ensure or facilitate tax compliance and administration within a domestic group. It therefore follows that the equal treatment principle has no application. For the same reasons, rules related to the distribution of the profits of a resident enterprise cannot be extended to a permanent establishment under paragraph 3 as they do not relate to the business activities of the permanent establishment (see paragraph 59 below).

42.   Also, it is clear that the application of transfer pricing rules based on the arm's length standard in the case of transfers from a permanent establishment to its head office (or vice versa) cannot be considered to be a violation of paragraph 3 even if such rules do not apply to transfers within an enterprise of the Contracting State where the permanent establishment is located. Indeed, the application of the arm's length standard to the determination of the profits attributable to a permanent establishment is mandated by paragraph 2 of Article 7 and that paragraph forms part of the context in which paragraph 3 of Article 24 must be read; also, since Article 9 would authorise the application of the arm's length standard to a transfer between a domestic enterprise and a foreign related enterprise, one cannot consider that its application in the case of a permanent establishment results in less favourable taxation than that levied on an enterprise of the Contracting State where the permanent establishment is located.

43.   Although the general rules mentioned above rarely give rise to any difficulties with regard to the principle of non-discrimination, they do not constitute an exhaustive list of the possible consequences of that principle with respect to the determination of the tax base. The application of that principle may be less clear in the case of tax incentive measures which most countries, faced with such problems as decentralisation of industry, development of economically backward regions, or the promotion of new activities necessary for the expansion of the economy, have introduced in order to facilitate the solution of these problems by means of tax exemptions, reductions or other tax advantages given to enterprises for investment which is in line with official objectives.

44.   As such measures are in furtherance of objectives directly related to the economic activity proper of the State concerned, it is right that the benefit of them should be extended to permanent establishments of enterprises of another State which has a double taxation convention with the first embodying the provisions of Article 24, once they have been accorded the right to engage in business activity in that

State, either under its legislation or under an international agreement (treaties of commerce, establishment conventions, etc.) concluded between the two States.

45.   It should, however, be noted that although non-resident enterprises are entitled to claim these tax advantages in the State concerned, they must fulfil the same conditions and requirements as resident enterprises. They may, therefore, be denied such advantages if their permanent establishments are unable or refuse to fulfil the special conditions and requirements attached to the granting of them.

46.   Also, it goes without saying that non-resident enterprises are not entitled to tax advantages attaching to activities the exercise of which is strictly reserved, on grounds of national interest, defence, protection of the national economy, etc., to domestic enterprises, since non-resident enterprises are not allowed to engage in such activities.

47.   Finally, the provisions of paragraph 3 should not be construed as obliging a State which accords special taxation privileges to non-profit institutions whose activities are performed for purposes of public benefit that are specific to that State, to extend the same privileges to permanent establishments of similar institutions of the other State whose activities are not exclusively for the first-mentioned State's public benefit.

B.   Special treatment of dividends received in respect of holdings owned by permanent establishments

48.   In many countries special rules exist for the taxation of dividends distributed between companies (parent company-subsidiary treatment, the *Schachtelprivileg*, the rule *non bis in idem*). The question arises whether such treatment should, by effect of the provisions of paragraph 3, also be enjoyed by permanent establishments in respect of dividends on holdings forming part of their assets.

49.   On this point opinions differ. Some States consider that such special treatment should be accorded to permanent establishments. They take the view that such treatment was enacted in order to avoid double taxation on profits made by a subsidiary and distributed to a parent company. In principle, profits tax should be levied once, in the hands of the subsidiary performing the profit-generating activities. The parent company should be exempted from tax on such profits when received from the subsidiary or should, under the indirect credit method, be given relief for the taxation borne by the subsidiary. In cases where shares are held as direct investment by a permanent establishment the same principle implies that such a permanent establishment receiving dividends from the subsidiary should likewise be granted the special treatment in view of the fact that a profits tax has already been levied in the hands of the subsidiary. On the other hand, it is hardly conceivable on this line of thought to leave it to the State where the head office of the parent company is situated to give relief from double taxation brought about by a second levying of tax in the State of the permanent establishment. The State of the parent company, in which no activities giving rise to the doubly taxed profits have taken place, will normally exempt the profits in question or will levy a profits tax which is not sufficient to bear a double credit (*i.e.* for the profits tax on the subsidiary as well as for such tax on the permanent

establishment). All this assumes that the shares held by the permanent establishment are effectively connected with its activity. Furthermore, an obvious additional condition is that the profits out of which the dividends are distributed should have borne a profits tax.

50.   Other States, on the contrary, consider that assimilating permanent establishments to their own enterprises does not entail any obligation to accord such special treatment to the former. They justify their position on various grounds. The purpose of such special treatment is to avoid economic double taxation of dividends and it should be for the recipient company's State of residence and not the permanent establishment's State to bear its cost, because it is more interested in the aim in view. Another reason put forward relates to the sharing of tax revenue between States. The loss of tax revenue incurred by a State in applying such special treatment is partly offset by the taxation of the dividends when they are redistributed by the parent company which has enjoyed such treatment (withholding tax on dividends, shareholder's tax). A State which accorded such treatment to permanent establishments would not have the benefit of such a compensation. Another argument made is that when such treatment is made conditional upon redistribution of the dividends, its extension to permanent establishments would not be justified, for in such a case the permanent establishment, which is only a part of a company of another State and does not distribute dividends, would be more favourably treated than a resident company. Finally, the States which feel that paragraph 3 does not entail any obligation to extend such treatment to permanent establishments argue that there is a risk that companies of one State might transfer their holdings in companies of another State to their permanent establishments in that other State for the sole purpose of availing themselves of such treatment.

51.   The fact remains that there can be very valid reasons for a holding being owned and managed by a permanent establishment rather than by the head office of the enterprise, *viz.*,

  — reasons of necessity arising principally from a legal or regulatory obligation on banks and financial institutions and insurance companies to keep deposited in countries where they operate a certain amount of assets, particularly shares, as security for the performance of their obligations;

  — or reasons of expediency, where the holdings are in companies which have business relations with the permanent establishment or whose head offices are situated in the same country as the permanent establishment;

  — or simple reasons of practical convenience, in line with the present tendency towards decentralisation of management functions in large enterprises.

52.   In view of these divergent attitudes, as well as of the existence of the situations just described, it would be advisable for States, when concluding bilateral conventions, to make clear the interpretation they give to the first sentence of paragraph 3. They can, if they so desire, explain their position, or change it as compared with their previous practice, in a protocol or any other document annexed to the convention.

53.   A solution could also be provided in such a document to meet the objection mentioned above that the extension of the treatment of holdings in a State (A) to permanent establishments of companies which are residents of another State (B) results in such companies unduly enjoying privileged treatment as compared with other companies which are residents of the same State and whose head offices own holdings in the capital of companies which are residents of State A, in that whereas the dividends on their holdings can be repatriated by the former companies without bearing withholding tax, such tax is levied on dividends distributed to the latter companies at the rate of 5 or 15 per cent as the case may be. Tax neutrality and the equality of tax burdens as between permanent establishments and subsidiary companies, as advocated by the States concerned, could be ensured by adapting, in the bilateral convention between States A and B, the provisions of paragraphs 2 and 4 of Article 10, so as to enable withholding tax to be levied in State A on dividends paid by companies which are residents of that State to permanent establishments of companies which are residents of State B in the same way as if they are received directly i.e. by the head offices of the latter companies, viz., at the rate of:

— 5 per cent in the case of a holding of at least 25 per cent;

— 15 per cent in all other cases.

54.   Should it not be possible, because of the absence of appropriate provisions in the domestic laws of the State concerned, to levy a withholding tax there on dividends paid to permanent establishments, the treatment of inter-company dividends could be extended to permanent establishments, as long as its application is limited in such manner that the tax levied by the State of source of the dividends is the same whether the dividends are received by a permanent establishment of a company which is a resident of the other State or are received directly by such a company.

C.   Structure and rate of tax

55.   In countries where enterprises, mainly companies, are charged a tax on their profits which is specific to them, the provisions of paragraph 3 raise, with regard to the rate applicable in the case of permanent establishments, some specific issues related to the fact that the permanent establishment is only a part of a legal entity which is not under the jurisdiction of the State where the permanent establishment is situated.

56.   When the taxation of profits made by companies which are residents of a given State is calculated according to a progressive scale of rates, such a scale should, in principle, be applied to permanent establishments situated in that State. If in applying the progressive scale, the permanent establishment's State takes into account the profits of the whole company to which such a permanent establishment belongs, such a rule would not appear to conflict with the equal treatment rule, since resident companies are in fact treated in the same way (see paragraphs 55, 56 and 79 of the Commentary on Articles 23 A and 23 B). States that tax their own companies in this way could therefore define in their bilateral conventions the treatment applicable to permanent establishments.

57.   When a system of taxation based on a progressive scale of rates includes a rule that a minimum rate is applicable to permanent establishments, it cannot be claimed *a priori* that such a rule is incompatible with the equal treatment principle. The profits of the whole enterprise to which the permanent establishment belongs should be taken into account in determining the rate applicable according to the progressive scale. The provisions of the first sentence of paragraph 3 are not observed only if the minimum rate is higher.

58.   However, even if the profits of the whole enterprise to which the permanent establishment belongs are taken into account when applying either a progressive scale of rates or a minimum rate, this should not conflict with the principle of the separate and independent enterprise, according to which the profits of the permanent establishment must be determined under paragraph 2 of Article 7. The minimum amount of the tax levied in the State where the permanent establishment is situated is, therefore, the amount which would be due if it were a separate and independent enterprise, without reference to the profits of the whole enterprise to which it belongs. The State where the permanent establishment is situated is, therefore, justified in applying the progressive scale applicable to resident enterprises solely to the profits of the permanent establishment, leaving aside the profits of the whole enterprise when the latter are less than those of the permanent establishment. This State may likewise tax the profits of the permanent establishment at a minimum rate, provided that the same rate applies also to resident enterprises, even if taking into account the profits of the whole enterprise to which it belongs would result in a lower amount of tax, or no tax at all.

59.   Since a permanent establishment, by its very nature, does not distribute dividends, the tax treatment of distributions made by the enterprise to which the permanent establishment belongs is therefore outside the scope of paragraph 3. Paragraph 3 is restricted to the taxation of the profits from the activities of the permanent establishment itself and does not extend to the taxation of the enterprise as a whole. This is confirmed by the second sentence of the paragraph, which confirms that tax aspects related to the taxpayer that owns the permanent establishment, such as personal allowances and deductions, are outside the scope of the paragraph. Thus, issues related to various systems for the integration of the corporate and shareholder's taxes (*e.g.* advance corporate tax, *précompte mobilier*, computation of franked income and related dividend tax credits) are outside the scope of the paragraph.

60.   In some States, the profits of a permanent establishment of an enterprise of another Contracting State are taxed at a higher rate than the profits of enterprises of that State. This additional tax, sometimes referred to as a "branch tax", may be explained by the fact that if a subsidiary of the foreign enterprise earned the same profits as the permanent establishment and subsequently distributed these profits as a dividend, an additional tax would be levied on these dividends in accordance with paragraph 2 of Article 10. Where such tax is simply expressed as an additional tax payable on the profits of the permanent establishment, it must be considered as a tax levied on the profits of the activities of the permanent establishment itself and not as

a tax on the enterprise in its capacity as owner of the permanent establishment. Such a tax would therefore be contrary to paragraph 3.

61.   That situation must, however, be distinguished from that of a tax that would be imposed on amounts deducted, for instance as interest, in computing the profits of a permanent establishments (e.g. "branch level interest tax"); in that case, the tax would not be levied on the permanent establishment itself but, rather, on the enterprise to which the interest is considered to be paid and would therefore be outside the scope of paragraph 3 (depending on the circumstances, however, other provisions, such as those of Articles 7 and 11, may be relevant in determining whether such a tax is allowed by the Convention; see the last sentence of paragraph 4).

D.   Withholding tax on dividends, interest and royalties received by a permanent establishment

62.   When permanent establishments receive dividends, interest, or royalties such income, by virtue of paragraph 4 of Articles 10 and 11 and paragraph 3 of Article 12, respectively, comes under the provisions of Article 7 and consequently — subject to the observations made in paragraph 53 above as regards dividends received on holdings of permanent establishment — falls to be included in the taxable profits of such permanent establishments (see paragraph 74 of the Commentary on Article 7).

63.   According to the respective Commentaries on the above-mentioned provisions of Articles 10, 11 and 12 (see respectively paragraphs 31, 24 and 20), these provisions dispense the State of source of the dividends, interest or royalties received by the permanent establishment from applying any limitation provided for in those Articles, which means — and this is the generally accepted interpretation — that they leave completely unaffected the right of the State of source, where the permanent establishment is situated, to apply its withholding tax at the full rate.

64.   While this approach does not create any problems with regard to the provisions of paragraph 3 of Article 24 in the case of countries where a withholding tax is levied on all such income, whether the latter be paid to residents (permanent establishments, like resident enterprises, being allowed to set such withholding tax off against the tax on profits due by virtue of Article 7) or to non residents (subject to the limitations provided for in Articles 10, 11 and 12), the position is different when withholding tax is applied exclusively to income paid to non-residents.

65.   In this latter case, in fact, it seems difficult to reconcile the levy of withholding tax with the principle set out in paragraph 3 that for the purpose of taxing the income which is derived from their activity, or which is normally connected with it — as is recognised to be the case with dividends, interest and royalties referred to in paragraph 4 of Articles 10 and 11 and in paragraph 3 of Article 12 — permanent establishments must be treated as resident enterprises and hence in respect of such income be subjected to tax on profits solely.

66.   In any case, it is for Contracting States which have this difficulty to settle it in bilateral negotiations in the light of their peculiar circumstances.

E. Credit for foreign tax

67.   In a related context, when foreign income is included in the profits attributable to a permanent establishment, it is right by virtue of the same principle to grant to the permanent establishment credit for foreign tax borne by such income when such credit is granted to resident enterprises under domestic laws.

68.   If in a Contracting State (A) in which is situated a permanent establishment of an enterprise of the other Contracting State (B), credit for tax levied in a third State (C) can be allowed only by virtue of a convention, then the more general question arises as to the extension to permanent establishments of the benefit of credit provisions included in tax conventions concluded with third States. Whilst the permanent establishment is not itself a person and is therefore not entitled to the benefits of these tax conventions, this issue is relevant to the taxation on the permanent establishment. This question is examined below in the particular case of dividends and interest.

F. Extension to permanent establishments of the benefit of the credit provisions of double taxation conventions concluded with third States

69.   When the permanent establishment in a Contracting State of a resident enterprise of another Contracting State receives dividends or interest from a third State, then the question arises as to whether and to what extent the Contracting State in which the permanent establishment is situated should credit the tax that cannot be recovered from the third State.

70.   There is agreement that double taxation arises in these situations and that some method of relief should be found. The majority of member countries are able to grant credit in these cases on the basis of their domestic law or under paragraph 3. States that cannot give credit in such a way or that wish to clarify the situation may wish to supplement the provision in their convention with the Contracting State in which the enterprise is resident by wording that allows the State in which the permanent establishment is situated to credit the tax liability in the State in which the income originates to an amount that does not exceed the amount that resident enterprises in the Contracting State in which the permanent establishment is situated can claim on the basis of the Contracting State's convention with the third State. If the tax that cannot be recovered under the convention between the third State and the State of residence of the enterprise which has a permanent establishment in the other Contracting State is lower than that under the convention between the third State and the Contracting State in which the permanent establishment is situated, then only the lower tax collected in the third State shall be credited. This result would be achieved by adding the following words after the first sentence of paragraph 3:

> When a permanent establishment in a Contracting State of an enterprise of the other Contracting State receives dividends or interest from a third State and the holding or debt-claim in respect of which the dividends or interest are paid is effectively connected with that permanent establishment, the first-mentioned State shall grant a tax credit in respect of the tax paid in the third State on the

MODEL TAX CONVENTION (CONDENSED VERSION) – ISBN 978-92-64-08948-8 – © OECD 2010

dividends or interest, as the case may be, by applying the rate of tax provided in the convention with respect to taxes on income and capital between the State of which the enterprise is a resident and the third State. However, the amount of the credit shall not exceed the amount that an enterprise that is a resident of the first-mentioned State can claim under that State's convention on income and capital with the third State.

If the convention also provides for other categories of income that may be taxed in the State in which they arise and for which credit should be given (e.g. royalties, in some conventions), the above provision should be amended to also cover these.

71.   Where a permanent establishment situated in a Contracting State of an enterprise resident of another Contracting State (the State of residence) receives dividends, interest or royalties from a third State (the State of source) and, according to the procedure agreed to between the State of residence and the State of source, a certificate of domicile is requested by the State of source for the application of the withholding tax at the rate provided for in the convention between the State of source and the State of residence, this certificate must be issued by the latter State. While this procedure may be useful where the State of residence employs the credit method, it seems to serve no purposes where that State uses the exemption method as the income from the third State is not liable to tax in the State of residence of the enterprise. On the other hand, the State in which the permanent establishment is located could benefit from being involved in the certification procedure as this procedure would provide useful information for audit purposes. Another question that arises with triangular cases is that of abuses. If the Contracting State of which the enterprise is a resident exempts from tax the profits of the permanent establishment located in the other Contracting State, there is a danger that the enterprise will transfer assets such as shares, bonds or patents to permanent establishments in States that offer very favourable tax treatment, and in certain circumstances the resulting income may not be taxed in any of the three States. To prevent such practices, which may be regarded as abusive, a provision can be included in the convention between the State of which the enterprise is a resident and the third State (the State of source) stating that an enterprise can claim the benefits of the convention only if the income obtained by the permanent establishment situated in the other State is taxed normally in the State of the permanent establishment.

72.   In addition to the typical triangular case considered here, other triangular cases arise, particularly that in which the State of the enterprise is also the State from which the income ascribable to the permanent establishment in the other State originates (see also paragraph 5 of the Commentary on Article 21). States can settle these matters in bilateral negotiations.

Paragraph 4

73.   This paragraph is designed to end a particular form of discrimination resulting from the fact that in certain countries the deduction of interest, royalties and other disbursements allowed without restriction when the recipient is resident, is restricted

or even prohibited when he is a non-resident. The same situation may also be found in the sphere of capital taxation, as regards debts contracted to a non-resident. It is however open to Contracting States to modify this provision in bilateral conventions to avoid its use for tax avoidance purposes.

74.   Paragraph 4 does not prohibit the country of the borrower from applying its domestic rules on thin capitalisation insofar as these are compatible with paragraph 1 of Article 9 or paragraph 6 of Article 11. However, if such treatment results from rules which are not compatible with the said Articles and which only apply to non-resident creditors (to the exclusion of resident creditors), then such treatment is prohibited by paragraph 4.

75.   Also, paragraph 4 does not prohibit additional information requirements with respect to payments made to non-residents since these requirements are intended to ensure similar levels of compliance and verification in the case of payments to residents and non-residents.

Paragraph 5

76.   This paragraph forbids a Contracting State to give less favourable treatment to an enterprise, the capital of which is owned or controlled, wholly or partly, directly or indirectly, by one or more residents of the other Contracting State. This provision, and the discrimination which it puts an end to, relates to the taxation only of enterprises and not of the persons owning or controlling their capital. Its object therefore is to ensure equal treatment for taxpayers residing in the same State, and not to subject foreign capital, in the hands of the partners or shareholders, to identical treatment to that applied to domestic capital.

77.   Since the paragraph relates only to the taxation of resident enterprises and not to that of the persons owning or controlling their capital, it follows that it cannot be interpreted to extend the benefits of rules that take account of the relationship between a resident enterprise and other resident enterprises (e.g. rules that allow consolidation, transfer of losses or tax-free transfer of property between companies under common ownership). For example, if the domestic tax law of one State allows a resident company to consolidate its income with that of a resident parent company, paragraph 5 cannot have the effect to force the State to allow such consolidation between a resident company and a non-resident parent company. This would require comparing the combined treatment of a resident enterprise and the non-resident that owns its capital with that of a resident enterprise of the same State and the resident that owns its capital, something that clearly goes beyond the taxation of the resident enterprise alone.

78.   Also, because paragraph 5 is aimed at ensuring that all resident companies are treated equally regardless of who owns or control their capital and does not seek to ensure that distributions to residents and non-residents are treated in the same way (see paragraph 76 above), it follows that withholding tax obligations that are imposed on a resident company with respect to dividends paid to non-resident shareholders but

not with respect to dividends paid to resident shareholders cannot be considered to violate paragraph 5. In that case, the different treatment is not dependent on the fact that the capital of the company is owned or controlled by non-residents but, rather, on the fact that dividends paid to non-residents are taxed differently. A similar example would be that of a State that levies a tax on resident companies that make distributions to their shareholders regardless of whether or not they are residents or non-residents, but which, in order to avoid a multiple application of that tax, would not apply it to distributions made to related resident companies that are themselves subject to the tax upon their own distributions. The fact that the latter exemption would not apply to distributions to non-resident companies should not be considered to violate paragraph 5. In that case, it is not because the capital of the resident company is owned or controlled by non-residents that it is treated differently; it is because it makes distributions to companies that, under the provisions of the treaty, cannot be subjected to the same tax when they re-distribute the dividends received from that resident company. In this example, all resident companies are treated the same way regardless of who owns or controls their capital and the different treatment is restricted to cases where distributions are made in circumstances where the distribution tax could be avoided.

79.   Since the paragraph prevents the discrimination of a resident enterprise that is solely based on who owns or controls the capital of that enterprise, it would not *prima facie* be relevant with respect to rules that provide for a different treatment of an enterprise based on whether it pays interest to resident or non-resident creditors. The paragraph is not concerned with rules based on a debtor-creditor relationship as long as the different treatment resulting from the rules is not based on whether or not non-residents own or control, wholly or partly, directly or indirectly, the capital of the enterprise. For example, if under a State's domestic thin capitalisation rules, a resident enterprise is not allowed to deduct interest paid to a non-resident associated enterprise, that rule would not be in violation of paragraph 5 even where it would be applied to payments of interest made to a creditor that would own or control the capital of the enterprise, provided that the treatment would be the same if the interest had been paid to a non-resident associated enterprise that did not itself own or control any of the capital of the payer. Clearly, however, such a domestic law rule could be in violation of paragraph 4 to the extent that different conditions would apply for the deduction of interest paid to residents and non-residents and it will therefore be important to determine, for purposes of that paragraph, whether the application of the rule is compatible with the provisions of paragraph 1 of Article 9 or paragraph 6 of Article 11 (see paragraph 74 above). This would also be important for purposes of paragraph 5 in the case of thin capitalisation rules that would apply only to enterprises of a Contracting State the capital of which is wholly or partly owned or controlled, directly or indirectly, by non-residents. Indeed, since the provisions of paragraph 1 of Article 9 or paragraph 6 of Article 11 form part of the context in which paragraph 5 must be read (as required by Article 31 of the *Vienna Convention on the Law of Treaties*), adjustments which are compatible with these provisions could not be considered to violate the provisions of paragraph 5.

80.   In the case of transfer pricing enquiries, almost all member countries consider that additional information requirements which would be more stringent than the normal requirements, or even a reversal of the burden of proof, would not constitute discrimination within the meaning of the Article.

Paragraph 6

81.   This paragraph states that the scope of the Article is not restricted by the provisions of Article 2. The Article therefore applies to taxes of every kind and description levied by, or on behalf of, the State, its political subdivisions or local authorities.

Observations on the Commentary

82.   The interpretation given in paragraphs 57 and 58 above is not endorsed by *Germany*, the tax laws of which require the application of a minimum rate on exclusively inbound sources with respect to non-residents; the minimum rate is close to the lower end of the progressive tax scale.

83.   The *United States* observes that its non-resident citizens are not in the same circumstances as other non-residents, since the United States taxes its non-resident citizens on their worldwide income.

84.   With respect to paragraph 71, the *Netherlands* acknowledges that States may wish to include in their bilateral conventions a provision to assure that the benefits of the Convention are denied in "triangular cases" which may be regarded as abusive. In drafting provisions like this, however, the starting point should always be that the benefits of the Convention can be claimed unless the situation is regarded to be abusive. Further the Netherlands would like to express the opinion that the notion "normally taxed" is too ambiguous to serve as a decisive landmark in determining whether a situation is abusive or not.

Reservations on the Article

85.   *Canada* and *New Zealand* reserve their positions on this Article.

86.   *Australia* reserves the right to propose amendments to ensure that Australia can continue to apply certain provisions of its domestic law relating to deductions for R&D and withholding tax collection.

87.   The *United States* reserves its right to apply its branch tax.

Paragraph 1

88.   *France* wishes to reserve the possibility of applying the provisions of paragraph 1 only to individuals, in view of the French case law and of the fact that paragraphs 3, 4 and 5 already provide companies with wide protection against discrimination.

89.   *Chile* and the *United Kingdom* reserve their position on the second sentence of paragraph 1.

Paragraph 2

90.   *Chile* and *Switzerland* reserve the right not to insert paragraph 2 in their conventions.

Paragraph 3

90.1   In view of its particular taxation system, *Chile* retains its freedom of action with regard to the provisions in the Convention relating to the rate and form of distribution of profits by permanent establishments.

Paragraph 4

91.   *France* accepts the provisions of paragraph 4 but wishes to reserve the possibility of applying the provisions in its domestic laws relative to the limitation to the deduction of interest paid by a French company to an associated or related company.

Paragraph 6

92.   *Chile*, *Greece*, *Ireland* and the *United Kingdom* reserve the right to restrict the application of the Article to the taxes covered by the Convention.

COMMENTARY ON ARTICLE 25
CONCERNING THE MUTUAL AGREEMENT PROCEDURE

I.   Preliminary remarks

1.   This Article institutes a mutual agreement procedure for resolving difficulties arising out of the application of the Convention in the broadest sense of the term.

2.   It provides first, in paragraphs 1 and 2, that the competent authorities shall endeavour by mutual agreement to resolve the situation of taxpayers subjected to taxation not in accordance with the provisions of the Convention.

3.   It also, in paragraph 3, invites and authorises the competent authorities of the two States to resolve by mutual agreement problems relating to the interpretation or application of the Convention and, furthermore, to consult together for the elimination of double taxation in cases not provided for in the Convention.

4.   As regards the practical operation of the mutual agreement procedure, the Article, in paragraph 4, merely authorises the competent authorities to communicate with each other directly, without going through diplomatic channels, and, if it seems advisable to them, to have an oral exchange of opinions through a joint commission appointed especially for the purpose. Article 26 applies to the exchange of information for the purposes of the provisions of this Article. The confidentiality of information exchanged for the purposes of a mutual agreement procedure is thus ensured.

5.   Finally, paragraph 5 provides a mechanism that allows a taxpayer to request the arbitration of unresolved issues that have prevented competent authorities from reaching a mutual agreement within two years. Whilst the mutual agreement procedure provides a generally effective and efficient method of resolving disputes arising under the Convention, there may be cases where the competent authorities are unable to agree that the taxation by both States is in accordance with the Convention. The arbitration process provided for under paragraph 5 allows such cases to be resolved by allowing an independent decision of the unresolved issues, thereby allowing a mutual agreement to be reached. This process is an integral part of the mutual agreement procedure and does not constitute an alternative route to solving disputes concerning the application of the Convention.

6.   Since the Article merely lays down general rules concerning the mutual agreement procedure, the comments below are intended to clarify the purpose of such rules, and also to amplify them, if necessary, by referring, in particular, to the rules and practices followed at international level in the conduct of mutual agreement procedures or at the internal level in the conduct of the procedures which exist in most OECD member countries for dealing with disputed claims regarding taxes. In particular, since paragraph 5 expressly requires the competent authorities to agree on the mode of application of the arbitration process that it provides, the comments below discuss in detail various procedural aspects of that process. An annex to this Commentary contains a sample form of agreement that the competent authorities may use as a basis for settling the mode of application of the arbitration process; that

MODEL TAX CONVENTION (CONDENSED VERSION) – ISBN 978-92-64-08948-8 – © OECD 2010

annex addresses various structural and procedural issues, discusses the various provisions of the sample agreement and, in some cases, puts forward alternatives.

II.   Commentary on the provisions of the Article

Paragraphs 1 and 2

7.   The rules laid down in paragraphs 1 and 2 provide for the elimination in a particular case of taxation which does not accord with the Convention. As is known, in such cases it is normally open to taxpayers to litigate in the tax court, either immediately or upon the dismissal of their objections by the taxation authorities. When taxation not in accordance with the Convention arises from an incorrect application of the Convention in both States, taxpayers are then obliged to litigate in each State, with all the disadvantages and uncertainties that such a situation entails. So paragraph 1 makes available to taxpayers affected, without depriving them of the ordinary legal remedies available, a procedure which is called the mutual agreement procedure because it is aimed, in its second stage, at resolving the dispute on an agreed basis, i.e. by agreement between competent authorities, the first stage being conducted exclusively in the State of residence (except where the procedure for the application of paragraph 1 of Article 24 is set in motion by the taxpayer in the State of which he is a national) from the presentation of the objection up to the decision taken regarding it by the competent authority on the matter.

8.   In any case, the mutual agreement procedure is clearly a special procedure outside the domestic law. It follows that it can be set in motion solely in cases coming within paragraph 1, i.e. cases where tax has been charged, or is going to be charged, in disregard of the provisions of the Convention. So where a charge of tax has been made contrary both to the Convention and the domestic law, this case is amenable to the mutual agreement procedure to the extent only that the Convention is affected, unless a connecting link exists between the rules of the Convention and the rules of the domestic law which have been misapplied.

9.   In practice, the procedure applies to cases — by far the most numerous — where the measure in question leads to double taxation which it is the specific purpose of the Convention to avoid. Among the most common cases, mention must be made of the following:

- questions relating to the attribution of profits to a permanent establishment under paragraph 2 of Article 7;
- the taxation in the State of the payer — in case of a special relationship between the payer and the beneficial owner — of the excess part of interest and royalties, under the provisions of Article 9, paragraph 6 of Article 11 or paragraph 4 of Article 12;
- cases of application of legislation to deal with thin capitalisation when the State of the debtor company has treated interest as dividends, insofar as such treatment is based on clauses of a convention corresponding for example to Article 9 or paragraph 6 of Article 11;

— cases where lack of information as to the taxpayer's actual situation has led to misapplication of the Convention, especially in regard to the determination of residence (paragraph 2 of Article 4), the existence of a permanent establishment (Article 5), or the temporary nature of the services performed by an employee (paragraph 2 of Article 15).

10.   Article 25 also provides machinery to enable competent authorities to consult with each other with a view to resolving, in the context of transfer pricing problems, not only problems of juridical double taxation but also those of economic double taxation, and especially those resulting from the inclusion of profits of associated enterprises under paragraph 1 of Article 9; the corresponding adjustments to be made in pursuance of paragraph 2 of the same Article thus fall within the scope of the mutual agreement procedure, both as concerns assessing whether they are well-founded and for determining their amount.

11.   This in fact is implicit in the wording of paragraph 2 of Article 9 when the bilateral convention in question contains a clause of this type. When the bilateral convention does not contain rules similar to those of paragraph 2 of Article 9 (as is usually the case for conventions signed before 1977) the mere fact that Contracting States inserted in the convention the text of Article 9, as limited to the text of paragraph 1 — which usually only confirms broadly similar rules existing in domestic laws — indicates that the intention was to have economic double taxation covered by the Convention. As a result, most member countries consider that economic double taxation resulting from adjustments made to profits by reason of transfer pricing is not in accordance with — at least — the spirit of the convention and falls within the scope of the mutual agreement procedure set up under Article 25.

12.   Whilst the mutual agreement procedure has a clear role in dealing with issues arising as to the sorts of adjustments referred to in paragraph 2 of Article 9, it follows that even in the absence of such a provision, States should be seeking to avoid double taxation, including by giving corresponding adjustments in cases of the type contemplated in paragraph 2. Whilst there may be some difference of view, States would therefore generally regard a taxpayer initiated mutual agreement procedure based upon economic double taxation contrary to the terms of Article 9 as encompassing issues of whether a corresponding adjustment should have been provided, even in the absence of a provision similar to paragraph 2 of Article 9. States which do not share this view do, however, in practice, find the means of remedying economic double taxation in most cases involving *bona fide* companies by making use of provisions in their domestic laws.

13.   The mutual agreement procedure is also applicable in the absence of any double taxation contrary to the Convention, once the taxation in dispute is in direct contravention of a rule in the Convention. Such is the case when one State taxes a particular class of income in respect of which the Convention gives an exclusive right to tax to the other State even though the latter is unable to exercise it owing to a gap in its domestic laws. Another category of cases concerns persons who, being nationals of one Contracting State but residents of the other State, are subjected in that other State

to taxation treatment which is discriminatory under the provisions of paragraph 1 of Article 24.

14.   It should be noted that the mutual agreement procedure, unlike the disputed claims procedure under domestic law, can be set in motion by a taxpayer without waiting until the taxation considered by him to be "not in accordance with the Convention" has been charged against or notified to him. To be able to set the procedure in motion, he must, and it is sufficient if he does, establish that the "actions of one or both of the Contracting States" will result in such taxation, and that this taxation appears as a risk which is not merely possible but probable. Such actions mean all acts or decisions, whether of a legislative or a regulatory nature, and whether of general or individual application, having as their direct and necessary consequence the charging of tax against the complainant contrary to the provisions of the Convention. Thus, for example, if a change to a Contracting State's tax law would result in a person deriving a particular type of income being subjected to taxation not in accordance with the Convention, that person could set the mutual agreement procedure in motion as soon as the law has been amended and that person has derived the relevant income or it becomes probable that the person will derive that income. Other examples include filing a return in a self assessment system or the active examination of a specific taxpayer reporting position in the course of an audit, to the extent that either event creates the probability of taxation not in accordance with the Convention (*e.g.* where the self assessment reporting position the taxpayer is required to take under a Contracting State's domestic law would, if proposed by that State as an assessment in a non-self assessment regime, give rise to the probability of taxation not in accordance with the Convention, or where circumstances such as a Contracting State's published positions or its audit practice create a significant likelihood that the active examination of a specific reporting position such as the taxpayer's will lead to proposed assessments that would give rise to the probability of taxation not in accordance with the Convention). Another example might be a case where a Contracting State's transfer pricing law requires a taxpayer to report taxable income in an amount greater than would result from the actual prices used by the taxpayer in its transactions with a related party, in order to comply with the arm's length principle, and where there is substantial doubt whether the taxpayer's related party will be able to obtain a corresponding adjustment in the other Contracting State in the absence of a mutual agreement procedure. As indicated by the opening words of paragraph 1, whether or not the actions of one or both of the Contracting States will result in taxation not in accordance with the Convention must be determined from the perspective of the taxpayer. Whilst the taxpayer's belief that there will be such taxation must be reasonable and must be based on facts that can be established, the tax authorities should not refuse to consider a request under paragraph 1 merely because they consider that it has not been proven (for example to domestic law standards of proof on the "balance of probabilities") that such taxation will occur.

15.   Since the first steps in a mutual agreement procedure may be set in motion at a very early stage based upon the mere probability of taxation not in accordance with the

Convention, the initiation of the procedure in this manner would not be considered the presentation of the case to the competent authority for the purposes of determining the start of the two year period referred to in paragraph 5 of the Article. Paragraph 8 of the annex to the Commentary on Article 25 describes the circumstances in which that two year period commences.

16.   To be admissible objections presented under paragraph 1 must first meet a twofold requirement expressly formulated in that paragraph: in principle, they must be presented to the competent authority of the taxpayer's State of residence (except where the procedure for the application of paragraph 1 of Article 24 is set in motion by the taxpayer in the State of which he is a national), and they must be so presented within three years of the first notification of the action which gives rise to taxation which is not in accordance with the Convention. The Convention does not lay down any special rule as to the form of the objections. The competent authorities may prescribe special procedures which they feel to be appropriate. If no special procedure has been specified, the objections may be presented in the same way as objections regarding taxes are presented to the tax authorities of the State concerned.

17.   The requirement laid on the taxpayer to present his case to the competent authority of the State of which he is a resident (except where the procedure for the application of paragraph 1 of Article 24 is set in motion by the taxpayer in the State of which he is a national) is of general application, regardless of whether the taxation objected to has been charged in that or the other State and regardless of whether it has given rise to double taxation or not. If the taxpayer should have transferred his residence to the other Contracting State subsequently to the measure or taxation objected to, he must nevertheless still present his objection to the competent authority of the State of which he was a resident during the year in respect of which such taxation has been or is going to be charged.

18.   However, in the case already alluded to where a person who is a national of one State but a resident of the other complains of having been subjected in that other State to an action or taxation which is discriminatory under paragraph 1 of Article 24, it appears more appropriate for obvious reasons to allow him, by way of exception to the general rule set forth above, to present his objection to the competent authority of the Contracting State of which he is a national. Finally, it is to the same competent authority that an objection has to be presented by a person who, while not being a resident of a Contracting State, is a national of a Contracting State, and whose case comes under paragraph 1 of Article 24.

19.   On the other hand, Contracting States may, if they consider it preferable, give taxpayers the option of presenting their cases to the competent authority of either State. In such a case, paragraph 1 would have to be modified as follows:

1.   Where a person considers that the actions of one or both of the Contracting States result or will result for him in taxation not in accordance with the provisions of this Convention, he may, irrespective of the remedies provided by the domestic law of those States, present his case to the competent authority of either Contracting State. The case must be presented within three years from the first

notification of the action resulting in taxation not in accordance with the provisions of the Convention.

20.   The time limit of three years set by the second sentence of paragraph 1 for presenting objections is intended to protect administrations against late objections. This time limit must be regarded as a minimum, so that Contracting States are left free to agree in their bilateral conventions upon a longer period in the interests of taxpayers, *e.g.* on the analogy in particular of the time limits laid down by their respective domestic regulations in regard to tax conventions. Contracting States may omit the second sentence of paragraph 1 if they concur that their respective domestic regulations apply automatically to such objections and are more favourable in their effects to the taxpayers affected, either because they allow a longer time for presenting objections or because they do not set any time limits for such purpose.

21.   The provision fixing the starting point of the three year time limit as the date of the "first notification of the action resulting in taxation not in accordance with the provisions of the Convention" should be interpreted in the way most favourable to the taxpayer. Thus, even if such taxation should be directly charged in pursuance of an administrative decision or action of general application, the time limit begins to run only from the date of the notification of the individual action giving rise to such taxation, that is to say, under the most favourable interpretation, from the act of taxation itself, as evidenced by a notice of assessment or an official demand or other instrument for the collection or levy of tax. Since a taxpayer has the right to present a case as soon as the taxpayer considers that taxation will result in taxation not in accordance with the provisions of the Convention, whilst the three year limit only begins when that result has materialised, there will be cases where the taxpayer will have the right to initiate the mutual agreement procedure before the three year time limit begins (see the examples of such a situation given in paragraph 14 above).

22.   In most cases it will be clear what constitutes the relevant notice of assessment, official demand or other instrument for the collection or levy of tax, and there will usually be domestic law rules governing when that notice is regarded as "given". Such domestic law will usually look to the time when the notice is sent (time of sending), a specific number of days after it is sent, the time when it would be expected to arrive at the address it is sent to (both of which are times of presumptive physical receipt), or the time when it is in fact physically received (time of actual physical receipt). Where there are no such rules, either the time of actual physical receipt or, where this is not sufficiently evidenced, the time when the notice would normally be expected to have arrived at the relevant address should usually be treated as the time of notification, bearing in mind that this provision should be interpreted in the way most favourable to the taxpayer.

23.   In self assessment cases, there will usually be some notification effecting that assessment (such as a notice of a liability or of denial or adjustment of a claim for refund), and generally the time of notification, rather than the time when the taxpayer lodges the self-assessed return, would be a starting point for the three year period to run. There may, however, be cases where there is no notice of a liability or the like. In

such cases, the relevant time of "notification" would be the time when the taxpayer would, in the normal course of events, be regarded as having been made aware of the taxation that is in fact not in accordance with the Convention. This could, for example, be when information recording the transfer of funds is first made available to a taxpayer, such as in a bank balance or statement. The time begins to run whether or not the taxpayer actually regards the taxation, at that stage, as contrary to the Convention, provided that a reasonably prudent person in the taxpayer's position would have been able to conclude at that stage that the taxation was not in accordance with the Convention. In such cases, notification of the fact of taxation to the taxpayer is enough. Where, however, it is only the combination of the self assessment with some other circumstance that would cause a reasonably prudent person in the taxpayer's position to conclude that the taxation was contrary to the Convention (such as a judicial decision determining the imposition of tax in a case similar to the taxpayer's to be contrary to the provisions of the Convention), the time begins to run only when the latter circumstance materialises.

24.   If the tax is levied by deduction at the source, the time limit begins to run from the moment when the income is paid; however, if the taxpayer proves that only at a later date did he know that the deduction had been made, the time limit will begin from that date. Where it is the combination of decisions or actions taken in both Contracting States that results in taxation not in accordance with the Convention, the time limit begins to run only from the first notification of the most recent decision or action. This means that where, for example, a Contracting State levies a tax that is not in accordance with the Convention but the other State provides relief for such tax pursuant to Article 23 A or Article 23 B so that there is no double taxation, a taxpayer will in practice often not initiate the mutual agreement procedure in relation to the action of the first State. If, however, the other State subsequently notifies the taxpayer that the relief is denied so that double taxation now arises, a new time limit begins from that notification, since the combined actions of both States then result in the taxpayer's being subjected to double taxation contrary to the provisions of the Convention. In some cases, especially of this type, the records held by taxing authorities may have been routinely destroyed before the period of the time limit ends, in accordance with the normal practice of one or both of the States. The Convention obligations do not prevent such destruction, or require a competent authority to accept the taxpayer's arguments without proof, but in such cases the taxpayer should be given the opportunity to supply the evidential deficiency, as the mutual agreement procedure continues, to the extent domestic law allows. In some cases, the other Contracting State may be able to provide sufficient evidence, in accordance with Article 26 of the Model Tax Convention. It is, of course, preferable that such records be retained by tax authorities for the full period during which a taxpayer is able to seek to initiate the mutual agreement procedure in relation to a particular matter.

25.   The three year period continues to run during any domestic law (including administrative) proceedings (e.g. a domestic appeal process). This could create difficulties by in effect requiring a taxpayer to choose between domestic law and

MODEL TAX CONVENTION (CONDENSED VERSION) – ISBN 978-92-64-08948-8 – © OECD 2010

mutual agreement procedure remedies. Some taxpayers may rely solely on the mutual agreement procedure, but many taxpayers will attempt to address these difficulties by initiating a mutual agreement procedure whilst simultaneously initiating domestic law action, even though the domestic law process is initially not actively pursued. This could result in mutual agreement procedure resources being inefficiently applied. Where domestic law allows, some States may wish to specifically deal with this issue by allowing for the three year (or longer) period to be suspended during the course of domestic law proceedings. Two approaches, each of which is consistent with Article 25 are, on one hand, requiring the taxpayer to initiate the mutual agreement procedure, with no suspension during domestic proceedings, but with the competent authorities not entering into talks in earnest until the domestic law action is finally determined, or else, on the other hand, having the competent authorities enter into talks, but without finally settling an agreement unless and until the taxpayer agrees to withdraw domestic law actions. This second possibility is discussed at paragraph 42 of this Commentary. In either of these cases, the taxpayer should be made aware that the relevant approach is being taken. Whether or not a taxpayer considers that there is a need to lodge a "protective" appeal under domestic law (because, for example, of domestic limitation requirements for instituting domestic law actions) the preferred approach for all parties is often that the mutual agreement procedure should be the initial focus for resolving the taxpayer's issues, and for doing so on a bilateral basis.

26.   Some States may deny the taxpayer the ability to initiate the mutual agreement procedure under paragraph 1 of Article 25 in cases where the transactions to which the request relates are regarded as abusive. This issue is closely related to the issue of "improper use of the Convention" discussed in paragraph 9.1 and the following paragraphs of the Commentary on Article 1. In the absence of a special provision, there is no general rule denying perceived abusive situations going to the mutual agreement procedure, however. The simple fact that a charge of tax is made under an avoidance provision of domestic law should not be a reason to deny access to mutual agreement. However, where serious violations of domestic laws resulting in significant penalties are involved, some States may wish to deny access to the mutual agreement procedure. The circumstances in which a State would deny access to the mutual agreement procedure should be made clear in the Convention.

27.   Some States regard certain issues as not susceptible to resolution by the mutual agreement procedure generally, or at least by taxpayer initiated mutual agreement procedure, because of constitutional or other domestic law provisions or decisions. An example would be a case where granting the taxpayer relief would be contrary to a final court decision that the tax authority is required to adhere to under that State's constitution. The recognised general principle for tax and other treaties is that domestic law, even domestic constitutional law, does not justify a failure to meet treaty obligations, however. Article 27 of the *Vienna Convention on the Law of Treaties* reflects this general principle of treaty law. It follows that any justification for what would otherwise be a breach of the Convention needs to be found in the terms of the Convention itself, as interpreted in accordance with accepted tax treaty interpretation

principles. Such a justification would be rare, because it would not merely govern how a matter will be dealt with by the two States once the matter is within the mutual agreement procedure, but would instead prevent the matter from even reaching the stage when it is considered by both States. Since such a determination might in practice be reached by one of the States without consultation with the other, and since there might be a bilateral solution that therefore remains unconsidered, the view that a matter is not susceptible of taxpayer initiated mutual agreement procedure should not be lightly made, and needs to be supported by the terms of the Convention as negotiated. A competent authority relying upon a domestic law impediment as the reason for not allowing the mutual agreement procedure to be initiated by a taxpayer should inform the other competent authority of this and duly explain the legal basis of its position. More usually, genuine domestic law impediments will not prevent a matter from entering into the mutual agreement procedure, but if they will clearly and unequivocally prevent a competent authority from resolving the issue in a way that avoids taxation of the taxpayer which is not in accordance with the Convention, and there is no realistic chance of the other State resolving the issue for the taxpayer, then that situation should be made public to taxpayers, so that taxpayers do not have false expectations as to the likely outcomes of the procedure.

28.   In other cases, initiation of the mutual agreement procedure may have been allowed but domestic law issues that have arisen since the negotiation of the treaty may prevent a competent authority from resolving, even in part, the issue raised by the taxpayer. Where such developments have a legally constraining effect on the competent authority, so that bilateral discussions can clearly not resolve the matter, most States would accept that this change of circumstances is of such significance as to allow that competent authority to withdraw from the procedure. In some cases, the difficulty may be only temporary however; such as whilst rectifying legislation is enacted, and in that case, the procedure should be suspended rather than terminated. The two competent authorities will need to discuss the difficulty and its possible effect on the mutual agreement procedure. There will also be situations where a decision wholly or partially in the taxpayer's favour is binding and must be followed by one of the competent authorities but where there is still scope for mutual agreement discussions, such as for example in one competent authority's demonstrating to the other that the latter should provide relief.

29.   There is less justification for relying on domestic law for not implementing an agreement reached as part of the mutual agreement procedure. The obligation of implementing such agreements is unequivocally stated in the last sentence of paragraph 2, and impediments to implementation that were already existing should generally be built into the terms of the agreement itself. As tax conventions are negotiated against a background of a changing body of domestic law that is sometimes difficult to predict, and as both parties are aware of this in negotiating the original Convention and in reaching mutual agreements, subsequent unexpected changes that alter the fundamental basis of a mutual agreement would generally be considered as requiring revision of the agreement to the extent necessary. Obviously where there is a

domestic law development of this type, something that should only rarely occur, good faith obligations require that it be notified as soon as possible, and there should be a good faith effort to seek a revised or new mutual agreement, to the extent the domestic law development allows. In these cases, the taxpayer's request should be regarded as still operative, rather than a new application's being required from that person.

30.   As regards the procedure itself, it is necessary to consider briefly the two distinct stages into which it is divided (see paragraph 7 above).

31.   In the first stage, which opens with the presentation of the taxpayer's objections, the procedure takes place exclusively at the level of dealings between him and the competent authorities of his State of residence (except where the procedure for the application of paragraph 1 of Article 24 is set in motion by the taxpayer in the State of which he is a national). The provisions of paragraph 1 give the taxpayer concerned the right to apply to the competent authority of the State of which he is a resident, whether or not he has exhausted all the remedies available to him under the domestic law of each of the two States. On the other hand, that competent authority is under an obligation to consider whether the objection is justified and, if it appears to be justified, take action on it in one of the two forms provided for in paragraph 2.

32.   If the competent authority duly approached recognises that the complaint is justified and considers that the taxation complained of is due wholly or in part to a measure taken in the taxpayer's State of residence, it must give the complainant satisfaction as speedily as possible by making such adjustments or allowing such reliefs as appear to be justified. In this situation, the issue can be resolved without resort to the mutual agreement procedure. On the other hand, it may be found useful to exchange views and information with the competent authority of the other Contracting State, in order, for example, to confirm a given interpretation of the Convention.

33.   If, however, it appears to that competent authority that the taxation complained of is due wholly or in part to a measure taken in the other State, it will be incumbent on it, indeed it will be its duty — as clearly appears by the terms of paragraph 2 — to set in motion the mutual agreement procedure proper. It is important that the authority in question carry out this duty as quickly as possible, especially in cases where the profits of associated enterprises have been adjusted as a result of transfer pricing adjustments.

34.   A taxpayer is entitled to present his case under paragraph 1 to the competent authority of the State of which he is a resident whether or not he may also have made a claim or commenced litigation under the domestic law of that State. If litigation is pending, the competent authority of the State of residence should not wait for the final adjudication, but should say whether it considers the case to be eligible for the mutual agreement procedure. If it so decides, it has to determine whether it is itself able to arrive at a satisfactory solution or whether the case has to be submitted to the competent authority of the other Contracting State. An application by a taxpayer to set

the mutual agreement procedure in motion should not be rejected without good reason.

35.   If a claim has been finally adjudicated by a court in the State of residence, a taxpayer may wish even so to present or pursue a claim under the mutual agreement procedure. In some States, the competent authority may be able to arrive at a satisfactory solution which departs from the court decision. In other States, the competent authority is bound by the court decision. It may nevertheless present the case to the competent authority of the other Contracting State and ask the latter to take measures for avoiding double taxation.

36.   In its second stage — which opens with the approach to the competent authority of the other State by the competent authority to which the taxpayer has applied — the procedure is henceforward at the level of dealings between States, as if, so to speak, the State to which the complaint was presented had given it its backing. But whilst this procedure is indisputably a procedure between States, it may, on the other hand, be asked:

— whether, as the title of the Article and the terms employed in the first sentence of paragraph 2 suggest, it is no more than a simple procedure of mutual agreement, or constitutes the implementation of a *pactum de contrahendo* laying on the parties a mere duty to negotiate but in no way laying on them a duty to reach agreement;

— or whether on the contrary, it is to be regarded (based on the existence of the arbitration process provided for in paragraph 5 to address unresolved issues or on the assumption that the procedure takes place within the framework of a joint commission) as a procedure of a jurisdictional nature laying on the parties a duty to resolve the dispute.

37.   Paragraph 2 no doubt entails a duty to negotiate; but as far as reaching mutual agreement through the procedure is concerned, the competent authorities are under a duty merely to use their best endeavours and not to achieve a result. Paragraph 5, however, provides a mechanism that will allow an agreement to be reached even if there are issues on which the competent authorities have been unable to reach agreement through negotiations.

38.   In seeking a mutual agreement, the competent authorities must first, of course, determine their position in the light of the rules of their respective taxation laws and of the provisions of the Convention, which are as binding on them as much as they are on the taxpayer. Should the strict application of such rules or provisions preclude any agreement, it may reasonably be held that the competent authorities, as in the case of international arbitration, can, subsidiarily, have regard to considerations of equity in order to give the taxpayer satisfaction.

39.   The purpose of the last sentence of paragraph 2 is to enable countries with time limits relating to adjustments of assessments and tax refunds in their domestic law to give effect to an agreement despite such time limits. This provision does not prevent, however, such States as are not, on constitutional or other legal grounds, able to

overrule the time limits in the domestic law from inserting in the mutual agreement itself such time limits as are adapted to their internal statute of limitation. In certain extreme cases, a Contracting State may prefer not to enter into a mutual agreement, the implementation of which would require that the internal statute of limitation had to be disregarded. Apart from time limits there may exist other obstacles such as "final court decisions" to giving effect to an agreement. Contracting States are free to agree on firm provisions for the removal of such obstacles. As regards the practical implementation of the procedure, it is generally recommended that every effort should be made by tax administrations to ensure that as far as possible the mutual agreement procedure is not in any case frustrated by operational delays or, where time limits would be in point, by the combined effects of time limits and operational delays.

40.   The Committee on Fiscal Affairs made a number of recommendations on the problems raised by corresponding adjustments of profits following transfer pricing adjustments (implementation of paragraphs 1 and 2 of Article 9) and of the difficulties of applying the mutual agreement procedure to such situations:

a) Tax authorities should notify taxpayers as soon as possible of their intention to make a transfer pricing adjustment (and, where the date of any such notification may be important, to ensure that a clear formal notification is given as soon as possible), since it is particularly useful to ensure as early and as full contacts as possible on all relevant matters between tax authorities and taxpayers within the same jurisdiction and, across national frontiers, between the associated enterprises and tax authorities concerned.

b) Competent authorities should communicate with each other in these matters in as flexible a manner as possible, whether in writing, by telephone, or by face-to-face or round-the-table discussion, whichever is most suitable, and should seek to develop the most effective ways of solving relevant problems. Use of the provisions of Article 26 on the exchange of information should be encouraged in order to assist the competent authority in having well-developed factual information on which a decision can be made.

c) In the course of mutual agreement proceedings on transfer pricing matters, the taxpayers concerned should be given every reasonable opportunity to present the relevant facts and arguments to the competent authorities both in writing and orally.

41.   As regards the mutual agreement procedure in general, the Committee recommended that:

a) The formalities involved in instituting and operating the mutual agreement procedure should be kept to a minimum and any unnecessary formalities eliminated.

b) Mutual agreement cases should each be settled on their individual merits and not by reference to any balance of the results in other cases.

c) Competent authorities should, where appropriate, formulate and publicise domestic rules, guidelines and procedures concerning use of the mutual agreement procedure.

42.   The case may arise where a mutual agreement is concluded in relation to a taxpayer who has brought a suit for the same purpose in the competent court of either Contracting State and such suit is still pending. In such a case, there would be no grounds for rejecting a request by a taxpayer that he be allowed to defer acceptance of the solution agreed upon as a result of the mutual agreement procedure until the court had delivered its judgment in that suit. Also, a view that competent authorities might reasonably take is that where the taxpayer's suit is ongoing as to the particular issue upon which mutual agreement is sought by that same taxpayer, discussions of any depth at the competent authority level should await a court decision. If the taxpayer's request for a mutual agreement procedure applied to different tax years than the court action, but to essentially the same factual and legal issues, so that the court outcome would in practice be expected to affect the treatment of the taxpayer in years not specifically the subject of litigation, the position might be the same, in practice, as for the cases just mentioned. In either case, awaiting a court decision or otherwise holding a mutual agreement procedure in abeyance whilst formalised domestic recourse proceedings are underway will not infringe upon, or cause time to expire from, the two year period referred to in paragraph 5 of the Article. Of course, if competent authorities consider, in either case, that the matter might be resolved notwithstanding the domestic law proceedings (because, for example, the competent authority where the court action is taken will not be bound or constrained by the court decision) then the mutual agreement procedure may proceed as normal.

43.   The situation is also different if there is a suit ongoing on an issue, but the suit has been taken by another taxpayer than the one who is seeking to initiate the mutual agreement procedure. In principle, if the case of the taxpayer seeking the mutual agreement procedure supports action by one or both competent authorities to prevent taxation not in accordance with the Convention, that should not be unduly delayed pending a general clarification of the law at the instance of another taxpayer, although the taxpayer seeking mutual agreement might agree to this if the clarification is likely to favour that taxpayer's case. In other cases, delaying competent authority discussions as part of a mutual agreement procedure may be justified in all the circumstances, but the competent authorities should as far as possible seek to prevent disadvantage to the taxpayer seeking mutual agreement in such a case. This could be done, where domestic law allows, by deferring payment of the amount outstanding during the course of the delay, or at least during that part of the delay which is beyond the taxpayer's control.

44.   Depending upon domestic procedures, the choice of redress is normally that of the taxpayer and in most cases it is the domestic recourse provisions such as appeals or court proceedings that are held in abeyance in favour of the less formal and bilateral nature of mutual agreement procedure.

45.   As noted above, there may be a pending suit by the taxpayer on an issue, or else the taxpayer may have preserved the right to take such domestic law action, yet the competent authorities might still consider that an agreement can be reached. In such cases, it is, however, necessary to take into account the concern of a particular competent authority to avoid any divergences or contradictions between the decision of the court and the mutual agreement that is being sought, with the difficulties or risks of abuse that these could entail. In short, therefore, the implementation of such a mutual agreement should normally be made subject:

— to the acceptance of such mutual agreement by the taxpayer, and

— to the taxpayer's withdrawal of the suit at law concerning those points settled in the mutual agreement.

46.   Some States take the view that a mutual agreement procedure may not be initiated by a taxpayer unless and until payment of all or a specified portion of the tax amount in dispute has been made. They consider that the requirement for payment of outstanding taxes, subject to repayment in whole or in part depending on the outcome of the procedure, is an essentially procedural matter not governed by Article 25, and is therefore consistent with it. A contrary view, held by many States, is that Article 25 indicates all that a taxpayer must do before the procedure is initiated, and that it imposes no such requirement. Those States find support for their view in the fact that the procedure may be implemented even before the taxpayer has been charged to tax or notified of a liability (as noted at paragraph 14 above) and in the acceptance that there is clearly no such requirement for a procedure initiated by a competent authority under paragraph 3.

47.   Article 25 gives no absolutely clear answer as to whether a taxpayer initiated mutual agreement procedure may be denied on the basis that there has not been the necessary payment of all or part of the tax in dispute. However, whatever view is taken on this point, in the implementation of the Article it should be recognised that the mutual agreement procedure supports the substantive provisions of the Convention and that the text of Article 25 should therefore be understood in its context and in the light of the object and purposes of the Convention, including avoiding double taxation and the prevention of fiscal evasion and avoidance. States therefore should as far as possible take into account the cash flow and possible double taxation issues in requiring advance payment of an amount that the taxpayer contends was at least in part levied contrary to the terms of the relevant Convention. As a minimum, payment of outstanding tax should not be a requirement to initiate the mutual agreement procedure if it is not a requirement before initiating domestic law review. It also appears, as a minimum, that if the mutual agreement procedure is initiated prior to the taxpayer's being charged to tax (such as by an assessment), a payment should only be required once that charge to tax has occurred.

48.   There are several reasons why suspension of the collection of tax pending resolution of a mutual agreement procedure can be a desirable policy, although many States may require legislative changes for the purpose of its implementation. Any requirement to pay a tax assessment specifically as a condition of obtaining access to

the mutual agreement procedure in order to get relief from that very tax would generally be inconsistent with the policy of making the mutual agreement procedure broadly available to resolve such disputes. Even if a mutual agreement procedure ultimately eliminates any double taxation or other taxation not in accordance with the Convention, the requirement to pay tax prior to the conclusion of the mutual agreement procedure may permanently cost the taxpayer the time value of the money represented by the amount inappropriately imposed for the period prior to the mutual agreement procedure resolution, at least in the fairly common case where the respective interest policies of the relevant Contracting States do not fully compensate the taxpayer for that cost. Thus, this means that in such cases the mutual agreement procedure would not achieve the goal of fully eliminating, as an economic matter, the burden of the double taxation or other taxation not in accordance with the Convention. Moreover, even if that economic burden is ultimately removed, a requirement on the taxpayer to pay taxes on the same income to two Contracting States can impose cash flow burdens that are inconsistent with the Convention's goals of eliminating barriers to cross border trade and investment. Finally, another unfortunate complication may be delays in the resolution of cases if a country is less willing to enter into good faith mutual agreement procedure discussions when a probable result could be the refunding of taxes already collected. Where States take the view that payment of outstanding tax is a precondition to the taxpayer initiated mutual agreement procedure, this should be notified to the treaty partner during negotiations on the terms of a Convention. Where both States party to a Convention take this view, there is a common understanding, but also the particular risk of the taxpayer's being required to pay an amount twice. Where domestic law allows it, one possibility which States might consider to deal with this would be for the higher of the two amounts to be held in trust, escrow or similar, pending the outcome of the mutual agreement procedure. Alternatively, a bank guarantee provided by the taxpayer's bank could be sufficient to meet the requirements of the competent authorities. As another approach, one State or the other (decided by time of assessment, for example, or by residence State status under the treaty) could agree to seek a payment of no more than the difference between the amount paid to the other State, and that which it claims, if any. Which of these possibilities is open will ultimately depend on the domestic law (including administrative requirements) of a particular State, but they are the sorts of options that should as far as possible be considered in seeking to have the mutual agreement procedure operate as effectively as possible. Where States require some payment of outstanding tax as a precondition to the taxpayer initiated mutual agreement procedure, or to the active consideration of an issue within that procedure, they should have a system in place for refunding an amount of interest on any underlying amount to be returned to the taxpayer as the result of a mutual agreement reached by the competent authorities. Any such interest payment should sufficiently reflect the value of the underlying amount and the period of time during which that amount has been unavailable to the taxpayer.

49.   States take differing views as to whether administrative interest and penalty charges are treated as taxes covered by Article 2 of the Convention. Some States treat

them as taking the character of the underlying amount in dispute, but other States do not. It follows that there will be different views as to whether such interest and penalties are subject to a taxpayer initiated mutual agreement procedure. Where they are covered by the Convention as taxes to which it applies, the object of the Convention in avoiding double taxation, and the requirement for States to implement conventions in good faith, suggest that as far as possible interest and penalty payments should not be imposed in a way that effectively discourages taxpayers from initiating a mutual agreement procedure, because of the cost and the cash flow impact that this would involve. Even when administrative interest and penalties are not regarded as taxes covered by the Convention under Article 2, they should not be applied in a way that severely discourages or nullifies taxpayer reliance upon the benefits of the Convention, including the right to initiate the mutual agreement procedure as provided by Article 25. For example, a State's requirements as to payment of outstanding penalties and interest should not be more onerous to taxpayers in the context of the mutual agreement procedure than they would be in the context of taxpayer initiated domestic law review.

Paragraph 3

50.   The first sentence of this paragraph invites and authorises the competent authorities to resolve, if possible, difficulties of interpretation or application by means of mutual agreement. These are essentially difficulties of a general nature which concern, or which may concern, a category of taxpayers, even if they have arisen in connection with an individual case normally coming under the procedure defined in paragraphs 1 and 2.

51.   This provision makes it possible to resolve difficulties arising from the application of the Convention. Such difficulties are not only those of a practical nature, which might arise in connection with the setting up and operation of procedures for the relief from tax deducted from dividends, interest and royalties in the Contracting State in which they arise, but also those which could impair or impede the normal operation of the clauses of the Convention as they were conceived by the negotiators, the solution of which does not depend on a prior agreement as to the interpretation of the Convention.

52.   Under this provision the competent authorities can, in particular:

— where a term has been incompletely or ambiguously defined in the Convention, complete or clarify its definition in order to obviate any difficulty;

— where the laws of a State have been changed without impairing the balance or affecting the substance of the Convention, settle any difficulties that may emerge from the new system of taxation arising out of such changes;

— determine whether, and if so under what conditions, interest may be treated as dividends under thin capitalisation rules in the country of the borrower and give rise to relief for double taxation in the country of residence of the lender in the same way as for dividends (for example relief under a parent/subsidiary regime when provision for such relief is made in the relevant bilateral convention).

53.   Paragraph 3 confers on the "competent authorities of the Contracting States", *i.e.* generally the Ministers of Finance or their authorised representatives normally responsible for the administration of the Convention, authority to resolve by mutual agreement any difficulties arising as to the interpretation of the Convention. However, it is important not to lose sight of the fact that, depending on the domestic law of Contracting States, other authorities (Ministry of Foreign Affairs, courts) have the right to interpret international treaties and agreements as well as the "competent authority" designated in the Convention, and that this is sometimes the exclusive right of such other authorities.

54.   Mutual agreements resolving general difficulties of interpretation or application are binding on administrations as long as the competent authorities do not agree to modify or rescind the mutual agreement.

55.   The second sentence of paragraph 3 enables the competent authorities to deal also with such cases of double taxation as do not come within the scope of the provisions of the Convention. Of special interest in this connection is the case of a resident of a third State having permanent establishments in both Contracting States. It is not merely desirable, but in most cases also will particularly reflect the role of Article 25 and the mutual agreement procedure in providing that the competent authorities may consult together as a way of ensuring the Convention as a whole operates effectively, that the mutual agreement procedure should result in the effective elimination of the double taxation which can occur in such a situation. The opportunity for such matters to be dealt with under the mutual agreement procedure becomes increasingly important as Contracting States seek more coherent frameworks for issues of profit allocation involving branches, and this is an issue that could usefully be discussed at the time of negotiating conventions or protocols to them. There will be Contracting States whose domestic law prevents the Convention from being complemented on points which are not explicitly or at least implicitly dealt with in the Convention, however, and in these situations the Convention could be complemented by a protocol dealing with this issue. In most cases, however, the terms of the Convention itself, as interpreted in accordance with accepted tax treaty interpretation principles, will sufficiently support issues involving two branches of a third state entity being subject to the paragraph 3 procedures.

Paragraph 4

56.   This paragraph determines how the competent authorities may consult together for the resolution by mutual agreement, either of an individual case coming under the procedure defined in paragraphs 1 and 2 or of general problems relating in particular to the interpretation or application of the Convention, and which are referred to in paragraph 3.

57.   It provides first that the competent authorities may communicate with each other directly. It would therefore not be necessary to go through diplomatic channels.

58.   The competent authorities may communicate with each other by letter, facsimile transmission, telephone, direct meetings, or any other convenient means. They may, if they wish, formally establish a joint commission for this purpose.

59.   As to this joint commission, paragraph 4 leaves it to the competent authorities of the Contracting States to determine the number of members and the rules of procedure of this body.

60.   However, whilst the Contracting States may avoid any formalism in this field, it is nevertheless their duty to give taxpayers whose cases are brought before the joint commission under paragraph 2 certain essential guarantees, namely:
   — the right to make representations in writing or orally, either in person or through a representative;
   — the right to be assisted by counsel.

61.   However, disclosure to the taxpayer or his representatives of the papers in the case does not seem to be warranted, in view of the special nature of the procedure.

62.   Without infringing upon the freedom of choice enjoyed in principle by the competent authorities in designating their representatives on the joint commission, it would be desirable for them to agree to entrust the chairmanship of each Delegation — which might include one or more representatives of the service responsible for the procedure — to a high official or judge chosen primarily on account of his special experience; it is reasonable to believe, in fact, that the participation of such persons would be likely to facilitate reaching an agreement.

Paragraph 5

63.   This paragraph provides that, in the cases where the competent authorities are unable to reach an agreement under paragraph 2 within two years, the unresolved issues will, at the request of the person who presented the case, be solved through an arbitration process. This process is not dependent on a prior authorization by the competent authorities: once the requisite procedural requirements have been met, the unresolved issues that prevent the conclusion of a mutual agreement must be submitted to arbitration.

64.   The arbitration process provided for by the paragraph is not an alternative or additional recourse: where the competent authorities have reached an agreement that does not leave any unresolved issues as regards the application of the Convention, there are no unresolved issues that can be brought to arbitration even if the person who made the mutual agreement request does not consider that the agreement reached by the competent authorities provides a correct solution to the case. The paragraph is, therefore, an extension of the mutual agreement procedure that serves to enhance the effectiveness of that procedure by ensuring that where the competent authorities cannot reach an agreement on one or more issues that prevent the resolution of a case, a resolution of the case will still be possible by submitting those issues to arbitration. Thus, under the paragraph, the resolution of the case continues to be reached through the mutual agreement procedure, whilst the resolution of a

COMMENTARY ON ARTICLE 25

particular issue which is preventing agreement in the case is handled through an arbitration process. This distinguishes the process established in paragraph 5 from other forms of commercial or government-private party arbitration where the jurisdiction of the arbitral panel extends to resolving the whole case.

65.   It is recognised, however, that in some States, national law, policy or administrative considerations may not allow or justify the type of arbitration process provided for in the paragraph. For example, there may be constitutional barriers preventing arbitrators from deciding tax issues. In addition, some countries may only be in a position to include this paragraph in treaties with particular States. For these reasons, the paragraph should only be included in the Convention where each State concludes that the process is capable of effective implementation.

66.   In addition, some States may wish to include paragraph 5 but limit its application to a more restricted range of cases. For example, access to arbitration could be restricted to cases involving issues which are primarily factual in nature. It could also be possible to provide that arbitration would always be available for issues arising in certain classes of cases, for example, highly factual cases such as those related to transfer pricing or the question of the existence of a permanent establishment, whilst extending arbitration to other issues on a case-by-case basis.

67.   States which are members of the European Union must co-ordinate the scope of paragraph 5 with their obligations under the European Arbitration Convention.

68.   The taxpayer should be able to request arbitration of unresolved issues in all cases dealt with under the mutual agreement procedure that have been presented under paragraph 1 on the basis that the actions of one or both of the Contracting States have resulted for a person in taxation not in accordance with the provisions of this Convention. Where the mutual agreement procedure is not available, for example because of the existence of serious violations involving significant penalties (see paragraph 26), it is clear that paragraph 5 is not applicable.

69.   Where two Contracting States that have not included the paragraph in their Convention wish to implement an arbitration process for general application or to deal with a specific case, it is still possible for them to do so by mutual agreement. In that case, the competent authorities can conclude a mutual agreement along the lines of the sample wording presented in the annex, to which they would add the following first paragraph:

1.   Where,

   a) under paragraph 1 of Article 25 of the Convention, a person has presented a case to the competent authority of a Contracting State on the basis that the actions of one or both of the Contracting States have resulted for that person in taxation not in accordance with the provisions of this Convention, and

   b) the competent authorities are unable to reach an agreement to resolve that case pursuant to paragraph 2 of the Article within two years from the presentation of the case to the competent authority of the other Contracting State,

MODEL TAX CONVENTION (CONDENSED VERSION) – ISBN 978-92-64-08948-8 – © OECD 2010

any unresolved issues arising from the case shall be submitted to arbitration in accordance with the following paragraphs if the person so requests. These unresolved issues shall not, however, be submitted to arbitration if a decision on these issues has already been rendered by a court or administrative tribunal of either State. Unless a person directly affected by the case does not accept the mutual agreement that implements the arbitration decision, the competent authorities hereby agree to consider themselves bound by the arbitration decision and to resolve the case pursuant to paragraph 2 of Article 25 on the basis of that decision.

This agreement would go on to address the various structural and procedural issues discussed in the annex. Whilst the competent authorities would thus be bound by such process, such agreement would be given as part of the mutual agreement procedure and would therefore only be effective as long as the competent authorities continue to agree to follow that process to solve cases that they have been unable to resolve through the traditional mutual agreement procedure.

70. Paragraph 5 provides that a person who has presented a case to the competent authority of a Contracting State pursuant to paragraph 1 on the basis that the actions of one or both of the Contracting States have resulted for that person in taxation not in accordance with the provisions of this Convention may request that any unresolved issues arising from the case be submitted to arbitration. This request may be made at any time after a period of two years that begins when the case is presented to the competent authority of the other Contracting State. Recourse to arbitration is therefore not automatic; the person who presented the case may prefer to wait beyond the end of the two year period (for example, to allow the competent authorities more time to resolve the case under paragraph 2) or simply not to pursue the case. States are free to provide that, in certain circumstances, a longer period of time will be required before the request can be made.

71. Under paragraph 2 of Article 25, the competent authorities must endeavour to resolve a case presented under paragraph 1 with a view to the avoidance of taxation not in accordance with the Convention. For the purposes of paragraph 5, a case should therefore not be considered to have been resolved as long as there is at least one issue on which the competent authorities disagree and which, according to one of the competent authorities, indicates that there has been taxation not in accordance with the Convention. One of the competent authorities could not, therefore, unilaterally decide that such a case is closed and that the person involved cannot request the arbitration of unresolved issues; similarly, the two competent authorities could not consider that the case has been resolved and deny the request for arbitration if there are still unresolved issues that prevent them from agreeing that there has not been taxation not in accordance with the Convention. Where, however, the two competent authorities agree that taxation by both States has been in accordance with the Convention, there are no unresolved issues and the case may be considered to have been resolved, even in the case where there might be double taxation that is not addressed by the provisions of the Convention.

72.   The arbitration process is only available in cases where the person considers that taxation not in accordance with the provisions of the Convention has actually resulted from the actions of one or both of the Contracting States; it is not available, however, in cases where it is argued that such taxation will eventually result from such actions even if the latter cases may be presented to the competent authorities under paragraph 1 of the Article (see paragraph 70 above). For that purpose, taxation should be considered to have resulted from the actions of one or both of the Contracting States as soon as, for example, tax has been paid, assessed or otherwise determined or even in cases where the taxpayer is officially notified by the tax authorities that they intend to tax him on a certain element of income.

73.   As drafted, paragraph 5 only provides for arbitration of unresolved issues arising from a request made under paragraph 1 of the Article. States wishing to extend the scope of the paragraph to also cover mutual agreement cases arising under paragraph 3 of the Article are free to do so. In some cases, a mutual agreement case may arise from other specific treaty provisions, such as subparagraph 2 d) of Article 4. Under that subparagraph, the competent authorities are, in certain cases, required to settle by mutual agreement the question of the status of an individual who is a resident of both Contracting States. As indicated in paragraph 20 of the Commentary on Article 4, such cases must be resolved according to the procedure established in Article 25. If the competent authorities fail to reach an agreement on such a case and this results in taxation not in accordance with the Convention (according to which the individual should be a resident of only one State for purposes of the Convention), the taxpayer's case comes under paragraph 1 of Article 25 and, therefore, paragraph 5 is applicable.

74.   In some States, it may be possible for the competent authorities to deviate from a court decision on a particular issue arising from the case presented to the competent authorities. Those States should therefore be able to omit the second sentence of the paragraph.

75.   The presentation of the case to the competent authority of the other State, which is the beginning of the two year period referred to in the paragraph, may be made by the person who presented the case to the competent authority of the first State under paragraph 1 of Article 25 (e.g. by presenting the case to the competent authority of the other State at the same time or at a later time) or by the competent authority of the first State, who would contact the competent authority of the other State pursuant to paragraph 2 if it is not itself able to arrive at a satisfactory solution of the case. For the purpose of determining the start of the two year period, a case will only be considered to have been presented to the competent authority of the other State if sufficient information has been presented to that competent authority to allow it to decide whether the objection underlying the case appears to be justified. The mutual agreement providing for the mode of application of paragraph 5 (see the annex) should specify which type of information will normally be sufficient for that purpose.

76.   The paragraph also deals with the relationship between the arbitration process and rights to domestic remedies. For the arbitration process to be effective and to avoid

the risk of conflicting decisions, a person should not be allowed to pursue the arbitration process if the issues submitted to arbitration have already been resolved through the domestic litigation process of either State (which means that any court or administrative tribunal of one of the Contracting States has already rendered a decision that deals with these issues and that applies to that person). This is consistent with the approach adopted by most countries as regards the mutual agreement procedure and according to which:

a) A person cannot pursue simultaneously the mutual agreement procedure and domestic legal remedies. Where domestic legal remedies are still available, the competent authorities will generally either require that the taxpayer agree to the suspension of these remedies or, if the taxpayer does not agree, will delay the mutual agreement procedure until these remedies are exhausted.

b) Where the mutual agreement procedure is first pursued and a mutual agreement has been reached, the taxpayer and other persons directly affected by the case are offered the possibility to reject the agreement and pursue the domestic remedies that had been suspended; conversely, if these persons prefer to have the agreement apply, they will have to renounce the exercise of domestic legal remedies as regards the issues covered by the agreement.

c) Where the domestic legal remedies are first pursued and are exhausted in a State, a person may only pursue the mutual agreement procedure in order to obtain relief of double taxation in the other State. Indeed, once a legal decision has been rendered in a particular case, most countries consider that it is impossible to override that decision through the mutual agreement procedure and would therefore restrict the subsequent application of the mutual agreement procedure to trying to obtain relief in the other State.

The same general principles should be applicable in the case of a mutual agreement procedure that would involve one or more issues submitted to arbitration. It would not be helpful to submit an issue to arbitration if it is known in advance that one of the countries is limited in the response that it could make to the arbitral decision. This, however, would not be the case if the country could, in a mutual agreement procedure, deviate from a court decision (see paragraph 74) and in that case paragraph 5 could be adjusted accordingly.

77.   A second issue involves the relationship between existing domestic legal remedies and arbitration where the taxpayer has not undertaken (or has not exhausted) these legal remedies. In that case, the approach that would be the most consistent with the basic structure of the mutual agreement procedure would be to apply the same general principles when arbitration is involved. Thus, the legal remedies would be suspended pending the outcome of the mutual agreement procedure involving the arbitration of the issues that the competent authorities are unable to resolve and a tentative mutual agreement would be reached on the basis of that decision. As in other mutual agreement procedure cases, that agreement would then be presented to the taxpayer who would have to choose to accept the agreement,

which would require abandoning any remaining domestic legal remedies, or reject the agreement to pursue these remedies.

78.   This approach is in line with the nature of the arbitration process set out in paragraph 5. The purpose of that process is to allow the competent authorities to reach a conclusion on the unresolved issues that prevent an agreement from being reached. When that agreement is achieved though the aid of arbitration, the essential character of the mutual agreement remains the same.

79.   In some cases, this approach will mean that the parties will have to expend time and resources in an arbitration process that will lead to a mutual agreement that will not be accepted by the taxpayer. As a practical matter, however, experience shows that there are very few cases where the taxpayer rejects a mutual agreement to resort to domestic legal remedies. Also, in these rare cases, one would expect the domestic courts or administrative tribunals to take note of the fact that the taxpayer had been offered an administrative solution to his case that would have bound both States.

80.   In some States, unresolved issues between competent authorities may only be submitted to arbitration if domestic legal remedies are no longer available. In order to implement an arbitration approach, these States could consider the alternative approach of requiring a person to waive the right to pursue domestic legal remedies before arbitration can take place. This could be done by replacing the second sentence of the paragraph by "these unresolved issues shall not, however, be submitted to arbitration if any person directly affected by the case is still entitled, under the domestic law of either State, to have courts or administrative tribunals of that State decide these issues or if a decision on these issues has already been rendered by such a court or administrative tribunal." To avoid a situation where a taxpayer would be required to waive domestic legal remedies without any assurance as to the outcome of the case, it would then be important to also modify the paragraph to include a mechanism that would guarantee, for example, that double taxation would in fact be relieved. Also, since the taxpayer would then renounce the right to be heard by domestic courts, the paragraph should also be modified to ensure that sufficient legal safeguards are granted to the taxpayer as regards his participation in the arbitration process to meet the requirements that may exist under domestic law for such a renunciation to be acceptable under the applicable legal system (e.g. in some countries, such renunciation might not be effective if the person were not guaranteed the right to be heard orally during the arbitration).

81.   Paragraph 5 provides that, unless a person directly affected by the case does not accept the mutual agreement that implements the arbitration decision, that decision shall be binding on both States. Thus, the taxation of any person directly affected by the case will have to conform with the decision reached on the issues submitted to arbitration and the decisions reached in the arbitral process will be reflected in the mutual agreement that will be presented to these persons.

82.   As noted in subparagraph 76 b) above, where a mutual agreement is reached before domestic legal remedies have been exhausted, it is normal for the competent

authorities to require, as a condition for the application of the agreement, that the persons affected renounce the exercise of domestic legal remedies that may still exist as regards the issues covered by the agreement. Without such renunciation, a subsequent court decision could indeed prevent the competent authorities from applying the agreement. Thus, for the purpose of paragraph 5, if a person to whom the mutual agreement that implements the arbitration decision has been presented does not agree to renounce the exercise of domestic legal remedies, that person must be considered not to have accepted that agreement.

83.   The arbitration decision is only binding with respect to the specific issues submitted to arbitration. Whilst nothing would prevent the competent authorities from solving other similar cases (including cases involving the same persons but different taxable periods) on the basis of the decision, there is no obligation to do so and each State therefore has the right to adopt a different approach to deal with these other cases.

84.   Some States may wish to allow the competent authorities to depart from the arbitration decision, provided that they can agree on a different solution (this, for example, is allowed under Article 12 of the EU Arbitration Convention). States wishing to do so are free to amend the third sentence of the paragraph as follows:

> ... Unless a person directly affected by the case does not accept the mutual agreement that implements the arbitration decision or the competent authorities and the persons directly affected by the case agree on a different solution within six months after the decision has been communicated to them, the arbitration decision shall be binding on both States and shall be implemented notwithstanding any time limits in the domestic laws of these States.

85.   The last sentence of the paragraph leaves the mode of application of the arbitration process to be settled by mutual agreement. Some aspects could also be covered in the Article itself, a protocol or through an exchange of diplomatic notes. Whatever form the agreement takes, it should set out the structural and procedural rules to be followed in applying the paragraph, taking into account the paragraph's requirement that the arbitration decision be binding on both States. Ideally, that agreement should be drafted at the same time as the Convention so as to be signed, and to apply, immediately after the paragraph becomes effective. Also, since the agreement will provide the details of the process to be followed to bring unresolved issues to arbitration, it would be important that this agreement be made public. A sample form of such agreement is provided in the annex together with comments on the procedural rules that it puts forward.

Use of other supplementary dispute resolution mechanisms

86.   Regardless of whether or not paragraph 5 is included in a Convention or an arbitration process is otherwise implemented using the procedure described in paragraph 69 above, it is clear that supplementary dispute resolution mechanisms other than arbitration can be implemented on an ad hoc basis as part of the mutual

agreement procedure. Where there is disagreement about the relative merits of the positions of the two competent authorities, the case may be helped if the issues are clarified by a mediator. In such situations the mediator listens to the positions of each party and then communicates a view of the strengths and weaknesses of each side. This helps each party to better understand its own position and that of the other party. Some tax administrations are now successfully using mediation to resolve internal disputes and the extension of such techniques to mutual agreement procedures could be useful.

87.   If the issue is a purely factual one, the case could be referred to an expert whose mandate would simply be to make the required factual determinations. This is often done in judicial procedures where factual matters are referred to an independent party who makes factual findings which are then submitted to the court. Unlike the dispute resolution mechanism which is established in paragraph 5, these procedures are not binding on the parties but nonetheless can be helpful in allowing them to reach a decision before an issue would have to be submitted to arbitration under that paragraph.

III. Interaction of the mutual agreement procedure with the dispute resolution mechanism provided by the General Agreement on Trade in Services

88.   The application of the General Agreement on Trade in Services (GATS), which entered into force on 1 January 1995 and which all member countries have signed, raises particular concerns in relation to the mutual agreement procedure.

89.   Paragraph 3 of Article XXII of the GATS provides that a dispute as to the application of Article XVII of the Agreement, a national treatment rule, may not be dealt with under the dispute resolution mechanisms provided by Articles XXII and XXIII of the Agreement if the disputed measure "falls within the scope of an international agreement between them relating to the avoidance of double taxation" (*e.g.* a tax convention). If there is disagreement over whether a measure "falls within the scope" of such an international agreement, paragraph 3 goes on to provide that either State involved in the dispute may bring the matter to the Council on Trade in Services, which shall refer the dispute for binding arbitration. A footnote to paragraph 3, however, contains the important exception that if the dispute relates to an international agreement "which exist[s] at the time of the entry into force" of the Agreement, the matter may not be brought to the Council on Trade in Services unless both States agree.

90.   That paragraph raises two particular problems with respect to tax treaties.

91.   First, the footnote thereto provides for the different treatment of tax conventions concluded before and after the entry into force of the GATS, something that may be considered inappropriate, in particular where a convention in existence at the time of the entry into force of the GATS is subsequently renegotiated or where a protocol is concluded after that time in relation to a convention existing at that time.

92.   Second, the phrase "falls within the scope" is inherently ambiguous, as indicated by the inclusion in paragraph 3 of Article XXII of the GATS of both an arbitration procedure and a clause exempting pre-existing conventions from its application in order to deal with disagreements related to its meaning. Whilst it seems clear that a country could not argue in good faith[1] that a measure relating to a tax to which no provision of a tax convention applied fell within the scope of that convention, it is unclear whether the phrase covers all measures that relate to taxes that are covered by all or only some provisions of the tax convention.

93.   Contracting States may wish to avoid these difficulties by extending bilaterally the application of the footnote to paragraph 3 of Article XXII of the GATS to conventions concluded after the entry into force of the GATS. Such a bilateral extension, which would supplement — but not violate in any way — the Contracting States' obligations under the GATS, could be incorporated in the convention by the addition of the following provision:

> For purposes of paragraph 3 of Article XXII (Consultation) of the General Agreement on Trade in Services, the Contracting States agree that, notwithstanding that paragraph, any dispute between them as to whether a measure falls within the scope of this Convention may be brought before the Council for Trade in Services, as provided by that paragraph, only with the consent of both Contracting States. Any doubt as to the interpretation of this paragraph shall be resolved under paragraph 3 of Article 25 or, failing agreement under that procedure, pursuant to any other procedure agreed to by both Contracting States.

94.   Problems similar to those discussed above may arise in relation with other bilateral or multilateral agreements related to trade or investment. Contracting States are free, in the course of their bilateral negotiations, to amend the provision suggested above so as to ensure that issues relating to the taxes covered by their tax convention are dealt with through the mutual agreement procedure rather than through the dispute settlement mechanism of such agreements.

Observation on the Commentary

95.   *Hungary* does not fully share the interpretation in paragraph 27 of the Commentary on Article 25 and is not in a position to pursue a mutual agreement procedure where a Hungarian court has already rendered a decision on the merits of the case.

Reservations on the Article

96.   With respect to paragraph 1 of the Article, *Turkey* reserves the right to provide that the case must be presented to its competent authority within a period of five years

---

1   The obligation of applying and interpreting treaties in good faith is expressly recognised in Articles 26 and 31 of the *Vienna Convention on the Law of Treaties*; thus, the exception in paragraph 3 of Article XXII of the GATS applies only to good faith disputes.

following the related taxation year. However, if the notification is made in the last year of that period, such application should be made within one year from the notification.

97.   The *United Kingdom* reserves its position on the last sentence of paragraph 1 on the grounds that it conflicts with the six year time limit under its domestic legislation.

98.   *Chile, Greece, Italy, Mexico, Poland, Portugal*, the *Slovak Republic* and *Switzerland* reserve their positions on the second sentence of paragraph 2. These countries consider that the implementation of reliefs and refunds following a mutual agreement ought to remain linked to time limits prescribed by their domestic laws.

99.   *Turkey* reserves its position on the second sentence of paragraph 2. Turkey's tax law provides that refunds of tax, like the assessment itself, must be made within a specific period. According to these provisions, if the administration finds an application for repayment acceptable, it must notify the fact to the taxpayer so that he can present his claim within a period of one year of such notification. If the taxpayer exceeds this time limit, his right to claim repayment lapses. The same procedure applies to the enforcement of judgements of courts under which repayments are required to be made. That is why Turkey is obliged to fix a time limit for the implementation of agreed mutual agreement procedures as is done for all repayments. For this reason Turkey wishes to reserve the right to mention in the text of bilateral conventions a definite time limit as regards their implementation.

100.   *Canada* reserves the right to include a provision, as referred to in paragraph 10 of the Commentary on Article 9, which effectively sets a time limit within which a Contracting State is under an obligation to make an appropriate adjustment following an upward adjustment of the profits of an enterprise in the other Contracting State.

101.   *Hungary* reserves its position on the last sentence of paragraph 1 as it could not agree to pursue a mutual agreement procedure in the case of a request that would be presented to its competent authority outside the prescription period provided for under its domestic legislation.

ANNEX

SAMPLE MUTUAL AGREEMENT ON ARBITRATION

1.   The following is a sample form of agreement that the competent authorities may use as a basis for a mutual agreement to implement the arbitration process provided for in paragraph 5 of the Article (see paragraph 85 above). Paragraphs 2 to 43 below discuss the various provisions of the agreement and, in some cases, put forward alternatives. Competent authorities are of course free to modify, add or delete any provisions of this sample agreement when concluding their bilateral agreement.

Mutual agreement on the implementation of paragraph 5 of Article 25

The competent authorities of [State A] and [State B] have entered into the following mutual agreement to establish the mode of application of the arbitration process provided for in paragraph 5 of Article 25 of the [title of the Convention], which entered into force on [date of entry into force]. The competent authorities may modify or supplement this agreement by an exchange of letters between them.

1. Request for submission of case to arbitration

A request that unresolved issues arising from a mutual agreement case be submitted to arbitration pursuant to paragraph 5 of Article 25 of the Convention (the "request for arbitration") shall be made in writing and sent to one of the competent authorities. The request shall contain sufficient information to identify the case. The request shall also be accompanied by a written statement by each of the persons who either made the request or is directly affected by the case that no decision on the same issues has already been rendered by a court or administrative tribunal of the States. Within 10 days of the receipt of the request, the competent authority who received it shall send a copy of the request and the accompanying statements to the other competent authority.

2. Time for submission of the case to arbitration

A request for arbitration may only be made after two years from the date on which a case presented to the competent authority of one Contracting State under paragraph 1 of Article 25 has also been presented to the competent authority of the other State. For this purpose, a case shall be considered to have been presented to the competent authority of the other State only if the following information has been presented: [the necessary information and documents will be specified in the agreement].

3. Terms of Reference

Within three months after the request for arbitration has been received by both competent authorities, the competent authorities shall agree on the questions to be resolved by the arbitration panel and communicate them in writing to the person who made the request for arbitration. This will constitute the "Terms of Reference" for the case. Notwithstanding the following paragraphs of this agreement, the competent authorities may also, in the Terms of Reference, provide procedural rules that are additional to, or different from, those included in these paragraphs and deal with such other matters as are deemed appropriate.

4. Failure to communicate the Terms of Reference

If the Terms of Reference have not been communicated to the person who made the request for arbitration within the period referred to in paragraph 3 above, that person and each competent authority may, within one month after the end of that period, communicate in writing to each other a list of issues to be resolved by the arbitration. All the lists so communicated during that period shall constitute the tentative Terms of Reference. Within one month after all the arbitrators have been appointed as provided in paragraph 5 below, the arbitrators shall communicate to the competent authorities and the person who made the request for arbitration a revised version of the tentative Terms of Reference based on the lists so communicated. Within one month after the revised version has been received by both of them, the competent authorities will have the possibility to agree on different Terms of Reference and to communicate them in writing to the arbitrators and the person who made the request for arbitration. If they do so within that period, these different Terms of Reference shall constitute the Terms of Reference for the case. If no different Terms of Reference have been agreed to between the competent authorities and communicated in writing within that period, the revised version of the tentative Terms of Reference prepared by the arbitrators shall constitute the Terms of Reference for the case.

5. Selection of arbitrators

Within three months after the Terms of Reference have been received by the person who made the request for arbitration or, where paragraph 4 applies, within four months after the request for arbitration has been received by both competent authorities, the competent authorities shall each appoint one arbitrator. Within two months of the latter appointment, the arbitrators so appointed will appoint a third arbitrator who will function as Chair. If any appointment is not made within the required time period, the arbitrator(s) not yet appointed shall be appointed by the Director of the OECD Centre for Tax Policy and Administration within 10 days of receiving a request to that effect from the person who made the request for arbitration. The same procedure shall apply with the necessary adaptations if for any reason it is necessary to replace an arbitrator after the arbitral process has begun. Unless the Terms of Reference provide otherwise, the remuneration of all arbitrators .... [the mode of remuneration should be described here; one possibility would be to refer to the method used in the Code of Conduct on the EC Arbitration Convention].

6. Streamlined arbitration process

If the competent authorities so indicate in the Terms of Reference (provided that these have not been agreed to after the selection of arbitrators pursuant to paragraph 4 above), the following rules shall apply to a particular case notwithstanding paragraphs 5, 11, 15, 16 and 17 of this agreement:

a) Within one month after the Terms of Reference have been received by the person who made the request for arbitration, the two competent authorities shall, by common consent, appoint one arbitrator. If, at the end of that period, the arbitrator has not yet been appointed, the arbitrator will be appointed by the Director of the OECD Centre for Tax Policy and Administration within 10 days of receiving a request to that effect from the person who made the request referred to in paragraph 1. The remuneration of the arbitrator shall be determined as follows ... [the mode of remuneration should be described here; one possibility would be to refer to the method used in the Code of Conduct on the EC Arbitration Convention].

b) Within two months from the appointment of the arbitrator, each competent authority will present in writing to the arbitrator its own reply to the questions contained in the Terms of Reference.

c) Within one month from having received the last of the replies from the competent authorities, the arbitrator will decide each question included in the Terms of Reference in accordance with one of the two replies received from the competent authorities as regards that question and will notify the competent authorities of the choice, together with short reasons explaining that choice. Such decision will be implemented as provided in paragraph 19.

7. Eligibility and appointment of arbitrators

Any person, including a government official of a Contracting State, may be appointed as an arbitrator, unless that person has been involved in prior stages of the case that results in the arbitration process. An arbitrator will be considered to have been appointed when a letter confirming that appointment has been signed both by the person or persons who have the power to appoint that arbitrator and by the arbitrator himself.

8. Communication of information and confidentiality

For the sole purposes of the application of the provisions of Articles 25 and 26, and of the domestic laws of the Contracting States, concerning the communication and the confidentiality of the information related to the case that results in the arbitration process, each arbitrator shall be designated as authorised representative of the competent authority that has appointed that arbitrator or, if that arbitrator has not been appointed exclusively by one competent authority, of the competent authority of the Contracting State to which the case giving rise to the arbitration was initially presented. For the purposes of this agreement, where a case giving rise to arbitration was initially presented simultaneously to both competent authorities, "the competent authority of the Contracting State to which the case giving rise to the arbitration was initially presented" means the competent authority referred to in paragraph 1 of Article 25.

9. Failure to provide information in a timely manner

Notwithstanding paragraphs 5 and 6, where both competent authorities agree that the failure to resolve an issue within the two year period provided in paragraph 5 of Article 25 is mainly attributable to the failure of a person directly affected by the case to provide relevant information in a timely manner, the competent authorities may postpone the nomination of the arbitrator for a period of time corresponding to the delay in providing that information.

10. Procedural and evidentiary rules

Subject to this agreement and the Terms of Reference, the arbitrators shall adopt those procedural and evidentiary rules that they deem necessary to answer the questions set out in the Terms of Reference. They will have access to all information necessary to decide the issues submitted to arbitration, including confidential information. Unless the competent authorities agree otherwise, any information that was not available to both competent authorities before the request for arbitration was received by both of them shall not be taken into account for purposes of the decision.

11. Participation of the person who requested the arbitration

The person who made the request for arbitration may, either directly or through his representatives, present his position to the arbitrators in writing to the same extent that he can do so during the mutual agreement procedure. In addition, with the permission of the arbitrators, the person may present his position orally during the arbitration proceedings.

12. Logistical arrangements

Unless agreed otherwise by the competent authorities, the competent authority to which the case giving rise to the arbitration was initially presented will be responsible for the logistical arrangements for the meetings of the arbitral panel and will provide the administrative personnel necessary for the conduct of the arbitration process. The administrative personnel so provided will report only to the Chair of the arbitration panel concerning any matter related to that process.

13. Costs

Unless agreed otherwise by the competent authorities:

a) each competent authority and the person who requested the arbitration will bear the costs related to his own participation in the arbitration proceedings (including travel costs and costs related to the preparation and presentation of his views);

b) each competent authority will bear the remuneration of the arbitrator appointed exclusively by that competent authority, or appointed by the Director of the OECD Centre for Tax Policy and Administration because of the failure of that competent authority to appoint that arbitrator, together with that arbitrator's travel, telecommunication and secretariat costs;

c) the remuneration of the other arbitrators and their travel, telecommunication and secretariat costs will be borne equally by the two Contracting States;

d) costs related to the meetings of the arbitral panel and to the administrative personnel necessary for the conduct of the arbitration process will be borne by the competent authority to which the case giving rise to the arbitration was initially presented, or if presented in both States, will be shared equally; and

e) all other costs (including costs of translation and of recording the proceedings) related to expenses that both competent authorities have agreed to incur, will be borne equally by the two Contracting States.

14. Applicable Legal Principles

The arbitrators shall decide the issues submitted to arbitration in accordance with the applicable provisions of the treaty and, subject to these provisions, of those of the domestic laws of the Contracting States. Issues of treaty interpretation will be decided by the arbitrators in the light of the principles of interpretation incorporated in Articles 31 to 33 of the *Vienna Convention on the Law of Treaties*, having regard to the Commentaries of the OECD Model Tax Convention as periodically amended, as explained in paragraphs 28 to 36.1 of the Introduction to the OECD Model Tax Convention. Issues related to the application of the arm's length principle should similarly be decided having regard to the OECD Transfer Pricing Guidelines for Multinational Enterprises and Tax Administrations. The arbitrators will also consider any other sources which the competent authorities may expressly identify in the Terms of Reference.

15. Arbitration decision

Where more than one arbitrator has been appointed, the arbitration decision will be determined by a simple majority of the arbitrators. Unless otherwise provided in the Terms of Reference, the decision of the arbitral panel will be presented in writing and shall indicate the sources of law relied upon and the reasoning which led to its result. With the permission of the person who made the request for arbitration and both competent authorities, the decision of the arbitral panel will be made public in redacted form without mentioning the names of the parties involved or any details that might disclose their identity and with the understanding that the decision has no formal precedential value.

16. Time allowed for communicating the arbitration decision

The arbitration decision must be communicated to the competent authorities and the person who made the request for arbitration within six months from the date on which the Chair notifies in writing the competent authorities and the person who made the request for arbitration that he has received all the information necessary to begin consideration of the case. Notwithstanding the first part of this paragraph, if at any time within two months from the date on which the last arbitrator was appointed, the Chair, with the consent of one of the competent authorities, notifies in writing the other competent authority and the person who made the request for arbitration that he has not received all the information necessary to begin consideration of the case, then

a) if the Chair receives the necessary information within two months after the date on which that notice was sent, the arbitration decision must be communicated to the competent authorities and the person who made the request for arbitration within six months from the date on which the information was received by the Chair, and

b) if the Chair has not received the necessary information within two months after the date on which that notice was sent, the arbitration decision must, unless the competent authorities agree otherwise, be reached without taking into account that information even if the Chair receives it later and the decision must be communicated to the competent authorities and the person who made the request for arbitration within eight months from the date on which the notice was sent.

17. Failure to communicate the decision within the required period

In the event that the decision has not been communicated to the competent authorities within the period provided for in paragraphs 6 c) or 16, the competent authorities may agree to extend that period for a period not exceeding six months or, if they fail to do so within one month from the end of the period provided for in paragraphs 6 c) or 16, they shall appoint a new arbitrator or arbitrators in accordance with paragraph 5 or 6 a), as the case may be.

18. Final decision

The arbitration decision shall be final, unless that decision is found to be unenforceable by the courts of one of the Contracting States because of a violation of paragraph 5 of Article 25 or of any procedural rule included in the Terms of Reference or in this agreement that may reasonably have affected the decision. If a decision is found to be unenforceable for one of these reasons, the request for arbitration shall be considered not to have been made and the arbitration process shall be considered not to have taken place (except for the purposes of paragraphs 8 "Communication of information and confidentiality" and 13 "Costs").

MODEL TAX CONVENTION (CONDENSED VERSION) – ISBN 978-92-64-08948-8 – © OECD 2010

19. Implementing the arbitration decision

The competent authorities will implement the arbitration decision within six months from the communication of the decision to them by reaching a mutual agreement on the case that led to the arbitration.

20. Where no arbitration decision will be provided

Notwithstanding paragraphs 6, 15, 16 and 17, where, at any time after a request for arbitration has been made and before the arbitrators have delivered a decision to the competent authorities and the person who made the request for arbitration, the competent authorities notify in writing the arbitrators and that person that they have solved all the unresolved issues described in the Terms of Reference, the case shall be considered as solved under the mutual agreement procedure and no arbitration decision shall be provided. This agreement applies to any request for arbitration made pursuant to paragraph 5 of Article 25 of the Convention after that provision has become effective.

[Date of signature of the agreement]

[Signature of the competent authority of each Contracting State]

General approach of the sample agreement

2.   A number of approaches can be taken to structuring the arbitral process which is used to supplement the mutual agreement procedure. Under one approach, which might be referred to as the "independent opinion" approach, the arbitrators would be presented with the facts and arguments by the parties based on the applicable law, and would then reach their own independent decision which would be based on a written, reasoned analysis of the facts involved and applicable legal sources.

3.   Alternatively, under the so-called "last best offer" or "final offer" approach, each competent authority would be required to give to the arbitral panel a proposed resolution of the issue involved and the arbitral panel would choose between the two proposals which were presented to it. There are obviously a number of variations between these two positions. For example, the arbitrators could reach an independent decision but would not be required to submit a written decision but simply their conclusions. To some extent, the appropriate method depends on the type of issue to be decided.

4.   The above sample agreement takes as its starting point the "independent opinion" approach which is thus the generally applicable process but, in recognition of the fact that many cases, especially those which involve primarily factual questions, may be best handled differently, it also provides for an alternative "streamlined" process, based on the "last best offer" or "final offer" approach. Competent authorities can therefore agree to use that streamlined process on a case-by-case basis. Competent authorities may of course adopt this combined approach, adopt the

streamlined process as the generally applicable process with the independent opinion as an option in some circumstances or limit themselves to only one of the two approaches.

The request for arbitration

5.   Paragraph 1 of the sample agreement provides the manner in which a request for arbitration should be made. Such request should be presented in writing to one of the competent authorities involved in the case. That competent authority should then inform the other competent authority within 10 days of the receipt of the request.

6.   In order to determine that the conditions of paragraph 5 of Article 25 have been met (see paragraph 76 of the Commentary on this Article) the request should be accompanied by statements indicating that no decision on these issues has already been rendered by domestic courts or administrative tribunals in either Contracting State.

7.   Since the arbitration process is an extension of the mutual agreement procedure that is intended to deal with cases that cannot be solved under that procedure, it would seem inappropriate to ask the person who makes the request to pay in order to make such request or to reimburse the expenses incurred by the competent authorities in the course of the arbitration proceedings. Unlike taxpayers' requests for rulings or other types of advance agreements, where a charge is sometimes made, providing a solution to disputes between the Contracting States is the responsibility of these States for which they in general should bear the costs.

8.   A request for arbitration may not be made before two years from the date when a mutual agreement case presented to the competent authority of a Contracting State has also been presented to the competent authority of the other Contracting State. Paragraph 2 of the sample agreement provides that for this purpose, a case shall only be considered to have been presented to the competent authority of that other State if the information specified in that paragraph has been so provided. The paragraph should therefore include a list of the information required; in general, that information will correspond to the information and documents that were required to initiate the mutual agreement procedure.

Terms of Reference

9.   Paragraph 3 of the sample agreement refers to the "Terms of Reference", which is the document that sets forth the questions to be resolved by the arbitrators. It establishes the jurisdictional basis for the issues which are to be decided by the arbitral panel. It is to be established by the competent authorities who may wish in that connection to consult with the person who made the request for arbitration. If the competent authorities cannot agree on the Terms of Reference within the period provided for in paragraph 3, some mechanism is necessary to ensure that the procedure goes forward. Paragraph 4 provides for that eventuality.

COMMENTARY ON ARTICLE 25

10.   Whilst the Terms of Reference will generally be limited to a particular issue or set of issues, it would be possible for the competent authorities, given the nature of the case and the interrelated nature of the issues, to draft the Terms of Reference so that the whole case (and not only certain specific issues) be submitted to arbitration.

11.   The procedural rules provided for in the sample agreement shall apply unless the competent authorities provide otherwise in the Terms of Reference. It is therefore possible for the competent authorities, through the Terms of Reference, to depart from any of these rules or to provide for additional rules in a particular case.

Streamlined process

12.   The normal process provided for by the sample agreement allows the consideration of questions of either law or fact, as well as of mixed questions of law and fact. Generally, it is important that the arbitrators support their decision with the reasoning leading to it. Showing the method through which the decision was reached may be important in assuring acceptance of the decision.

13.   In some cases, however, the unresolved issues will be primarily factual and the decision may be simply a statement of the final disposition, for example a determination of the amount of adjustments to the income and deductions of the respective related parties. Such circumstances will often arise in transfer pricing cases, where the unresolved issue may be simply the determination of an arm's length transfer price or range of prices (although there are other transfer pricing cases that involve complex factual issues); there are also cases in which an analogous principle may apply, for example, the determination of the existence of a permanent establishment. In some cases, the decision may be a statement of the factual premises on which the appropriate legal principles should then be applied by the competent authorities. Paragraph 5 of the sample agreement provides a streamlined process which the competent authorities may wish to apply in these types of cases. That process, which will then override other procedural rules of the sample agreement, takes the form of the so-called "last best offer" or "final offer" arbitration, under which each competent authority is required to give to an arbitrator appointed by common consent that competent authority's own reply to the questions included in the Terms of Reference and the arbitrator simply chooses one of the submitted replies. The competent authorities may, as for most procedural rules, amend or supplement the streamlined process through the Terms of Reference applicable to a particular case.

Selection of arbitrators

14.   Paragraph 5 of the sample agreement describes how arbitrators will be selected unless the Terms of Reference drafted for a particular case provide otherwise (for instance, by opting for the streamlined process described in the preceding paragraph or by providing for more than one arbitrator to be appointed by each competent authority). Normally, the two competent authorities will each appoint one arbitrator. These appointments must be made within three months after the Terms of Reference

have been received by the person who made the request for arbitration (a different deadline is provided for cases where the competent authorities do not agree on the Terms of Reference within the required period). The arbitrators thus appointed will select a Chair who must be appointed within two months of the time at which the last of the initial appointments was made. If the competent authorities do not appoint an arbitrator during the required period, or if the arbitrators so appointed do not appoint the third arbitrator within the required period, the paragraph provides that the appointment will be made by the Director of the OECD Centre for Tax Policy and Administration. The competent authorities may, of course, provide for other ways to address these rare situations but it seems important to provide for an independent appointing authority to solve any deadlock in the selection of the arbitrators.

15.   There is no need for the agreement to stipulate any particular qualifications for an arbitrator as it will be in the interests of the competent authorities to have qualified and suitable persons act as arbitrators and in the interests of the arbitrators to have a qualified Chair. However, it might be possible to develop a list of qualified persons to facilitate the appointment process and this function could be developed by the Committee on Fiscal Affairs. It is important that the Chair of the panel have experience with the types of procedural, evidentiary and logistical issues which are likely to arise in the course of the arbitral proceedings as well as having familiarity with tax issues. There may be advantages in having representatives of each Contracting State appointed as arbitrators as they would be familiar with this type of issue. Thus it should be possible to appoint to the panel governmental officials who have not been directly involved in the case. Once an arbitrator has been appointed, it should be clear that his role is to decide the case on a neutral and objective basis; he is no longer functioning as an advocate for the country that appointed him.

16.   Paragraph 9 of the sample agreement provides that the appointment of the arbitrators may be postponed where both competent authorities agree that the failure to reach a mutual agreement within the two year period is mainly attributable to the lack of cooperation by a person directly affected by the case. In that case, the approach taken by the sample agreement is to allow the competent authorities to postpone the appointment of the arbitrators by a period of time corresponding to the undue delay in providing them with the relevant information. If that information has not yet been provided when the request for arbitration is submitted, the period of time corresponding to the delay in providing the information continues to run until such information is finally provided. Where, however, the competent authorities are not provided with the information necessary to solve a particular case, there is nothing that prevents them from resolving the case on the basis of the limited information that is at their disposal, thereby preventing any access to arbitration. Also, it would be possible to provide in the agreement that if within an additional period (*e.g.* one year), the taxpayer still had not provided the necessary information for the competent authorities to properly evaluate the issue, the issue would no longer be required to be submitted to arbitration.

Communication of information and confidentiality

17. It is important that arbitrators be allowed full access to the information needed to resolve the issues submitted to arbitration but, at the same time, be subjected to the same strict confidentiality requirements as regards that information as apply to the competent authorities themselves. The proposed approach to ensure that result, which is incorporated in paragraph 8 of the sample agreement, is to make the arbitrators authorised representatives of the competent authorities. This, however, will only be for the purposes of the application of the relevant provisions of the Convention (i.e. Articles 25 and 26) and of the provisions of the domestic laws of the Contracting States, which would normally include the sanctions applicable in case of a breach of confidentiality. The designation of the arbitrator as authorised representative of a competent authority would typically be confirmed in the letter of appointment but may need to be done differently if domestic law requires otherwise or if the arbitrator is not appointed by a competent authority.

Procedural and evidentiary rules

18. The simplest way to establish the evidentiary and other procedural rules that will govern the arbitration process and that have not already been provided in the agreement or the Terms of Reference is to leave it to the arbitrators to develop these rules on an ad hoc basis. In doing so, the arbitrators are free to refer to existing arbitration procedures, such as the International Chamber of Commerce Rules which deal with many of these questions. It should be made clear in the procedural rules that as general matter, the factual material on which the arbitral panel will base its decision will be that developed in the mutual agreement procedure. Only in special situations would the panel be allowed to investigate factual issues which had not been developed in the earlier stages of the case.

19. Paragraph 10 of the sample agreement follows that approach. Thus, decisions as regards the dates and format of arbitration meetings will be made by the arbitrators unless the agreement or Terms of Reference provide otherwise. Also, whilst the arbitrators will have access to all information necessary to decide the issues submitted to arbitration, including confidential information, any information that was not available to both competent authorities shall not be taken into account by the arbitrators unless the competent authorities agree otherwise.

Taxpayer participation in the supplementary dispute resolution process

20. Paragraph 11 of the sample agreement provides that the person requesting arbitration, either directly or through his representatives, is entitled to present a written submission to the arbitrators and, if the arbitrators agree, to make an oral presentation during a meeting of the arbitrators.

Practical arrangements

21.   A number of practical arrangements will need to be made in connection with the actual functioning of the arbitral process. They include the location of the meetings, the language of the proceedings and possible translation facilities, the keeping of a record, dealing with practical details such as filing etc.

22.   As regards the location and the logistical arrangements for the arbitral meetings, the easiest solution is to leave the matter to be dealt with by the competent authority to which the case giving rise to the arbitration was initially presented. That competent authority should also provide the administrative personnel necessary for the conduct of the arbitration process. This is the approach put forward in paragraph 12 of the sample agreement. It is expected that, for these purposes, the competent authority will use meeting facilities and personnel that it already has at its disposal. The two competent authorities are, however, entitled to agree otherwise (*e.g.* to take advantage of another meeting in a different location that would be attended by both competent authorities and the arbitrators).

23.   It is provided that the administrative personnel provided for the conduct of the arbitration process will report only to the Chair of the arbitration panel concerning any matter related to that procedure.

24.   The language of the proceedings and whether, and which, translation facilities should be provided is a matter that should normally be dealt with in the Terms of Reference. It may be, however, that a need for translation or recording will only arise after the beginning of the proceedings. In that case, the competent authorities are entitled to reach agreement for that purpose. In the absence of such agreement, the arbitrators could, at the request of one competent authority and pursuant to paragraph 10 of the sample agreement, decide to provide such translation or recording; in that case, however, the costs thereof would have to be borne by the requesting party (see under "Costs" below).

25.   Other practical details (*e.g.* notice and filing of documents) should be similarly dealt with. Thus, any such matter should be decided by agreement between the competent authorities (ideally, included in the Terms of Reference) and, failing such agreement, by decision of the arbitrators.

Costs

26.   Different costs may arise in relation to the arbitration process and it should be clear who should bear these costs. Paragraph 13 of the sample agreement, which deals with this issue, is based on the principle that where a competent authority or a person involved in the case can control the amount of a particular cost, this cost should be borne by that party and that other costs should be borne equally by the two competent authorities.

27.   Thus, it seems logical to provide that each competent authority, as well as the person who requested the arbitration, should pay for its own participation in the

arbitration proceedings. This would include costs of being represented at the meetings and of preparing and presenting a position and arguments, whether in writing or orally.

28. The fees to be paid to the arbitrators are likely to be one of the major costs of the arbitration process. Each competent authority will bear the remuneration of the arbitrator appointed exclusively by that competent authority (or appointed by the Director of the OECD Centre for Tax Policy and Administration because of the failure of that competent authority to appoint that arbitrator), together with that arbitrator's travel, telecommunication and secretariat costs.

29. The fees and the travel, telecommunication and secretariat costs of the other arbitrators will, however, be shared equally by the competent authorities. The competent authorities will normally agree to incur these costs at the time that the arbitrators are appointed and this would typically be confirmed in the letter of appointment. The fees should be large enough to ensure that appropriately qualified experts could be recruited. One possibility would be to use a fee structure similar to that established under the EU Arbitration Convention Code of Conduct.

30. The costs related to the meetings of the arbitral panel, including those of the administrative personnel necessary for the conduct of the arbitration process, should be borne by the competent authority to which the case giving rise to the arbitration was initially presented, as long as that competent authority is required to arrange such meetings and provide the administrative personnel (see paragraph 12 of the sample agreement). In most cases, that competent authority will use meeting facilities and personnel that it already has at its disposal and it would seem inappropriate to try to allocate part of the costs thereof to the other competent authority. Clearly, the reference to "costs related to the meetings" does not include the travel and accommodation costs incurred by the participants; these are dealt with above.

31. The other costs (not including any costs resulting from the taxpayers' participation in the process) should be borne equally by the two competent authorities as long as they have agreed to incur the relevant expenses. This would include costs related to translation and recording that both competent authorities have agreed to provide. In the absence of such agreement, the party that has requested that particular costs be incurred should pay for these.

32. As indicated in paragraph 13 of the sample agreement, the competent authorities may, however, agree to a different allocation of costs. Such agreement can be included in the Terms of Reference or be made afterwards (e.g. when unforeseen expenses arise).

Applicable legal principles

33. An examination of the issues on which competent authorities have had difficulties reaching an agreement shows that these are typically matters of treaty interpretation or of applying the arm's length principle underlying Article 9 and paragraph 2 of Article 7. As provided in paragraph 14 of the sample agreement, matters

of treaty interpretation should be decided by the arbitrators in the light of the principles of interpretation incorporated in Articles 31 to 33 of the *Vienna Convention on the Law of Treaties*, having regard to these Commentaries as periodically amended, as explained in paragraphs 28 to 36.1 of the Introduction. Issues related to the application of the arm's length principle should similarly be decided in the light of the OECD *Transfer Pricing Guidelines for Multinational Enterprises and Tax Administrations*. Since Article 32 of the *Vienna Convention on the Law of Treaties* permits a wide access to supplementary means of interpretation, arbitrators will, in practice, have considerable latitude in determining relevant sources for the interpretation of treaty provisions.

34.   In many cases, the application of the provisions of a tax convention depends on issues of domestic law (for example, the definition of immovable property in paragraph 2 of Article 6 depends primarily on the domestic law meaning of that term). As a general rule, it would seem inappropriate to ask arbitrators to make an independent determination of purely domestic legal issues and the description of the issues to be resolved, which will be included in the Terms of Reference, should take this into account. There may be cases, however, where there would be legitimate differences of views on a matter of domestic law and in such cases, the competent authorities may wish to leave that matter to be decided by an arbitrator who is an expert in the relevant area.

35.   Also, there may be cases where the competent authorities agree that the interpretation or application of a provision of a tax treaty depends on a particular document (*e.g.* a memorandum of understanding or mutual agreement concluded after the entry into force of a treaty) but may disagree about the interpretation of that document. In such a case, the competent authorities may wish to make express reference to that document in the Terms of Reference.

Arbitration decision

36.   Paragraph 15 of the sample agreement provides that where more than one arbitrator has been appointed, the arbitration decision will be determined by a simple majority of the arbitrators. Unless otherwise provided in the Terms of Reference, the decision is presented in writing and indicates the sources of law relied upon and the reasoning which led to its result. It is important that the arbitrators support their decision with the reasoning leading to it. Showing the method through which the decision was reached is important in assuring acceptance of the decision by all relevant participants.

37.   Pursuant to paragraph 16, the arbitration decision must be communicated to the competent authorities and the person who made the request for arbitration within six months from the date on which the Chair notifies in writing the competent authorities and the person who made the request for arbitration that he has received all of the information necessary to begin consideration of the case. However, at any time within two months from the date on which the last arbitrator was appointed, the Chair, with the consent of one of the competent authorities, may notify in writing the other

competent authority and the person who made the request for arbitration that he has not received all the information necessary to begin consideration of the case. In that case, a further two months will be given for the necessary information to be sent to the Chair. If the information is not received by the Chair within that period, it is provided that the decision will be rendered within the next six months without taking that information into account (unless both competent authorities agree otherwise). If, on the other hand, the information is received by the Chair within the two month period, that information will be taken into account and the decision will be communicated within six months from the reception of that information.

38.   In order to deal with the unusual circumstances in which the arbitrators may be unable or unwilling to present an arbitration decision, paragraph 17 provides that if the decision is not communicated within the relevant period, the competent authorities may agree to extend the period for presenting the arbitration decision or, if they fail to reach such agreement within one month, appoint new arbitrators to deal with the case. In the case of the appointment of new arbitrators, the arbitration process would go back to the point where the original arbitrators were appointed and will continue with the new arbitrators.

Publication of the decision

39.   Decisions on individual cases reached under the mutual agreement procedure are generally not made public. In the case of reasoned arbitral decisions, however, publishing the decisions would lend additional transparency to the process. Also, whilst the decision would not be in any sense a formal precedent, having the material in the public domain could influence the course of other cases so as to avoid subsequent disputes and lead to a more uniform approach to the same issue.

40.   Paragraph 15 of the sample agreement therefore provides for the possibility to publish the decision. Such publication, however, should only be made if both competent authorities and the person who made the arbitration request so agree. Also, in order to maintain the confidentiality of information communicated to the competent authorities, the publication should be made in a form that would not disclose the names of the parties nor any element that would help to identify them.

Implementing the decision

41.   Once the arbitration process has provided a binding solution to the issues that the competent authorities have been unable to resolve, the competent authorities will proceed to conclude a mutual agreement that reflects that decision and that will be presented to the persons directly affected by the case. In order to avoid further delays, it is suggested that the mutual agreement that incorporates the solution arrived at should be completed and presented to the taxpayer within six months from the date of the communication of the decision. This is provided in paragraph 19 of the sample agreement.

42.   Paragraph 2 of Article 25 provides that the competent authorities have the obligation to implement the agreement reached notwithstanding any time limit in their domestic law. Paragraph 5 of the Article also provides that the arbitration decision is binding on both Contracting States. Failure to assess taxpayers in accordance with the agreement or to implement the arbitration decision through the conclusion of a mutual agreement would therefore result in taxation not in accordance with the Convention and, as such, would allow the person whose taxation is affected to seek relief through domestic legal remedies or by making a new request pursuant to paragraph 1 of the Article.

43.   Paragraph 20 of the sample agreement deals with the case where the competent authorities are able to solve the unresolved issues that led to arbitration before the decision is rendered. Since the arbitration process is an exceptional mechanism to deal with issues that cannot be solved under the usual mutual agreement procedure, it is appropriate to put an end to that exceptional mechanism if the competent authorities are able to resolve these issues by themselves. The competent authorities may agree on a resolution of these issues as long as the arbitration decision has not been rendered.

MODEL TAX CONVENTION (CONDENSED VERSION) – ISBN 978-92-64-08948-8 – © OECD 2010

COMMENTARY ON ARTICLE 26
CONCERNING THE EXCHANGE OF INFORMATION

I. Preliminary remarks

1. There are good grounds for including in a convention for the avoidance of double taxation provisions concerning co-operation between the tax administrations of the two Contracting States. In the first place it appears to be desirable to give administrative assistance for the purpose of ascertaining facts in relation to which the rules of the convention are to be applied. Moreover, in view of the increasing internationalisation of economic relations, the Contracting States have a growing interest in the reciprocal supply of information on the basis of which domestic taxation laws have to be administered, even if there is no question of the application of any particular article of the Convention.

2. Therefore the present Article embodies the rules under which information may be exchanged to the widest possible extent, with a view to laying the proper basis for the implementation of the domestic tax laws of the Contracting States and for the application of specific provisions of the Convention. The text of the Article makes it clear that the exchange of information is not restricted by Articles 1 and 2, so that the information may include particulars about non-residents and may relate to the administration or enforcement of taxes not referred to in Article 2.

3. The matter of administrative assistance for the purpose of tax collection is dealt with in Article 27.

4. In 2002, the Committee on Fiscal Affairs undertook a comprehensive review of Article 26 to ensure that it reflects current country practices. That review also took into account recent developments such as the *Model Agreement on Exchange of Information on Tax Matters*[1] developed by the OECD Global Forum Working Group on Effective Exchange of Information and the ideal standard of access to bank information as described in the report *Improving Access to Bank Information for Tax Purposes.*[2] As a result, several changes to both the text of the Article and the Commentary were made in 2005.

4.1 Many of the changes that were then made to the Article were not intended to alter its substance, but instead were made to remove doubts as to its proper interpretation. For instance, the change from "necessary" to "foreseeably relevant" and the insertion of the words "to the administration or enforcement" in paragraph 1 were made to achieve consistency with the *Model Agreement on Exchange of Information on Tax Matters* and were not intended to alter the effect of the provision. New paragraph 4 was added to incorporate into the text of the Article the general understanding previously expressed in the Commentary (see paragraph 19.6). New paragraph 5 was added to reflect current practices among the vast majority of OECD member countries (see

---

1 Available on *www.oecd.org/taxation*.
2 OECD, Paris, 2000. Available on *www.oecd.org/taxation*.

paragraph 19.10). The insertion of the words "or the oversight of the above" into new paragraph 2, on the other hand, constitutes a reversal of the previous rule.

4.2   The Commentary also has been expanded considerably. This expansion in part reflects the addition of new paragraphs 4 and 5 to the Article. Other changes were made to the Commentary to take into account recent developments and current country practices and more generally to remove doubts as to the proper interpretation of the Article.

II.   Commentary on the provisions of the Article

Paragraph 1

5.   The main rule concerning the exchange of information is contained in the first sentence of the paragraph. The competent authorities of the Contracting States shall exchange such information as is foreseeably relevant to secure the correct application of the provisions of the Convention or of the domestic laws of the Contracting States concerning taxes of every kind and description imposed in these States even if, in the latter case, a particular Article of the Convention need not be applied. The standard of "foreseeable relevance" is intended to provide for exchange of information in tax matters to the widest possible extent and, at the same time, to clarify that Contracting States are not at liberty to engage in "fishing expeditions" or to request information that is unlikely to be relevant to the tax affairs of a given taxpayer. Contracting States may agree to an alternative formulation of this standard that is consistent with the scope of the Article (*e.g.* by replacing, "foreseeably relevant" with "necessary" or "relevant"). The scope of exchange of information covers all tax matters without prejudice to the general rules and legal provisions governing the rights of defendants and witnesses in judicial proceedings. Exchange of information for criminal tax matters can also be based on bilateral or multilateral treaties on mutual legal assistance (to the extent they also apply to tax crimes). In order to keep the exchange of information within the framework of the Convention, a limitation to the exchange of information is set so that information should be given only insofar as the taxation under the domestic taxation laws concerned is not contrary to the Convention.

5.1   The information covered by paragraph 1 is not limited to taxpayer-specific information. The competent authorities may also exchange other sensitive information related to tax administration and compliance improvement, for example risk analysis techniques or tax avoidance or evasion schemes.

5.2   The possibilities of assistance provided by the Article do not limit, nor are they limited by, those contained in existing international agreements or other arrangements between the Contracting States which relate to co-operation in tax matters. Since the exchange of information concerning the application of custom duties has a legal basis in other international instruments, the provisions of these more specialised instruments will generally prevail and the exchange of information concerning custom duties will not, in practice, be governed by the Article.

6.   The following examples may clarify the principle dealt with in paragraph 5 above. In all such cases information can be exchanged under paragraph 1.

7.   Application of the Convention

   a) When applying Article 12, State A where the beneficiary is resident asks State B where the payer is resident, for information concerning the amount of royalty transmitted.

   b) Conversely, in order to grant the exemption provided for in Article 12, State B asks State A whether the recipient of the amounts paid is in fact a resident of the last-mentioned State and the beneficial owner of the royalties.

   c) Similarly, information may be needed with a view to the proper allocation of profits between associated enterprises in different States or the proper determination of the profits attributable to a permanent establishment situated in one State of an enterprise of the other State (Articles 7, 9, 23 A and 23 B).

   d) Information may be needed for the purposes of applying Article 25.

   e) When applying Articles 15 and 23 A, State A, where the employee is resident, informs State B, where the employment is exercised for more than 183 days, of the amount exempted from taxation in State A.

8.   Implementation of the domestic laws

   a) A company in State A supplies goods to an independent company in State B. State A wishes to know from State B what price the company in State B paid for the goods with a view to a correct application of the provisions of its domestic laws.

   b) A company in State A sells goods through a company in State C (possibly a low-tax country) to a company in State B. The companies may or may not be associated. There is no convention between State A and State C, nor between State B and State C. Under the convention between A and B, State A, with a view to ensuring the correct application of the provisions of its domestic laws to the profits made by the company situated in its territory, asks State B what price the company in State B paid for the goods.

   c) State A, for the purpose of taxing a company situated in its territory, asks State B, under the convention between A and B, for information about the prices charged by a company in State B, or a group of companies in State B with which the company in State A has no business contacts in order to enable it to check the prices charged by the company in State A by direct comparison (e.g. prices charged by a company or a group of companies in a dominant position). It should be borne in mind that the exchange of information in this case might be a difficult and delicate matter owing in particular to the provisions of subparagraph c) of paragraph 3 relating to business and other secrets.

   d) State A, for the purpose of verifying VAT input tax credits claimed by a company situated in its territory for services performed by a company resident in State B, requests confirmation that the cost of services was properly entered into the books and records of the company in State B.

9.   The rule laid down in paragraph 1 allows information to be exchanged in three different ways:

a) on request, with a special case in mind, it being understood that the regular sources of information available under the internal taxation procedure should be relied upon in the first place before a request for information is made to the other State;

b) automatically, for example when information about one or various categories of income having their source in one Contracting State and received in the other Contracting State is transmitted systematically to the other State (see the OECD Council Recommendation C(81)39, dated 5 May 1981, entitled *Recommendation of the Council concerning a standardised form for automatic exchanges of information under international tax agreements*, the OECD Council Recommendation C(92)50, dated 23 July 1992, entitled *Recommendation of the Council concerning a standard magnetic format for automatic exchange of tax information*, the OECD Council Recommendation on the use of *Tax Identification Numbers in an international context* C(97)29/FINAL dated 13 March 1997, the OECD Council Recommendation C(97)30/FINAL dated 10 July 1997 entitled *Recommendation of the Council of the OECD on the Use of the Revised Standard Magnetic Format for Automatic Exchange of Information* and the OECD Council Recommendation on the use of the OECD *Model Memorandum of Understanding on Automatic Exchange of Information for Tax Purposes* C(2001)28/FINAL);[1]

c) spontaneously, for example in the case of a State having acquired through certain investigations, information which it supposes to be of interest to the other State.

9.1   These three forms of exchange (on request, automatic and spontaneous) may also be combined. It should also be stressed that the Article does not restrict the possibilities of exchanging information to these methods and that the Contracting States may use other techniques to obtain information which may be relevant to both Contracting States such as simultaneous examinations, tax examinations abroad and industry-wide exchange of information. These techniques are fully described in the publication *Tax Information Exchange between OECD Member Countries: A Survey of Current Practices*[2] and can be summarised as follows:

— a simultaneous examination is an arrangement between two or more parties to examine simultaneously each in its own territory, the tax affairs of (a) taxpayer(s) in which they have a common or related interest, with a view of exchanging any relevant information which they so obtain (see the OECD Council Recommendation C(92)81, dated 23 July 1992, on an OECD Model agreement for the undertaking of simultaneous examinations);

— a tax examination abroad allows for the possibility to obtain information through the presence of representatives of the competent authority of the requesting Contracting State. To the extent allowed by its domestic law, a Contracting State

---

1   OECD Recommendations are available on *www.oecd.org/taxation*.
2   OECD, Paris, 1994.

may permit authorised representatives of the other Contracting State to enter the first Contracting State to interview individuals or examine a person's books and records, — or to be present at such interviews or examinations carried out by the tax authorities of the first Contracting State — in accordance with procedures mutually agreed upon by the competent authorities. Such a request might arise, for example, where the taxpayer in a Contracting State is permitted to keep records in the other Contracting State. This type of assistance is granted on a reciprocal basis. Countries' laws and practices differ as to the scope of rights granted to foreign tax officials. For instance, there are States where a foreign tax official will be prevented from any active participation in an investigation or examination on the territory of a country; there are also States where such participation is only possible with the taxpayer's consent. The Joint Council of Europe/OECD Convention on Mutual Administrative Assistance in Tax Matters specifically addresses tax examinations abroad in its Article 9;

— an industry-wide exchange of information is the exchange of tax information especially concerning a whole economic sector (e.g. the oil or pharmaceutical industry, the banking sector, etc.) and not taxpayers in particular.

10.   The manner in which the exchange of information agreed to in the Convention will finally be effected can be decided upon by the competent authorities of the Contracting States. For example, Contracting States may wish to use electronic or other communication and information technologies, including appropriate security systems, to improve the timeliness and quality of exchanges of information. Contracting States which are required, according to their law, to observe data protection laws, may wish to include provisions in their bilateral conventions concerning the protection of personal data exchanged. Data protection concerns the rights and fundamental freedoms of an individual, and in particular, the right to privacy, with regard to automatic processing of personal data. See, for example, the *Council of Europe Convention for the Protection of Individuals with regard to Automatic Processing of Personal Data* of 28 January 1981.[1]

10.1 Before 2000, the paragraph only authorised the exchange of information, and the use of the information exchanged, in relation to the taxes covered by the Convention under the general rules of Article 2. As drafted, the paragraph did not oblige the requested State to comply with a request for information concerning the imposition of a sales tax as such a tax was not covered by the Convention. The paragraph was then amended so as to apply to the exchange of information concerning any tax imposed on behalf of the Contracting States, or of their political subdivisions or local authorities, and to allow the use of the information exchanged for purposes of the application of all such taxes. Some Contracting States may not, however, be in a position to exchange information, or to use the information obtained from a treaty partner, in relation to taxes that are not covered by the Convention under the general rules of Article 2. Such

---

1   See *http://conventions.coe.int.*

States are free to restrict the scope of paragraph 1 of the Article to the taxes covered by the Convention.

10.2 In some cases, a Contracting State may need to receive information in a particular form to satisfy its evidentiary or other legal requirements. Such forms may include depositions of witnesses and authenticated copies of original records. Contracting States should endeavour as far as possible to accommodate such requests. Under paragraph 3, the requested State may decline to provide the information in the specific form requested if, for instance, the requested form is not known or permitted under its law or administrative practice. A refusal to provide the information in the form requested does not affect the obligation to provide the information.

10.3 Nothing in the Convention prevents the application of the provisions of the Article to the exchange of information that existed prior to the entry into force of the Convention, as long as the assistance with respect to this information is provided after the Convention has entered into force and the provisions of the Article have become effective. Contracting States may find it useful, however, to clarify the extent to which the provisions of the Article are applicable to such information, in particular when the provisions of that convention will have effect with respect to taxes arising or levied from a certain time.

Paragraph 2

11. Reciprocal assistance between tax administrations is feasible only if each administration is assured that the other administration will treat with proper confidence the information which it will receive in the course of their co-operation. The confidentiality rules of paragraph 2 apply to all types of information received under paragraph 1, including both information provided in a request and information transmitted in response to a request. The maintenance of secrecy in the receiving Contracting State is a matter of domestic laws. It is therefore provided in paragraph 2 that information communicated under the provisions of the Convention shall be treated as secret in the receiving State in the same manner as information obtained under the domestic laws of that State. Sanctions for the violation of such secrecy in that State will be governed by the administrative and penal laws of that State.

12. The information obtained may be disclosed only to persons and authorities involved in the assessment or collection of, the enforcement or prosecution in respect of, the determination of appeals in relation to the taxes with respect to which information may be exchanged according to the first sentence of paragraph 1, or the oversight of the above. This means that the information may also be communicated to the taxpayer, his proxy or to the witnesses. This also means that information can be disclosed to governmental or judicial authorities charged with deciding whether such information should be released to the taxpayer, his proxy or to the witnesses. The information received by a Contracting State may be used by such persons or authorities only for the purposes mentioned in paragraph 2. Furthermore, information covered by paragraph 1, whether taxpayer-specific or not, should not be disclosed to persons or authorities not mentioned in paragraph 2, regardless of domestic information

disclosure laws such as freedom of information or other legislation that allows greater access to governmental documents.

12.1 Information can also be disclosed to oversight bodies. Such oversight bodies include authorities that supervise tax administration and enforcement authorities as part of the general administration of the Government of a Contracting State. In their bilateral negotiations, however, Contracting States may depart from this principle and agree to exclude the disclosure of information to such supervisory bodies.

12.2 The information received by a Contracting State may not be disclosed to a third country unless there is an express provision in the bilateral treaty between the Contracting States allowing such disclosure.

12.3 Similarly, if the information appears to be of value to the receiving State for other purposes than those referred to in paragraph 12, that State may not use the information for such other purposes but it must resort to means specifically designed for those purposes (e.g. in case of a non-fiscal crime, to a treaty concerning judicial assistance). However, Contracting States may wish to allow the sharing of tax information by tax authorities with other law enforcement agencies and judicial authorities on certain high priority matters (e.g. to combat money laundering, corruption, terrorism financing). Contracting States wishing to broaden the purposes for which they may use information exchanged under this Article may do so by adding the following text to the end of paragraph 2:

> Notwithstanding the foregoing, information received by a Contracting State may be used for other purposes when such information may be used for such other purposes under the laws of both States and the competent authority of the supplying State authorises such use.

13. As stated in paragraph 12, the information obtained can be communicated to the persons and authorities mentioned and on the basis of the last sentence of paragraph 2 of the Article can be disclosed by them in court sessions held in public or in decisions which reveal the name of the taxpayer. Once information is used in public court proceedings or in court decisions and thus rendered public, it is clear that from that moment such information can be quoted from the court files or decisions for other purposes even as possible evidence. But this does not mean that the persons and authorities mentioned in paragraph 2 are allowed to provide on request additional information received. If either or both of the Contracting States object to the information being made public by courts in this way, or, once the information has been made public in this way, to the information being used for other purposes, because this is not the normal procedure under their domestic laws, they should state this expressly in their convention.

Paragraph 3

14. This paragraph contains certain limitations to the main rule in favour of the requested State. In the first place, the paragraph contains the clarification that a Contracting State is not bound to go beyond its own internal laws and administrative

practice in putting information at the disposal of the other Contracting State. However, internal provisions concerning tax secrecy should not be interpreted as constituting an obstacle to the exchange of information under the present Article. As mentioned above, the authorities of the requesting State are obliged to observe secrecy with regard to information received under this Article.

14.1 Some countries' laws include procedures for notifying the person who provided the information and/or the taxpayer that is subject to the enquiry prior to the supply of information. Such notification procedures may be an important aspect of the rights provided under domestic law. They can help prevent mistakes (e.g. in cases of mistaken identity) and facilitate exchange (by allowing taxpayers who are notified to co-operate voluntarily with the tax authorities in the requesting State). Notification procedures should not, however, be applied in a manner that, in the particular circumstances of the request, would frustrate the efforts of the requesting State. In other words, they should not prevent or unduly delay effective exchange of information. For instance, notification procedures should permit exceptions from prior notification, e.g. in cases in which the information request is of a very urgent nature or the notification is likely to undermine the chance of success of the investigation conducted by the requesting State. A Contracting State that under its domestic law is required to notify the person who provided the information and/or the taxpayer that an exchange of information is proposed should inform its treaty partners in writing that it has this requirement and what the consequences are for its obligations in relation to mutual assistance. Such information should be provided to the other Contracting State when a convention is concluded and thereafter whenever the relevant rules are modified.

15.   Furthermore, the requested State does not need to go so far as to carry out administrative measures that are not permitted under the laws or practice of the requesting State or to supply items of information that are not obtainable under the laws or in the normal course of administration of the requesting State. It follows that a Contracting State cannot take advantage of the information system of the other Contracting State if it is wider than its own system. Thus, a State may refuse to provide information where the requesting State would be precluded by law from obtaining or providing the information or where the requesting State's administrative practices (e.g. failure to provide sufficient administrative resources) result in a lack of reciprocity. However, it is recognised that too rigorous an application of the principle of reciprocity could frustrate effective exchange of information and that reciprocity should be interpreted in a broad and pragmatic manner. Different countries will necessarily have different mechanisms for obtaining and providing information. Variations in practices and procedures should not be used as a basis for denying a request unless the effect of these variations would be to limit in a significant way the requesting State's overall ability to obtain and provide the information if the requesting State itself received a legitimate request from the requested State.

15.1 The principle of reciprocity has no application where the legal system or administrative practice of only one country provides for a specific procedure. For instance, a country requested to provide information could not point to the absence of a ruling regime in the country requesting information and decline to provide information on a ruling it has granted, based on a reciprocity argument. Of course, where the requested information itself is not obtainable under the laws or in the normal course of the administrative practice of the requesting State, a requested State may decline such a request.

15.2 Most countries recognise under their domestic laws that information cannot be obtained from a person to the extent that such person can claim the privilege against self-incrimination. A requested State may, therefore, decline to provide information if the requesting State would have been precluded by its own self-incrimination rules from obtaining the information under similar circumstances. In practice, however, the privilege against self-incrimination should have little, if any, application in connection with most information requests. The privilege against self-incrimination is personal and cannot be claimed by an individual who himself is not at risk of criminal prosecution. The overwhelming majority of information requests seek to obtain information from third parties such as banks, intermediaries or the other party to a contract and not from the individual under investigation. Furthermore, the privilege against self-incrimination generally does not attach to persons other than natural persons.

16. Information is deemed to be obtainable in the normal course of administration if it is in the possession of the tax authorities or can be obtained by them in the normal procedure of tax determination, which may include special investigations or special examination of the business accounts kept by the taxpayer or other persons, provided that the tax authorities would make similar investigations or examinations for their own purposes.

17. The requested State is at liberty to refuse to give information in the cases referred to in the paragraphs above. However if it does give the requested information, it remains within the framework of the agreement on the exchange of information which is laid down in the Convention; consequently it cannot be objected that this State has failed to observe the obligation to secrecy.

18. If the structure of the information systems of two Contracting States is very different, the conditions under subparagraphs a) and b) of paragraph 3 will lead to the result that the Contracting States exchange very little information or perhaps none at all. In such a case, the Contracting States may find it appropriate to broaden the scope of the exchange of information.

18.1 Unless otherwise agreed to by the Contracting States, it can be assumed that the requested information could be obtained by the requesting State in a similar situation if that State has not indicated to the contrary.

19. In addition to the limitations referred to above, subparagraph c) of paragraph 3 contains a reservation concerning the disclosure of certain secret information. Secrets mentioned in this subparagraph should not be taken in too wide a sense. Before invoking this provision, a Contracting State should carefully weigh if the interests of the taxpayer really justify its application. Otherwise it is clear that too wide an

interpretation would in many cases render ineffective the exchange of information provided for in the Convention. The observations made in paragraph 17 above apply here as well. The requested State in protecting the interests of its taxpayers is given a certain discretion to refuse the requested information, but if it does supply the information deliberately the taxpayer cannot allege an infraction of the rules of secrecy.

19.1 In its deliberations regarding the application of secrecy rules, the Contracting State should also take into account the confidentiality rules of paragraph 2 of the Article. The domestic laws and practices of the requesting State together with the obligations imposed under paragraph 2, may ensure that the information cannot be used for the types of unauthorised purposes against which the trade or other secrecy rules are intended to protect. Thus, a Contracting State may decide to supply the information where it finds that there is no reasonable basis for assuming that a taxpayer involved may suffer any adverse consequences incompatible with information exchange.

19.2 In most cases of information exchange no issue of trade, business or other secret will arise. A trade or business secret is generally understood to mean facts and circumstances that are of considerable economic importance and that can be exploited practically and the unauthorised use of which may lead to serious damage (e.g. may lead to severe financial hardship). The determination, assessment or collection of taxes as such could not be considered to result in serious damage. Financial information, including books and records, does not by its nature constitute a trade, business or other secret. In certain limited cases, however, the disclosure of financial information might reveal a trade, business or other secret. For instance, a request for information on certain purchase records may raise such an issue if the disclosure of such information revealed the proprietary formula used in the manufacture of a product. The protection of such information may also extend to information in the possession of third persons. For instance, a bank might hold a pending patent application for safe keeping or a secret trade process or formula might be described in a loan application or in a contract held by a bank. In such circumstances, details of the trade, business or other secret should be excised from the documents and the remaining financial information exchanged accordingly.

19.3 A requested State may decline to disclose information relating to confidential communications between attorneys, solicitors or other admitted legal representatives in their role as such and their clients to the extent that the communications are protected from disclosure under domestic law. However, the scope of protection afforded to such confidential communications should be narrowly defined. Such protection does not attach to documents or records delivered to an attorney, solicitor or other admitted legal representative in an attempt to protect such documents or records from disclosure required by law. Also, information on the identity of a person such as a director or beneficial owner of a company is typically not protected as a confidential communication. Whilst the scope of protection afforded to confidential communications might differ among states, it should not be overly broad so as to hamper effective exchange of information. Communications between attorneys, solicitors or other admitted legal representatives and their clients are only confidential if, and to the extent that, such representatives act in their capacity as attorneys, solicitors or other admitted legal representatives and not in a different capacity, such as nominee shareholders, trustees, settlors, company directors or under a power of attorney to represent a company in its business affairs. An assertion that information is protected as a confidential communication between an attorney, solicitor or other admitted legal representative and its client should be adjudicated exclusively in the Contracting State under the laws of which it arises. Thus, it is not intended that the courts of the requested State should adjudicate claims based on the laws of the requesting State.

19.4 Contracting States wishing to refer expressly to the protection afforded to confidential communications between a client and an attorney, solicitor or other admitted legal representative may do so by adding the following text at the end of paragraph 3:

  d) to obtain or provide information which would reveal confidential communications between a client and an attorney, solicitor or other admitted legal representative where such communications are:

  (i) produced for the purposes of seeking or providing legal advice or

  (ii) produced for the purposes of use in existing or contemplated legal proceedings.

19.5 Paragraph 3 also includes a limitation with regard to information which concerns the vital interests of the State itself. To this end, it is stipulated that Contracting States do not have to supply information the disclosure of which would be contrary to public policy (*ordre public*). However, this limitation should only become relevant in extreme cases. For instance, such a case could arise if a tax investigation in the requesting State were motivated by political, racial, or religious persecution. The limitation may also be invoked where the information constitutes a state secret, for instance sensitive information held by secret services the disclosure of which would be contrary to the vital interests of the requested State. Thus, issues of public policy (*ordre public*) rarely arise in the context of information exchange between treaty partners.

Paragraph 4

19.6 Paragraph 4 was added in 2005 to deal explicitly with the obligation to exchange information in situations where the requested information is not needed by the requested State for domestic tax purposes. Prior to the addition of paragraph 4 this obligation was not expressly stated in the Article, but was clearly evidenced by the practices followed by member countries which showed that, when collecting information requested by a treaty partner, Contracting States often use the special examining or investigative powers provided by their laws for purposes of levying their domestic taxes even though they do not themselves need the information for these purposes. This principle is also stated in the report *Improving Access to Bank Information for Tax Purposes.*[1]

19.7 According to paragraph 4, Contracting States must use their information gathering measures, even though invoked solely to provide information to the other Contracting State. The term "information gathering measures" means laws and administrative or judicial procedures that enable a Contracting State to obtain and provide the requested information.

19.8 The second sentence of paragraph 4 makes clear that the obligation contained in paragraph 4 is subject to the limitations of paragraph 3 but also provides that such limitations cannot be construed to form the basis for declining to supply information where a country's laws or practices include a domestic tax interest requirement. Thus, whilst a requested State cannot invoke paragraph 3 and argue that under its domestic laws or practices it only supplies information in which it has an interest for its own tax purposes, it may, for instance, decline to supply the information to the extent that the provision of the information would disclose a trade secret.

19.9 For many countries the combination of paragraph 4 and their domestic law provide a sufficient basis for using their information gathering measures to obtain the requested information even in the absence of a domestic tax interest in the information. Other countries, however, may wish to clarify expressly in the convention that Contracting States must ensure that their competent authorities have the necessary powers to do so. Contracting States wishing to clarify this point may replace paragraph 4 with the following text:

> 4. In order to effectuate the exchange of information as provided in paragraph 1, each Contracting State shall take the necessary measures, including legislation, rule-making, or administrative arrangements, to ensure that its competent authority has sufficient powers under its domestic law to obtain information for the exchange of information regardless of whether that Contracting State may need such information for its own tax purposes.

Paragraph 5

19.10 Paragraph 1 imposes a positive obligation on a Contracting State to exchange all types of information. Paragraph 5 is intended to ensure that the limitations of paragraph 3 cannot be used to prevent the exchange of information held by banks, other financial institutions, nominees, agents and fiduciaries as well as ownership information. Whilst paragraph 5, which was added in 2005, represents a change in the structure of the Article it should not be interpreted as suggesting that the previous version of the Article did not authorise the exchange of such information. The vast majority of OECD member countries already exchanged such information under the previous version of the Article and the addition of paragraph 5 merely reflects current practice.

---

1   OECD, Paris, 2000 (at paragraph 21 *b*).

19.11 Paragraph 5 stipulates that a Contracting State shall not decline to supply information to a treaty partner solely because the information is held by a bank or other financial institution. Thus, paragraph 5 overrides paragraph 3 to the extent that paragraph 3 would otherwise permit a requested Contracting State to decline to supply information on grounds of bank secrecy. The addition of this paragraph to the Article reflects the international trend in this area as reflected in the *Model Agreement on Exchange of Information on Tax Matters*[1] and as described in the report, *Improving Access to Bank Information for Tax Purposes.*[2] In accordance with that report, access to information held by banks or other financial institutions may be by direct means or indirectly through a judicial or administrative process. The procedure for indirect access should not be so burdensome and time-consuming as to act as an impediment to access to bank information.

19.12 Paragraph 5 also provides that a Contracting State shall not decline to supply information solely because the information is held by persons acting in an agency or fiduciary capacity. For instance, if a Contracting State had a law under which all information held by a fiduciary was treated as a "professional secret" merely because it was held by a fiduciary, such State could not use such law as a basis for declining to provide the information to the other Contracting State. A person is generally said to act in a "fiduciary capacity" when the business which the person transacts, or the money or property which the person handles, is not its own or for its own benefit, but for the benefit of another person as to whom the fiduciary stands in a relation implying and necessitating confidence and trust on the one part and good faith on the other part, such as a trustee. The term "agency" is very broad and includes all forms of corporate service providers (*e.g.* company formation agents, trust companies, registered agents, lawyers).

19.13 Finally, paragraph 5 states that a Contracting State shall not decline to supply information solely because it relates to an ownership interest in a person, including companies and partnerships, foundations or similar organisational structures. Information requests cannot be declined merely because domestic laws or practices may treat ownership information as a trade or other secret.

19.14 Paragraph 5 does not preclude a Contracting State from invoking paragraph 3 to refuse to supply information held by a bank, financial institution, a person acting in an agency or fiduciary capacity or information relating to ownership interests. However, such refusal must be based on reasons unrelated to the person's status as a bank, financial institution, agent, fiduciary or nominee, or the fact that the information relates to ownership interests. For instance, a legal representative acting for a client may be acting in an agency capacity but for any information protected as a confidential communication between attorneys, solicitors or other admitted legal representatives and their clients, paragraph 3 continues to provide a possible basis for declining to supply the information.

---

1   OECD, Paris, 2000. Available on *www.oecd.org/taxation*.

2   OECD, Paris, 2000.

19.15   The following examples illustrate the application of paragraph 5:

a) Company X owns a majority of the stock in a subsidiary company Y, and both companies are incorporated under the laws of State A. State B is conducting a tax examination of business operations of company Y in State B. In the course of this examination the question of both direct and indirect ownership in company Y becomes relevant and State B makes a request to State A for ownership information of any person in company Y's chain of ownership. In its reply State A should provide to State B ownership information for both company X and Y.

b) An individual subject to tax in State A maintains a bank account with Bank B in State B. State A is examining the income tax return of the individual and makes a request to State B for all bank account income and asset information held by Bank B in order to determine whether there were deposits of untaxed earned income. State B should provide the requested bank information to State A.

Observation on the Commentary

20.   [Deleted]

21.   In connection with paragraph 15.1, *Greece* wishes to clarify that according to Article 28 of the Greek Constitution international tax treaties are applied under the terms of reciprocity.

COMMENTARY ON ARTICLE 27
CONCERNING THE ASSISTANCE IN THE COLLECTION OF TAXES

1.   This Article provides the rules under which Contracting States[1] may agree to provide each other assistance in the collection of taxes. In some States, national law or policy may prevent this form of assistance or set limitations to it. Also, in some cases, administrative considerations may not justify providing assistance in the collection of taxes to another State or may similarly limit it. During the negotiations, each Contracting State will therefore need to decide whether and to what extent assistance should be given to the other State based on various factors, including

— the stance taken in national law to providing assistance in the collection of other States' taxes;

— whether and to what extent the tax systems, tax administrations and legal standards of the two States are similar, particularly as concerns the protection of fundamental taxpayers' rights (e.g. timely and adequate notice of claims against the taxpayer, the right to confidentiality of taxpayer information, the right to appeal, the right to be heard and present argument and evidence, the right to be assisted by a counsel of the taxpayer's choice, the right to a fair trial, etc.);

— whether assistance in the collection of taxes will provide balanced and reciprocal benefits to both States;

— whether each State's tax administration will be able to effectively provide such assistance;

— whether trade and investment flows between the two States are sufficient to justify this form of assistance;

— whether for constitutional or other reasons the taxes to which the Article applies should be limited.

The Article should only be included in the Convention where each State concludes that, based on these factors, they can agree to provide assistance in the collection of taxes levied by the other State.

2.   The Article provides for comprehensive collection assistance. Some States may prefer to provide a more limited type of collection assistance. This may be the only form of collection assistance that they are generally able to provide or that they may agree to in a particular convention. For instance, a State may want to limit assistance to cases where the benefits of the Convention (e.g. a reduction of taxes in the State where income such as interest arises) have been claimed by persons not entitled to them. States wishing to provide such limited collection assistance are free to adopt bilaterally an alternative Article drafted along the following lines:

---

1   Throughout this Commentary on Article 27, the State making a request for assistance is referred to as the "requesting State" whilst the State from which assistance is requested is referred to as the "requested State".

Article 27
Assistance in the collection of taxes

1.   The Contracting States shall lend assistance to each other in the collection of tax to the extent needed to ensure that any exemption or reduced rate of tax granted under this Convention shall not be enjoyed by persons not entitled to such benefits. The competent authorities of the Contracting States may by mutual agreement settle the mode of application of this Article.

2.   In no case shall the provisions of this Article be construed so as to impose on a Contracting State the obligation:

  a) to carry out administrative measures at variance with the laws and administrative practice of that or of the other Contracting State;

  b) to carry out measures which would be contrary to public policy (*ordre public*).

Paragraph 1

3.   This paragraph contains the principle that a Contracting State is obliged to assist the other State in the collection of taxes owed to it, provided that the conditions of the Article are met. Paragraphs 3 and 4 provide the two forms that this assistance will take.

4.   The paragraph also provides that assistance under the Article is not restricted by Articles 1 and 2. Assistance must therefore be provided as regards a revenue claim owed to a Contracting State by any person, whether or not a resident of a Contracting State. Some Contracting States may, however, wish to limit assistance to taxes owed by residents of either Contracting State. Such States are free to restrict the scope of the Article by omitting the reference to Article 1 from the paragraph.

5.   Article 26 applies to the exchange of information for purposes of the provisions of this Article. The confidentiality of information exchanged for purposes of assistance in collection is thus ensured.

6.   The paragraph finally provides that the competent authorities of the Contracting States may, by mutual agreement, decide the details of the practical application of the provisions of the Article.

7.   Such agreement should, in particular, deal with the documentation that should accompany a request made pursuant to paragraph 3 or 4. It is common practice to agree that a request for assistance will be accompanied by such documentation as is required by the law of the requested State, or has been agreed to by the competent authorities of the Contracting States, and that is necessary to undertake, as the case may be, collection of the revenue claim or measures of conservancy. Such documentation may include, for example, a declaration that the revenue claim is enforceable and is owed by a person who cannot, under the law of the requesting State, prevent its collection or an official copy of the instrument permitting enforcement in the requesting State. An official translation of the documentation in the language of the requested State should also be provided. It could also be agreed, where appropriate, that the instrument permitting enforcement in the requesting State shall, where appropriate and in accordance with the provisions in force in the requested State, be

MODEL TAX CONVENTION (CONDENSED VERSION) – ISBN 978-92-64-08948-8 – © OECD 2010

accepted, recognised, supplemented or replaced, as soon as possible after the date of the receipt of the request for assistance, by an instrument permitting enforcement in the latter State.

8.   The agreement should also deal with the issue of the costs that will be incurred by the requested State in satisfying a request made under paragraph 3 or 4. In general, the costs of collecting a revenue claim are charged to the debtor but it is necessary to determine which State will bear costs that cannot be recovered from that person. The usual practice, in this respect, is to provide that in the absence of an agreement specific to a particular case, ordinary costs incurred by a State in providing assistance to the other State will not be reimbursed by that other State. Ordinary costs are those directly and normally related to the collection, i.e. those expected in normal domestic collection proceedings. In the case of extraordinary costs, however, the practice is to provide that these will be borne by the requesting State, unless otherwise agreed bilaterally. Such costs would cover, for instance, costs incurred when a particular type of procedure has been used at the request of the other State, or supplementary costs of experts, interpreters, or translators. Most States also consider as extraordinary costs the costs of judicial and bankruptcy proceedings. The agreement should provide a definition of extraordinary costs and consultation between the Contracting States should take place in any particular case where extraordinary costs are likely to be involved. It should also be agreed that, as soon as a Contracting State anticipates that extraordinary costs may be incurred, it will inform the other Contracting State and indicate the estimated amount of such costs so that the other State may decide whether such costs should be incurred. It is, of course, also possible for the Contracting States to provide that costs will be allocated on a basis different from what is described above; this may be necessary, for instance, where a request for assistance in collection is suspended or withdrawn under paragraph 7 or where the issue of costs incurred in providing assistance in collection is already dealt with in another legal instrument applicable to these States.

9.   In the agreement, the competent authorities may also deal with other practical issues such as:

— whether there should be a limit of time after which a request for assistance could no longer be made as regards a particular revenue claim;
— what should be the applicable exchange rate when a revenue claim is collected in a currency that differs from the one which is used in the requesting State;
— how should any amount collected pursuant to a request under paragraph 3 be remitted to the requesting State.

Paragraph 2

10.   Paragraph 2 defines the term "revenue claim" for purposes of the Article. The definition applies to any amount owed in respect of all taxes that are imposed on behalf of the Contracting States, or of their political subdivisions or local authorities, but only insofar as the imposition of such taxes is not contrary to the Convention or other instrument in force between the Contracting States. It also applies to the

interest, administrative penalties and costs of collection or conservancy that are related to such an amount. Assistance is therefore not restricted to taxes to which the Convention generally applies pursuant to Article 2, as is confirmed in paragraph 1.

11.   Some Contracting States may prefer to limit the application of the Article to taxes that are covered by the Convention under the general rules of Article 2. States wishing to do so should replace paragraphs 1 and 2 by the following:

1.   The Contracting States shall lend assistance to each other in the collection of revenue claims. This assistance is not restricted by Article 1. The competent authorities of the Contracting States may by mutual agreement settle the mode of application of this Article.

2.   The term "revenue claim" as used in this Article means any amount owed in respect of taxes covered by the Convention together with interest, administrative penalties and costs of collection or conservancy related to such amount.

12.   Similarly, some Contracting States may wish to limit the types of tax to which the provisions of the Article will apply or to clarify the scope of application of these provisions by including in the definition a detailed list of the taxes. States wishing to do so are free to adopt bilaterally the following definition:

The term "revenue claim" as used in this Article means any amount owed in respect of the following taxes imposed by the Contracting States, together with interest, administrative penalties and costs of collection or conservancy related to such amount:

a) (in State A): ...

b) (in State B): ...

13.   In order to make sure that the competent authorities can freely communicate information for purposes of the Article, Contracting States should ensure that the Article 26 is drafted in a way that allows exchanges of information with respect to any tax to which this Article applies.

14.   Nothing in the Convention prevents the application of the provisions of the Article to revenue claims that arise before the Convention enters into force, as long as assistance with respect to these claims is provided after the treaty has entered into force and the provisions of the Article have become effective. Contracting States may find it useful, however, to clarify the extent to which the provisions of the Article are applicable to such revenue claims, in particular when the provisions concerning the entry into force of their convention provide that the provisions of that convention will have effect with respect to taxes arising or levied from a certain time. States wishing to restrict the application of the Article to claims arising after the Convention enters into force are also free to do so in the course of bilateral negotiations.

Paragraph 3

15.   This paragraph stipulates the conditions under which a request for assistance in collection can be made. The revenue claim has to be enforceable under the law of the requesting State and be owed by a person who, at that time, cannot, under the law of

that State, prevent its collection. This will be the case where the requesting State has the right, under its internal law, to collect the revenue claim and the person owing the amount has no administrative or judicial rights to prevent such collection.

16.   In many States, a revenue claim can be collected even though there is still a right to appeal to an administrative body or a court as regards the validity or the amount of the claim. If, however, the internal law of the requested State does not allow it to collect its own revenue claims when appeals are still pending, the paragraph does not authorise it to do so in the case of revenue claims of the other State in respect of which such appeal rights still exist even if this does not prevent collection in that other State. Indeed, the phrase "collected by that other State in accordance with the provisions of its laws applicable to the enforcement and collection of its own taxes as if the revenue claim were a revenue claim of that other State" has the effect of making that requested State's internal law restriction applicable to the collection of the revenue claim of the other State. Many States, however, may wish to allow collection assistance where a revenue claim may be collected in the requesting State notwithstanding the existence of appeal rights even though the requested State's own law prevents collection in that case. States wishing to do so are free to modify paragraph 3 to read as follows:

> When a revenue claim of a Contracting State is enforceable under the laws of that State and is owed by a person who, at that time, cannot, under the laws of that State, prevent its collection, that revenue claim shall, at the request of the competent authority of that State, be accepted for purposes of collection by the competent authority of the other Contracting State. That revenue claim shall be collected by that other State in accordance with the provisions of its laws applicable to the enforcement and collection of its own taxes as if the revenue claim were a revenue claim of that other State that met the conditions allowing that other State to make a request under this paragraph.

17.   Paragraph 3 also regulates the way in which the revenue claim of the requesting State is to be collected by the requested State. Except with respect to time limits and priority (see the Commentary on paragraph 5), the requested State is obliged to collect the revenue claim of the requesting State as though it were the requested State's own revenue claim even if, at the time, it has no need to undertake collection actions related to that taxpayer for its own purposes. As already mentioned, the phrase "in accordance with the provisions of its law applicable to the enforcement and collection of its own taxes" has the effect of limiting collection assistance to claims with respect to which no further appeal rights exist if, under the requested State's internal law, collection of that State's own revenue claims are not permitted as long as such rights still exist.

18.   It is possible that the request may concern a tax that does not exist in the requested State. The requesting State shall indicate where appropriate the nature of the revenue claim, the components of the revenue claim, the date of expiry of the claim and the assets from which the revenue claim may be recovered. The requested State will then follow the procedure applicable to a claim for a tax of its own which is similar

to that of the requesting State or any other appropriate procedure if no similar tax exists.

Paragraph 4

19.   In order to safeguard the collection rights of a Contracting State, this paragraph enables it to request the other State to take measures of conservancy even where it cannot yet ask for assistance in collection, *e.g.* when the revenue claim is not yet enforceable or when the debtor still has the right to prevent its collection. This paragraph should only be included in conventions between States that are able to take measures of conservancy under their own laws. Also, States that consider that it is not appropriate to take measures of conservancy in respect of taxes owed to another State may decide not to include the paragraph in their conventions or to restrict its scope. In some States, measures of conservancy are referred to as "interim measures" and such States are free to add these words to the paragraph to clarify its scope in relation to their own terminology.

20.   One example of measures to which the paragraph applies is the seizure or the freezing of assets before final judgement to guarantee that these assets will still be available when collection can subsequently take place. The conditions required for the taking of measures of conservancy may vary from one State to another but in all cases the amount of the revenue claim should be determined beforehand, if only provisionally or partially. A request for measures of conservancy as regards a particular revenue claim cannot be made unless the requesting State can itself take such measures with respect to that claim (see the Commentary on paragraph 8).

21.   In making a request for measures of conservancy the requesting State should indicate in each case what stage in the process of assessment or collection has been reached. The requested State will then have to consider whether in such a case its own laws and administrative practice permit it to take measures of conservancy.

Paragraph 5

22.   Paragraph 5 first provides that the time limits of the requested State, *i.e.* time limitations beyond which a revenue claim cannot be enforced or collected, shall not apply to a revenue claim in respect of which the other State has made a request under paragraph 3 or 4. Since paragraph 3 refers to revenue claims that are enforceable in the requesting State and paragraph 4 to revenue claims in respect of which the requesting State can take measures of conservancy, it follows that it is the time limits of the requesting State that are solely applicable.

23.   Thus, as long as a revenue claim can still be enforced or collected (paragraph 3) or give rise to measures of conservancy (paragraph 4) in the requesting State, no objection based on the time limits provided under the laws of the requested State may be made to the application of paragraph 3 or 4 to that revenue claim. States which cannot agree to disregard their own domestic time limits should amend paragraph 5 accordingly.

24.   The Contracting States may agree that after a certain period of time the obligation to assist in the collection of the revenue claim no longer exists. The period should run from the date of the original instrument permitting enforcement. Legislation in some States requires renewal of the enforcement instrument, in which case the first instrument is the one that counts for purposes of calculating the time period after which the obligation to provide assistance ends.

25.   Paragraph 5 also provides that the rules of both the requested (first sentence) and requesting (second sentence) States giving their own revenue claims priority over the claims of other creditors shall not apply to a revenue claim in respect of which a request has been made under paragraph 3 or 4. Such rules are often included in domestic laws to ensure that tax authorities can collect taxes to the fullest possible extent.

26.   The rule according to which the priority rules of the requested State do not apply to a revenue claim of the other State in respect of which a request for assistance has been made applies even if the requested State must generally treat that claim as its own revenue claim pursuant to paragraphs 3 and 4. States wishing to provide that revenue claims of the other State should have the same priority as is applicable to their own revenue claims are free to amend the paragraph by deleting the words "or accorded any priority" in the first sentence.

27.   The words "by reason of their nature as such", which are found at the end of the first sentence, indicate that the time limits and priority rules of the requested State to which the paragraph applies are only those that are specific to unpaid taxes. Thus, the paragraph does not prevent the application of general rules concerning time limits or priority which would apply to all debts (*e.g.* rules giving priority to a claim by reason of that claim having arisen or having been registered before another one).

Paragraph 6

28.   This paragraph ensures that any legal or administrative objection concerning the existence, validity or the amount of a revenue claim of the requesting State shall not be dealt with by the requested State's courts and administrative bodies. Thus, no legal or administrative proceedings, such as a request for judicial review, shall be undertaken in the requested State with respect to these matters. The main purpose of this rule is to prevent administrative or judicial bodies of the requested State from being asked to decide matters which concern whether an amount, or part thereof, is owed under the internal law of the other State. States in which the paragraph may raise constitutional or legal difficulties may amend or omit it in the course of bilateral negotiations.

Paragraph 7

29.   This paragraph provides that if, after a request has been made under paragraph 3 or 4, the conditions that applied when such request was made cease to apply (*e.g.* a revenue claim ceases to be enforceable in the requesting State), the State that made the request must promptly notify the other State of this change of situation. Following the receipt of such a notice, the requested State has the option to ask the requesting

State to either suspend or withdraw the request. If the request is suspended, the suspension should apply until such time as the State that made the request informs the other State that the conditions necessary for making a request as regards the relevant revenue claim are again satisfied or that it withdraws its request.

Paragraph 8

30.   This paragraph contains certain limitations to the obligations imposed on the State which receives a request for assistance.

31.   The requested State is at liberty to refuse to provide assistance in the cases referred to in the paragraph. However if it does provide assistance in these cases, it remains within the framework of the Article and it cannot be objected that this State has failed to observe the provisions of the Article.

32.   In the first place, the paragraph contains the clarification that a Contracting State is not bound to go beyond its own internal laws and administrative practice or those of the other State in fulfilling its obligations under the Article. Thus, if the requesting State has no domestic power to take measures of conservancy, the requested State could decline to take such measures on behalf of the requesting State. Similarly, if the seizure of assets to satisfy a revenue claim is not permitted in the requested State, that State is not obliged to seize assets when providing assistance in collection under the provisions of the Article. However, types of administrative measures authorised for the purpose of the requested State's tax must be utilised, even though invoked solely to provide assistance in the collection of taxes owed to the requesting State.

33.   Paragraph 5 of the Article provides that a Contracting State's time limits will not apply to a revenue claim in respect of which the other State has requested assistance. Subparagraph a) is not intended to defeat that principle. Providing assistance with respect to a revenue claim after the requested State's time limits have expired will not, therefore, be considered to be at variance with the laws and administrative practice of that or of the other Contracting State in cases where the time limits applicable to that claim have not expired in the requesting State.

34.   Subparagraph b) includes a limitation to carrying out measures contrary to public policy (*ordre public*). As is the case under Article 26 (see paragraph 19 of the Commentary on Article 26), it has been felt necessary to prescribe a limitation with regard to assistance which may affect the vital interests of the State itself.

35.   Under subparagraph c), a Contracting State is not obliged to satisfy the request if the other State has not pursued all reasonable measures of collection or conservancy, as the case may be, available under its laws or administrative practice.

36.   Finally, under subparagraph d), the requested State may also reject the request for practical considerations, for instance if the costs that it would incur in collecting a revenue claim of the requesting State would exceed the amount of the revenue claim.

37.   Some States may wish to add to the paragraph a further limitation, already found in the joint Council of Europe-OECD multilateral Convention on Mutual Administrative Assistance in Tax Matters, which would allow a State not to provide assistance if it considers that the taxes with respect to which assistance is requested are imposed contrary to generally accepted taxation principles.

COMMENTARY ON ARTICLE 28
CONCERNING MEMBERS OF DIPLOMATIC MISSIONS AND CONSULAR POSTS

1. The aim of the provision is to secure that members of diplomatic missions and consular posts shall, under the provisions of a double taxation convention, receive no less favourable treatment than that to which they are entitled under international law or under special international agreements.

2. The simultaneous application of the provisions of a double taxation convention and of diplomatic and consular privileges conferred by virtue of the general rules of international law, or under a special international agreement may, under certain circumstances, have the result of discharging, in both Contracting States, tax that would otherwise have been due. As an illustration, it may be mentioned that *e.g.* a diplomatic agent who is accredited by State A to State B and derives royalties, or dividends from sources in State A will not, owing to international law, be subject to tax in State B in respect of this income and may also, depending upon the provisions of the bilateral convention between the two States, be entitled as a resident of State B to an exemption from, or a reduction of, the tax imposed on the income in State A. In order to avoid tax reliefs that are not intended, the Contracting States are free to adopt bilaterally an additional provision which may be drafted on the following lines:

> Insofar as, due to fiscal privileges granted to members of diplomatic missions and consular posts under the general rules of international law or under the provisions of special international agreements, income or capital are not subject to tax in the receiving State, the right to tax shall be reserved to the sending State.

3. In many OECD member countries, the domestic laws contain provisions to the effect that members of diplomatic missions and consular posts whilst abroad shall for tax purposes be deemed to be residents of the sending State. In the bilateral relations between member countries in which provisions of this kind are operative internally, a further step may be taken by including in the Convention specific rules that establish, for purposes of the Convention, the sending State as the State of residence of the members of the diplomatic missions and consular posts of the Contracting States. The special provision suggested here could be drafted as follows:

> Notwithstanding the provisions of Article 4, an individual who is a member of a diplomatic mission or a consular post of a Contracting State which is situated in the other Contracting State or in a third State shall be deemed for the purposes of the Convention to be a resident of the sending State if:
>
> a) in accordance with international law he is not liable to tax in the receiving State in respect of income from sources outside that State or on capital situated outside that State, and
>
> b) he is liable in the sending State to the same obligations in relation to tax on his total income or on capital as are residents of that State.

MODEL TAX CONVENTION (CONDENSED VERSION) – ISBN 978-92-64-08948-8 – © OECD 2010

4.   By virtue of paragraph 1 of Article 4 the members of diplomatic missions and consular posts of a third State accredited to a Contracting State, are not deemed to be residents of the receiving State if they are only subject to a limited taxation in that State (see paragraph 8 of the Commentary on Article 4). This consideration also holds true of the international organisations established in a Contracting State and their officials as they usually benefit from certain fiscal privileges either under the convention or treaty establishing the organisation or under a treaty between the organisation and the State in which it is established. Contracting States wishing to settle expressly this question, or to prevent undesirable tax reliefs, may add the following provision to this Article:

> The Convention shall not apply to international organisations, to organs or officials thereof and to persons who are members of a diplomatic mission or a consular post of a third State, being present in a Contracting State and not treated in either Contracting State as residents in respect of taxes on income or on capital.

This means that international organisations, organs or officials who are liable in a Contracting State in respect only of income from sources therein should not have the benefit of the Convention.

5.   Although honorary consular officers cannot derive from the provisions of the Article any privileges to which they are not entitled under the general rules of international law (there commonly exists only tax exemption for payments received as consideration for expenses honorary consuls have on behalf of the sending State), the Contracting States are free to exclude, by bilateral agreement, expressly honorary consular officers from the application of the Article.

COMMENTARY ON ARTICLE 29
CONCERNING THE TERRITORIAL EXTENSION OF THE CONVENTION

1. Certain double taxation conventions state to what territories they apply. Some of them also provide that their provisions may be extended to other territories and define when and how this may be done. A clause of this kind is of particular value to States which have territories overseas or are responsible for the international relations of other States or territories, especially as it recognises that the extension may be effected by an exchange of diplomatic notes. It is also of value when the provisions of the Convention are to be extended to a part of the territory of a Contracting State which was, by special provision, excluded from the application of the Convention. The Article, which provides that the extension may also be effected in any other manner in accordance with the constitutional procedure of the States, is drafted in a form acceptable from the constitutional point of view of all OECD member countries affected by the provision in question. The only prior condition for the extension of a convention to any States or territories is that they must impose taxes substantially similar in character to those to which the convention applies.

2. The Article provides that the Convention may be extended either in its entirety or with any necessary modifications, that the extension takes effect from such date and subject to such conditions as may be agreed between the Contracting States and, finally, that the termination of the Convention automatically terminates its application to any States or territories to which it has been extended, unless otherwise agreed by the Contracting States.

MODEL TAX CONVENTION (CONDENSED VERSION) – ISBN 978-92-64-08948-8 – © OECD 2010

COMMENTARY ON ARTICLES 30 AND 31 CONCERNING THE ENTRY INTO FORCE AND THE TERMINATION OF THE CONVENTION

1.   The present provisions on the procedure for entry into force, ratification and termination are drafted for bilateral conventions and correspond to the rules usually contained in international treaties.

2.   Some Contracting States may need an additional provision in the first paragraph of Article 30 indicating the authorities which have to give their consent to the ratification. Other Contracting States may agree that the Article should indicate that the entry into force takes place after an exchange of notes confirming that each State has completed the procedures required for such entry into force.

3.   It is open to Contracting States to agree that the Convention shall enter into force when a specified period has elapsed after the exchange of the instruments of ratification or after the confirmation that each State has completed the procedures required for such entry into force.

4.   No provisions have been drafted as to the date on which the Convention shall have effect or cease to have effect, since such provisions would largely depend on the domestic laws of the Contracting States concerned. Some of the States assess tax on the income received during the current year, others on the income received during the previous year, others again have a fiscal year which differs from the calendar year. Furthermore, some conventions provide, as regards taxes levied by deduction at the source, a date for the application or termination which differs from the date applying to taxes levied by assessment.

5.   As it is of advantage that the Convention should remain in force at least for a certain period, the Article on termination provides that notice of termination can only be given after a certain year, to be fixed by bilateral agreement. It is open to the Contracting States to decide upon the earliest year during which such notice can be given or even to agree not to fix any such year, if they so desire.

NON-OECD ECONOMIES' POSITIONS ON THE OECD MODEL TAX CONVENTION

INTRODUCTION

1.   When, in 1991, the Committee on Fiscal Affairs adopted the concept of an ambulatory Model Tax Convention, it also decided that because the influence of the Model Tax Convention had extended far beyond the OECD member countries, the ongoing process through which the Model Tax Convention would be updated should be opened up to benefit from the input of non-OECD economies.

2.   Pursuant to that decision, the Committee on Fiscal Affairs decided, in 1996, to organise annual meetings that would allow experts of member countries and some non-OECD economies to discuss issues related to the negotiation, application and interpretation of tax conventions. Recognising that non-OECD economies could only be expected to associate themselves to the development of the Model Tax Convention if they could retain their freedom to disagree with its contents, the Committee also decided that these countries should, like member countries, have the possibility to identify the areas where they are unable to agree with the text of an Article or with an interpretation given in the Commentary.

3.   This has led to the inclusion in the Model Tax Convention of this section, which sets out the positions of a number of non-OECD economies on the Articles of the Model and the Commentary thereon. It is intended that this document will be periodically updated, like the rest of the Model Tax Convention, to reflect changes in the views of participating economies.

4.   This section reflects the following non-OECD economies' positions on the Model Tax Convention:

Albania	Argentina	Armenia
Belarus	Brazil	Bulgaria
Croatia	Democratic Republic of the Congo	Estonia
Gabon	Hong Kong, China	India
Indonesia	Israel	Ivory Coast
Kazakhstan	Latvia	Lithuania
Malaysia	Morocco	People's Republic of China
Philippines	Romania	Russia
Serbia	South Africa	Thailand
Tunisia	Ukraine	United Arab Emirates
Vietnam		

5.   Whilst these economies generally agree with the text of the Articles of the Model Tax Convention and with the interpretations put forward in the Commentary, there are for each economy some areas of disagreement. For each Article of the Model Tax Convention, the positions that are presented in this section indicate where a country disagrees with the text of the Article and where it disagrees with an interpretation

given in the Commentary in relation to the Article.[1] As is the case with the observations and reservations of member countries, no reference is made to cases where an economy would like to supplement the text of an Article with provisions that do not conflict with the Article, especially if these provisions are offered as alternatives in the Commentary, or would like to put forward an interpretation that does not conflict with the Commentary.

1　Indonesia and the People's Republic of China wish to clarify expressly that in the course of negotiations with other countries, they will not be bound by their stated positions included in this section.

POSITIONS ON ARTICLE 1
(PERSONS COVERED)
AND ITS COMMENTARY

Positions on the Article

1.   The *Philippines* reserves the right to tax its citizens in accordance with its domestic law.

2.   *Brazil* reserves the right to extend coverage of the Convention to partnerships since partnerships are considered to be legal entities under its legislation.

Position on the Commentary

3.   *Gabon, India, Ivory Coast, Morocco* and *Tunisia* do not agree with the interpretation put forward in paragraphs 5 and 6 of the Commentary on Article 1 (and in the case of India, the corresponding interpretation in paragraph 8.8 of the Commentary on Article 4) according to which if a partnership is denied the benefits of a tax convention, its members are entitled to the benefits of the tax conventions entered into by their State of residence. They believe that this result is only possible, to a certain extent, if provisions to that effect are included in the convention entered into with the State where the partnership is situated.

POSITIONS ON ARTICLE 2
(TAXES COVERED)
AND ITS COMMENTARY

Positions on the Article

Paragraph 1

1.   Wherever the terms "capital" and "movable property" appear in the Convention, *Belarus* reserves the right to replace these terms, which do not exist in its domestic law, by "property" and "property other than immovable property" respectively.

2.   *Brazil* reserves its position on that part of paragraph 1 which states that the Convention should apply to taxes of political subdivisions or local authorities, as well as on the final part of the paragraph which reads "irrespective of the manner in which they are levied".

3.   Since they have no tax on capital, *Brazil* and *Indonesia* reserve the right not to include any reference to such tax in paragraph 1.

4.   *Romania* reserves the right to include taxes imposed on behalf of administrative-territorial units.

5.	*South Africa* reserves its position on that part of paragraph 1 which states that the Convention should apply to taxes of local authorities.

Paragraph 2

6.	*Brazil* wishes to use, in its conventions, a definition of income tax that is in accordance with its constitutional legislation. Accordingly, it reserves the right not to include paragraph 2 in its conventions.

7.	*Armenia, Latvia, Lithuania, Romania* and *Tunisia* hold the view that "taxes on the total amounts of wages or salaries paid by enterprises" should not be regarded as taxes on income and therefore reserve the right not to include these words in paragraph 2.

8.	*Ukraine* reserves its position on that part of paragraph 2 which states that the Convention shall apply to taxes on capital appreciation.

POSITIONS ON ARTICLE 3
(GENERAL DEFINITIONS)
AND ITS COMMENTARY

Positions on the Article

1.	With respect to the definition of "company", *Albania* and *Belarus* reserve the right to replace the concept of "body corporate", which does not exist in their domestic law, by "any legal person or any entity which is treated as a separate entity for tax purposes".

2.	*Israel* reserves the right to include a trust within the definition of a "person".

3.	With respect to the definition of "national", *Albania, Romania* and *Russia* reserve the right to replace the term "nationality" by "citizenship" as the term "nationality" does not mean "citizenship" under their law.

4.	*Bulgaria* reserves the right to propose in bilateral negotiations to include a definition of the term "business profits", which covers both profits of a company and income of an individual, derived from carrying on of a business through a permanent establishment. This inclusion is a consequence of the deletion of Article 14 and results in the possibility of applying Article 7 in conformity with Bulgarian internal legislation as regards income, derived by individuals.

4.1	*Brazil* reserves the right not to include the definitions of "enterprise" and "business" in paragraph 1 of Article 3 because it reserves the right to include an article concerning the taxation of independent personal services.

5.	With respect to the definition of "international traffic", *Bulgaria* and *Croatia* reserve the right to extend the scope of the definition to cover road and railway transportation in bilateral conventions.

6.   *Serbia* reserves the right to extend the scope of the definition of "international traffic" to cover road transportation in bilateral conventions.

7.   *Thailand* reserves the right to include in the definition of "person" any entity treated as a taxable unit under the taxation laws in force in either Contracting State.

8.   *India* reserves the right to include in the definition of "person" only those entities which are treated as taxable unit under the taxation laws in force in the respective Contracting States.

9.   *India* reserves the right to include definitions of "tax" and "fiscal year".

10.   *Hong Kong, China* reserves the right to omit the phrase "operated by an enterprise that has its place of effective management in a Contracting State" from the definition of "international traffic" in subparagraph *e*) of paragraph 1.

11.   *Hong Kong, China* reserves its position with respect to the definition of "national" in subparagraph *g*) of paragraph 1, because Hong Kong, China is not a sovereign state. Where the term "national" appears in Articles 4, 19, 24 and 25, Hong Kong, China reserves the right to use alternative provisions based on the concepts of "right of abode" and "incorporated or constituted in".

POSITIONS ON ARTICLE 4
(RESIDENT)
AND ITS COMMENTARY

Positions on the Article

Paragraph 1

1.   *Albania, Armenia, Belarus, Estonia, Indonesia, Latvia, Lithuania, Russia, Thailand, Ukraine* and *Vietnam* reserve the right to include the place of incorporation or a similar criterion (registration for Belarus and Vietnam) in paragraph 1.

2.   The *United Arab Emirates* reserves the right to adopt its own definition of residence in its bilateral conventions and not necessarily follow Article 4.

2.1   *Hong Kong, China* reserves the right to modify the definition of "resident" in its bilateral agreements because it is not a sovereign state and it taxes on a territorial basis.

3.   *Brazil* reserves the right not to include the second sentence of paragraph 1 in its conventions as the position of diplomatic staff is dealt with under its domestic law.

4.   *India* and *Russia* reserve the right to amend the Article in their tax conventions in order to specify that their partnerships must be considered as residents of their respective countries in view of their legal and tax characteristics.

4.1   *Gabon, Ivory Coast, Morocco* and *Tunisia* do not agree with the general principle according to which if tax owed by a partnership is determined on the basis of the personal characteristics of the partners, these partners are entitled to the benefits of tax conventions entered into by the States of which they are residents as regards income that "flows through" that partnership. Under their domestic law, a partnership is considered to be liable to tax even though, technically, that tax is collected from the partners or in the case of Morocco from the principal partner; for that reason, Gabon, Ivory Coast, Morocco and Tunisia reserve the right to amend the Article in their tax conventions in order to specify that their partnerships must be considered as residents of their country in view of their legal and tax characteristics.

Paragraph 3

5. *Armenia, Bulgaria, Russia, Thailand* and *Vietnam* reserve the right to use the place of incorporation (registration for Vietnam) as the test for paragraph 3.

6. [Deleted]

7. *Israel* reserves the right to include a separate provision regarding a trust that is a resident of both Contracting States.

8. *India* and *Kazakhstan* reserve the right to include a provision that will refer to a mutual agreement procedure for determination of the country of residence in case of a dual resident person other than an individual if the State in which its effective place of management is situated cannot be determined.

8.1 *Bulgaria* reserves the right to include a provision that will refer to the State of derivation of the legal status and, in case this State could not be determined, to the mutual agreement procedure, for the determination of the country of residence in the case of a dual resident person other than an individual and a company and, in the absence of such an agreement, it will deny benefits under the Convention to this person.

Positions on the Commentary

Paragraph 2

9. In the opinion of *Vietnam* the personal relations and economic relations mentioned in paragraphs 14 and 15 of the Commentary should be separated and one given priority over the other. For Vietnam, economic relations, particularly the criterion of the country where employment is exercised, is more important to determine the country of residence for treaty purposes in the case of a dual resident individual.

9.1 In the case of *Gabon*, since the phrase "and economic relations" used in paragraphs 13, 14 and 15 of the Commentary is ambiguous, these two types of relations should be distinguished and one type may have priority over the other. The State in which employment is exercised should therefore prevail over the personal relations for purposes of determining the State of residence of an individual.

MODEL TAX CONVENTION (CONDENSED VERSION) – ISBN 978-92-64-08948-8 – © OECD 2010

9.2   *Kazakhstan* reserves the right to replace subparagraph *d)* by: "*d)* if the individual's status cannot be determined by reason of subparagraphs *a)* to *c)* of this paragraph, the competent authorities of the Contracting States shall settle the question by mutual agreement."

9.3   *Indonesia* is of the opinion that in considering the dual residence of an individual, economic relations shall have priority over personal relations.

Paragraph 3

10.   The interpretation by *Argentina, Armenia, Russia, Ukraine* and *Vietnam* of the term "place of effective management" is practical day to day management, irrespective of where the overriding control is exercised.

11.   *India* does not adhere to the interpretation given in paragraph 24 that the place of effective management is the place where key management and commercial decisions that are necessary for the conduct of the entity's business as a whole are in substance made. It is of the view that the place where the main and substantial activity of the entity is carried on is also to be taken into account when determining the place of effective management.

12.   *Brazil* does not adhere to the interpretation given in paragraph 24 of the Commentary since it considers that such definition is an issue to be dealt with by domestic law and domestic court decisions.

POSITIONS ON ARTICLE 5
(PERMANENT ESTABLISHMENT)
AND ITS COMMENTARY

Positions on the Article

1.   Considering the special problems in applying the provisions of the Model Convention to activities carried on offshore in a Contracting State in connection with the exploration or exploitation of the sea bed, its subsoil and their natural resources, *Latvia* and *Lithuania* reserve the right to insert in a special Article provisions relating to such activities.

Paragraph 2

2.   In paragraph 2, in addition to "the extraction of" natural resources, *Argentina, Brazil, Gabon, Ivory Coast, Morocco,* the *Philippines, Russia, Thailand, Tunisia* and the *United Arab Emirates* reserve the right to refer to the "exploration for" such resources.

2.1   *Indonesia* reserves the right to add to paragraph 2 the exploration and exploitation of natural resources and a drilling rig or working ship used for exploration and exploitation of natural resources.

3. *India* and *Indonesia* reserve the right to add to paragraph 2 additional subparagraphs that would cover a sales outlet and a farm, plantation or other place where agricultural, forestry, plantation or related activities are carried on.

4. *India, Indonesia, Thailand* and *Vietnam* reserve the right to add to paragraph 2 an additional subparagraph that would cover a warehouse in relation to a person supplying storage facilities for others.

5. *Armenia* and *Ukraine* reserve the right to add to paragraph 2 an additional subparagraph that would cover an installation, or structure for the exploration for natural resources and a warehouse or other structure used for the sale of goods.

6. *Gabon* and *Vietnam* reserve the right to add to paragraph 2 an additional subparagraph that would cover an installation structure or equipment used for the exploration for natural resources.

6.1 *Argentina, Gabon* and *Ivory Coast* reserve the right to add to paragraph 2 an additional subparagraph that would cover places where fishing activities take place.

6.2 *Kazakhstan* reserves the right to add to paragraph 2 an additional subparagraph that would cover a pit, an installation and a structure for the exploration for natural resources.

Paragraph 3

7. *Argentina* reserves its position on paragraph 3 and considers that any building site or construction, assembly, or installation project that lasts more than three months should be regarded as a permanent establishment.

8. *Armenia, Brazil, Thailand* and *Vietnam* reserve their position on paragraph 3 as they consider that any building site or construction, assembly or installation project which lasts more than six months should be regarded as a permanent establishment.

9. *Albania*, the *Democratic Republic of the Congo, Lithuania* and *Hong Kong, China* reserve their position on paragraph 3 and consider that any building site, construction, assembly or installation project or a supervisory or consultancy activity connected therewith constitutes a permanent establishment if such site, project or activity lasts for a period of more than six months.

9.1 *Serbia* reserves the right to treat any building site, construction, assembly or installation project or a supervisory or consultancy activity connected therewith as constituting a permanent establishment only if such site, project or activity lasts for a period of more than twelve months.

10. *Bulgaria, Gabon, Ivory Coast, Malaysia, Morocco*, the *People's Republic of China, South Africa* and *Tunisia* reserve their right to negotiate the period of time after which a building site or construction, assembly, or installation project should be regarded as a permanent establishment under paragraph 3.

11. *Argentina, Malaysia*, the *People's Republic of China, South Africa, Thailand* and *Vietnam* reserve the right to treat an enterprise as having a permanent establishment if the

enterprise carries on supervisory activities in connection with a building site or a construction, assembly, or installation project that constitute a permanent establishment under paragraph 3 (in the case of Malaysia, the period for this permanent establishment is negotiated separately).

11.1 *India* and *Indonesia* reserve the right to replace "construction or installation project" with "construction, installation or assembly project or supervisory activities in connection therewith" and reserve the right to negotiate the period of time for which these should last to be regarded as a permanent establishment.

12. *Argentina* reserves the right to treat an enterprise as having a permanent establishment if the enterprise furnishes services, including consultancy services, through employees or other personnel engaged by the enterprise for such purpose, but only where activities of that nature continue (for the same or a connected project) within the country for a period or periods aggregating more than three months.

13. *Gabon, India, Indonesia, Ivory Coast, Morocco,* and *Tunisia* reserve the right to treat an enterprise as having a permanent establishment if the enterprise furnishes services, including consultancy services through employees or other personnel engaged by the enterprise for such purpose but only where such activities continue for the same project or a connected project for a period or periods aggregating more than a period to be negotiated.

14. *Albania, Armenia, Lithuania, Serbia, South Africa, Thailand, Vietnam* and *Hong Kong, China* reserve the right to treat an enterprise as having a permanent establishment if the enterprise furnishes services, including consultancy services, through employees or other personnel engaged by the enterprise for such purpose, but only where activities of that nature continue (for the same or a connected project [other than in the case of Armenia]), within the country for a period or periods aggregating more than six months within any twelve month period.

14.1 The *Democratic Republic of the Congo, Gabon, Ivory Coast, Latvia, Morocco, South Africa* and *Tunisia* reserve the right to deem any person performing professional services or other activities of an independent character to have a permanent establishment if that person is present in the State for a period or periods exceeding in the aggregate 183 days in any twelve month period.

14.2 *Bulgaria* and *Estonia* reserve the right to deem an individual performing professional services or other services of an independent character to have a permanent establishment for the purposes of the Convention if they are present in the other State for a period or periods exceeding in the aggregate 183 days in any twelve month period.

14.3 *Bulgaria* reserves the right to treat an enterprise as having a permanent establishment if the enterprise furnishes services, including consultancy services, through employees or other personnel engaged by the enterprise for such purpose, where activities of that nature continue (for the same or a connected project) within the country for a period or periods aggregating more than six months within any twelve month period.

14.4 *Bulgaria* and *Indonesia* reserve the right to insert a provision that deems a permanent establishment to exist if, for more than a negotiated period, an installation, drilling rig or ship is used for the exploration of natural resources.

14.5 *Indonesia*, the *United Arab Emirates* and *Vietnam* reserve the right to tax income derived from activities relating to exploration and exploitation of natural resources.

14.6 *South Africa* reserves the right to insert a provision that deems a permanent establishment to exist if, for more than six months, an enterprise conducts activities relating to the exploration or exploitation of natural resources.

14.7 *Israel* reserves the right to insert a provision according to which an installation, drilling rig or ship used for activities connected with the exploration of natural resources shall be treated as constituting a permanent establishment in a Contracting State if those activities last in aggregate more than 365 days in that State in any two year period.

Paragraph 4

15. *Albania, Argentina, Armenia, Gabon, India, Indonesia, Ivory Coast, Malaysia, Morocco, Russia, Thailand, Tunisia, Ukraine* and *Vietnam* reserve their position on paragraph 4 as they consider that the term "delivery" should be deleted from subparagraphs a) and b).

16. *Albania, Argentina* and *Thailand* reserve their position on subparagraph 4 f).

16.1 [Deleted]

16.2 The *Democratic Republic of the Congo* reserves its position on subparagraphs 4 d), e) and f).

Paragraph 5

17. *Albania, Armenia, Gabon, India, Indonesia, Ivory Coast, Morocco, Russia, Thailand, Tunisia, Ukraine* and *Vietnam* reserve the right to treat an enterprise as having a permanent establishment if a person acting on behalf of the enterprise habitually maintains a stock of goods or merchandise in a Contracting State from which the person regularly delivers goods or merchandise on behalf of the enterprise.

17.1 *India, Malaysia* and *Thailand* reserve the right to treat an enterprise of a Contracting State as having a permanent establishment in the other Contracting State if a person habitually secures orders in the other Contracting State wholly or almost wholly for the enterprise.

17.2 *Indonesia* reserves the right to treat an enterprise as having a permanent establishment if a person acting on behalf of the enterprise, other than an independent agent, manufactures or processes for the enterprise goods or merchandise belonging to the enterprise.

Paragraph 6

18. *Albania, Gabon, Estonia, Ivory Coast, Lithuania, Morocco, Serbia, Thailand, Tunisia* and *Vietnam* reserve the right to make clear that an agent whose activities are conducted

wholly or almost wholly on behalf of a single enterprise will not be considered an agent of an independent status.

19.   Gabon, India, Indonesia, Ivory Coast, Morocco, Russia, Thailand, Tunisia and Vietnam reserve the right to provide that an insurance enterprise of a Contracting State shall, except with respect to re-insurance (other than in the case of India), be deemed to have a permanent establishment in the other Contracting State if it collects premiums in the territory of that other state or insures risks situated therein through a person other than an agent of an independent status to whom paragraph 6 applies.

19.1   India reserves the right to make it clear that an agent whose activities are conducted wholly or almost wholly on behalf of a single enterprise will not be considered an agent of an independent status.

Positions on the Commentary

20.   India, Morocco and Vietnam do not agree with the words "The twelve month test applies to each individual site or project" found in paragraph 18 of the Commentary. They consider that a series of consecutive short term sites or projects operated by a contractor would give rise to the existence of a permanent establishment in the country concerned.

21.   Bulgaria and Serbia would add to paragraph 33 of the Commentary on Article 5 their views that a person, who is authorised to negotiate the essential elements of the contract, and not necessarily all the elements and details of the contract, on behalf of a foreign resident, can be said to exercise the authority to conclude contracts.

22.   Bulgaria does not adhere to the interpretation, given in paragraph 17 of the Commentary on Article 5, and is of the opinion that on-site planning and supervision of the erection of a building, where carried on by another person, are not covered by paragraph 3 of the Article, if not expressly provided for.

23.   Brazil does not agree with the interpretation provided in paragraphs 42.1 to 42.10 on electronic commerce, especially in view of the principle of taxation at the source of payments in its legislation.

24.   India deems as essential to take into consideration that irrespective of the meaning given to the third sentence of paragraph 1.1 — as far as the method for computing taxes is concerned, national systems are not affected by the new wording of the model i.e. by the elimination of Article 14.

25.   India and Malaysia do not agree with the interpretation given in paragraph 5.3 (first part of the paragraph) and 5.4 (first part of the paragraph); they are of the view that these examples could also be regarded as constituting permanent establishments.

26.   India does not agree with the interpretation given in paragraph 8; it is of the view that tangible or intangible properties by themselves may constitute a permanent establishment of the lessor in certain circumstances.

27. *India* does not agree with the interpretation given in paragraph 10; it is of the view that ICS equipment may constitute a permanent establishment of the lessor in certain circumstances.

28. *India* does not adhere to the interpretation given in paragraphs 12 and 42.25 concerning the list of examples of paragraph 2 of the Article; it is of the view that the examples can always be regarded as constituting *a priori* permanent establishments.

29. *India* does not agree with the interpretation given in paragraph 23; it would not include scientific research in the list of examples of activities indicative of preparatory or auxiliary nature.

30. *India* does not agree with the interpretation given in paragraph 25; it is of the view that when an enterprise has established an office (such as a commercial representation office) in a country, and the employees working at that office are substantially involved in the negotiation of contracts for the import of products or services into that country, the office will in most cases not fall within paragraph 4 of Article 5. Substantial involvement in the negotiations exists when the essential parts of the contract — the type, quality, and amount of goods, for example, and the time and terms of delivery are determined by the office. These activities form a separate and indispensable part of the business activities of the foreign enterprise, and are not simply activities of an auxiliary or preparatory character.

31. *India* does not agree with the interpretation given in paragraph 33; it is of the view that the mere fact that a person has attended or participated in negotiations in a State between an enterprise and a client, can in certain circumstances, be sufficient, by itself, to conclude that the person has exercised in that State an authority to conclude contracts in the name of the enterprise. India is also of the view that a person, who is authorised to negotiate the essential elements of the contract, and not necessarily all the elements and details of the contract, on behalf of a foreign resident, can be said to exercise the authority to conclude contracts.

32. *India* does not agree with the interpretation given in paragraph 42; it is of the view that where a company (enterprise) resident of a State is a member of a multinational group and is engaged in manufacture or providing services for and on behalf of another company (enterprise) of the same group which is resident of the other State, then the first company may constitute a permanent establishment of the latter if other requirements of Article 5 are satisfied.

33. *India* does not agree with the interpretation given in paragraph 42.2; it is of the view that website may constitute a permanent establishment in certain circumstances.

34. *India* does not agree with the interpretation given in paragraph 42.3; it is of the view that, depending on the facts, an enterprise can be considered to have acquired a place of business by virtue of hosting its website on a particular server at a particular location.

35.   *India* does not agree with the interpretation given in paragraphs 42.14 and 42.15 that a service permanent establishment will be created only if services are performed in the source State. It is of the view that furnishing of services is sufficient for creation of a service permanent establishment.

36.   *India* does not agree with the interpretation given in paragraphs 42.18 and 42.46, it is of the view that taxation rights may exist in a state even when services are furnished by the non-residents from outside that State. It is also of the view that the taxation principle applicable to the profits from sale of goods may not apply to the income from furnishing of services.

37.   *India* does not agree with the interpretation given in paragraph 42.19 that only the profits derived from services should be taxed and the provisions that are included in bilateral Conventions which allow a State to tax the gross amount of the fees paid for certain services is not an appropriate way of taxing services.

38.   *India* does not agree with the conclusions given in paragraph 42.22 that taxation should not extend to services performed outside the territory of a State; that taxation should apply only to the profits from these services rather than to the payments for them, and that there should be a minimum level of presence in a State before such taxation is allowed.

39.   *India* does not agree with the interpretation given in paragraph 42.31; it is of the view that for furnishing services in a State, physical presence of an individual is not essential.

40.   *India* does not agree with the interpretation given in paragraphs 42.40 and 42.43.

41.   *India* does not agree with the interpretation given in example 3 of paragraph 42.44 concerning the taxability of ZCO.

42.   *Brazil* does not agree with the interpretation provided for in paragraphs 42.11 to 42.48 of the Commentary on the taxation of services, especially in view of the principle of taxation at source of payments in its legislation.

43.   *India* does not agree with the interpretation in paragraph 5.5 of the Commentary on Article 5 according to which a satellite's footprint in the space of a source country cannot be treated as a permanent establishment. India is of the view that in such a case, the source state not only contributes its customer base but also provides infrastructure for reception of the satellite telecast or telecommunication process. India is also of the view that a satellite's footprint falls both in the international and national space. The footprint has a fixed location, has a value and can be used for commercial purposes. Accordingly, it can be treated as a fixed place of business in the space in the jurisdiction of a source country.

44.   *India* does not agree with the interpretation in paragraph 9.1 of the Commentary on Article 5 as it considers that a roaming call is a composite process which requires a composite use of various pieces of equipment located in the source and residence countries and the distinction proposed in paragraph 9.1 was neither intended by the wording of Article 5 nor logical.

45. *India* does not agree with the interpretation in the last two sentences of paragraph 26.1 of the Commentary on Article 5 according to which even undersea cables and pipelines lying in the territorial jurisdiction of a source country cannot be considered as permanent establishment of an enterprise.

POSITIONS ON ARTICLE 6
(INCOME FROM IMMOVABLE PROPERTY)
AND ITS COMMENTARY

Positions on the Article

Paragraph 1

1.   *India* and *Indonesia* wish to address the issue of the inclusion of the words "including income from agriculture or forestry" through bilateral negotiations.

Paragraph 2

2.   Given the meaning of the term "immovable property" under its domestic law, *Belarus* reserves the right to omit the second sentence of this paragraph.

2.1   *Latvia* and *Lithuania* reserve the right to include in the definition of the term "immovable property" any option or similar right to acquire immovable property.

2.2   *Estonia* reserves the right to include in the definition of the term "immovable property" any right of claim in respect of immovable property because such right of claim may not be included in its domestic law's meaning of the term.

3.   *Lithuania* reserves the right to modify the second sentence of the definition of the term "immovable property" to make clear that the sentence does not apply for domestic law purposes.

3.1   *Morocco* wishes to retain the possibility of applying the provisions in its domestic laws relative to the taxation of income from shares or rights, which are treated therein as income from immovable property.

Paragraph 3

4.   *Latvia* and *Lithuania* reserve the right to include in paragraph 3 a reference to income from the alienation of immovable property.

5.   *Latvia* and *Lithuania* also reserve the right to tax income of shareholders in resident companies from the direct use, letting, or use in any other form of the right to enjoyment of immovable property situated in their country and held by the company, where such right is based on the ownership of shares or other corporate rights in the company.

POSITIONS ON ARTICLE 7
(BUSINESS PROFITS)
AND ITS COMMENTARY

Positions on the Article

1.   Argentina, Brazil, Indonesia, Latvia, Malaysia, Romania, Serbia, South Africa, Thailand and Hong Kong, China reserve the right to use the previous version of Article 7, i.e. the version that was included in the Model Tax Convention immediately before the 2010 Update, subject to their positions on that previous version (see annex below).

1.1   India reserves the right to use the previous version of Article 7, i.e. the version that was included in the Model Tax Convention immediately before the 2010 update, subject to its positions on that previous version (see annex below). It does not agree with the approach to the attribution of profits to permanent establishments in general that is reflected in the revised Article, in its Commentary and in the consequential changes to the Commentary on other Articles (i.e. paragraph 21 of the Commentary on Article 8, paragraphs 32.1 and 32.2 of the Commentary on Article 10, paragraphs 25.1 and 25.2 of the Commentary on Article 11, paragraphs 21.1 and 21.2 of the Commentary on Article 12, paragraphs 27.1 and 27.2 of the Commentary on Article 13, paragraph 7.2 of the Commentary on Article 15, paragraphs 5.1 and 5.2 of the Commentary on Article 21, paragraphs 3.1 and 3.2 of the Commentary on Article 22 and subparagraph 40 a) of the Commentary on Article 24).

1.2   Argentina and Indonesia reserve the right to include a special provision in the Convention that will permit them to apply their domestic law in relation to the taxation of the profits of an insurance and re-insurance enterprise.

1.3   Whilst the People's Republic of China understands and respects the separate and independent enterprise principle underlying the new version of Article 7, due to its tax administration capacity it reserves the right to adopt the previous version of the Article and, in some cases, to resort to simpler methods for calculating the profits attributable to a permanent establishment.

2.   Malaysia, Thailand and Ukraine reserve the right to add a provision to the effect that, if the information available to the competent authority of a Contracting State is inadequate to determine the profits to be attributed to the permanent establishment of an enterprise, the competent authority may apply to that enterprise the provisions of the taxation law of that State, subject to the qualification that such law will be applied, so far as the information available to the competent authority permits, in accordance with the principles of this Article.

2.1   Albania, Argentina, Brazil, Croatia, Gabon, Indonesia, Ivory Coast, Malaysia, Morocco, the People's Republic of China, Russia, Serbia, Thailand, Tunisia and Vietnam reserve the right to maintain in their conventions a specific article dealing with the taxation of "independent personal services". Accordingly, reservation is also made with respect to all the corresponding modifications in the Articles and the Commentaries, which have been modified as a result of the elimination of Article 14.

2.2   *Bulgaria* reserves the right to propose in bilateral negotiations the replacement, in this Article, of the term "profits" with the term "business profits", provided that it is defined in Article 3.

2.3   *Tunisia* reserves the right to propose in bilateral negotiations to add a criterion for the taxation in the Source State of the independent personal services, under the former Article 14, based on the amount (to be established through bilateral negotiations) of the remuneration paid.

3.   *Argentina, Morocco* and *Thailand* reserve the right to tax in the State where the permanent establishment is situated business profits derived from the sale of goods or merchandise which are the same as or of a similar kind to the ones sold through a permanent establishment situated in that State or from other business activities carried on in that State of the same or similar kind as those effected through that permanent establishment. They will apply this rule only as a safeguard against abuse and not as a general "force of attraction principle". Thus, the rule will not apply when the enterprise proves that the sales or activities have been carried out for reasons other than obtaining a benefit under the Convention.

3.1   *Indonesia* reserves the right to tax, in the State where the permanent establishment is situated, business profits derived from the sale of goods or merchandise which are the same as or of a similar kind to the ones sold through that permanent establishment or from other business activities carried on in that State of the same or similar kind as those carried on through that permanent establishment.

4.   *Albania* and *Vietnam* reserve the right to tax in the State where the permanent establishment is situated business profits derived from the sale of goods or merchandise which are the same as or of a similar kind to the ones sold through a permanent establishment situated in that State or from other business activities carried on in that State of the same or similar kind as those effected through that permanent establishment.

4.1   *Morocco* and the *Philippines* reserve the right to adopt a length of stay and fixed base criteria in determining whether an individual rendering personal services is taxable.

4.2   The *United Arab Emirates* reserves the right to include a special provision in its conventions that will permit its domestic law to apply to all activities that are related to the exploration, extraction or exploitation of natural resources, including petroleum activities as well as rendering services in connection with these activities, when these activities are carried out on its territory.

5.   *Argentina* reserves the right to provide that a Contracting State shall not be obliged to allow the deduction of expenses incurred abroad which are not reasonably attributable to the activity carried on by the permanent establishment, taking into account the general principles contained in its domestic legislation concerning executive and administrative expenses for assistance services.

6.   [Deleted]

7.   *Armenia, Lithuania* and *Serbia* reserve the right to add to paragraph 2 a clarification that expenses to be allowed as deductions by a Contracting State shall include only expenses that are deductible under the domestic laws of that State.

8.   *Serbia* reserves the right to specify that a potential adjustment will be made only if it is considered justified.

9.   [Deleted]

10.   [Deleted]

11.   [Deleted]

Position on the Commentary

12.   *Argentina, Brazil, Indonesia, Latvia, Malaysia, Romania, Serbia, South Africa, Thailand* and *Hong Kong, China* will interpret Article 7 as it read before the 2010 Update in line with the relevant Commentary as it stood prior to that update.

ANNEX

POSITIONS ON THE PREVIOUS VERSION OF ARTICLE 7 AND ITS COMMENTARY

The following is the text of the non-OECD economies' positions on Article 7 and its Commentary as it read before 22 July 2010. That previous version of the positions on Article 7 and its Commentary is provided for historical reference as it will continue to be relevant for the application and interpretation of bilateral tax conventions that use the previous version of the Article.

Positions on the Article

1.   *Argentina* and *Chile* reserve the right to include a special provision in the Convention that will permit them to apply their domestic law in relation to the taxation of the profits of an insurance and re-insurance enterprise.

2.   *Malaysia, Thailand* and *Ukraine* reserve the right to add a provision to the effect that, if the information available to the competent authority of a Contracting State is inadequate to determine the profits to be attributed to the permanent establishment of an enterprise, the competent authority may apply to that enterprise the provisions of the taxation law of that State, subject to the qualification that such law will be applied, so far as the information available to the competent authority permits, in accordance with the principles of this Article.

2.1   *Albania, Argentina, Brazil, Chile, Croatia, Gabon, India, Ivory Coast, Malaysia, Morocco,* the *People's Republic of China, Russia, Serbia, Tunisia* and *Vietnam* reserve the right to maintain in their conventions a specific article dealing with the taxation of "independent personal services". Accordingly, reservation is also made with respect to all the corresponding modifications in the Articles and the Commentaries, which have been modified as a result of the elimination of Article 14.

2.2   *Bulgaria* reserves the right to propose in bilateral negotiations the replacement, in this Article, of the term "profits" with the term "business profits", provided that it is defined in Article 3.

2.3   *Tunisia* reserves the right to propose in bilateral negotiations to add a criterion for the taxation in the Source State of the independent personal services, under the former Article 14, based on the amount (to be established through bilateral negotiations) of the remuneration paid.

Paragraphs 1 and 2

3.   *Argentina, Morocco* and *Thailand* reserve the right to tax in the State where the permanent establishment is situated business profits derived from the sale of goods or merchandise which are the same as or of a similar kind to the ones sold through a permanent establishment situated in that State or from other business activities carried on in that State of the same or similar kind as those effected through that permanent establishment. They will apply this rule only as a safeguard against abuse and not as a general "force of attraction principle". Thus, the rule will not apply when the enterprise proves that the sales or activities have been carried out for reasons other than obtaining a benefit under the Convention.

4.   *Albania* and *Vietnam* reserve the right to tax in the State where the permanent establishment is situated business profits derived from the sale of goods or merchandise which are the same as or of a similar kind to the ones sold through a permanent establishment situated in that State or from other business activities carried on in that State of the same or similar kind as those effected through that permanent establishment.

4.1   *Morocco* and the *Philippines* reserve the right to adopt a length of stay and fixed base criteria in determining whether an individual rendering personal services is taxable.

4.2   *Chile* and *India* reserve the right to amend Article 7 to provide that, in applying paragraphs 1 and 2 of the Article, any income or gain attributable to a permanent establishment during its existence may be taxable by the Contracting State in which the permanent establishment exists even if the payments are deferred until after the permanent establishment has ceased to exist. Furthermore, India also reserves the right to apply such a rule under Articles 11, 12, 13 and 21.

Paragraph 3

5.   With respect to paragraph 3, *Argentina* reserves the right to provide that a Contracting State shall not be obliged to allow the deduction of expenses incurred abroad which are not reasonably attributable to the activity carried on by the permanent establishment, taking into account the general principles contained in domestic legislation concerning executive and administrative expenses for assistance services.

6.   *Brazil* reserves its position on the words "whether in the State in which the permanent establishment is situated or elsewhere" found in paragraph 3.

7.   *Armenia, India, Lithuania* and *Slovenia* reserve the right to add to paragraph 3 a clarification that expenses to be allowed as deductions by a Contracting State shall include only expenses that are deductible under the domestic laws of that State.

7.1   *Estonia* and *Latvia* reserve the right to add to paragraph 3 a clarification that expenses to be allowed as deductions by a Contracting State shall include only expenses that would be deductible if the permanent establishment were a separate enterprise of that Contracting State.

8.   *Ukraine* and *Vietnam* reserve the right to add to paragraph 3 a clarification to the effect that the paragraph refers to actual expenses incurred by the enterprise (other than interest in the case of a banking enterprise).

Paragraph 4

9.   *Brazil* reserves the right not to adopt paragraph 4.

Paragraph 5

10.   *Vietnam* reserves the right not to adopt paragraph 5.

Paragraph 6

11.   *Brazil* reserves the right not to adopt paragraph 6.

Positions on the previous Commentary

12.   *India* does not agree with the interpretation given in paragraph 25.

13.   As regards paragraphs 41-50 of the Commentary on Article 7, *Chile* does not adhere to the specific methods provided as the rules on the amount of profit attributable to a permanent establishment; these must be established in and follow domestic law (including foreign exchange legislation).

POSITIONS ON ARTICLE 8
(SHIPPING, INLAND WATERWAYS
TRANSPORT AND AIR TRANSPORT)
AND ITS COMMENTARY

Positions on the Article

1.   *Armenia*, *Latvia* and *Lithuania* reserve the right in exceptional cases to apply the permanent establishment rule in relation to profits derived from the operation of ships in international traffic.

Paragraph 1

2.   The *Philippines* reserves the right to provide for taxation of the profits from shipping and air transport in accordance with domestic law.

2.1   *Indonesia* reserves the right to allow the State of source to tax profits from the operation of ships in international traffic provided that the shipping activities arising from such operation in that State are more than casual and subject to certain limits.

3.   *Albania* and *Bulgaria* reserve the right to tax profits from the carriage of passengers or cargo taken on board at one place in a respective country for discharge at another place in the same country.

4.   *South Africa* reserves the right to include in paragraph 1 profits from the leasing of containers.

5.   *Thailand* reserves the right to provide for taxation of the profits from shipping in accordance with domestic law.

5.1   *India* reserves the right to apply Article 12 and not Article 8 to profits from leasing ships or aircraft on a bare charter basis.

6.   *Bulgaria, Latvia, South Africa* and *Ukraine* reserve the right to include a provision that will ensure that profits from the leasing of ships or aircraft on a bare boat basis and, in the case of Bulgaria, Latvia and Ukraine, from the leasing of containers, will be treated in the same way as income covered by paragraph 1 when such profits are incidental to international transportation.

6.1   *Bulgaria, Croatia, Russia* and *South Africa* reserve the right to extend the scope of the Article to cover international road and railway transportation in bilateral conventions.

6.2   *Morocco* reserves the right to provide for taxation of profits derived by an enterprise engaged in international transport from the lease of containers which is supplementary or incidental to its international operation of ships or aircraft fall within the scope of this Article.

6.3   *Serbia* reserves the right, in the course of negotiations, to propose that the leasing of containers, even if directly connected or ancillary, be regarded as an activity separate from international shipping or aircraft operations, and consequently be excluded from the scope of the Article.

6.4   *Serbia* reserves the right to extend the scope of the Article to cover international road transportation in bilateral conventions.

6.5   *Vietnam* reserves the right to provide that the taxing right with respect to income derived from international transportation shall be shared 50/50.

6.6   The *United Arab Emirates* reserves the right to include in its bilateral conventions a provision to confirm that income from selling tickets on behalf of other enterprises, income derived from selling technical services to third parties, income from bank deposits and other investments, such as bonds, shares and other debentures, are covered by Article 8 provided that this income is incidental to the operation of air transport enterprises operating in international traffic.

Paragraph 2

7.   *Albania, Argentina, Brazil, Estonia, Gabon, India, Latvia, Malaysia, Morocco*, the *People's Republic of China, South Africa* and *Hong Kong, China* reserve the right not to extend the scope of the Article to cover inland waterways transportation in bilateral conventions and are free to make corresponding modifications to paragraph 3 of Articles 13, 15 and 22.

Positions on the Commentary

8.   *Vietnam* disagrees with the interpretation presented in paragraph 5 of the Commentary.

9.   *Vietnam* disagrees with the interpretation presented in paragraph 10 of the Commentary in relation to the incidental leasing of containers.

10.   *Brazil, India* and *Malaysia* reserve their position on the application of this Article to income from ancillary activities (see paragraphs 4 to 10.1).

POSITIONS ON ARTICLE 9
(ASSOCIATED ENTERPRISES)
AND ITS COMMENTARY

Positions on the Article

1.   *Brazil, Russia, Thailand* and *Vietnam* reserve the right not to insert paragraph 2 in their conventions.

2.   *Bulgaria, Lithuania, Russia* and *South Africa* reserve the right to replace "shall" by "may" in the first sentence of paragraph 2 in their conventions.

3.   *Malaysia* and *Serbia* reserve the right to specify in paragraph 2 that a correlative adjustment will be made if the adjustment is considered to be justified.

4.   *Ivory Coast, Morocco* and *Tunisia* reserve the right not to insert paragraph 2 in their conventions unless the commitment to make an adjustment does not apply in the case of fraud, wilful default or neglect. In such a case Tunisia reserves the right to limit the adjustment to periods not covered by its internal statute of limitation.

5.   *Israel* reserves its right to insert a provision according to which any appropriate adjustment to the amount of the tax charged therein on those profits shall be implemented notwithstanding any time limits or other procedural limitations in the domestic law of the Contracting States, except such limitations as apply to claims made in pursuance of such an agreement.

POSITIONS ON ARTICLE 10
(DIVIDENDS)
AND ITS COMMENTARY

Positions on the Article

1.   *Argentina* and *Thailand* reserve the right to apply a 10 per cent rate of tax at source in the case referred to in subparagraph *a)*.

2.   [Deleted]

3.   *Bulgaria, Estonia, India, Latvia, Lithuania, Russia* and *Serbia* reserve the right not to include the requirement for the competent authorities to settle by mutual agreement the mode of application of paragraph 2.

4.   *Israel* reserves its position on the rates provided for in paragraph 2.

5.   *Romania* reserves the right to tax at a uniform rate to be negotiated all dividends referred to in this paragraph.

6.   Gabon, Ivory Coast, Morocco, Russia, South Africa and Tunisia reserve their position on the rates of tax in paragraph 2 and the minimum percentage for the holding in subparagraph a).

7.   Serbia and Vietnam reserve the right to tax, at a uniform rate of not less than 10 per cent, all dividends referred to in paragraph 2.

7.1   Latvia reserves the right to reduce to 10 per cent the minimum percentage for the holding in subparagraph a) and to apply a 10 per cent rate of tax at source in the case referred to in subparagraph b).

7.2   India reserves the right to settle the rate of tax in bilateral negotiations.

Paragraph 3

8.   Argentina, Russia and Tunisia reserve the right to include a provision that will allow them to apply the thin capitalisation measures of their domestic law notwithstanding any other provisions of the Convention.

9.   As their legislation does not provide for such concepts as "jouissance" shares, "jouissance" rights, mining shares and founders' shares, Albania, Armenia, Bulgaria, Belarus and Serbia reserve the right to omit them from paragraph 3.

10.   Bulgaria, Estonia, Latvia and Lithuania reserve the right to replace, in paragraph 3, the words "income from other corporate rights" by "income from other rights".

10.1   Morocco reserves the right to amplify the definition of dividends in paragraph 3 by adding the words "and other assimilated income" after the words "as well as income from other corporate rights" and before the words "which is subjected to the same taxation treatment...".

10.2   India reserves the right to modify the definition of the term "dividends".

10.3   Israel reserves the right to exclude payments made by a Real Estate Investment Trust which is a resident of Israel from the definition of dividends in paragraph 3 and to tax those payments according to its domestic law.

Paragraph 5

11.   Argentina, Kazakhstan, Morocco, Russia and Tunisia reserve the right to apply a branch profits tax.

12.   Brazil reserves the right to levy withholding tax on profits of a permanent establishment at the same rate of tax as is provided in paragraph 2, as is the traditional rule in the Brazilian income tax system.

13.   Thailand reserves the right to levy a profit remittance tax on a permanent establishment at the same rate as is provided for in subparagraph 2 a).

14.   Indonesia reserves the right to apply a branch profits tax, but that branch profits tax shall not affect the provisions contained in any production sharing contracts relating to oil and gas and contracts of works for other mining sectors.

Position on the Commentary

15.   *India* does not adhere to the interpretation set out in paragraph 24. Under the domestic law certain payments are treated as distributions and are therefore included in the definition of dividends.

POSITIONS ON ARTICLE 11
(INTEREST)
AND ITS COMMENTARY

Positions on the Article

1.   *Bulgaria* and *Ukraine* reserve the right to exclude from the scope of the Article interest on a debt-claim where the main purpose or one of the main purposes of any person concerned with the creation or assignment of the debt-claim in respect of which the interest is paid is to take advantage of this Article and not for *bona fide* commercial reasons.

Paragraph 2

2.   *Argentina, Brazil, India, Israel, Ivory Coast*, the *Philippines, Romania, Thailand* and *Ukraine* reserve their positions on the rate provided for in paragraph 2.

3.   *Brazil* reserves the right to add to its conventions a paragraph dealing with interest paid to a government of a Contracting State or one of its political subdivisions or a local authority thereof or any agency (including a financial institution) wholly owned by the said government and stating that such interest is taxable only in the State of residence of the creditor. However, if interest is paid by a government of a Contracting State or one of its political subdivisions or a local authority thereof or any agency (including a financial institution) wholly owned by the said government, such interest shall be taxable only in that Contracting State (*i.e.* in the State of source).

4.   *Bulgaria, Estonia, India, Latvia, Lithuania, Russia* and *Serbia* reserve the right not to include the requirement for the competent authorities to settle by mutual agreement the mode of application of paragraph 2.

Paragraph 3

5.   *Brazil, Thailand* and *Ukraine* reserve the right to regard penalty charges for late payment as interest for the purposes of this Article, in accordance with their domestic law.

6.   *Malaysia* reserves the right to exclude premiums or prizes from the definition of interest, in accordance with the treatment of such payments under its domestic law.

7.   *Brazil* and *Thailand* reserve the right to consider as interest any other income assimilated to income from money lent by the tax law of the Contracting State in which the income arises.

7.1   Estonia, Latvia, Lithuania, Morocco and Tunisia reserve the right to amend the definition of interest to clarify that interest payments treated as distributions under its domestic law fall within Article 10.

Paragraph 4

8.   Brazil reserves the right to provide that where interest is paid to a permanent establishment of a resident of the other Contracting State situated in a third State, the limit on the rate of taxation of interest in paragraph 2 shall not apply.

8.1   Morocco reserves the right to include in paragraph 4 a reference to other business activities carried on in the other State of the same and similar kind as those effected through a permanent establishment.

Paragraph 5

8.2   Israel reserves the right to include a provision that would allow interest income to be taxed under Article 7 if the taxpayer so elects.

Positions on the Commentary

9.   Malaysia does not agree with paragraph 20 of the Commentary as under Malaysian domestic legislation, premiums or prizes are not taxable.

10.   India reserves its right to treat the interest element of sales on credit (described in paragraphs 7.8 and 7.9) as interest.

11.   India does not adhere to the interpretation set out in paragraph 20, it reserves the right to treat the difference between redemption value and issue price in accordance with its domestic law.

POSITIONS ON ARTICLE 12
(ROYALTIES)
AND ITS COMMENTARY

Positions on the Article

1.   Bulgaria and Ukraine reserve the right to exclude from the scope of this Article royalties arising from property or rights created or assigned mainly for the purpose of taking advantage of this Article and not for bona fide commercial reasons.

2.   [Deleted]

Paragraph 1

3.   Albania, Argentina, Armenia, Belarus, Brazil, Bulgaria, Croatia, the Democratic Republic of the Congo, Gabon, Indonesia, Ivory Coast, Kazakhstan, Latvia, Lithuania, Malaysia, Morocco, the People's Republic of China, the Philippines, Romania, Russia, Serbia, South Africa,

Thailand, Tunisia, Ukraine, Vietnam and *Hong Kong, China* reserve the right to tax royalties at source.

4.   *Armenia* reserves the right to tax copyright royalties for literary, scientific and artistic work at a reduced tax rate.

4.1   *India* reserves the right to: tax royalties and fees for technical services at source; define these, particularly by reference to its domestic law; define the source of such payments, which may extend beyond the source defined in paragraph 5 of Article 11, and modify paragraphs 3 and 4 accordingly.

Paragraph 2

5.   *Argentina, Brazil, Gabon, Ivory Coast, Morocco, Russia, Thailand* and *Tunisia* reserve the right to continue to include in the definition of royalties income derived from the leasing of industrial, commercial or scientific equipment and of containers, as provided for in paragraph 2 of Article 12 of the 1977 Model Double Taxation Convention.

6.   *Argentina*, the *Philippines, Thailand* and *Vietnam* reserve the right to include fees for technical services in the definition of royalties.

7.   *Brazil, Gabon, Ivory Coast* and *Tunisia* reserve the right to include fees for technical assistance and technical services in the definition of "royalties".

7.1   *Morocco* reserves the right to include in the definition of the royalties, payments for services, technical assistance, technical and economic studies and all kind of services fees.

8.   *Albania, Armenia, Belarus, Brazil, Bulgaria, India, Indonesia, Kazakhstan, Latvia, Lithuania, Malaysia,* the *People's Republic of China,* the *Philippines, Romania, Russia, Serbia, Thailand* and *Vietnam* reserve the right to include in the definition of royalties payments for the use of, or the right to use, industrial, commercial or scientific equipment. Bulgaria intends to propose in bilateral negotiations the source taxation of royalties on industrial, commercial or scientific equipment at a lower rate than the rate applied to the rest of the royalty payments.

8.1   *Serbia* reserves the right to include in the definition of royalties income derived from the leasing of ships or aircraft on a bare boat charter basis and containers.

8.2   *Malaysia* reserves the right to include in the definition of royalties income derived from the leasing of containers and ships or aircraft, including on a slot hire, time charter, voyage charter, or a bare boat charter basis, whether or not such charters are crewed, equipped or provisioned.

9.   *Belarus* reserves the right to include a reference to transport vehicles in the definition of royalties.

10.   *Brazil, Bulgaria, Morocco* and *Romania* reserve the right to include in the definition of the royalties payments for transmissions by satellite, cable, optic fibre or similar technology.

10.1 *Vietnam* reserves the right to include in the definition of royalties, payments for the use of or the right to use of "films, tapes or digital media used for radio or television broadcasting".

11. *Albania, Malaysia, Serbia* and *Vietnam* reserve the right to deal with fees for technical services in a separate Article similar to Article 12.

12. *Albania, Argentina, Armenia, Belarus, Brazil, Bulgaria, Croatia, Estonia, Gabon, Indonesia, Ivory Coast, Kazakhstan, Latvia, Lithuania, Malaysia, Morocco,* the *People's Republic of China,* the *Philippines, Romania, Serbia, South Africa, Thailand, Tunisia, Ukraine, Vietnam* and *Hong Kong, China* reserve the right, in order to fill what they consider as a gap in the Article, to add a provision defining the source of royalties by analogy with the provisions of paragraph 5 of Article 11, which deals with the same issue in the case of interest.

12.1 *Morocco* reserves the right to include in the paragraph a reference to other business activities carried on in the other State of the same and similar kind as those effected through a permanent establishment.

12.2 The *Democratic Republic of the Congo* and *Malaysia* reserve their position on the treatment of software.

12.3 *Kazakhstan* reserves the right to include in the definition of royalties payments for the use of, or the right to use, software.

Positions on the Commentary

13. *Argentina, Morocco, Serbia* and *Tunisia* do not adhere to the interpretation in paragraphs 14 and 15 of the Commentary. They hold the view that payments relating to software fall within the scope of the Article where less than the full rights to software are transferred, either if the payments are in consideration for the right to use a copyright on software for commercial exploitation or if they relate to software acquired for the personal or business use of the purchaser.

14. *Vietnam* does not agree with paragraph 9 of the Commentary. Even if the phrase "for the use of, or the right to use, industrial, commercial or scientific equipment" is not included in paragraph 2 and income from the leasing of equipment falls under Article 7, the fact that an enterprise of a Contracting State leases heavy equipment to a person resident in Vietnam will constitute a permanent establishment of that enterprise in Vietnam.

15. *Brazil* does not agree with the interpretation provided in paragraphs 17.1 to 17.4, especially in view of the principle of taxation at the source of payments in its legislation.

16. *Malaysia* cannot adhere to the new additional sentence in paragraph 11.2, i.e. "Payments made under the latter contracts generally fall under Article 7". Malaysia treats payments for the provision of services as Special Classes of Income under her domestic law and not as business income.

17.   *India* reserves its position on the interpretations provided in paragraphs 8.2, 10.1, 10.2, 14, 14.1, 14.2, 14.4, 15, 16 and 17.3; it is of the view that some of the payments referred to may constitute royalties.

18.   *India* does not agree with the interpretation that information concerning industrial, commercial or scientific experience is confined to only previous experience.

19.   *Malaysia* does not adhere to the interpretation in paragraph 14.2 because Malaysia is of the view that licence fees for rights to distribute software constitute royalties.

20.   *India* does not agree with the interpretation in paragraph 9.1 of the Commentary on Article 12 according to which a payment for transponder leasing will not constitute royalty. This notion is contrary to the Indian position that income from transponder leasing constitutes an equipment royalty taxable both under India's domestic law and its treaties with many countries. It is also contrary to India's position that a payment for the use of a transponder is a payment for the use of a process resulting in a royalty under Article 12. India also does not agree with the conclusion included in the paragraph concerning undersea cables and pipelines as it considers that undersea cables and pipelines are industrial, commercial or scientific equipment and that payments made for their use constitute equipment royalties.

21.   *India* does not agree with the interpretation in paragraph 9.2 of the Commentary on Article 12. It considers that a roaming call constitutes the use of a process. Accordingly, the payment made for the use of that process constitutes a royalty for the purposes of Article 12. It is also the position of India that a payment for a roaming call constitutes a royalty since it is a payment for the use of industrial, commercial or scientific equipment.

22.   *India* does not agree with the interpretation in paragraph 9.3 of the Commentary on Article 12. It considers that a payment for spectrum license constitutes a royalty taxable both under India's domestic law and its treaties with many countries.

23.   The *People's Republic of China* does not adhere to the interpretation in paragraph 10.1 because it takes the view that some payments for the exclusive distribution rights of a product or a service in a given territory may be treated as royalties.

POSITIONS ON ARTICLE 13
(CAPITAL GAINS)
AND ITS COMMENTARY

Positions on the Article

1.   *Argentina* and *Brazil* reserve the right to tax at source gains from the alienation of property situated in a Contracting State other than property mentioned in paragraphs 1, 2, 3 and 4.

2. The *People's Republic of China*, *Serbia* and *Thailand* reserve the right to tax gains from the alienation of shares or rights that are part of a substantial participation in a resident company.

3. *Latvia* and *Lithuania* reserve the right to insert in a special Article provisions regarding capital gains relating to activities carried on offshore in a Contracting State in connection with the exploration or exploitation of the sea bed, its subsoil and their natural resources.

4. *Estonia* and *Lithuania* reserve the right to limit the application of paragraph 3 to enterprises operating ships and aircraft in international traffic.

5. *India* and *Vietnam* reserve the right to tax gains from the alienation of shares or rights in a company that is a resident of their respective country.

6. *Bulgaria* reserves the right to tax gains from the alienation of shares or rights in a company that is a resident of Bulgaria other than shares quoted on a regulated stock exchange.

7. *Bulgaria* reserves the right to extend the scope of the provision to cover gains from the alienation of railway and road transport vehicles.

8. *Vietnam* reserves the right to modify paragraph 4 so that the immovable property in question need only be 30 per cent of all assets owned by the company.

9. *Serbia* reserves the right to extend the scope of the provision to cover gains from the alienation of road transport vehicles operated in international traffic.

10. *India* reserves its position on paragraph 4.

11. *Israel* reserves its right to insert a provision according to which where a person, who was a resident of a Contracting State, has become a resident of the other Contracting State, this Article shall not prevent the first-mentioned State from taxing under its domestic law the capital gains on the property of that person at the time of change of residence. In the case of the alienation of property dealt with in paragraphs 1, 2, 3 and 4 made after the change of residence, double taxation will be eliminated by the first-mentioned Contracting State. In the case of the alienation of property dealt with in paragraph 5 made after the change of residence, double taxation will be eliminated by the other Contracting State.

POSITIONS ON ARTICLE 14
(INDEPENDENT PERSONAL SERVICES)
AND ITS COMMENTARY

Positions on the Article

[All the positions on Article 14 were deleted when, on 29 April 2000, Article 14 itself was deleted from the Model Tax Convention pursuant to the report entitled "Issues

Related to Article 14 of the OECD Model Tax Convention", which had been adopted by the OECD Committee on Fiscal Affairs on 27 January 2000.]

POSITIONS ON ARTICLE 15
(INCOME FROM EMPLOYMENT)
AND ITS COMMENTARY

Positions on the Article

1. *Argentina* reserves its position on subparagraph *a*) of paragraph 2 and wishes to insert in its conventions the words "in the fiscal year concerned" instead of the words "in any twelve month period commencing or ending in the fiscal year concerned".

2. *Latvia* and *Lithuania* reserve the right to insert in a special Article provisions regarding income derived from dependent personal services relating to activities carried on offshore in a Contracting State in connection with the exploration or exploitation of the sea bed, its subsoil and their natural resources.

3. *Argentina* reserves the right to insert in a special article provisions regarding income derived from dependent personal services relating to offshore hydrocarbon exploration and exploitation and related activities.

4. *Serbia* reserves the right to propose a separate paragraph which provides that remuneration derived by a resident of a Contracting State shall be taxable only in that State if the remuneration is paid in respect of an employment exercised in the other Contracting State in connection with a building site, a construction or installation project, for an agreed period during which the site or project does not constitute a permanent establishment in that other State.

5. *India* reserves the right to decide the period of stay referred in this paragraph through bilateral negotiations.

5.1 The *United Arab Emirates* reserves the right to modify paragraph 3 to provide that remuneration derived in respect of an employment exercised in connection with an aircraft operated in international traffic (including the crew of the aircraft and ground staff) shall be taxed exclusively in the country of residence of the operator of that aircraft.

Position on the Commentary

6. *India* does not adhere to the interpretation set out in paragraph 6.2, because it does not recognise the concept of a partner being treated as an employer in the case of fiscally transparent partnership.

POSITIONS ON ARTICLE 16
(DIRECTORS' FEES)
AND ITS COMMENTARY

Positions on the Article

1. *Albania*, *Bulgaria*, the *Democratic Republic of the Congo*, *Estonia*, *Indonesia*, *Latvia*, *Lithuania* and *Serbia* reserve the right to tax under this Article any remuneration of a member of a board of directors or any other similar organ of a resident company.

2. [Deleted]

3. *Morocco* reserves the right to tax under this Article any remuneration of a member of a board of directors or any other similar organ of a resident company. Morocco also reserves the right to extend the Article to cover the remuneration of senior employees.

4. *Indonesia*, *Malaysia* and *Vietnam* reserve the right to extend the Article to cover the remuneration of top-level managerial officials.

POSITIONS ON ARTICLE 17
(ARTISTES AND SPORTSMEN)
AND ITS COMMENTARY

Positions on the Article

1. The *Philippines* and *Russia* reserve the right to exclude from the application of paragraph 1 artistes and sportsmen employed in organisations which are subsidised out of public funds.

2. *India* and *Thailand* reserve the right to exclude from the application of paragraphs 1 and 2 the income from activities performed in a Contracting State by entertainers or sportspersons if the activities are substantially supported by public funds and to provide for residence based taxation of such income.

POSITIONS ON ARTICLE 18
(PENSIONS)
AND ITS COMMENTARY

Position on the Article

1. [Deleted]

2. *Brazil*, *Bulgaria*, *Ivory Coast*, *South Africa* and *Ukraine* reserve the right to include in paragraph 1 an explicit reference to annuities.

 MODEL TAX CONVENTION (CONDENSED VERSION) – ISBN 978-92-64-08948-8 – © OECD 2010

POSITIONS ON ARTICLE 19
(GOVERNMENT SERVICE)
AND ITS COMMENTARY

Position on the Commentary

1.   *India* does not agree that public bodies like State Railways and Post Offices are performing business activities.

POSITIONS ON ARTICLE 20
(STUDENTS)
AND ITS COMMENTARY

Positions on the Article

1.   *Albania, Brazil* and *Serbia* reserve the right to add a second paragraph providing for the granting to visiting students of the same tax exemptions, reliefs or reductions as are granted to residents in respect of any subsidies, grants and payments for dependent personal services.

2.   *Estonia, Latvia, Lithuania* and *Morocco* reserve the right to refer to any apprentice and to a trainee in this Article.

3.   [Deleted]

4.   *Vietnam* reserves the right to provide that remuneration for services rendered by a student or business apprentice in a Contracting State shall not be taxed in that State, provided that such services are in connection with his studies or training.

5.   *Thailand* reserves the right to provide that remuneration for services rendered by a student or business apprentice in a Contracting State shall not be taxed in that State if such remuneration does not exceed a certain amount to be negotiated, provided that such services are in connection with his studies or training.

6.   *Brazil, Bulgaria, India, Ivory Coast, Morocco,* the *People's Republic of China,* the *Philippines, Serbia, Thailand, Tunisia* and *Vietnam* reserve the right to add an article which addresses the situation of teachers, professors and researchers, subject to various conditions and are free to make a corresponding modification to paragraph 1 of Article 15.

7.   *Gabon, Ivory Coast* and *Tunisia* reserve the right to provide that remuneration for services rendered by a student or business apprentice in the visiting State shall not be taxed in that State, provided that such remuneration was received for the purpose of his maintenance, studies or training.

8.   *Morocco* reserves the right to add a second paragraph providing that the remuneration from employment derived from the visiting State shall not be taxed in

that State, or, in case of taxation, the granting to visiting students of the same tax exemptions, reliefs or reductions as are granted to residents.

9.   *India* and *Hong Kong, China* reserve the right to exclude "business apprentice" from this Article.

10.   *India* reserves the right to provide that remuneration for services rendered by a student in a Contracting State shall not be taxed in that State provided that such services are directly related to his studies and is free to make a corresponding modification to paragraph 1 of Article 15.

11.   *India* reserves the right to limit the exemption provided for in the Article to a period of six years.

POSITIONS ON ARTICLE 21
(OTHER INCOME)
AND ITS COMMENTARY

Position on the Article

1.   *Albania, Argentina, Belarus, Brazil, Bulgaria, Gabon, India, Indonesia, Ivory Coast, Malaysia, Morocco, Russia, Serbia, South Africa, Thailand* and *Vietnam* reserve their positions on this Article as they wish to maintain the right to tax income arising from sources in their own country.

POSITIONS ON ARTICLE 22
(CAPITAL)
AND ITS COMMENTARY

Positions on the Article

1.   *Argentina* reserves the right to tax capital, other than property mentioned in paragraph 3, that is situated on its territory.

2.   *Brazil, Bulgaria, Indonesia, Malaysia,* the *People's Republic of China, Thailand* and *Vietnam* reserve their positions on the Article if and when they impose taxes on capital.

3.   *India* reserves the right to tax capital as per domestic law.

POSITIONS ON ARTICLES 23 A AND 23 B
(EXEMPTION METHOD AND CREDIT METHOD)
AND ITS COMMENTARY

Positions on the Article

1.   Albania, Argentina, Brazil, India, Ivory Coast, Malaysia, Morocco, the People's Republic of China, Serbia, Thailand, Tunisia and Vietnam reserve the right to add tax sparing provisions in relation to the tax incentives that are provided for under their respective national laws.

2.   Argentina and Vietnam reserve the right to add a matching credit for some or all of the income covered under Articles 10, 11 and 12 with the result that tax shall be deemed to have been paid, for purposes of the Article on elimination of double taxation, at a certain rate, to be negotiated, of the gross income.

3.   Brazil reserves the right to add a matching credit for some or all of the income covered under Articles 11 and 12 with the result that tax shall be deemed to have been paid, for purposes of the Article on elimination of double taxation, at a certain rate, to be negotiated, of the gross income.

4.   Brazil and Tunisia reserve the right to provide that income covered under Article 10 shall be exempt or entitled to a matching credit in the other Contracting State.

5.   Argentina and Brazil reserve their position on paragraph 4 of Article 23 A.

POSITIONS ON ARTICLE 24
(NON-DISCRIMINATION)
AND ITS COMMENTARY

Positions on the Article

Paragraph 1

1.   [Deleted]

2.   Brazil, Romania, Russia, Thailand and Vietnam reserve their position on the second sentence of paragraph 1.

2.1   Bulgaria reserves the right to omit the words "other or" in the first sentence of paragraph 1.

2.2   Indonesia, Malaysia and Tunisia reserve the right to restrict the scope of the Article to residents of the Contracting States.

Paragraph 2

3.   [Deleted]

4.   *Albania, Bulgaria, Estonia, India, Malaysia, the Philippines, Russia, Serbia* and *Vietnam* reserve the right not to insert paragraph 2 in their conventions.

Paragraph 3

5.   *Argentina* reserves the right to apply a branch profits tax.

6.   *Brazil* reserves its position on paragraph 3 since royalties paid by a permanent establishment situated in Brazil to its head office abroad are not deductible under its law.

7.   *Thailand* reserves the right to apply a profit remittance tax and a special taxation regime in respect of agricultural production activities.

7.1   *Morocco* reserves the right to add a paragraph stating that nothing in this article can be interpreted as prohibiting Morocco to apply its branch tax, its domestic thin-capitalisation and transfer-pricing legislation.

7.2   *South Africa* reserves the right to add a paragraph stating that nothing in the Article will prevent South Africa from imposing on the profits attributable to a permanent establishment in South Africa of a company that is not a resident, a tax at a rate that does not exceed the rate of normal tax on companies by more than five percentage points.

Paragraph 4

8.   *Vietnam* reserves its position on this paragraph in the case of interest paid to non-residents that is not subject to a withholding tax.

8.1   *Malaysia* reserves its position on this paragraph in the case of interest, royalties, or fees for technical services paid to non-residents where withholding tax has not been deducted.

Paragraph 5

9.   *Brazil* reserves the right to include, after the words "other similar enterprises of the first-mentioned State", the words "whose capital is totally or partially, directly or indirectly, held or controlled by one or several residents of a third State".

Paragraph 6

10.   *Albania, Brazil, Bulgaria, Malaysia, the Philippines, Romania, Serbia, Thailand, Tunisia, Vietnam* and *Ukraine* reserve the right to restrict the scope of the Article to the taxes covered by the Convention.

Positions on the Commentary

11.   *India* and *Malaysia* reserve their position on the interpretation set out in paragraph 44.

12.   *India* reserves the right to add a paragraph to clarify that this provision can neither be construed as preventing a Contracting State from charging the profits of a

permanent establishment which a company of the other Contracting State has in the first-mentioned State at a rate of tax which is higher than that imposed on the profits of a similar company of the first-mentioned Contracting State, nor as being in conflict with the provisions of paragraph 3 of Article 7 (as it read before the 2010 update to the Model Tax Convention).

POSITIONS ON ARTICLE 25
(MUTUAL AGREEMENT PROCEDURE)
AND ITS COMMENTARY

Positions on the Article

Paragraph 1

1.   Brazil, the Philippines and Thailand reserve their positions on the last sentence of paragraph 1.

1.1   Kazakhstan reserves its position on the second sentence of paragraph 1 and reserves its right to supplement the paragraph with the following sentence: "In the case of judicial proceedings, a court decision cannot be reconsidered by the competent authority of Kazakhstan."

Paragraph 2

2.   Brazil, the Philippines and Thailand reserve their positions on the second sentence of paragraph 2. These countries consider that the implementation of reliefs and refunds following a mutual agreement ought to remain linked to time limits prescribed by their domestic laws.

Paragraph 3

3.   Brazil, Thailand, Tunisia and Ukraine reserve their position on the second sentence of paragraph 3 on the grounds that they have no authority under their respective laws to eliminate double taxation in cases not provided for in the Convention.

Paragraph 4

4.   Brazil, Malaysia, the People's Republic of China, the Philippines, Thailand and Ukraine reserve the right to omit the words "including through a joint commission consisting of themselves or their representatives".

Positions on the Commentary

5.   Brazil and India do not agree with the interpretation given in paragraphs 11 and 12; they are of the view that in the absence of paragraph 2 in Article 9, economic double taxation arising from transfer pricing adjustments does not fall within the scope of mutual agreement procedure set up in Article 25.

6.   Concerning paragraph 14, *Argentina* reserves its right not to commence or accept a mutual agreement procedure case if taxation not in accordance with the Convention has not been charged or notified to the taxpayer.

7.   In relation to paragraph 25, *India* is of the view that the competent authorities can reach an agreement under Article 25 during pendency of domestic law action. However, the taxpayer has an option to either accept or reject the resolution order. If the taxpayer accepts the resolution order, he has to withdraw domestic law action.

8.   *India* does not agree with the view expressed in paragraph 42 that a taxpayer may be permitted to defer acceptance of the solution agreed upon as a result of the mutual agreement procedure until the court had delivered its judgement in that suit.

POSITIONS ON ARTICLE 26
(EXCHANGE OF INFORMATION)
AND ITS COMMENTARY

Positions on the Article

1.   [Deleted]

2.   *India* reserves the right to include documents or certified copies of the documents within the scope of this Article.

2.1   *Morocco* and *Thailand* reserve the right not to include the words "The exchange of information is not restricted by Articles 1 and 2" in paragraph 1.

Position on the Commentary

3.   As regards paragraph 10.3 of the Commentary, *Hong Kong, China* wishes to clarify its position on the exchange of information that existed prior to the entry into force of the bilateral agreement. In view of its domestic law requirements, Hong Kong, China will only exchange information relating to taxable periods after the agreement came into operation.

POSITIONS ON ARTICLE 28
(MEMBERS OF DIPLOMATIC MISSIONS AND CONSULAR POSTS)
AND ITS COMMENTARY

Position on the Article

1.   Considering that *Hong Kong, China* is not a sovereign state but a special administrative region of the People's Republic of China, Hong Kong, China reserves the right to replace "diplomatic missions" by "government missions" in this Article.

POSITIONS ON ARTICLE 29
(TERRITORIAL EXTENSION)
AND ITS COMMENTARY

Position on the Article

1.   *Indonesia*, the *People's Republic of China* and *Thailand* reserve their position on this Article.

ANNEX

RECOMMENDATION OF THE OECD COUNCIL CONCERNING THE MODEL TAX CONVENTION ON INCOME AND ON CAPITAL

(Adopted by the Council on 23 October 1997)

THE COUNCIL,

Having regard to Article 5(b) of the Convention on the Organisation for Economic Co-operation and Development of the 14 December 1960;

Having regard to the Recommendation of the Council dated 31 March 1994 concerning the Model Tax Convention on Income and Capital [C(94)11/FINAL] and the Recommendation of the Council dated 21 September 1995 amending the Appendix to that previous Recommendation [C(95)132/FINAL];

Having regard to the Report of the Committee on Fiscal Affairs of 24 June 1997 entitled "The 1997 Update to the Model Tax Convention" [DAFFE/CFA/WP1(97)10/REV2] (hereinafter referred to as "the 1997 Report");

Considering the need to remove the obstacles that international juridical double taxation presents to the free movement of goods, services, capital, and persons between countries by the conclusion of conventions for that purpose;

Considering also the need to harmonise existing bilateral conventions on the basis of uniform principles, definitions, rules, and methods and to extend the existing network of such conventions to all member countries and where appropriate to non-member countries;

Considering further the need to encourage the common application and interpretation of the provisions of tax conventions that are based on those of the Model Tax Convention on Income and on Capital (hereinafter referred to as the "Model Tax Convention");

Considering that efforts made in this direction by member countries have already produced substantial results and that the proposed revisions to the Model Tax Convention will make it possible to confirm and extend existing international co-operation on tax matters;

Taking note of the Model Tax Convention and the Commentaries thereon (as last modified by the 1997 Report), which may be amended from time to time hereafter;

I.   RECOMMENDS the Governments of member countries:

1. to pursue their efforts to conclude bilateral tax conventions on income and on capital with those member countries, and where appropriate with non-member countries, with which they have not yet entered into such conventions, and to revise those of the existing conventions that may no longer reflect present-day needs;

2. when concluding new bilateral conventions or revising existing bilateral conventions, to conform to the Model Tax Convention, as interpreted by the Commentaries thereon;

3. that their tax administrations follow the Commentaries on the Articles of the Model Tax Convention, as modified from time to time, when applying and interpreting the provisions of their bilateral tax conventions that are based on these Articles.

II.   INVITES the Governments of member countries to continue to notify the Committee on Fiscal Affairs of their reservations on the Articles and observations on the Commentaries.

III.   INSTRUCTS the Committee on Fiscal Affairs to continue its ongoing review of situations where the provisions set out in the Model Tax Convention or the Commentaries thereon may require modification in the light of experience gained by member countries, and to make appropriate proposals for periodic updates.

IV.   DECIDES to repeal the Recommendations of the Council C(94)11/FINAL (31 March 1994) and C(95)132/FINAL (21 September 1995).

MODEL TAX CONVENTION (CONDENSED VERSION) – ISBN 978-92-64-08948-8 – © OECD 2010

OECD PUBLICATIONS, 2, rue André-Pascal, 75775 PARIS CEDEX 16
PRINTED IN FRANCE
(23 2010 08 1 P) ISBN 978-92-64-08948-8 – No. 57501 2010

Lightning Source UK Ltd.
Milton Keynes UK
UKOW031240240112

185970UK00001B/6/P